D0420397

IMPORTANT:

HERE IS YOUR REGISTRATION CODE TO ACCESS
YOUR PREMIUM McGRAW-HILL ONLINE RESOURCES.

For key premium online resources you need THIS CODE to gain access. Once the code is entered, you will be able to use the Web resources for the length of your course.

If your course is using **WebCT** or **Blackboard**, you'll be able to use this code to access the McGraw-Hill content within your instructor's online course.

Access is provided if you have purchased a new book. If the registration code is missing from this book, the registration screen on our Website, and within your WebCT or Blackboard course, will tell you how to obtain your new code.

Registering for McGraw-Hill Online Resources

TO gain access to your McGraw-Hill web resources simply follow the steps below:

1. USE YOUR WEB BROWSER TO GO TO: **www.mhhe.com/fahnestock**
2. CLICK ON **FIRST TIME USER**.
3. ENTER THE REGISTRATION CODE* PRINTED ON THE TEAR-OFF BOOKMARK ON THE RIGHT.
4. AFTER YOU HAVE ENTERED YOUR REGISTRATION CODE, CLICK **REGISTER**.
5. FOLLOW THE INSTRUCTIONS TO SET-UP YOUR PERSONAL UserID AND PASSWORD.
6. WRITE YOUR UserID AND PASSWORD DOWN FOR FUTURE REFERENCE. KEEP IT IN A SAFE PLACE.

TO GAIN ACCESS to the McGraw-Hill content in your instructor's **WebCT** or **Blackboard** course simply log in to the course with the UserID and Password provided by your instructor. Enter the registration code exactly as it appears in the box to the right when prompted by the system. You will only need to use the code the first time you click on McGraw-Hill content.

Thank you, and welcome to your McGraw-Hill online Resources!

0-07-293616-9 T/A FAHNESTOCK: A RHETORIC OF ARGUMENT, 3/E

MCGRAW-HILL
ONLINE RESOURCES

REGISTRATION CODE

FL86-OWZU-S38M-I4JL-26MS

A Rhetoric of Argument

A Text and Reader
Third Edition

Jeanne Fahnestock
University of Maryland

Marie Secor
Pennsylvania State University

Boston Burr Ridge, IL Dubuque, IA Madison, WI New York
San Francisco St. Louis Bangkok Bogotá Caracas Kuala Lumpur
Lisbon Lon Montreal New Delhi
Santi aipei Toronto

Higher Education

President of McGraw-Hill Humanities/Social Sciences: *Steve Debow*
Executive editor: *Lisa Moore*
Director of development: *Carla Kay Samodulski*
Executive marketing manager: *David S. Patterson*
Senior media producer: *Todd Vaccaro*
Project manager: *Ruth Smith*
Production supervisor: *Carol A. Bielski*
Freelance design coordinator: *Gino Cieslik*
Lead supplement producer: *Marc Mattson*
Photo research coordinator: *Alexandra Ambrose*
Associate art editor: *Cristin Yancey*
Photo researcher: *David Tietz*
Permissions: *Marty Granahan*
Cover and interior design: *Maureen McCutcheon*
Typeface: *10/12 Janson*
Compositor: *G&S Typesetters*
Printer: *R.R. Donnelley and Sons Inc.*

Library of Congress Cataloging-in-Publication Data

Fahnestock, Jeanne, (date)–
   A rhetoric of argument/Jeanne Fahnestock, Marie Secor.—3rd ed.
      p. cm.
   Includes index.
   ISBN 0-07-303616-1 (soft cover: alk. paper)—ISBN 0-07-303617-X (brief ed.: alk. paper)
   1. English language—Rhetoric. 2. Persuasion (Rhetoric) I. Secor, Marie, (date)– II. Title.
PE1431.F3 2004
808'.042—dc21

2003045916

www.mhhe.com

To Anna, Laura, Peter, and Derek

CONTENTS

Preface   xvii
Introduction for Students   xxv

PART ONE   READING AND WRITING ARGUMENTS

CHAPTER 1   An Introduction to the Study of Argument   3

In the Media: We Encourage You to Vote Today *The Indianapolis Star*   3
Analyzing "We Encourage You to Vote Today"   4
Expanding Your Definition of Argument   7
Contexts for Argument   8
    Personal   8
    Interpersonal   9
    Professional   9
    Public   10
The Rhetorical Situation   11
    Audience   12
    Exigence   12
    Constraints   14

CHAPTER 2   Building the Case: Logos   16

In the Media: An Ad for Purina One "Beef Jerky Strips"   16
Analyzing the Advertisement for Beef Jerky Strips   17
The Materials of Argument   19
Building the Logos   19
    One-Part Argument: The Claim Alone   21
    Two-Part Argument: The Enthymeme   21
    Expanding Arguments: Branching Support   22
    Expanding Arguments: Chains of Support   23
    Writing Your Argument: Building an Argument from
    Claim-Reason Pairs   26
    Expanding the Three-Part Argument: The Full Toulmin Model   27
Building Arguments with Other Positions in Mind   29
    Writing Your Argument: Taking Account of Other Positions   30
The Building Blocks of Arguments: Values and Facts   31
    Values   32
    Facts   33
    Using Sources   34
    Determining the Reliability of a Source   37
Visual Rhetoric: Arguing with Images   38
    The Specter of Global Aging   Robert Samuelson (Article with Photograph)   38

v

For You to Analyze   41
Advertisement for Kleenex Cold Care Tissues   42
Don't Legalize Those Drugs   BARRY R. McCAFFREY   43
The former head of the Office of National Drug Control Policy argues against the legalization of drugs because "[i]n general, our laws indicate that self-destructive activity should not be permitted or condoned."

CHAPTER 3   Establishing Credibility and Appealing to Emotion: Ethos and Pathos   45

In the Media: While the Children Sleep   *A. M. Rosenthal*   45

Analyzing "While the Children Sleep"   46

Ethos   48
The Elements of Ethos   49
Types of Ethos   51

Pathos   53

Ethos and Pathos Combine in Identification   55

Establishing Ethos in Writing   56
The Intellectual Virtue of Reasonableness   56
The Overall Effects of Conviction and Moderation   59
Disclaimers: Don't Get the Wrong Idea about Me or My Argument   59

Writing Your Argument: Establishing Your Ethos   60

Evoking Pathos in Argument   60
Choosing Words Carefully   61
Choosing Powerful Examples   63

Writing Your Argument: Evoking Pathos   65

Fallacies   65

Visual Rhetoric: Emotion in Images   72
Twin Towers   Jack Ohman (Political Cartoon)   72

For You to Analyze   74
Pay Your Own Way! (Then Thank Mom)
AUDREY ROCK-RICHARDSON   74
In a "My Turn" column for *Newsweek*, Rock-Richardson maintains that "the notion that parents must finance their children's education is ridiculous."

A Letter to the Terrorists   LEONARD PITTS   75
In an article published on September 12, 2001, syndicated columnist Leonard Pitts assures the terrorists who were behind the attacks on the World Trade Center and Pentagon that "[a]s Americans we will weep, as Americans we will mourn, and as Americans we will rise in defense of all we cherish."

For You to Write   76

CHAPTER 4   Generating the Argument: Questions and Claims   77

In the Media: Drug Tests Backed for Broader Pool of Students
St. Louis Post-Dispatch   77

Analyzing "Drug Tests Backed for Broader Pool of Students"   78

Finding Issues to Argue   81
Answering Questions with Claims   81
The Four Basic Questions   83

Warrants and the Four Basic Questions   86
Combining the Questions   88
Finding the Key Questions at Issue   88

The Basic Questions as a Research Strategy   90

Writing Your Argument: Using the Basic Questions to Organize Your Research   91

Reading for Questions   92

Japan's Modern Women Living Single and Loving It
KATHRYN TOLBERT   93

A reporter for the *Washington Post* discovers a trend among Japanese women: "the number of women in their late twenties who have not married has risen from 30 percent to about 50 percent in the last 15 years."

Crucifix Can Reflect on Good Moral Character of School . . .
JOSETTE SHINER   97

Defending the presence of crucifixes in the classrooms of Georgetown University, Shiner writes, "[T]he diverse expression of religious values can play a tremendous role in the healthy civic life of our nation."

It Would Drive Away Students   BONNIE ERBE   98

Objecting to the presence of crucifixes in Georgetown University's classrooms, Erbe writes, "If the handful of students who want to place crucifixes in each classroom succeeds, they will drive many students who might otherwise have attended Georgetown to other institutions."

For You to Write   99

CHAPTER 5   Expressing Appeals: Language and Voice   101

In the Media: Subsidizing Illegal Residents   *Ward Connerly*   101
Analyzing "Subsidizing Illegal Residents"   102
Choosing a Voice   104
   Using *I* or Not Using *I*   104
   Using *You* or Not Using *You*   108
   Dialogue Building with Questions   115
   Using *We* or Not Using *We*   117
   Other Ways of Creating and Appealing to Groups   120

Visual Rhetoric: Visuals Involve the Viewer   122
   "I Want You for the U.S. Army" (Recruiting poster)   122

Writing Your Argument: Finding an Effective Stance   124

For You to Analyze   124

The Face of Welfare   SHAWNTELLE SANTAS   125

"You click into judgment mode and see WELFARE MOM flashing above my head in neon lights," Santas writes. She goes on to show, however, that "[t]he only safe assumption about someone else's life is that there *are* no safe assumptions."

"Better Safe . . . ? Diary of a Mad Law Professor"
PATRICIA J. WILLIAMS   126

A professor of law at Columbia University, Williams asks about increased attempts to profile possible terrorists, "How can we be putting all this work into appearances when appearances bear no necessary relation to intent?"

For You to Write   128

PART TWO TYPES OF ARGUMENTS

CHAPTER 6   Definition: What Is It?   131

In the Media: Scientists Determine Chimpanzees Have "Culture"
AP News Service   131

Analyzing "Scientists Determine Chimpanzees Have 'Culture'"   132

Definition: Arguing about the Nature of Things   135
   Types of Definition Arguments   136

Constructing a Definition Argument   137
  Support by Example   138
  Support by Definition   143
  Support by Comparison   153

Visual Rhetoric: Neil Armstrong Walks on the Moon   158
Astronaut Neil Armstrong Steps on the Moon's Surface (Photo)

Writing Your Own Definition Argument: Answering the Question
"What Is It?"   160
  Drafting Your "What Is It" Argument   161
  Reviewing and Revising Your Definition   161
  Writing Suggestions   162
  Comparison/Contrast Assignment   164

Readings

Cheerleading: A Sport or an Activity?   JILL HENKEL   165
"A cheerleader for three years" while in high school, college student Jill Henkel maintains that
"[a]lthough many people disagree, cheerleading is clearly a sport."

One Vet's Mission to Set the Record Straight   MICHAEL KELLEY   169
Kelley, himself a Vietnam veteran, questions the commonly accepted idea that 160,000 Vietnam
veterans have committed suicide. "What became a protracted and stupefying journey into this
fantasy world of wholesale veterans' suicides began for me with the realization that what I was
hearing and reading did not square with my experience."

The Myth of the Fading Family   E. J. DIONNE   172
Dionne, a columnist for the *Washington Post*, argues for the persistence of the two-parent
family, despite headlines to the contrary. "[I]t would . . . be wrong if ideology led us to
exaggerate the problem with the family in America. If the family has begun to come back
together, at least a little bit, we need to figure out why, and how to nurture the forces making
it happen."

Much Ado about Friends: *What Pop Culture Offers Literature*
RICHARD KELLER SIMON   174
An English professor argues that the television program is part of a tradition in comedy that
goes back hundreds of years: "The popular situation comedy *Friends* . . . is a contemporary
variation on Shakespeare's melodramatic comedy *Much Ado about Nothing*. . . . The core
characters, plots, and themes are almost the same."

CHAPTER 7   Causal Argument: How Did It Get That Way?   179

In the Media: Harness Fire? Mother Nature Begs to Differ
George Johnson   179
Analyzing "Harness Fire? Mother Nature Begs to Differ"   181
Causal Arguments: Determining Why or How Something Happened   182
Constructing a Causal Argument   183
  Framing Narratives for Causal Analysis   184
  Considering Other Causal Models   190
  Fitting a Narrative to a Purpose   195
  Establishing Causal Relationships   196
  Supporting a Causal Relationship   199
  Other Types of Causal Arguments   207

Visual Rhetoric: Cause and Effect for the Eye   210
  "Crude Male Death Rate for Lung Cancer in 1950 and Per Capita Consumption of
    Cigarettes in 1930 in Various Countries" (Line Graph)   210
  "20-Year Lag Time between Smoking and Lung Cancer" (Line Graph)   211

Writing Your Own Causal Argument: Answering the Question "How
Did It Get That Way?"   214
  Drafting Your Causal Argument   216
  Reviewing and Revising Your Causal Argument   216
  Writing Suggestions   217

Readings

Spandex Nation   HINDA GONCHOR   217
Gonchor identifies the culprit behind Americans' expanding waistlines: "With the addition of Lycra or Spandex to fabrics—3 percent, 10 percent, 44 percent, 100 percent—everything always fits."

Study: Beer Taxes Reduce STD Rates   DAVID PITT   218
Pitt reports on an interesting correlation: "The CDC analyzed the drops in gonorrhea rates following different tax increases and came up with the estimate that a 20 cent increase per six-pack would lead to a 9 percent drop in gonorrhea rates."

Expert Report Disputes U.S. on Trade Center Collapse
JAMES GLANZ AND ERIC LIPTON   220
Two *New York Times* reporters explore conflicting analyses of the cause of the collapse of the World Trade Center and the parties that have a stake in the rival explanations: "Experts commissioned in a $4 billion insurance case involving the World Trade Center have come to conclusions that fundamentally contradict a federal investigation into what caused the twin towers to collapse."

Successful Inner-City Schools Share Common Traits
SAMUEL CASEY CARTER   224
Carter offers "seven common traits" of successful schools, and asserts, "Outstanding principals know that all children can excel academically regardless of race, income level or family background. Studying their success should be the highest priority of educators in a country where more than half of all low-income 4th-graders cannot even read."

CHAPTER 8   Evaluation: Is It Good or Bad?   228

In the Media: Why Generation X Is Embracing Morality
Stacey Felzenberg   228
Analyzing "Why Generation X Is Embracing Morality"   229
Evaluation: Determining the Value of Something   231
Constructing a Sound Evaluation   232
  Supporting Criteria with a Specific Audience in Mind   233
  Possible Subjects for Evaluation   234
  The Evaluation as Comparison   251
  Superlative Evaluation   252

Visual Rhetoric: The Eye of a Dying Whale   254
  Close-up of the Eye of a Dying Whale (Photo)   255

Writing Your Own Evaluation: Answering the Question "Is It Good or Bad?"   256
  Drafting Your Evaluation   257
  Reviewing and Revising Your Evaluation   257
  Writing Suggestions   258

Readings

Harvest the Whales, with Letters to the Editor in Response
NICHOLAS D. KRISTOF   260
In his *New York Times* column, Kristof takes a controversial stand on the hunting of a beloved mammal: "There is no longer a 'save the whales' imperative for a moratorium on commercial whaling of all species." Writing in response to Kristof, Fred O'Regan, president of the International Fund for Animal Welfare, writes, "Commercial whaling is an inherently cruel practice that represents a significant threat to the conservation status of whales, both rare and abundant."

Editorial: Leave the Flicks Alone   DES MOINES REGISTER EDITORIAL BOARD   264
Some video stores' practice of censoring films to remove possibly objectionable scenes and dialogue "is trespassing on the director's intellectual property."

The Best   JONATHAN V. LAST   266

According to Last, a reporter for the *Weekly Standard,* "The secret of Michael Jordan's greatness—of all competitive greatness—is not merely . . . to *do your best.* It is to make your best superior to everyone else's. . . . Somebody must lose so you can win."

Yes, Gambling Is Productive and Rational   DAVID RAMSAY STEELE   270

Economist Steele takes on foes of legalized gambling: "The fundamental argument for legalizing gambling is not that it will bring in business from elsewhere, but rather that people are entitled to do whatever they please with their own lives as long as they don't invade other people's rights."

CHAPTER 9   Proposal: What Should We Do about It?   283

In the Media: Hollywood Simply Can No Longer Abdicate Its Responsibility to Kids   283

Analyzing "Hollywood Simply Can No Longer Abdicate Its Responsibility to Kids"   285

Proposals: Arguing for Action   289
Convincing an Audience   289
Kinds of Proposals   291

Constructing a Full Proposal   292
Preliminary Arguments   292
Evaluating the Consequences   294
Proposal Statement   297
Supporting Arguments   299
Feasibility: "It Can Be Done"   302
Anticipating Difficult Questions   305

Visual Rhetoric: Before and After: The Visual Proposal   308
Advertisement for Allegra-D   308

Writing Your Own Proposal: Answering the Question "What Should We Do about It?"   310
Drafting Your Proposal   312
Reviewing and Revising Your Proposal   312
Writing Suggestions   313

Readings

With Liberty and Prayer for All   MICHAEL NOVAK   314

Novak, a theologian at the American Enterprise Institute, maintains that the prohibition of prayer in the public schools is "a great sin against pluralism." He proposes that "a blue-ribbon committee could create a book of 200 or so 'Favorite Prayers of the American People,' one for each day of the school year, representing every religious and ethnic tradition, including Ethical Humanists."

My 60-Second Protest from the Hallway   EMILY LESK   317

In a "My Turn" column for *Newsweek,* Emily Lesk states the reason that she protested the state-mandated minute of silence in her high school: "My objection to Virginia's Minute of Silence law is very simple. I see the policy as an attempt to bring organized prayer into the public schools, thus violating the United States Constitution."

Vote, or Else   JOHN SOLOMON   319

Journalist Solomon offers a drastic solution to the problem of low voter turnout: "If voting is viewed as an obligation of citizenship, then why not use the straightforward ('Vote, it's the law') approach?"

Let Teen-Agers Try Adulthood   LEON BOTSTEIN   322

Botstein, the president of Bard College, suggests that "[w]e should entirely abandon the concept of the middle school and junior high school. Beginning with the seventh grade, there should be four years of secondary education that we may call high school. Young people should graduate at 16 rather than 18."

PART THREE RESEARCHING ARGUMENTS

CHAPTER 10   Finding Sources to Support Your Claim   327

An Overview of Sources   327
Primary Sources That Serve as Direct Evidence in Different Fields   328
Secondary Sources That Offer Analysis, Interpretation, Evaluation, and
    Commentary   333
Sources That Help Answer Specific Questions   334

Locating Sources   337
Searching for Sources by Keyword   339
Searching for Library Sources   346
Searching for Electronic Sources   349
Evaluating Internet Sources   358

Web Pages of Interest to Researchers   360

CHAPTER 11   Using Sources to Support Your Claim   372

Taking Effective Notes   372

Integrating Sources   374
Quoting   374
Paraphrasing   377
Summarizing   379

Avoiding Plagiarism   382
When to Document Your Sources   383

Citing Sources in Your Paper   385
Using MLA Style   385
A Student Paper in MLA Style: Add a New Clause to the American Society for
    Interior Designers' Code of Ethics   *Meaghan O'Keefe*   392
Using APA Style   406
A Student Paper in APA Style: Manic Depression: A Diagnostic Challenge
    Daniel M. Pulver   412

PART FOUR AN ANTHOLOGY OF ARGUMENTS

CHAPTER 12   The Promise and Perils of Globalization   419

I Love Global Capitalism—and I'm under 30   AARON LUKAS   419
An analyst for the Cato Institute, Lukas announces, "I'm in my '20s and I like global capitalism. And here's some more news: Most people my age agree with me."

French Food vs. Fast Food   MICHELLE MARTIN   420
After French farmer Jose Bové led an attack on a McDonald's restaurant, he "quickly became France's newest national hero." Bové and his followers were protesting U.S. sanctions on French products, but "[t]hey [were also] fighting what Bové calls 'a global problem' . . . industrialized food production, which is crowding out France's small farmers and their distinctive products."

A World Not Neatly Divided   AMARTYA SEN   422
A Nobel laureate in economics, Sen questions the idea of a clash of civilizations between the Islamic world and the West: "The basic weakness of the theory lies in its program of categorizing people of the world according to a unique, allegedly commanding system of classification."

A New Ethics for a New World   PAUL R. EHRLICH   424
Ehrlich, the author of several influential books on overpopulation, writes that "[i]n 10,000 years, an evolutionary eye-blink, humanity has been transformed from an extremely clever great ape living in groups of six to 600 individuals, to the very same ape dominating Earth, living in a global group of 6 billion."

Veil of Fears STANLEY KURTZ 426

"The veil was never the nightmare American feminists make it out to be," claims Kurtz, an anthropologist. "In a world where satisfaction in life is predicated on the honor, strength, and unity of the kin group, the veil makes sense. Although the oppressive impositions of the Taliban have rightly been abolished, the United States ought not to be in the business of browbeating Muslim women out of their veils, much less reforming the Middle Eastern kinship system."

Beauty and the Beast of Intolerance WOLE SOYINKA 430

Reacting to horrendous violence in his country, which was allegedly caused by the presence of the Miss World contest, the Nobel prize–winning writer declares, "Destruction of property and human massacres are always traumatic events in a community, saddening and enraging, but the organizers of the beauty contest, as well as the participants, must understand that they are totally free of guilt. The guilty are the storm troopers of intolerance, the manipulators of the feeble-minded but murderous hordes of fanaticism."

Questions for Discussion 433

Writing Suggestions 433

CHAPTER 13 The Revolution in Biotechnology 435

Closing In on Cloning WESLEY J. SMITH 435

Supporting a ban on all cloning, lawyer Smith writes, "When the Senate takes up the cloning debate later this year, we will confront the most fundamental of issues: Does individual human life have inherent value simply because it is human?"

Fatalist Attraction VIRGINIA I. POSTREL 440

The former editor of *Reason* magazine, Postrel reminds opponents of cloning research about the benefits of biomedical research, claiming that debates over cloning "are really about whether centralized powers will wrest hold of scientists' freedom of inquiry and patients' freedom to choose."

Growing More Food COUNCIL FOR BIOTECHNOLOGY INFORMATION 442

The Council was founded in 2000 by biotechnology companies and other interested parties. This article from the Council's web site outlines the benefits to humanity of plant biotechnology: "World crop productivity could increase by as much as 25 percent through the use of biotechnology to grow plants that resist pests and diseases, tolerate harsh growing conditions, and delay ripening to reduce spoilage."

A Personal Note JEREMY RIFKIN 445

A prominent thinker and writer on the topics of science and technology, Rifkin has serious misgivings about "the emerging biotech revolution." He warns, "The biotechnology revolution will affect each of us more directly, forcefully, and intimately than any other technology revolution in history. For that reason alone every human being has a direct and immediate stake in the direction biotechnology will take in the coming century."

Remarks by the President on Stem Cell Research GEORGE W. BUSH 451

In a nationally televised speech delivered in August 2001, President Bush gives the reasoning behind his decision on federal funding for research on stem cells derived from human embryos, which could potentially help to ameliorate or cure a number of diseases and injuries. "At its core, this issue forces us to confront fundamental questions about the beginnings of life and the ends of science."

The Political Control of Biotechnology FRANCIS FUKUYAMA 454

Fukuyama, a best-selling author and a member of the President's Council on Bioethics, proposes a middle ground between opposition to biotechnology and a wholesale embrace of it. He writes, "In the face of the challenge from a technology like this, where good and bad are intimately connected, it seems to me that there can be only one possible response: countries must regulate the development and use of technology politically, setting up institutions that will discriminate between those technological advances that promote human flourishing, and those that pose a threat to human dignity and well-being."

Questions for Discussion 463

Writing Suggestions 464

CHAPTER 14   The Challenge of Dealing with Juvenile Crime   465

The Killer Narcissists   BARBARA LERNER   465
Reacting to the shootings at Columbine High School in Colorado in April 1999, Lerner asserts, "We have more wanton schoolboy killers today because we have more narcissists, and the step from being a narcissist to being a wanton killer is a short one, especially in adolescence."

Violence by Young People: Why the Deadly Nexus?
ALFRED BLUMSTEIN   467
Blumstein analyzes a disturbing trend in the national crime rate in the late 1980s and early 1990s, and speculates on its causes, finding a strong correlation with the growth of the market for crack cocaine in the mid-1980s: "To service that growth, juveniles were recruited, they were armed with the guns that are standard tools of the drug trade, and these guns then were diffused into the larger community of juveniles."

They Do What They See   JOHN R. LION AND JONAS R. RAPPEPORT   476
Psychiatrists Lion and Rappeport note that violent behavior often follows highly publicized crimes such as the shootings at Columbine High School. "For those struggling with urges to harm or kill, saturation coverage of violent events — especially on television — becomes a disinhibitor, like alcohol."

Preventing School Violence: No Easy Answers   LYNNE LAMBERG   480
"Psychiatrists and other mental health professionals know how to identify and treat young people at risk for violent behavior, and they have a good handle on primary prevention of violence, too. . . . Implementing this knowledge is the tough part: that takes money, a network of support services, and physicians and others committed to voluntary service in their communities."

Juvenile Offenders: Should They Be Tried in Adult Courts?
MICHAEL P. BROWN   485
Brown, a professor of criminal justice, discusses the practice of trying juvenile offenders as adults, including the justifications for it, and questions its effectiveness. "At best, waivers are a short-term solution to a complex social condition that will not be simplified by transferring juveniles to the jurisdiction of the criminal court." He maintains that "juvenile court intervention holds the most promise for transforming troubled youths into productive, law-abiding adults."

Injustice and Ice Cream   BOB HERBERT   489
Herbert, a columnist for the *New York Times*, writes about a 17-year-old boy sentenced to three years in prison for stealing a box of ice cream bars. He asks, "[W]hat do we do about a criminal justice system that readily opens up a cell for Dehundra Caldwell while waving goodbye to murderers and rapists because of overcrowding?"

Questions for Discussion   491
Writing Suggestions   492

CHAPTER 15   The Meaning of Sports in Our Society   493

Where Have All The Young Men Gone?   PAUL AUSTER   493
Writing about the popularity of soccer in Europe, Auster claims that "[c]ountries now wage their battles on the soccer field with surrogate armies in short pants. It's supposed to be a game, and it's supposed to be fun, but an eerie memory of past antagonisms hovers over each match, and every time a goal is scored, one hears an echo of old victories and old defeats."

Celebration or Exploitation? Women Athletes Pose Question   LINDA ROBERTSON   494
Robertson, a sports columnist for the *Miami Herald,* writes about women athletes and body image. "While women have progressed from corsets and swim bloomers and ankle-length tennis dresses to Lycra athletic apparel, there remains a level of skepticism — or disapproval or fear — about women's display of strength."

Don't Call Jocks Sports "Heroes"   GEORGE J. BRYJAK   496
According to Bryjak, a sociologist, "Athletes should be accorded the respect and admiration they deserve. However, to speak of All-Pro quarterbacks or home-run hitters as heroes trivializes the activity of those truly deserving the title."

"What Tiger Does Best Is Golf"   JOSEPH H. BROWN   **497**

Brown, an editorial writer for the *Tampa Tribune*, doesn't think that Tiger Woods should be asked to take a stand on the controversy over the exclusion of women at the Augusta National Golf Course. "The most revealing thing about this whole episode is the double standard placed on black athletes in the spotlight, like Woods and Michael Jordan. White athletes are never asked to 'speak out' on issues or expected to 'give back' to their communities, as almost all black athletes are."

The Indian Wars   S. L. PRICE   **499**

Citing the results of a poll, Price questions the notion that Native Americans are offended by team names and team mascots based on Indian culture or stereotypes of Indians, noting that "for three out of four Native Americans, even a nickname such as Redskins, which many whites consider racist, isn't objectionable."

Polls Apart   ANDREA WOO   **503**

Published as a sidebar to Price's article, Woo's brief article presents the results of the poll of "Native Americans and sports fans in general on the use of Indian nicknames."

Mascot Supporters Insult Native Peoples   REBECCA L. ADAMSON   **504**

A Native American activist, Adamson takes issue with Price's article: "The use of polling and backroom deals at the SEC [Securities and Exchange Commission] to stop the movement against the derogatory and demeaning use of Indian names, logos and mascots can only be called what it is—greedy racism."

Questions for Discussion   **505**

Writing Suggestions   **506**

CHAPTER 16 Public Taste   **508**

Statement Concerning the Recent Actions of Abercrombie and Fitch
JAMIE CHAN, DARREN JOE, JUNG JU   **508**

Three Princeton University students speak out about a line of T-shirts that they consider offensive. "With such a powerful influence on American youth, what message does Abercrombie convey about cultural diversity, minority issues, racism, and stereotypes when it issues racially offensive shirts and then excuses them merely as an attempt at humor?"

A Small Plea to Delete a Ubiquitous Expletive   ELIZABETH AUSTIN   **510**

Austin protests the widespread use of "the 'F' word" and calls for its elimination in public discourse. "When we put private frustrations and the right to be foulmouthed ahead of public order and civility, we coarsen society and risk an avalanche of rage and violence."

A Parent's View   JOHN A. YAHNER   **512**

As a parent, Yahner struggles with the issue of how to react to, and control, the music his children listen to: "[O]ne person's junk is another person's jewel. So who's to decide what music is acceptable? In our house, with our kids, my wife and I. We are the censors; we set the limits. That's our job. It is not the government's job."

Music Censorship Limits Rights   JENNY LEETE   **514**

Jenny Leete thinks both parents and the government should keep music with offensive lyrics away from children: "It is the responsibility of parents and the government to make sure children at a young age are not purchasing and listening to music with offensive lyrics."

Breaking a Taboo, Editors Turn to Images of Death
FELICITY BARRINGER   **515**

Barringer, a media reporter for the *New York Times*, considers the issue of how the print and broadcast media should present graphic images of the dead. "In fits and starts, the reflexes that made graphic death a rarity in newspapers in the generation after the Vietnam War are being supplanted by a willingness to use such images for their emotional impact."

The Kitschification of Sept. 11   DANIEL HARRIS   **518**

Writing for the online magazine *Salon*, Harris complains about the "rhetoric of kitsch" and the way it "makes the unsaid permissible and silences dissenting opinions, which cannot withstand the emotional vehemence of its rhetoric."

Questions for Discussion   **526**

Writing Suggestions   **527**

CHAPTER 17 The Debate on the Meaning of the First Amendment   528

Bill of Rights (The First Ten Amendments to the U.S. Constitution)   528

Sometimes Freedom Is a Necessary Nuisance   CLARENCE PAGE   529
Concerned that Americans seem too willing to give up precious freedoms following the terrorist attacks on September 11, 2001, Page stresses the importance of a free, and skeptical, press. "We all have a responsibility to keep our leaders accountable because we will all share the blame when our leaders mess up."

The (No) Free Speech Movement   JULIE BOSMAN   531
In 2001, demonstrations followed the decision to run a controversial advertisement opposing reparations for slavery in the *Badger Herald,* the student newspaper at the University of Wisconsin–Madison. In an op-ed piece that was published in the *Wall Street Journal,* Bosman, the paper's editor, writes that "[t]he issues raised here go to the heart of a critical question: Are American university campuses free and open to a spirit of inquiry, or closed places where activist cohorts can determine what is, or isn't, acceptable?"

Once Nailed to the Door, Now Shuffled Out of Sight   HOWARD TROXLER   532
Troxler, a columnist for the *St. Petersburg Times,* objects to the use of "Designated Protest Areas" to keep protesters away from politicians: "[W]hen today's government claims that it has the power to keep dissent at a remote physical distance from the thing being protested—and when the police claim the power to arrest citizens who refuse to obey—it is an anti-American suppression of free speech."

The "Separation of Church and State" Myth   LINDA CHAVEZ   533
Chavez disputes the idea that the Constitution "guarantees the separation of church and state." Instead, she maintains that "[t]he First Amendment guarantees the freedom of religion, not from religion."

Going Overboard, with letters to the editor in response
ST. LOUIS POST-DISPATCH   535
Objecting to a recent court ruling that the words "under God" in the Pledge of Allegiance violate the First Amendment, the editorial claims that "even cherished legal principles, such as the separation of church and state, can be taken to absurd lengths." Although several letter writers agree, others support the court's position: "When did we become a nation that cared more about its symbols of democracy than the truths those symbols represent?"

Free Speech in the Sky   ROBIN CHARLOW   538
Cherlow writes about her reaction to the image of an aborted fetus flown overhead on a banner while her family was enjoying a day at the beach, an image that she felt crossed the line. "Well, some kind of line. But, as a constitutional law professor, I had to admit, not the legal line. To paraphrase a Supreme Court justice, one man's vulgarity is another's free speech."

Questions for Discussion   539

Writing Suggestions   540

Credits   C-1

Index   I-1

PREFACE

When the first edition of *A Rhetoric of Argument* appeared in 1982, few writing courses were devoted to teaching the skills of written argument. But in the last twenty years writing teachers have recognized the importance of these skills, both for helping students succeed at the academic writing they do in their courses and for enhancing their lives as citizens beyond the classroom. Argument is now routinely taught at all levels in the composition classroom, from first year to advanced, and many textbooks incorporating various approaches to the teaching of argument are now available. Even writing courses that are not structured around the teaching of argument include it. Courses that teach students to do cultural analyses emphasize the argumentative skills of interpretation and evaluation, courses that focus on writing across the disciplines spend time showing how issues are formed and developed in specific fields, and courses that ask students to write from personal experience link those narratives with issues of broader concern. Argument is even entering the high school curriculum since the results of national testing in the nineties demonstrated the need for teaching high school students to write persuasive essays.

The first edition of *A Rhetoric of Argument* developed an approach to teaching argument that was new in writing pedagogy at that time. It distinguished among the various kinds of questions that students were addressing in their papers—questions of definition, cause, value, and action—and linked specific ways of developing arguments with each of these questions. This approach was developed out of classroom practice in a program at Penn State University initiated by Professor Wilma Ebbitt, formerly of the University of Chicago. It is based ultimately on what are known in classical rhetorical theory as the stases, the general issues identified in Greek and Roman courtroom practice. After we worked out the pedagogy of this approach in our textbook, we introduced it in an article that appeared in *College Composition and Communication* in 1983 and applied it in other joint work. Most argument textbooks for writing courses now incorporate some form of the *stases* or questions.

The Basic Approach

Our approach has stayed the same through all three editions of *A Rhetoric of Argument*. We identify the fixed types of questions that an argument can address, helping students build their writing projects around the need to develop answers to significant questions concerning facts, definitions, causes, values and actions. These questions form a logical progression—questions of fact and definition must be settled before questions of cause can be addressed, and so on—which means that they can serve as the basis of a sequence of assignments. By executing this sequence of assignments, students can acquire and build on skills that they will use in all their writing.

An approach to argument through the basic questions is uniquely productive because it occupies a space halfway between the highly abstract identification of formal features, which is difficult to translate into specific instruction for writing, and the wholly concrete discussion of particular instances, which is difficult to generalize. The question or stasis approach begins by examining the actual arguments that develop around particular issues through the lens of general types, sorting out and identifying the kinds of questions that are considered.

Hallmarks of *A Rhetoric of Argument*

In all three editions, the following features have given students a theoretically sound, practical way to understand the arguments of others and to build their own arguments.

- **The Stasis Approach.** The third edition of *A Rhetoric of Argument* retains its emphasis on the four types of question that form the basis of the student's inquiry in every writing assignment. Indeed, the four issues or questions, developed in our adaptation of stasis theory, still constitute the backbone of the book and can easily lead to a sequence of assignments for the students. We break down each issue into its components and then suggest how these are handled as we "talk" students through the process of inventing various kinds of arguments. The advantage of this basic approach is that it teaches argument constructively rather than confrontationally. It treats arguments as positions to be developed rather than as face-offs with adversaries who are to be defeated.

- **A Wealth of Examples.** We believe that detailed examples on many different subjects, ranging from the everyday to the globally significant, are the best way both to clarify an abstract feature of argument and to strengthen the point that argument is utterly common and pervasive in all human activities. We have found in our own classroom practice, as have many others, that shared examples begin the teaching process by showing the relevance of abstract ideas, and they end the teaching process by bringing ideas down to practical applications. We have drawn illustrations from many sources and scenes of argument, including advertisements for popular products, conversational exchanges and news articles (which are not often seen as arguments), as well as popular culture, academic inquiry, and professional practice. This constant reference to examples is designed to inspire students and teachers to bring their own examples to the discussion of arguments.

- **Provocative and Contemporary Readings.** Almost every chapter in parts 1 and 2 ends with illustrative readings drawn from a range of different sources, all of them accessible to student writers. These selections offer still more examples of how arguments are developed in real situations on a variety of subjects. These readings can serve as models for analysis, reinforcing the contents of each chapter, as well as prompts for further investigation and argument on their subjects.

- **Suggestions for Writing and Class Activities.** As in the earlier editions of *A Rhetoric of Argument*, each chapter in parts 1 and 2 contains a rich variety of suggestions for classroom activity and writing assignments, and we have added even more to the third edition. Many of our classroom activities and out-of-class assignments encourage students to work in groups in order to discover how arguments work in many different contexts. Our suggestions for writing include a wide range of disciplinary issues as well as many issues of enduring public and personal interest. We explicitly encourage the treatment of argument as a collaborative and cooperative activity.

New Features of the Third Edition

While retaining our core approach, we have added many new features to the third edition, additions that reflect the considerable changes in writing instruction in the last twenty years as well as our own varied teaching experience. With the increase in training programs for teachers of rhetoric and composition, writing instructors are now much more familiar with basic rhetorical terminology than they were when the first edition of this book appeared. The new features of the third edition are meant to address this new state of familiarity among instructors at all levels, as well as new developments in the teaching of argument.

- **Organization.** Part 1 now provides a thorough introduction to the elements of arguments, with chapters on building the case (logos) and establishing credibility and appealing to emotion (ethos and pathos), along with chapters on generating claims and using language in argument. Each of the chapters in Part 2 covers one of the four basic issues in argument: definition, cause, value, and policy. Part 3 offers two chapters on conducting research and writing arguments that draw on sources, and Part 4 provides an anthology of readings on six themes of current interest to students. An alternative version of *A Rhetoric of Argument*, consisting of parts 1–3 and omitting the anthology of arguments, is also available.
- **Coverage of the Three Aristotelian Appeals.** The first two editions of *A Rhetoric of Argument* incorporated discussion of the three appeals derived from Aristotle's *Rhetoric*, but we did not use the labels *logos, pathos,* and *ethos* because at the time this descriptive terminology was not in widespread classroom use. *Logos* was and still is covered implicitly in all the sections devoted to building arguments according to issues; it is now also discussed more directly in sections on argument analysis. *Pathos* and *ethos* were addressed in former editions under the general rubric of "Accommodation," the art of shaping an argument from a particular speaker to a particular audience. The material on accommodation, concerned

with building author credibility and audience engagement, has been moved to the front of the book to reflect the classroom practice of most teachers, and it is now presented in Aristotelian terms as integral to the construction of arguments.

- **"In the Media" Arguments.** This edition uses arguments from a wide range of newspapers to introduce each chapter in parts 1 and 2. These arguments on contemporary public issues are all taken from readily accessible sources. They are short, readable, complete, and designed to simulate the way they looked when they were first published, which gives them a sense of immediacy. We think that these short pieces represent the current, widely accepted standard of public argument addressed to large, mixed audiences. These arguments are more detailed than our quick exchanges of informal, everyday conversation, but they are certainly less developed and documented than academic arguments are expected to be. As such they are a kind of approachable medium that is highly useful for introducing the basic concepts of argumentation. Each facsimile argument is followed by a rhetorical analysis in nontechnical language focusing on the argumentative feature being taught and previewing the contents of the chapter. The same points and similar analyses can be readily applied to editorials and op-ed pieces taken from current, local newspapers, and the instructor can easily find similar examples that students will find interesting.

  We should emphasize that these samples are not specially constructed idealized models. They are snatches from the art of argument as it is currently practiced, and they are certainly flawed. But we believe that their defects are a virtue, for they should lead students to question what arguers in the public media routinely offer in exchange for our adherence. They should see how these typical arguments appeal to widely held beliefs that may not be so widely held, and how in the process they construct those beliefs. And they should notice how authorities and studies are cited without the specific references that would allow readers to verify their methods and conclusions. Most instructors would demand that student writers in a classroom context produce greater detail and more specific documentation in a similar argument. This contrast between the standards of academic and public argumentation should lead students to appreciate how, as Chaim Perelman and Lucie Olbrechts-Tyteca point out, an audience is ultimately responsible for the standard of argument it accepts.

- **Attention to Analysis, Including the Toulmin Model.** New features in this revised edition are meant to teach the reciprocal processes of analyzing as well as constructing arguments. The strength of the first edition was its attention to the construction of arguments, a much more difficult task than analysis. However, this revised edition includes many aids to analyzing arguments without sacrificing the explanations that help students construct sound arguments themselves. Our discussions of arguments emphasize the skill that students need to extract the point and the major structural elements of an argument when reading, thus helping them to become stronger critical thinkers.

The Toulmin model, for example, was not widely used in composition textbooks when the first edition of *A Rhetoric of Argument* was published. It is now a routine feature of argument texts, and we have included it here as an aid to the analysis of arguments. Although we know very little about how people actually read arguments in natural situations (as opposed to the analytic approach developed in the pedagogy of critical thinking and argument instruction), if one is going to analyze arguments, one needs some kind of scheme to identify their parts. We have also added a section on logical fallacies that shows how the identification of fallacies can enhance rather than inhibit argumentative exchange.

- **More Help with Writing Arguments Throughout.** "Writing Your Argument" boxes in the chapters in Part 1 offer students practical advice on applying the instruction on constructing arguments to their own writing. In addition, the "Writing Your Own [type of argument]" sections at the end of each chapter in Part 2 give students step-by-step advice as they construct their own definition, causal, evaluation, and proposal arguments.

- **Improved Treatment of the Rhetorical Situation.** While earlier editions of *A Rhetoric of Argument* did discuss the situations in which argument occurs, this edition draws more explicitly upon the work of Lloyd Bitzer and other rhetoricians on rhetorical situation, a concept that can be applied just as fruitfully to written discourse as to oral. We present in Chapter 1 detailed consideration of the contexts in which argument occurs and how various aspects of that context influence the construction of any argument.

- **A Completely New Selection of Readings.** The readings in the third edition are completely new, with most of them published in 2000 or later. On topics of current interest such as the state of marriage and the family, gambling, responses to the attacks on September 11 and to terrorism, and prayer in the schools, they offer compelling examples of how arguments at each stasis are developed in real situations on a variety of subjects.

- **A New Anthology of Arguments.** The third edition now includes an anthology of arguments in Part 4. The readings, on the broad themes of globalization, biotechnology, juvenile justice, sports, public taste, and the First Amendment, offer instructors and students more examples of arguments at each stasis as well as additional prompts for discussion and for writing. Each chapter in Part 4 ends with a series of questions that encourage students to analyze strategies used in the readings and make connections among them.

- **Chapters on Conducting Research.** The two chapters in Part 3, Researching Arguments, provide students with ample advice on conducting primary and secondary research, locating sources in the library and on the Internet, evaluating sources found on the Internet, and integrating and documenting sources. Chapter 10 ends with a comprehensive list of web resources from across the disciplines. Chapter 11 includes guidelines and models for both the MLA and APA systems of documentation, as well as sample student arguments in both styles.

- **Attention to Visual Argument.** Students today confront an ever-increasing array of arguments in visual form. To help them learn to analyze these arguments, new Visual Rhetoric sections near the end of most chapters in parts 1 and 2 provide analyses of photographs, a political cartoon, line graphs, a recruiting poster, and an advertisement, among other images.
- **Attention to the Internet.** In addition to the coverage of Internet research in the chapters in Part 3, "For You to Discover Online" activities with the readings in Part 2 give students suggestions for conducting online research on a topic related to the reading, thus giving them a means of expanding their investigation of the issue involved. No treatment of student writing can ignore the importance of the Internet as a place to find evidence and as a means of participating in ongoing conversations about significant issues.

We offer this third edition of *A Rhetoric of Argument* as a text that brings together the best of current theory and instructional practice in written argument. It presents a tested sequence of assignments for constructing arguments along with the pedagogical support and elaboration that instructors need to bring liveliness and engagement to the classroom.

Supplements for Students and Instructors

- **Website for *A Rhetoric of Argument*** (www.mhhe.com/fahnestock). The website includes links on issues included in *A Rhetoric of Argument*, URLs from the text, a web-tutorial on evaluating sources, and free access to a search engine.
- **Instructor's Manual to accompany *A Rhetoric of Argument*.** Available for downloading at www.mhhe.com/fahnestock, the instructor's manual by Linda Macri of the University of Maryland includes overviews of each chapter, suggestions for using the exercises and activities in class, suggestions for using the reading selections, and sample syllabi.
- **Teaching Composition Faculty Listserv** (www.mhhe.com/tcomp). Moderated by Chris Anson at North Carolina State University and offered by McGraw-Hill as a service to the composition community, this listserv brings together senior members of the college composition community with new members—junior faculty, adjuncts, and teaching assistants—through an online newsletter and accompanying discussion group to address issues of pedagogy, both in theory and practice.

Acknowledgements

Beth Colson and Sonya Brown from the University of Maryland drew on their expertise with the Internet and library research to prepare chapters 10 and 11 on finding and using sources. We want to acknowledge and thank them for their significant contribution to the third edition. We also want to thank Linda Macri for drawing on her superb teaching skills in creating the online Instructor's Manual.

Many dedicated people at McGraw Hill helped us to prepare this third edition and we would like to take this opportunity to thank them. Lisa Moore, Executive Editor, remained committed to this project and brought her energy and her vision to its development. David Patterson, Executive Marketing Manager, along with field publishers Ray Kelley, Lori DeShazo, Paula Radosevich, and Byron Hopkins, developed and implemented a strong marketing plan for the text. Carolyn Lengel prepared questions, made useful suggestions, helped with the editing and, along with Meg Botteon, prepared apparatus for the readings. Laura Barthule gave us her guidance in early stages of the project. Marty Granahan handled the permissions, and Ruth Smith saw the manuscript with its many formatting challenges through production. Gino Cieslik oversaw the design of the text and cover.

Finally, we would like to thank Carla Samodulski, whose guidance and encouragement have been extraordinary. Her suggestions and advice kept us on track and helped us find better ways to present our material. She sets the standard for editors not only because of her deep understanding of the field of composition, but also because of her skill in helping this project develop in ways that enhanced its usefulness to teachers and students.

We would also like to thank the following instructors, who provided us with useful advice as we developed the third edition.

Larry Beason, *Eastern Washington University*

L. Bensel-Meyers, *University of Tennessee*

Bill Bolin, *Texas A&M University*

Vincent Casaregola, *Saint Louis University*

James Crosswhite, *University of Oregon*

Marnie Dresser, *University of Wisconsin*

Michael Alan Foster, *Illinois Central College*

Steven Frye, *Antelope Valley College*

Gil Harootunian, *Syracuse University*

David Hawes, *Owens Community College*

Paul Heilker, *Virginia Tech*

Dan Holt, *Lansing Community College*

Richard Johnson, *Kirkwood Community College*

Eleanor Latham, *Central Oregon Community College*

Jennifer Lehman, *University of Texas-Austin*

Rhonda Lemke Sanford, *Fairmont State College*

Nancy Lowe, *Pennsylvania State University*

Nancy A. Mace, *United States Naval Academy*

Pat Medeiros, *Scottsdale Community College*

Alan Merickel, *Tallahassee Community College*

Jeff Morris, *Texas A&M University*

Carol Poster, *University of Northern Iowa*

Peggy L. Richards, *University of Akron*

Carol Rodriguez, *Northern Arizona University*

Cynthia Sheard, *University of Kentucky*

Glenn A. Steinberg, *College of New Jersey*

John K. Swensson, *De Anza College*

Todd Travaille, *Buena Vista University*

Tim Twohill, *Kent State University*

Thomas A. Wallis, *North Carolina State University*

Thomas West, *Modesto Junior College*

We also thank our many students over the years, graduate and undergraduate, who have sustained our interest in teaching argument and provided countless examples of interesting topics for discussion. And as always, we thank our husbands, Stephen Fahnestock and Robert Secor, who have continued to provide many opportunities for honing our skills in argument.

Jeanne Fahnestock
Marie Secor

The further along you go in your education, the more papers you will be asked to write. Typical writing assignments will ask you to interpret works of literature, to take a stand on contemporary issues, to express your personal beliefs, to report on your research into a topic, to outline a plan of action in a hypothetical case study. All of these kinds of assignments can be looked on as invitations to argue, and all of them share certain features. You will be asked to reach a conclusion or select a preferable alternative and to give reasons for your position. Since your school practice and later life experiences will continually ask you to make a case for your view of things, one of the best ways to improve your writing is to study the art and discipline of argument.

A Rhetoric of Argument is designed to improve your skills at putting together an argument. We say improve, not develop or create, because making arguments is as natural as breathing. You already take in and produce arguments on many different occasions for many different reasons. This book aims to help you do better what you do already by making you more conscious of how you are doing it and more controlled in the choices that you make. Arguing thus resembles a physical skill like running: even if you already know how to run, instruction will help you refine your stride and do it better. We focus especially on the skill of producing an extended written argument rather than the skills of interpersonal negotiation through speaking and listening, though there are certainly overlaps and we draw many examples from conversational exchanges.

You already hear and read arguments, and you already make them frequently. You make arguments in your daily life, you make them as a member of every community you belong to, from the classroom to the home to the workplace to the special interest group, and you will make them in every aspect of your chosen field. The kinds of arguing you will be asked to do in your classes differs only in its fullness and detail from the arguments you have already been reading and making. Every discussion you have in the classroom is an argument, as people articulate and test their interpretations of what they are learning. Every report and paper you write is an argument, with a point to be made and supported. Even the lecture your teacher gives is a kind of argument, presenting a point and offering some evidence for you to consider and to learn. We would even argue that your textbook itself is an argument, presenting its explanation of the way things are and supporting its view of reality with evidence and explanation.

This book assumes that you are already skillful at arguing, and it builds on the skills you already possess in several ways.

1. Because you are already familiar with arguments in the media, whether in movie or music reviews, on talk shows, or on panel discussions, we build on your skills at reading and analyzing arguments. Each chapter in parts 1 and 2 of this book begins with a brief argument taken from a large circulation newspaper or magazine. These "In the Media" arguments are used to highlight the feature of argument under discussion in the chapter. They are real, published arguments, not cooked-up or perfected models. They have their flaws, as do all real arguments, but those flaws make them more interesting. We also conclude each chapter in parts 1 and 2 with a varied selection of readings, and these too are drawn from contemporary published arguments. These reading selections allow you to practice your analytical skills and extend your familiarity with the kinds of subjects people argue about.

2. Throughout this book you will find examples of informal, interpersonal arguing, the kind that occurs in spontaneous situations. Everyone has had the experience of trying to persuade friends and family on a variety of topics, and these little encounters exhibit many of the characteristics of more developed arguments. The extensive examples referred to in this book are meant to talk you through the process of building arguments, inviting you to take the same techniques you use in conversation and apply them to different kinds of situations and subjects.

3. The aim of this kind of approach to argument is constructive rather than negative. We want you to become careful consumers and creators of arguments, not rejecters of everything you hear and read. By learning how arguments are constructed and how they appeal to their audiences, you will come to understand how unavoidable argument is and how arguments create our beliefs and our understanding of everything we know about, from the most trivial subjects to the most profound.

4. The notion of argument that you will learn about in this book may differ somewhat from the everyday use of the term. Argument as you will learn about it here is not adversarial. Its purpose is not to win by defeating the person who represents the other side. In some situations, to be sure, issues are presented in two-sided conflict: a defendant will be acquitted or convicted; in a two-party election, one party will win and the other lose; and debates are contests between pro and con positions with clear rules for deciding a winner. But most of the situations in which arguments occur do not resemble that model. We do not assume that there are only two sides to every issue. There may be multiple positions on a subject for which one could develop a convincing argument. The purpose of argument emphasized here, rather, is inquiry. The aim is to learn how to find a position that is supportable and to construct an argument for it.

5. The skills of argument that you will learn from this book will prepare you for academic argument. You will encounter some examples of the

kinds of arguments you will read in your various classes, and you may be asked to write arguments resembling those in different fields of study. In your other classes, you will learn about the subjects that people in those fields study and the standards of evidence appropriate for different disciplines. But what you learn about constructing arguments from this book will help you, no matter what your field of study is.

6. No treatment of how arguments are constructed can ignore the explosion of argument on the Internet. Everywhere you turn, every time you click on your computer and access your browser, arguments clamor for your attention in chat rooms, advertisements, and Web sites of every description. We all need to become intelligent consumers and evaluators of the words and pictures that invite our assent. We need to learn how to recognize reputable authorities and how to argue so that *we* can become reputable authorities in whatever media we use. In this book you will find advice for conducting research on the Internet in Chapter 10, suggestions for exploring topics on the World Wide Web following the readings in Part 2, as well as ongoing discussions of how to evaluate arguments, including visual ones, wherever they are found.

7. Argument is an active process, one you can learn only by doing. This book is filled with suggestions for small- and large-scale activities that will help you learn how to make arguments. Some of these are quite informal, many of them involve collaborating with others; some can be done in class, while others send you out looking for arguments. The aim is to sharpen your sense of the world of argument that surrounds you.

Reading and Writing Arguments

Part One

1. An Introduction to the Study of Argument 3

2. Building the Case: Logos 16

3. Establishing Credibility and Appealing to Emotion: Ethos and Pathos 45

4. Generating the Argument: Questions and Claims 77

5. Expressing Appeals: Language and Voice 101

An Introduction to the Study of Argument

Chapter 1

We Encourage You to Vote Today

The Indianapolis Star

If you are looking for a reason to vote today, here are a few: sheriff, prosecutor, secretary of state, member of Congress, judge, constable, assessor.

Electing the folks who hold these offices is a fundamental task of U.S. citizenship—the one way every American adult can be part of the government that we have charged with securing our common defense, our general welfare and the blessings of liberty.

This privilege we exercise today has not always been universal, of course. Blacks were denied the right to vote until 1870 when the 15th Amendment was adopted. Women had to wait 50 more years after that.

The fact that we didn't all always get to vote is a sure sign that voting means power. Election Day is a rare opportunity not only to change our leaders but refocus our government.

Unfortunately, a solid majority of U.S. citizens do not take advantage of Election Day. If one counts both its presidential and mid-term elections in recent years, the United States has had one of the poorest voter turnout records among democracies and democratic republics across the globe. Non-voters say such things as, "My vote won't make a difference" or "It doesn't really matter who gets elected." Those excuses hold no weight, as we have seen in history that individual votes do make a difference and our

leaders make decisions that can drastically affect our future.

Why else does it matter? "Since most voting studies show that the act of voting is a lowest-common-denominator political act—that if one does not vote, one tends not to participate in any other form of constructive civic and social activity—the decline in voter participation robs the nation of its social capital, the human resources needed for the constructive pursuit of a better society," according to the Committee for the Study of the American Electorate.

By voting today, you'll set a good example for others. While you're at it, take your children with you to the polling site, as urged by the National PTA, Kids Voting USA and Council for Excellence in Government.

According to a 2002 survey by the council, 45 percent of people registered to vote said their parents took them to the polls when they were young.

The trends are worrisome; voting by young adults has dropped steadily for the past three decades. Only 42 percent of eligible 18- to 24-year-olds voted in 2000.

Because parental voting patterns are such a strong predictor of children's voting habits, we have the power to reverse the trend quickly. So vote today. And take your kids.

ANALYZING "We Encourage You to Vote Today"

We can begin our study of argument by analyzing a simple example. This argument appeared as an editorial in *The Indianapolis Star* on November 5, 2002, an election day in the city of Indianapolis and all over the country. It illustrates some of the basic features of all arguments that are worth keeping in mind as you develop your skills at constructing your own arguments.

1. An Argument Is Addressed to a Specific Audience at a Particular Time

Because this argument appeared on the editorial page of a widely read newspaper, it naturally addressed the readers of that newspaper. They are the "you" of the editorial's title, the citizens of Indianapolis referred to in the first line.

This argument was useless the day after it appeared when it was too late to vote in the 2002 election. But some parts of it are less time sensitive than others. The reminders that American citizens have a duty to vote and that some Americans have not always had that right would be relevant in 1902 or 2022. But the references to specific offices on the November 5 ballot (member of Congress, county assessor) would not apply to every election or every part of the country. This editorial was written to have an effect on a particular day. Not all arguments lose their "ripeness" immediately, but all arguments respond to their cultural and historical moment.

2. An Argument Wants Something from Its Audience

Our sample editorial wants something very specific from its readers. It wants them to go out and vote that day. That goal is obvious in the title and again in the ending with its imperative, "So vote today." The editorial also recommends that voters who are parents take their children along to the polls. Arguments differ in what they want from readers: some want to introduce ideas; some want to correct misconceptions; some want to shape attitudes and beliefs; some want money, votes, and action; and some want all of these results at once. Arguments also differ in how explicitly they ask for what they want. Some are as clear as this editorial, whereas others never get directly to the point. But like all acts of communication, they want something, even if it is only to be heard.

3. An Argument Gives Its Audience Reasons for What It Wants

The *Indianapolis Star* editorial writer does much more than simply repeat the overall claim "Vote, vote, vote." The arguer also provides many other claims that are intended to operate on readers as inducements or reasons, encouraging them to have the proper attitude that will lead to their taking the recommended action.

One line of support in this editorial comes from historical facts about extensions of the right to vote by the Fifteenth Amendment to the U.S. Constitution in 1870 and the Nineteenth Amendment in 1920. (You might be interested to see what additional voting rights were secured in the Twenty-Fourth and Twenty-Sixth Amendments.) Readers are also told that the United States has had "one of the poorest voter turnout records among democracies and democratic republics across the globe," a claim consistent with the statistic also cited that only 42 percent of eligible 18- to 24-year-olds voted in the 2000 election.

In addition to these facts about voting rights and turnout, readers are also presented with statements about values, about what is worthwhile or deserving of praise. Individual votes are called a way to "make a difference"; voting also "means power," certainly a good thing, and it is labeled the "fundamental task of U.S. citizenship." All these claims refer to the values that democratic governments are built on.

4. Not All the Reasons Are Stated Openly

An argument depends for its effect on more than the facts and values that it mentions explicitly. It also depends on elements that are not mentioned but that are brought into play by active participation from its audience. Readers (or listeners to a speech) bring their assumptions—about values and about the way things work in the world—and their reasoning abilities to the activity of taking in an argument. Many of the explicit reasons the arguer offers will work only if readers mentally draw on their implicit beliefs and assumptions to complete the arguer's case.

Take for example the second paragraph claiming that Americans who vote can be part of a government "that we have charged with securing our common defense, our general welfare and the blessings of liberty." The editorial writer assumes agreement with this list of the goals of our government, and that is hardly surprising since this list comes from the Preamble to the U.S. Constitution.

Or consider the opening sentence of the fourth paragraph: "The fact that we didn't always get to vote is a sure sign that voting means power." This claim assumes readers agree that the right to vote places power in the hands of those who exercise it, certainly a fundamental assumption in a participatory democracy. In later paragraphs, the editorial calls on widely held beliefs about parents as role models for their children and about voting as a sign of willingness to be an active citizen.

Beliefs like those just listed are suggested in almost every sentence of the editorial. In its dependence on unstated assumptions, this argument is completely typical. All arguments appeal to or evoke the assumptions and beliefs of their audiences. Nor is it necessary for the arguer to plan all of these unstated appeals. An arguer who knows an audience and its cultural context inevitably draws on shared assumptions and calls on common reasoning processes. The more successfully an argument invites an audience's cooperative participation—the more an audience completes the argument for the arguer—the more likely it is to be persuasive.

5. Arguments Are Also Supported by Calling on Readers' Attitudes and Feelings

If this article convinced anyone to vote on the day it appeared, it would certainly be because those readers who chose to act accepted the reasons it offered as support for its goal of encouraging voter turnout. Among the explicit arguments offered in the editorial are the following:

1. On the November 5 ballot there are many important offices open for voters' choices. You should vote to have an impact on the outcome of these races.
2. The right to vote has not always been available to all Americans. You should vote to exercise a once-denied privilege.

3. The United States has one of the poorest rates of voter turnout among countries where voting matters. You should vote to correct that shameful imbalance.
4. Voting sets an example of good citizenship. You should vote and take your children along.

However, if this argument works effectively on members of its audience, it will not only have established these reasons as convincing. It will also have created the attitudes, perceptions, or feelings in those readers that lead to their taking action. The word "feeling," or its synonym "emotion," can be particularly misleading here. You may think that emotion has no place in argument. What role emotions can and should play in argument will be discussed in detail in Chapter Three. For now we can recognize that a cooperative reader of this editorial is encouraged to respond with feelings appropriate to the argument, including some patriotism, some anxiety about the future, and perhaps even some guilt.

The notion that voting is a hard-won "privilege" and that it allows Americans to take part in their government should call upon feelings of pride and patriotism. The fact that Americans consistently neglect to exercise this privilege should create some shame, especially for non-voting parents who fail to set an example of good citizenship for their children. The editorial calls on other emotions when it describes the trends in low voter turnout as "worrisome." If the youngest voters do not show up at the polls, we have reason to feel some anxiety about the future of our democracy. Altogether, then, the editorial evokes a mix of positive and negative emotions and attitudes that reinforce its recommendation.

6. The Source of an Argument Matters

Unlike most of the arguments we read, no individual is given credit for writing this editorial. It appears in a daily column of editorials, the kind of column that is produced every day in every newspaper. It was probably written by a member of the editorial staff and approved by others. Because it appears where it does, we can say that it is authored by the newspaper itself, and the newspaper in this case, *The Indianapolis Star,* is a well-known and respected daily. So the source of this argument is highly credible. We trust the facts cited without further confirmation because we assume that *The Indianapolis Star* has the resources to check its facts and that it practices responsible journalism and would not knowingly print a falsehood. We also trust that the paper's editors have a sense of civic responsibility. So the source of this argument is part of what makes it convincing. If the same argument appeared in an anonymous pamphlet distributed on a street corner, it would not have the same credibility.

Most of the arguments you read will be attributed to specific authors. Sometimes the authors will have well-deserved reputations; often brief biographical entries will help you assess the qualifications of the arguer, and the place of publication will also help you determine the argument's credibility.

But even without any external props of credibility—a famous author and a prestigious place of publication—the way an argument is written, the quality of its arguments, and the sources provided for its information can go a long way to give a piece the credibility that comes from a trustworthy source.

7. A Counterargument Is Always in the Background

Nowhere in this editorial is there any suggestion that anyone has ever made the counterargument to it: Don't vote today. The editorial writer is not arguing against another stated position. This is not a "pro" argument in response to a "con" argument.

Nevertheless, some of the arguments used in this editorial were constructed to answer the typical excuses for not voting. To a claim that "My vote won't make a difference," the writer reminds readers that "we have seen in history that individual votes do make a difference." Anyone remembering the closeness of the 2000 presidential election will agree with this response. To the claim that "It doesn't really matter who gets elected," the editorial answers that "leaders make decisions that can drastically affect our future." Indeed, any claim about lack of time, energy, interest, or commitment on the part of indifferent voters is answered by the editorial's many references to what good citizenship demands.

EXPANDING YOUR DEFINITION OF ARGUMENT

The sample editorial from *The Indianapolis Star* satisfies our common understanding of what an argument is. It offers reasons urging readers who have not yet voted to go out and vote, attempting to reverse their attitudes from apathy to action. Typically we think that arguments have strong goals like this one, trying to reverse beliefs and behavior. But ask yourself how often your mind has been completely changed, your thinking and action totally altered from one position to its opposite, by an argument you read or heard. Though such complete reversals do happen, they are not common and they are not the goal of most arguments.

Far more common than arguments that change minds are arguments that increase or decrease an already existing belief or inclination. This observation about the goals of argument was emphasized by two Belgian rhetoricians, Chaim Perelman and Lucie Olbrechts-Tyteca, in 1958. They pointed out that conviction comes in different strengths. We stick to ideas and behaviors more or less firmly. Therefore strengthening or weakening rather than overturning convictions is the actual goal of many arguments. Think, for example, of candidates who address political rallies; their goal is to strengthen their supporters, not convert their opponents. Or think of courtroom defense attorneys who confront a strong case against their clients; their goal may simply be to weaken the prosecution's case by planting doubts about it in the minds of jury members. Taking existing notions and then trying to affirm or strengthen them is also a way of testing out a case to see whether it deserves our adherence.

Still another widespread and powerful purpose needs to be added to an expanded notion of what arguments can accomplish. In addition to changing minds and strengthening or weakening already existing beliefs, arguments can also construct beliefs and attitudes where none existed before. These are knowledge-forming arguments. The TV anchor who reports a study claiming that one-half of all Americans are overweight, that day-trading in stocks is a growing trend, or that relations between China and Taiwan are improving is constructing perceptions and information for us. If we accept these accounts, and we usually do, then we have some new beliefs about the world. These new beliefs may or may not contradict existing notions (usually they do not), but taking in such claims from numerous sources over the years (friends, family, teachers, reading, the media) has filled our minds.

When you limit the goal of argument to changing minds, a goal that often requires a confrontation resulting in a winner and a loser, argument becomes something to avoid whenever possible. People who are "having an argument" are angry and shouting, belligerently defending their own point of view and not listening to anyone else. But given our expanded definition of argument as a way of establishing and testing out ideas, we can see its usefulness in everything from academic inquiry to practical decision making. When argument is used for inquiry, it is a way of finding the most convincing set of beliefs about an issue. Consider the example of historians debating the causes of a war, interpreting and reinterpreting the available documents and artifacts. When argument is used for practical decision making, it is a way of deciding on the best possible course of action. Consider legislators debating new laws or even families deciding where to take their next vacation.

In our expanded sense then, argument is an activity that helps us form our beliefs and determine our actions. While we are making up our minds about what to think or do, we ought to hear whatever can be said on an issue, from every possible perspective. We may even deliberately take a position and support it when we do not particularly believe it, just to hear what the case sounds like and what others say in response. Argument is thus more a process of discussion and deliberation than a contest of opposites. Furthermore, the quality of our deliberations can be measured by how open they are and how fully those who have a stake in the outcome participate. Learning how to participate, how to argue, is important for everyone and even more important for those who feel powerless or reluctant to present their views, for whatever reason. The ability to argue helps to equalize the unequal distribution of power that exists in every institution and situation.

CONTEXTS FOR ARGUMENT

Argument in our expanded sense, as deliberation about ideas and actions, exists everywhere in our culture. Here is a brief review of different contexts in which argument occurs.

Personal

We all carry on continuing internal conversations in our heads, sometimes splitting ourselves into different voices that answer back and forth: Am I more like my father or my mother? Have I really been a good friend to X? Am I really happy in this job? Prospective college students consider choices of school and major. Prospective car buyers mull over choices of model and color. Young people obsess over relationships, old people over retirement plans, vain people over cosmetic surgery, poor people over how they are going to pay their bills, and affluent people over how they are going to invest their money. And all people turn over in their minds, sometimes for many years, philosophical issues and matters of personal faith.

Though they certainly affect our actions and what we say about them, none of these internal musings necessarily leads to a speech or a piece of writing. Yet they are all instances of argument, the stuff that makes up the fabric of our minds. Thus the move to spoken or written argument is less of a leap than you might think. You have been making internal mental arguments all your life, ever since you wondered whether grabbing your preschool playmate's cookie was going to be worth having your hair pulled.

Interpersonal

We usually think of argument not as personal debates carried on in our heads but as an exchange, more or less confrontational, with one or more other people. You can easily imagine examples of this kind of interpersonal argument: You have just seen *Spider Man* with a friend and you disagree over whether it was a good movie. You and your parents have several "conversations" over whether you should have a car at college. You try to convince a salesperson to give you a refund for the CD you didn't like. Or you find yourself at a crowded lunch table or on a long car trip with friends participating in a heated discussion about anything from politics to popular music. These are all situations in which you may try to convince someone else who disagrees with your ideas, or you may propose ideas to discover what can be said for or against them.

Many of these interpersonal arguments are, in fact, more cooperative than confrontational. We often refer to them as decision making or negotiation rather than argument. Team members working on a group project, for example, meet to determine the division of tasks. A committee formed to run an event gets together to decide on location, price of tickets, and what band to hire. An extended family has a phone conference to plan the next reunion. An Internet chat room of fans of the same team support each other through the latest losing streak. As all these examples illustrate, like-minded people, sharing a passion or an identity, can get together and create groups, more or less formal, to plan ways to promote their interests. In all these situations, along with the introductions, smiles, and chitchat, there will be issues raised, different positions offered, and agreements reached. Thus there is argument.

Professional

Another context for argument includes the interpersonal but emphasizes the creation and communication of expert knowledge. Professional communities are far more formal and structured than the shifting groups we form and the

occasional meetings we attend. Professions have entrance or license requirements, special training, gate-keeping rituals, and hierarchies in their membership. Such professional communities include medicine, the law, and the
academic disciplines as well as various business communities, from the international banking industry to the local trade association.

Because members of a profession hold common interests despite being scat-
tered geographically, they create publications or occasions for meeting and
face-to-face exchanges. In their publications and meetings they argue with
each other over the best possible beliefs to have in their area of expertise.
A history professor publishes an article in a scholarly journal on the nature of
fire companies in the nineteenth century; an astronomer announces the discovery of a planet in another star system at a professional meeting; a lawyer reviews lapses in ethical standards at a bar association meeting; a doctor tells
other specialists about a new procedure; a computer consultant reviews print-
ers for a trade magazine; a contractor writes a treatise on heat pumps for other
builders. All of these professionals are engaged in knowledge-forming and
knowledge-spreading arguments.

The writing that you do as a student in high school and college can be
thought of as a kind of professional writing. It is what you do when your job is
being a student. Some of it rehearses the types of writing you will encounter
in the working world, but much of it gives you practice in the skills that go into
that kind of writing: the ability to do research, to think critically, to select appropriate evidence, to plan a text, to express ideas clearly, and even to design
the method of presentation, verbal or visual. Competence at these skills will
serve you in any field.

Public

The final context for argument is a familiar one, a single speaker addressing a
large public audience, whether in person or on the radio or television. You may
have heard a celebrity giving a graduation speech, a politician persuading
potential voters, an award recipient addressing a banquet, a CEO speaking
to stockholders. Few of us listen to live public speeches these days; usually
we consume these speeches through print, film, television, radio, and on the
Internet. In public arguments we are not direct participants as we are in
interpersonal argument, and we need no special expertise to be part of the
audience, unlike the professional argument situation.

Public arguments can take many forms, and one form we all know is advertising. The entire advertising industry convinces us to part with our cash for
goods like BMWs and services like the psychic hot line. Some ads are entirely
visual, but these too are arguments. Web sites, whether published by an individual, an institution, a business, or a government bureau, are also public arguments about the nature, value, and significance of their subject. Arguments
on television and radio take a variety of unusual forms. On an infomercial the
viewing audience watches a representative buyer "oohing" and "aahing" over
a cubic zirconium brooch. On a political discussion show like *Crossfire*, the

audience witnesses strong presentations of incompatible positions. On a radio talk show, listeners absorb the host's commentary and a whole spectrum of callers agreeing and disagreeing. What about our daily newspapers? The editorial pages of a newspaper, as we saw above, obviously contain arguments, and in some ways the news too, which poses as information (whether presented in the paper, on TV, or on the radio), is really argument constructing the audience's preferences and world view. Similarly, the nature of arguing in the arts—in films, literature, music, and other visual media—may be indirect, but nonetheless powerful.

After reading through the above description of four contexts for argument, you will no doubt think of many cases where the distinctions overlap. People at work in an office engage in both interpersonal and professional arguments, at their desks, around the conference table, and at lunch. Many editorials appearing in mass circulation newspapers are written by professionals assuming the voice of the "public intellectual." And the arguments we consume or overhear—from the news snippet in the media, to the issue of the day in the office, to the casual conversation in the coffee bar—may find their way into our continuing internal mental conversation, where they become matters of personal argument.

SUGGESTED ACTIVITY

1. Keep an argument diary for a day. Record all the instances of personal decision making you engage in, the ads you read on public transportation, your conversations, the news reports you read or hear that catch your attention, the speeches you are exposed to from politicians on television, and so on. How many of these instances of argument added to your beliefs about the world, reinforced a belief you already held, changed your mind about something, helped you decide on a course of action?

2. In a class, each participant can present a candidate for "argument of the day" drawn from any or all of the four contexts for argument.

THE RHETORICAL SITUATION

The variety of contexts in which argument can occur should convince you how common argument is and how much practice we have all our lives in listening to and forming arguments. But though the situations are diverse, all of them, from the personal to the public, share common elements. As Lloyd Bitzer observed in an influential article in 1968 (*Philosophy and Rhetoric* vol. I, pp. 1–14), all arguments need an audience, they need an exigence or reason to come into being, and they must observe certain constraints, determining or limiting their features. Together these three elements—audience, exigence, and constraints—constitute the rhetorical situation of an argument.

Audience

Every argument is addressed to someone, even if that someone is only an aspect of oneself. Audiences vary greatly in size, from the single conversational partner to the worldwide television audience of 2 billion for the Olympics, from the handful of readers interested in a professional article to the thousands of hits on a popular web site. Audiences also vary in nearness and accessibility. The speaker before a small group can see if someone in the audience looks confused or has fallen asleep. Student writers learn, sometimes too precisely, what the teacher as audience thinks of their papers. Flaming e-mailers may be quickly singed with a response. But there is one difference in kind of audience that we need to examine more closely, the difference between listeners to a spoken argument and readers of a written argument.

Because the writer's audience is so different from the speaker's, and because this book primarily concerns written argument, we need to think about the special circumstances of the writer's audience. First, though some forms of writing, like the editorial to the citizens of Indianapolis, are targeted to specific readers, writers have no absolute control over who will pick up their texts or when. Second, in all writing situations, the "now" of the writer is never the "now" of the reader. The writer can never make moment-to-moment adjustments to the perplexities and gleams that cross a reader's face. Third, the writer can rarely be sure of the reader's background information or interest in a topic. For these reasons, Plato distrusted writing and made Socrates complain, "once a thing is committed to writing it circulates equally among those who understand the subject and those who have no business with it; a writing cannot distinguish between suitable and unsuitable readers. And if it is illtreated or unfairly abused it always needs its parent to come to its rescue; it is quite incapable of defending or helping itself" (*Phaedrus*, translated Walter Hamilton. London: Penguin, 1973, p. 97).

Because of the distance in space and time separating writer and reader, written arguments have special constraints. Writers have to work harder to imagine and anticipate audience reaction since they will not see or hear it as speakers do. Writers may have to explicitly address a smaller group among their readers since they cannot turn toward them as a speaker can. Writers sometimes become less "time bound" in their references if their piece is supposed to be read in the coming years and not just in the coming days. But even though some pieces of writing seem to address anyone at any time, all arguments are always addressed to an audience. There is an "other" out there, and that possibility of an audience affects every choice that an arguer makes.

Exigence

All arguments have another requirement, one so obvious that it is almost invisible. Arguments need a reason to exist. We do not just begin to make a case to another person unless we have a reason to make one and we can convince the other person or persons that they have a reason to listen. Often that reason is a problem that needs to be solved (what candidate to choose) or an event that needs to be responded to (an accident), or a circumstance that requires speech (a wedding toast). Furthermore, there must be some forum and occasion like a town meeting, or some demand and deadline like a research paper assignment, to bring the argument into existence. In other words, there must be some push in the circumstances and some way to respond to that push. The combination of these factors creates what can be called *exigence*.

In order to appreciate the need for exigence in argument, think of the need for appropriateness in everyday conversation. Imagine a very imperfect stranger stopping you in the street and forcefully detaining you with a harangue on an absurd topic like the merits of plastic toothpicks. You would assume the stranger was drunk or insane to speak to an unknown person at an inconvenient time about an irrelevant subject. Our irritation with such uncalled-for discourse reveals the social requirements for appropriate communication. We instinctively assume that communications addressed to us have a purpose, even if that purpose is maintaining friendships. In the same way, we expect arguments addressed to us to justify their demands on our attention—in other words to have exigence.

Exigence in Writing

In speaking situations, where the factors of time and place are powerful and inescapable, exigence is easy to understand. On the day of your "retro" party, you walk into a store and ask "Do you sell toothpicks?" and the salesperson launches into a discussion of the merits of plastic over wood toothpicks. Perfectly appropriate.

But in writing situations exigence can be harder to invoke. You could not write an essay on plastic toothpicks for a general circulation magazine without giving people a reason to want to read it. To compensate for the greater separation of writing from its audience and occasion, a written argument must frequently create its own exigence. It must give its readers a reason for reading, an answer to their fatal question "So what? Why should I be reading this? Why should anyone care about what this writer cares about?"

To solve the exigence problem, writers can always try to put their texts in the hands of only interested readers. The writer of the editorial that opens this chapter knew that its argument addressed to Indianapolis voters was going to appear in an Indianapolis newspaper. Furthermore, the editorialist could take advantage of timeliness to create exigence. The editorial urging readers to vote appeared on the very day of the election.

Without the possibility of such direct appeals to the features of an immediate rhetorical situation, writers can also try less direct means to construct reader interest. They can, in effect, preface their main argument with a mini-argument about its importance, interest, curiosity value, significance, and so on. To do so they find some feature in their material that links to the known interests and concerns of their audience. The writer with plastic toothpicks to sell may appeal to the nostalgia of an older audience or the desire to awaken interest in the styles of the 1940s in a younger audience. A clever writer can construct exigence for almost any case.

Constraints

Arguments are affected by another common element, namely the constraints or limits that shape what one can say or write to an audience in a particular situation or format. Sometimes these constraints are announced: in academic writing, students are usually told how long an essay should be, what conventions and formats it should observe, and how research should be incorporated. But unannounced constraints are no less real: if you submit a résumé and cover letter when applying for a job, you will not scribble a summary of your recent activities on a piece of torn note paper. These announced or understood constraints operate in public, professional, and interpersonal situations. After-dinner speakers sense how serious or humorous their remarks should be, professionals invariably check out their target journal to find out what articles in it look like, and even class discussions follow understood guidelines about how one enters the conversation and responds to the comments of others. Constraints are influenced by the genre, time, and place of an argument.

Genre

A *genre* is a recognized type of writing or speaking. Comic books, speeches of introduction, sports columns, commencement addresses, and research articles are examples of genres. Often the constraints that govern a type of discourse can be explained in terms of the genre conventions it follows. Formal reports have abstracts, executive summaries, and often appendices. Newspaper articles follow a predictable order in the presentation of information. Advertising copy will often include sentence fragments. Even greeting card verses are predictable in the kinds of language, appeals, and type fonts they use. Once writers choose an appropriate genre, the constraints they have to observe simplify the writing process. We pick up on these genre characteristics easily and eagerly. Often when you are given a writing assignment by a teacher, you ask to see a model of the type of paper expected so that you can reproduce its features.

Time and Place

Constraints of time are also inevitable. In speeches, time constraints operate very strongly, and we all know what it is like to be in the audience for a speech that continues when it is supposed to stop. In written texts, time means length, a feature often determined by genre. The targeted length of a piece of writing will determine how elaborate its argument can be and how much and what kinds of evidence it can incorporate. A 250-word abstract will summarize the data in a study, while the entire 250-page report will present it in great detail, with qualifications and complications. A newspaper editorial will be long enough to present some evidence for its case, but given its length constraints, it will rarely go into details that verify its evidence.

Other constraints are created by place. Again, the limits imposed by place are easy to understand in spoken argument, where something as basic as the size of a room will determine whether a speaker can be heard without amplification. Similarly, in written argument, the "place" of publication determines how widely an argument will be read depending on how, when, and where the publication is disseminated. Place of publication brings us back to target audience again since all the features that make up a rhetorical situation are intimately connected. As both reader and writer, you always need to be aware of audience, exigence, and constraints.

SUGGESTED ACTIVITIES

1. The sample argument that opens this chapter is an editorial from a large-circulation daily newspaper. Pick an editorial from any newspaper and identify the seven characteristic features of an argument in your sample.

2. Examine the opening paragraphs of the articles in a large-circulation magazine such as *Sports Illustrated, Vanity Fair,* or *Glamour.* How have the authors tried to create exigence for (that is, interest in) their subjects? Look at samples of e-mail or letters to the editor in a newspaper. How do the letter writers establish exigence?

3. Are some topics less time bound than others? For example, an argument about candidates for the 1998 election is hardly worth reading in 2001, but what about an argument about spiritual well-being? Make a list of at least five topics that do not seem time sensitive, and then construct at least one appeal that would connect one of these perennial topics to a current public preoccupation.

4. Organize a genre search. List the different genres of written texts that you encounter in a single day. How did you identify the genre of a piece of writing? By its place of publication? Its appearance on the page? Were there any texts that you could not categorize as belonging to a particular genre?

Building the Case: Logos

Chapter 2

**An Ad for Purina One
Beef Jerky Strips**

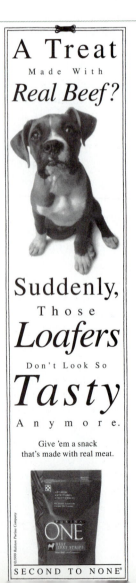

ANALYZING the Advertisement for Beef Jerky Strips

Because we are surrounded by them—on TV, on the radio, on the sides of buses, on the pages of our magazines and even on the Internet—the arguments we know best are advertisements. Ads always want us to do or buy something, and they use sophisticated appeals in words, images, and sounds to persuade us. Ads have the seven characteristics of all arguments that we outlined in Chapter 1. But in our analysis of the ad for Purina's Beef Jerky Strips, we are going to focus only on the main point and how it is supported.

Every argument has a bottom line, a main point. We can call this main point the argument's overall **claim.** The basic claim of most ads is "Buy this product." Though some ads are so indirect that they hold our attention by making us guess, eventually we figure out what the ad is selling. What product does the Purina ad want us to buy? The name of the product is not featured, but we do have a picture of it, and we can read the name on the package. The overall claim of this ad, its bottom line, is "Buy Purina One Beef Jerky Strips." We understand that bottom line, even though the ad does not use those exact words.

Why should we go along with the ad and buy this product? Why, in other words, should we find the claim convincing? We can call any statement that supports the claim a **reason.** A reason makes a claim more believable. Where in the few sentences of this ad do we find a reason for buying the product? The ad certainly lets us know Purina's dog snacks are made with "real beef" or "real meat." We are likely to accept this information as a fact about the product, even though it comes first in the form of a question presumably asked by the dog. This fact seems to offer a reason for buying the product. To test how the claim and reason work together, we can try connecting them with a "because," the word we often use to link claims and reasons.

Claim: Buy Purina One's Beef Jerky Strips
Reason: [because] they are made with real beef.

Does that fact about the product provide a reason for buying it? If we accept the connection, we must also hold another belief, a belief that makes the connection possible. We can reconstruct this connecting belief from the parts of the argument that are given. It must be some belief or assumption like the following: "You should buy dog snacks made with real beef" or "Dog snacks made with real beef are worth buying." We need some general belief about the wisdom of buying dog snacks made with real beef if we are going to agree that we should buy a particular brand because it is made with real beef. When we reconstruct this connecting belief, we see that a version of it does appear in the ad just above the picture of the product: "Give 'em a snack that's made with real meat." (We take it that "real beef" and "real meat" mean roughly the same thing.)

The statement or belief that allows us to link the reason and the claim can be called the **warrant.** A warrant allows us to make an inference, a rational connection, between a reason and a claim. An argument needs all three parts to be complete: a claim, a supporting reason, and a linking warrant, even if some of these parts are not written down but are only understood.

We could paraphrase the core argument in the Purina ad as follows. We are going to put the general belief first and the claim last, though that is not their order in the text.

Warrant: You should buy a dog snack that is made with real beef.
Reason: Purina One's Beef Jerky Strips are a dog snack made with real beef.
Claim: You should buy Purina One's Beef Jerky Strips.

We now have an argument for the main claim. But what about the reason and the warrant? Why should we agree to them any more than to the main claim itself? Do they need their own support? When we ask that question, we discover an important principle about building arguments: **Any statement offered as a reason or warrant can in turn become a claim requiring further support.** There is nothing special about a statement in itself that makes it a claim or a reason or a warrant. Instead, the role a statement plays in an argument depends on how it is used, and the same statement can have different roles, serving as a reason at one point and then as a claim requiring further support in another. In this manner, an argument grows like a chain with overlapping links, as a reason or a warrant becomes a claim requiring a further reason and warrant.

Does the ad offer further support for the reason or warrant identified above? Nothing apparently supports the reason, "Purina One is made of real beef," except perhaps the repetition of that fact. As it is, we just have to trust the company and the ad writers, and perhaps ultimately the government agencies that enforce truthful labels on products.

But what about that other key piece of support, the warrant? Why should we believe that we need to give our dogs snacks that are made with real beef? Here at last we find a use for the sentence that occupies the middle of the ad. We can paraphrase how it works to support the warrant, which is now a claim in its own argument:

Claim: You should give your dog a snack made with real beef.
Reason: Suddenly those loafers don't look so tasty anymore. (*Translated: You want your dog to stop chewing shoes.*)

This pair requires its own connecting warrant, which would be something like the following: *Dogs who are given snacks made with real beef stop chewing on shoes.* Sound plausible? The ad writers hope so. Notice, however, that they never explicitly state any beliefs about dogs and shoes. They are not writing a treatise on dog behavior. In the few seconds that any reader may spend glancing at this ad, they hope to call on many widely held beliefs about dogs and their owners: that dogs like to chew on things, that their owners do not like them to chew on shoes, that a substitute for shoes is a good idea, and that leathery snacks like Purina beef jerky strips are a good substitute. Ideally some such complex set of beliefs will be invoked by the explicit argument in the text of this ad.

Of course this ad contains additional "arguments" that are not expressed in words. The pictures could also be said to argue. That tough little dog with the "I want some" stare is another reason for buying the product. We want to give that dog a snack, and it might as well be Purina One's Beef Jerky Strips. The picture of the product facilitates the main claim; it is easier to buy a product when we know what it looks like. The distinctive size and font of the letters also assist the argument. (Consider why certain words are highlighted the way they are and why 'em is used instead of *them*.) Even that final slogan, "Second to None," is an inducement. "Second to None" rhymes with "Purina One" and helps to fix the product name in our minds. It takes great skill to craft concentrated packages of persuasion like this simple ad.

THE MATERIALS OF ARGUMENT

In the analysis of the Purina ad, we identified the parts of an argument put together by someone else. Now suppose you have to build your own argument, not just take another person's argument apart. What materials can you draw on to persuade others to believe what you want them to believe or to act the way you want them to act?

This question has been asked for thousands of years, and some of the best answers are the oldest. In ancient Greece, Aristotle identified three basic sources of appeal that can combine into an effective argument; these are known by the Greek terms *logos, ethos,* and *pathos.* To begin with rough distinctions, we can define **logos** as the basic case made in an argument, namely the claims, and the facts, beliefs, and values offered to support them. **Ethos** stands for the appeal that comes from the arguer's character, including the arguer's recognized social roles and revealed personal qualities. **Pathos** refers to appeals based on the audience for the argument, on who they are and what touches them. We will look at each of these appeals separately, starting with logos in this chapter. But keep in mind that these three appeals blend and reinforce each other, and in every actual argument they are intertwined.

BUILDING THE LOGOS

To look at the process of building the logos, the basic case, from the bottom up, we can take ourselves through an imaginary situation that calls for an argument. In doing so, we will again use the terms introduced in the sample analysis at the beginning of the chapter.

Suppose you and a friend (your audience) are in a video store selecting a movie (your exigence) when a title in the Classics section catches your eye and you say, "Let's see *Rear Window.*" Your friend asks, "Why that one?" and you reply "It was directed by Alfred Hitchcock."

Brief as it is, this exchange is an argument. It is not, of course, an argument in the popular sense of "angry confrontation"; it is an argument in the general sense of trying to convince someone about something. You want to persuade your friend to take action—to rent and watch *Rear Window* with you. This goal can be called your main point, conclusion, thesis or, sticking with the term we used before, your **claim.** The answer you provide to your friend's question ("Why that one?") can be called the grounds, premise, support or, again as above, the **reason** for your claim. If what you offer in response to your friend's question works as a reason, you should be able to connect it to your claim with the word "because." Try it.

But if your friend is convinced by your argument and watches *Rear Window* with you, it is also because he or she has agreed to something you never mentioned. Look again at the claim/reason pair you produced in your conversation:

Claim: Let's see *Rear Window*

Reason: [because] it was directed by Alfred Hitchcock.

What else do you have to believe in order to be convinced that the fact that Alfred Hitchcock directed a movie is a reason for seeing it? If you were to express the missing belief here it would be something like the following: "Any movie directed by Alfred Hitchcock should be seen or is worth seeing." We can call this missing piece, as we did in our analysis above, a **warrant**. The warrant "connects" the claim to the reason. It makes an inference between the claim and the reason possible.

A simple argument, then, actually involves three elements. We can rearrange them with the claim last, adding the word "therefore" to show how our claim is drawn from the warrant and the reason together.

Warrant: Any movie directed by Hitchcock should be seen.

Reason: *Rear Window* was directed by Hitchcock.

Claim: [Therefore] let's see *Rear Window*.

In Aristotelian logic, such a three-part argument is called a syllogism, and its parts carry different labels. The warrant is called the *major premise*, the reason is called the *minor premise*, and the claim is called the *conclusion*. If you have taken a course in logic, chances are you have been introduced to syllogisms like the following famous example:

Major premise (Warrant): All men are mortal.

Minor premise (Reason): Socrates is a man.

Conclusion (Claim): Therefore, Socrates is mortal.

We can also lay out the three-part structure of our argument using a scheme adapted from the British philosopher Stephen Toulmin (whose views on expanding arguments will be discussed below). In a Toulmin diagram of a three-part argument, reasons are on the left, claims are on the right, and linking warrants, which make the connection between the claim and reason possible, are placed below.

[Reason] Rear Window was directed by Hitchcock. → **[Claim]** Let's see Rear Window.

↑

[Warrant] Any movie directed by Hitchcock should be seen.

Ways of schematizing an argument like the syllogism or the Toulmin model will help you see the relationships among its parts. But in ordinary speaking and writing, the order of the elements can vary greatly. When all three parts of an argument are present, the reason and the warrant can come before, after, or on both sides of the claim.

1. *Rear Window* was directed by Hitchcock and his movies are always worth seeing. Let's see *Rear Window*.
2. Let's see *Rear Window*. It was directed by Hitchcock, and all his movies are worth seeing.
3. *Rear Window* was directed by Hitchcock. Let's see it. Any movie of his should be seen.

In any order, all three parts make up the basic elements of a simple argument. Furthermore, in everyday arguments, repeating precisely the same words from one part of an argument to another is not necessary, as long as the substitutions used are basically synonymous. For example, we have used "worth seeing" and "should be seen" as equivalents in our versions of the video store argument.

Working either alone or with a group of your classmates, supply a reason and warrant for each of the claims listed below.

1. Campus parking for students should be expanded.
2. National parks should be off limits to snowmobilers.
3. Let's take a vacation at the beach this year.
4. Buy a car that gets at least 26 miles per gallon.
5. You should study at least three hours a day.

EXERCISE 2.1

One-Part Argument: The Claim Alone

Once we have a simple three-part model in place, we can do some interesting things with it by taking away, multiplying, or adding parts. These variations on the basic three-part argument are possible because arguments are made by real people in real situations. Since different kinds of speakers adjust to different audiences and circumstances, arguments exist in a variety of forms.

A basic argument may have three parts, but which parts need to be expressed will depend on the situation and audience. Sometimes only one part of an argument is needed: the claim itself. All arguers make statements that they expect readers to agree to without added reasons or linking warrants. If you suddenly found yourself in a burning building, smelling smoke and seeing flames, and you heard someone yell "Let's get out of here!" you would not wait for an explicit reason before following that recommendation. The situation and your beliefs about fire, danger, and self-preservation would convince you quickly.

Even in less dramatic situations, arguments cannot go on forever. They all come down to some bottom-line statements that are claimed without further support. If you and your friend in the video store shared a long history as movie buffs, just the statement "Let's see *Rear Window*" might be convincing. You could count on your friend's knowing enough movie history to recognize that *Rear Window* was directed by Alfred Hitchcock and that a movie by Hitchcock is worth seeing. It may seem strange to think that just stating a claim is a kind of arguing, but that is what happens when an arguer merely makes a statement in a way that assumes the audience's agreement.

Two-Part Argument: The Enthymeme

When you sense that your audience will not immediately accept a claim, you will naturally offer at least one supporting point or reason for it. By offering a reason, you are trying to get your audience to agree with your claim while demonstrating that you have a reason for your claim in the first place. The "claim + reason" unit is very common in everyday arguments. People usually provide only those two parts, drawing on shared knowledge or values to connect them.

Aristotle pointed out in his *Rhetoric* that all three basic parts of an argument are rarely expressed in informal or public situations. Traditionally, a two-part argument has been given Aristotle's label, **enthymeme.** A reason plus a claim forms the typical enthymeme; warrants can often be left out because they often seem redundant or obvious. Readers or listeners can supply the missing warrant from their own stock of knowledge or values. The fact that audience members must, in a sense, participate in completing a two-part argument by supplying the third part is an advantage to this form. Because audience members have to draw on or construct the beliefs that will round out the argument, they are participants in their own persuasion.

Though typically an enthymeme consists of a claim and a reason, actually any two parts from a full three-part argument can be used. In the video store example, the imaginary speaker used the typical "claim + reason" pair: "Let's take out *Rear Window*. It was directed by Hitchcock." But the speaker could have used the warrant in place of the reason: "Let's see *Rear Window*. Hitchcock's movies are always worth seeing." In this case, the listener has to infer that *Rear Window* was directed by Hitchcock. Or the speaker might even have left out the claim itself and offered the warrant and reason instead: "*Rear Window* was directed by Hitchcock. His movies are always worth seeing." This time, the listener constructs the claim that follows from these two statements. In each case, the two-part argument depends on the audience for completion.

Expanding Arguments: Branching Support

As we have seen, although there are three basic parts in an argument—a claim plus a reason, linked by a warrant—usually just two parts, claim and reason, appear. The basic three-part model can be expanded, though, to adjust to the audience you are trying to convince. For example, when arguers sense resistance to a claim, they often provide more than one supporting reason for it. To return to the video example, you can imagine yourself introducing a whole new line of support to convince your friend to agree to your choice of movies: "Let's see *Rear Window*," you say, "because it was directed by Alfred Hitchcock **and** it stars James Stewart." We can schematize the argument as follows:

Let's see *Rear Window*.

↗   ↖

Rear Window was directed   It stars James Stewart.
by Hitchcock.

You now have a single claim supported by two reasons. Your argument is growing by branching out. Of course your new reason, "It stars James Stewart," also requires its own warrant, "A movie starring James Stewart is worth seeing." You have started a separate line of argument. Each claim-reason pair (enthymeme) could be expanded into three-part form, repeating the claim each time. But it is usual in actual arguments for the claim to appear once, followed by the reasons that support it independently. And you could go on adding reasons: because it is a good mystery; because the hero is confined in a wheel chair; because it is so classically "fifties." Each new reason requires its own new linking warrant, stated or not. Your argument expands as you branch out to new reasons for the same claim.

Working either alone or with a group of your classmates, supply at least two reasons for each claim listed below.

1. The situation comedy *Friends* provides a realistic/unrealistic view of city life.
2. Manned space flight with the shuttle should continue.
3. Wild animals should not be kept in cages.
4. Internet providers should ban pop-up ads.
5. Free downloading of music actually helps bands on independent labels.

Expanding Arguments: Chains of Support

Arguments expand not only when you add new reasons and invoke new warrants, but also when you support the ones you have already supplied. Let's look again at the core three-part argument above: "Let's see *Rear Window* because it was directed by Alfred Hitchcock and a movie by Alfred Hitchcock is worth seeing." A skeptical friend could question either your reason or your warrant. When that happens, each has to be treated as a claim requiring *its own* further support.

Whether a reason or a warrant or both need further support depends, as usual, on the audience. Suppose in response to your reason, that *Rear Window* was directed by Hitchcock, your doubting friend asks, "How do you know that?" You point to the DVD case and answer, "The label says the film was directed by Hitchcock." Your new claim-reason pair ("*Rear Window* was directed by Hitchcock because the label on the DVD case says so") depends of course on its own warrant, "The labels on DVD cases are a reliable source of factual information about who directs a film." The warrant in this case is a basic belief about the credibility of a source of evidence.

Now suppose that your friend (who is becoming rather tiresome) challenges your warrant that "A film directed by Hitchcock is worth seeing." That warrant in turn becomes a claim. You might offer as support that "Film critics and historians have almost unanimously praised Hitchcock's movies." This new claim-reason pair requires its own warrant that might be phrased as follows: "The opinions of film critics are reliable indicators of what is worth seeing." This warrant expresses a widely held belief in the trustworthiness of authorities.

To satisfy a more demanding audience, then, our argument begins to grow like a chain, where a claim is supported by a reason and warrant which in turn become claims supported by further reasons and warrants. To diagram this expanding structure, we can add on to the basic Toulmin scheme used above.

Reason: *Rear Window* was directed by Hitchcock.   →   **Claim:** Let's see *Rear Window.*

↑   ↑

The DVD label lists Hitchcock
as the director.   **Warrant:** A movie by Hitchcock is worth seeing.

↑

Film critics and historians have almost unanimously
praised Hitchcock's films.

If we were to fill out this structure with the warrants that link all the claim-reason pairs, we could produce a diagram like the following. Notice that we have highlighted each three-part unit by arranging it in a Toulmin diagram. Both the reason and the warrant in our main argument become claims in the subsidiary arguments.

Reason: The label on the DVD   →   **Reason:** *Rear Window* was   →   **Claim:** *Rear Window*
says it was directed by Hitchcock.   directed by Alfred Hitchcock.   is worth seeing.
                                          [becomes a claim requiring   [Let's see it!]
                                          its own support]

Warrant: Labels on DVDs are reliable sources of
information about a film, including the director.

Reason: Film critics praise   →   **Warrant:** A movie directed by
Hitchcock as a director.   Hitchcock is worth seeing. [becomes
                                        a claim requiring its own support]

Warrant: Film critics are reliable authorities
on what movies are worth seeing.

EXERCISE 2.3

Go through any of the sample arguments about *Rear Window* provided above and replace *Rear Window* with your favorite movie or with a recent video release that you want to see. Now imagine yourself in a video store trying to convince a friend to see this movie. What is the first reason you will give to create a two-part argument? What warrant will connect that reason with the claim? Next branch out and provide more reasons for your choice. Then imagine that your friend is somewhat skeptical and locate places where you will have to provide additional arguments for your reasons or warrants.

EXERCISE 2.4

Working either alone or with a group of your classmates, identify the claim-reason pairs (the enthymemes) in the following short arguments. In each case, write out a three-part version of the argument, supplying the missing part, if any. Remember that in real arguments, claims and reasons can be stated more than once, and they do not necessarily come close to each other.

1. The national outpouring after the Littleton shootings has forced us to confront something we have suspected for a long time: the American high school is obsolete and should be abolished. In the last month, high school students present and past have come forward with stories about the cliques and the artificial intensity of a world defined by insiders and outsiders, in which the insiders hold sway because of superficial definitions of good looks and attractiveness, popularity and sports prowess.

   —Leon Botstein, "Let Teen-Agers Try Adulthood," *New York Times*, May 17, 1999, p. A26.

2. The statistics are undeniable: As motorists advance through their 70s they are increasingly likely to have accidents. The incidence increases between 75 and 79 and climbs steeply after that. The accident rate for drivers 85 and older is far higher than that of teenagers.

   Considering that record, it's reasonable to subject older drivers to more frequent and intense examinations.

   —"Yes, Do Test Elderly Drivers," *Los Angeles Times*, August 8, 1999, p. 4.

3. Solving our region's growing traffic problems is an urgent priority for all of us. For some, however, the urgency is even greater. A few extra minutes shaved off a working parent's commuting time is important, but a few extra minutes shaved off the response time of an ambulance crew can make the difference between life and death.

   —"This Is an Emergency Situation," *Washington Post*, June 6, 1999, p. B8.

EXERCISE 2.5

Search through the pages of your local newspaper to find a news story about an improvement scheme that is currently being proposed in your area. Generate at least three claim-reason pairs for going ahead with this proposal. Then construct the warrants that make these claim-reason pairs possible.

EXERCISE 2.6

Working either alone or with a group of classmates, write down several statements that you would agree with about any of the following topics, or a similar one of your own. Then see what claims you could support with these statements. Expand each reason-claim pair into a three-part argument by supplying the missing warrant. (You may go on to use these three-part arguments as building blocks for a written argument.)

1. Students working and going to school at the same time
2. The science courses you took in high school
3. Your friends' beliefs about politicians

⎡ WRITING YOUR ARGUMENT ⎤

**BUILDING AN ARGUMENT FROM
CLAIM-REASON PAIRS**

When you are analyzing a written argument, like our opening example, you should always try to identify the claim-reason pairs, or enthymemes, that the writer offers. When you are constructing your own argument, the need for claim-reason pairs can guide you in two ways.

1. If you already know the claim you are supporting, you can generate reasons by imagining that your intended readers are asking you, "Why do you believe that?" Suppose you think a new stadium should be built for a team you support. What reasons can you think of that fit this situation? Knowing that you have to come up with reasons will stimulate your thinking and lead you to conduct further research. You can help this process along by writing your claim at the top of a sheet of paper or typing it into a new computer document and then writing "because" three or four times on separate lines below it. Then fill in the blanks behind each "because." Next look over the reasons you have generated and decide which might need to be treated as claims requiring their own support. For each one, write another "because" indented on the next line and try to fill in the blank. Your brainstorming sheet will look like the following:

Claim: _____

Reason: [because] _____

Reason: [because] _____

Reason: [because] _____

Reason for the reason* [because] _____

Now go back, review your individual claim-reason pairs, and construct the warrant that is necessary to connect them. For convenience you can use a diagram like the following:

Reason _____ →   Claim _____

↑

Warrant _____

After you have identified the warrants that connect each reason with its claim, consider whether your audience might need to have any of the warrants supported as well.

2. If you know what subject interests you, or what subject you have been assigned to investigate, but you are not sure what claims you could make about it, the need to generate claim-reason pairs can still guide you. This situation is common when you are first researching a subject.

　　Based on the reading and thinking you have done, write down several statements about your subject that you consider believable. Treat these as "reasons" (you can

---

*Provide further support wherever you judge that your audience needs it.

even put a "because" in front of them). Then see what claim they can support. You can use the word "therefore" as a prompt to help you invent a potential claim. For example, suppose that you are undecided about whether your team should build a new stadium. You could list several facts and beliefs that seem relevant to this proposal, and then see what overall claim they can support.

Reason: [because of] _____

Reason: [and because of] _____

Reason: [and because of] _____

Claim: [Therefore] _____

Remember that in building up to a claim in this way, you may also have to supply reasons for your reasons.

After you have your reasons and claim, review your individual reason-claim pairs and supply the necessary warrant for each so that you can assess the plausibility of the case you are building, for yourself and your potential audience.

Reason _____   →   Claim _____

↑

Warrant _____

You can use either of these two methods—claim first or reasons first—when constructing an argument. Some people believe that the first method is actually more common, that researchers usually start with a potential claim or claims in mind and see what support is available, abandoning claims with insufficient support and keeping only those with the strongest support. Whichever process you follow, though, remember that the core of your developing argument will be the claim-reason pairs you can generate.

Expanding the Three-Part Argument: The Full Toulmin Model

As you have seen, the three-part model of a basic argument—claim, reason, and warrant—can be expanded when more reasons are added or when a reason and warrant are treated as claims requiring further support. This three-part model can also be expanded in still another way. To understand this new direction we have to introduce another aspect of argument.

Qualifiers

People make claims with varying degrees of certainty or conviction. They often qualify their claims, offering them boldly or tentatively, depending on what seems to be at stake in the situation and how compelling their reasons are. Our movie rental claim, for example, could be qualified in the following ways:

We absolutely have to see this movie.
We probably should see this movie.

We might enjoy this movie.

We could take this movie out if there's nothing better available.

Most claims are hedged in ways like these because we know that special circumstances or possible counterarguments could weaken our case. So we add a **qualifier** to the claim, adjusting the certainty according to the strength of our support and the amount of resistance we expect. The Toulmin scheme for laying out arguments includes a place for the qualifier in the claim. (In an actual claim, the qualifier may appear in a different place from the one suggested by the diagram.)

$$\text{Reason} \quad \rightarrow \quad \text{[Qualifier] Claim}$$
$$\uparrow$$
$$\text{Warrant}$$

The qualifier in a claim is often directly tied to circumstances that can affect the argument. To return to our video store example, suppose your friend has heard your reasons for taking out *Rear Window* and is inclined to agree. But your friend dislikes older movies in black and white and so will agree to rent *Rear Window* only if it is in color. We can call your friend's stipulation the **rebuttal condition** in the argument. If this condition is present, if *Rear Window* is in black and white, then the claim no longer holds. We can add the rebuttal condition (and there could be more than one) to the Toulmin scheme in a way that shows its impact on the claim.

Counterarguments

The qualifier in a claim is also affected by potential counterarguments. To return to our example, suppose your friend has an irrational dislike of Grace Kelly, the beautiful actress who left Hollywood in the 1950s to marry the Prince of Monaco. It happens that the female lead in *Rear Window* is played by Grace Kelly. Your friend's dislike of Kelly is an argument against seeing the movie. You can deal with this argument by acknowledging it and then setting it aside; it weakens the case and increases the hedging but doesn't destroy it. You maintain that the argument based on the director is stronger than the counterargument based on dislike of Grace Kelly.

It was directed by Alfred Hitchcock. $\quad \rightarrow \quad$ [Probably] Let's see *Rear Window*.
$$\uparrow$$
A Hitchcock film is worth seeing

although it stars Grace Kelly.

When you add a counterargument in this schematic way, you can see that one way to strengthen the argument would be to answer the counterargument.

Thus an argument recommending *Rear Window* could turn into a defense of Grace Kelly as an actress.

This fuller scheme for laying out the parts of an argument, developed by the British philosopher Stephen Toulmin, is widely used in the teaching of writing and critical thinking. Qualifying a claim according to the strength of the reasons or the rebuttal conditions is a wise practice in everyday argument since we can rarely prove our claims; we can only make them more probable.

EXERCISE 2.7

Working either alone or with a group of classmates, expand one of the three-part arguments you developed for Exercise 2.6 by supplying a rebuttal condition or counterargument. Depending on your rebuttal condition or counterargument, add an appropriate qualifier to your claim. (You may go on to use this expanded argument as part of a written argument.)

BUILDING ARGUMENTS WITH OTHER POSITIONS IN MIND

In our long-playing example of two people deciding what DVD to rent, one speaker already had a course of action in mind. The only problem was how to convince a friend to go along. But while this simple example is typical of the many little daily arguments we make, it does not reflect the processes we go through to help us make up our minds in the first place. In more complex situations—how to respond to an assignment, whom to vote for in an election, what position to take in a controversy—we usually do not know immediately what to believe or do. In cases like these, we use the process of argument itself to help us think through an issue and form a claim. We try out the arguments for various positions, testing to see which seem the strongest to us or to the audience we want to persuade.

An extended example will show how the process of examining arguments on at least two sides of an issue can help you decide what claim to support and how to put together a case for it. Suppose that for a film course you have been assigned to assess the practice of colorizing black and white films and broadcasting them on television in the new colorized format. You can easily find many published arguments on this issue. Reading through them, you can list the various reasons for approving or disapproving of colorization. You can also come up with reasons of your own. The reasons on either side can then be lined up according to whether they directly answer each other.

Colorizing rejuvenates black and white movies.	**Colorizing ruins black and white movies.**
1. The technology of computer colorization is good and getting better.	1. The colors imposed on movies look unnatural and bleed into one another.
2. Colorization improves the TV and DVD markets for old movies.	

3. The original directors would have used color had it been available.

3. Black and white film is an aesthetic medium in its own right.

4. Colorizing makes movies accessible to audiences that would otherwise not see them.

4. These audiences are not seeing the movies as they were meant to be seen.

5. Colorization makes movies appear less dated.

5. Colorization distorts film history.

6. Prominent directors, actors, and critics object to colorization.

7. You can always turn the color off.

You could support each individual reason in these lists with additional reasons, of course. For example, you could support the point about black and white being an artistic medium in its own right by citing Stephen Spielberg's choice of this medium for substantial parts of one of his most important movies, *Schindler's List*.

One side may have more reasons than the other, but arguments are not decided just by counting the reasons. One reason on one side may seem to outweigh all the others. In our example here, the appeal to film history, to being faithful to the original artistic form of a movie, would be more convincing to some audiences than any other reason. For others, the strength of the overall case on one side or the other, without weighting the individual points, could seem decisive. It is even possible that someone who has gone through the process of making the case for each side will conclude that neither position is stronger than the other. Whatever conclusion you reach, conducting this kind of analysis, carefully compiling all the reasons for different positions, improves your chances of reaching a considered position and finally producing a fair and thorough argument. Since the process of making up one's mind depends on knowing whatever can be said on all sides of an issue, it makes sense to be patient and willing to take into account whatever and whoever can contribute to a debate.

WRITING YOUR ARGUMENT

TAKING ACCOUNT OF OTHER POSITIONS

The full Toulmin diagram of an argument includes a place for you to fill in the conditions and counterarguments in the minds of your audience that could weaken your claim. The diagram provides a visual scheme that can help you put together your response to other positions.

Begin by identifying competing claims about the topic you are investigating. It is common to form claims that are opposed to each other, pro and con, but you can also create positive claims that cannot be maintained simultaneously by the same person. They cancel each other out in a sense; you cannot hold both or all of them at the same time. The two claims in the example above, "Colorizing rejuvenates black and white movies" and "Colorizing ruins black and white movies," are incompatible. If you come up with incompatible claims, write each one at the top of a piece of paper or a computer screen and list reasons for each underneath. Where possible, line up the reasons that contradict each other.

Claim A _____   Claim B _____

Reason _____   Reason _____

Reason _____   Reason _____

Reason _____   Reason _____

and so on as needed.

Following this process should help you determine which position deserves your adherence overall. You can also use it to strengthen the claim you finally choose by dealing directly with any reason that seems to weaken your claim. To help you in this process, fill in the slots in the full Toulmin diagram to help you visualize how a claim-reason pair can be strengthened by taking a counterargument into account. For example, you can concede the validity of the counterargument by qualifying your claim to accommodate it, or you can argue against (refute) the counterargument. (For more on dealing with other positions, see Chapter 3, pp. 56–58.)

Reason _____   →   [Qualifier] Claim _____

        ↑

Warrant _____

                    Rebuttal Condition/
                    Counterargument _____

Working either alone or with a group of your classmates, identify competing claims about one of the following topics, then list reasons for each claim underneath. Line up any reasons that contradict each other. Then decide how you would weight the reasons you have listed. Which claim is stronger?

1. Reality television shows such as *Survivor* and *The Bachelor*
2. State lotteries
3. School vouchers
4. Privacy on the Internet
5. Peace-keeping role of the United Nations

EXERCISE 2.8

THE BUILDING BLOCKS OF ARGUMENTS: VALUES AND FACTS

In the sample arguments we have worked through so far in this chapter, we have stressed the importance of the basic three-part structure: claim, reason, and warrant. Claims are either given and then supported by reasons and warrants, or they are discovered from the available reasons and warrants.

Where do these building blocks, reasons and warrants, come from? The fundamental building blocks, the sources or bases of all of the types of arguments discussed in this book, are values and facts.

Let's focus on reasons for the moment to see how facts and values can be drawn on to support them. Compare the following two reason-claim pairs.

EXAMPLE A:

Reason: The disabled elderly confined in long-term care facilities deserve to be treated humanely and generously.

Claim: Therefore we should carefully inspect and control long-term care facilities for the elderly.

EXAMPLE B:

Reason: There are almost 3 million disabled elderly in long-term care facilities in the United States today [1999].

Claim: Therefore we should carefully inspect and control long-term care facilities for the elderly.

Both these examples argue for the same claim, but in the first the reason offered is a value and in the second the reason is a fact. You can see the difference between these two reasons by considering the different kinds of additional support each would need. You could support the statement of fact, reason B, by citing a credible source for statistics about residents in long-term care facilities. You could not, however, support Reason A by turning to census data. It is not a fact that can be verified; it is a value judgment. It can still be supported or strengthened, but it offers a different kind of basis for building a case.

The Belgian rhetoricians Chaim Perelman and Lucie Olbrechts-Tyteca were the first to emphasize the categories of values and facts as the building blocks of arguments. In their joint work, *The New Rhetoric*, they described values and facts as "sources of agreement," the materials that can be used as common ground between the arguer and the audience. Since arguments cannot go on forever, they have to stop (or begin) somewhere, and Perelman and Olbrechts-Tyteca believed that these stopping (or starting) points are always the values and facts that an arguer judges an audience will accept. We will review briefly the differences between these two broad categories and then discuss the special problem of finding or verifying facts for an argument.

EXERCISE 2.9

Consider the reasons that you came up with for Exercise 2.6 or 2.8 and decide whether each reason is a fact or a value.

Values

Values are beliefs about what is good or bad, moral or immoral, right or wrong, beautiful or ugly. Our values determine the attitudes that we hold toward ideas, goals, actions, people, and things. The sample argument above calling for inspection of long-term care facilities invoked a certain attitude toward the elderly based on their value as people deserving special care and respect. The argument at the beginning of Chapter 1, which urges citizens of Indianapolis to go to the polls, invokes the value of voting in a democracy ("Election Day is a rare opportunity not only to change our leaders but refocus our government"). Even our video store example relies on both a fact as a reason (*"Rear Window* was directed by Alfred Hitchcock") and a value judgment about artistic works as a warrant ("A movie by Hitchcock is worth seeing"). Values can also be thought of as motives for action. If you value something strongly and positively, then you will act to acquire or preserve it. In fact, the strength of a value can be measured by what you are willing to sacrifice for it, by how much you are willing to pay in time, money, or energy to acquire or preserve it.

Values will be discussed in greater detail in Chapter 8 on evaluation arguments. Here we simply want to stress one important feature of values as sources of agreement. Perelman and Olbrechts-Tyteca pointed out that the values appealed to in an argument depend greatly on the particular audience being persuaded. A value appeal that one audience responds to strongly might have little force with another audience. An audience of British citizens, for example, will tend to have a different attitude toward, or evaluation of, their Queen than an audience of American citizens will. Perelman and Olbrechts-Tyteca also stressed that while many people may share the same basic "list" of values, they do not prioritize the values on that list in the same way, and they do not always agree about which value from the list is the most important one to call on in a particular case. So arguments have to be introduced that weight one value over another and these, in turn, will depend on still other values that the audience will acknowledge. The bottom line is that arguers have to be very sensitive to their audience's particular values.

Facts

Unlike values, which may have limited appeal, facts are by definition the kind of statements that we imagine everyone will agree with. **Facts** can be defined as answers to the basic questions about reality involving who, what, where, when, how many, and so on. Who won the Super Bowl in 1977? Where is Botany Bay? When was the Treaty of Utrecht signed? How many stocks posted gains in today's trading on the NASDAQ? We label as facts any answers to such questions that we believe should meet with unanimous agreement, whether that agreement is given immediately or after verification. So strong is our assumption that "facts" should command everyone's agreement that when we encounter someone whose recognition of facts is radically different from our own, we tend to consider that person not just ill informed but abnormal.

Facts need to be considered from two perspectives. First, there are those facts that you count on your readers agreeing to immediately. Facts treated as unproblematic should be phrased in a way that makes them easy to accept; the precise wording of such a statement is critical if is to be recognized as obvious fact. Second, arguers often need to use sources to verify their facts and to discover them in the first place. Such sources can include personal experience, the testimony of others, and authoritative sources in print or on the Internet.

Stating Facts

Think about how you respond to statements presented to you as facts. Whether or not you accept a statement as a fact depends on what is already in your mind. Suppose, for example, you read that Abraham Lincoln is buried in Springfield, Illinois. Although you have never heard that fact before, you probably do not doubt it because this new fact lines up with your existing knowledge of Lincoln's associations with Illinois. The new fact fits, so you accept it readily. But if someone told you Lincoln is buried in Hawaii, your reaction would be quite different.

Whether a new fact passes without a challenge depends in part on how it is worded. Suppose you hear or read the statement that "the opossum is a marsupial." At first, the word *marsupial* may make you think of Australia, kangaroos, and koala bears, while the word *opossum*, on the contrary, suggests an animal that can be found in your own backyard. Because these bits of information seem to contradict each other, you may tend to doubt the new fact. How can an Australian animal wind up on your side of the world? However, if the statement had been worded differently—"The opossum is the only North American marsupial"—this new fact might have met with less resistance. Those careful qualifications, "only" and "North American," show that the framer of the statement knew the audience's predictable previous knowledge might make the simple assertion "The opossum is a marsupial" difficult to accept.

Since wording can be so important, you, as an arguer, should try to anticipate your readers' reaction to any statement you present as a fact. Are they likely to know it already? If they are, then you can simply assert the fact. The earth revolves around the sun, hot air rises, and some people lose money on the stock market. The barest prose suffices for simple, well-known facts. At the same time, as a reader you should be careful of statements that are presented as patently obvious facts. Any writer can make a clear, absolute statement about anything, and one way to make a controversial statement appear to be a widely accepted fact is to state it in a simple, direct way.

Using Sources

Sources for Verifying Facts

Sometimes you need more than careful wording to make your readers accept a statement as a fact. They are not going to accept it just because you state it. You have to verify it. To "verify" a fact usually requires citing the source where you found it in the first place. Ideally, this source should be accessible to your readers so that if they want to go and check it for themselves, they can.

The sources you used to find the information in the first place are also the means for verifying facts. To verify, you acknowledge in your argument whatever source convinced you of your facts in the first place. In general, the more crucial a fact is to your argument, the less you should rely on a single or questionable source to verify it.

Basically, people are convinced of facts from four sources:

1. They have seen and experienced the facts firsthand.
2. Others whom they trust have told them about what they have seen and experienced.
3. They have gathered facts from experts in the media, in books or articles, or in reference books such as encyclopedias or dictionaries.
4. They have found a source of information on the Internet that they consider reliable.

Each of these four has special advantages and disadvantages as sources of information and verification.

Personal Experience   Many of the arguments you write will arise from situations in your own life: your dorm needs better security; the library should be open for more hours; your community needs a new parking lot or swimming pool and does not need a new prison or another shopping mall. You select these subjects for argument because you have been frightened by a stranger in the dorm, unable to study in the library on a Saturday night, frustrated looking for a parking place, or sweltering on a hot summer afternoon with no place to swim. All of these experiences are facts. They have actually happened; they happened to you. When the topic of your argument grows out of personal experience, you can regard your experiences as facts and use them in your argument.

The Testimony of Others   The word "testimony" suggests the evidence provided by a witness in a trial, a special example of a widely used source of information: what another person tells you. A person can make a factual claim to you directly, or you can hear someone's testimony on the news or read it in the paper or in some other printed or online source. Most of the information that stocks our minds comes to us not through our own experience but from the reported experience of others.

If you are going to use personal testimony, the witness of others, as verification, you have to make sure that your source is trustworthy and competent, with no obvious motives to deceive. A witness may need many kinds of competence simply to take in and comprehend what happens. You could have a medical examination, for example, and not be able later to give a clear report of what was done to you, or you could be in the control room of a nuclear power plant when an accident occurs and not even realize it. A great deal of prior knowledge may be necessary simply to be aware of what is happening.

Testimony is usually more believable when the source is named. Journalists, however, will sometimes credit "a White House source who asked to remain anonymous" or "a Pentagon informant who did not wish to be identified." This questionable practice may increase the credibility of testimony as verification;

it is so true, the reasoning goes, that the informant could be fired for disclosing it and so has asked to remain anonymous. In a courtroom, where the standard of evidence is higher, evidence from an unnamed source is inadmissible. Whenever you have reason to doubt your informant, their testimony needs further verification. When, for example, Peter Habeler and Reinhold Messner claimed to have climbed Mt. Everest together without oxygen, they were asked to produce evidence other than their mutual corroboration.

Authority   An authority is a person or publication that is widely trusted to give accurate information and is therefore a reliable source of verification. *The Statistical Abstract, The Handbook of Chemistry and Physics, The Oxford English Dictionary, Encyclopedia Britannica*—these are famous, authoritative reference books, and there are hundreds of others, compendiums of information on everything from abacus to zygote. These sources are never 100 percent accurate—that is an impossible state of perfection—but those that have been continually updated and corrected have been acknowledged as trustworthy over the years. You can verify basic information in these printed sources or consult them in CD-ROM versions or online.

When you need information that is too current to have found its way into the thin pages of a reference book, you must turn to more frequently published newspapers and journals or to continually updated online sources (see the following section). Newspapers and magazines differ greatly in their credibility or authoritativeness. You would not usually verify facts from the latest edition of a supermarket tabloid instead of a widely distributed national newspaper like *The New York Times* or *The Wall Street Journal*. Your local newspaper may not be as reliable or detailed on national events as the national newspapers are, but it may be your only source of information on events in your community. You may also verify facts about current events from magazines like *Time* or *Newsweek* or *Sports Illustrated*. But keep in mind that mass-circulation magazines, like newspapers, often bend and color facts, or leave out tedious but important details and qualifications in order to entertain. Such magazines should not be used alone as sources of verification.

Television is in the same somewhat unreliable category as mass circulation publications. An enormous amount of information is presented on television, but it is very difficult to trust it implicitly or to use any of it authoritatively. The time restrictions of television programs create more distortions than are found in print. The format of some television shows also makes them problematic as sources of verification. When the famous talk show host Oprah Winfrey was on trial for "defaming" beef, she explained that her show would invite people on different sides of the issue to participate, but would not independently check the veracity of their accounts. Thus the show gave license to claims that could not be verified. Winfrey claimed that her show was entertainment, "not the evening news," and that her audience knew the difference. Yet many people do absorb their information about the world from talk shows like Winfrey's. They assume that the people making claims on such shows have a certain authority because they are appearing on television.

So just as distinctions have to be made among publications, they have to be made among television shows. To check what you have heard and seen on a television show, interview, or documentary, you can often request a transcript and tapes from Journal Graphics or directly from many online sources such as C-Span.

So far we have considered certain publications as possible authorities on current topics. But another very obvious meaning of the word *authority* is a person who is an expert on a subject. Experts often present their information in books and articles, so when you want to know anything about a field, you find out who the experts are. Do not assume, however, that anyone who has written a book about a subject is an expert. At first glance, books may look equally authoritative, but not all of them are written by conscientious and thoughtful scholars.

How do you tell the difference between authors who are reliable sources of verification and those who are not? The following suggestions will help you.

Determining the Reliability of a Source

1. Check the credentials of an author by noting other books and articles that he or she has published. If a previous book was an exposé of the secret life of Elvis Presley and the most recent a harangue on the dangers of cloning, you might doubt your author's credibility. But if the author has published other reputable books, you can feel more confident.
2. Check the credibility of a book by looking up reviews of it in journals and newspapers that send books to other experts for assessment.
3. The book itself will provide some clues as to its credibility, and the more you know the subject, the more the quality of a book on that subject will be evident to you. Most importantly, does the book show its sources of verification, just as you are required to do when you write a paper for an academic course?

When you want to verify a fact for readers, cite the authority that verified it for you in footnotes, in-text citations, or the very wording of your argument. Accurate documentation is not only a matter of intellectual honesty; it is also a mark of respect for your audience as alert, intelligent readers.

Online Sources   Access to the Internet allows us to do everything from ordering vitamins to checking sports scores to looking up encyclopedia entries to keeping up with the headlines to finding bibliography entries for a research project. This wonderful resource has made the raw materials of argument more available than ever before in history. But are Internet sources the ultimate answer to problems of finding and verifying information?

Consider again the purpose of verifying the facts you use in an argument. You want to give your audience directions to the sources of your information

Arguing with Images

The Specter of Global Aging

Robert J. Samuelson

The art of prophecy is very difficult—especially with respect to the future.

—Mark Twain

Some things we can glimpse, and one of them is global aging. It is a specter that stalks most advanced societies. During the next half-century, most wealthy societies—the United States is a conspicuous exception—will lose population; all will have older populations. This is a collective change that will profoundly influence the world economy, the future of democracy and relations between nations with declining populations (generally richer countries) and those with expanding populations (generally poorer countries).

"By 2014, Europe's entire population will be shrinking, as will Japan's," says Paul Hewitt of the Center for Strategic and International Studies in Washington. "After 2010, the working-age populations decline by a little less than 1 percent a year. That will cause most of the rich world to grow much more slowly economically." Hewitt also foresees a global scarcity of savings and investment. Government budget deficits may rise to pay for increasing pension and health benefits, draining funds from private investment. Private pension funds and retirement accounts will sell stocks and bonds, also depleting savings.

Just how large these effects might be is anyone's guess. But the driving forces behind aging and population decline—low birthrates and longer life expectancy—seem fairly fixed. The table below, based on U.S. Census Bureau projections, shows what may lie ahead. The first column estimates total population change between 2000 and 2050 for six rich countries. The second and third columns provide estimates for the traditional working age population (20–64) and those over 65.

Population Change, 2000–2050
(Percent Change)

	Total Population	Working-Age	Over 65
France	−18%	−26%	+60%
Germany	−30	−43	+53
Italy	−32	−47	+41
Japan	−20	−36	+51
United Kingdom	−9	−15	+61
United States	+43	+29	+127

Only the United States—with higher birthrates and immigration—escapes population decline. But even in the United States, there are fewer potential workers for each potential retiree. As long as retirees are supported by taxpayers, through Social Security and health insurance, the economic burden on workers will rise. In most countries, the shifts would be stark and possibly unworkable. Gemany's working age population is projected to drop from 51 million in 2000 to 29 million in 2050; meanwhile, the 65-and-over population rises from 14 million to 21 million.

Although these precise predictions may prove wrong, the central truth is that "the natural growth of population in the more developed countries has essentially ceased," writes population expert Nicholas Eberstadt in the current issue of *Foreign Policy* magazine. In Germany and Japan, the fertility rate is 1.4, meaning that women on average have slightly more than one child each. At 2.1, the United States is roughly at the replacement rate.

Americans may have succeeded better in mixing family and work. Or immigrants may have more children than other Americans. Regardless, all rich nations will feel the pressures of aging—or declining—populations. And there's a perverse possibility that more old people will further reduce the number of young people. If taxes on workers increase to cover higher retirement benefits, families' willingness to have children may diminish, because it would be harder to pay for them.

Immigration is one possible safety valve. But to Europe and Japan, the increases needed to avert population declines would be huge. For Europe, including Russia, a doubling of present immigration levels to 1.8 million annually would be required, writes Eberstadt. Japan—with little immigration now—would have to accept 350,000 newcomers a year. By 2050, a sixth of its population would be of immigrant stock. In Europe, the comparable share would be about 20 percent. Given the social tensions caused by massive immigration, these increases would be difficult.

As Hewitt notes, richer countries could also prepare for their aging by investing in poorer countries. Trade could substitute for immigration. Investments from wealthier countries would enable developing nations to build up their industries. As people retire in the rich world, they could use some of the dividends and interest from their investments to buy imports from poorer countries. Both developed and developing countries would benefit. But this bargain assumes, Hewitt says, that "globalization" works smoothly—an iffy assumption.

To predict the future is (as Twain said) always iffy. But few rich countries are anticipating it. They should be tempering the vicious circle of higher retirement spending, heavier taxes on workers and fewer children. This means gradually raising retirement ages and scaling back benefits, especially for wealthier retirees. It isn't happening. In the United States, it has (so far) been impossible to make basic changes in Social Security and Medicare. In France, Germany and Italy, the average retirement age is 59, says Hewitt. Democracies have trouble facing the future when powerful constituents in the present have so little stake in it.

Robert Samuelson's editorial appeared in the *Washington Post* on February 28, 2001, along with an illustration, a photo, to capture the attention of page turners and reinforce its message. Browsing readers who took in only the title, "The Specter of Global Aging," and the picture probably gained a sense that the editorial is about some impending threat from the elderly. And this negative impression certainly supports Samuelson's point. But in addition to conveying a negative attitude, does the picture also communicate the points in the argument, its logos?

The actual argument in Samuelson's editorial predicts a coming population trend in "most wealthy societies" (that is, Japan and some countries in western Europe). People are living longer in these countries and having smaller families. The result of these two trends is a declining population and a greater percentage of elderly people in the population that remains. The table that follows the third paragraph forecasts the changes over the next 50 years. Notably, the United States is predicted to have an increasing population overall, but it too will have a dramatic increase in the percentage of elderly. Samuelson bases his argument on the projections reported by authorities: Paul Hewitt of the Center for Strategic and International Studies, the U.S. Census Bureau, and Nicholas Eberstadt writing in *Foreign Policy* magazine. He emphasizes that "these precise predictions may prove wrong," but that the overall trend in declining and aging populations looks firm. This trend will have serious consequences as a dwindling proportion of workers tries to support a growing proportion of dependent old people.

How does the image communicate Samuelson's prediction about population trends and their consequences? First of all, note that the accompanying illustration is a photo, not

—Continued

a drawing. Even though we know that photos can be doctored, we still tend to believe in their truthfulness. This photo, therefore, bears the stamp of reality. It looks like the kind of scene that could occur on any given day, and we cannot imagine any reason for faking it. It represents an event or circumstance that actually happened, just as Samuelson's prediction is based on actual figures. However, unlike news photos whose purpose is to substantiate an event at a particular moment and place, this photo, credited to the Associated Press, has no identifying caption. We recognize that the people in it are probably European, not Asian or African. Their dress and their circumstances—they seem to be shopping in some kind of open-air market—do not suggest an American scene. Because it is obviously an actual photo and yet does not show a specific event, it can stand for a real scene from any of the countries in Europe mentioned in Samuelson's article. It is both an example and a generalization.

Samuelson's main prediction is that the dependent elderly will constitute a greater portion of the population of wealthy societies than younger workers. That point is dramatically illustrated in the photograph, which includes six recognizable figures, four of them aged (one man and three women) and two younger. If we focus just on the four figures in the foreground, we have a proportion of 3 older people to 1 younger person. The picture therefore depicts a future when the elderly will outnumber the young, actually an exaggeration of the available statistics. Furthermore, the small, elderly woman in the middle is squeezed between two others, and all the figures are packed together. The proportion of elderly to younger people and their density may be the result of cropping: the scene shown here may have been selected from a larger picture. We have no idea what is going on around this scene, but we assume it is more of the same. Though Samuelson's text actually talks about declining populations, the photo conveys an impression of crowding.

That crowding and the fact that the scene in this photo seems to be an open-air food market also help to render one of Samuelson's points in visual terms. This shoulder-to-shoulder press in a marketplace implies competition over food, and indeed Samuelson's argument does suggest that the demands of the elderly for retirement benefits will be a harmful burden in the future because of the need to increase taxes on those still in the workforce. So though population density is not the point, competition for resources is. The younger woman on the left is frowning, her purse, with its strap slipping off her shoulder, is visible, and she is turned away from the food. Though the elderly women have no visible purses, it looks as if they will get most of the potatoes.

Perhaps the strongest visual reinforcement of Samuelson's argument comes from the placement of the figures. When we look at pictures of people, we pay attention to the way they are interacting with each other. We follow the lines of their vision and get a sense of a story by noticing who is looking at whom. The positions of the people in this picture convey conflict or antagonism between people of different age groups. The two elderly women in the middle of the photo look anxious, and the small one in the foreground has her gaze fixed on the food. Her back or shoulder is touching the younger woman on the left, but they are not interacting. Furthermore, if we look at the whole picture, we see the conflict between age groups depicted by its symmetry: the younger woman to the far left and the older woman to the far right are looking in opposite directions. Their bodies are as opposed to each other as the interests of the young and elderly are, according to Samuelson's predictions.

Although Robert Samuelson probably did not select the picture that accompanied his editorial, whoever did choose it found a powerful means of conveying and reinforcing the points raised in the editorial. But could the photograph have communicated his argument on its own? Scholars have debated the extent to which images can argue without accompanying words. It seems unlikely that Samuelson's premises could be accurately interpreted from the visual that illustrates them. But taken together, the text and visual make a stronger case than would the text alone.

so that they can check for themselves, if they so desire. But the very nature of Internet sites and web pages makes it difficult for readers to consult them as sources of verification. Internet and World Wide Web sites change frequently. You may find a piece of information on a site one day that will be gone when the site is updated. Or the site itself may disappear. Someone could type in the URL you provide and access the site but not find the same information that you found there. How then can you feel confident in using the Internet as a source of verification?

To get around this problem, the conventions for citing web sources require you to include not only the URL address but also the date of access. Some web sites keep an archive of past postings so that users can find out what was on the site at a specific date in the past. But these archives are by no means widely available. If an archive is not available, the very purpose of citing a source for verification, to give your readers the chance to check what you checked, cannot be fulfilled.

This problem with access is only a small part of the issue of verification from the Internet. The World Wide Web has been celebrated for its openness, for the possibility it offers for anyone to enter dialogue and share perspectives. But that very openness creates problems of reliability. Anyone with the appropriate software and access to a server can set up a web site and say anything whatsoever on it. Someone surfing the World Wide Web can access the genome database from the National Institutes of Health and promotional literature from Heaven's Gate, the cult that committed mass suicide to join its extraterrestrial friends. For more on evaluating and citing Internet resources, see Chapters 10 and 11.

FOR YOU TO ANALYZE

Use the two arguments that follow to practice your skills as a critical reader of arguments. For each argument, identify the following:

1. The main claim.
2. The reasons given to support the main claim. You can use a simple tree-diagram to show when the argument branches out with several reasons to support one claim.
3. The warrants that link the reasons and claims. If they are not included, reconstruct them as necessary.
4. The chaining of arguments. Where are reasons given to support other reasons or warrants?
5. The qualifications in the claim.
6. The rebuttal conditions or counterarguments. How are they answered?
7. The basic building blocks of the argument. What facts are used? Are they verified, and if so how? What values are appealed to?

Advertisement for Kleenex ColdCare Tissues

Don't Legalize Those Drugs

BARRY R. McCAFFREY

Barry R. McCaffrey was the director of the Office of National Drug Control Policy, a position popularly known as "drug czar," from 1996 to 2001. Before joining the executive branch, McCaffrey was a highly decorated general in the U.S. Army and a veteran of the Vietnam and Desert Storm Wars. This article first appeared in the *Washington Post* in June 1999.

Three-quarters of the U.S. population opposes the legalization of psychoactive drugs   1 such as heroin, cocaine, LSD, methamphetamine, and marijuana. Therefore, the term "drug legalization" has rightfully acquired pejorative connotations. Many supporters of this position have adopted the label "harm reduction" to soften the impact of an un-popular proposal that, if passed, would encourage greater availability and use of drugs—especially among children. The euphemism of "harm reduction" implies that legalizing dangerous substances would reduce the harm these substances cause. In fact, condoning drugs would increase their use and hence their harm. Drug use imposes an unacceptable risk of harm on the user and others. The evidence supporting this view-point is chilling:

Substance abuse wrecks families. A survey of state child-welfare agencies found sub-stance abuse to be one of the top two problems exhibited by 81 percent of families re-ported for child maltreatment. Researchers estimate that chemical dependence is pres-ent in at least half of the families involved in the child welfare system. One study published in the *Journal of the American Medical Association* revealed that non-drug users who live in households where drugs are used are 11 times more likely to be killed than individuals from drug-free households.

Drug-dependent individuals are responsible for a disproportionate percentage of our nation's violent and income-generating crimes such as robbery, burglary or theft. National Institute of Justice surveys consistently find that between one-half and three-quarters of all arrestees have drugs in their system at the time of arrest. In 1997, a third of state prisoners and about one in five federal prisoners said they had committed the crimes that led to incarceration while under the influence of drugs.

Injection-drug users place themselves at great risk. A University of Pennsylvania study of Philadelphia injection-drug users found that four times as many addicts died from overdose, homicide, heart disease, renal failure and liver disease as did from causes associated with HIV disease. Dr. James Curtis, director of addiction services at Harlem Hospital Center, explains: "It is false, misleading and unethical to give addicts the idea that they can be intravenous drug abusers without suffering serious self-injury."

Clearly, drugs themselves harm users. A significant percentage of all current drug   5 users are addicted to illegal substances. Addiction is a brain disease that changes a per-son's neurochemistry. For 4 million chronically addicted people, drug use is not a choice and hence has little to do with personal liberty. Removing the threat of crimi-nal sanctions would eliminate the possibility of forced treatment and condemn count-less addicts to miserable lives.

One argument given for drug legalization by harm-reduction advocates is that the "war against drugs has been lost." Aside from the fact that this is not a war, much progress has been made. Current drug policies are reducing drug use and its conse-quences. Drug use in this country has declined by half since 1979. The number of cur-rent users dropped from 25 million in 1979 to 13 million in 1996. The decrease in cur-rent use of cocaine has been even more dramatic.

This is not to say that drug policies cannot be improved. The 1999 National Drug Control Strategy is implementing important changes. The stategy's number one goal is prevention. In the past four years, the administration increased spending on prevention by 55 percent while spending on treatment rose 25 percent. The strategy calls for more treatment in the criminal justice system to break the cycle of drugs and crime.

At root, the debate over drug legalization boils down to a question of risk. Studies show that the more a product is available and legitimized, the greater will be its use. If drugs were legalized, the cost to the individual and society would grow astronomically. Removing the criminal status associated with drug use and sale would not make such activity less criminal when drug abuse wrecks young lives. It is criminal that more money is spent on illegal drugs than on art or higher education; it is criminal that crack babies are born addicted and in pain; it is criminal that thousands of adolescents lose their health and the freedom to create a bright future.

Harm-reduction advocates tolerate drug use because they consider it part of the human condition that will always be with us. Many other perennial problems such as racism, theft and aggression cannot be extinguished entirely, but we still resist their damage and criminalize the practices. No one argues that we should legalize these activities to make them more sanitary or provide tax revenues.

On a judicial level, the question of drug legalization comes down to whether we   10 should legalize destructive behavior. With respect to the individual, society at large and the environment, American jurisprudence has run in the opposite direction. Americans have decided that people do not have a right to ride motorcycles without wearing helmets, drive cars without using seat belts, pollute the environment at will, or endanger the self and others by refusing vaccination or similar life-saving health measures. In general, our laws indicate that self-destructive activity should not be permitted or condoned. Drug consumption damages the brain, which in turn produces other forms of destructive behavior. U.S. law does not grant people the right to destroy themselves or others. Addictive drugs were criminalized because they are harmful; they are not harmful because they were criminalized.

Establishing Credibility and Appealing to Emotion: Ethos and Pathos

Chapter 3

While the Children Sleep

A. M. Rosenthal

He strolled out of his apartment in Manhattan. He knew where to get what he wanted, no problem. He was back soon with his packages, the way some husbands come home with ice cream or flowers.

He took some of the contents, and so did his wife. She died. The two little kids were asleep. They found out in the morning.

Happens all the time—heroin overdose, dead on arrival. But he was a young magazine publisher and she a stockbroker—both up and coming and everything to live for. How could they do this to themselves and the kids?

Soon somebody wrote a letter to *The Times* explaining how it happened. U.S. anti-drug policies are to blame. The "demonization" of drugs prevented people from learning how much heroin at what potency was O.K. for holding good jobs without dropping dead. That failure to acknowledge the enduring appeal of drugs is the "larger tragedy."

This was from a professor. He also is a senior fellow at one of those pro-legalization groups supported by tax-free foundation money.

This column is not directed to people like that. They make their reputations and living by being professional legalization pushers; they are gone, goodbye. It is addressed to other people, in academia, or journalism, some lawyers, who simply believe that making drugs legally available would reduce drug crime and save the billions spent on fighting drugs.

They are worth arguing with because they are people of influence. Their activities, writing, their money to pro-drug foundations, help create a casualness, an acceptance, toward drugs that increases their use.

I ask them to rethink the consequences of what they do. Start by calling the Center on Addiction and Substance Abuse, (212) 841-5227, to get its new report, "Legalization: Panacea or Pandora's Box?"

I have read myself groggy with studies on drugs. This one by the center—at Columbia University and headed by Joseph A. Califano Jr.—is one of the most valuable. From now on, the legalizers will have to deal with it.

Briefly, with only a taste of the evidence the report presents, these are some of the points it makes:

The drug war has made substantial progress that would have been impossible without laws and public support. The number of "current" users—those who used drugs within the last month—has dropped from 24.8 million in 1979 to 13 million last year, nearly 50 percent—but not evenly in all cities and neighborhoods. The number of hard addicts has stayed steady at about 6 million. Wrestling with them is the job ahead.

Marijuana is the growing enemy of American youth. It not only weakens them physically and mentally in their growing years, and reduces the I.Q. of babies if used by pregnant women, but also is the gateway to harder drugs. Teen-agers who use it are 85 times more likely also to use cocaine than those who do not, 17 times more likely to use cocaine in their adulthood. Almost all Americans who use drugs begin before they are 21. And youngsters say that the major deterrent to use of marijuana and other drugs is legal penalty.

More access to drugs through legalization or permissiveness will hugely increase consumption and addiction. That will cost far more than the $13 billion spent to fight drugs — in increased hospital costs, spread of disease, and drop in economic productivity and student learning abilities.

Drug-gang crimes would decrease only if drugs could be bought almost everywhere by grown-ups and kids, wiping out all black markets. Even so crime would increase — by drug-related crimes not related to the drug trade, like murder, rape and assault.

Foreign experiments in legalization or permissiveness have failed. In the Netherlands, for instance, adolescent marijuana use has increased 250 percent. Registered harder-drug addicts have increased by 22 percent. Italy has the highest rate in Europe of addicts enjoying the "enduring appeal" of heroin.

I'm a little sick of trying to persuade pro-legalizers by statistics and money talk. Leave your pocket calculator home, just go out and look at the shaking people with shaking brains.

But reading this report should be the ticket to talking about legalization. Go argue with it. If you still want more access to drugs, stroll down to buy a few packets for yourself and your wife, while the children sleep. No problem.

ANALYZING "While the Children Sleep"

When people speak directly to us, we respond to more than just the claims they make and the support they offer for them. Human beings are much more than data-processing machines. We often react emotionally to the words a speaker uses and the pictures those words create in our minds, and at the same time we assess the speaker's credibility—the manner, the body language, the authority that is projected, and the attitude toward the audience. We bring our previous knowledge, values, and attitudes to the situation, and we respond to the clues the speaker presents to us as we react to what is said and the person saying it. In other words, we respond to the **ethos,** or character of the writer or speaker, and we respond to appeals to our own feelings and identity, to the **pathos** projected in an argument. Ethos and pathos are intertwined with **logos** in every argument, but we have chosen an obvious example of how these two appeals work in the selection above, which appeared as a column in the *New York Times.* For purposes of discussion, we will separate the appeals to ethos and those to pathos, although you will notice how they work closely together.

Ethos, the character of the writer, can be established externally, by the reputation that the writer brings to the situation, and internally, by the text at hand. If a reader knows A. M. Rosenthal personally or knows his work from reading his columns, that accumulated knowledge and reputation will affect the reader's sense of his character. For our purposes, we will concentrate on what A. M. Rosenthal reveals about himself in his writing. From the beginning of the column, it is clear that he is passionate about his subject, upset about the death of the young mother from a heroin overdose, and angry—very angry, with the people he calls "professional legalization pushers." These emotions are established as he starkly recounts the story of the mother's death and dismisses the argument of the professor who favors legalization with withering irony. Rosenthal is direct and urgent, announcing to his readers what he wants them to do and even instructing them how to do it. He wants his readers to "rethink the consequences" of believing that drugs should be legally available, and "Start by calling the Center on Addiction and Substance Abuse." He reveals his sincere commitment by including the phone number to call.

But if Rosenthal were only angry and urgent, he might appear unreasonable or out of control. He also wants us to realize that he "knows his stuff" and has done his homework on this topic. He tells us directly that "I have read myself groggy with studies on drugs" and assures us that the study he is recommending is "one of the most valuable." Then he offers a summary of some of the evidence from the report, which he wants us to believe both because it was conducted by a reputable center at Columbia University, a prestigious school, and because he believes it after doing a great deal of reading on his own.

He ends his column by returning to the impatient voice he established at the beginning: "I'm a little sick of trying to persuade pro-legalizers by statistics and money talk." In contrast to the cool language he uses when summarizing the evidence from authorities, Rosenthal's voice here is much more informal—even colloquial—and intense. Once again he grabs his readers by the lapels and tells them what to do: "Leave your pocket calculator home, just go out and look at the shaking people with shaking brains." He challenges them to argue with the report, even dares them to "stroll down to buy a few packets for yourself and your wife." The character he has established here is that of someone who is well informed, upset at the havoc wrought by drug use, and furious at those who support legalization.

Rosenthal presents himself as a passionate crusader against drug legalization, a well-informed person with an intense commitment. That is his ethos, his character as revealed in his writing. What does he want from us? Clearly, he wants us not only to know what he knows, but also to feel what he feels. He wants us to share his attitudes in the hope that we too will become passionately committed to his position. Thus he makes strong appeals to the emotions of his readers, to pathos. The story of the young mother who died of an overdose conveys the first emotional appeal. Rosenthal relates it starkly, in short, punchy sentences: "She died. The two little kids were asleep. They found out in the morning." The style resembles that of tough-guy fiction, direct but tight-lipped and restrained. We feel that the emotion is being held back. The story is followed by a rhetorical question: "How could they do this to themselves and the kids?" We can imagine readers shaking their heads in outrage and disbelief. The question does not call for an answer; it assumes our agreement that what happened was awful, even unthinkable. The story, the word choice, the sentence structure all convey strong feelings that are barely kept in check.

Rosenthal introduces a new emotional appeal in the next part of the column. Here he describes the letter blaming government anti-drug policies. He quotes selectively from it, referring to the "demonization" of drugs and the "larger tragedy" of not acknowledging the enduring appeal of drugs. The words he puts in quotes are high-sounding and academic, and he juxtaposes them with his own strong language about "how much heroin was O.K. for holding good jobs without dropping dead." His slangy language is meant to shock us into agreement. Rosenthal also constructs the audience he is persuading. He casts people who use fancy language to advocate legalization out of his audience. The letter writer is a professor, "a senior fellow at one of those pro-legalization groups supported by tax-free foundation money." These are not the people he is talking to; they take "tax-free" money to make arguments that do not take account of brutal reality. Presumably, we want to be straight-talking realists like him, not like them.

After he isolates those whom he is not addressing, he dismisses them forcefully: "they are gone, goodbye." Who is left? An audience he characterizes more neutrally as academics, journalists, and lawyers "who simply believe that making drugs legally available would reduce drug crime and save the billions spent on fighting drugs." He compliments these people as influential and asks them "to rethink the consequences of what they do." Thus he positions himself as addressing not a group of extremists, but a middle group who can be reasonable and listen to his argument. If we have responded to his emotional appeals, we are now upset by the waste of life caused by drugs and impatient with "ivory-tower" dwellers who miss the whole point. Thus Rosenthal has identified an audience that will listen to reason as he presents it.

At the end of the column, Rosenthal returns to making strong emotional appeals, abandoning in disgust "trying to persuade pro-legalizers by statistics and money talk." He addresses his readers directly as "you," ordering us to "look at the shaking people with shaking brains." The repetition of "shaking," applied first to people and then to brains, conjures up a picture of a drug addict right before our eyes. Rosenthal assumes that if we are made to feel, we will be ready to act. He concludes by daring us to step into the shoes of the potential drug user: "stroll down to buy a few packets for yourself and your wife, while the children sleep. No problem." The fact that drugs are so readily available, that it is "no problem" to purchase them, is meant to jolt us out of complacency into action.

The above analysis shows how a writer can reinforce an argument with appeals to the readers' emotions and sense of identity and with appeals that come from our awareness of his own character. Rosenthal's appeals are very strong, and by writing his argument the way he does he takes a risk. If he fails to convince us of his own good sense, good will toward us, and good moral character (in other words, if he does not project his ethos effectively), we will not be moved by other appeals. He is asking for a very strong commitment from his readers, and his appeals to our feelings are correspondingly intense. Not all arguments are as emotionally intense as this one, but all of them project the author's ethos and invoke pathos to engage the audience. It is up to the reader to determine whether these appeals are used effectively. Only a strong sense of audience will help you make effective choices about conveying your own character and appealing to your reader's feelings.

ETHOS

The analysis of A. M. Rosenthal's column illustrates an important lesson about arguments: the character of the arguer is a factor in persuasion. We see this in every context where arguments occur, whether commercial (the famous athlete endorses sneakers), legal (the lawyer wants the witness in a trial to appear reliable to the jury), public (the Nobel Prize winner signs a letter on an environmental issue), or personal (you accept your best friend's advice because you trust her). The importance of character in argument leads to an important question. If the claim, supporting statements, and warrants are the same in two arguments, but the two people making the arguments are different, will one argument be more convincing to an audience than the other one? To answer that question, consider how expertise or advice is sought out or marketed. Suppose you need to find out something about sound technology in order to produce a demo album for your musical group. You would be more inclined to believe advice from someone who had experience with the equipment and process than advice from someone who is trying to sell you his old equipment. In fact, you would probably try to find an expert who could confirm the advice offered by someone whose knowledge or motive you didn't quite trust. Common sense always leads us to seek out an authority, someone with knowledge of the subject, a reputation for dealing honestly and fairly with others, and no conceivable reason to mislead us. So character always matters in argument.

The Elements of Ethos

Rhetoricians have long recognized the importance of the speaker's perceived character to the persuasiveness of an argument. The speaker, as Aristotle points out, must exhibit "good sense, good moral character, and good will." We can group these qualities under the general term *ethos*. If we trust a speaker or an author—that is, if we believe that he or she knows the subject, has no reason to deceive us, and has no ulterior motives—we are more likely to pay attention, to be favorably disposed toward what he or she says, and perhaps, finally, to be convinced. A speaker or an author who has an effective ethos exhibits all three qualities.

Good Sense

By "good sense" we mean that the writer displays sound knowledge of his or her subject, knowledge sufficient for the purpose at hand. Clearly, as a student, you cannot be expected to know everything about a subject you write about, but you can still project the ethos of "good sense" by being in command of your material. Have you read everything you need to read about your subject? Have you quoted from recognized experts in the area you are writing about? Have you made sure that your knowledge of your subject is up to date? Have you drawn on reputable, well-documented sources? Have you presented your argument as fully and as fairly as possible?

Good Will

In addition to the knowledge that you reveal in your writing, another element of effective ethos is your "good will" toward the reader. You may wonder how you reveal good will simply by what you choose to put on a page. If you think about it, though, there are actually many ways to do so. You show good will toward your reader by writing in language that your audience understands. We all have been annoyed by writers who seem condescending, treating us as if we were stupid or gullible. Some writers exclude readers by making references to people and terms that only insiders understand. You can also show good will toward your readers by anticipating their need for explanation and clear examples. Finally you can show good will by conveying your enthusiasm for your subject in such a way that your readers can share it. In short, you can convey good will by treating your readers exactly as you would want to be treated if you were in their shoes.

Good Moral Character

The third element of effective ethos is "good moral character." Like good sense and good will, it too is conveyed by the choices, both conscious and unconscious, that you make as a writer. Any argument reveals something about the character of the arguer: is the person open-minded or rigid, generous or mean-spirited, honest or deceptive, sincere or hypocritical? We all know that character shows in what we say and do. It is equally obvious in what we write. We are inclined to believe the arguments of people who have a reputation for good character and to doubt people we distrust, no matter what the subject. Like good sense and good will, good character is something one brings to one's writing and, at the same time, something one reveals in it.

Working either alone or with a group of classmates, decide whether the writer of each of the following extracts is displaying the elements of ethos—good sense, good moral character, and good will. If so, how does he or she convey these qualities? If not, how could the passage be revised to convey these qualities?

1. The nation will need two million new teachers over the next decade, and nobody has any clear idea of where they're going to come from. The passage of the big education initiative in Washington last week marked the federal government's greatest leap yet into establishing standards and requiring testing in the public schools. This is swell, but unfortunately it's also the easiest part of the package. The toughest part is finding qualified people to do the teaching that raises the scores and meets the standards. Neither Congress nor the Bush administration has had nearly as many helpful suggestions on that subject.
   —Gail Collins, "Taking the Cure," *New York Times,* June 19, 2001, p. A23.

2. The question of whether animals have culture is a bit like asking whether chickens can fly. Compared with an albatross or a falcon, perhaps not, but chickens do have wings, they do flap them, and they can get up in the trees. Similarly, viewed from the cultural heights achieved by humans in art, cuisine, science and politics, other animals seem to be nowhere in sight. But what if we change perspective, and don't measure them by our standards? This is what Kinji Imanishi, a Japanese anthropologist, proposed in the early 1950s. In an imaginary debate between an evolutionist, a layman, a monkey and a wasp, Imanishi suggested that culture—defined as the non-genetic transmission of habits—was entirely possible, and even likely, for animals other than humans.
   —Frans B. M. de Waal, "Cultural Primatology Comes of Age," *Nature* 399 (1999), p. 635.

3. Barring technological breakthroughs—ways of producing cheap energy with few emissions or capturing today's emissions—it's hard to see how the

world can deal with global warming. Developing countries sensibly insist on the right to reduce poverty through economic growth, which means more energy use and emissions. (Much is made of China's recent drop in emissions; this is probably a one-time decline, reflecting the shutdown of inefficient factories. In 1999 China had eight cars per 1,000 people compared with 767 per 1,000 for the United States. Does anyone really believe that more cars, computers and consumer goods will cut China's emissions?) Meanwhile, industrialized countries won't reduce emissions if it means reducing living standards. There is a natural stalemate.

—Robert Samuelson, "The Kyoto Delusion,"
Washington Post, June 21, 2001, p. A25.

Types of Ethos

As noted in the analysis of A. M. Rosenthal's column, there are two kinds of *ethos* in argument, the extrinsic and the intrinsic.

Extrinsic Ethos

Extrinsic ethos derives from the reputation that the speaker or writer brings to the occasion. It is what the audience believes about the speaker or writer before a word is uttered or a page read. You will go to hear a lecture delivered by someone recognized as an internationally famous authority on a subject. Similarly, you will be favorably disposed toward a novel by a Nobel Prize winner or a film by an Oscar-winning director. Where does extrinsic ethos come from? It can come from expertise or professional qualifications, as established by advanced degrees, training, or certification: You are inclined to believe what your doctor tells you about your health and what your auto mechanic tells you about your car. It can come from a person's position in a hierarchy. When the president or CEO of an organization makes a claim, we are more inclined to accept it than when a subordinate makes the same claim. And it can come from personal experience. The women who formed the organization Mothers Against Drunk Driving all had children who were killed in accidents caused by drunk driving.

Intrinsic Ethos

Whether or not we know anything about the speaker or writer ahead of time, the actual text we hear or read, the way it is written or spoken and what it says, always conveys an impression of the author's character. This impression of the person writing or speaking created by the text itself is called the author's **intrinsic ethos,** and every arguer has the opportunity to create a favorable or unfavorable ethos. Like a voice with a reassuring or an irritating tone, the intrinsic ethos can either enhance or destroy the author's extrinsic ethos. Imagine listening to a lecturer with a reputation as the originator of a brilliant new theory and hearing a confused, bumbling talk, full of obvious statements and unsurprising conclusions. This poor performance will cause you to reassess the speaker's reputation and probably weaken the speaker's case considerably.

Working either alone or with a group of classmates, discuss how the writer of each of the following passages establishes his or her ethos. Is that ethos extrinsic, intrinsic, or both?

1. "Pearl Harbor," the movie, is an engagingly ramshackle mess of comical improbabilities, '40s clichés and dialogue so corny it must have been (was it?) deliberate. It is entertaining enough but would hardly merit serious attention were it not for one scene too egregious to go unremarked.

   It is the scene of FDR convening his military advisers after the attack. Finding them depressed and defeatist, FDR makes a melodramatic "when I had the use of my legs" speech and then, to illustrate the point, rises from his chair—theatrically, clumsily, angrily struggling to stand using leg braces and cane—with the ringing admonition: "Don't tell me it can't be done."

   I've been in a wheelchair about as long as FDR and I cannot think of a more grotesque abuse of his disability. FDR would never have said or done anything remotely like this. He never talked about his disability with anyone—his family, his wife, even his mother—let alone did stunts for war counselors and generals. If anyone dared broach the subject with him, FDR would freeze him out.

   —Charles Krauthammer, "The Campaign to Undo FDR,"
   Washington Post, June 15, 2001, p. A33.

2. I found the European mood to be mellower in Provence (French for "Province"), an extremely picturesque sector of southern France filled with picturesque houses and fields and little picturesque towns connected by winding roads upon which the French whiz around at speeds upwards of 17 million kilograms per hour in cute French cars the size of an Altoids tin.

   Provence was once occupied by the Romans, who built picturesque ruins until their empire collapsed as a result of eating too much cheese. The same thing happened to us. We consumed cheese by the metric ton. We bought it at open-air markets, which are held in certain towns on certain days. The rest of the time, France is closed. (You think I'm joking.)

   On market day, all the residents of Provence get into their Altoidsmobiles and whiz to the same town, where they form a massive traffic jam and park in every conceivable place, including on top of other cars. Then they walk around the market and buy delicious, inexpensive cheeses, sausages, breads, pastries, candies and other delicacies. Then they go home and throw all the food away. At least that's what I assume they do, because, despite living in Cholesterol World, they're all thin. The entire population of France weighs less than a standard American softball team.

   —Dave Barry, "Americans in Paris May Face Waiters Who Are 'Les Snobs,'"
   Miami Herald, July 1, 2001.

3. Today, education is perhaps the most important function of state and local governments. Compulsory school attendance laws and the great expenditures for education both demonstrate our recognition of the importance of education to our democratic society. It is required in the performance of our most basic public responsibilities, even service in the armed forces. It is the very foundation of good citizenship. Today it is a principal instrument in awakening the child to cultural values, in preparing him for later professional training, and in helping him to adjust normally to his environment. In these days, it is doubtful that any child may reasonably be expected to succeed in life if he is denied the opportunity of an education. Such an opportunity, where the state has undertaken to provide it, is a right which must be made available to all on equal terms.

   We come then to the question presented: Does segregation of children in public schools solely on the basis of race, even though the physical facilities and other "tangible" factors may be equal, deprive the children of the minority group of equal educational opportunities? We believe that it does.

   —Chief Justice Earl Warren, U.S. Supreme Court Decision in *Brown v. Board of Education* (1954)

PATHOS

The final kind of appeal does not depend on the writer's character or the subject matter, but on the audience that receives the argument. The appeal to *pathos* is sometimes defined as an appeal that incites the audience's emotions, rousing their pity or indignation or hopefulness or fear. These powerful incentives to belief and action are often delivered through pictures, film, and sound as well as through words. Think of ads for charities that show appealing children in rags or ads for pet adoptions with pictures of baby animals.

How are emotions incited in an audience? Direct appeals to the reader to feel an emotion (for example, "You should be crying now") are rarely effective. None of us wants to be told what we should be feeling. Instead, to create an emotion with words an arguer usually needs to recreate the scene or event that would in "real" circumstances arouse the emotion. Thus the story of the young mother who died of a drug overdose in the example that begins this chapter works on our emotions. Or the arguer can work on the natural "trigger" of the emotion. If, for example, we usually feel sympathy toward someone who, we believe, has suffered undeserved hardship, then an arguer who wants to make us sympathetic might make a case that a person has suffered unfairly.

In addition to appeals to the emotions that all humans share, arguers can also invoke their readers' self-interest and their sense of identity. Arguers often take the time to "tell" the members of an audience who they are, consciously creating in them a sense of belonging to a group. They can then use that group identity as a factor in favor of their claim. People think of themselves as members of groups on the basis of their age (Gen X-ers, senior citizens), race or ethnicity (African-Americans, Asian-Americans), occupation (teachers, health-care workers), religious belief (Muslim, atheist), and many other categories that we are used to hearing about in a pluralistic society like the United States. Of course, the same person can be placed into an endless variety of less obvious groups: alumni of a school, residents of an apartment complex, natives of a county, listeners to a certain radio station, readers of a popular author, travelers who have vacationed in the same place, and on and on. Readers can be appealed to as unique individuals, the sole member of a group of one, or as members of the same human race throughout the history of the planet. Once audience members imagine themselves into a group, they can then respond to what the arguer presents as advancing or threatening the interests of that group. Thus appeals to group membership can become powerful triggers of the emotions.

Are Emotional Appeals Legitimate?

Some people believe that emotional appeals have no place in valid argument, that all appeals to the emotions are to be regarded with suspicion. According to this view, appeals to reason are rational and appeals to the emotions are irrational, amounting to manipulation or even propaganda. Underlying this common belief is the assumption that reason and the emotions, the head and the heart, work against each other, and that when people's feelings are touched, their brains must be turned off.

This belief in the illegitimacy of emotional appeals has a long history in the western tradition. It was especially strong in the decades after World War II when people recalled the propaganda techniques used by the Nazi party in Germany to inspire devotion to its programs and leader. In the 1950s, people also became convinced that subliminal messages, segments of film too short to be consciously noticed, were being used in movie theaters to convince patrons to buy popcorn and soda. Humans, it was widely believed, give in to conditioning that works against their conscious will; they respond to sounds and images without thinking. Some research supports this common belief. Wine merchants have discovered that if they play French music in the background, their customers buy more French wine, and if they play German music, they buy more German wine. Young people are assumed to be particularly vulnerable to this kind of irrational persuasion; thus in the 1990s a cigarette company was accused of manipulating young people's emotions through the use of a cartoon camel in cigarette ads.

Emotion seems particularly out of place in the arguments that scholars and scientists publish to establish new knowledge. Scholarly arguments presumably do not depend on emotional appeals to their readers. It is commonly accepted that historians should study the past without passion; scientists should not contaminate their investigations with their own likes and dislikes. When people make these claims about the irrelevance of emotions, they are thinking about the most dramatic emotions, such as hate or fear. But not all emotions are so intense. Milder emotions such as commitment, dedication, curiosity, and allegiance to a school of thought all play a part in scholarly arguments. Because the works of historians, anthropologists, psychologists, and literary critics deal with human emotions and actions, they inevitably invoke emotions. It is in fact impossible to imagine any argument, or indeed any human activity, without an emotional dimension.

Working either alone or with a group of classmates, decide on an appropriate emotional appeal for each of the following claims and audiences.

1. The school year should be extended to 12 months. (audience: parents)
2. Smoking should be allowed in designated areas in public buildings. (audience: nonsmokers)
3. Carefully regulated logging should be allowed on public land. (audience: members of a wilderness preservation group)
4. The drinking age should be kept at 21 to prevent accidents caused by drunk driving. (audience: college students)
5. Gun owners should be required to buy liability insurance, like car owners. (audience: people who enjoy hunting and target shooting)

EXERCISE 3.3

ETHOS AND PATHOS COMBINE IN IDENTIFICATION

Since arguments are human events, not diagrams, the dimensions of speaker and listener, writer and reader, are always present. A skillful arguer can make the appeals in an argument reinforce each other. One of the most powerful combinations happens when the appeals of *ethos* and *pathos* are joined. Remember that audiences are persuaded by the speaker's character (*ethos*) and by the image of themselves created in the argument (*pathos*). What happens when arguers identify with an audience, when they present themselves as representatives of and indeed as people who are speaking *for* the audience? When the characters of speaker and audience combine in this way, an arguer can be especially persuasive. Listening to such a speaker, audience members find themselves looking into a mirror, hearing their own interests and beliefs expressed powerfully—or perhaps they hear interests and beliefs they did not know they had until they heard them expressed by their representative. This powerful tactic of unifying speaker and listener, writer and reader—called "identification"—was described by the twentieth-century rhetorician Kenneth Burke. Politicians use this tactic when they change or enhance their regional dialect depending on their audience, or when they find some tenuous family connection with the part of the country they are visiting. They identify with their audience, and they want that audience, in turn, to identify with their positions.

ESTABLISHING ETHOS IN WRITING

The Intellectual Virtue of Reasonableness

So far we have established that *ethos* and *pathos* are important in writing arguments. But what are the qualities of mind that you, as a good arguer, should exhibit? We can call these qualities intellectual virtues, as Aristotle did over 2,000 years ago. Virtues are not only habits of good behavior; they are also habits of good thought. Like all virtues, the intellectual virtues are resolutions of extremes, midpoints between opposite tendencies. Perhaps the greatest intellectual virtue in argument is reasonableness, a moderation of mind that occupies the middle ground between the extremes of stubbornness and spinelessness. Reasonable people are open to reason. They are not so intransigent that they dig in against the other side, nor are they so weak-minded that they refuse to take a stand at all. Reasonableness in argument can take many forms. For convenience we have represented these forms in the following imaginary self-declarations.

I Am Not an Extremist

Most of us carefully avoid walking close to, or engaging in an argument with, a wild orator on a soapbox. We discard without reading polemical pamphlets thrust into our hands. We tend to shun extremism and like to think of ourselves as moderate, sane, and balanced. Given this predisposition, a moderate *ethos* can be effective in an argument. But it is not something you can fake. You must really have established other positions as too extreme, too strained, or too far-fetched. If you can locate your own position between two more extreme ones, then it may be convincing to point out its moderateness to your readers.

I Know the Other Side and They Are Wrong

In most issues involving action and value, there are several competing points of view. Often you need to argue not only *for* your own position but also *against* competing positions. But you cannot argue against them until you understand them, even if you see them as wrong. And since you need to show your reader that you understand the other positions, you should present them in your argument.

The least you can do is mention competing positions without giving them any credit at all. In effect, you say, "I know my opposition, and they are wrong." In the following excerpt from his book-length argument on the nature of evolution, the English zoologist Richard Dawkins fulfills this minimum requirement of reasonableness.

> My purpose is to examine the biology of selfishness and altruism. Apart from its academic interest, the human importance of this subject is obvious. It touches every aspect of our social lives, our loving and hating, fighting and cooperating, giving and stealing, our greed and our generosity. These are claims which could have been made for Lorenz's *On Aggression*, Ardrey's *The Social Contract*, and Eibl-Eibesfeldt's *Love and Hate*. The trouble with these books is their authors got it totally and utterly wrong. They got it wrong because they

misunderstood how evolution works. They made the erroneous assumption that the important thing in evolution is the good of the *species* (or the group) rather than the good of the *individual* (or the gene).

—Richard Dawkins, *The Selfish Gene*
(New York: Oxford University Press, 1976), pp. 1–2.

I See Merit in the Other Side

Often, you can do more than just acknowledge the existence of the other position. You can even be sympathetic toward it. Without conceding to the opposition, you can show your audience that you treat other positions with respect, understanding, and even kindness. You can compliment the opposition on their reasoning, acknowledge their good faith, appreciate their perspective—anything short of conceding that they are right and you wrong.

Seeing merit in the other position is a middle road between cold acknowledgment and concession. It may be the only civilized position you can take when your opposition is strong and your audience will not allow you to rebuff them outright. For example, in his review of *Good Cop, Bad Cop* by Henry Ruth and Kevin Reitz, James Q. Wilson approves of several positions in a book he otherwise criticizes.

This book offers many sensible, thoughtful suggestions on specific issues related to crime. Its authors call attention to some interesting crime-prevention and crime-reduction policies, accurately criticize certain antidrug programs like DARE and boot camps, and properly oppose the current tendency to convert every street crime into a federal offense.

Why, then, do I not like *The Challenge of Crime* as much as I should?

—James Q. Wilson, review in *Commentary*, June 2003, p. 59.

To approve these points is certainly to see merit in them, though offering such a compliment does not mean that you agree with them.

I Concede One or More Points to the Other Side

Rarely is an issue so clear that one side is completely right and the other totally wrong. Of course, you must be convinced that your side has better arguments, or you would not bother to maintain it. But other positions may be right about some aspects of the issue; in fact, they may even be right about all but one. You do not have to demonstrate that they are totally wrong in order to show that you are right.

When arguments are mixed on your opponent's side, the indispensable gesture from your side is **concession,** the graceful acknowledgment that "on this point" or "in that matter" some other argument has merit. Intellectually, concession contributes to an ethos of honesty, precision, moderation, and thoroughness. When you concede one or more points to the opposition, your readers perceive you as gracious and reasonable as well as intellectually honest. In the following passage from an essay against political nepotism, the author concedes that nepotism, which he defines elsewhere as "favoring one's kin in the apportionment of power," is widespread in many walks of life:

Sure, a certain amount of nepotism has always been a feature of American life. Many of the former captains of industry passed their companies on to their sons; the entertainment industry is riddled with the offspring and spouses of established stars.

Although conceding a point shows intellectual honesty and moderation, a concession cannot go unanswered. It has to be downplayed or discounted in some way. The acknowledgment of widespread nepotism in business and entertainment is followed with this retort:

> But politics is different. Unlike business or entertainment, it is supposed to be the arena in which our democratic values are secured and preserved. It is more important in politics than almost anywhere else that the system be open to all, and be seen to be open to all.
>
> —Andrew Sullivan, "All in the Family," *New York Times Magazine,*
> September 9, 2000, p. 26

The indispensable accompaniment of a concession, then, is a *but*.

I May Be Wrong, But . . .

Another way to show moderation is to admit openly the potential problems of your own position. By doing so you are not necessarily confessing weakness or incompetence. Not every position can or need be held as though it were the one correct view, the only perfect solution. Nor can you be sure that you know everything about an issue or that you will never change your mind. Arguing from a temporary or tentative position is often the best anyone can do in specific circumstances. When you honestly find yourself somewhat uncertain on an issue, even after thinking through some arguments, you can shift into a lower gear by admitting your own uncertainty, the tentative nature of some of your conclusions, your openness to new ideas. Notice how paleontologist and science writer Stephen Jay Gould qualifies his indictment of anthropologist and theologian Teilhard de Chardin, whom he accuses of fraud:

> Perhaps I am now too blinded by my own attraction to the hypothesis of Teilhard's complicity. Perhaps all these points are minor and unrelated, testifying only to the faulty memory of an aging man. But they do form an undeniable pattern. Still, I would not now come forward with my case were it not for a second argument, more circumstantial to be sure, but somehow more compelling in its persistent pattern of forty years—the record of Teilhard's letters and publications.
>
> —Stephen Jay Gould, "The Piltdown Conspiracy," *Hens Teeth and Horse's Toes*
> (New York: W. W. Norton, 1983), p. 213.

The modesty of Gould's opening admission is appealing, and in the face of strong opposition, such tentativeness may be the only sensible stance, a way to at least get a hearing.

However, a claim of modesty will not excuse inadequate or sloppy research, failure to think carefully about the issues, or a refusal to listen to all sides of the argument. Yet even after we have done all the work that an honest conscience demands, most of us still have much to be modest about.

The Overall Effects of Conviction and Moderation

In conveying *ethos*, every gain has a corresponding loss. The stronger the conviction you convey, the less moderate you will seem. When an audience senses intransigence or stubbornness, they perceive you as extreme. And when you open your arms to every point of view, your commitment to your own becomes questionable. Striking a balance is possible when the arguer, poised in the middle, is thoroughly convinced of his or her own position while understanding and acknowledging other positions.

But a middle-of-the-road stance is not always the best. It is often legitimate to tip the balance in one way or the other. For some audiences and subjects, it may be wiser to display strong conviction rather than moderation, especially when you have strong evidence or willing readers. The best advice, then, is to be aware that moderation and conviction create very different effects. Since you gain an excess of one only at the expense of the other, you should know what the trade-offs are.

Disclaimers: Don't Get the Wrong Idea about Me or My Argument

What would people think of you if you proposed cross-country travel by pneumatic tube? Or advocated mile-high skyscrapers? Or mandatory vegetarianism? They would think you a dreamer or a fool. If you ever wanted to argue seriously for such fanciful ideas, you would have to begin by convincing your audience that you are sane and realistic.

A claim that anticipates and answers an audience's negative reaction is called a **disclaimer.** It is a denial, a repudiation of what your audience is likely to think. Disclaimers are useful even in arguments far less fanciful than the ones above. Any time your audience would be likely to think ill of you, to slap a label on you, or to attribute a position to you that you do not hold, you may need to anticipate their reaction and deny before being accused.

Disclaimers resemble concessions. When you concede a point, you anticipate a reader's assumption that your argument differs in every way from that of your opposition and let your reader know that on some points, at least, it does not differ. In a similar way, a disclaimer dissociates you from a predictable position, but it is usually personal. Suppose you wanted to tell your friends how exciting the last golf championship match was, but didn't want them to think you are the kind of person who would watch any and every sports competition with equal enthusiasm. You might say, "I'm not a big fan of TV sports and I hardly ever watch golf, but you really should have seen the last U.S. Open." Or you might dissociate yourself from the technologically adept to strengthen your argument that online shopping is really very easy: "I'm no techie, and it usually takes me a long time to catch on to new ways of doing things, but I now do almost all my shopping online."

Is there danger in making a disclaimer? Yes, if you disclaim an accusation that your audience would never have thought of. In applying for a job as a bank teller, you would not deny being an embezzler if your prospective employer had no reason to suspect you. You would not tell readers that your proposal is not unrealistic if your audience is not likely to think it so. When making a disclaimer, then, be sure you have an accurate sense of what your audience might think of you and your argument.

EXERCISE 3.4

In newspapers, on television news programs, or on the Internet, look for examples of arguers using the techniques described in this section to establish themselves as reasonable, and bring at least three examples to class (you can jot down notes on any examples you find on TV news programs). In a group with two or three of your classmates, discuss the examples you have each found and decide on two or three that you consider especially effective. Be prepared to present your most effective examples to the class and explain why they are successful.

WRITING YOUR ARGUMENT

ESTABLISHING YOUR ETHOS

Since projecting an appropriate ethos requires balancing effects, you can experiment with different stances:

1. Take the opening paragraph of an argument you are working on and rewrite it in the following two ways:
   - With no mention of yourself.
   - With an introduction that features yourself and your commitment and involvement with your subject.

   Given your audience and purpose, which projection is likely to be more effective? Ask your classmates for their judgment.

2. Take one of the arguments opposed to your own position and frame it in the following ways:
   - As wrong and misguided.
   - As well-meaning but flawed.
   - As a point that has to be conceded.

   Again, which stance is the most effective?

EVOKING PATHOS IN ARGUMENT

The *ethos* of reasonableness that we have been advocating need not be a cold virtue. The good person who argues well may also be the sensitive person who has emotional convictions, who feels anger, pity, fear, or warmth over an issue and evokes those same feelings in the reader. An arguer can convey such emotions and deliberately arouse them in the reader as a way of reinforcing rational conviction. Reinforcing emotions can be conveyed through carefully chosen words and examples.

Choosing Words Carefully

Many words are bristly. They have a core of meaning and a surface that produces feelings or sensations in the reader. The simple term *ice cream* refers to a frozen confection of cream, sugar, and flavoring and for most of us evokes pleasant memories and happy anticipations. The word *cancer*, on the other hand, produces as much fear as meaning. In writing you can make the positive and negative associations of words work for you to transfer appropriate emotions to your readers.

You can often choose from among a group of words that have approximately the same meaning but different associations. Naturally, you will want to choose words with appropriate associations for your audience and your argument. If, for example, you are advocating milder punishment for teenagers who break the law, you would not refer to them as "juvenile delinquents" or "young criminals." You would do better to call them "youthful offenders" or "teenagers with problems," terms with more neutral associations, or even "disturbed children," a term that calls for sympathy.

Euphemism

If you want to avoid a certain word, you can usually substitute a more neutral or more attractive word. The substitute word is called a **euphemism.** Euphemisms abound whenever the subject is diplomacy, politics, human categorization, death, or private bodily functions. Direct or embarrassing references to these subjects can hurt or disgust readers. To show consideration for an audience, you often will need to sweeten a reference to a controversial, disturbing, or embarrassing subject; the reader eats it anyway, but it tastes better.

When is it legitimate to use a euphemism and when is it not? It all depends on the situation, the purpose, and the audience. Euphemisms often replace words that an audience would find crude or socially taboo. For example, faced with a grieving friend, you probably would not say, "I heard your father died yesterday." Your sympathy would lead you to make some less direct statement like "Sorry to hear about your father." On the other hand, when the situation is impersonal, you can usually be more direct. For instance, you would not write, "Thomas Jefferson and John Adams both passed to the great beyond on July 4, 1826." Every era has its taboo words. In the nineteenth century, women were not referred to as "pregnant." Instead, they were "soon to be confined." We laugh at these euphemisms now while we respect our own taboos.

Similarly, speakers and writers commonly use certain euphemisms for groups of human beings to replace labels that have offensive connotations. For example, we now prefer to call people over 65 "senior citizens" or "older Americans" rather than "the elderly" or "old people." Similarly, a garbage collector is a "sanitation worker," a janitor a "custodian," and an old-fashioned undertaker a "funeral director." Because language changes over time, a term that is merely descriptive to one generation may become offensive to the next. Some of the newer labels may sound strained or stilted at first, but in time they will either become part of common usage or they will be discarded.

Although many euphemisms are meant to protect readers' feelings and sensitivities, euphemisms that conceal the ugly realities of oppression or underhanded dealings of any kind should be challenged. It is inexcusable to call concentration camps "temporary detainment centers" when in fact innocent civilians are forcibly incarcerated for undefined periods of time in them, and politicians should not call their vacations at taxpayer expense "fact-finding missions." If your argument requires you to justify ugly realities by renaming them, or to cover up moral shadiness through the use of euphemisms, then it is an argument you should not be making.

Perhaps this advice sounds excessively idealistic. You may agree that individuals, responsible to their own consciences, can take high moral stands. But, you might ask, what about people who are speaking not for themselves but for a nation? Wouldn't such a spokesperson be justified in concealing ugly realities for the sake of a higher aim such as national security? If a country is at war, for example, wouldn't it be wiser to call a lost battle a "strategic withdrawal" rather than a "defeat"?

This is a tough example, but even a nation at war, and by extension any arguer who has a great deal at stake, should tell the truth. The term "strategic withdrawal" implies an intentional retreat or a planned regrouping of forces rather than a military loss. To be sure, a government that has to admit a lost battle is probably torn between giving accurate information and sustaining the wartime morale of its people. Yet it can do both with careful word choice. The lost battle might honestly be termed a "temporary setback," a phrase that admits defeat but not its finality. Clearly, such ethical matters require patient untangling and careful word choice. Nevertheless, lies are unacceptable. Carefully choosing words that do not lie is always possible and in the long run always wiser. When citizens are well informed, they can make wiser choices, engage in more productive public debate, and have more confidence in their government than when they are deliberately kept in the dark. And it is possible to be honest without giving away details of national security. A public that knows that its government has strategic missiles in place, for example, does not need to know exactly where they are. What holds true for government spokespeople, who carry heavy responsibilities, also holds true for individual arguers.

Periphrasis or Circumlocution: Taking the Long Way Around

Sometimes when you are trying to avoid a sensitive word or phrase or issue in an argument, no direct verbal substitute will help. Instead, you must take the long way around the matter in a series of sentences. The Greek word *periphrasis* and the Latin word *circumlocution* both mean using many words to say what could be said in a few. Such wordiness is not necessarily dishonest. Meaning is not hidden, but drawn out and softened. Periphrasis can be pompous and long-winded, but it can also be useful in a situation in which a single word or short phrase would be counterproductive.

Imagine that you are the personnel director in a company, and you have evaluated a good friend's qualifications for a job and found them wanting. You could just blurt out "You're not going to get the job" and get it over with, but another choice is available. Instead of being cruelly blunt, you could give your friend a lengthy explanation in which you talk about the qualifications of other candidates, the budget constraints you are working with, your plans for the future, and how much she has always meant to you. By letting the truth slowly emerge in this way, you are using periphrasis.

Descriptive Language

Effective arguers show sensitivity to their audience's feelings by avoiding words that will offend them and choosing words that will inspire them. You can create direct emotional labels by adding words such as *unfair, disgusting, cruel, pitiful, joyous,* or *generous* to shape an emotional reaction to what the words describe. There is quite a difference between a "police officer," a "jolly neighborhood police officer," and a "menacing police officer," or a meeting described as "angry," "tense," or "cooperative."

You can also choose words that do not describe an emotion directly but are nonetheless charged with emotional associations. For some audiences, terms such as *left wing, right wing, mother, home,* and *school* are as emotional as *pain* and *joy*. We are not recommending that you sprinkle your argument with emotional sugar or salt, however. But you should be aware of the choices that are available—and the choices that other writers have made as they work on your emotions.

Choosing Powerful Examples

Examples or stories are another important means of conveying pathos in any argument. Examples tie your claim or thesis to reality, and they can have another function as well. They are the best means of making a direct appeal to your audience's emotions, and these appeals to the audience's fear, pity, anger, love, disgust, pride, and laughter are ways of involving an audience in an argument.

Examples are effective magnets for the various emotions because we all respond directly to anything made present to our sight, hearing, touch, smell, and taste. In the argument that opens this chapter, notice how Rosenthal begins with the example of the young mother who died of a drug overdose in order to evoke an immediate emotional response. You can count on the general effectiveness of some emotional appeals. Images of starving refugees facing winter without adequate shelter arouse pity for them and anger at those who caused their plight. Examples of homeless children and lonely old people upset anyone who reads about them, and many people who have little sympathy for members of their own species respond to bedraggled kittens, loyal dogs, and noble horses. On the positive side, you can count on examples of chortling babies, sunny days, colorful flowers, plentiful food, and warm homes to delight most people.

Whenever you use an example that appeals to the emotions, you are trying not only to gain your audience's mental assent to your argument, but also to reinforce their emotional conviction. This "yes" of the heart is no replacement for the "yes" of the head, but it is a powerful aid to agreement, and to action if that is what you are recommending. So by all means use examples when you can be sure that the emotion they evoke will work for you.

You cannot, however, count on readers sharing your emotions just because you feel intensely. Emotional appeals can backfire. If, for example, you are trying to persuade hunters that their sport is cruel and should be prohibited, they will probably be unmoved by an example of a deer shot down and dying, bleeding in the snow, and not at all disgusted by graphic descriptions of field dressing. When you use examples of less extreme forms of suffering, some audiences may remain unmoved by the emotional appeal. Veteran teachers feel little pity when bleary-eyed students tell them they have studied all night for an exam or stayed up late to write a paper.

The positive reactions inspired by examples with emotional appeal are even less predictable. You probably know what it is like to have a joke fall flat, to have a pleasant story shrugged off, to have a double meaning taken in only one way. Suppose you are evaluating different kinds of classrooms, the traditional and the open. You might argue that the traditional classroom is best, describing the orderly rows of desks, the quiet of children absorbed in their work, the way they all lift their heads and look at the teacher when he or she is talking, and the A papers tacked up neatly on bulletin boards. You hope that your readers will find this example pleasant and agree with your evaluation. But many prefer the kind of classroom where children are moving around, where the noise level is many decibels above silence, where the teacher is not easy to find, and where the room is a bit cluttered with projects at various stages of completion. Your example of the traditional classroom might strike them as authoritarian and cold.

It is important to choose examples whose emotional appeal you can count on for a particular audience, but remember that many audiences are mixed, and they may have a wide range of attitudes toward your issue. Some readers are ready to agree with you before you start, whereas others might be far, far away from your position. But because those who disagree are hardest to convince, it is best to aim your examples at them. Those who agree will come along anyway.

EXERCISE 3.5

In newspapers, on television or radio talk shows, or on the Internet, look for examples of arguers using the techniques described in this section to appeal to their readers', listeners', or viewers' emotions, and bring at least three examples to class (you can jot down notes on any examples you find on TV or radio talk shows). In a group with two or three classmates, discuss the examples you have each found and decide on two or three that you consider especially effective. Be prepared to present your most effective examples to the class and explain why they are successful.

┌───┐

WRITING YOUR ARGUMENT

EVOKING PATHOS

1. Take the draft of an argument you are working on and circle every word that has a strong positive or negative connotation.

   • Ask yourself if these connotations support the position you are arguing for. Should any be changed given your audience and purpose?

   • Try replacing several of the emotionally charged words with neutral choices. What is the effect likely to be with your intended audience?

   • Try replacing several of the neutral terms with emotionally charged choices. Again, what is the effect likely to be?

2. Insert a paragraph into your argument that includes a vivid example likely to arouse your readers' emotions in a way that reinforces your argument. What would make this example too weak or too strong for your audience?

3. Have you addressed your readers directly anywhere in your draft? Try inserting direct appeals to "you" the reader, and then assess whether such directness might hurt or help.

└───┘

FALLACIES

We have been offering a great deal of advice about how to construct arguments. But since people make arguments in response to questions to which there can be more than one answer, someone else's argument often answers a question in a way that you just do not agree with, or that you consider flawed in either principle or presentation. Often when you encounter another argument, you find yourself answering back: "No, that's just not so." "That just doesn't follow." "That's an unfair tactic." "That point is completely irrelevant." Thus an important part of responding to arguments and constructing your own position is figuring out when and why someone else's argument doesn't work.

As a logician as well as a rhetorician, Aristotle was well aware that people make mistakes in reasoning, and he was also aware that we tend to seize on the mistakes that others make while we fail to see the flaws in our own arguments. Some of these mistakes may be formal, lapses in the logical structure of an argument. But since we usually argue in everyday language rather than in chains of logical statements or with diagrams, these kinds of errors may be hard to detect. Other more common lapses may consist of false, misleading, or imprecise statements: statements that appear to be true but aren't, statements that make illegitimate appeals, statements that don't fit in an argument. We can debate about whether such errors are the result of deception, carelessness, or misunderstanding. As we interact with others, it may be important to make such distinctions because our assessment of motive certainly affects our responses to arguments made by others. However, if our purpose is solely to identify such errors, we may not need to consider the motives behind them. We will use the catchall term **fallacy** to describe all such errors in argument, regardless of their source.

Logicians and rhetoricians have identified scores of different fallacies and classified them in many different ways. The identification of fallacies is an imprecise art for several reasons. First, most of us do not consider our own arguments fallacious, only those that other people make. So people will disagree about whether any particular statement or argument is fallacious. You might consider it wholly reasonable to set aside someone's argument because of that person's character; someone else might accuse you of the fallacy of making an *ad hominem* argument. Second, the kinds of fallacies overlap. For example, what one person might label a *non sequitur*, someone else might see as an attribution of false cause. Finally, accusing someone else's argument of fallacy does not mean that you have settled an issue or trumped—and therefore defeated—the other party. Even if you intend your accusation of fallacy to defeat the other person's argument, the game of "gotcha" is not so easily won. Given the opportunity, the other person will usually deny your accusation, and then further discussion can ensue. Still, if you can see the places where a given argument is weak, you will be better able both to build your own arguments so that they stand up to criticism and to identify the weak points of other arguments in order to shape your response to them.

The following list of fallacies identifies some of the most common mistakes in argument. It defines each one briefly and offers illustrations what such a fallacy might look like. (Of course, made-up examples are much easier to identify than real ones because arguments are rarely stripped to their bare bones.) Each example is followed by a parenthetical explanation of why the argument might be considered fallacious.

Hasty Generalization   Making a general statement on the basis of an inadequate sample of evidence.

EXAMPLES

My friend Ellen lives in a small town and is afraid of big cities. I guess that's what people who live in small towns are like. (Not necessarily; a sample of one does not allow you to make such a generalization.)

I saw a bluebird last week. They must be common around here. (Not necessarily; you might have had a rare sighting.)

Ten students in my class of 30 are returning adult students. Thirty percent of our students at this college must be returning adults. (That statement would be true only if you can be certain that the proportions in your class are typical of the entire student population at your institution.)

False Cause (Post Hoc)   *Post hoc, ergo propter hoc*, literally "after this, therefore because of this." Assuming that one event caused another because it preceded it in time.

EXAMPLES

The water pipe in my garage exploded the day after I sold my house. I guess my house
   didn't like being sold. (Said in jest, but surely your house does not know that it was sold.)
The stock market crashed in 1929 and the Great Depression followed. The crash of the
   stock market caused the Great Depression. (Maybe both events happened because of
   other causes.)
Peppered moths are normally white-winged. Since dark-winged variants appeared near
   the smokestacks of the industrial city of Manchester, industrial pollution must have
   caused the variation. (Maybe the variation was caused by some other agent, or perhaps
   the sample was inadequate.)

Slippery Slope   Assuming that if a certain step is taken, a whole series of undesirable consequences will follow.

EXAMPLES

If students are allowed to drop courses without penalty late in the semester, there will be
   huge drop rates and pretty soon everyone will want to drop any course in which he or
   she does not receive an A. (The consequences may not be so dire; maybe only a few
   students will take advantage of the option.)
If we allow any logging at all in national parks, pretty soon our parks will be nothing but
   lumberyards. (Assumes that if any amount of logging is allowed, there will soon be
   successful pressure for much more of it.)
If Elizabeth stops eating meat, pretty soon she will waste away from malnourishment.
   (Not if she obtains the right kind of protein from other foods.)
If we allow solicitors on campus, they will soon be making commercial pitches in our
   classrooms. (Not necessarily; allowing them on campus does not mean we have to allow
   them in the classrooms.)

Straw Man   Presenting an extreme or a very weak case as an example of the argument you want to refute.

EXAMPLES

My opponent, who supports legalized marijuana, wants to live in a society in which people
   are spaced out on drugs all the time. (A supporter of marijuana legalization would be
   very unlikely to make this argument.)
Those who argue for the elimination of the SAT want to fill our colleges with unqualified
   students. (That is probably not their aim; they may well favor other means of
   evaluation.)
Anyone who supports the proposal to build the new highway through our county is
   voting for the end of our rural way of life. (That may not be the aim of supporters of
   this policy, and it may not even be an effect of it.)

False Analogy   Going beyond simply pointing out a resemblance between two things or situations to claim that the things or situations are the same or call for the same response.

EXAMPLES

In World War I and World War II, Congress declared war; therefore, Congress should
   always declare war before the country takes up arms. (None of the wars since WWII

have been preceded by declarations of war; perhaps current practice does not require a formal declaration of war.)

Rhetoric is like cooking; both arts pander to the consumer's appetite for pleasure rather than nourishing his or her mind. (Perhaps pleasing and nourishing can both occur at the same time; perhaps rhetoric is a much more substantial art than cookery; perhaps cookery is more worthy of praise than this comparison suggests.)

The legal penalties for the mistreatment of animals should be as severe as the legal penalties for the mistreatment of children. Both animals and children depend on humans for kindness and nurturing. (It might be argued that animals and children are essentially different and what is owed to them may differ.)

False Dilemma (Either/Or)   Arguing that there are only two choices in a situation and that your choice is the correct one because the other is unthinkable.

EXAMPLES

Either we attack our enemy or our enemy will attack us. (Maybe those aren't the only alternatives. A course of action short of all-out attack may be possible, and perhaps a counterattack can be prevented in other ways.)

We're damned if we do and we're damned if we don't. (Which is worse?)

We can either raise taxes or reduce spending. (Maybe there is a third alternative; maybe we need to do both; maybe we don't need to do either.)

Begging the Question   Often called "circular argument," begging the question refers to an argument that either assumes exactly what is to be established or restates its conclusion in different words so that it looks like a reason. This kind of fallacy is most deceptive when it occurs over a long text and the similarities between premises and conclusions are obscured, but here are some short samples.

EXAMPLES

Rich people have a right to tax-free inheritance because it is the duty of government to protect the property of those to whom it is passed by inheritance. (Both the claim and the reason supporting it say just about the same thing.)

I know Jimmy stole my bicycle because I know he's just the kind of person who would do that. (What needs to be established is exactly that Jimmy is the kind of person who would—and did—commit the crime.)

Pete Rose should not be admitted to the Baseball Hall of Fame because Pete Rose is banned from baseball. (The reason Pete Rose is not in the Hall of Fame is that he was banned from baseball. Whether the fact that he has been banned *should* prevent his admission is the relevant question.)

Non Sequitur   Literally, "it does not follow." This is a catchall category, referring to an unconvincing pairing of a claim and premise.

EXAMPLES

My client is innocent of fraud because she didn't know that what she was doing is illegal. (Ignorance of the law does not excuse illegal behavior.)

I need to be paid more for doing this job because I want to take a vacation in Hawaii this year. (Your desire for a tropical vacation is not a reason to raise your salary.)

Moses is a very good-natured cat because he's orange. (There is no known link between the color of cats and their dispositions.)

Red Herring   An argument that is intended to divert attention from the real issue at hand, a false clue that is intended to mislead.

EXAMPLES

You should eat all the vegetables on your plate because some children don't have enough to eat every day. (The issue is not whether some children don't have enough food but whether there is a good reason for you to eat vegetables.)

This bill calling for welfare reform legislation should not be supported because we need to pay much more attention to environmental issues. (The issue is not whether we need to pay attention to environmental issues but whether the proposed idea for welfare reform is a good one.)

I really can't start writing this paper until I do something about choosing my major. (The need to decide on a major may be a very important matter, but at the moment thinking about it may just be a distraction from starting your paper.)

Complex Question   Literally, two questions. This fallacy usually takes the form of a question that will make you look bad no matter how you answer it because buried in the question is the assumption of some undesirable precondition.

EXAMPLES

When are you going to start acting like a responsible adult? (By asking for an answer that names a time when change will occur, the questioner assumes that you are not at present acting like a responsible adult and that you need to change.)

How can we conserve our dwindling coal supply? (Do we know that the supply of coal is really dwindling? Perhaps new deposits are being discovered. Do we have to conserve it? Perhaps other kinds of energy make the need less pressing.)

What should we do about our corrupt city council? (There are two issues here: is the city council corrupt, and if so, what should we do about it?)

Equivocation   Shifting the definition of a key term within an argument. Usually equivocation occurs over an extended text and may not be immediately obvious. But sometimes you can recognize a shift even in a short argument.

EXAMPLES

In our society everyone needs to be literate. You would be surprised by how many people are so illiterate that they use the word "like" in every other sentence. (Ordinarily, literacy means the ability to read and write well enough to function in our society, but here people who have a certain verbal tic are being accused of illiteracy.)

I know that everyone is in favor of keeping our neighborhood safe. So I'm sure you will all agree with me that we need to put a chain link fence around it to ensure safety. (We may share a commonsense definition of what it means to keep our neighborhood safe, but that definition might not include an action as extreme as fencing it in.)

I know that John Keats is one of the Romantic poets. It's surprising, then, that his "Ode to Autumn" is all about the season and has nothing to do with relationships between men and women. (Two different meanings of the word "romantic" are operating here: one is the popular name for English poetry of the early nineteenth century, the other refers to relations between people who are attracted to each another.)

Ad Populum Argument   Literally, *ad populum* means "to the people," and it refers to an argument that appeals to popular opinion or popular belief or the opinions of those who are popular rather than those who are particularly knowledgeable about an issue.

EXAMPLES

You should buy this kind of car because several top NASCAR drivers make commercials for it. (Race-car drivers are experts on racing cars, but probably not on the kind of car you need to buy.)

Sam's ideas are really bad because he's a radical. (You should consider Sam's ideas on the subject at hand, not some general notion of what approved or unapproved group he belongs to.)

It's all right to cheat on your income taxes because everyone does it. (The fact that many people engage in this illegal action, if true, does not make the action legal.)

Appeal to Ignorance   Basing an argument on the absence of evidence or on evidence that can't be examined.

EXAMPLES

That can't be lightning. I don't hear any thunder. (Maybe you are hard of hearing and just didn't hear the thunder. Maybe the lightning is too far away for you to hear the thunder.)

Annie must be a vegetarian; she didn't order the roast beef at the wedding. (Maybe Annie doesn't care for roast beef; maybe she prefers salmon.)

I'm sure that Joe has no school spirit at all; he didn't attend the pep rally last weekend. (Joe's absence may not be evidence of his indifference. Maybe he was sick; maybe he forgot about it; maybe he had an exam at that time.)

Ad Hominem Appeal   Literally, *ad hominem* means "to the man" or, we might say, "to the person." It refers to any argument that attacks the character of a person rather than the substance of what the person has said on an issue. The problem with *ad hominem* arguments is always the relevance of the personal attack to the argument the accuser is calling into question.

EXAMPLES

Dr. X's advice about stopping smoking is worthless. He smokes himself. (His advice about quitting smoking may be perfectly sound, though his personal behavior may be inconsistent with his scientific awareness.)

You should never vote for Joe. His supporters include some people who are known libertarians. (The statement implies guilt by association; people should not be judged by their association with people or groups assumed to be unpopular.)

You can expect rude behavior from Sue. She's a feminist. (The author is accusing Sue of bad behavior because of her association with a point of view that the author doesn't care for.)

Faulty Emotional Appeals   Relying on emotional appeals in the absence of reason.

EXAMPLES

My client should not be sentenced to a jail term even though he was convicted of murder. Look at how devastated his mother is. (The fact that the client's mother feels sad has nothing to do with the kind of punishment he deserves.)

"I really need that toy," screams the child in the toy store, stamping her feet. (The child's tantrum is not a reason to buy the toy if the parent is convinced that it is dangerous, unnecessary, or too expensive.)

I am going to have to give Tom the promotion he wants because if he doesn't get it he will just make my life miserable every day of the week with his hostile attitude. (The supervisor should make the decision based on Tom's performance, not on his anticipated emotional reaction.)

As you can see from the parenthetical comments following each example of a fallacy, all of these brief sample arguments can be seen as wrong, or false, or inadequate, or misleading. It is easy to say that we should not be distracted by irrelevancies or moved by inadequate reasons. When you point out the fallacy of someone's argument, however, that person probably won't reply, "Oh, I see the error of my ways. I am indeed guilty of a *non sequitur*. I stand corrected and will never make such a poor argument again." Usually, given the opportunity, most people will insist that although there may be such a thing as a fallacious argument, theirs is not one of them. What may seem a faulty emotional appeal to you may seem perfectly reasonable to the person making it and may even convince someone else. Just for the fun of it, put yourself in the place of the person making one of the arguments we have identified as fallacious, and try to defend yourself against the accusation of fallacy to one or more of your classmates. You will probably initiate some lively discussion.

Why, then, is it important to be aware of fallacies? Because looking for fallacies in arguments helps you understand how the reasons people offer for their conclusions are related to evidence and to the mental process of creating an argument. If you study fallacies, even examples as brief as the ones presented here, you start thinking about why and how one statement follows from another. Every time you ask yourself, "What must I believe in order to accept this argument?" you are on the way to becoming a more astute critical thinker.

Emotion in Images

Political cartoons have a long history as vehicles of persuasion in our country. Cartoonists are able to express complex ideas in exaggerated images that argue for their point of view. In political cartoons, famous people, especially politicians, are lampooned in stinging carica-tures, and cultural symbols are used to represent groups, institutions, and even abstract ideas. A donkey, for example, stands for the Democratic party and an elephant for the Re-publicans, and both animals are often depicted doing and saying ridiculous things. The Statue of Liberty, Uncle Sam, and an occasional eagle are pressed into service to stand for the United States. Viewers of political cartoons need both cultural and current knowledge to "read" the images.

Political cartoons are an especially powerful means of creating or drawing out and fo-cusing the emotional responses of an audience. Usually their goal is to induce scorn in all its varieties, from amused contempt to bitter outrage. Cartoonists deflate pomposity with em-barrassing depictions and tame their enemies with visual mockery. But political cartoons can also evoke other emotional responses and, by doing so, try to express the current feelings of a community.

The cartoon reprinted here appeared shortly after the terrorist attacks of September 11, 2001. Perhaps no event in recent U.S. history has produced such an outpouring of dif-ferent emotions: horror, grief, anger, and eventually pride, patriotism, resolve, and other feelings "too deep for words." Cartoonists used their special medium to try to express the reactions of citizens across the country. (For an archive of selected responses, see http://cagle.slate.msn.com/news/9-11Remembered.) In *The Portland Oregonian,* Jack Ohman produced a drawing that seems to communicate several emotions at once. Of the many as-pects of 9/11 that could be focused on, Ohman chose one that has been especially power-ful for Americans—the deaths of hundreds of fire fighters and police officers in the act of trying to rescue people from the burning towers of the World Trade Center. In addition to their shock and horror in the days following the attack, many Americans also came to admire and even identify with and take comfort from the gritty determination of rescue personnel from police and fire departments who, out of dedication to their fallen comrades, searched the rubble of the collapsed buildings for survivors and later for the remains of victims.

To capture something of this mixture of emotions, Ohman created an image that expresses both the grief of a funeral and the admiration of a memorial. Perhaps drawing inspiration from the common description of someone enduring trouble and exhibiting fortitude as a "tower of strength," Ohman depicts a fire fighter and a police officer as "Twin Towers." They stand in the New York skyline where the buildings of the World Trade Center once stood, and they are huge and monumental, dwarfing the remaining buildings. Their exaggerated scale expresses Ohman's, and presumably his audience's, estimation of their heroism. But the picture also conveys the horrendous loss of 9/11 since these figures now stand in a schematic urban cityscape where the buildings once stood. They are forever associated with the towers that, in this image, they have replaced.

Political or editorial cartoons are traditionally printed in black and white. Using this restricted medium dramatically, Ohman depicts a dark sky, which has connotations of mourning. Everything else in the image is light and, as a result, the two figures seem to be made of stone, as though they were statues in a park or graveyard. In real life, they would be wearing dark coats, but now they are made of the same material as the other buildings. They are permanent fixtures, immovable and solid.

But why are their backs turned to the audience? On the backs of their coats, fire fighters and police rescue personnel wear identifying logos, so the initials NYPD (New York Police Department) and NYFD (New York Fire Department) inform the audience who these figures are—a task that the visual alone might not be able to do, especially in the case of the police officer whose hat is not recognizable from behind. Presenting these figures from the back also solves the problem of depicting a representative fire fighter or police officer since the personnel in these departments are both men and women and come from all racial and ethnic groups. No choices need be made. These generic figures can stand for everyone who serves the public in these saving and protecting professions.

All of these visual features together communicate an emotional message powerfully and immediately. A message of admiration and sorrow could be put into words, but it is one thing to describe emotions, another to *evoke* an emotional response in an audience. Images can arouse a viewer's emotions directly, even bypassing their conscious resistance to the message behind the image.

Cartoons that make argumentative claims are as old as drawing and printing itself. Even during the American Revolution, colonial cartoonists ridiculed the British and King George III in exaggerated and mocking drawings. Political cartoons are not, however, common on television, for obvious reasons, and as more and more Americans bypass daily newspapers, the familiar fixture of the cartoon on the editorial page may soon be a thing of the past. But newer media, including web sites devoted exclusively to political cartoons, may continue this centuries-old tradition.

FOR YOU TO ANALYZE

The first essay that follows appeared in a national magazine. Its author has worked her way through college without any financial assistance from her family. The second essay was written by a nationally syndicated columnist on the day after the terrorist attacks on the World Trade Center and the Pentagon. How would you describe the ethos these authors create in their pieces, and how do they create it? To what emotions in their audiences do they appeal? What strategies of identification do they use?

Pay Your Own Way! (Then Thank Mom)

AUDREY ROCK-RICHARDSON

Audrey Rock-Richardson lives in Stansbury Park, Utah. The following essay was published in *Newsweek* in September 2000.

Is it me, or are students these days lazy? I'm not talking about tweens who don't want to do their homework or make their bed. I'm referring to people in legal adulthood who are in the process of making hugely consequential life decisions. And collectively, their attitude is that they simply cannot pay for college.

Don't get me wrong. I realize that there are people out there who pay their own tuition. I know that some cannot put themselves through school because of disabilities or extenuating circumstances. But I have to say: the notion that parents must finance their children's education is ridiculous.

During college I consistently endured comments from peers with scholarships and loans, peers who had new Jeeps and expensive apartments, all who would say to me, eyes bulging, "You mean your parents didn't help you at *all?*"

I resented my fellow students for asking this, first because they made it sound like my parents were demons, and second because they were insinuating that I wasn't capable of paying my own way. "How did you pay tuition?" they'd ask. My response was simple: "I worked." They would look at me blankly, as though I had told them I'd gone to the moon.

As an undergrad (University of Utah, 1998), I put myself through two solid years of 5 full-tuition college by working as a day-care provider for $4.75 an hour. I then married and finished out seven more quarters by working as an interpreter for the deaf and a tutor in a private school.

I didn't work during high school or save for years. I simply got a job the summer following graduation and worked 40 hours a week. I didn't eat out every weekend, shop a lot or own a car. I sacrificed. I was striving for something bigger and longer-lasting than the next kegger.

Looking at the numbers now, I'm not sure how I managed to cover all the costs of my education. But I did. And I bought every single textbook and pencil myself, too.

I remember sitting in a classroom one afternoon during my senior year, listening to everyone introduce themselves. Many students mentioned their part-time jobs. There were several members of a sorority in the class. When it came to the first girl, she told us her name and that she was a sophomore. "Oh," she added, "I major in communications." After an awkward silence, the teacher asked, "Do you work?"

"Oh, no," she said emphatically, "I go to school full time." (As if those of us who were employed weren't really serious about our classes.)

The girl went on to explain that her parents were paying tuition and for her to live 10
in a sorority house (complete with a cook, I later found out). She was taking roughly
13 credit hours. And she was too busy to work.

I, on the other hand, was taking 18, count 'em, 18 credit hours so I could graduate
within four years. I worked 25 hours a week so my husband and I could pay tuition
without future loan debt. And here's the kicker: I pulled straight A's.

I caught a glimpse of that same girl's report card at the end of the quarter, and she
pulled C's and a few B's, which didn't surprise me. Having to juggle tasks forces you to
prioritize, a skill she hadn't learned.

I'm weary of hearing kids talk about getting financial help from their parents as
though they're entitled to it. I am equally tired of hearing stressed-out parents groan-
ing, "How are we going to pay for his/her college?" Why do they feel obligated?

I do not feel responsible for my daughter's education. She'll find a way to put herself through if she wants to go badly enough. And (I'm risking sounding like my mom
here), she'll thank me later. I can say this because I honestly, wholeheartedly thank my
parents for giving me that experience.

I'm not saying that it's fun. It's not. I spent the first two years of school cleaning up 15
after 4-year-olds for the aforementioned $4.75 an hour and taking a public bus to cam-
pus. My husband and I spent the second two struggling to pay out our tuition. We lived
in a cinder-block apartment with little privacy and no dishwasher.

Lest I sound like a hypocrite, yes, I would have taken free college money had the
opportunity presented itself. However, because my parents put themselves through
school they expected me to do the same. And, frankly, I'm proud of myself. I feel a
sense of accomplishment that I believe I couldn't have gained from 50 college degrees
all paid for by someone else.

Getting through school on our own paid off in every way. My husband runs his own
business, a demanding but profitable job. I write part time and work as a mother full
time. I believe the fact that we are happy and financially stable is a direct result of our
learning how to manage time and money in college.

So, kids, give your parents a break. Contrary to popular belief, you can pay tuition
by yourself. And you might just thank your mother for it, too.

A Letter to the Terrorists

LEONARD PITTS, JR.

A nationally syndicated columnist, Leonard Pitts is on the staff of the *Miami Herald*. He is also the author
of *Becoming Dad: Black Men and the Journey to Fatherhood*. The following article was published on
September 12, 2001.

They pay me to tease shades of meaning from social and cultural issues, to provide words 1
that help make sense of that which troubles the American soul. But in this moment of airless shock when hot tears sting disbelieving eyes, the only thing I can find to say, the only
words that seem to fit, must be addressed to the unknown author of this suffering.

You monster, you beast. You unspeakable bastards.

What lesson did you hope to teach us by your coward's attack on our World Trade
Center, our Pentagon, us? What was it you hoped we would learn? Whatever it was,
know that you failed.

Did you want us to respect your cause? You just damned it.

Did you want to make us fear? You just steeled our resolve. 5

Did you want to tear us apart? You just brought us together.

Let me tell you about my people. We are a vast and quarrelsome family, a family rent by racial, cultural, political and class division, but a family nonetheless. We're frivolous, yes, capable of expending tremendous emotional energy on pop cultural minutiae—a singer's revealing dress, a ball team's misfortune, a cartoon mouse.

We're wealthy, too, spoiled by the ready availability of trinkets and material goods, and maybe because of that, we walk through life with a certain sense of blithe entitlement. We are fundamentally decent, though—peace-loving and compassionate. We struggle to know the right thing and to do it. And we are, the overwhelming majority of us, people of faith, believers in a just and loving God.

Some people—you, perhaps—think that any or all of this makes us weak. You're mistaken. We are not weak. Indeed, we are strong in ways that cannot be measured by arsenals.

Yes, we're in pain now. We are in mourning, and we are in shock. We're still grappling with the unreality of the awful thing you did, still working to make ourselves understand that this isn't a special effect from some Hollywood blockbuster, isn't the plot from a Tom Clancy novel.   10

Both in terms of the awful scope of its ambition and the probable final death toll, your attacks are likely to go down as the worst acts of terrorism in the history of the United States and, indeed, the history of the world. You've bloodied us as we have never been bloodied before.

But there's a gulf of difference between making us bloody and making us fall. This is the lesson Japan was taught to its bitter sorrow the last time anyone hit us this hard, the last time anyone brought us such abrupt and monumental pain. When roused, we are righteous in our outrage, terrible in our force. When provoked by this level of barbarism, we will bear any suffering, pay any cost, go to any length, in the pursuit of justice.

I tell you this without fear of contradiction. I know my people, as you do not. What I know reassures me. It also causes me to tremble with dread of the future.

In days to come, there will be recrimination and accusation, fingers pointing to determine whose failure allowed this to happen and what can be done to prevent it from happening again. There will be heightened security, misguided talk of revoking basic freedoms. We'll go forward from this moment sobered, chastened, sad. But determined, too.

Unimaginably determined.   15

There is steel beneath this velvet. That aspect of our character is seldom understood by those who don't know us well. On this day, the family's bickering is put on hold. As Americans we will weep, as Americans we will mourn, and as Americans we will rise in defense of all that we cherish.

Still, I keep wondering what it was you hoped to teach us. It occurs to me that maybe you just wanted us to know the depths of your hatred.

If that's the case, consider the message received. And take this message in exchange: You don't know my people. You don't know what we're about. You don't know what you just started.

But you're about to learn.

   FOR YOU TO WRITE

1. Write a column in response to Rock-Richardson's essay, either agreeing or disagreeing with it. Pay special attention to the ethos and pathos that you create for yourself.

2. Write your own letter to the perpetrators of a recent terrorist attack or other notorious crime.

Generating the Argument:
Questions and Claims

Chapter 4

Drug Tests Backed for Broader Pool of Students

St. Louis Post-Dispatch

By Charles Lane
The Washington Post
Carolyn Bower and Imran Vittachi of the *Post-Dispatch* contributed to this report.
WASHINGTON—The Supreme Court approved on Thursday random drug testing of public high school students in extracurricular activities. The ruling increases the tools available to 14,700 public school systems to fight illegal drug use.

By a vote of 5–4, the court ruled that local school officials' responsibility for the health and safety of their students can outweigh those students' concerns about privacy. Mandatory drug testing of students in activities such as band, Future Farmers of America and chess does not violate the constitutional prohibition on "unreasonable" searches, the court said.

The court had already authorized mandatory random drug testing for student athletes in a 1995 case that noted the special safety risks and lower expectation of privacy inherent in sports, as well as the fact that athletes are role models for other students.

But, writing for the majority Thursday, Justice Clarence Thomas made clear the court had a much broader rationale in mind—the schools' quasi-parental role with regard to their young charges.

"A student's privacy interest is limited in a public school environment where the state is responsible for maintaining discipline, health and safety," Thomas wrote. "School children are routinely required to submit to physical examinations and vaccinations against disease. Securing order in the school environment sometimes requires that students be subjected to greater controls than those appropriate for adults."

Under the Tecumseh, Okla., policy at issue Thursday, students can neither be prosecuted nor expelled from school.

Thomas was joined by Chief Justice William Rehnquist and Justices Antonin Scalia, Anthony Kennedy and Stephen Breyer.

The decision could encourage more school districts to try policies similar to the one in rural Tecumseh, which school authorities instituted in 1998. Under that policy, students who refuse to take the test, or test positive more than twice, face banishment from extracurricular activities for the rest of the school year.

In dissent, Justice Ruth Bader Ginsburg, joined by Justices John Paul Stevens, Sandra Day O'Connor and David Souter, wrote that "the particular testing program upheld today is not reasonable, it is capricious, even perverse: (It) targets for testing a student population least likely to be at risk for illicit drugs and their damaging effects."

Bernard DuBray, superintendent of the Fort Zumwalt School District in St. Charles County, welcomed the Supreme Court's ruling. But he said his district does not need a mandatory drug testing policy.

"I think it's good that the Supreme Court gave schools another tool to eradicate the drug problem," he said.

The district's three high schools test athletes and members of the cheerleading squad and pompon club voluntarily—and only with the consent of parents or guardians.

He says this approach has worked because people don't feel coerced or intimidated.

In this past academic year, he said, five students had tested positive for drugs. Students who test positive are not punished. Instead, DuBray said, the district enrolls them in substance abuse counseling.

The test screens urine for traces of 10 drugs, including cocaine, marijuana and amphetamines.

The Kirkwood schools do not test students for drugs.

"It's not that some of our kids don't have a problem with drugs," Superintendent David Damerall said. "Our philosophy is to work more with the prevention angle."

Damerall said the downside to drug testing is that it's intrusive.

"It makes the assumption that some kids are using drugs even if there is no evidence that they are," he said.

Leo Hefner, superintendent of Belleville High School District 201, said the district has not considered any regular drug testing of athletes or other students.

"I doubt our policy will change," he said.

Drug or alcohol offenses result in a 10-day suspension, which can be shortened to three days if the student and a parent agree to a six-week educational program about drug and alcohol use.

ANALYZING "Drug Tests Backed for Broader Pool of Students"

On any day of the week, you will watch reports about major news stories on TV or read about them in the newspaper. This particular example appeared in the *St. Louis Post-Dispatch* on June 28, 2002; versions of the same story were published in every major newspaper on the same day, while cable and network news shows also mentioned the event. Most news items like this one probably fade quickly from your notice. But a few catch your attention, and you read or listen further to satisfy your curiosity. If you took the time to put your curiosity into words, it would shape itself into questions like the following: *What happened here? Who or what was involved? Why did this occur? How should I react to this news? Do I need to do something about this? How is this going to affect me or the people and places and causes I know and care about?* Some of your questions will be answered by the information you read or hear, but some details will be unclear or even contradictory, and other questions will remain unanswered. If your interest is stimulated, you will have to seek out additional sources of information.

The event reported in this article is a ruling by the Supreme Court on one school district's policy of testing students for drug use. **What are the facts? What exactly was involved in this decision?** The article explains that the ruling now makes it "legal" for school officials to administer drug tests to high school students who are involved in extracurricular activities. In other words, if officials choose to institute such tests, they are not likely to be sued successfully for doing so. The Supreme Court's decision was given in a case brought by a student in an Oklahoma high school, Lindsey Earls, who objected to having to pass a drug test before she could participate in a competitive singing group. Her lawyers labeled the test an invasion of her "right to privacy" based on the Fourth Amendment to the Constitution. They sued her school district and lost. The American Civil Liberties Union took the case to a higher court, the U.S. Court of Appeals for the Tenth District, and won. The school district then appealed to the U.S. Supreme Court, which overturned the decision of the Appeals Court, once more restoring the right of the school district to test for drugs students who want to participate in extracurricular activities.

Why are Supreme Court rulings like this one so important? As the highest court in the United States, the Supreme Court determines whether decisions made by lower courts violate the basic principles of our Constitution. The status of the Supreme Court as final arbiter is a basic feature of our government. U.S. citizens who disagree with one another about the issues before the court must nevertheless accept the force of a Supreme Court ruling in our system. When the court rules against a person or group, the losing party can always keep trying to bring a case involving the same issue before the court again, but that party still has to accept the existing decision. That acceptance, as well as seeking legal remedies and refusing to resort to violence, is what it means to live in a system where there are procedures to manage disagreement and the rule of law.

Why did the Supreme Court make this ruling? We are always curious about the causes of or explanations behind events. A Supreme Court ruling is not an event that occurs because of some combination of physical causes or human errors, like a train derailment or a plane crash. Instead, in a decision made by a court or an institution or a government authority, the "cause" will be, to begin with, some official explanation of the reasoning behind it. When we hear about a plane crash, we are not satisfied unless we eventually receive a plausible explanation of its causes. In the same way, we are not satisfied with the announcement of a government ruling unless we are offered some rationale for it, some account of the reasoning behind it.

As in all Supreme Court decisions, in this case two justices, one writing for the majority and one for the minority, published their reasoning for and against. Fortunately for all concerned citizens, the full texts of Supreme Court decisions are available on the Court's web site (www.supremecourt.gov). The *Post-Dispatch* article cites some of the supporting arguments the justices offered. According to this account, the court did not define the case before them as one involving a significant invasion of the right of Americans to be protected from unwarrantable searches under the Fourth Amendment. Instead, the majority reasoned that a public school is, by definition, a special kind of institution with parental responsibilities. In this special setting where they are responsible for minors, public school officials can take actions that secure the "discipline, health, and safety" of the students. Using an analogy to support this decision, Clarence Thomas, writing for the majority, also pointed out that since public schools can require students to have health examinations and vaccinations, they can also require drug tests.

The *Post-Dispatch* article suggests other explanations for the decision as well. In an earlier 1995 ruling on a similar issue, the justices upheld the testing of student athletes for drugs by reasoning that athletes are role models for other students and so can be held to a higher standard of accountability. They also cited a potential danger to other students engaged in sports if some players are on drugs. These same reasons (being role models or causing danger) could extend to the case of students involved in other extracurricular activities. (Evidently, no one is concerned about the drug habits of disengaged students who play no sports and participate in no activities.)

Was this decision a good one? How should we evaluate it? Obviously the nine members of the court were divided over the wisdom of this ruling. Five favored this decision and four did not, so evidently there are substantial arguments on both sides. As this chapter explains, making a judgment about whether an event or a policy is good or bad always involves two broad categories of argument: one type of argument considers the potential consequences and the other its moral dimensions.

The five judges who supported the ruling evidently believe that random drug testing has the good consequence of discouraging students from using drugs. They also do not think that the school board's policy has any serious negative consequences. The most serious penalty that students face if they refuse testing or test positive twice is expulsion from an activity, not from school. Nor, presumably, can they face any other kind of prosecution. (Is this confidence in the limited penalties justified?)

Writing for the four dissenting justices, Ruth Bader Ginsburg objected to the ruling on the grounds of consequence, namely the uselessness of the policy at issue. The testing, she pointed out, will not be a significant weapon in the war on drugs since it targets a population of students who, in her assessment, are not likely to use drugs anyway. And although Ginsburg agreed with the 1995 decision that allows testing student athletes on the basis of safety considerations, she did not see potential dangers in extracurricular activities like band or chess. So according to the four dissenting justices, the majority's decision is not a good one because they predict that it will not have the consequences the majority expects: it will not discourage drug use and it may even discourage participation in extracurricular activities that might prevent drug use.

Notice that in the reasoning provided in the article, neither group of justices disagrees about the negative evaluation of drug use itself (Thomas referred to the "war against drugs as a pressing concern" and Ginsburg mentioned their "damaging effects"). Both agree that illegal drug use in the schools is a serious problem, though they disagree about the means for addressing it.

Of course, how people judge the potential consequences of a decision like this one strongly depends on how they might be personally affected by it. If you are not a high school student, chances are this decision will have no practical consequences in your life, and those who are unaffected are more likely to remain neutral. But considering the number of high school students in the country and their parents and relatives, the number of people who could be affected and who will make a value judgment is large.

What action will or should follow from this decision? The writers of the article predict that this "decision could encourage more school districts to try policies similar to the one in rural Tecumseh [Oklahoma]." However, although one local school official quoted in the article approves of the ruling, there is no clear prediction of a change in local high schools. In fact, the two other local officials quoted in the article are not inclined to introduce a drug-testing policy in their schools.

An article like this one often raises more questions than it answers. What, for instance, motivated Ms. Earls to bring the suit in the first place? Not everyone who is subjected to an irritating procedure goes to court over it, so there may be specific causes behind this case. When the event and the issues involved are at all important to us, we need to find more than one account and source of information. Any single source is by definition limited, and that observation definitely includes all newspapers, including the most prestigious. While newspapers may not print deliberate lies, they are often misinformed, or they quote sources who are. There is also always a "slant" based on what is selected and what is omitted. It is therefore always wise to sample several news sources, an activity that the web has made possible and even easy.

Though every news story about an event or policy is different, the questions aroused by our curiosity are always the same. We want to know what happened, why it happened, whether what occurred is good or bad, and what, if anything, should be done about it.

These are the four basic questions that drive our inquiry, and we are rarely satisfied until we can answer all of them. And we tend to ask them in the order given here—fact, cause, value, and action. After all it makes no sense to investigate the causes of an event if we are not sure exactly what occurred.

As a story develops in the news, any of these four issues can lead to conflicting accounts or disagreements. In 1996, TWA Flight 800, bound for Paris, crashed into the ocean shortly after taking off from New York's Kennedy Airport. Questions about what happened on board and why it crashed have never been answered. In the sample news story here on the Supreme Court's drug testing decision, there is no disagreement about the facts of the case (who brought it and where) or about the Court's reasoning for its decision (available in their own words in their written opinions). However, the motivations behind this case are not clear, and reasonable people can certainly disagree about whether the decision was a good one and what consequences it will actually have in the schools. Where there are disagreements, there are opportunities for argument.

FINDING ISSUES TO ARGUE

So far we have looked at the building blocks of all arguments, at how they are put together with a basic case (logos: claims, reasons, warrants) and with appeals based on the arguer and the audience (ethos and pathos). Now we want to take a larger view and ask where the subjects of arguments come from in the first place. How do the writers whose arguments you read find their topics? How can you find your own? In particular, since arguments form around claims, where do claims come from?

Informal arguments develop naturally from everyday situations that raise questions and demand decisions. The car breaks down and a family has to decide, "Should we buy a new one or sink more money into the old one?" Two friends in a video store debate, "What movie should we see tonight?" An election is coming up and every voter wonders, "Which candidate deserves my vote?" Colleagues at work have to choose: "What is the best software on the market for this application?" Students in a history course are given a writing assignment, "What was President Andrew Johnson's reconstruction policy for the former Confederate states?" Questions like these are motives for arguments (see "Contexts for Argument," Chapter 1, pp. 8–11).

Answering Questions with Claims

When you are asked a question, you try to answer it. The answer you come up with, whether simple or complex, certain or qualified, is a claim. Here are some examples of questions and the claims that answer them.

> **Question:** Who won the Bulls-Jazz game last night?
> **Answering Claim:** The Bulls won, 106 to 98.

Question: Is it wrong to eat animal products?

Answering Claim: It is not wrong to eat animal products.

Question: Is the gray wolf an endangered species in the continental United States?

Answering Claim: The gray wolf is not really an endangered species in the continental United States.

Question: Why were there so many more school shootings by students in the 1990s?

Answering Claim: The increase in school shootings by students in the 1990s was caused primarily by the increase in violent video games played by teenagers.

Question: Should we send astronauts to Mars?

Answering Claim: We probably should not send astronauts to Mars.

Each question, then, invites a statement in response, a claim that can be supported for an audience when the occasion requires. The question about the Bulls-Jazz game, however, probably strikes you as somewhat different from the others. If you want to know the score of a basketball game, you can check ESPN online, turn on a sports show, or look in the newspaper. If you can answer a question to the satisfaction of yourself and your audience, with no ambiguity or uncertainty left over, there is no need for an argument.

But none of the other questions in the list above has an easy or obvious single answer. Each has several possible answers, and convincing an audience that your answer is the best one for a particular situation requires an argument. Consider the example "Is it wrong to eat animal products?" A question like this one could generate many possible claims, with different qualifications, as answers.

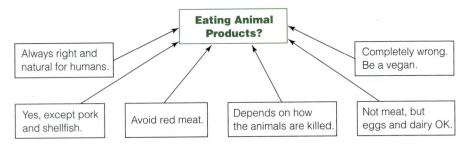

When a question remains open over time, when it attracts different answers from different groups, we think of it as an **issue**. An issue is a debated question, a problem that has not been solved or put to rest to the satisfaction of everyone involved, and perhaps cannot be resolved. In the United States, perennial and divisive issues include abortion, capital punishment, and gun control. No single claim answering questions like "Is capital punishment justified?" has ever satisfied all of the people all of the time.

Working either alone or with a group of classmates, generate a question and at least two claims about each of the following issues.

1. Fingerprinting visitors from other countries
2. Tuition support based on family income
3. Compulsory service in the military
4. Privacy on the Internet
5. Mandatory sentencing for drug offenses

The Four Basic Questions

In our examples so far, we have started with clear questions. But sometimes, when you first consider a subject, or when an event first happens, the questions that have to be answered are not immediately clear, or there are so many of them it is hard to know where to begin. An instructor gives a class a subject to write on, but no particular question to answer. A breaking story in the news becomes more complicated every hour. A business is having so many problems, it is hard to know where to begin taking action to improve things.

When you need or want to find a position on a subject, then, you first need to identify the questions that have to be answered. In the opening example about drug testing, we see how this process of question formation occurs. As in every story that dominates the news media, there is a natural sequence of questions to consider. This natural sequence gives us a way of organizing our study of argument. We can understand the claims we are making by the *kind* of question we are trying to answer. The specific questions and claims that respond to them can concern any subject in the world. But we can reduce the *kinds of questions* to the following four:

- What is it?
- How did it get that way?
- Is it good or bad?
- What should we do about it?

These questions work not only for breaking news stories, but also for the kind of topics that one just "hears about"; subjects that are mentioned here and there as though they were well-established phenomena. Take the subject of so-called "student apathy," the supposed lack of interest in public issues among current college students compared to the college students of a generation ago. If you were interested in pursuing this subject, you would naturally investigate it by seeking answers to the four basic questions. First, does this apathy about political issues among current college students really exist? How is "apathy" defined so that it can be recognized or measured? If there is evidence of apathy, what brought it about among the current generation of students? Is this political apathy a good or bad trend? "Apathy" is a negative word, but this question deserves another look. If this trend seems to exist and if it is arguably negative, how could this state of political apathy be changed? An attempted answer to any of these questions will be a claim requiring an argument. For example, the question "Is political apathy among college students a good or bad trend?" could generate this answering claim: "Political apathy among college students is actually a good trend." Of course if your answer to the first question was "No, the supposed political apathy among current college students does not exist," then there would be no point in asking the rest of the questions in the series.

Each type of question calls for a different type of claim in response. Questions about causes are answered with claims about causes; questions about what to do are answered by claims proposing a course of action, and so on. Thus the overall pattern of these recurring basic questions provides us with a simple approach to studying argument. We use them as the organizing principle of Part Two of this book, devoting a chapter to each one. They help us take arguments apart or put them together. When you are analyzing someone else's argument, identifying the kind of question the arguer is addressing gives you insight into what to expect. When you are building your own argument, identifying the kind of question you are answering tells you what kind of claim you need, and this awareness can help you see how to put your case together. The rest of this chapter examines each of the four basic questions in more detail and then considers how these questions help you find and refine arguments on complex subjects.

The First Question: What Is It?

When we ask this first question, we want an answer in the form of a claim that establishes or **defines** the nature of our subject. In the case of an event, we want to know whether it happened and what exactly happened. Did the President have sexual relations with a White House intern? In the case of a trend, we want to know what is or was happening. Is drug abuse increasing or decreasing in the United States? Sometimes we want a label that allows us to define or characterize our subject. Was the Unabomber, Ted Kacyzinski, mentally unfit to stand trial? Are Americans cynical about politicians?

Claims answering such questions, as Chapter 6 explains, always involve facts and definitions, and matters of fact and definition are always related. Whether or not a defendant is "mentally unfit," for example, depends on the definition of "mentally unfit" that the court will accept even though common opinion may not, and whether Americans are "cynical about politicians" depends on how "cynical" is defined in terms of opinions and assumptions that can be sampled or surveyed. Even apparently simple questions about whether or not something happened can depend on a key term: lawyers involved in accusations against President Clinton had different definitions of "sexual relations." And there have been conflicting reports on trends in drug abuse in the United States because of different ways of defining "drug abuse." Statistics may show, for example, that the use of marijuana is declining but the use of inhaled heroin, a far more serious drug, is increasing. Although the total number of drug users, including those using the less addictive drugs, may be down, the number of those using more dangerous drugs has gone up. Is "drug abuse" the number of people abusing serious drugs, in which case drug abuse has increased, or the number abusing illegal substance, in which case drug abuse has decreased? The same numbers can be characterized in very different ways. All these examples show how critical definition is in these kinds of arguments.

The Second Question: How Did It Get That Way?

To answer questions of this type, we start with situations, events, or trends and look for their **causes.** Why did the Soviet Union collapse in the late 1980s? What caused the crash of John F. Kennedy Jr.'s plane in 1999? Why has the number of abortions declined in the last five years? We can also ask more general questions about causes, questions not tied to specific people or events: What role does negative press coverage play in weakening a political candidate? What are the roots of Islamic terrorism?

We can also start with situations, events, or trends and look for their **consequences and effects.** What have been the effects of the increase in heroin use in the United States in the last 20 years? What are the consequences of home schooling on the social skills of a child? Questions about consequences and effects are still basically causal questions, only now we are asking what something causes, not what caused it. We can also add to this category all questions about future consequences. What will computers be able to accomplish 10 years from now? What will be the results of the "flight to small towns" that began in the 1990s? Questions like these are answered by predictions and so also lead to causal claims and arguments. Chapter 7 explains the many types and tactics of causal arguments.

The Third Question: Is It Good or Bad?

Under this general question we can group all the particular questions that concern how something should be valued: whether an action is right or wrong, moral or immoral; whether a thing is beautiful or ugly, good or bad of its kind; whether a person is worthy of praise or blame. Any time a word expressing a judgment appears in a claim, we are dealing with a question about values. Such claims are quite common in all the contexts of argument, as the following examples demonstrate: "The extension of legalized gambling is an unfortunate trend." "A hybrid car is the buyer's best choice." "*Titanic*, winner of the Academy Award for Best Picture in 1997, was actually a terrible movie." "The coverage of Princess Diana's death was absurdly overdone." "There are too many emotional appeals in politics today." "Profiling groups that may support terrorists is justified." "The EEOC did the right thing in restoring the gold medal despite the fact that the athlete tested positive for steroids."

Claims like these are supported by **evaluation** arguments and, as Chapter 8 will explain, evaluation arguments are either based on the nature of something or on its causes and effects. If you make a judgment about the quality of a movie or an acoustic guitar, for example, you probably have in mind what qualities a good movie or a great acoustic guitar should have. The object in question is then measured against those qualities or criteria. Other evaluations may use causal arguments, pointing out consequences as a way of supporting a judgment; things are judged negatively when they have bad effects, positively when they have good ones. Someone arguing that legalized gambling is a bad trend might point out the increase in personal bankruptcies caused by addictive gambling.

The Fourth Question: What Should We Do about It?

The final common question "What should we do about it?" follows naturally from the third. If we decide that something is bad, we want to stop it, and if we decide that something is good, we want to bring it about. Claims that answer the question, "What should we do about it?" are called **proposals,** and they are among the most common that we make and hear every day: "We should find a diplomatic solution to the problems with North Korea," "Congress should restructure the tax code," "People need to eat five servings of fruits and vegetables every day," "Recovered memory testimony should not be admitted in court."

As you will learn in Chapter 9, when we argue for a proposal, we build on claims answering the first three questions. A proposal to solve a problem, for example, can go through several stages, arguing that a situation exists, that it is wrong because it violates a moral standard or leads to bad consequences, and that the course of action recommended will satisfy a moral standard and have good consequences. The "we" in this general question is also important because it reminds us how much proposals depend on the particular people and circumstances involved in an action.

EXERCISE 4.2

Working either alone or with a group of your classmates, review the questions that you came up with for Exercise 4.1 and decide which kind of question you generated for each issue. Choose one issue and develop a question for each of the three other basic types of questions. Finally, choose one question from among the four you have generated and construct a claim answering it. (You may go on to use this as the claim for a written argument.)

Warrants and the Four Basic Questions

In Chapter 2, we discussed how to build a basic case in an argument. Arguers make claims and offer reasons to support them in order to make them more believable to an audience. Whenever a reason is offered to support a claim, a warrant—sometimes expressed but more usually left unstated—links the reason and claim. For example, if you argue for the claim "The income tax should be abolished" with the reason "because it is unconstitutional," your connecting warrant, whether explicit or not, has to be that "An unconstitutional tax should be abolished." Or, to take a personal example, if you argue to yourself, "I should study Latin" because "Latin will help me to improve my vocabulary," you must also believe in the linking warrant, "I should do something to improve my vocabulary."

Now we can combine these basic building blocks of all arguments with the new perspective that arguments can be grouped according to the type of question they try to answer. The type of question determines the type of warrant. If you make a claim about the nature of something, your warrant will be a definition. A causal claim needs a causal warrant, a belief about what can cause what. When you want to evaluate, you will have to assume or state a value. And when you want to urge a course of action, you will build on a warrant providing some motive for action. Here are examples of each of the four kinds of questions presented in Toulmin diagrams.

Definition Warrant
Reason: He has a Body Mass Index → *Claim:* My friend is obese.
above 30.
↑
Warrant: Anyone with a body mass index above 30 is obese.

Causal Warrant
Reason: Her opponent engaged in → *Claim:* Negative campaigning negative campaigning. defeated Senator X.
↑
Warrant: Negative campaigning by an opponent can defeat a candidate.

Value Warrant
Reason: Home theater systems → *Claim:* Home theater systems are a produce movielike sound. good purchase.
↑
Warrant: Any TV system that imitates the movies is a good purchase.

Proposal Warrant
Reason: Success in today's → *Claim:* All high school students technological society should be required to take requires computer literacy. courses in computer literacy.
↑
Warrant: High school students should be required to take courses that will help them succeed in today's technological society.

When a basic three-part argument is laid out in this way, you can see the kinds of additional arguments that might be required by an audience. In each case the warrants require different support. The definition warrant would require some authority for a definition of obesity in terms of a score on a Body Mass Index. The authority in this case is the U.S. Department of Agriculture and the American Medical Association. The second warrant posits an established causal connection between negative press coverage and a candidate's defeat. How firm is that assumption? The third warrant states the criterion for a certain kind of consumer item and the fourth an imperative for decisions on course requirements in high schools. Each warrant could be treated as a claim requiring its own support. Chapters 6–9 examine in detail arguments that answer each of the four basic questions and provide strategies for supporting each kind of warrant.

Combining the Questions

When we consider the series of four basic questions, we notice that the first and second represent the fundamental questions we ask when we begin to investigate a subject: "What is the nature of this thing and what has brought it about?" What is happening and why is it happening and what effects is it having? Consider, for example, a pair of questions like the following: "What is the nature of population movement in the United States and what factors are responsible for any changes?" In the 1990s, demographers identified a new population trend. If the United States is divided into four regions (Northeast, South, Midwest, and West), population statistics show that the Northeast is "exporting" people and the other three regions are "importing" them, though at different rates. Of course different population trends can be created by different geographical divisions. But once a pattern like this is identified, people naturally ask, "Why should this trend occur?" "What will its results be?"

If you are investigating a subject, whether for a class or work or to satisfy your own curiosity, the first two questions can guide your research, leading you to find the information that will help you support answering claims about the nature of your subject and its causes and effects. Of course you should have a positive answer to the first question before you can ask the second. Why look into the reasons for a decrease in the size of women's purses if this trend cannot be established in the first place? Though some arguers try to short-circuit the process, you should be convinced that an event happened or that a situation or trend exists or existed before you look for its causes and effects.

Finding the Key Questions at Issue

Almost any complex event or problem that occupies public attention can be understood in terms of the questions asked and the answers offered. To find a specific topic for an argument about one of these complex subjects, you need to focus on one of these questions.

Take for example the recent debates about reintroducing predators such as wolves and grizzly bears into selected sites in the "lower 48" states (excluding Alaska, where large predators abound). This topic presents important issues concerning any one of the four basic questions. To begin with, nothing would seem less problematic than defining the animals themselves and how they are identified. A wolf is a wolf, a grizzly is a grizzly. But there is debate over whether a population of wolves once common around the Mexican border is a special subspecies, the Mexican wolf, or a population of the most common species, the gray wolf. And if gray wolves have reintroduced themselves "naturally" in Montana and Idaho, where they migrated from Canada, is it also necessary to introduce wolves into national parks? These questions concern matters of definition, and they are critical in arguing over whether the gray wolf can be defined as "endangered," the status a species must have if it is to be protected or reintroduced into an area.

Obviously the debate over wolves has also concerned their effects. What will the consequences of reintroduction be? Those who favor reintroduction point out a good consequence: wolves can help control proliferating herds of deer and elk. Those who oppose reintroduction point out the negative consequences: wolves can pose a danger to domestic animals, pets, and humans. Citizens in Idaho objected to the danger of reintroducing grizzlies in their national forests. Are their fears for public safety justified? Or is the real purpose of reintroducing predators the desire to create fears that will reduce human use of wilderness areas?

Questions have also been raised about who should fund or carry out the reestablishment of predators: government, environmental groups, or private individuals? The reintroduction of wolves into Yellowstone by the Natural Park Service and into the Apache National Forest by the U.S. Fish and Wildlife Service cost taxpayers millions of dollars. Was this cost justified? CNN mogul Ted Turner, the largest private landowner in New Mexico, has bred wolves on his property at his own expense. Does he have the right to do so? Can the government tell a private landowner what animals to raise or not to raise on his or her property? What if these privately raised animals migrate to public lands and cause damage? What are the legal issues involved?

If you read arguments about the reintroduction of predators, you will also come across other issues: aesthetic issues about the beauty of the wilderness and ethical issues about the responsibility of Americans to preserve ecosystems as they existed before the nineteenth century. Any one of the many issues that have already been raised in the public debate on this complex problem could be the subject of an argument. It is also possible that any one of these issues will lead to new questions that are worth arguing about.

While some subjects raise many demanding questions, for others there is one key question that focuses the controversy, one question that attracts the most serious disagreements and creates a deadlock. The abortion debate in the United States has long been deadlocked over the definition of the fetus either as an individual human being or as a part of its mother's body. The gun control issue has been deadlocked over interpretations of the Second Amendment. The debate over a Homeland Security Department was stalled over whether employees in national security agencies should be unionized. The question of how to interpret voter intent divided people over the issue of which candidate won the most votes in Florida in the disputed presidential election of 2000. These key questions persist even after legal decisions may have settled a matter. They continue as long as the dissatisfied group is large enough and powerful enough to express its views and call for the issue to be opened again. If you can find the key question at issue in a subject, therefore, you will always have an issue worth arguing over.

In the process of trying to address a key question, a group of subsidiary questions will also develop. These may have to be answered in order to address the key question. In the aftermath of 9/11, the number of questions that demanded answers expanded with each passing day. How did the terrorists get control of the planes? Was airport security inadequate? How did they coordinate their activities and communicate with one another? How was money transferred to them and what were its sources? Did they have co-conspirators in the United States? Since several had illegal driver's licenses, how were these obtained? How was it possible for them to receive pilot training at U.S. flight schools? Did they violate existing laws for foreign nationals on student visas? Why wasn't the FBI or the CIA aware of the developing plot? Was key information available but misinterpreted? Memos from FBI field offices did warn of the possible scenario of hijacked planes being flown into buildings, but these memos remained unanswered. Why? Singling out any thread in this tangled story will bring with it a connected set of questions.

When you are either assigned a subject to write about or choose one that interests you, your first step in doing research is to find the question or questions that remain open and that have attracted different responses. A question invites an answering claim, and a claim invites an argument.

EXERCISE 4.3

Working either alone or with a group of your classmates, decide on the key question for each of the following controversial issues. (You may go on to use this key question to generate a claim for a written argument.)

1. The drinking age
2. Affirmative action
3. Income tax rates
4. Animal rights
5. The death penalty

THE BASIC QUESTIONS AS A RESEARCH STRATEGY

When you begin to research a subject, you will retrieve bibliographical sources and Internet postings and plunge into the process of reading and taking notes. You may also find people to interview, places to visit, databases to consult, experiments to perform. At first the information you discover is not likely to come in any kind of order; each piece will offer a different perspective on your subject, and although some details will be repeated, you will also find new nuggets from source to source. Later, as you refine the question you are pursuing, your research will narrow. But for now we can look at the process of going from a general subject to a particular question to address on that subject.

You can divide the material you read during your preliminary research into two rough categories. In the first category are the "factual" reports on your topic such as news stories about an event, entries in encyclopedias or textbooks on a subject, data on a web site. These sources review a subject and will often explicitly point out the questions that are causing disagreements about it. While these sources seem to avoid taking a position on a subject, they actually argue implicitly by what they include or leave out, by what they put first or last, and by the language they use. If you read more than one news report on a subject you are researching, you will see how the differences among them reveal implicit arguments. Sometimes you will even find the basic facts reported differently.

In the second category are sources that openly take a position on an issue, such as editorials in a newspaper, statements from advocacy groups, or scholarly articles. These are explicit arguments, and as argument they have inevitably identified a question worth addressing. If you find several arguments tackling the same question from different sides and reaching different conclusions, you have certainly identified a key issue.

WRITING YOUR ARGUMENT

USING THE BASIC QUESTIONS TO ORGANIZE YOUR RESEARCH

Once you have identified a subject to investigate, you can use the four basic questions to organize your inquiry. You can be fairly certain that you want to find the best possible answers to the first two questions about the nature of your subject and its causes and effects. The other two questions usually follow, especially the third on the value and importance of your subject. As you continue to read "around" a complex subject, you will begin to see the points of disagreement among those who have already thought and written about your topic. A good strategy for organizing your reading is to look for the problems or points of disagreement according to the kind of basic question involved.

Use the following headings to organize your notes, either by making a list for each or putting the headings on separate pages of a computer file. Under each, write down the agreements and disagreements that emerge from your reading and other research.

Questions about Facts and Definitions

What are the agreements and disagreements about the facts of the subject and about the meaning of key terms? Differences in facts may show up only when you compare different sources. Such disagreements about facts can come when your sources disagree about how to verify them, but they can also occur when your sources are using different definitions to generate the facts in the first place. So pay particular attention to the meanings of words and phrases that might be at issue.

Questions about Causes and Consequences

Have your sources investigated causes and do they agree about them? Sources may disagree about how many factors contributed to an event, or they may disagree about which cause is the most important. Do your sources disagree about the consequences of your subject, about what it caused or will cause? Claims about causes and consequences often take the form of narratives about a subject, so see if the stories about your subject agree from source to source.

Questions of Value

Do your sources value your subject in the same way and to the same degree, or do they offer different judgments about its morality, rightness, seriousness and so on? If your subject is a work of art or entertainment, you will certainly find claims, and often subtle disagreements, about the value of the work. The overall significance of a subject may also be at issue. Some arguers may want to claim that an event has great significance; others will want to diminish its importance.

Questions about What Action to Take

Are your sources raising questions about what should be done? About who should do it? About where it should be done? About how much it should cost? About how much time it should take? About whether a proposal will actually fix something? These are all questions concerning what action should be taken. When you are finding questions about your subject under this heading, you can be sure that questions under the previous three headings have already been answered, or the answers have been assumed. So an issue at this level may take you back through the first three levels of questions again.

Reading for Questions

We can practice the process of reading with the four basic questions in mind with an easily accessible piece from a newspaper, the kind of article that might spark your interest in a subject in the first place and lead to more serious research. A newspaper story belongs to that rough category of "factual" reports on a subject described above. The purpose of the following piece is to convince American readers about the existence of a trend and its impact in Japan: "Japan's Modern Women Living Single and Loving It." While the author of the article does not take a stand, she does note what has been controversial about this trend, at least in Japan. We can organize the relevant material from this reading according to the headings suggested in the Writing Your Argument box above. Instead of taking notes on the information provided in the article in the order in which it is presented, we have rearranged paraphrased and quoted material under the types of questions this material helps to answer and noted other questions that the material raises. We have also included commentary in these notes to suggest how the material is being interpreted.

▌ Japan's Modern Women Living Single and Loving It

KATHRYN TOLBERT

The following article was published in *The Washington Post Sunday News Journal* on February 13, 2000.

Miki Takasu is 26 years old, drives a BMW and carries a $2,800 Chanel handbag—   1
when she is not using her Gucci, Prada or Louis Vuitton purses. She vacations in
Switzerland, Thailand, Los Angeles, New York and Hawaii.

Happily unmarried, living with her parents while working as a bank teller, she is
what people here call a "parasite single."

There are so many women like Takasu that they have become the focus of a heated
controversy.

Depending on whom you ask, they are good for the economy because they spend
their salaries on clothes, cars and dining out, or they are destroying society by refusing to get married and have children. They are young women with no responsibilities,
or they are trailblazers, trying to find a path different from their mothers'.

They are the first significant group of women in Japan to stay single beyond their   5
early twenties—the number of women in their late twenties who have not married has
risen from 30 percent to about 50 percent in the last 15 years.

Takasu and her girlfriends have formed a social circle they laughingly dubbed with
an English acronym—DSS, for Darling Searching Society—but none of them wants
to get married, for now. Takasu said she wants to get married and have children. But
the ideal age to get married, she said, is 30.

"It's not necessary to be in a hurry about marriage," she said. "If I have my first child
by the time I'm 35, that's early enough."

Editorials here talk about the need to spiff up the image of marriage and child-
rearing. But single women don't frown on married life. Rather, they are content with
the status quo and feel the possibilities open to them now will be closed later on.

They study. English conversation schools are filled with women, and the boom in
special skills courses, from computing to accounting, is fueled by women.

They shop. Rings and watches by Cartier, Bulgari and Hermes costing $2,000 to   10
$3,000 are particularly popular among working women, who buy themselves presents
for special occasions—to celebrate her 10th anniversary on the job, or turning 30.

They travel. Takasu, who earns about $28,000 a year, has been to Hawaii three
times and Malaysia and Egypt as well—all with girlfriends.

They can afford this lifestyle because they have jobs, live with their parents and
treat most of their income as spending money.

They also have been less affected by Japan's economic downturn. While the recession pushed the average unemployment rate to 4.7 percent last year, the number of
contract and part-time jobs, usually filled by women, has been increasing.

Fewer women than men are out of work. Visitors to Tokyo looking for signs of recession are struck by the crowded department stores, due in large part to single women.

The ease of a social life among girlfriends is one of the striking aspects of life in   15
Tokyo. In restaurants, particularly the upscale French and Italian ones, more women
than couples are dining together. Hotels offer special packages for women traveling
together.

"In Japan we treat our girlfriends well. Boyfriends come and go, but girlfriends are
your sustenance, your life," Takasu said.

Mariko Kawana, 31, organized a Christmas millennium party for her girlfriends.
She and seven friends rented a suite for a night at the Park Hyatt Hotel—cost: about

$750—had dinner from their favorite Italian restaurant brought in and partied until 4 a.m.

The money Kawana spends on going out with girlfriends is her biggest monthly expense. The second is the payment on her BMW.

She isn't sure why she's still single.

"I used to think I would marry early, but somehow it just didn't happen," she said.　20

She lives at home, works as an assistant to traders at an international investment bank and takes frequent trips abroad—half the time with her mother, the rest with her girlfriends.

She talks a lot about uncertainties in her life—how she would like to have a career in finance but is not sure how to advance; how she wants to get married but hasn't been able to meet the right person.

The widely held image of life after marriage, among both women and men, is that the wife will look after the child and the home and be supported by her husband. For so many women it seems like an either/or situation—work and do things for themselves or get married and take care of a house and children.

"In the United States and Europe, it's possible to pursue a career even after marriage, even after having a baby," said Tamako Sarada, a writer. But in Japan, she said, "if after marrying, a woman then realizes there is something she wants to do, she has almost no chance to come back to it."

Sarada takes issue with the label "parasite single" and its negative connotation.　25

"Deep in their hearts, single women think there is something they can do and want to do," she said.

More than 70 percent of the single women in Tokyo live at home, according to surveys, and about half pay rent to their parents. Masahiro Yamada, a sociology professor at Tokyo Gakugei University who coined the term "parasite single," said the main reason women are delaying marriage is that life at home is too comfortable. They don't cook or do housework or laundry.

Most young women in Japan feel that their current situations are defined by their parents' affluence, and that their future lives will be defined by the husband's job, Yamada said.

"Parasitic singles feel that whatever they do is not going to make any difference," he said. "So they might as well relax and enjoy themselves."

Questions about Facts and Definitions

What event or trend or situation has occurred? Answering claim: "the number of women in their late twenties who have not married has risen from 30 percent to about 50 percent in the last 15 years." These young unmarried women are "the first significant group of women in Japan to stay single beyond their early twenties." The article does not indicate or suggest that the existence of this trend has been debated. Social statistics are usually considered reliable in developed nations. What we do not learn is whether there are any significant class or geographical patterns in this trend.

Are there any significant patterns in this trend? In other words, does the trend vary according to family income, rural versus urban residence, level of education, and so on?

What about young Japanese men in the same age group, 25–30? Presumably if the young women are not marrying, neither are the young men.

Would statistics in the United States show the same trend over the last 15 years for women between 25 and 30?

Also convincing readers that the trend exists are the colorful details of the lifestyles pursued by Miki Takasu, 26, and Mariko Kawana, 31. These details strongly suggest the additional claim that this new group of single women in Japan is affluent.

Are most of these single women affluent consumers? A key term is "parasite singles," coined by Masahiro Yamada, a sociology professor at Tokyo Gakugei University. This is an evaluative label and will be discussed below under "Questions of Value."

Meanwhile, is this term applied only to unmarried women in their twenties?

Questions about Causes and Consequences

What have been the consequences of this increase in the number of affluent unmarried young women? The article suggests several *consequences*, or parallel trends, that have resulted from the increase in the number of single women. These subsequent trends also tend to support the claim that these single women are affluent.

- A boom in special skills courses.
- Increased consumption of luxury items (watches, designer accessories, and so on).
- Increased travel, especially by groups of women.
- Increased upscale dining.
- Increased social bonding among women. ("In Japan, we treat our girlfriends well. Boyfriends come and go, but girlfriends are your sustenance, your life.")

What changes in dating habits and young men's lifestyles have also occurred as a consequence of this changing pattern of marriage? What will the long-term consequences of this pattern be for Japanese society?

Next, what has caused this trend among young women to postpone marriage? One would expect that many factors contribute to it. Evidently, according to interviews with the women in Takasu's "Darling Searching Society," "none of them wants to get married for now." The details in the article strongly suggest that their lives as single women are very enjoyable and they do not want to give them up. So we want to look for the causes that contribute to this attitude.

Why do they have these enjoyable lifestyles? "They can afford this lifestyle because they have jobs, live with their parents and treat most of their income as spending money."

Why do they have these jobs? They have jobs because Japan's recent recession has raised unemployment but increased "the number of contract and part-time jobs, usually filled by women." In other words, they are in a unique position to profit from the changing nature of the job market in a weak economy. The reported boom in special skills courses may suggest that these women have prepared themselves for the available jobs.

Why do they have money to spend on luxury items? They can spend money on luxuries because they "treat most of their income as spending money" (a claim supported by the example of Kawana's spending), and that behavior in turn is caused by the fact that many of them (70% in Tokyo) live at home, don't pay rent, and don't have to cook or clean. If these young women find their single lives enjoyable, they must also find the alternative, marriage in their twenties, less attractive.

Why is marriage not an attractive alternative for young women? The article suggests that the answer can be found in the rigid separation of gender roles in Japanese marriages: "The widely held image of life after marriage, among both women and men, is that the wife will look after the child and the home and be supported by her husband. For so many women it seems like an either/or situation—work and do things for themselves or get married and take care of a house and children." This claim is supported by a quotation from a Japanese writer, Tamako Sarada, who contrasts the situation in Japan with that in Europe and the United States where women can pursue careers after marriage and children.

This answer is certainly consistent with Western views about the conservative nature of Japanese society and the natural aspirations of women for an identity and career outside the family. It may not, however, be consistent with Japanese views since, according to the sociologist quoted at the end of the article, "Most young women in Japan feel that their current situations are defined by their parents' affluence, and that their future lives will be defined by the husband's job." In other words, according to this view, they are not challenging a Japanese woman's traditional role but merely postponing it. Hence they take temporary rather than career-building jobs. Some day they will do the laundry for their working daughters and go on vacation with them occasionally.

Which causal explanation seems most probable?

Questions of Value

Is this trend among young women to postpone marriage a good one or a bad one? According to the article, this question has sparked a controversy among the Japanese. It is an open question that has been answered by conflicting claims. "Depending on whom you ask, they are good for the economy because they spend their salaries on clothes, cars and dining out, or they are destroying society by refusing to get married and have children." The terms of this disagreement are based on the consequences, good or bad, of the trend. There is no evidence in the article to suggest negative consequences.

There is also evidence of a negative moral judgment in that evaluative label, "parasite singles." This term suggests that these women are living and enjoying themselves at the expense of others, an immoral thing to do.

Does this negative judgment seem justified? How would readers in the United States tend to evaluate this trend? Would they also split along the same lines as the Japanese commentators? Would they find something else about this new group and its lifestyle to judge either positively or negatively?

Questions about What Action to Take

What actions, if any, have been or should be taken in response to this trend? This article does not indicate that any groups or government agencies have acted or proposed an action in response to this trend. The only stirring mentioned here has been in editorials talking "about the need to spiff up the image of marriage and child-rearing." The lack of proposed responses that would either encourage or discourage this new pattern is not surprising since the Japanese are evidently still debating what to think about it. If it isn't really a problem, why "solve" it?

If it is, what actions by the Japanese government or some other group could either increase or decrease the average age at which people marry? What changes in Japanese culture would be required?

SUGGESTED ACTIVITIES

1. Each of the following two editorials was written in response to the same issue, *Should Georgetown University, a school affiliated with the Catholic church, place crucifixes in its classrooms as some students at the school have suggested?* This question obviously concerns what action should be taken in a specific situation, but each editorial makes points that could go under the four basic questions. Read these two conflicting pieces and, using the procedure demonstrated above, list the agreements and disagreements under each of the four basic questions.

2. Select several readings on a subject you are researching and organize your notes for all of them together under the same four headings. Give yourself room by putting each question at the top of a separate sheet or on a separate page in a computer file.

Crucifix Can Reflect on Good Moral Character of School

JOSETTE SHINER

This article and the following one were both published in the *News Journal*, a daily newspaper in Wilmington, Delaware, in November 1997.

I certainly cannot deny my colleague the right to be offended by the placement of a crucifix in each classroom at a Catholic university. But one wonders if there is any room left for the public display of religion in our society if a Catholic university, headed by a priest and still proudly connected to the church, cannot display this most important symbol of its faith.

It is true that some may be so repelled by different symbols of faith that they will choose only schools founded by their own religion or secular institutions. They are free to do so. But there are others who celebrate the contribution that Yeshivas, Christian colleges and Catholic universities make to our civic life. In fact, it is a unique strength of American society that we promote not only tolerance of our private differences of faith, but a public appreciation of them.

Justice Scalia wrote in his dissent to Lee v. Weisman of the contribution public expressions of faith, such as diverse prayers at graduation ceremonies, can make.

"To deprive our society of that important unifying mechanism, in order to spare the non-believer of what seems to me the minimal inconvenience of standing or even sitting in respectful non-participation, is as senseless in policy as it is unsupported in law," he wrote. And he was right.

Students attending Georgetown make "genuinely independent and private choices" (to quote one Supreme Court criterion regarding religion) to attend a Catholic institution. They knowingly attend such a university because of its good academic reputation—and perhaps even because of their admiration of the moral principles at the foundation of the university.

In fact, the head of the Jewish ministry at Georgetown has said in published reports 5 that he is not offended by the crucifixes. "It's good for our students, through the crucifix, to know that suffering exists in our world," said Rabbi Harold White. He, for one, seems to understand a common message of our founding fathers: that the diverse expression of religious values can play a tremendous role in the healthy civic life of our nation.

It Would Drive Away Students

BONNIE ERBE

As a proud, non-Jesuit alumna of Georgetown University, I treasured my educational 1 experience there for its pluralism. I attended Georgetown Law School's evening program. My fellow students included men, women, whites, blacks, Asians, Hispanics, Catholics, Jews, Buddhists and Muslims—all manner of Americans and foreign students. It was a wonderful microcosm of the pastiche that makes up American society.

The only reminder of the law school's religious base that I can recall is the chapel on the bottom floor of the building. Students who wished to intersperse their studies with religious contemplation or prayer were perfectly free to do so. Those of us who did not share those beliefs were free from compulsion to observe them.

Only about half of Georgetown's student body is Catholic. If the handful of students who want to place crucifixes in each classroom succeeds, they will drive many students who might otherwise have attended Georgetown to other institutions. I, for one, would have felt extremely out of place and would have taken my tuition dollars and myself elsewhere.

In some older classrooms on the main campus crucifixes still hang. But years ago Georgetown officials stopped the practice of hanging them in new buildings, because they wanted to attract a diverse student body.

Student association President John Crondan, a wise man for his 21 years, says that, 5 personally, he would welcome the placement of crucifixes in classrooms, but that as an officer of the entire student body association, he opposes the suggestion because "I do not believe I have the right to use my position in student government to force my own religious beliefs on the entire student body."

His fellow students should be as Solomonic. My advice to those leading the pro-crucifix movement: go ahead with your plan. If you succeed, prepare to take responsibility for a drastic drop in the size and caliber of the student body. Watch the school's income base decline, and its prestige plummet. Then pat yourselves on the back as being great religious crusaders.

FOR YOU TO WRITE: A "WHAT'S AT ISSUE" PAPER

When you first investigate a subject, you will probably begin with some vague ideas about it and perhaps a few details. You need to fill in the gaps, to set boundaries to your inquiry and to identify problems and issues to write about. This assignment will help you get an overview of "what is at issue" on a subject.

Suppose, for example, that during a museum visit you were fascinated by a diorama of a Neanderthal family and intrigued by questions about their nature and fate. If you begin by reading the most recent, reputable, accessible sources on Neanderthals (working backwards to earlier sources), you will discover debates about where and when they lived, about their social organization, about what caused their extinction, and about whether they were a distinct species in the first place (a question whose answer could make some of the other questions irrelevant). Or suppose some news articles on the return of refugees to Haiti have captured your interest. Sampling the flood of articles, editorials, and letters to the editor on this subject, you discover differing definitions of "economic" versus "political" refugees as well as controversies over interpretations of U.S. and international law concerning refugees, over the moral dimensions and practical consequences of U.S. refugee policy, over the causes of the Haitian exodus in the first place. Or suppose you were investigating "Attention Deficit Disorder," perhaps because a family member has been diagnosed with this condition. You would discover many competing definitions and significant disagreements about identifying and responding to this disorder.

In each of these cases, your initial investigation would require you to sort through the questions at issue. You will do this same sorting of issues whenever you take up a topic. One of the issues you identify, or perhaps a new one that you discover, can become the focus of a targeted argument. But before you get to that stage, it is often helpful to write a preliminary paper that provides an overview of the questions being raised about a subject.

To get an idea of your rhetorical situation in this paper, imagine a room full of people, conversing in pairs and groups, sometimes heatedly, all talking on different aspects of the same subject. That room is what your sources are like. Meanwhile, your reader is out in the hallway. You enter the room, sample the conversations, and then come out and give your reader a coherent account of what you have overheard.

Select a subject that interests you, perhaps one you have been assigned in another course or have developed in response to an exercise or activity in this book or in the classroom. Select the most credible sources available. In addition to using standard reference sources and databases to compile a bibliography, use the references cited in one book or article to lead you to others. If you read an article summarizing someone else's position, try to find the original argument. Pay attention to clues revealing alternative perspectives, and try to track those perspectives down. If possible, you should also interview people who can contribute to your understanding.

Remember that you will confuse your reader if you begin too abruptly with one of the issues you identified in your research. Instead, start out by providing enough background or history to make your analysis comprehensible. When you turn to the analysis of issues, you can use the standard order of the four basic questions. Or you can find an alternative order, perhaps beginning with or leading up to the most important question at issue and showing what other questions have to be answered before that one can be addressed.

Of course you are arguing in this paper, not simply informing, because you are selecting, defining, and shaping material for your reader. Such shaping will be obvious in the way you explain the background of your subject. A debate about the "language of the bees," for example, can be cast as a fairly recent controversy about just that, bee communication, or it can be seen as part of a larger, longer controversy about communication in animal species. Even though you are arguing, and even though bias is inevitable in your review, try to control it. Bias comes in degrees. Try to project an attitude of neutrality in your presentation of debated points.

This paper will also give you practice in using and citing sources according to the conventions required in academic writing. Using sources with skill for your own rhetorical purposes—sometimes quoting, sometimes paraphrasing, sometimes summarizing—helps create a credible ethos. (See Chapter 11 for a review of these skills.) In addition to the appropriate in-text citations, your paper must also include a bibliography of the material you consulted. (For more on locating print and online sources, see Chapter 10.)

Expressing Appeals: Language and Voice

Chapter 5

Subsidizing Illegal Residents

Ward Connerly

My sense of fairness was shaped by my Uncle James, the man who raised me after my grandmother and I moved to California in the late 1940s. Uncle James made most of his important decisions in life based on what a college professor of mine, Dr. Robert Thompson, called his "knower." A "knower" is that part of your psyche that just knows what is right and what is wrong. All of us have one, but sometimes we choose to ignore what it is telling us.

And it seems to me that California Governor Gray Davis, members of the California Legislature, and the regents of the University of California system are ignoring their knowers over the issue of college tuition breaks for illegal aliens.

Here's what's happened: Guided by a desire to give "equitable treatment" to the sons and daughters of illegal immigrants, on the rationale that children should not be held responsible for the conduct of their parents, the regents voted 17-5 (with yours truly being in the minority of that vote) to charge illegal immigrants less to attend California public universities than U.S. citizens who live in, say, Phoenix or Denver. The requirements to qualify for this subsidy are that the student must have attended a California high school for three years, graduated from high school, and filed an affidavit declaring intent to seek American citizenship.

That's right. Every citizen living legally in the other 49 states will be charged a higher tuition rate in California than illegal immigrants who happen to be in California. My knower knows this is just flat wrong.

As a regent of the University of California system, I know that the citizens of my state, as well as federal taxpayers, subsidize each graduate and undergraduate student's tuition to the tune of thousands of dollars each year. That is a price California citizens, largely, must pay in state taxes to ensure a top-notch university system — one that is envied throughout the country. California residents pay $3,859 in yearly tuition to attend UC, while out-of-state students pay nearly $15,000 for the same education.

I am not unsympathetic to the millions of individuals throughout the world who want to come to California to earn a decent living and pursue opportunity and freedom. But our federal laws are crystal clear about illegal immigration. These laws should not be cavalierly ignored or even given a big wink. It is wrong to confer a benefit on illegal residents that we do not confer on our own citizens. This is a shameful devaluation of the privilege of American citizenship, to say nothing of the inducement to greater illegal entry into the United States.

How can we ask the working families of California — many of whom have taken out sizable loans to finance their children's college education, and many of whom will never be able to afford to send their children to college — to subsidize the education of those who should not be in our country at all?

Not to be overlooked is the fact that hundreds of thousands of Californians are unemployed, due in large part to the attack against our nation by individuals who were in our country as a result of lax immigration policies and controls. Haven't we learned anything at all from the events of September 11, 2001, and subsequent thereto?

Furthermore, why would any legal foreign student pay out-of-state tuition at a UC campus when by becoming illegal he or she can get a huge annual tuition cut of about $11,000?

Few are suggesting that the children of illegal residents shouldn't be allowed to attend college in California, provided that they are not a threat to national security. However, they should play by the same rules as American citizens who live in other states and simply pay out-of state tuition. This is not much to ask.

Our state has spent billions of dollars—that's right, billions—providing illegal residents with emergency and preventative health care and other public benefits through an enormous network of hospitals and medical clinics and other taxpayer-financed expenditures. These subsidies are appropriate because our nation has a commitment to provide relief to any man, woman, or child whose life and health is endangered. These are the Judeo-Christian tenets on which our culture is founded.

But college tuition subsidies are different from health care, primarily because no one needs a college degree to sustain health and welfare. And, education is not a "human right," as some of the proponents of this goofy attitude about tuition subsidies for illegals suggest.

At the end of the day, the implementation of this policy means the state of California gets to write its own, unique immigration laws.

Funny! I don't recall the United States Constitution providing such an exemption.

ANALYZING "Subsidizing Illegal Residents"

This web editorial was published on February 5, 2002, on www.townhall.com. Its author, Ward Connerly, makes an argument with all the typical parts. He has an overall claim—that illegal residents should not be charged less tuition than out-of-state students in the University of California system—and several premises, among them that illegal residents should not receive benefits that citizens do not receive and that legal foreign students will not want to pay higher tuition when illegal residents pay less. He concedes the right of illegal residents to attend college and their right to health care, but he believes that tuition benefits are in a different category.

But in this argument, as in every argument expressed in ordinary language and addressed to a diverse audience, Connerly chooses language to make himself come alive as the arguer and to create links for his audience's involvement. One of the ways to appreciate this lively dimension of written argument, the impression of a human speaking to humans, is to pay attention to the pronouns Connerly uses.

Connerly puts himself in his argument with the **first person pronoun I.** In the first paragraph he creates a point of view from biographical details. Readers learn that both his uncle and a former professor believed in something called a personal "knower," an internal sense of right and wrong. This "knower" represents a kind of folksy wisdom. Having learned this wisdom from his family, Connerly presents himself as an "ordinary" person grounded in common sense. In paragraph 3, readers also learn another dimension of the "I" writing this argument; Connerly is one of the regents of the University of California, someone in a position to know about the tuition requirements and decisions in the university system. He is not just an "ordinary *I*"; he is also an "authoritative *I*" on the subject of his argument.

In addition to referring to himself, Connerly also addresses his readers in several different ways. Very briefly in the first paragraph, Connerly uses **direct address to readers as you.** He places that "knower" in every reader by defining it as "that part of *your* psyche that just knows what is right and what is wrong." This brief personal address to the individual reader comes right in the opening and concerns a point that few would be likely to dispute.

However, more common than *you* in this piece as a way to involve readers is the use of the **first person plural pronoun we.** Connerly's use of *we* is extremely important in this argument because it creates a sense of the groups that both he and his readers belong to. In the opening paragraph, the group is as broad as possible; it is everyone, since "all of us" have a "knower" though "we" sometimes choose to ignore it. Later in the argument, "we" are in effect American citizens and "our federal laws" are clear about immigration and about the rights of "our own citizens." In "our nation" we also share "our culture," which commits us to help anyone whose life and health is endangered. At one point, however, the group suggested by "we" is much smaller than all U.S. citizens. When Connerly writes about "our state," he is talking only to Californians.

Just as important as these constructed roles for writer and readers—roles constructed using *I, you,* and *we*—are the other groups that Connerly creates with his language choices. Clearly his argument is about illegal residents, a group formed by this very label and other synonyms in the piece. People presumably fitting this legal definition are always referred to in the **third person, sometimes as they.** However, and here is an important exception, a group that is named in an argument may also be the group addressed in the argument. Actual readers may then identify with that named group or not. Connerly, for example, often talks about "California citizens" and "California residents" and "Californians" who make up the group that should be the most interested in this argument about the tuition practices of the University system in their state. Connerly could have talked more directly *to* rather than *about* California citizens, and perhaps he should have. But since his argument appears on a web site that has potential readers across the nation, Connerly does not focus on his fellow Californians. In fact, in the final few lines he points out that California might be in violation of the Constitution.

Readers can be involved in an argument even when they are not addressed directly by *you* or *we* or offered a group to identify with. Any **question** that a writer asks is a natural invitation for an answer. Sometimes writers go on to answer their own questions, but more often, as in several questions that Connerly asks, readers are invited to supply the obvious answers that support the writer's case. These unanswered questions, called *rhetorical questions,* can be seen as a way the writer "speaks" a point and the reader "hears" it. The question mark at the end creates a rising intonation that puts emotion in the writer's voice.

In addition to personal pronouns and named groups, Connerly also refers to rather undefined groups at strategic points. The notion that illegal residents should not be allowed to attend college is one that "few" suggest. And a college education is something that "no one" needs for health and welfare; this point applies to everyone. Other groups are mentioned in this article, and as a useful exercise you might ask how each of these characterizations could either enhance or detract from Connerly's case. (How and why, for instance, does Connerly refer to those responsible for the terrorist acts on 9/11?) Altogether Connerly's editorial is typical of arguments addressed to wide audiences in the popular media. It draws on all the rich resources in the language to create a human encounter on the page.

CHOOSING A VOICE

Once an arguer has researched the questions surrounding an issue, decided on a claim, and come up with reasons, warrants, and counterarguments, how does he or she appeal to the readers' emotions and project character, let alone a good character, in the final written argument? *Ethos* and *pathos*, which were discussed in Chapter 3, are produced by careful language choices, especially those words and phrases that speakers or writers use to refer to themselves. In this chapter, we offer some advice about creating a personality by the voice you choose. You are immediately present to your reader in your words when you use the pronoun of self-reference, *I.* You create closeness with your audience when you use *you* (as in this sentence), and still another effect when you choose *we.* Finally, you can diminish the presence of your personality (though never eliminate it entirely) by writing impersonally. You can and should move in and out of these voices in different parts of your argument. You may have been told at some point in your education that you should never use *I* in your writing. We will complicate that advice and discuss the effects of using different personal pronouns in your writing. The following discussion should help you make successful choices and create an effective relationship with your audience.

Using *I* or Not Using *I*

Pick up a newspaper and read the articles on the front page. Is there an *I* in any of them? Probably not. Do you have a sense of a distinctive individual talking to you in any of those "*I*-less" articles? If you read closely, you may notice differences. Now turn to the signed columns on the editorial page and find one that does use *I.* Suddenly the voice has a personality that can project anything from the stern wisdom of the political commentator to the racy wit of a satirical columnist.

Of course, the news is conventionally presented in the voice of objective authority. When a journalist wants to convey an impression of fact not influenced by personal experience or point of view, then it is most effective to write impersonally, to leave out the *I.* Indeed, the conventions of news reporting as well as other kinds of writing (like technical reports) forbid the use of *I.* But in other situations certain effects can be achieved only by writing in your own voice, by appearing in your own writing as *I.*

The *I* of Personal Experience

Some writers avoid references to personal experience in written argument because they think using the pronoun *I* is improper. Somewhere they have heard that "one" doesn't refer to "oneself" as "I" in anything more formal than a letter home. There is some justification for this belief because in some writing situations (such as history papers or lab reports) no personal experience is significant. You wouldn't write, ". . . and then I spilled the acid" or "I feel that World War II was an unfortunate occurrence."

But in other, less formal writing situations, if a personal experience is in any way important to your argument—something that happened to you or put you on the track of a conclusion—it need not be left out. Although it may have only a small place in your argument, it can have a large effect on your audience.

The *I* of Authority

I can be used even when you are not talking about your personal experiences. You can also bring yourself into an argument as an authority who believes, thinks, claims, or asserts. Columnists who write week after week on politics, economics, sports, or the arts have authoritative personal voices that go easily into *I*. Notice the claim to professional authority in this excerpt from a newspaper column:

> For years I sat by quietly as I read negative articles and letters about the poor quality of our educational system. After experiencing a wonderful Friday in-service day, listening to great achievements made by my peers, helping children believe in themselves and urging them to become doctors, lawyers, financiers, nurses, teachers, great parents, and so on, I read Larry Bachman's opinion, "Who Benefits Most from Current Education System?"
>
> I certainly am not here to say all is perfect in the field of education, but at least listen to my perspective as a teacher with 37 years of experience and many years as an industrial consultant in the field of career development and electronics manufacturing.
>
> —Centre Daily Times [*CDT*], June 4, 2000, p. 11A.

If you are a student you are probably thinking, "That's fine for the expert who can use *I* any time, but what about me? I'm no famous expert with a lifetime of experience." The *I* of authority does need to be earned, and few things sound worse than an unjustified claim to it. Yet anyone who puts forth an argument should acquire at least a modest authority on that subject, should have conscientiously read much on the topic, interviewed people concerned, or collected reliable evidence. The authority earned by background work can give an arguer an *I* to stand on.

Authority can come not only from recognized professional expertise or research in a discipline, but also from bringing a unique point of view to an issue. The business expert who proposes a new scheme for running a family efficiently, the biologist who brings the ideas of that field to another, or the classical musician who evaluates jazz—all of these bring a kind of authority from a fresh point of view. Such authority can be claimed by a vigorous *I*.

The Ordinary *I*

Odd as it may sound, you can sometimes establish your *ethos* effectively by *not* claiming authority. If your point of view on an issue is that of an average citizen, a typical college student, a representative suburbanite, an ordinary American, a typical taxpayer, you can identify yourself in that role. The reasoning behind the appeal of the "ordinary *I*" is something like this: "If an average person like me can hold this position, so can an average person like you. If something is good or appealing to ordinary me, it can be good for ordinary you too." The effect is to put the writer on the same level as the audience, not on a platform looking down at them. Sometimes a strong ethos comes from identifying yourself not as an authority but simply as someone who will be affected by a policy proposal, like the student who began his letter to the local newspaper, "As a member of the Mount Nittany Middle School student body, I disagree with making students wear uniforms" (*CDT*, June 4, 2000, p.11A). Your evaluation of that appeal will depend on the degree to which you believe that the "ordinary" student should have a voice in the decision.

The *I* of Method

You can also speak in your own voice in order to let your reader know what the method of your argument is. In other words, you can guide your readers through your own argument, stopping now and then to describe insights or to give encouragement or to explain your organization. You can say things like "First I will trace the history of the Amish in America," "I found such austerity difficult to understand until I had seen an Amish house," and so on.

What do you gain by using *I* to convey information that could be written impersonally? There are several advantages. First, you can highlight the organization of your argument if it is at all extended or complicated or difficult. To be sure, sentences that reveal structure can be written without *I*, but they gain emphasis and contribute to the ethos of the writer when *I* speaks them. Second, you can establish the ethos of a person going through a process and inviting readers to join in, in effect saying, "If I went through all these steps and came to this conclusion, so can you." Finally, there are sometimes rough spots in your argument where you might lose, confuse, or alienate your readers. You want to carry them over such spots so they will continue reading, and you can do that by having *I* helpfully forecast the coming trouble. It's like posting a sign on a trail warning hikers of rough terrain; people are grateful when they know what to expect. Here is an example of such a warning worded in different ways.

1. Impersonal: "This is a difficult concept to grasp until the Russian meaning of 'science' is understood."
2. Using *You*: "You will find this concept difficult to grasp until you understand what the Russians mean by 'science.'"
3. Using *I*: "I found this concept difficult to grasp until I understood what the Russians mean by 'science.'"

Version 1 is perfectly acceptable, and it might be the preferred choice in some circumstances, but it doesn't call attention to itself as dramatically as 2 or 3. Version 2 is certainly emphatic, but it also risks sounding like an insult to the reader's intelligence, quite the opposite of what you want to do in argument. Version 3 gets the reader's attention without talking down. *I* admits to the difficulty, thereby conveying an ethos of modesty, making the author seem more human and the reader smarter. The rhetorical situation will determine which choice is most effective.

The Dangers of *I*

The ethos created by the use of *I* can work for you, but it can also hurt you. The advantages of using the *I* of personal experience, of authority, and of method have corresponding disadvantages.

1. The personal experience of *I* can sometimes be set aside by readers as untypical. Your readers could say, "This incident might have happened to you, but you can't draw any general conclusions from it." The more personal the experience seems, the less it may seem to the reader to represent a large number of similar experiences. Instead of an ethos that invites others to identify with you, you might create one that isolates you from your readers.

2. Your reader might find your claims to authority—your "I think" and "I believe"—arrogant. It is one thing for a seasoned diplomat with strong external ethos to make statements about foreign policy that begin with "I think" or "I believe," but quite another for someone with no obvious expertise.

3. The *I* of method is emphatic, but that emphasis can work against you. If, for instance, *I* points out all the procedures followed, the reader can more easily criticize what was or was not done. "I take my figures from a newly published study," brags the writer. "You mean you didn't run your own survey?" replies the reader.

4. In some situations, calling attention to oneself by using *I* is inappropriate or foolish. If the use of *I* gives your reader an opening to question your judgment, then be very cautious. Although you must admit anything that if found out would damage you, you need not dwell on the problems or the benefits for yourself. Or if your argument includes a severe criticism of someone else's actions or arguments, such an attack should never seem as personal as the use of *I* would make it.

5. A letter or a signed article or a single-authored paper is often a legitimate occasion for the author's *I*. But if you are writing as the representative of a group or as the chair of a committee, and if what you write is not going to appear under your own name alone, the unexplained presence of *I* might confuse your reader. Can you imagine an official report from a Planning Commission including a sentence like this: "I have done some research, and, although my results were ambiguous, I still think that the highway should not be built"?

We have given you two kinds of advice about how to create an effective *ethos*, some of it urging you to use the first person and some of it warning you against it. We have not proclaimed a rule. When you are trying to create a strong *ethos* in writing, you have to choose for yourself, taking into account your audience, your subject, and yourself. The benefit of *I* is that it can humanize your argument and convey your own character. The danger of *I* is that it can undermine the very basis of argument by suggesting a perspective that is too personal or too limited.

Working either alone or with a group of classmates, identify the type of *I* used in each of the following extracts. Decide whether the *I* is effective. If it is not, what would have been a better choice?

1. The particular story that came most often to my attention shortly before *The Vanishing Hitchhiker* got into print was the one about the choking dog. It had a plot that sounded as fresh as this morning's headlines, and plenty of true believers passing it along as gospel. The story of the dog—usually a Doberman—that was choking on fingers bitten off an intruder turned out to be a fine example of a "new" urban legend sweeping the country, but its apparent newness just thinly masked much older folklore elements.

   In order to expose this new legend as the old story it is, and also to demonstrate how folklore research sometimes works, I give in this chapter the history of the choking dog plot, insofar as it can be written, plus an account of my detective work that established its sources. Unlike most other new urban legends that spring up, for this one a fairly complete genealogy can be traced.
   —Jan Harold Brunvand, *The Choking Doberman and Other "New" Urban Legends* (New York: W. W. Norton, 1984) pp. 5–6.

2. Seriously, I guess people collect shotguns. Which is great. I used to collect baseball cards. You know, when I was a kid. The thing about baseball cards is that each one is different; you get a Don Mattingly or a Frank Thomas. Is there that big a difference between shotguns? Somebody enlighten me because I'm operating out of ignorance here.
   —Al Franken, "Phil Gramm, Gun Lover," *Rush Limbaugh Is a Big Fat Idiot* (New York: Delacorte Press, 1996) p. 84.

3. The John Cusack character is someone I have known all my life. He is assembled out of my college friends, the guys at work, people I used to drink with. I also recognize Barry, the character played by Jack Black; he's a type so universal it's a wonder he hasn't been pinned down in a movie before: a blowhard, a self-appointed expert on all matters of musical taste, a monologuist, a guy who would rather tell you his opinion than take your money.
   —Roger Ebert, review of *High Fidelity*, *Suntimes.com* (www.suntimes.com/ ebert/ebert_reviews/2000/03/033102.html) March 2000.

4. The greater part of what my neighbors call good I believe in my soul to be bad, and if I repent of anything, it is very likely to be my good behavior. What demon possessed me that I behaved so well? You may say the wisest thing you can, old man,—you who have lived seventy years, not without honor of a kind,—I hear an irresistible voice which invites me away from all that. One generation abandons the enterprises of another like stranded vessels.
   —Henry David Thoreau, *Walden* (New York: Macmillan Publishing Co., 1962) p. 20.

Using *You* or Not Using *You*

As we have seen, *ethos* consists of both the character of the writer as revealed in the text and the attitude of good will that the writer establishes toward the reader. In conveying good will, the writer needs to draw the reader into a relationship with herself, to get the reader's attention. Think of what happens in a live situation. If you want to get the attention of someone near you, you call her name or tap someone on his shoulder. Keeping the attention of a listener who is within reach is easy in face-to-face interaction, and even when you are speaking before an audience, you can pull their attention toward you by maintaining eye contact and addressing them collectively as *you*. But it is more difficult to maintain a relationship with a reader who can drop your pages without the slightest twinge of conscience.

One way of establishing a relationship with the reader is to use the written equivalent of the hand on the shoulder or eye contact. You can address your audience as *you*. Unless you are writing an argument addressed to only one person, your audience will usually be many people. Yet, paradoxically, the act of reading is solitary and any piece of writing is taken in by only one person at a time. So the indefinite *you* can be a way of establishing a relationship with an entire audience as though you meant only one person.

Addressing your reader establishes a relationship in two ways. First, it helps capture and keep attention. Just as we perk up when we hear our own names, so also do we respond with extra attention when addressed directly. Second, using *you* makes it easier to apply an argument to your audience. When *you* have seen how difficult the problem is, when *your* future is involved, when *you* will profit, the *you* being addressed—actually any reader—will feel the impact of an argument's appeals more forcefully. Readers will not have to work to imagine themselves in the situation of the argument; you, the writer, can do that for them.

Opening with an Attention-Getting *You*

Experienced writers often begin with a direct address or invitation to *you*. This attention-getting *you* appears even when the subject of an argument is far removed from the reader's experience. The professional writer tries to draw a reader to a subject not normally interesting, so a hook is dangled for *you*. The direct address is often dropped once the writer gets down to business. Here is an example of a *you* opening in an otherwise impersonal argument:

> Would you rather have botulism or cancer?
>   That's essentially the question federal regulators are asking in formulating policy on the hazard of sodium nitrite in cured meats, fish and poultry.
> —Jean Carper, "Stop Playing Politics with the
> Nitrite Issue," *The Washington Post*.

After that collar-grabbing opening, the author never uses *you* again.

Audience Creation

An opening *you* can be more than just a hook to grab the uninterested. It can also single out just those to whom an argument is directed and help define or create the audience for it. Of course, this very specific audience creation may also drive away those unconcerned with your argument, but that may be no loss. Those who are concerned will feel that they are being singled out for special attention and will read more attentively.

Here is an example of audience creation from the opening of a proposal on how to prepare a preschool child for kindergarten:

> If you have a 4-year-old who will begin school in September, what can you do *now*—every day—to help the child get a good start? You can do what the kindergarten teachers do—recognize that learning comes through experience and that all experiences come through the senses.
>
> —Bernard Ryan, Jr., "Helping Your Child
> Get a Start in School," *The New York Times*.

This argument is directed to parents of four-year-olds. Others might read the proposal as well, but they become the overhearers rather than the target audience for the essay.

A Scene Starring *You*

The next step after identifying the role of *you* is having *you* act out that role. A writer can go beyond talking directly to a reader to imagining the reader involved in a scene. *You* then becomes more than just a reader; *you* is a doer involved in some action that draws *you* into the argument. Notice how the opening lines of the following argument create a scene pulling the reader into the argument:

> You pause for a moment in a shop where a sealskin coat is on display. You admire its rich and perfect texture. Expensive, yes; but oh, so handsome. Then a troubling thought: Is it right to want luxury at the cost of wildlife? You remember the ads and articles and television shows that deplore the killing of seals. You hesitate—then drift on. Maybe you'll return, but for the moment, you're overwhelmed by an odd sense of guilt.

The writer, Victor B. Scheffer, takes *you* on a shopping trip and imagines even *your* innermost thoughts. He skillfully (though perhaps to some tastes excessively) identifies the points of contact between the average reader's life and the subject of his argument. Most of us have nothing to do with seals, but we have heard of the controversy about killing them in ads and articles and television shows, as the author reminds us, as he gets us to contemplate whether to buy a sealskin coat.

Giving Directions to *You*

This whole book repeatedly addresses the reader as *you*. We are always suggesting that *you* consider this point or avoid that tactic. We hope we have avoided the dangers of sounding either too tentative or too dictatorial. How can those dangers be avoided? Perhaps the best way is not to give a direction without including the reasons for giving it or the consequences of following or not following it. That is, never command your reader, "Don't you ever buy a sealskin coat," without giving a reason like "If you do, you will be contributing to the deaths of innocent animals." And now that we have offered you that advice we will give *you* a reason for it. Most people prefer to move themselves by the force of their own conviction rather than to be moved by the force of external authority. No one responds well to a list of unexplained *do's* and *don'ts.* As a writer, you can show your respect and good will toward your readers by treating them as people who respond to reasons rather than orders.

Directions appear naturally in arguments supporting a proposal, particularly in the description of the first step the reader is supposed to take. Notice how this passage from a popular book about leadership directs the reader and indicates the consequences of following a certain course of action:

> "Inside-out" means to start first with self; even more fundamentally, to start with the most *inside* part of self—with your paradigms, your character, and your motives.
>
> It says if you want to *have* a happy marriage, *be* the kind of person who generates positive energy and sidesteps negative energy rather than empowering it. If you want to *have* a more pleasant, cooperative teenager, *be* a more understanding, empathic, consistent, loving parent. If you want to *have* more freedom, more latitude in your job, *be* a more responsible, a more helpful, a more contributing employee. If you want to be trusted, *be* trustworthy. If you want the secondary greatness of recognized talent, focus first on primary greatness of character.
>
> —Stephen R. Covey, *The 7 Habits of Highly Effective People*
> (New York: Simon & Schuster, 1989), p. 43.

Often in giving directions, writers include sentences in which *you* does not appear but is understood, as in the following example.

> Leave [*you* understood] babies and eggs alone. Any adult alligator will respond to a distress call from any youngster. Mother alligators defending nests and babies will defend them.
>
> —Joshue Piven and David Borgenicht, *The Worst Case Scenario Survival Handbook*
> (San Francisco: Chronicle Books, 1999) p. 59.

Talking to *You* about the Argument

Throughout this book we talk about the importance of imagining the response of your readers to your writing. Consideration of audience is important at every stage of writing. As you write, you are in effect always putting yourself in your reader's mind, anticipating reactions, overcoming inertia, and arousing emotions. One way to show that you have put yourself in your reader's mind is to use direct address. In effect, you articulate the thoughts in your reader's mind and use those thoughts as structuring devices in your argument. Here are some examples of this use of direct address from Martin Luther King, Jr.'s "Letter from Birmingham Jail." We are quoting only the first sentences from several different paragraphs:

> You may well ask, "Why direct action?" [The answer to this anticipated question follows.]

You express a great deal of anxiety over our willingness to break the law.
[In this case, King is about to answer an objection that was verbalized by
his audience of clergymen.]

I hope you are able to see the distinction I am trying to point out. [Here
King senses that his point is a difficult one for his audience, and he warns
them to give it special attention.]

The Pitfalls of Using *You*

You is a very powerful audience grabber, sometimes too powerful. If readers
sense that they are being bullied, their reaction will be negative. They may not
fling your pages across the room, but they will feel uncomfortable in the presence of someone who is coming on too strong. The excessive use of *you* can
undercut the *ethos* of good will.

Here is an example of excessively strong *you* language from a brochure
soliciting subscriptions to a magazine.

> I have reason to believe that you are part of an important minority in this
> country . . . that you are politically alert, independent and more than a wee bit
> suspicious of power . . . that you won't be lured by high-sounding but mean-
> ingless political rhetoric . . . that you are concerned about trends in govern-
> ment that threaten certain inalienable rights like liberty and the pursuit of hap-
> piness . . . that you cherish old-fashioned liberal ideals but are suspicious of
> mounting government intervention in our lives . . . that you try to read be-
> tween the headlines of newspapers . . . that you don't want your issues spoon-
> fed and predigested . . . that you don't want other people to do your thinking
> for you . . . that bungling bureaucracy in government angers you . . . that you
> believe well-informed, responsible, involved citizens can bring about much-
> needed changes in our system . . . that you inquire.
>
> If you can say, "Yes, that's me," allow me to say thank you. It's people like
> you who helped create and build this nation. And we need more of you if our
> democratic system is to survive.
>
> That's why I urge you to stand up and be counted—to make your voice
> heard on important matters—to keep yourself continually informed about the
> issues—to keep your mind open without losing sight of your principles.

This kind of "hard sell" probably repels more than it convinces. The repetition of *you* throughout the piece is aggressive and manipulative. The writer
seems to be bullying or flattering readers instead of treating them with respect
by allowing them to make up their own minds.

The *you* of direct address can also be ineffective if it is used to characterize
an audience negatively. To accuse readers, to make them feel guilty, lazy, stupid, inadequate, bigoted, uninformed, immoral, or insensitive, arouses un-
pleasant feelings and is no way to show good will. Some arguments do require
that people become aware of their own shortcomings, but that does not mean
that the writer should address them harshly about their failures. For example,
unless the circumstances were exceptional, a writer trying to persuade adults
to enroll for courses in a community night school would not motivate them
with insults: "You are stupid and lazy. You sit in front of the television, drinking

beer, while your mind rots away." Instead, bringing readers to some state of self-criticism in order to motivate them might be done in one of the following ways:

1. One can include oneself in the accusations, using *we* instead of *you:* "We all spend too much time in front of the television set while the exciting world of new knowledge and ideas passes us by."
2. Or the writer can be impersonal, creating a group to which neither writer nor readers belong. Then readers have the freedom to decide whether they fit into this group: "Many people think their education is over when they finish school. They settle in front of the television set and allow their minds to go idle, losing the opportunity to keep learning."

Either of these tactics might work better than an insulting or condescending direct address that is in effect an attack. Direct address is most effective when it attracts readers into an argument and guides them through it, not when it pulls them by the hair. Notice how the author of the following advice for college students avoids direct address when he characterizes students negatively, but switches to *you* when he offers them positive suggestions:

> Few students recognize the importance of self-conditioning in their examination attitudes (remember Dr. Pavlov, who was trained by his dogs to ring a bell whenever they salivated?). One who prepares thoroughly for tests is usually relaxed and confident. Luck has little to do with his or her performance. This student quickly becomes "test-wise."
>
> The poor student relies heavily on cramming and luck and hopes for the "right questions." Despite his surface bravado, he senses the dangers ahead, and "psyched out," does poorly. Each "blown" exam makes the next one more important and the student more tense and forgetful. By the end of the semester, when the low grades arrive, he has conditioned himself to be a poor test taker.
>
> The sense of well-being conferred by good grades makes it easier and more rewarding to maintain them, while failure breeds an avoidance pattern. So a good start in college is vital for the conditioning process. Pulling up low grades is a powerful test of self-discipline, and one that many fail.
>
> Learn [*you* understood] the required material through scheduled reviews. Your first college crisis will be midterm week, when every professor seems to assign a major exam simultaneously, so plan your reviews carefully. Avoid or minimize [*you* understood] cramming, a common but poor study technique.
>
> If the test in a given subject covers, for example, the notes from three weeks' classes, and you need five reviews, space them equidistantly over the study period. Do [*you* understood] the final review just before the test.
>
> Check [*you* understood] previous examinations, often available from student organization files, the library, or friends who have taken the course. Evaluate [*you* understood] their overall format and the kinds of questions asked. What are the professor's thought patterns? Which elements of the course does he emphasize? The answers should shape your preparations.
>
> —Lance Trusty, "College Students: Test-Taking Advice for the Wise," *The Christian Science Monitor* October 2, 1978.

EXERCISE 5.2

Working either alone or with a group of classmates, identify the way *you* is used in each of the following extracts. Decide whether the *you* is effective. If it is not, what would have been a better choice?

1. A tax subsidy is any deduction or exemption that you oppose. In the abstract, it is possible to separate tax-code complications that relate to fairness in the tax system from complications that have some nontax-related purpose, and to call the second type a subsidy. In practice, the distinction is harder. If a person earns $100,000 and has $20,000 in medical expenses, should he or she be taxed as someone who earns $100,000 or as someone who earns $80,000? Likewise, what about a person who earns $100,000 and gives $20,000 to charity? If you think the answer is $80,000, then allowing this person a $20,000 deduction is not a subsidy. If you think the answer is $100,000, then any special treatment is a tax subsidy, and you must decide whether the subsidy is justified. If you think the answer is, "Well, I dunno, maybe somewhere in between, depending on this and that," you are probably right. And you can see why the income tax form will never be a postcard.

   —Michael Kinsley, "Tax Reform in Plain English. Honest!"
   Time, December 9, 2002, p. 58.

2. New Yorkers seem to think the best thing two people can do is talk. Silence is OK when you're watching a movie (although it might be better if punctuated by clever asides) or when you're asleep (collecting dreams to tell when you're awake). Talking is a New Yorker's way of showing friendship, especially to strangers.

   —Deborah Tannen, as quoted in *How to Talk American* by Jim Crotty (Boston: Houghton Mifflin, 1997) p. 224.

3. Show me a cultural relativist at thirty thousand feet and I'll show you a hypocrite. Airplanes built according to scientific principles work. They stay aloft, and they get you to a chosen destination. Airplanes built to tribal or mythological specifications, such as the dummy planes of the cargo cults in jungle clearings or the beeswaxed wings of Icarus, don't. If you are flying to an international congress of anthropologists and literary critics, the reason you will probably get there—the reason you don't plummet into a ploughed field—is that a lot of Western scientifically trained engineers have got their sums right. Western science, acting on good evidence that the moon orbits the Earth a quarter of a million miles away, using Western-designed computers and rockets, has succeeded in placing people on its surface. Tribal science, believing that the moon is just above the treetops, will never touch it outside of dreams.

   —Richard Dawkins, "All Africa and Her Progenies" *River Out of Eden: A Darwinian View of Life* (New York: Basic Books, 1995), pp. 31–32.

4. As a creative person, you naturally want to write clever copy and produce fancy promotions. But as a professional, your obligation to your client is to *increase sales at the lowest possible cost*. If a classified ad works better than a full-page ad, use it. If a simple typewritten letter gets more business than a four-color brochure, mail the letter.

   —Robert W. Bly, *The Copywriter's Handbook: A Step-by-Step Guide to Writing Copy That Sells* (New York: Henry Holt, 1985), p. 5.

Dialogue Building with Questions

Questions are another excellent way of establishing a good relationship with readers by bringing them into dialogue with you. When you are interested in what you are reading, don't questions about the material occur to you? And when someone asks you a question, don't you have a natural impulse to answer it? (Didn't you have a natural impulse to answer that question?) When you write arguments, you should anticipate and build upon your readers' natural instinct to ask and answer questions.

Questions That You Answer

Suppose you are developing an argument in favor of changing the parking regulations where you work. In the course of your research, you ask many questions: "What are the legal ordinances governing parking near a building with a certain occupancy? What inconveniences do the current regulations create?" After investigating the issue, you have answered these questions for yourself.

When you write your argument, remember that your readers will most likely be asking the same questions that you did. If you want to adjust your argument to their mental processes and pull them into dialogue with you, ask the questions for them. Anticipate the questions, articulate them, and then answer them. If you include these *structuring questions*, readers may follow your argument more easily because it duplicates their own reasoning process.

Asking and answering questions can help you to structure your argument, to decide what parts go in what order. Suppose, for instance, you think of an objection or a question that readers are likely to raise at a particular point. If you ask that question yourself and then deal with it satisfactorily, you may forestall the objection and strengthen your argument. Notice how Frans DeWaal, the author of a study of animal behavior, predicts a question in his discussion of the development of moral ability in animals and humans:

> The criminal justice system of course encounters . . . serious deviations, and these too can often be traced to lessons received, or not received, during sensitive phases of moral development.
>
> Does this make morality a biological or a cultural phenomenon? There really is no simple answer to this sort of question, which has been compared to asking whether percussive sounds are produced by drummers or by drums. If we have learned anything from the debate between ethologists and behaviorists, it is that nature and nurture can be only partially disentangled.
>
> —Frans DeWaal, *Good Natured: The Origins of Right and Wrong in Humans and Other Animals* (Cambridge, MA: Harvard University Press, 1996), pp. 36–37.

The question DeWaal asks here is one that any intelligent reader might raise. And by drawing readers into the discussion and addressing their questions, DeWaal establishes his ethos as a writer.

Rhetorical Questions: Questions That You Don't Answer

Unlike the structuring question that you ask and answer for your readers, the *rhetorical question* is one that you ask but don't answer. In a sense, your readers answer it themselves, in their own heads. Thus rhetorical questions are an excellent device for involving readers in a dialogue with writers. When readers find themselves mentally answering your questions, they are in effect conversing with you.

Since a rhetorical question is really a way of making a statement that your audience will agree with, it should be worded so that it requires only a short predictable answer. You ask, "Do we want our school to have a bad reputation?" The readers feel compelled to answer, "No, of course not." You ask, "What kind of parent allows a 10-year-old child to be out until 2 A.M.?" Your readers quickly reply, "A bad one." Even if readers do not consciously verbalize the short answer that is required, the question itself seems to provide it.

Any question requiring a lengthy, complicated answer, however—"Why do some teenagers dye their hair bright green?" "What are the qualities of an effective political leader?"—should not be left unanswered by the writer. Questions of this kind, which call for detailed answers, are the structuring questions we talked about above.

Of course, the rhetorical question works only if readers answer it in exactly the way that will support your argument. If they answer it in any other way, it is working against you. So the rhetorical question must be framed and asked in such a way that the right answer is the only one that occurs to readers. The writer of the following proposal that drug addicts receive free drugs knows exactly what answer to expect from the final rhetorical question in the paragraph:

> [E]ven in what people do for pleasure, conformity is the first thing thought of; they like in crowds; they exercise choice only among things commonly done; peculiarity of taste, eccentricity of conduct are shunned equally with crimes, until by dint of not following their own nature they have no nature to follow: their human capacities are withered and starved; they become incapable of any strong wishes or native pleasure, and are generally without either opinions or feelings of home growth, or properly their own. Now is this, or is it not, the desirable condition of human nature?
>
> —John Stuart Mill, *On Liberty*, ed. Elizabeth Rapaport (Indianapolis, IN: Hackett Publishing Co., 1978), pp. 58–59.

Readers are supposed to answer the last question with a resounding "No!" A contradictory "Yes" would be disastrous and even a doubtful "Maybe" would be damaging. But with a "No" in mind, readers will be more receptive to the proposal that follows. The rhetorical question can also be a vehicle or outlet for some of the emotion the writer feels about the topic and wants to convey. It is especially effective for communicating feelings like anger or defiance or exasperation.

Rhetorical questions are effective when you feel confident that your readers will answer in the way you want and feel just as you do. But use the rhetorical question sparingly. An argument that throws one question after another at its readers, that keeps readers answering "Yes," "No," "No," "Yes," will simply bewilder or irritate them.

In newspapers and newsmagazines, look for an article in which a writer asks and answers questions and an article in which a writer uses at least one rhetorical question. Bring the two articles to class and share them with other members of your group. As a group, decide which writers are successful in using these questioning strategies and why.

Using *We* or Not Using *We*

We have already discussed the effect of speaking of yourself as *I* and to your reader as *you* in an argument. Another possible voice is *we*. When *we* is used as the voice speaking in an argument, it can have one of several different meanings, and these different meanings say different things about the character of the writer and the reader.

The Genuine Plural *We*: *I* + *I* = *We*

The least common *we* in written argument is the one that stands literally for two or more writers. That is the *we* that we (Fahnestock and Secor) use frequently in this book. It is the voice of two or more authors who have produced one work and therefore sensibly refer to themselves as *we*. This *we* is simply the plural of *I*. It has all the same benefits of *I* (personality and informality) as well as the same drawbacks. If you look at the preface to this book, you will find the *we* of plural authors. Elsewhere, *we* occasionally means ourselves, the writers of the book, but more often means the *we* of the next category.

The *We* That Unites Reader and Writer: *I* + *You* = *We*

A commonly used *we* is simply a combination of *I* and *you*, writer and reader. This *we* is a particularly accommodating choice. When *we* talks in an argument, writer and reader are invited to get together in a friendly way. The potential egotism of *I* and the unwelcome bullying of *you* are replaced by identification between writer and reader. Can you sense the difference pronoun choice makes in the following statements?

> I believe in the U.S. Constitution, and I assume that you do too.
> We believe in the U.S. Constitution.

Both sentences say basically the same thing, but the first version seems to build a barrier between the writer and reader and at worst even challenges the reader. The second, however, unites writer and reader in agreement and suggests that the two are part of the same group.

We is a wise choice when your argument builds on values and assumptions that the reader and writer share. Speaking as *we*, you can remind your reader of beliefs you have in common. Notice how the writers Anne Moir and David Jessel use *we* to unite themselves and readers in a common failing and a mutual plea for improvement:

> The truth is that for virtually our entire tenancy of the planet, we have been a sexist species. Our biology assigned separate functions to the male and female

of Homo sapiens. Our evolution strengthened and refined those differences. Our civilisation reflected them. Our religion and our education reinforced them.

Yes we both fear, and defy, history. We fear it, because we are afraid of seeming to be in complicity with the centuries old crimes of sexual prejudice. We defy it, because we want to believe that mankind has at last achieved escape velocity, released from the muddy gravity of our animal past and neanderthal assumptions.

—Anne Moir and David Jessel "Brain Sex," from *Conversations*, 2nd ed., 1991, p. 359.

Here the *we* includes the writers, the readers, and by extension everyone else who acknowledges the self-evidence of what the writers assert.

This inclusive *we* stands for the writer and any member of the audience who would plausibly be reading the argument. That audience always has characteristics, of course, even if it is as large and vague a group as the American public or the "general audience" that writers often imagine themselves addressing. After all, the American public does not include the Iranian public or the Indonesian public. The *we* used in the quotation above does not really include everyone. It assumes that readers share with the writers the values of gender equity.

The Position Speaks as We

Legend has it that when someone commented on how short Britain's Queen Victoria was, she drew herself up to her full 4 feet and 11 inches and replied frostily, "We are rather small for a Queen." Queen Victoria quite properly used what is often called the "royal *we*" to refer to herself, because even as a small queen she was more than a single short person. She represented a ruling house, a church, a nation.

In much the same way, when the pope speaks for the entire Roman Catholic Church, he speaks as *we*. *We* is not limited, however, to use by heads of church or state. Anyone who represents the authority of a group, an organization, a team, a corporation, an institution, can speak as *we*. A person can be chosen to speak for many, not simply to represent a personal point of view. Not "I, the president of the corporation," but "We at Microsoft." Not "I, the editor of the *Daily Sentinel*," but the editorial "we."

The official *we* can be used only in sanctioned situations. It conveys arrogance if its authority is not earned and if the position it is taking does not represent the position of its audience. We all resent partisans who claim to speak for "we, the American people" when representing views we do not share.

The We of Well-Defined Groups

No clear line separates the *we* that stands for a large, inclusive group and the *we* that stands for a well-defined group. It is difficult to say exactly where a *we* that includes any plausible reader of an argument turns into a *we* that excludes some readers. But when that zone is crossed, when *we* excludes as well as includes, a significantly different picture of the writer emerges.

It is possible to create a group to which writer and reader can belong but from which others are eliminated. The writer may want the reader to join in a circle of insiders who share an interest, an occupation, something in common. Such appeals to group identity can be effective when the group has something to do with the argument and the writer wants readers to be associated with it. If, for instance, you were proposing ways to prevent credit-card fraud in on-line shopping, it would make sense to create a *we* as "those of us who have shopped online and worried about the security of our transactions." Members of that group can talk about the experiences and concerns that *we* share.

In the following example, the author uses *we* to announce her community with others of her ethnic background, the well-defined group she addresses:

> What do you want to be called, American Indian or Native American? This is the most common question other people ask us. This is not a question we ask each other and there is no pressing need for us to answer it right now. It is a good question to mull over, if only to let others know what we'd rather not be called.
> —Suzan Shown Harjo, "What Do You Want to Be Called?" *Indian Country Today* (www.indiancountry.com/?2692), July 25, 2001.

Since arguments generally aim to make writer and reader identify with each other, to agree like members of the same group, it may seem that *we* is always a wise choice. But not always. *We* has pitfalls just as *I* and *you* have, and once again knowledge of your relationship with your audience can help you determine the best choice. Some audiences will resist the arm-around-the-shoulder chumminess of *we*.

Working either alone or with a group of your classmates, identify the types of *we* used in the following extract by columnist Molly Ivins. Ivins wrote the article the extract comes from in response to the publication in 1995 of a book by Robert McNamara, who was Secretary of Defense during the Kennedy and Johnson administrations in the 1960s. For each use of *we*, decide why Ivins is using it in that way and whether another voice (*I* or *you*) would have been an equally effective, or a better, choice.

> There it is. Thank you, Mr. McNamara.
> "Stop the presses!" is the way we in the newspaper business say, "This is *really* important." I wish there were some way to stop all the presses—to get all the spin doctors and O.J. media hypesters and smug Republicans and backpedaling Democrats and busy moms and teens who only read about Madonna to sit down, be quiet, and listen to Robert McNamara for a little while.
> Odd but appropriate that as we celebrate the fiftieth anniversary of our victory in the Good War, we should also be reminded of the one we mucked up. Important, so important, for everyone holding public office, everyone, to consider the possibility that twenty years hence they, too, might have to sit down and write: "We were wrong, terribly wrong."

EXERCISE 5.4

And for those of us who were outside the Pentagon, on the other side of those fences and police lines, trying to scream truth to power, we, too, have something to learn from McNamara's confession.

Unless we understand how we got from the end of World War II—when we were the good guys, when we liked ourselves and stood for the right stuff, not to mention free chewing gum for foreign kids—to the end of the Vietnam War, then we cannot understand how we got from the end of 'Nam to where we are now. All this distrust and dislike that Americans now have for one another—all this cynicism. How did we get from raising the flag at Iwo Jima to My Lai?

—Molly Ivins, "'We Were Wrong'—This Time He's Right," *Fort Worth Star Telegram*, April 11, 1995, p. 17.

Other Ways of Creating and Appealing to Groups

As we have suggested, the *we* that forcefully unites writer and reader can be inappropriately personal. There are other ways of creating groups that do not necessarily include reader and writer, but do not exclude them either. These groups seem open for the reader to join if he or she chooses. If, for instance, the writer refers to "everyone who is concerned about higher education," readers can nominate themselves for membership in that group. Of course, no one would want to join a group that sounds undesirable—"anyone who has lice," "everyone of below average intelligence," "all those who never read books." A skillful arguer mentions an undesirable group only as one to be avoided.

You can also create desirable groups for your readers to join by naming them and giving them attractive attributes. "The sensitive person," "generous people," "those in the know," "successful young professionals"—all these labels describe categories most people want to belong to. Think of the advertisements that bombard us with glitzy images of attractive groups whose lives we are invited to share, if only we buy the right products.

Putting the Opposition in a Group

Another way to pull your readers toward you is to push the opposition away. This effect can be accomplished by identifying the opposition with groups that you present as undesirable. We are *not* talking here about creating scapegoats or calling names or stereotyping people. Such labeling is always unethical. Rather, we are talking about characterizing groups by the positions they hold on a certain issue or the consequences of those positions.

Suppose, for example, that you are offering an argument against airline regulation to a largely uncommitted audience. You can talk about the opposition as "those who support airline regulation," as though they were not present among your readers. That identification is quite neutral, but it still has the effect of separating your opposition from you and your readers. They become "those out there." Of course, your argument cannot stop merely with identifying "them" as the opposition; you must honestly deal with their position.

You can also characterize your opposition or their position in negative ways. Those who haven't considered the consequences of a policy you are critical of may be "short-sighted" or "impractical." Those whose ethical assumptions differ from your own might be characterized as "insensitive" or "unfair." Those who don't know what they should know can be called "poorly informed." Of course, any label you apply to others should come from your considered evaluation of their position, not from any automatic, emotional rejection.

Using an Impersonal Voice

Any sentence without a pronoun or any other reference to writer or reader is written in an impersonal voice. Most sentences in an argument are written in this background voice. The other voices of *I*, *you*, and *we* are used for special effects, mainly in the opening passages, where writers establish their *ethos*, and in the closing passages, where they may make a final emotional appeal to their readers. But this other, transparent voice predominates in written argument, and understandably so.

Even an impersonal voice creates certain effects or impressions on the reader, and it can often speak powerfully. First, it offers no competition to the content of the argument, but allows the subject matter to claim all the reader's attention. Second, it diffuses, though it does not eliminate, the appeal to *pathos*. And third, it downplays any egotism in the argument, replacing it with a voice that the audience is likely to perceive as impartial and authoritative.

An impersonal voice will usually dominate in direct proportion to the verifiability of the argument's content. In other words, the more information conveyed, the more impersonal the writing is likely to be. Textbooks and scholarly articles are usually written impersonally. The impersonal voice dominates in science, where the criteria of verification are most precise and where the personality of whoever performed the experiment, designed the computer operation, interpreted the data, or wrote the paper should be of no importance.

When to use the impersonal voice depends on the writer's authority, the subject of the argument, and the audience. Some disciplines and writing situations demand impersonality; others permit more variation. When scientists write on current research in professional journals, they often speak impersonally. But when they turn to address the public on scientific issues, they may refer to themselves with personal pronouns.

Inexperienced writers often believe that the exclusive use of an impersonal voice is a mark of mature writing, but in fact accomplished writers often alternate voices. A more personal voice is appropriate when the writer is demonstrating thought processes, staking out the territory of a definition, trying to draw in the audience, and certainly when he or she is narrating personal experience. An impersonal voice can take over when the writer presents verifiable information or sets out an evaluation.

In newspapers and newsmagazines, look for an article in which a writer creates groups, either for readers to join or for the opposition. Working in your group, decide which writers have used this technique fairly and effectively and which writers, if any, have used it unfairly.

EXERCISE 5.5

WRITING YOUR ARGUMENT

FINDING AN EFFECTIVE STANCE

In addition to the choices you need to make in order to put together the premises of an effective argument, you have many options for expressing that argument in a way that will have an impact on your audience.

People who are reading your argument will gain an impression of you, the author, based in part on how you represent yourself in your writing, and they will also respond to how you refer to them and to other groups.

You can experiment with different stances for yourself by, first, using different pronouns. Select a paragraph from the draft of a paper in progress (or use a paper already completed and graded that nevertheless could use "re-visioning").

1. Write the paragraph putting yourself in the paper as *I*. (Even if this paragraph does not express a personal experience, put yourself in it as the writer who has done the research, thought through the issues, and reached a certain perspective.)

2. Rewrite the same paragraph without *I*. (Is it possible to describe a personal experience without using *I* and without falsifying the story?)

Which version seems more effective given your audience? *Remember that many teachers do not want students to use* I *unless they are writing personal narratives or responses.*

Next, experiment with ways of representing your audience through pronoun choices. Take another paragraph from your paper and try out the following variations.

1. Phrase your points using *you*, talking directly to your readers. (You may find that it is possible to make some points with this choice that are otherwise difficult to express. You can try this with a paragraph that presents a positive point and one that presents a negative point. See also suggestions in the chapter for using *you*.)

2. Next, rewrite the same paragraph using *we* instead of *you*.

3. Finally, write the paragraph with no reference to the readers at all.

Which version seems most effective, given your audience? *Remember once again that some instructors feel strongly that academic writing should contain no pronouns referring to the audience.*

There are other ways of putting yourself and your audience into a text. Try these out on your draft.

1. Phrase the opening of one or more paragraphs as a question. The rest of the paragraph answers the question.

2. Rephrase one or more of your points as a rhetorical question, a question you do not answer but that invites your readers' response.

3. Finally, try to construct a group that your readers can identify with or that they can separate themselves from. Does this tactic create an ethical problem? Does it lead to an unfair characterization?

Read the two short arguments that follow and, for each one, analyze the author's use of language to establish her ethos and appeal to readers' emotions.

1. What pronouns is the writer using, and in what way does she use each one?
2. Where does the writer use questions? Are these questions effective—do they help draw the reader into the argument?
3. Has the writer constructed a group to which both the writer and readers belong? Or has the writer constructed a group for the opposition? If so, is the writer fair to the views of the opposing group?

The Face of Welfare: Not Quite What You Pictured, Am I?

SHAWNTELLE SANTAS

The following article appeared in *Woman's Day* in April 1999.

I'm ahead of you in the checkout line at the grocery store. With me are my four chil- 1 dren, chattering as they unload groceries from the cart. When the last item has been scanned, I count out food stamps to the cashier.

You click into judgment mode and see WELFARE MOM flashing above my head in neon lights. You monitor each item as the cashier bags it. I get demerits for the 2-liter bottle of soda, but no credit for the fresh tomatoes.

You survey my children. If they're dressed in school clothes, faces freshly washed, you'll be convinced it's possible to live the good life on welfare. If, instead, the children are in play clothes and smudgy with dirt, you'll be sure they haven't washed in a week. You won't consider that *all* children are dirt magnets in the same annoying yet innocent way.

Because I'm a welfare mother, you feel it's safe to assume a few things about me and my life. For instance, that I'm probably immune to any of the less charitable names that flash into your head, along with "welfare mother." And if, on a particularly stressful day, you let one of those names slip out in a mumbled whisper, you can be sure it won't affect me at all. The most popular of those words in our neighborhood is "wellie." Compared with options like "scum" or "white trash," wellie may not seem so bad, but tone of voice is everything and, laced with contempt, any word can sting as sharply as any other.

It's a safe bet I was too busy being delinquent to finish high school—you know, with 5 drinking, drugs, unprotected sex, vandalism and petty theft. You've also concluded that each of my children has a different father and, of course, that I've never been married. Surely my own unwed mother was on welfare most of her life as well.

Here are a few facts about me you probably *won't* assume: I was raised by two parents who were never on welfare. I was a virgin when I graduated high school with a high B average. I never drank and never even saw an illegal drug.

After graduation I intended to work a year to save for college. I met my future husband at my job. Our decision to marry after six months was an impulsive one. Contrary to prevailing assumptions (then and now), I wasn't pregnant until six months after our wedding.

Six years later, when our fourth child was born, we were both working full-time and making slow, steady progress, even making land contract payments on a house. You may expect now to hear how I became a victim of circumstance. And, yes, the bookstore I managed closed four months after my husband and I decided we could live on my income alone so he could stay home with the baby. The stress took its toll on our relationship in tabloid-worthy ways. And eventually my husband left. Still, I'm only a victim if where I am is where I plan to stay.

In line behind me at the grocery store, you might not imagine I'm well-read enough to understand the politics behind welfare reform. You might think a five-year lifetime limit on cash benefits seems fair, and you'd probably be surprised to know I agree with you, though I doubt you've considered, as I have, what the effects will be on women and children.

In the western New York county where I live, strict conditions must be met to re-   10
ceive assistance. A person working fewer than 30 hours per week must be looking for additional employment and be able to *prove* it. The unemployed must perform community service and attend classes on interviewing and job application techniques to earn benefits. No exceptions are made for recipients without access to reliable child care or transportation.

If there was ever any truth in the stereotype of the welfare mother who spends her days sprawled on a couch ingesting chips and tabloid TV, surely that truth is changing. I'm working as if my life, my children's lives, depended on it. I write for the local newspaper. I submit essays to one magazine after another until they are sold. I am even writing greeting-card ideas.

Someday soon, you'll see me at the grocery store paying with cash and you won't give me another thought. Until then, when you see me, remember: The only safe assumption about someone else's life is that there *are* no safe assumptions.

Better Safe . . . ? Diary of a Mad Law Professor

PATRICIA J. WILLIAMS

Patricia J. Williams is the James L. Dohr Professor of Law at Columbia University and writes a regular column, titled "Diary of a Mad Law Professor," for *The Nation*, where the following article was first published in March 2002. Books she has written include *The Alchemy of Race and Rights* (1991), *The Rooster's Egg* (1995), and *Seeing a ColorBlind Future: The Paradox of Race* (1998).

In my last column, I called the expansion of profiling that has occurred since   1
September 11 "equal opportunity." I meant it ironically, but a surprising number of people took me literally. So I want to make clear that I don't consider this upgraded frisking any kind of opportunity, nor do I think that its expansion is really the same as equality. I am also aware, as was pointed out to me, that there are people in the world who might appreciate a good cavity search, confident that this is all for their benefit. And while I understand that we have all become subject to "nothing more than" the same ministrations that visitors to maximum security prisoners go through, the fact that some think this is the best of all possible worlds strikes me as fatuous.

The billions of dollars currently being pumped into police and surveillance budgets represent an unprecedented investment in a heavily patrolled world. Such an extraordinary buildup will inevitably exacerbate questions about the limits of state force; it will require the greatest vigilance to prevent our turning into not just a police state but one big global military base. Specific categories of us will probably continue to bear a special burden—black women in airports are, according to some figures, searched more than anyone else because I, as Typical Black Everywoman, meet the description of a drug courier better than you—as in You, profiled *Nation* reader and Typical Ungendered White Person.

Blacks and Latinos are the profiled shape of the "war on drugs," even though the majority of actual drug abusers are young white people like Governor Jeb Bush's poor daughter, Noelle. The "war on terror" promises to be even more sweeping. For the time being, our new international, militarized police force has increased its scrutiny, from black women in airports and black men in cars, to include Middle Eastern men anywhere, Asian people who look vaguely Filipino, as well as ample Minnesota housewives actually armed with sets of silver fondue forks.

Is this better or worse? I think it's a misuse of data, often creating a false sense of security. The kind of profiling that seems to inform the majority of stops and searches is usually based on statistical relations so vague as to be useless. Such profiling, premised on diffuse probabilities about looks and dress, ethnicity or nationality, class or educational status, begs for more analysis. Otherwise it can be defeated on the one hand by guards and gatekeepers whose interpretation of looks or class status is skewed by selective and subjective prejudice and on the other hand by travelers committed to the art of disguise.

The attacks on the Pentagon and the World Trade Center were carried out by 5 deeply rational and well-trained operatives whose tactics defied easy profiling. They looked—and were—well educated; they dressed professionally. The fact that the FBI actually had information that some of them had been involved in terrorist networks counted less in the real world than that they looked good. After all, it is true that in a very large sense sleek, well-dressed professionals commit fewer crimes than the hungry, grumpy lower classes. I have this painful recurring dream of the security guards at Logan on September 11, carelessly waving all eighteen men through, while strip searching long lines of black women having bad hair days.

I worry that we're doing the same thing with shoes: Richard Reid was able to board an airplane because he played against the expectation embedded in profiles. He looked odd enough to have been stopped and questioned, but ultimately looks had little to do with what made him dangerous. Although they were suspicious, security officials did not discover his criminal record, surely better evidence of his propensities than whether he wore a ponytail. He was finally allowed on board; he was a British citizen, and British citizens were not the subject of any profile. They searched his bag but not his shoes, because shoes were not at that point the subject of any profile. Now that we know thick-soled sneakers can be turned into weapons of mass destruction, airports spend a lot of time removing and examining them. It's likely to catch copycats, I suppose, which is not a problem to be ignored, but does anyone really believe that Al Qaeda would use shoes again? In other words, while there is, after Richard Reid, a marginal relation between shoes and bombs, the actual odds of it ever happening precisely like that again are slim to nonexistent. Indeed, what distinguishes professional operatives who calculatedly sow terror is that they take the time to play against type.

So I worry when I hear about plans to expand profiling as we now seem to practice it. I worry when I hear about plans to have our thumb prints taken, our irises scanned, our DNA plotted. How can we be putting all this work into appearances when appearances bear no necessary relation to intent? The risk of this is not just one of diminished dignity or privacy. The problem ought to have been made clear to us in the wake of "accidents" like Amadou Diallo.* The problem ought to be apparent in recent news stories about the CIA having flown an unmanned surveillance craft over a street in Afghanistan. It had a night vision camera on it that caught in its scope a group of men conversing who fit a profile because one of their number was unusually tall, as is Osama bin Laden. After some consultation at the remote site where the CIA officers and their telemonitors were located, the CIA decided to bomb the group. The men were killed, but as of this writing, the CIA admits it still doesn't know who the men were. Civilians on the ground claimed that the men were townspeople scavenging for scrap metal.

This death by actuary. This profiled guilt. The trial by night vision drone. Our superlative technology permits us to listen, scan, survey and X-ray anybody and everybody in the world. But a sea of data alone won't help us if there is no higher wisdom in the final analysis. Good "intelligence" means more than eyes and ears—there must be a heart and a brain, or we will never achieve the global stability we all so desperately desire.

---

*Amadou Diallo was killed by police officers in New York City who assumed—incorrectly—that he was reaching for a gun.

FOR YOU TO WRITE

Write your own argument on a topic about which you possess more information than many readers do (as Santas, a welfare recipient, does about the circumstances that can lead to dependence on public assistance, and Williams, a law professor and an African-American woman, does about the subject of ethnic profiling). In your argument, use *I* and *we,* as well as questions, in ways that will establish your credibility with your readers and appeal to their emotions and group identifications.

Types of Arguments

Part Two

6. Definition: What Is It? 131

7. Causal Argument: How Did It Get That Way? 179

8. Evaluation: Is It Good or Bad? 228

9. Proposal: What Should We Do about It? 281

Definition: What Is It?

Chapter 6

Scientists Determine Chimpanzees Have "Culture"

AP News Service

Some chimpanzees greedily slurp ants off a stick as if it were a wriggling lollipop, while others daintily pluck them, one by one.

Some chimps mop their brows with leaves; others demurely raise their arms while companions groom them.

Researchers now agree that the variety of behavior exhibited by mankind's closest relative can be summed up in a single word: culture.

It is the first time scientists have concluded that a species other than humans has a culture, or a way of life based on customs that are learned and shared rather than genetically programmed.

"The evidence is overwhelming that chimpanzees have a remarkable ability to invent new customs and technologies, and they pass these on socially," said primatologist Frans de Waal of Emory University.

The study, conducted by primatologist Andrew Whiten of the University of St. Andrews in Scotland and others, was published Thursday in the journal *Nature*.

The findings are based on an analysis of chimp data spanning five decades.

Jane Goodall, the world-renowned scientist who has been observing primates at Gombe Stream in Tanzania since 1960 in the longest-running animal behavior project, co-wrote the study.

The research found at least 39 customs related to chimps' tool use, grooming and courtship. The customs vary widely from group to group, much as they do in humans. The scientists said it is too early to tell if some chimp cultures are more advanced than others.

"What we see in wild chimps, on a lesser scale, is the sort of cultural diversity that we would see in traditional human societies," said primatologist Craig Stanford of the University of Southern California.

Chimps and ancestral humans split on the evolutionary tree more than 4 million years ago, but the ape's genetic code still overlaps ours by more than 98 percent.

Primatologists generally consider chimps to be as mentally capable as a 4-year-old child, and they share many practices with primitive human cultures, including social bonds, certain hunting habits and the use of plants for medicinal purposes.

Many animal species learn fundamental survival skills from their parents, and their habits differ depending on where they live. Songbirds, for example, learn local dialects of their species' song.

Dolphins swim in groups and have a complex communications system, while elephants display a range of emotions, including grief.

But the extensive types of behavior among chimps are unparalleled and are not necessarily dictated by particular boundaries or environments.

In Tanzania, chimps at Gombe routinely use sticks to probe the ground for termites, but chimps 100 miles away in the Mahale Mountains do not.

Gombe chimps don't use stones to crack nuts, even though their terrain is strewn with rocks. But Tai rainforest chimps in the Ivory Coast use stone tools even though rocks are scarce.

At Tai, grooming chimps wipe parasites on their forearms before mashing them with their forefingers. At Gombe, groomers mash parasites on a leaf.

What remains unresolved is the origins of chimp customs and precisely how they are shared.

"We're just now beginning to videotape families to see how they acquire these behaviors," said Ann Pusey of the University of Minnesota.

The findings raise an important new consideration in the conservation of chimpanzees' rapidly dwindling populations across Africa. Logging, hunting and farming have reduced the chimp population to less than 200,000, down from the millions of chimpanzees 100 years ago.

"We are not just losing chimpanzees," Whiten said, "We are losing the diversity of chimpanzee cultures."

ANALYZING "Scientists Determine Chimpanzees Have 'Culture'"

The sample offered here is a news article released by the Associated Press on June 16, 1999. You may think that this piece cannot be an argument because it is just a news story, but look again. This report has all the features of an argument: a claim, reasons for believing the claim, and connecting warrants. Furthermore, it is an argument on the first of the issues described in Chapter 4. It makes a claim about the nature of things, answering a "What is it?" question.

Readers need look no further for the **claim** than the title, or headline: "Scientists Determine Chimpanzees Have 'Culture.'" The first part of this sentence gives the source of the claim; removing that, we have the basic claim: "Chimpanzees have culture." This claim is repeated in the third, fourth, and fifth paragraphs, each time with greater specificity. These restatements or clarifications of the basic claim are crucial to the argument, and we will come back to them.

If you came across this headline, would you stop to read the article because the claim struck you as unusual or intriguing: Chimpanzees have—"culture"? We are used to seeing discussions about human culture, but not about animal culture. Other claims about chimpanzees would not surprise us: "Chimpanzees eat bananas," "Chimpanzees live in trees." But "Chimpanzees have culture" is newsworthy because it strikes us as surprising and intriguing. The fourth paragraph also tells us that we have a "first" here, the "first time scientists have concluded that a species other than humans has a culture." That detail, in addition to the surprise value of the claim, provides exigence for the piece, a nudge about its importance. Since most of us find this claim unusual to begin with, and since we are told that it is a kind of breakthrough as well, we may be interested. But for the very same reasons that the claim arouses our curiosity, we require some convincing before we are likely to accept it.

What reasons **support** this claim? To answer that question, let's first consider what the argument here is trying to do. It is taking some facts or data from the world—observations, objects, or events—and trying to apply a label to them, to fit them into a category. There are, according to the claim, some things that chimpanzees do that we can call "culture." The claim, then, essentially has two parts: its *subject* (chimpanzees or chimpanzee behavior, things chimps do) and *what is said about this subject* (culture exists among chimps). Support for this argument, as for all arguments about the nature of things, comes from working on these two parts.

The most important part, however, is not, as you might think, the data about chimpanzee behavior. The critical part is calling such behavior "culture." What do the originators of this claim mean by using the term "culture"? How is "culture" being defined here? "Culture" is a somewhat vague term that we may have seen in relation to the fine arts (a *cultured* person); that is certainly not the sense used here. It is also a term used in descriptions of human behavior and of human-made objects by anthropologists and archaeologists (*cultural* practices; material *culture*). That meaning seems closer to the one intended in this argument. To limit the audience's understanding of this crucial term, we need a definition of "culture" that will help the argument, and we find it in both the fourth and fifth paragraphs when the claim is restated.

> It is the first time scientists have concluded that a species other than humans has *a culture, or a way of life based on customs that are learned and shared rather than genetically programmed.*
>
> "The evidence is overwhelming that chimpanzees have *a remarkable ability to invent new customs and technologies, and they pass these on socially,*" said primatologist Frans de Waal of Emory University. [italics added]

Readers now have a working **definition** of culture for purposes of this argument. A culture includes customs, varying ways of doing things, that chimps are not born with but learn from each other and can even invent. This definition is the crucial warrant in the argument, the link between the reasons and the claim (see Chapter 2). Later in this chapter we will go into the techniques for constructing such definitions. For now, we simply note that a crucial piece of an argument about what something is, about its nature, has been put into place.

With this definition of "culture" (assuming readers accept it as plausible), the scientists have a principle for selecting the data, or facts, about chimpanzees to offer as reasons or evidence for the overall claim. The facts will have to be about things that chimps do not do instinctively, by nature. Since anything that *all* chimps do is probably genetically determined, only things that some chimps do and some do not can be offered as evidence of behavior that fits under the argument's definition of the term "culture."

The first two paragraphs offer striking **examples** of varying chimp behavior: slurping versus plucking ants; mopping brows and raising arms. (How good is this second example?) Furthermore, as is typical in the fluid arrangement of real arguments, these supporting examples appear first in the text, after the headline but before the claim is clarified. Later in the article we are offered more examples: some chimps use sticks and stones in food gathering while others do not; some mash parasites with their fingers while others use leaves. If this evidence were offered in a multi-media format, we could see brief videos of these chimp behaviors. These examples come from the raw descriptions made by scientists observing chimps in the wild. They constitute the chimp behavior that deserves the label "culture."

But notice that these raw data, these striking examples that the reader virtually "sees," are not offered in great quantity. Instead, the report summarizes much of the data under a subsidiary claim:

> The research found at least 39 customs related to chimps' tool use, grooming and courtship. The customs vary widely from group to group, much as they do in humans.

We might combine these two sentences into one as follows: "At least 39 customs related to chimps' tool use, grooming and courtship vary widely from group to group." This summary is important because it tells the reader two things: that the arguers have much more evidence than the specific examples given, and that the examples that are given are *typical* of all the data on chimp behavior collected.

Bringing this summary about the data together with the overall claim and the definition, we can construct a simplified Toulmin diagram to represent the argument reported on in this news piece.

Reason: Chimps have at least 39 customs related to tool use, grooming, and courtship that vary widely from group to group.   →   **Claim:** Chimpanzees have culture.

↑

Warrant: A culture is a way of life based on customs that are invented, learned, and shared; they vary from group to group and are passed on socially rather than genetically.

The overall claim about chimp culture is not, however, supported only by direct evidence from watching chimps. As often happens in arguments about the nature of things, **comparison** is also brought in to help convince the audience. Comparisons branch in two directions in this argument, to other species and to humans. Examples about other species' behavior (songbirds, dolphins, and elephants) are offered as a contrast. Unlike chimp behavior, their actions depend on the animal's locale. (Does the detail about elephants really fit?) These contrasts are probably included because readers may have heard of these behaviors, and they may seem to contradict the claim about chimpanzee culture itself, or its status as a "first."

The comparisons to humans are more important because the term "culture" has in the past been reserved for humans, and this argument wants to stretch the term to fit chimpanzee behavior. So readers are told that chimps have the mental capabilities of four-year-olds and that humans and chimps share 98 percent of their genetic code. Given these points of comparison, it becomes less surprising that "'What we see in wild chimps, on a lesser scale, is the sort of cultural diversity that we would see in traditional human societies.'"

The claim that chimps have culture is based on reported examples of chimp behavior. Why should we find this data credible? How is it verified? The answer is obvious. The article cites the authorities who generated the data in the first place, providing names and credentials of these sources: primatologists Frans de Waal of Emory University, Andrew Whiten of the University of St. Andrews in Scotland, and Jane Goodall, a famous chimpanzee researcher whose name we might recognize (though just in case we have never heard of her before, the article reminds us of her reputation and the basis of her work). Furthermore, we learn that this study was published in the journal *Nature.* Its appearance in what we assume is a reputable scientific journal also vouches for its credibility. The evidence, then, is verified by citing sources and their institutional affiliations. No further arguments on why such sources should be trusted are provided. An argument cannot back up everything; it has to rely on some assumptions shared with the audience.

The critical definition of "culture" is also not supported by anything else in the article. It could be backed up by quoting another expert or by the authority of a dictionary. But the writers assume that the definition offered, "a way of life based on customs that are learned and shared rather than genetically programmed," needs no further support. They count on its being accepted as uncontroversial, even by readers who find that applying "culture" to chimpanzee behavior is a challenging stretch.

Who is the intended audience for this piece, and what are the exigence and constraints involved in its appearance in a news story? As Chapter 1 explains, every argument is influenced by features of its **rhetorical situation.** This piece is directed at a wide, general audience, people who read a daily newspaper. It has to capture the interest of this audience, and it tries to do so with its title and with the colorful opening examples. If this material required a specialist's vocabulary, it would probably never appear in a publication for general readers. As a news release, it has further requirements: It must be fairly short, and it must deliver the gist of the piece in the beginning. News stories, even when they resemble feature stories like this one, are usually written so that the main points can be gathered in the first few sentences; the last paragraphs contain details that could be cut off by an editor trying to fit an article on a page or by a reader.

But the question of the **exigence** for this piece, the *why* of its appearance, is a bit more complicated. Where did the Associated Press get the story? Most likely they acquired it as a press release either from the authors of the study or from the journal *Nature.* Why was it important to the scientists that their work reach a wide public audience? The answer to that question, and to the ultimate "So what?" of this piece for the public, is provided in the final paragraphs. The claim about cultural diversity among chimpanzees depends on the chance to observe different populations in geographically separated communities. But native chimpanzee populations are dwindling in Africa, if not to the point of endangering the species, certainly to the point of endangering its variety. Therefore, their various habitats need to be protected, and public pressure, depending on an aroused public consciousness about the unique "culture" of each group, could help.

DEFINITION: ARGUING ABOUT THE NATURE OF THINGS

Every day, newspapers, magazines, television, and web sites fill our eyes and ears with reports about the state of the world: The unemployment rate is down four-tenths of a percent; another candidate has declared her intention to run; a civil war is raging in a distant country. We rarely question such reports; instead, we grant them the status of fact by making two crucial assumptions: that such stories could be verified if we wanted to check into them, and that the sources who deliver these stories have no intent to deceive us.

Yet behind the simplest news story lie definitions, perceptions, and categories that could become sources of different views held by equally competent observers and interpreters—that could, in other words, spawn arguments offering different answers to "What is it?" questions. The unemployment rate, for example, is an extremely complex indicator; reporting procedures can and do change such a figure. If, for instance, only those actively looking for work are counted, the figure will not indicate those who have given up, those who have never tried, or those who are working part-time and wish to work full time. Thus the number of the unemployed defined narrowly may have decreased, but under a fuller definition, the number may actually have gone up. The best way to count the unemployed can be a debatable issue.

We need to appreciate the richness and variety of arguments in this category since they contribute to our construction and understanding of the worlds we inhabit. We encounter a variety of arguments about the nature of things in every situation and type of publication. For example, when the Food and Drug Administration (FDA) claimed that cigarettes were an addictive substance and took over the right to control cigarette sales, this change in the definition of cigarettes had a sweeping effect on their marketing and distribution until March 2000, when the Supreme Court declared this unilateral redefinition unconstitutional. William Arens's 1979 book, *The Man-Eating Myth: Anthropology and Anthropophagy*, claimed that extensive, institutionalized cannibalism has never occurred among humans; his claim led to a raging anthropological debate, which has inspired a reassessment of documentary and scientific evidence about cultures said to be cannibalistic. An article in the January 1998 *Smithsonian* magazine redefined chess not as a game engaging cool and elevated intellects but as a "violent sport." Such arguments about the nature of things surround us on all sides and help form what we believe about our world.

Types of Definition Arguments

Definition arguments answer fundamental questions about what things are, what they can be called, and how they may be changing. They include the following types of arguments:

Arguments Identifying Trends and Describing States of Public Taste and Opinion

These point to patterns in events or track them over time. Such arguments are particularly important in business and marketing, where trends in the economy and consumer buying habits are constantly assessed: "An increasing number of Americans are shopping on the Internet." "The market for designer foods has increased dramatically in the last five years." Claims about public opinion are also extremely important in politics, the art of marketing candidates and policies: "Most Americans support the president's War on Terror." "Few Americans would support a constitutional amendment on flag burning." Often, the critical element in arguments about trends is whether the sample chosen as evidence of the opinions and behavior of millions of people is really representative.

Arguments Claiming That Events Have or Have Not Occurred

These arguments constitute most of the fare of newspapers. The standard news story is actually an argument for the reality of the events reported: Russian troops invade Grozny; a hurricane devastates the coast of Texas and Louisiana; five people are found shot to death in a bank in Iowa. The mere presence of such stories in newspapers constitutes an argument from authority for the reality of these events. But if you look at these pieces as arguments, you will also see how your belief in the news report's account of an event is encouraged by supporting details such as the interviews and quotations cited, the pictures offered, or the reporters' claims of being on the scene.

Arguments Claiming That Things Exist or Do Not Exist

Obviously, we mount arguments in this category only if it is difficult to produce the thing itself or verifiable evidence of it. So arguments of this type often use indirect or "sign" arguments, offering traces of the existence at issue, like the tracks of Bigfoot or the recovered memories of alien abductees. There is a whole cottage industry in this category for arguments about alien visitors and UFOs of extraterrestrial origin. More commonly, we might argue for the presence of a bear from tracks and an overturned garbage can.

Arguments Placing a Topic (a Person, an Event, an Object, a Trend) in a Category or Applying a Label to It

Our opening argument, "Chimpanzees Have Culture," is an example of this type. When we ask "What can we call this?" we are interested in coming to terms with something by labeling it: "The governor is a Libertarian," "Symbolic logic is a form of mathematics," "Vegetarianism is a religion." Such claims call for supporting arguments only when they are likely to strike an audience as implausible or surprising. You wouldn't mount an argument for "The governor is a Libertarian" unless people thought he was something else.

Arguments Interpreting Works of Art

Like arguments in the preceding category, these offer an overall characterization or label suggesting the essence or significance of a subject. Many arguments of this type attempt to clarify or determine the meaning of works of literature, art, and film. Hence, they are essentially arguments about the nature of the objects under study: "This novel is a study in the failure of a young man to break away from the overwhelming control of his parents." "This movie uncovers the complexities that all of us face when we consider the effects of our personal choices on others." "This painting expresses the peace and stability of Flemish home life in the seventeenth century." Such claims often seem to pass judgment on a work of art, but they are usually preliminary to assessing the quality of a work. They are instead concerned with arguing for a view of what the work is "really" about, what its "essence" is.

CONSTRUCTING A DEFINITION ARGUMENT

Our analysis of the sample argument that opens this chapter explains the basic features of arguments about the nature of things. Now we want to turn from taking such arguments apart to the task of putting them together. How do you go about convincing yourself or someone else to believe a claim that answers some version of the question "What is it?" To understand the features of these arguments, we can look at the process of arriving at and supporting a claim about the nature of something in an informal social context.

Support by Example

Suppose you share an apartment or dorm room, and you cannot help but notice the following actions on the part of your roommate.

> Last night he put a half-eaten Big Mac in his desk drawer.
>
> He has left a pile of dirty laundry sitting on the foot of his bed for three weeks.
>
> He hasn't showered for three days.

While having lunch with a friend, you complain, "My roommate is a slob," and you go on to describe, in vivid language, the three behaviors listed above. It was these observations that led to your labeling your roommate a slob in the first place. Now you offer them to your friend as reasons for your label. You are trying to convince your friend to agree with you about your roommate's nature.

The three facts listed above describe situations, events, or objects connected with a specific time, place, and person. They are as close as language can come to real experience, and they are backed up by your testimony. Such verifiable particular examples are effective in an argument for just that reason. They create a sharable reality for other eyes (or noses) and help readers become aware of the experiences, the evidence, that inspired your claim.

Specific and Iterative Examples

Now the examples you have offered so far may show that your roommate has done some odd things recently. But do they add up to a continuing pattern of behavior that says something about your roommate's basic habits and personality? Anyone defending your roommate's character might say that these examples are unusual and not typical actions on his part. So in addition to such particular or unique instances, you might also use **repetitive** or **iterative** ones, citing things that happen frequently or consistently. Using the present tense suggests habit.

> He leaves his shoes on his pillow.

Putting in a word that suggests repetition is another way.

> He often stores used gum on his computer monitor.

Without better evidence of recurring habits, you would have to hedge your claim with a qualifier, "My roommate is sometimes a slob" or "During finals week, my roommate is a slob."

Examples then may be specific (single and not recurring) or iterative (occurring frequently over time). In the argument about chimpanzees that opened this chapter, the examples of chimp behavior were certainly presented as recurring, not as things that a few chimps did once. The difference in the nature of the claim that can be supported with iterative versus specific examples can be significant.

Typicality: "It's Not the Number of Examples That Matters"

As the distinction between specific and iterative examples indicates, the evidence you provide to support a broad claim like "My roommate is a slob" has to meet certain requirements. First, the evidence must actually represent facts and deeds really associated with the subject; in the case of the roommate, it would have to represent things he did, not things that others did with his possessions. Second, those facts and deeds have to be genuinely representative. If the details about your roommate were gathered over four years, each an isolated incident in the life of an otherwise neat and tidy person, they would not be a fair sampling of this roommate's behavior.

How many examples or pieces of evidence does it take to support a claim about the nature of something? Does it take three, or four, or ten? Could one ever be enough? Actually, no magic number of examples adds up to sufficient support for an argument about what something is or whether something is happening. It is not the quantity of the evidence that counts, but rather how typical it is. No matter how many specific or iterative instances you use, if they do not convincingly represent your subject, your argument is insufficiently supported.

But if the typicality is strong enough, even one example can suffice. Consider the paleontologist who concluded, "Some dinosaurs exhibited parenting behavior," a claim that contradicted the once-prevailing belief that dinosaurs simply laid their eggs and then abandoned them. He had discovered one eggshell-littered nest containing the remains of baby dinosaurs. Since the teeth of these babies were worn, he reasoned that food had been brought to them. Who else but the adult dinosaurs would have brought the food? He then drew the conclusion that a whole species of dinosaur cared for their young on the basis of this one nest. He was building on an assumption about the uniformity of behavior among members of the same species in matters dictated by instinct and related to their survival, so the evidence from one nest could be used to support a claim about the nature of an entire species. But an assumption of typicality this strong can rarely be used in generalizing about human behavior. The behavior of one person is rarely seen as typical of all humans, nor is a single act usually sufficient evidence of a person's character. One half-eaten Big Mac in a desk drawer does not necessarily make a person always and essentially a slob.

Working either alone or with a group of your classmates, think of a particular person, trend, or thing that would fit each of the following categories. Then, for one category, come up with specific or iterative details that would convincingly support placing that person, trend, or thing in that category. You may go on to use these examples in a full argument.

- A musical group whose work fits a certain style
- A political figure who made a difference (for better or worse)
- A fashion that was the typical "look" of a time and place
- A sports figure who was seen as a hero or villain
- An idea or trend that affected your life

EXERCISE 6.1

Modifying Your Subject to Fit Your Evidence

The subjects in arguments about the nature of things range from the individual (my lab partner) through the many (the students in my class) to all (every student), and from the specific (students taking Organic Chemistry I this semester) to the abstract (the pre-nursing major). These different kinds of subjects impose different requirements on the selection of evidence in an argument.

Abstractions   An abstraction is something you cannot put your hands on easily. Ask anyone to show you *knowledge, business, the national interest,* or an *energy crisis.* An abstraction is an umbrella that can shelter a variety of examples. If you are constructing an argument about an abstraction, you have to adopt a strategy for selecting evidence.

Suppose, for example, you are supporting a claim about the existence of a trend, "Organized athletics is expanding." "Organized athletics" is an abstract term, potentially covering everything except the chance meeting of five people in a playground who start up a spontaneous game of touch football. It can include sports from Little League baseball to the World Cup soccer play-offs, from intramurals to the Olympics. If you want to say something convincing about organized athletics in general, you would have to draw your examples from several categories or levels of participation. However, you might find it more convenient, as well as more accurate, to replace such a large abstraction with a more modest term that fits your examples better. For instance, if your examples are limited to intramurals, your proposition should read "Intramural athletics are expanding." "Intramural athletics" is still an abstraction, standing for a number of sports organized in a school, but it is less abstract than "organized athletics."

Individual Subjects   A claim with a single subject makes an assertion about a single thing ("My Chippendale sofa is probably a fake"), a single person ("The author of this book really understands gardening"), or a single entity ("The 101st Congress is deadlocked on gun control").

A single subject must be identified for any audience that would not recognize it immediately. Otherwise, the evidence that you select to make a claim about a single subject must follow the constraints we discussed above; it must actually belong to the subject and represent it fairly.

Subjects with Definite Numbers   A claim about the nature of things can be about a group with a definite number of members, and the claim can assert something about all of them: "Eighteen states are overrepresented in Congress," "The seven liberal arts are still the core of a college education."

If the definite number of items in your subject is small, you must consider each member individually. If you talked about six liberal arts but didn't mention the seventh, readers would find the omission strange. You would not construct a claim with a definite number unless your evidence supported such a claim in the first place.

However, a large definite number in the subject ("Eighteen states are overrepresented in Congress") can create certain problems in managing evidence. In a relatively brief argument, you would probably not be able to give each state separate attention, so you must adopt a strategy for covering them all. You can at least name all 18 to satisfy your reader's curiosity, but you might select two or three to discuss in detail, assuring your readers that those three states were typical of the 18. Another tactic would be to classify the 18 states into smaller groups—the old, tiny colonies; the big, empty western states, and the noncontiguous newcomers—and discuss a single representative example of each of these groups, such as Delaware, Wyoming, and Alaska, in detail.

Subjects with Indefinite Numbers   When we argue about the nature of things, we often refer to part but not all of a group. We use an indefinite plural like *some* or *many* when we know that our claim does not hold for all the possible members of a group, but we do not or cannot know how many it does hold for. We may know that it would be incorrect to say, "All students at Wilson Community College need career counseling," yet we cannot say that precisely 837 need career counseling. So we settle on a rough approximation like "Many students at Wilson Community College need career counseling."

We have the following indefinite number markers at our disposal to suggest shades of proportion, ranging from a few isolated members of a group to all the members: *a couple, a few, several, few, some, many, a lot, most, almost all, all.* We can also use adverbs such as *rarely, occasionally, sometimes, frequently, often,* and *usually* as indefinite quantifiers. Indefinite markers of quantity can be ordered in relation to one another almost like numbers. Choosing a quantifying adjective requires us to assess what kind of support we have for a claim. The term *a few* stands for some small number and is used in written argument when a specific number is inaccessible, inappropriate, or unnecessary: "A few students in my biology class failed the midterm."

- The term *few* (without the article "a") is different: "Few students in my biology class failed the midterm" means, in effect, "Isn't it surprising that more did not?" You might mention the few who failed, but most of your attention will be devoted to the most who did not. We might even say that *few* and *most* are corollaries; a claim about "few" implies the opposite claim about "most."

- *Some* is a safe choice in a claim. You can use it when you have a number of examples or indirect evidence about a group fitting your case, but no way or need to assess what proportion of the whole that number represents.

- *Many* means more than *some*: "Many Americans distrust the government" makes a stronger claim than "Some Americans distrust the government." A *many* argument may use the same number of examples or the same survey data as a *some* argument, but there is a greater assumption of typicality behind the evidence offered; thus the reader is asked to take a bigger leap between the evidence and the claim in the *many* argument.

- In written argument, *most* is usually taken to stand for more than half of a group (at least 51 percent), and often for much more than half. In fact, a "most" proposition may even suggest a cautious *all*. Prefacing a claim with *most* protects against overstatement and easy refutation. Our experience rarely takes in all the possible members of the group we are generalizing about. A *most* statement may use the same number of examples as a *some* or a *many* argument, but *most* makes an even stronger assumption that the examples are typical of the whole subject. To support the typicality of your examples when you are claiming more from them, a new tactic may be called for—an appeal, stated or unstated, to the essence or defining characteristics of a thing.

- A claim with "all" makes a statement about an entire subject. If the subject is a group, then every single member is involved. Claims about all or every or any or no member of a group are called *universal* statements or generalizations. A statement about an individual, such as "My roommate is a slob," is also universal if it always holds. If you are making a claim about a small group, you must examine or account for each member in order to make such a generalization, but *all* is not reserved for small, countable groups. You can use it even when you don't know how large the group you are talking about is, but you must present your subject in such a way that what you say about it in your claim becomes one of its necessary features. Your subject must include in its very nature what you are saying about it, and it must have this feature all the time.

An Invisible *All* Formal universal claims, carefully marked with *all* or *none*, seldom appear in ordinary writing. But that does not mean that arguments for universal claims are rare. Instead, such arguments are often presented inconspicuously. Often, arguers use a collective or plural noun with no quantifier in front of it, so universal claims may look like the following: "Coastal wetlands are a renewable resource," "Sports fans are fed up with high ticket prices," "Americans distrust the media."

Whenever we generalize without specifying *some, most, few,* or *many*, we imply *all*. The naked subject stands for the entire group. This kind of invisible or "silent" universal is more common in informal writing and speaking, and it is very common in newspaper headlines. The argument analyzed in the opening of this chapter was an implied universal: [all] chimpanzees have culture. The arguers were making a claim about an essential attribute of chimpanzees.

We are likely to slip into an invisible universal when we want emphasis or when not much is at stake in an argument. We tend not to recognize our own state of uncertainty about how strong our argument is unless someone challenges us. Then we either admit exceptions ("Well, I don't really mean *all*"), or we stand our ground and make the necessary definition argument.

Though many of the claims you read and hear are expressed as silent universals, as an arguer you should not be confused about the strength of your evidence and your claim. If you really mean *all*, you must be prepared to support your claim in the way described above if it might be challenged. If you cannot support it that way, you should modify your claim with a *most* or a *many*, taking account of qualifications and exceptions.

Working either alone or with a group of your classmates, suggest a way to modify the claims below to make them easier to support, and then describe the evidence you might use. You may go on to use one of these modified claims and the supporting evidence in a full argument.

- No religious practices are illegal in the United States.
- The beauty standards depicted in fashion magazines are European, not American.
- Professional sports are losing fan support.
- Americans spend most of their leisure time in front of the television.
- In most action movies, government officials are the villains.

EXERCISE 6.2

Support by Definition

So far, then, the basic tactic for supporting a claim about the nature of something is providing evidence that actually comes from that something and is typical of it. But that is not all there is to this basic type of argument. Consider the following.

> My roommate is a slob. After he makes his bed in the morning, his bedspread hangs two inches lower at the foot of his bed than at the head. His desk blotter is off center and its edge is not parallel to the edge of his desk. What's more, there's an ink stain approximately two centimeters in diameter in the upper right-hand corner. One of the books on his shelf has a piece of paper sticking out of it, and the spare push pins on his bulletin board don't line up evenly across the bottom. Even more disgusting, he does his laundry only once a week, and he actually failed to brush his teeth after lunch today.

The examples offered as evidence in this short argument could certainly represent the person described and be typical of his behavior. But something else is seriously wrong. The person who wrote this paragraph obviously has a definition of "slob" in mind that is nothing like the commonly accepted definition. It might pass in a military academy or a monk's dormitory, but nowhere else. If this arguer were backed into a corner and asked for his definition of a "slob," he might straighten his collar and declare, "A slob is anyone who does not meet my high standards of order and cleanliness." But even if he puts this definition into his argument, at the head of his examples, no one would be convinced that his roommate is a slob according to the common meaning of the term. The writer's definition of "slob" is too personal and idiosyncratic.

This odd argument illustrates another requirement in supporting a claim about the nature of something. Not only does the evidence offered have to represent the subject fairly and typically, but it must also reasonably fit what is being said about the subject. The arguer must adjust these two parts to fit together: evidence from the subject and what is said about the subject. Thus, constructing an argument about the nature of something is a process of finding the best possible fit between the available evidence from your subject and what you are saying about that subject, and this fit must be convincing to your audience.

The Balancing Act between Definition and Evidence

Arguments about the nature of things build on both evidence about the subject and an acceptable definition of what is claimed about it. Does this simple two-part requirement hold for all the types of arguments listed above, including claims about trends, about labels, about interpretations?

We can test out this double requirement on a claim about the existence of a trend. In March 2000, an article in the *Journal of the American Medical Association* argued that winners of the Miss America pageant have become skinnier over the contest's 78-year history. How was "skinnier" defined so that facts about the winners could be collected and used? After all, the weights of Miss Americas vary from year to year, but then so do their heights; a trend in weights alone would not substantiate a trend to skinnier Miss Americas.

To generate evidence supporting their claim, the arguers used data about the heights and the weights of Miss Americas to calculate their Body Mass Index (BMI). The BMI is calculated by squaring the height in meters (that is, multiplying the height in meters by itself), and dividing the weight in kilograms by the square of the height in meters.

The resulting number, the BMI, allows comparison of people of different heights and weights. Since the BMIs of Miss Americas have declined from the 1920s through the 80s, a claim that Miss Americas have been getting skinnier can be supported. The authors could also claim a more sinister trend; a BMI between 20 and 25 is considered normal, but many Miss Americas in the last 30 years have had BMIs below 18.5, the World Health Organization's standard for malnutrition. Overall, this example illustrates how the evidence representing the subject fits and is even generated by the way the key term in the claim is defined: "skinnier" here means "a declining body mass index."

Statements claiming that something exists or that an event happened might seem to be the least concerned with an adjustment between definition and the evidence available in the real world. But the fit between evidence and definition is critical in these claims too, especially when the audience's resistance to the claim is high. Take, for instance, the sort of headline frequently displayed in tabloids at the supermarket checkout counter: "Bigfoot seen in Superior National Forest." Despite the frequency of stories like these and documentaries on odd cable channels, most Americans do not believe that Bigfoot exists (a claim in itself !). The problem is insufficient evidence to meet most people's standard of what it takes to prove the "existence" of a new species, as well as the questionable credibility of the sources. Resistance is high to a claim that a hitherto unknown large animal exists in places visited by thousands of people for hundreds of years. Obviously the personal testimony of witnesses ("I saw the thing") or the evidence from signs (footprints and tufts of hair) is not going to do it. It will take a specimen, dead or alive.

Relying on Accepted Definitions

A definition of what you are claiming about your subject is always a necessary part of an argument about the nature of things. But the question you face as the writer of such an argument is whether to make that definition an explicit part of your argument or to rely on your audience's already having the same definition in mind, or at least not resisting the way you are implicitly defining a term.

When your audience will readily accept the way you are using key terms in your claim, you will usually not need an explicit definition. You can always put in a definition for emphasis or clarification, as the writer of the "Chimpanzees Have Culture" argument did. But your audience's inclination to agree with you will probably not be damaged if you omit the definition of an unproblematic term. Arguments for claims like "My uncle is a cheapskate," "Weightlifting is a strenuous activity," and "Most Americans support the United Nations" could go right to the evidence because what is being said about the subject is likely to seem obvious to most audiences. A "cheapskate" is someone who won't spend his or her money in the ways that others do, and a "strenuous activity" is one that would quickly tire most people. What it means to "support the United Nations" could be more complicated, but it could also mean that in a poll, more than 50 percent of respondents answered yes to the question, "Do you support the United Nations?"

Using Explicit Definitions

Since an argument should always be shaped for its rhetorical situation—its audience, its place of publication, its moment—few absolute rules can be offered to writers about when definitions should or should not appear. But in general, explicit definition is more common when a claim is more arguable, that is, when it is more likely to meet with scrutiny or resistance. In demanding situations, it may be necessary not only to include an explicit definition, but also to defend it. The following is a list of rhetorical situations that usually require explicit definition and of the kinds of claims that tend to meet with resistance.

Arguments Made in Academic and Professional Settings   Since academic disciplines are, by definition, research communities trying to advance knowledge in an area, they require the highest, toughest standards of arguing. Ideally, all key terms in an argument published in a research journal should be defined. Even when knowledgeable readers can be counted on to understand key terms, they may be defined as part of the gesture of making everything explicit.

Arguments in many professional settings, such as legal arguments, usually include explicit definitions of key terms. Contracts or rental agreements, legislation presented to governing bodies, regulations put out by an institution—all of these require explicit definitions of critical terms. If, for example, a college declares as a requirement for enrollment that "All degree-seeking students must have a high school diploma or its equivalent," it will have to define what counts as the equivalent of a high school diploma.

Arguments That Make a Surprising or Implausible Characterization

If a claim puts an unusual label on its subject or places it in an unexpected category, chances are that an explicit definition will be called for as part of the support. Of course, claims can be implausible to an audience for a wide variety of reasons, but in general arguments will strike readers as challenging if they

- Go against prevailing beliefs ("The United States is not a democratic society").
- Make very broad, unqualified claims ("All politicians are narcissists").
- Use invented terms ("Most perfume ads on television are a form of psychosocial pollution").
- Use terms metaphorically ("Children are an endangered species").
- Appear paradoxical ("Doing nothing is creative").
- Suggest the redefinition of a common term ("Community colleges employ real teachers").

Arguments for claims like these usually require explicit definitions of what is being said about the subject. According to what definition of a democratic society is the United States not one? What is a *real teacher* as opposed, evidently, to other teachers who are not real? And since "creative" usually means creating something, how can doing nothing lead to creating something? Whenever your audience is likely to respond to your claim with a question like one of these, you have a challenging claim and in most cases a need for explicit definition.

Arguments in Which a Decision about the Nature of a Thing Will Have Serious Consequences

An argument for a claim like "Alcohol is a drug" seems to involve terms with widely understood meanings, and a case for this claim could certainly be made informally, by building on the commonly accepted definition of non-medicinal drugs as addictive and physically damaging substances. However, making the case that alcohol is a drug could have some serious consequences in our society. For starters, if alcohol belongs in the same category as heroin and cocaine, then why doesn't it fall under the same restrictions? Also, since the federal government has mandated an anti-drug advertising campaign, why aren't ads against alcohol part of the campaign? Since what is at stake in acceptance of this claim is so high, it is going to have to be argued carefully, and careful argument usually requires explicit definition.

Working either alone or with a group of your classmates, find ways to add explicit definitions to the following claims as needed to make the claims less challenging and less likely to provoke audience resistance. You may go on to use one of these claims in a full argument.

- Organic food is not healthy.
- Vaccinations are a game of Russian roulette.
- The great apes deserve human rights.
- Being laid off can be the key to a successful career.
- Soap operas are pornographic.
- Cable news shows exaggerate the news.

Where to Put the Definition

If you judge that an explicit definition should be part of your argument, how can you work it in? In a textbook, definitions are often underlined, boxed, or starred, making them as obtrusive as possible. Similarly, in a scientific or legal document, definition is often blunt. In such situations, an explicit, isolated definition is usually the best tactic.

But in other situations—an essay about literature, a paper for a history course, an article for a general audience, a play review—the argument requires that definition be present, but the style demands that the elements of the argument be less obtrusive. In these cases, the gradual clarification of a key concept, or a dispersed definition, can be used.

Isolated Definition   The isolated definition is a definition given all at once and by itself. It can be as brief as a synonym or it can be extended for several paragraphs. But no matter the length, it is delivered whole, in one installment:

> Culture, as traditionally understood, is a "matrix" of beliefs and ways, of heritable artifacts and ideas. Most importantly, culture makes and enforces demands. To a greater or lesser extent, it tells you who you are, and what your possibilities are or should be.
>
> —*Washington Times* (weekly edition), May 15–21, 2000, p. 28.

Dispersed Definition   A dispersed definition is worked into an argument in several places. It may consist of phrases repeated throughout an argument that define the meaning of a term as it is being used in a particular instance. Or the definition may have many parts which are then dispersed throughout the argument, satisfying the requirement for a definition and, at the same time, organizing the essay. Suppose, for example, that you are arguing that Stephen King writes sensation novels. As is often the case when you place a work of art in a specific category, "sensation novel" is best defined by a list of features: the plot concerns a mystery or secret, often involving a crime; the characters (if not always the reader) are kept in suspense; the setting is threatening; the characterizations are exaggerated; and the subject matter may suggest the supernatural, but the supernatural may be explained away.

Here is both a definition of a "sensation novel" and the beginning of an outline for an argument. Each of these features could begin a paragraph that would then present supporting evidence from King's books. You could begin your essay by giving this list of the features of sensation novels before dispersing it, including a defense of this particular definition, perhaps by citing the source it came from. Or you could end your essay by pulling the parts of the definition together, providing a summary.

Dispersing a definition works well with terms whose meanings can be given as a list of features. However, defining what you are claiming about your subject and finding evidence that fits the definition are reciprocal processes. Each feeds the other. You won't know what evidence or examples to look for unless you know what the examples might be evidence of; on the other hand, a bag full of examples won't mean anything without the organizing principle of a definition.

PROJECT FOR CLASS DISCUSSION

As a group, come up with a subject that can be defined by a list of features (e.g., a career, a political party, a city or town, a type of movie). Working on your own or with a small group of classmates, create a list of the features that define the subject. Discuss the lists that your classmates have made. Are there features common to all or most lists? Why do you think those features are important? Are there features that spark a debate? Why? Can a convincing definition argument be made from the material on the lists? Why or why not?

Ways to Define

Explicit definition is critical in many arguments, especially high stakes arguments. If you use any term that your audience will not recognize, either because it is unfamiliar to them or because you are using it in an unfamiliar way, you must define it. If you are constructing an argument about the nature of things, definition of a key term can determine the very structure of your argument.

Keep in mind that your purpose in including a definition in an argument is not to account for every meaning a word can have, but only to construct a definition of the one meaning that will work in your argument and be acceptable to your readers. The more ways of defining you know, the better your chance of constructing a definition that both fits your argument and is accepted by your audience. You can even use several techniques of definition on the same word and shed light on it from different perspectives. What follows is a list of common tactics of definition.

Synonyms   Using a synonym is the fastest way to define. You simply follow the word to be defined with another word or phrase that means roughly the same thing but is more familiar to your audience.

litotes = understatement
dour = gloomy, sullen, severe
dolce far niente = it is sweet to do nothing
madrassah = Islamic school
chad = ballot waste

The terms in the above list are probably unfamiliar enough to most audiences to need definition. Technical, obsolete, and foreign words or phrases are often easily translated by a synonym.

Sometimes in an argument a phrase, a combination of words that no one would ever look up in the dictionary, needs the same kind of clarification that a synonym brings to a single word. Since a stipulated, author-provided meaning is so important in argument, you may also use synonymous phrases to define a group of words in just the way you mean them. You might, for instance, describe an upcoming primary as "a crucial test for the president," and follow that phrase with the explanation, "one that will determine whether the president runs for re-election."

The Genus/Difference Definition   This kind of definition has two parts. First, the word to be defined is placed in a *genus*, a larger class, category, or group. Second, the qualities that distinguish it from other members of that genus or class are named. Those other qualities are called the *difference*. In the examples that follow, the genus occurs in bold type and the difference in italics.

> Linguine is a type of **pasta** *shaped into long, slender, flat pieces.*
>
> An asteroid is a *minor* **planet.** (Here the differentiating term, *minor*, is just an adjective modifying the genus.)
>
> A tabloid is a **newspaper** *whose pages, usually about five columns wide, are about one-half the size of the standard newspaper page laid flat.*

Constructing a useful genus/difference definition requires, first, finding a genus that is not too broad or too obscure. If your genus is too broad, you need too many distinguishing qualities. "Rigatoni is a kind of **food** *made from a paste of wheat and egg forming an unleavened dough which is then rolled thin and shaped in short, ridged tubes*" is more cumbersome than "Rigatoni is a type of **pasta** *shaped into short, ridged or smooth tubes.*" (Of course, for an audience unfamiliar with the term "pasta," you would have no choice but to use a genus term they did recognize.)

Second, constructing a useful genus/difference definition also requires finding the right distinctions to separate the term at issue from other members of the genus. In a crowded genus, this shaping requires considerable skill, but of course it will be guided by what is most useful for your argument. In general, you can distinguish one member of a genus from others with information along the following lines.

- What it looks, sounds, feels, tastes, or smells like: Polynosic is a type of **fabric** *that is shiny and feels like silk.*

- How to make or do it: Pointillism is a technique of **painting** *by applying small, single dots of paint.*
- What it does or is supposed to do: A satire is a **literary work** *that attacks human folly or vice in a witty, ironic, or derisive way.*
- What it is made of or what its parts are: Pemican is a Native American **food** *made from dried meat mixed into a paste with fat and berries.*

Definition by Example   Since many words stand for collections of things, they can be defined by singling out one or more examples from that collection. The chosen example must be recognized by an audience or it will clarify nothing. Suppose you defined *entrepreneur* as *"someone like Colonel Sanders."* Ideally, your audience should immediately recognize who Colonel Sanders was and what he is famous for. If there is a chance they won't, you can include key details when you mention your example: "An entrepreneur is someone like Colonel Sanders, who turned a single chicken store into the Kentucky Fried Chicken empire." Here we get the sense that an entrepreneur is someone who starts small and builds up a large, successful business.

An extended example can also be used to pin down the sense in which you are using a word, even when the example is unknown to readers beforehand. If, for instance, you were trying to define the "typical NRA (National Rifle Association) member" you might produce a thumbnail sketch of one person. The details of this person's gun ownership and voting record would help define the group and its goals. (Needless to say, these representative examples will be presented in a way that serves the writer's overall purpose.)

Etymological Definition   An etymological definition clarifies a word by taking it apart and defining what those parts mean. The parts or syllables of many words can be traced back to their roots in the languages that have contributed to English, especially German, Latin, French (also from Latin sources), and Greek. The word *philogyny*, for example, comes from two Greek roots, *philo* meaning "love" and *gyne* meaning "woman." So *philogyny* means "love of women." Words that are not widely used tend to stay true to their roots. Words in common usage may have altered their meanings. The word *republic*, for example, comes from two Latin words, *res* for "things or matters" and *publica*, having to do with "the people." Hence, by its roots, republic means something like "matters of/for the people."

Genetic or Historical Definition   The genetic or historical definition gives the origin of the thing rather than the origin of the word that stands for it. It is a way of defining something by relating its history, how it came about, or how it was developed. In form, genetic or historical definitions often resemble extended genus/difference definitions. The "difference" part of the definition is simply expanded into a story, as in the following definition of the Conestoga wagon used for westward migration.

During the early 1700s English and German traditional craftsmen— wheelwrights, blacksmiths, joiners, and turners—in the Conestoga valley of Lancaster County [Pennsylvania] began to combine features of earlier European wagons—the road wagons of England and the large farm wagons of western Germany—to produce familiar but new styles of freight-bearing vehicles. By mid-century these wagons were generally known as Conestoga wagons.

> —Robert Secor, ed. *Pennsylvania 1776* (University Park, PA: Pennsylvania State University Press, 1975), p. 119.

Note that the etymology of the word *Conestoga* itself, a Native American place name, is irrelevant to the definition of "Conestoga wagon."

Genetic and historical definitions are obviously most useful for defining terms from the past when readers have lost their original meanings or have no idea what they mean. You could not define words like *Schwenkfelder* or *phlogiston* or *orrery*—concepts and objects from the past—without describing the historical origins of what they stand for.

Negative Definition   Sometimes the best way to say what a word means is to say what it does not mean. This technique is often preliminary to another method of defining; we use it to eliminate rival meanings that our audience may confuse with the meaning that we want to isolate and use.

> An antique is not something of a certain age, that is, made before 1830, as some scholars claim, not necessarily something intrinsically precious, like gold or diamonds, not something of high style or artistic merit. An antique, rather, is anything that people consider worth collecting, so long as it is not still being made. Some people collect the baseball cards of ten years ago, and since they are not still being made, they are antiques.

In this example, negative definition is a kind of ground clearing that removes the mistaken meanings readers may have for "antique." Once these are out of the way, the writer turns to genus/difference definition and definition by example.

Related to the negative definition is the **contrast definition.** In this technique, a writer discriminates between two words or two senses of a word that are often confused by readers. Suppose you want to characterize someone as *frugal*. On your way to defining *frugal* so that your examples will fit the term as you want to use it, you can distinguish it from a word close in meaning, *stingy*. *Frugal* and *stingy* both describe a scrupulous caring for one's resources (usually money), but stingy suggests meanness as well, an unwillingness to spend even what is necessary. *Frugal* does not have the same negative connotations, and one of the best ways to point out that difference is to say, in effect, "When I say *frugal* I do not mean *stingy*."

Figurative Definition   When Karl Marx defined religion as the "opium of the people," he created a figurative definition, a definition that makes a creative comparison between the term under scrutiny and some other thing or quality that literally has nothing to do with it. Religion is not a drug derived from poppies, but, as Marx saw it, religion acts like a narcotic, dulling the believer's sense of outrage.

Figurative definitions are usually constructed for purposes of evaluation. Obviously, Marx had a very dim view of religion. But occasionally a figurative definition is used for clarification, as in "DNA is the code of life." For either purpose, figurative definitions can be memorable ways of constructing the meaning of and attitude toward a word in a way that will support your argument.

Ostensive Definition   An ostensive definition is simply definition by listing. If the term you are defining stands for a limited group, you can simply define it by naming the members of that group.

> The Beatles (John Lennon, Paul McCartney, George Harrison, Ringo Starr)
>
> The Republican presidents since World War II (Eisenhower, Nixon, Ford, Reagan, George H.W. Bush, and George W. Bush)

The gesture behind the ostensive definition is, obviously, to construct the group you are listing in a way that helps your argument. Thus, ostensive definitions are very useful for saying, in effect, that *for purposes of this argument*, a term stands for these members.

Operational Definition   An operational definition is sometimes described as a scientific method of defining, but it actually uses a tactic of defining common in everyday life. Suppose your mother asks you to weed her newly planted flower garden, and you are not sure which of the sprouting green things is a weed and which is a flower-to-be. To protect her chrysanthemums from your indiscriminate hand, she had better tell you that anything that does not have a dark green multi-lobed leaf is a weed. That description is an operational definition, one that defines *weed* for one particular time and place. This operational definition is nothing like the definition of *weed* in a dictionary. It is, rather, a definition you can operate or act on.

An operational definition is particularly useful for setting boundaries. The definition of a "child" who qualifies for free admission to the circus as "anyone who can walk under the turnstile" sets an upper limit for which there is an easy, immediate test. The Motion Picture Association of America defines an "appropriate audience member for a movie rated NC-17" as "anyone who is at least seventeen years old," setting in this case a lower limit. An employer can define "eligibility for a three-week vacation" as "more than five but fewer than fifteen years of employment," setting both an upper and a lower limit. Once an operational definition is in place, whether anyone or anything belongs in the category so defined can be a matter of fact. You either are or are not old enough to see an NC-17 movie.

An operational definition is also a test that can yield data. Operational definitions are frequently employed in research designed to yield a claim about a state of affairs. If the Department of Labor wants to know whether the assembly workers in an industry are satisfied with their jobs, a social scientist may create an operational definition of "job satisfaction" as, in part, "showing up for work." Job satisfaction cannot be directly measured, but "coming to work" can be measured precisely by absenteeism or by worker turnover. However, some of the general meaning of job satisfaction has also been lost. "Satisfaction" is not always precisely assessed even by the person who feels it, and it is possible for a worker to show up faithfully for a job he or she loathes.

Many public debates revolve around operational definitions. For example, the current definition of "high school graduate" in many places is "someone who has a diploma from a secondary school or its equivalent, such as a GED diploma." There is, however, a movement to add another operational test, a passing grade on tests of reading and math skills. This additional operational definition could remove many people from the category "high school graduate."

PROJECT FOR CLASS DISCUSSION

Use at least three of the tactics of definition explained above to construct an extended definition of any of the following terms.

xenotransplant	menial job
shyness	jihad
phrenology	infatuation
terrorist	Weltanschauung
quality control	avatar

Compare your definitions with those of your classmates. Can the class agree on which tactic seems to work best for each term? Why or why not? Are there any tactics of definition that no one used on a given term? Which definition for each term would support an argument going against a common belief?

Support by Comparison

Another way of getting at the nature of something is to compare it to something else that is more familiar to an audience. A comparison can involve likenesses as well as differences, so we are using the one umbrella term, *comparison*, for setting things side by side.

Comparisons differ greatly in how plausible they appear to an audience when they are simply stated. The most plausible comparisons point out a likeness between things that an audience believes are similar to start with: "Ohio State University resembles the University of Illinois." What else would anyone expect about two large midwestern land grant universities in the Big Ten?

Of course, using a comparison that confirms an existing assumption can provide useful support in an argument. You attach the less familiar to the more familiar; you assure an audience that their expectations hold. But an obvious comparison is sometimes less useful when you are trying to convince an audience to see something in a new way. Then it might be useful to incorporate an implausible comparison, one that has to be not merely stated but also argued for in itself.

Neil Armstrong Walks on the Moon

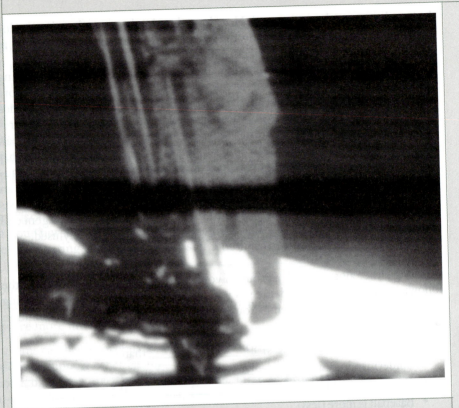

An old proverb acknowledges that "Seeing is believing." If you wanted to convince a friend that something incredible had happened—say a meteorite had crashed through your roof and smashed into your computer, destroying all the drafts of your papers—you would simply take your friend to the scene of the disaster. If transporting your audience physically was not possible, the next best thing would be to show pictures of the hole in your roof and the large oddly shaped rock now sitting in the debris that once was your computer. With no pictures, you could tell your friend in many excited words what happened, and chances are a friend would believe you, though a teacher might not. The moral of the story is that we have a natural hierarchy of evidence for convincing ourselves and others of the reality of an event or situation: being there to witness it, seeing a picture of it, hearing about it.

On July 20, 1969, the first human walked on the moon. Watching on TV, a worldwide audience received real-time audio of the moment the lunar module touched down and then saw flickering images of astronaut Neil Armstrong descending the ladder to the moon's surface. The image reproduced here is a photo of a TV screen displaying this historic video feed. It was taken by a video camera, a 1960s prototype far less advanced than those available today, that was mounted on the side of the lunar module; this camera is visible on the left side of the picture. Using remote control, Armstrong swung the camera into place from its storage compartment before his descent. The black band across the image is interference. Because the moon lacks an atmosphere to filter the reflected light of the sun, its surface is excessively bright. Though the image was certainly enhanced before it was broadcast, its indistinctness seems fitting given the extraordinary circumstances. Its imperfections are, in other words, the markers of its authenticity. Not only was the actuality of the first moon landing substantiated by these images, but the emotional power of this event, the sense of history in the making, was greatly enhanced.

Over the last 150 years, documentary photography has had a history of persuading viewers of the existence and nature of many events and circumstances such as the moon landing. In the early twentieth century, for example, Jacob Riis raised the consciousness of the nation to the plight of the urban poor with his gritty photographs of inner city slums. During the Civil Rights Movement of the 1960s, photographs taken by Charles Moore provided evidence of police violence against demonstrators, who were sprayed with fire hoses and attacked by dogs. Published in *Life* magazine, these photos persuaded many Americans to support civil rights legislation. Because of the tradition of black and white news photos and documentary films, some people actually have a cultural bias toward black and white images, which they find more believable than color images.

Photos in newspapers, film and video clips on TV, videophone images and the stills made from them are routinely used to provide evidence for the reality of the events that are being reported on. Critics have pointed out that people consider photos believable because they seem to be "written" by the objects themselves; the camera merely records the light. And the scenes they depict usually seem to continue beyond the frame of the image. Photos are, however, subject to enhancements that affect their persuasive value. Editors will usually select one photo from many others taken of the same event on the basis of its expressive qualities. An individual photo is often cropped; that is, parts are cut off to produce an effective composition out of what remains, or to focus viewers' attention on a particular part of the scene. Techniques used in developing photos can alter the tone of black and white photos and the saturation values in color ones, producing final prints that are darkened or lightened or color-enhanced in ways that can add an emotional connotation to a photo.

In fact, from the moment that photography was invented, so were techniques that allowed photographers to doctor and fake images. With the advent of digital cameras and computer processing, the potential to alter photographs—to produce documentary evidence of events and circumstances that never existed—is greater than it has ever been before. But even in the 1960s, before much of this technology was available, some people claimed that the photos of the moon landing were faked and that Armstrong, Buzz Aldrin, and all the subsequent astronauts never walked on the moon. The poor quality of the early images, taken by some as evidence of their truthfulness, struck others as evidence of their faking. The superb quality of photos of later moon missions also confirmed their authenticity for believers and seemed "too good to be true" to the suspicious.

While photographs have often served as key pieces of evidence, the absence of photographic documentation has also been used to deny the reality or the particular nature of an event. On the morning of September 11, 2001, many cameras recorded the hideous spectacle of planes flying into the twin towers of the World Trade Center. But no one actually filmed the plane flying into the Pentagon a short time later. In 2002 a French writer published a best-selling book in France that claimed that no plane ever flew into the Pentagon but that instead the U.S. government itself blew up the building with a guided missile. This author used photographs of the gaping hole in the building to support his case because these photos of the damage (at least the ones released to the public) did not show recognizable pieces of the plane. Hence photographs, whether they exist or not, have by no means eliminated the need for arguing about the reality and nature of things. They have become subjects of argument themselves.

Writing Your Own Definition Argument

ANSWERING THE QUESTION →

"What Is It?"

The art of shaping an argument to answer this kind of question depends on refining and adjusting what your claim is about and what you can say about it that your audience could also believe. To begin with, you need an idea of what you are examining and what precisely you are asking about it. You may have developed ideas for a definition argument from one of the exercises in this chapter, or you may decide to develop a topic suggested by one of the writing ideas on pp. 162–63. Whatever topic you choose, the following steps will help you construct a convincing definition.

1. Think about a Subject You Might Want to Investigate

Write down your first attempt at naming your subject. Is it a person, a trend, a work of art? Choose a subject that interests you, one that you know something about or would like to learn more about. If you are stuck on this step, try writing down several options and working through the following steps for each one to see which will work best.

2. Ask a General Question about the Subject

Which of the following questions most closely matches what you want to know about your subject? Did it happen or does it exist? If it is a trend, a change over time, what kind of trend is it? What category does it belong in, or what kind of label would best describe it? What is it similar to or different from? Write down a first attempt at the question you are asking about your subject.

3. Make a Preliminary Claim Answering the Question

If you already have an idea what an answer to this question might be, you could write it down as a preliminary claim, a working thesis for your argument. If you have absolutely no idea, you need to do some research until you can write down a tentative claim. You can also adopt the strategy of wording your preliminary claim with the options that seem possible. Whichever way you get to it, this step is important because it gets you started on the necessary process of fitting together your claim and your research.

4. Think of Ways to Clarify and/or Define Key Terms in the Claim

Your preliminary claim will contain a key term or phrase that is critical for your argument. That key term will appear in what you say about your subject. Your definition of this critical term will give you a principle for your selection of evidence. Think of the most useful way to define your terms, looking at the ways to define provided in this chapter. The subject of your claim will probably also need to be clarified along with what you are saying about it.

But once you have adjusted these two parts of your claim, you will have a better idea of the kinds of evidence you are looking for and, therefore, of the sources you should investigate.

5. Look for Appropriate Kinds and Sources of Evidence

When you have some idea of the kinds of evidence you are looking for, you can begin a more directed research process, building on your research skills (see the review of sources in Chapter 10). You can support your definition argument by example, by definition, and/or by comparison.

6. Revise Your Claim as Needed

Once you have done your research based on an improved version of your subject and a working definition of what you are saying about it, you can revise your claim to represent more accurately the position you are prepared to argue for. Does your subject fit your evidence? Do the definition and the evidence match up?

7. Consider the Counter-Evidence and Claims against Your Position

With a revised version of your claim, based on refining your subject and assessing your evidence, you are in a better position to consider the weak points in your developing argument and the arguments that could be made for contrary positions. Write down the evidence that works against your case and the counterclaims that it might support. (Remember that if the evidence against your revised working claim gets too strong, you may need to change positions.)

8. Assess the Audience's Response to the Claim

While you are revising your case to fit your key definitions and your evidence, as well as your awareness of weak points and counterclaims, you will also, in effect, be assessing how acceptable your claim is going to seem to your intended audience. Are they likely to believe your claim easily, or are they likely to resist it as far-fetched? Keeping the prevailing attitude of your audience in mind will help you assess how much and what kinds of evidence you will need to support your claim.

DRAFTING YOUR "WHAT IS IT?" ARGUMENT

As you draft a full version of your argument, pay special attention to your definition of key terms, which should guide the construction of your argument, and the fit between that definition and the evidence. All your preliminary work in the previous steps—defining, narrowing, researching, and considering other positions—will make the actual writing much easier. But nothing can substitute for the force of your argument as it develops in a more complete form. Remember, as always, to keep your audience and purpose in mind as you shape your argument.

REVIEWING AND REVISING YOUR DEFINITION

Once you have completed a draft of your definition, set it aside for a while. Then read through it carefully, looking for weaknesses in your argument. The following section will help you analyze your definition argument and solicit helpful comments from your classmates. Remember that successive drafts, improving the presentation and arrangement of

—Continued

evidence, may require continued fine tuning of your claim. But make sure that you do not alter the question your claim answers in the course of making your case. Or if you do, realize that now you need a different kind of supporting argument.

Questions to Ask about a "What Is It?" Argument

Whether you are reviewing your own definition argument or one written by a classmate, ask yourself the following questions and write down the answers. Make your answers as detailed as possible, pointing out specific places in the draft that are problematic. (Skip any questions that do not apply to the definition argument you are evaluating.) When you have done your own analysis and gone over any comments from your classmates, use these comments and suggestions to revise and refine your definition argument and make it stronger.

1. *Has the argument maintained a clear, consistent audience and purpose?* Who is the audience for this argument, and what is its purpose? Is the purpose appropriate for this audience? If the audience is a general one, is the language too specialized? What type of definition argument is this?

2. *Are the examples appropriate?* Do the examples support the claim? Are they typical? If specific examples are used, are they sufficient to prove the claim? Can you think of ways to argue against any of the examples? How could the examples be strengthened?

3. *Does the subject fit the evidence?* Is the claim too broad or too narrow? Do subjects with definite numbers receive appropriate coverage, depending on the size of the sample? Do modifiers like *some, many,* or *most* accurately reflect the evidence? If the claim is an invisible *all,* does the evidence support it?

4. *Does the argument define key terms clearly?* Are there any terms left undefined that should be defined? How would you define them? Are the definitions appropriate and convincing? If the argument relies on accepted definitions, do you accept them as presented? Does the argument require explicit definitions? If so, are all the necessary definitions included? Do any definitions work against the argument? How? Are there better ways to define any key terms?

5. *Is the definition in an appropriate place (or appropriate places) in the argument?* If the definition is isolated, do you agree that it should be? If the definition is dispersed, does it contribute to the organization of the paper? Is any part of the definition out of place? Where would you put the definition?

6. *Are comparisons convincing?* Do comparisons confirm an existing assumption? If so, are they useful? Does the argument include enough points of similarity or difference to make a persuasive comparison? Are the points defined and argued carefully? Are the things being compared comparable? Is there any other problem with the comparisons? How could they be improved?

7. *Are counterclaims considered?* Does the argument have any weak points that it does not address? Has opposition been anticipated appropriately? Can you think of any ways to refute this argument?

WRITING SUGGESTIONS

A claim about the nature of things can be made and supported in any context. Below are some broad suggestions of areas where you can form and defend such claims.

1. Social sciences: Make a claim about the existence or nonexistence of a psychological or sociological phenomenon or trend. (Examples: "More Americans in their twenties are postponing marriage." "Support for the death penalty is declining all over the world.")

2. History: Make a comparison involving a historical event, period, or person. (Examples: "The 2000 Presidential election was the beginning of a new era in American politics." "The South before the Civil War resembled ancient Rome.")

3. Arts: Make a claim about the nature of an artist, a movement, or a work. (Examples: "Jim Carrey's recent movies are not funny." "Eminem is not a true rap artist.")

4. Sports: Take an unexamined assumption that you hold about a state of affairs in present-day professional sports and see if you can actually support it by selecting and gathering appropriate evidence. (Examples: "Basketball is now America's national pastime." "Many men are fans of women's sports.")

5. Business: Identify a trend in marketing or consumption. (Examples: "Americans are willing to pay more for environmentally friendly products." "Business schools are paying increased attention to ethics.")

Comparison/Contrast Assignment

Comparisons and contrasts are usually used to support claims about the nature of things. But many essay tests and writing assignments ask students to "Compare/contrast X with Y" as an end in itself. It can, therefore, be useful to practice writing arguments whose purpose is to establish a convincing likeness or difference between two or more items.

To add a challenge to a comparison argument:

- Select two objects, people, events, or concepts that people usually consider quite different (for example, Islam/Judaism or Bill Clinton/ George W. Bush).
- Make a list of features of your two subjects that can be constructed into sentences like the following:
Both x and y ___.
This sentence can be broken down into two sentences with different subjects or with the same or similar wording in a way that is faithful to complications in the evidence:

   EXAMPLE:
   Both Judaism and Islam claim Abraham as their ancestor.

- Each of these "both" claims can be the topic sentence for a paragraph that discusses the key term and supporting evidence.

    ↙   ↘

Judaism claims   Islam claims
Abraham as its ancestor.   Abraham as its ancestor.

To add a challenge to a contrast argument:

- Select two objects, people, events, concepts that people might consider similar (for example, Operation Desert Storm/Operation Iraqi Freedom; *Good Morning America/The Today Show*).
- Make a list of paired positive and negative claims like the following:
X has _____ but Y does not.
Y has more _____ than X.

   EXAMPLE:
   Unlike Desert Storm, in Operation Iraqi Freedom troops entered Iraq in the first days of the conflict.

It is always possible to combine comparisons and contrasts in a single argument as a rich way of exploring the connections between two or even more subjects. Usually, however, in the beginning, either the differences or the similarities between your subjects will seem more plausible to your audience. Start with whichever seems more believable and then move on to the less initially plausible view, whether likeness or difference.

Cheerleading: A Sport or an Activity?

JILL HENKEL

Jill Henkel graduated from Penn State University in 2003. She was a cheerleader for seven years. This article first appeared in *Penn Statements* in 2001.

Dear Woodland Hills High School Yearbook Committee,

I was recently watching an old episode of "Designing Women" when something that the character Anthony said struck me. In trying to persuade one of the women to go bowling, he said, "If you can eat a hot dog while competing, it isn't a sport—it's a game." Very few people agree on what constitutes a sport. I'm sure that many professional bowlers would have something to say to Anthony's comment. According to the *Official Encyclopedia of Sports*, bowling is indeed a sport, as is billiards (Pratt, pp. 73-74, 81-82).

I would like to address the issue of the cheerleaders' pictures appearing in the Activities section rather than the Sports section of our yearbook. Each year, the members of your committee are bombarded with questions concerning this issue. As a recent graduate of Woodland Hills and a cheerleader for three years, I have many times joined in this questioning. But now I realize why you cannot answer these questions. No one has taken the opportunity to explain cheerleading to you. I would like to do so now. Although many people disagree, cheerleading is clearly a sport.

First of all, allow me to define the word *sport*. A sport is a physical activity that requires its participants to be healthy and physically able, strong, and skilled. A sport requires commitment from its participants and, in many cases, teamwork. Competition, either with oneself or with others, is also a key part of sports. Cheerleading more than adequately fits these criteria.

Until rather recently, cheerleading was no more than a popularity contest. As pointed out in an article by Diane Divorky and Peter Schrag in 1972, girls knew "whether they were popular enough to try out" for the squad (Divorky and Schrag, p. 61). In some high schools, the situation may still be this way. But for the most part, cheerleaders are picked based on ability rather than popularity. I was always the nerd who stayed home on Saturday nights to read or do homework, and I still got on the squad. I was not well known in Woodland Hills, and I certainly didn't date a football player, but I was willing and able to cheer, an attitude that merited me a spot among the varsity cheerleaders.

In talking with members of other squads at games and competitions, I've found that 5 most cheerleaders practice at least three times a week for about two hours each time during football and basketball seasons. If they are involved in competitions, they most likely practice every day. During the summer, practice often continues in preparation for the following year and usually includes some weight training and running. Practice is many times a seemingly nonstop drill of cheers, dances, stunts, and jumps, with short two-minute water breaks every so often. In order to keep up with these practice sessions, cheerleaders have to be physically fit. They have to eat properly and keep their bodies hydrated. They must be able to continue shouting out their cheers while engaging in very tiring moves. A not-so-rare sight at practice is girls getting ill or fainting because they didn't get a chance to eat breakfast or lunch. During games, the only breaks are during halftime. Other than that, the cheerleaders are on the football field or basketball court, continuously cheering on their team. Cardiovascular exercise is necessary in order to build up endurance for these games, as well as for competitions.

Besides being physically fit, strength and skill are also important. Our squad used to do weight training at least two times a week in the summer in order to increase arm and leg strength, which are necessary for jumps and stunts. We also used to do our motions for our cheers while holding soup cans, in order to build arm muscle. Stunts, especially those done in competitions, require a lot of strength because cheerleaders who serve as bases often have to lift other cheerleaders up over their heads, sometimes by just one foot. Pushing and holding up all that weight requires a lot of muscle and special technique. I was always on the top of the mounts, but once I became a senior, I had to become a base and hold other girls up. Only then did I realize how difficult it really is to do. Skill is required not only in stunting but also in doing cheers and jumps. Cheers have to be learned and then practiced repeatedly for games and especially for competitions. Jumps require flexibility and extensive stretching, as well as the building of leg muscle. Today, more than ever, gymnastics is becoming a big part of cheerleading. Although my squad didn't have many girls who could do flips, they are necessary for big competitions like the nationals held in Florida every year. Handsprings and tucks require very special ability and a lot of gymnastics training.

Maybe even more important than physical ability, cheerleading requires commitment. In the three years that I've cheered, I've seen many girls give up after the first month because they didn't feel like putting their time into practicing, or they hated cheering at the football games instead of being in the stands. In order to build a close-knit squad with good motions and solid stunts, the desire to cheer is key. Many people become cheerleaders because they believe it will be all fun. Like your committee, they misunderstand what it means to be a cheerleader. Once they are exposed to the hard work and vigorous training, they decide cheerleading just isn't for them. The most commitment I've seen from the Woodland Hills cheerleaders came from the girls with whom I was on the competition squad. We were working toward a goal and we were all really excited about competing. Therefore, we all went through the hard work together and eventually formed a really solid routine. The commitment of each girl was very important to the overall success of the squad. Each girl on the competition squad made great sacrifices, such as giving up a greatly needed after-school job or other extracurricular activities, in order to devote her full attention and time to practicing for competition.

A couple of weeks ago, I was watching a special called "Inside Cheerleading" on The Learning Channel. It featured two squads, one all-girl squad and one co-ed squad, that had made it to a national competition. During the preliminary routine of the all-girl squad, one of the bases for a stunt got her two front teeth knocked out by a girl she was holding in the stunt. This occurred in the first ten seconds of the routine, but the girl, while bleeding profusely from the mouth, finished the final two minutes of the routine. I was amazed. Someone got her on tape afterwards and, although she was crying because the injury hurt a lot, she wasn't the least bit angry with the girl who hit her. She went on to the final round without her front teeth, and her squad took third place. This was truly the most courageous and selfless act I have ever heard about. She should be a model for all cheerleaders, and better yet, all the athletes of the world. She truly exemplifies the type of committed person that cheerleading, as well as all other sports, requires.

In addition to the commitment of each individual person, cheerleading also requires the cheerleaders to work together as a team. Whether it be out on the field, cheering on another sports team, or out on the competition floor being cheered on by parents and friends, the cheerleaders have to be dedicated to each other and willing to give up individual comfort for the good of the squad. At competitions, knee and wrist braces are not uncommon sights. Many cheerleaders continue participating in their sport even when they are hurt because they know they are an integral part of the team. They don't focus on their pain but rather on hitting their jumps and stunts. Just like the girl who got her teeth knocked out, cheerleaders understand the meaning of team-work, and each member of the squad looks out for all the other members. They work together to help each other perfect motions, jumps, flips, and stunts.

I was involved in an accident at competition practice that almost stopped me from   10 ever stunting again. I was up in a very high stunt, extended above my bases' heads, and I began to fall. As I was falling, the girls didn't let go of my feet. I landed on my back and got the wind knocked out of me. In those few brief seconds, as I was scrambling around on the floor, I thought I would never breathe again and that I would die right there on the mat. For a couple of practices afterwards, I refused to do that stunt. But my coach had a talk with me and stressed the importance of my position in the squad and my need to work on the stunt and perfect it before the competition. I knew I had to try again for the sake of the other girls because everybody had already put so much time and effort into the routine. They would have been highly disappointed if I gave up and quit on them. Of course, after that incident, everyone was more careful and nothing like that ever happened again. It was a learning experience, just like all mis-takes are. I learned an important lesson in commitment, not only to my sport, but to my team members as well.

Finally, cheerleaders compete, often in two senses of the word. The most obvious way they compete is by going to formal competitions and performing routines. They are often put into divisions based on the size of the squad and whether the squad is co-ed or not. After performing their routines, each lasting about two-and-a-half minutes, they are judged and first, second, and third places are awarded. These competitions take place across the nation at all different levels, including junior high, high school, and college. They start out with local squads competing and then the winners go to national competitions with people from all over the nation competing. At nationals, the competition is very stiff, and just getting into a national competition is quite an ac-complishment. These national competitions are shown on ESPN (which also proves that cheerleading is a sport). My squad never made it to nationals, although we made a huge effort to get there. Cheerleaders also compete informally with the other team's cheerleaders at football and basketball games. They often chant back and forth, claim-ing that they have more spirit than the other team. The victors of these informal com-petitions are almost always the cheerleaders of the team that wins. These mini-competitions serve to increase the spirit of the cheerleaders and the fans.

Although you may still not agree with me that cheerleading is a sport, I strongly urge you to stop by one of the Woodland Hills cheerleading practices after school and see these athletes in action. Talk with them about the requirements of their sport. I'm sure they will be very willing to further enlighten you about what cheerleaders actu-ally do. If that doesn't convince you, check out one of the local cheerleading competi-tions or catch one of the national competitions on ESPN. I assure you that cheerlead-ers cannot eat a hot dog while they are competing.

Sincerely,
Jill Henkel
Woodland Hills Alumni
And current Penn State
University Freshman

FOR YOU TO ANALYZE

1. In the third paragraph, the author uses an explicit definition of the term "sport." In the fourth paragraph, she suggests a negative definition of "cheerleading." What risk might she be taking with this strategy? What preconceived notions is she assuming that her audience holds?

2. The author's argument places her topic (cheerleading) in the larger category of sport. What features connecting "cheerleading" and "sport" support her claim? Does she provide adequate evidence for each point?

3. Although the author wants her audience to take one specific action, the scope of her argument seems to be much larger. What is the exigence for this author's letter? What specific changes—large and small—does she hope to accomplish?

4. How effective is the author's use of anecdote in appealing to her reader's emotions?

FOR YOU TO WRITE

1. The author describes the changes in cheerleading from the early 1970s (paragraph 4) to now. Think of another traditionally female sport, activity, job, or social role that has changed dramatically over the last few years or decades. Write a brief contrast definition of this subject: what was the traditional understanding of this term, and what does it mean now?

2. In paragraph 8, the author describes one cheerleader's performance as an exemplification of athleticism. In a brief essay, describe how one specific person exemplifies (that is, embodies your specific definition of) a particular trait, such as heroism, generosity, sportsmanship, or grace.

3. Think of a particular sport or activity that does not get the respect you think it deserves. In a letter to a national sports magazine or sports cable channel, argue for better understanding and more coverage of this sport or activity.

FOR YOU TO DISCOVER ONLINE

In 1972, legislation that prohibited discrimination on the basis of sex in any educational program receiving federal aid was signed into law. Commonly known as Title IX, this legislation had an especially positive impact for young women who wished to participate in athletic activities in secondary schools and colleges. In 2002, however, the United States Department of Education undertook a review of Title IX, a review that many women's groups see as undermining equal access to athletic opportunity. For a report on the successes of Title IX on its twenty-fifth anniversary, go to www.ed.gov/pubs/TitleIX. For more information on current challenges to Title IX, go to www.womenssportsfoundation.org, and click on "issues and action." Based on your understanding of Title IX, how compliant is your own college with this legislation? How would you define "equal access" to athletic opportunities according to Title IX?

▌ *One Vet's Mission to Set the Record Straight*

MICHAEL KELLEY

Michael Kelley, an artist in Sacramento, California, won the Purple Heart and the Bronze Star in Vietnam. This article first appeared in the *Washington Post* in August 1999.

One hundred and sixty thousand Vietnam veterans have committed suicide since returning from the war. Or so said one reputable veterans' publication. If true, that's nearly three times as many as died in the war itself.

I called the editor. "What was your source?"

His reporter found a mention of 150,000 suicides in a 1990 book, he explained to me, "and then added 10,000 to reflect the probable increase between 1990 and 1995."

"Great science there," I said. "But what would you say if I told you there is absolutely no scientific evidence to support 150,000, or even as many as 20,000 suicides?"

"Well in that case, I'd say you were full of . . . ."   5

At the time, I thought he and other veterans would be overjoyed to learn the suicide myth was untrue, and that they would share my relief at finding that we are not, after all, such a twisted, tormented and damaged group that 15 or so of us have taken our own lives every single day for the past 30 years.

Since then, I have learned that a substantial number of veterans want to believe the myth. Some veterans and veterans organizations have simply enshrined it as fact, institutionalizing the Vietnam veteran as victim, promoting the idea that after losing 58,000 men in the war we had lost that many again—or two or three times that many—who fell into such desperation after coming home that they killed themselves.

What became a protracted and stupefying journey into this fantasy world of wholesale veterans' suicides began for me with the realization that what I was hearing and reading did not square with my experience.

I thought about the infantry unit I served with for 11 months: Delta Company, 1st Battalion of the 502nd Infantry, 101st Airborne Division. About 45 men from that company were killed in action during its four and a half years in Vietnam. If as many vets killed themselves later as died during the war, then 45 of the company's approximately 800 veterans would have committed suicide—or 135, if suicides were three or more times the number of wartime deaths. But in fact, as far as the unit's association can determine, not a single one of those veterans has died by suicide.

Struck by the huge discrepancy between the supposed suicide statistics and my   10 knowledge of the veterans' community, I went to a local library and spent a few hours thumbing through bibliographies related to veterans' mortality. What I found then and in subsequent research left me reeling. The first surprise was that there already existed a substantial body of scientific literature on the subject. The second surprise was that none of it remotely supported the numbers I saw being published as fact.

What on earth brought this plague upon us?

The assertion of 58,000 suicides appears to have drawn its first breath in a 1980 manual titled "Post-Traumatic Stress Disorders of the Vietnam Veteran." Published by the Disabled American Veterans, the manual was used widely throughout the Veterans Administration (VA). Its first edition (but none after) noted that "more Vietnam combat veterans have died since the war by their own hands than were actually killed in Vietnam."

That statement was credited to an unpublished paper written in April 1979 by one Tom Williams, who was also the editor of the manual. Curiously, his claim came a full eight years before the first comprehensive study of Vietnam veterans' mortality was published. Just where Williams divined his data remains a mystery. (I have made several attempts to find out, but he's never responded to my queries.)

From there the suicide story, with numbers ranging up to 200,000, spread to news reports, books, television documentaries and news magazines, and the World Wide Web.

Actual mortality studies tell a completely different story.   15

No one knows precisely how many Vietnam veterans have committed suicide. Nor does anyone know how many have died from all causes. We do have information, though, that points to what is possible and what is not.

Approximately 3.1 million Americans served in Southeast Asia during the Vietnam War. On average, suicides have accounted for just over 1.1 percent of all U.S. male deaths during the last half of this century. According to research done by the Centers for Disease Control (CDC) in the 1980s, suicides were somewhat more elevated for Vietnam veterans than for non-veterans in the same age group during the veterans' first five years after discharge. After five years, though, the differences disappeared.

A projection based on the CDC findings shows suicides would represent a shade over 1.2 percent of veterans' deaths from 1967 to 1996. VA data indicate that total postwar deaths among Vietnam vets had reached roughly 305,000 by January 1996, so if the percentage suggested by the CDC data is correct, the number of suicides over those 30 years would have been about 3,750.

Over several months, I examined all the other relevant studies I could find. Different analyses led to different estimates of the actual number of suicides, but none came remotely close to the fantastic numbers so many have accepted as truth. The highest estimates I could find that were based in any way on actual mortality data were in the neighborhood of 20,000; the bulk of the evidence suggested total suicides were somewhere between 2,000 and 5,000.

I was excited by what I found and wanted to share it. It was very important to me   20 that an assault on the myth should be launched in a veterans' publication, so, after distilling my research into a reasonably solid, if overly zealous monograph, I sent it off to a number of veterans' magazines.

Most seemed startled but enthusiastic, and my spirits rose. This is important stuff, I was told, and we'll do our best to get it published. But weeks stretched into months, months into a year, and one by one the submissions were returned with polite rejections.

Either what I'd written was very bad, or these publications had no spine for the potential storm the article might evoke from part of their constituency. Perhaps some hesitated for fear of endangering worthwhile veterans assistance programs—the apparent assumption being that the suicide myth was helpful in showing why those programs were needed and why funding agencies should keep supporting them. I didn't want to harm veterans programs, but I didn't think that risk should outweigh the benefit of honestly assessing our mental health.

But it can't just be bureaucratic reasons that explain why many veterans and their organizations are so unwilling to let go of the myth. I'm not sure I know all the reasons, but it is worth remembering that back in 1980 or so, when the suicide story first surfaced, Vietnam vets as a group were introverted and isolated from society, much more so than we are now. News reports and artistic portrayals of us were often negative. I don't think we thought much of ourselves back then, either. Losing was embarrassing. Abandoning the Vietnamese was embarrassing. Being rejected was painful. So we all just tried to blend into the woodwork and stay as invisible as possible.

Many of us knew veterans who were troubled—or were troubled ourselves—by drinking, drug use and divorce. And when we began to hear that more of us were killing ourselves than had died in the war, we may have subconsciously found the story plausible.

At another level, I know there are some veterans who want to believe the myth be- 25 cause it validates their view of themselves as victims of an inept and evil government. I have been accused of being part of a government conspiracy for suggesting that our suicide rate was not astronomical.

But the facts should not be dismissed so easily. I served in Vietnam with many honorable, very brave and decent men. I also served with some of the most despicable scumbags you could imagine. I have no illusions about who we were or what we did and do not wish to represent veterans as anything other than what we are and were. All I ask is that people tell the truth about us. And everything I have learned persuades me that the truth is what a buddy of mine, a Marine veteran of Vietnam, once said when we were chewing the fat about the suicide story. I didn't write down his exact words but this is close:

"They're trying to tell me that my buddies are killing themselves faster than Charlie could? Guys who fought tooth and nail to stay alive? Guys who would have sold their mothers to get out of 'Nam in one piece? They're trying to say we're coming home and standing in line to blow our brains out? What a crock!"

FOR YOU TO ANALYZE

1. What type of argument is Kelley making? Do you think his argument is convincing? Why or why not?

2. How does Kelley's autobiographical material help to support his argument? How would you categorize this supporting material? Does it make the argument more or less persuasive? Why?

3. Why do you think Kelley mentions his unsuccessful attempts to get this information published previously? How does this information affect his argument?

4. How would you characterize Kelley's purpose in making this argument, and for what audience is it intended? How do you know?

FOR YOU TO WRITE

1. Kelley tries to convince his audience to reconsider accepted stereotypes of Vietnam veterans. Think of a group that is commonly portrayed as victimized; write a brief argument against viewing the members of this group as victims.

2. Kelley uses his own experiences and the quotation from his fellow veteran that closes the article to help define a typical Vietnam veteran as someone unlikely to commit suicide. Use an experience of your own to define some characteristic of a group of which you are a member.

3. Kelley says that "a substantial number of veterans want to believe the myth." What is another myth or urban legend that you think many people want to believe? How would you convince them that the belief is a myth?

The Myth of the Fading Family

E. J. DIONNE, JR.

E. J. Dionne, Jr., has been a columnist since 1993 for the *Washington Post,* where this article first appeared in May 2001. He is a senior fellow in government studies at the Brookings Institution.

You would think from reading the headlines that the mom-and-dad-and-kids family is in a state of total collapse in America. Those headlines are based on accurate reporting of certain data from the 2000 Census.

But the headlines are wrong. The two-parent family is still the norm in America.

Among households with children, according to the new Census Bureau figures, 71.8 percent are led by *married couples.* That's down from 76.1 percent a decade ago and 93 percent in 1960. So, yes, the two-parent family has had its problems in the past 40 years. But if a household includes children, the odds are nearly 3 to 1 that it will be led by a couple rather than by a single parent.

And the Census Bureau's Current Population Survey offers evidence that the decline of the two-parent family stopped in the mid-1990s. That is big, underreported—and heartening—news, especially if it is confirmed in the coming years.

Between 1990 and 1996, there was a continuing decline in the proportion of households with children headed by couples. But there has been no decline since then. In fact, between 1999 and 2000, there was a modest—though perhaps statistically insignificant—increase in the proportion of households with children headed by two parents.   5

"When you look at just two points in time," says Jason Fields, a family demographer in the Census Bureau's population division, referring to 1990 and 2000, "you miss the fact that the trends have leveled off in the late 1990s. The increase in single-mother families has really leveled off. Divorce has really leveled off."

How does this square with what you've been reading and hearing? Among the typical headlines that turn up in a Web search of newspapers and news broadcasts: "Is the Traditional American Family Heading Toward Extinction?" And a cover line on *Newsweek* this week: "Why the Traditional Family Is Fading Fast."

Most of these stories focus on the decline in the proportion of all households that consist of two parents with children. Here are the numbers:

- In 1960, 45 percent of American households consisted of married couples with kids.
- In 1970, the proportion dropped to 38.8 percent.
- In 1980, it was down to 30.8 percent.

- In 1990, it was 25.6 percent.
- In 2000, it was 23.5 percent.

The much-repeated line, entirely true, is that for the first time, married-couples-with-kids families represent less than a quarter of all American households.

But notice a few things about these numbers. First, the married-couples-with-kids homes did not constitute a majority of households even in 1960, the age of "Ozzie and Harriet" and "Father Knows Best." That's because kids grow up and move out. Our grandparents, if they lived long enough, knew what it was like to be "empty-nesters."

Second, the big declines in the proportion of households made up of married 10 couples with kids *had already occurred by 1990.* The decline in the past 10 years is quite modest.

Third, part of the decline in mom-and-dad-and-kids households as a proportion of the whole has to do with the fact that people are living longer. There are not a lot of people over 65 whose kids still live with them. This fact of life has nothing to do with "the decline of the family." My mother-in-law, one of the most family-oriented people I know, lives in an apartment upstairs from one of her sons. Yet her "household" would be counted against the family because, technically, she lives alone.

None of this should diminish our concern for the difficulties faced by children in single-parent households. You don't have to be a conservative to believe that on the whole, two parents are far better than one. As Jonathan Rauch argues in the current issue of *National Journal,* "children raised in single parent homes are at greater risk of poverty, school dropout, delinquency, teen pregnancy and adult joblessness." We can debate how to help those kids, but we shouldn't let ideology blind us to their problems.

But it would also be wrong if ideology led us to exaggerate the problem with the family in America. If the family has begun to come back together, at least a little bit, we need to figure out why, and how to nurture the forces making it happen.

It makes better copy and probably boosts talk-show ratings to say that the two-parent family is going the way of the Oldsmobile. The happier but more prosaic truth is that while the family does face large new challenges, most Americans still believe that kids need two parents. And most of them still try hard to behave as they believe.

FOR YOU TO ANALYZE

1. What does Dionne mean by the term "family" in the headline? How do you know what his definition is? Is this a definition that would probably be accepted without proof? Why or why not?

2. Dionne's article argues that something does not exist—that, as the title says, the "fading family" is a myth. What kinds of evidence does he use to support this claim? Is it convincing? Why or why not?

3. Who is the audience for this piece? What is the purpose of trying to convince them that the "fading family" is a myth?

4. How well do the subject and the evidence fit? Could you strengthen Dionne's argument? Could you refute it?

FOR YOU TO WRITE

1. How would you define "family"? If your definition is different from Dionne's, write a brief argument supporting your definition.

2. Dionne uses the census information to discuss a trend in American households. Write a brief definition of a trend you see in the population of your own community (however you choose to define it). What does this trend mean, in your view?

3. In Dionne's argument, statistics usually interpreted negatively (in this case, the decline in the number of American households containing two parents and at least one child) can also have a positive interpretation. Think of an event or trend about which you have heard mainly negative reports. How could you convince an audience to view the event or trend more positively?

FOR YOU TO DISCOVER ONLINE

Go to the U.S. Census site, www.census.gov, to get data from the 2000 Census. What kinds of information are available? Look at the report on families (use the alphabetic subject index to find this information). How does the Census Bureau's report compare to Dionne's argument? Is the Bureau's interpretation of the data on family makeup different from Dionne's? What do you think accounts for any difference in interpretation? Which is more convincing? Why?

Much Ado about Friends: What Pop Culture Offers Literature

RICHARD KELLER SIMON

Richard Keller Simon teaches English literature at California Polytechnic State University, where he is also the chairman of humanities. He is the author of *Trash Culture: Popular Culture and the Great Tradition* (1999). The following selection is excerpted from an article that appeared in the *Chronicle of Higher Education* in June 2000.

Identical twins enter the university. Literatura is a bright, hard-working student who loves stories and majors in English. Vulgara is just as bright and hard working, and also loves stories, but gets her fill of them from movies and television programs, forms that Literatura detests. Vulgara majors in business. My challenge is to teach both of them.

Literatura lives in Culture House, reading happily. Vulgara rooms in Aaron Spelling Hall, writing marketing plans for her seminar in product placement. In her spare time, she stares, entranced, at television shows—when she isn't scurrying over to the multiplex to be passively entertained in wider, louder dimensions.

What will become of them? Literatura eventually will turn her academic skills and love of literature into a position as a temporary, part-time, adjunct lecturer in English. Vulgara will turn her business skills and love of commercial entertainment into a position as senior vice president for programming at a major communications conglomerate.

The English department will fawn over Vulgara, hoping for a large donation for a new building, while denying Literatura a secure, full-time job. Such are the realities of modern university life. But Literatura is the one doing the heavy lifting, the one scrutinizing and absorbing the timeless tales of the ages. Right?

In a course on the great books of the classical world, Literatura reads in the *Iliad* 5
about the fury of Achilles on and off the battlefield. Vulgara watches *Rambo: First Blood
Part II* and sees a contemporary variation on the same story. Literatura reads Aeschylus'
Oresteia trilogy while Vulgara watches Francis Ford Coppola's *Godfather* trilogy; Euripides' *Hippolytus* while Vulgara watches *Jerry Springer;* Aristophanes' *The Clouds*
while Vulgara watches Rodney Dangerfield in *Back to School;* Plato's *Symposium*, a dialogue on sex and love, while Vulgara pores over her boyfriend's copy of *Playboy.*

The rival forms of storytelling are put before Literatura and Vulgara quite differently, the one as literature that demands careful study, the other as entertainment that
exists solely for our pleasure. But that distinction has more to do with context than
with any inherent quality of the stories. In dismissing Stallone's translation and abridgment of the *Iliad* as beneath the versions we find in literary anthologies, we lose sight
of popular culture as a potentially powerful teaching tool.

A literature course that took popular culture seriously might inspire Vulgara to
change her major. Perhaps such a background would make her look twice, when she
becomes an entertainment executive, at that proposed biopic about Caravaggio instead
of the treatment for a new game show. At the very least, it might compel her to earmark her donation to the university for an endowed chair to be filled by her sister. . . .

In his 1998 *The Rise and Fall of English,* Robert Scholes expressed the fear that
English departments were about to go the way of classics departments, shrinking into
insignificance, unless they learned how to change. The answer, I would argue, is hidden
in plain sight: on TV and at the movies.

What our students love, and what we know how to teach, after all, are almost the
same. And while this may outrage some literary purists, the future of English departments depends on our ability to link the two kinds of stories.

The popular television sitcom *Friends,* for example, is a contemporary variation on 10
Shakespeare's melodramatic comedy *Much Ado About Nothing.* Never mind that the
settings are different (Renaissance Italy, contemporary Manhattan), or that one is written in poetry and the other in the language of everyday life. The core characters, plots,
and themes are almost the same.

One reason for the parallels is that all comedies share certain qualities, especially
those written on the pattern established by Roman New Comedy. Young lovers get together over the objections of their parents or their community, usually by clever trickery, and at the end there is a wedding or weddings, when everybody and everything is
reconciled. Many sitcoms and movies are just as dependent on this Plautine form as
are the great dramatic comedies of the past, although in those meant for family audiences, young children trick their parents to garner more age-appropriate rewards.
(The twins in *The Parent Trap,* for instance, have as their goal getting their estranged
parents back together.)

But *Friends* shares much more with Shakespeare than the tradition of New Comedy. It is *Much Ado* adapted to current economic and cultural conditions, and to the demands of the half-hour sitcom.

In *Friends,* as in *Much Ado,* a small group of unmarried young men and women flirt
with each other, play a series of tricks on each other, and fall in and out of love. Some
characters are apprehensive and fearful about marriage and commitment, others more
enthusiastic, but all are torn between the conflicting obligations of love and friendship.

Weddings end in disaster (Rachel's and Ross's, to name only . . . five). A man
(Chandler) keeps women at a distance with his compulsive joking. Men and women
(Ross and Rachel, Chandler and Monica) become romantically involved only when they
learn by accident or unplanned confession how much each loves the other. A woman

(Rachel) who has been badly hurt by the man she loves (Ross) requires that he suffer in abject humiliation before she will accept him again. A young couple are torn apart by jealousy (Ross, Rachel, and the infamous "break" in their dating). A woman who is quiet and conventional (Rachel, in the show's first season) slowly begins to gain confidence and, with it, her voice.

Ross loves Rachel in the first few seasons of the sitcom just as Claudio loves Hero 15 in Shakespeare's comedy. The men are painfully shy, unsure of themselves because of their limited experience with love and sexuality, and more than a little awkward. The women are young, beautiful, and gradually getting to understand and accept their qualities beyond that beauty.

In both cases, the characters are contrasted with their opposites. In Shakespeare, Claudio's comrades are the sexually active and witty Benedick, and Don Pedro, a man expert at wooing women and eager to help his friends; in *Friends*, Ross's pals are the sexually active, goofy Joey, who is usually successful with women, and the witty Chandler, who seldom is. Among *Much Ado*'s women, Hero is complemented by the outspoken, independent Beatrice. In *Friends*', Rachel has the outspoken, offbeat Phoebe and the independent Monica.

Four friends in Shakespeare become six on prime time, but the dynamics among them are similar. Chandler is the sitcom's version of Benedick—the witty, sarcastic bachelor who keeps himself from getting attached to women by obsessing over their faults. Benedick finally meets his match in the strong and clever Beatrice, who trades jibes with him and ultimately marries him, just as Chandler finally finds Monica. And through it all, Phoebe wanders like a typical Shakespearean fool, making off-the-wall comments and singing wacky songs that contain more than their share of truth.

In my classes, I grant equal time to *Much Ado* and *Friends*, even though it means I will have that much less time to devote to some other literary masterpiece. My students love *Friends*. When I show brief excerpts, their faces light up. Many of them talk about the major characters as if they were close personal friends. They remember the names of minor characters who have appeared in no more than one or two episodes.

The students are more apprehensive about Shakespeare, concerned as they are about the language they must master, the characters to keep straight, and the exam looming on the horizon. What they most want to talk about and understand is the television program, while what I want to talk about and have them understand is Shakespeare. We meet in the middle.

I'm not tricking my students. *Friends* isn't simply an entree into Shakespeare. 20 Shakespeare is also an entree into *Friends*. Shakespeare is the best way for them to fully appreciate something that enchants them and is an important part of their lives.

"The students who come to us now exist in the most manipulative culture human beings have ever experienced," Robert Scholes wrote in his 1985 book, *Textual Power: Literary Theory and the Teaching of English*. "They are bombarded with signs, with rhetoric, from their daily awakenings until their troubled sleep, especially with signs transmitted by the audio-visual media. And, for a variety of reasons, they are relatively deprived of experience in the thoughtful reading and writing of verbal texts. They are also sadly deficient in certain kinds of historical knowledge that might give them some perspective on the manipulations that they currently encounter."

This statement, which I reproduce for my students and ask that they place in some spot that they will look at every day—like a bathroom mirror or the front of their television set—is my critical starting point. I tell them that I have a skill to teach them that will be essential to their well-being for the rest of their lives—literary criticism—for with it they will be able to understand the stories they love as well as the stories their parents and their professors worry so much about. And then I lecture on Shakespeare, but only after they know that there will be a paper to write on *Friends*, or a group discussion of the show.

After dissecting both works, I ask my students the toughest question I know: Who gets the better story, the Elizabethan who attended a production at the Globe 400 years ago, or someone who watches the American sitcom on a regular basis? Are we being cheated today?

My students are divided on the issue: Some are clearly disappointed in *Friends*, say they can watch TV no more, and feel distressed at the loss of language in the past 400 years. Others are enchanted by *Friends* and say they have recruited others to watch it as well, so impressed are they by the ways in which Shakespeare can be adapted to the demands of contemporary American television. But in either case, I've won a victory: I have shown them that literary criticism is not simply a skill that allows them to get good grades in English courses, and that the great tradition of literature is alive and well, and worth knowing. . . .

FOR YOU TO ANALYZE

1. What type of argument is Simon making? Why does he choose to make this type of argument?

2. Simon uses comparisons in paragraphs 1–5 and in paragraphs 10–17. How does the comparison in the opening paragraphs prepare readers for his argument?

3. What points of similarity does Simon present in paragraphs 10–17? Does he offer enough support for his claim about *Friends* and *Much Ado about Nothing?* Why or why not?

4. Where does Simon answer an objection? Is his answer satisfactory? Why or why not?

FOR YOU TO WRITE

1. Simon describes two types of students at the beginning of his essay. Which type of student are you? Do you think his categories are mutually exclusive? Write a brief argument agreeing with, or taking issue with, Simon's characterization of these two types.

2. In paragraph 21, Simon quotes Robert Scholes. Do you agree with Scholes's statement? Write a brief argument in which you define "manipulative culture" and explain how the culture you live in manipulates you or fails to manipulate you.

3. Simon maintains that he has "a skill to teach [students] that will be essential to their well-being for the rest of their lives—literary criticism." In a brief argument, agree or disagree with Simon's claim.

FOR YOU TO DISCOVER ONLINE

You have probably heard of *urban legends*—the often outrageous stories that people relate to one another as actual incidents that happened to a "friend of a friend." Some urban legends have long histories. Visit a web site that collects and/or debunks urban legends, such as www.snopes.com, and choose one legend that has been in circulation recently. Compare it to other stories that you are familiar with. Why do the same story elements keep showing up? What does the urban legend you have chosen—and other, similar stories—tell us about our culture?

Causal Argument: How Did It Get That Way?

Chapter 7

Harness Fire? Mother Nature Begs to Differ

George Johnson

As the site of secret workshops of the Manhattan Project, Los Alamos, N.M., is known to history as "the atomic city"—the place where scientists harnessed nuclear power, building the bomb that destroyed Hiroshima. The Cerro Grande fire, which burned on last week, was a reminder of how absurd it is to believe that mankind can ever harness a force of nature. Los Alamos learned to tap the power of nuclear energy. But it was brought to a standstill by a different kind of chain reaction: ordinary fire.

For decades the Los Alamos National Laboratory has steeled itself against the possibility of a nuclear missile strike. It has guarded against terrorists, spies and computer hackers. But the threat that turned out to be most immediate was disquietingly familiar: the tens of thousands of acres of neighboring Ponderosa forests that crowd the Pajarito plateau and the adjacent Jemez mountains, and which exploded, as had long been feared, into a firestorm.

A small "controlled burn"—in Cerro Grande's aftermath, the very term has become, suspect—was lit May 4 in a remote corner of Bandelier National Monument, a canyon wilderness sheltering cliff dwellings and stone-walled ruins of the ancient people called Anasazi. The idea was to clear encroaching pines and other combustible debris from an overgrown mountain meadow, making it safer from fire. But winds unexpectedly pushed the flames beyond the prescribed perimeter, and ultimately beyond imagination and control.

Within hours the fire had overwhelmed the small team assigned to it. A "back burn" lit three days later to control the first blaze—literally fighting fire with fire—raced out of control and began sweeping toward Los Alamos. Before it was over, more than 47,000 acres of forest—roughly three times the size of Manhattan—had been consumed in the biggest fire in the history of New Mexico, a dry, heavily timbered state that has become accustomed to mammoth conflagrations. Los Alamos was evacuated, its residents returning to find more than 200 residences destroyed. Late last week, the fire was on its way to being contained, but firefighters predicted that it would continue burning for many days.

Theorists at the lab who study complex systems like whirlpools and thunderstorms—not everyone there designs bombs—often refer to a phenomenon called "sensitive dependence on initial conditions." Chaos, for short. Tiny actions, the theory goes, can have enormous, unforeseeable consequences. The idea has entered the culture of popular science as "the butterfly effect." A mythological insect flapping its wings in Rio de Janiero causes a hurricane off the coast of Louisiana. A small fire routinely lit to clear a few hundred acres of tinder closes down a nuclear research center.

Foresters try to plan their intentional burns like lab technicians preparing for an experiment.

The Los Alamos National Laboratory surrounded by smoke from the Cerro Grande fire last week.

They gather data—the moisture content of the wood, the wind speed, the relative humidity and temperature of the air. They plug the factors into a computer model—those assemblages of software that spin the comforting illusion that nature can be contained by numbers. They take into account the lay of the land, whether natural features like cliffs and streams will help enclose the burning. And they consider how likely it is that the plan could go awry (a factor crucial in the postmortem of Cerro Grande) and what it would take to set it right again.

But one can never know how the butterfly will flap its wings. A sudden wind or a moment of inattention can make the calculations irrelevant. Whipped by gales like the ones that overtook Cerro Grande, the fire creates its own weather, becoming so large that, like a hurricane, it is given its own name.

Results from a preliminary Department of Interior investigation laid the blame not on the precision of the data or the accuracy of the calculcations but on matters of human judgment. The fact that strong prevailing winds were on the horizon was left out of a National Weather Service report, and no one asked for the missing data. Compounding this oversight, planners at Bandelier underestimated the potential complexity of the situation—how many people and how much equipment they would need if the fire didn't behave as it was supposed to.

There was a list of other deviations as well, the seriousness of which will be evaluated as investigators try to determine which butterflies' flapping did most to spread the flames. Taken together they tell a familiar story: there was a gulf between the way the fire played out in the calculations of the planners and the way it unfolded in the unforgiving real world.

Some politicians and homeowners were eager to have a specific villain to blame, but the culpability was far more diffuse. Large-scale cattle grazing and the clear-cutting of timber in the 19th century, followed by decades of dutiful suppression of natural wildfires, have conspired to produce thickets of highly combustible pines all over the region. A 1998 National Forest Service report warned that during the next five years there was a 30 percent chance of a large fire striking the woods around Los Alamos, sparked perhaps by one of the numerous summer lightning storms. And a Department of Energy report published last year concluded that "a major fire moving up to the edge of Los Alamos National Laboratory is not only credible but likely."

The same danger threatens forests all over the West. At the same time as Cerro Grande, two major fires in southern New Mexico were burning, one ignited by a downed power line, the other by a campfire. Two devastating fires had come dangerously close to Los Alamos in 1977 and 1996.

After the second one, tinder was cleared to create firebreaks. But protecting the town from something like Cerro Grande would have taken a huge public works program—a kind of Manhattan Project involving saws and axes. Whether that would have been as costly as the estimated billion dollars in damage the fire has caused is now a matter of historical curiosity. . . .

ANALYZING "Harness Fire? Mother Nature Begs to Differ"

In May 2000, the largest forest fire in the history of New Mexico burned out of control for over a week. When it was over, people wanted a complete account of what caused a fire that had destroyed 47,000 acres of forest and threatened the Los Alamos nuclear lab. The argument here, which appeared in the "Week in Review" section of the *Sunday New York Times* on May 21, 2000, attempts to give such an explanation for this unique event. In doing so, it provides several examples of the typical causal stories we use in our culture. The key words that we use in these stories are highlighted in the analysis that follows.

The article opens by reminding readers of the event that requires explanation, and this event is characterized by its most extreme consequences, the explosive firestorm ripping through tens of thousands of acres and the threat to Los Alamos. In paragraphs 3 and 4, the author backs up to what could be called the **precipitating or initiating event** that caused the fire, the setting of a "small 'controlled burn'" that foresters wanted to use to clear an overgrown area. Ironically, these forest rangers wanted to prevent exactly the kind of fire they started. This small initiating fire is also **remote** in location from the most devastating effects of the blaze. We are given a brief **chain of events:** the controlled burn, the unexpected winds, the overwhelming expansion of the fire within hours, the attempt at a "back burn," and then the uncontrolled expansion of that second set fire. The remote cause is linked to the final effect, and the wind is an **influence,** speeding up the rate and extent of the fire.

In these two paragraphs, we are also given all the **necessary** ingredients that together would be required to bring about a forest fire: a "dry, heavily timbered state" and a precipitating spark. But on their own, these ingredients would not have been sufficient to cause the massive fire that resulted. The **sufficient causes** of the disaster, according to this account, were the necessary ingredients *and* the wind. Add the wind to dry timber and a small starting fire, and together these causes are both necessary and sufficient to produce the devastating effect. We do not have an effect with mysterious causes here but rather causes that are already highly plausible. Everyone knows the "usual suspects," the **agents** or **agency** that can cause a forest fire. Agents function as **warrants** in causal arguments:

Reason: The wind increased in strength after a controlled burn was set in Bandelier National Monument. → **Claim:** The New Mexico Cerro Grande fire of May 2000 was brought about by strong winds whipping up a controlled burn when other factors or conditions required for a fire were present.

↑

Warrant: Winds can cause a small fire to spread quickly when conditions are right.

Since most complex effects like forest fires have multiple contributing causes, different causes can function as warrants as a causal argument builds a comprehensive explanation of an event.

Paragraph 6 lists some of the data behind the planning for the controlled burn. All the necessary and sufficient causes were considered and plugged into a computer model to produce a prediction. When we can list the multiple necessary and sufficient causes that are required to bring about an effect, we often refer to them as **factors.** But since one of the factors, the wind, cannot be controlled, or perhaps even sufficiently predicted, there was an element of chaos or **chance** in this event, a massive, unpredictable consequence from a small initiating event. We can look at this event in yet another way, suggested at the end of paragraph 7: it was not just the wind that whipped up the fire, but also the fire that "creates its own weather," becoming like a hurricane. Here is an element that could be described as **reciprocal causality,** a cause and effect that increase each other. The wind creates a huge fire, and a huge fire creates its own wind.

The wind and Mother Nature may be well past the control of humans. But humans did set the initial fire, so not surprisingly, part of a causal explanation of this event has to consider what role **human responsibility** played in the outcome. In fact, the Department of the Interior, the institution responsible for the national forests and national monuments, initiated an investigation to find the responsible human agents. Three points of human responsibility are mentioned in paragraph 8, and notably all of these concern not things that were done, but things that were not done: the National Weather Service report provided no wind data, no one asked for the missing data, and the planners did not provide enough people and equipment to rush in if the fire got out of hand, as it did. All the other causal factors, the temperature, the dryness of the wood, and the prevailing wind, might have gone for nothing if something like a fire brigade had been standing by when the first controlled burn got out of hand. At this point we have a different causal story on our hands, one with human rather than natural agents.

However, the article does not stop here, blaming the planners. In the final two paragraphs, the writer switches to yet another causal model or story. Changing the scale and the time frame, the Cerro Grande fire becomes the consequence of **conditions** that have developed for over a century: large-scale cattle grazing, clear cutting of timber, and the forest service's previous policy of fighting all forest fires, presumably preventing the frequent natural fires that would burn off the undergrowth. As a result of these misguided practices of the past, there are "thickets of highly combustible pines all over the region," only waiting for a precipitating cause, like a lightning strike or a deliberately set controlled burn, to start a large fire. Furthermore, as the last paragraph warns, there are really no feasible **blocking causes** that could be put in place to prevent fires like Cerro Grande anywhere in the West. A fire break around Los Alamos alone would have cost perhaps as much as the damage inflicted by the fire. So we end this causal explanation with a warning that conditions are ripe for disaster and a prediction that another destructive firestorm like the one just suffered could happen at any time. The devastating Western fires of the summer of 2002 fulfilled this prediction.

CAUSAL ARGUMENTS: DETERMINING WHY OR HOW SOMETHING HAPPENED

Our most basic questions about the world ask, "What is happening?" "What am I encountering?" "What is this thing?" "What is it like?" Answers to questions like these, as the previous chapter explained, produce claims about the nature of things. But we rarely stop with these answers, satisfied that we know all there is to know.

After answering our "What?" questions, we may begin to wonder "Why?" or "How?" We see things come into being or pass out of existence. We see a change from a before to an after and we ask "Why? What brought that about?" Or we imagine a new object or a possible future and we ask, "How can we make that happen?" Answers to questions like these involve *causes*, and since there are often competing answers to these questions, we need causal arguments to convince others to accept our account of what did or could bring something about.

The kind of causal argument we produce depends very much on our purpose and rhetorical situation. There are several motives, or exigencies, for causal arguments. First, we may want to explain the causes, to figure out how an effect came about to satisfy our own and others' curiosity. Such explanations are still arguments because competing versions can be constructed. Second, we may construct a causal argument because we want to repeat an effect or improve it or make something new happen; in this case, our argument will seek to separate essential causes from mere accessories and causes that we can act on from those we cannot alter. Third, we may want to stop an effect. Then our causal argument will emphasize causes that can be blocked or changed. And finally, we may want to predict the future, and to do so requires causal argument, identifying the forces in place now that will lead to coming effects. To achieve any of these purposes, it helps to understand the features of causal arguments and the way we build causal models or stories.

CONSTRUCTING A CAUSAL ARGUMENT

Though all arguments share the features outlined in the opening chapters, arguments about causes differ in some fundamental ways from arguments about the nature of things. An argument about the nature of things depends on an assumed or accepted definition as a principle for selecting evidence. A causal argument, on the other hand, relies on an assumed or accepted *agency*. Agency will be explained in greater detail below, but for now we can simply describe it as a shared belief about what can cause what. Although we do not always voice such beliefs, they are fundamental to much of our thinking, and they are absorbed almost unconsciously from our culture. If someone tells us that a murder was committed out of jealousy, that a fire started because of faulty wiring, or that a young woman chose a career because she was inspired by a teacher, we have no trouble believing these causal claims. The causes they identify are all plausible; they all depend on causal agencies most people in our culture find believable. A causal agency, then, works as a warrant in a causal argument.

Reason: The wiring in the building was faulty.   →   **Claim:** The fire in the building was started by faulty wiring.

↑

Warrant [Agency]: Faulty wiring in a building can cause fires.

The art of supporting causal arguments is the art of finding agencies that arguer and audience can share and that also fit the evidence. Even a cause that sounds convincing may not be supported by the facts of the case. It may, for instance, sound very plausible to say that a fire was started by faulty wiring, but if the wiring had just been inspected and was up to code, that cause will have to be abandoned and other possible causal explanations tried out. Every case whose causes we wonder about both suggests and limits the agencies we can employ in argument. Thus, in understanding and constructing causal arguments, we should know the variety of causes at our disposal so that we can find the best fit between agency and evidence.

Framing Narratives for Causal Analysis

Before beginning to construct a causal argument, we need an opening idea of what we are investigating. Is it a physical object? an isolated event? a state of affairs? a trend or pattern of events? And we need to be convinced that the effect we are examining really exists. There is no sense investigating the causes of an effect that never happened.

But once we are convinced that an effect has occurred and we have clarified it, we can begin to shape a causal argument. To fit agency to evidence, we can draw on the common terms we use for describing causes, including words like *influence*, *chance*, and *responsibility*. To make these common labels usable in our thinking about causes, we can organize them into sets representing the common *stories* we tell ourselves about how things come about. We can investigate possible causes by trying out a set of causes the way we try out a frame for a picture. This frame can work in two ways: It can impose an order on whatever information we already have, or it can send us looking, doing further research, for the material that will complete the causal story. Often more than one frame will fit. The terms listed below overlap, and the same cause might be called by several names. But some terms will fit the evidence better than others and, depending on the purpose of our causal argument, will produce the most convincing account. Think, then, of the following list as a stimulus for causal brainstorming, for building a convincing account about the relationships among the possible causes suggested by the facts of the case.

Frame I: Conditions, Influences, and Precipitating Causes

In the first frame for causal analysis, the first type of story we tell ourselves about causes and effects, we construct a set of background circumstances that make a result possible or even likely. We often call these *conditions* or *influences*. When we group them together, they are sometimes called *factors*. We can picture them as the setting, like a scene on a stage, waiting for an actor who will use that setting to make something happen.

Conditions   Conditions include the physical setting of an event, the historical time, the social climate or any other feature that seems to make an event more likely. The Protestant Reformation in Europe, for example, has been associated with the invention of the printing press in the fifteenth century, a condition or circumstance that made new religious ideas spread much more easily than ever before. Similarly, the fall of communist regimes in Eastern Europe in the 1980s has been linked to the new availability of fax machines and copiers among reformers, machines that made the dissemination of information easier and less susceptible to control. However, no one would claim that background conditions like printing presses and fax machines were the only causes of the religious or political changes they helped to bring about.

Some conditions may be crucial, while others may not be worth mentioning given your audience and purpose. If you are explaining the causes of a forest fire, you would mention the crucial condition of a prolonged dry spell as a background condition that made the fire more likely. But if you are talking about a freak accident, someone killed by a cornice falling off a tall building, you would not mention gravity as an important condition behind the event. Gravity is the condition for every event on earth.

Conditions will usually be part of your causal argument when your main purpose is *explanation,* an attempt at a full accounting of how an event or situation came about. Thus conditions figure in historical arguments and arguments about the success or failure of a person, or business, or other social enterprise.

Influences   In everyday language, an "influence" is really just another word for a condition. But we can reserve the term *influence* for those conditions affecting the rate at which an effect takes place or the degree to which it happens. That is, an influence cannot bring about or prevent an effect, but it can intensify or diminish it, make it happen more quickly or more slowly.

Think of influences as cheerleaders at a football game. They do not really cause the cheering; spectators always do some cheering. But cheerleaders do intensify the cheering and speed it up, prompting cheers from a crowd even before the game begins.

Causal arguments in the sciences often involve the identification of influences on an outcome. To return to our forest fire example, a prolonged drought and the resulting dryness of a forest certainly set the stage for a fire, but once a small fire starts, a prevailing wind can influence its spread and cause a small fire to become a devastating one.

Precipitating Causes   Conditions and influences prepare for an effect, but a precipitating cause comes along and actually forces it to happen. A precipitating cause is like that one extra salt crystal that makes a solid form out of a saturated solution; one minute you have a clear solution and the next minute there is gunk on the bottom of the beaker. The precipitating or triggering cause usually happens right before the effect. It is the famous "last straw that breaks the camel's back."

Remember the conditions for a forest fire—a drought and parched vegetation. A bolt of lightning could act on these conditions as a precipitating cause, igniting the combustible materials. It is the last thing that needs to happen before the event itself.

We usually think of wars as having precipitating causes that act on ripe conditions. The abduction of Helen of Troy was the precipitating cause of the Trojan War; the NATO bombing of the former Yugoslavia was cited as triggering the expulsion of ethnic Albanians from Kosovo. Trends can also be described in terms of conditions acted on by precipitating causes. The Beatles' long hair presumably precipitated a decade of changes in the appearance of young people. But it is easier to see precipitating causes when they themselves are dramatic events and when they precede events with clear beginnings.

Precipitating causes are not by nature different from any other kind of cause. You cannot say with certainty that any particular kind of event is a precipitating cause. A border skirmish between India and Pakistan, for instance, may or may not precipitate a wider conflict. In the case of a war, we can identify a precipitating cause only by hindsight. But in cases where nature's laws take over, we can have more confidence in labeling precipitating causes. Sparks from pyrotechnic devices precipitated a deadly fire in a Rhode Island night club.

EXERCISE 7.1

Working either alone or with a group of your classmates, select a particular event and think up some of the plausible conditions or influences behind it and the precipitating causes that could have acted to bring it about. You may go on to use these examples in a full causal argument. The list below may also jog your memory into recalling other events, perhaps personal ones, whose causes can be examined usefully this way and used in a causal argument: any election outcome, any sports victory or defeat, any business success or failure, any sudden fame or disgrace.

1. A war
2. A political scandal
3. A breakthrough in the treatment of a disease
4. The sudden rise or fall in the price of a stock
5. A marriage proposal

Frame 2: Near and Remote Causes

Unlike the model presented in Frame 1, which sees background conditions operated on by a sudden precipitating cause, the next framework creates a continuing story line. It distinguishes causes in terms of their separation in time or place or kind from an effect. Near causes are close to an effect in time or space, and remote causes are distant.

Near Causes   A near or "proximate" cause is one that comes close to an effect in time and place. It can be useful to distinguish passive persistent conditions from close-in-time causes that are unique, separate events in themselves. Suppose we are looking for the causes of the final selection of a presidential candidate. The choice is not only the result of conditions that have built up over the last four years or even longer—the economy, foreign relations, domestic crises—but also the result of the events that happen in the months and even days before the party's final choice is announced at a convention—the various primary victories, media disasters, deals, endorsements, and withdrawals that lock up delegates' votes. These happenings can be labeled proximate causes because they occur relatively close in time (within months or weeks) to the final effect, the choice of a particular candidate.

Remote Causes   A near cause operates close to its effect in time or place; a remote cause is distant in time or place or both from its result. In another sense, a cause can seem "remote" if it comes from a source quite different from its effect. Recently an interest in "chaos theory" has popularized the idea that very minor, remote causes, perhaps the flapping of a butterfly's wings in the Amazon rain forest, can lead to a series of occurrences culminating in a major event, such as a hurricane, weeks later. In general, causes are "remote" because their link to an event seems surprising until someone successfully argues for them. Since we tend to think that causes occur immediately before and physically near their effects, remote causes are often more challenging to argue for.

A remote cause can often be linked to its effect by a *chain of events.* It has been argued, for example, that the building of the Great Wall of China was a cause of the fall of Rome. That is about as remote as a cause can be, both in place and time, but these two events can be connected by identifying the links between them. The nomadic tribes of central Asia, stopped from invading China by the Wall, turned west and began pushing other tribes westward, until those tribes, like dominoes falling, fell on Rome.

When do we think in terms of remote causes? Historians often go back in time to identify the possible origins of events and trends. An account of both near and remote causes can produce a sense of convincing completeness by tracing a chain of events, trends, and ideas through time.

We often search for remote causes when we want to understand the sources of an individual's achievements or failures: the starting points of a successful career, the breakdown of a marriage, the roots of a neurosis, or the drive behind an Olympic gold medal. To explain such later effects in an individual's life, we often search out causes in childhood events. We also search for remote causes when considering natural phenomena like geological formations; we go back until we have a full set of causes that would allow us to reconstruct in our imaginations how the effect, the mountain chain or canyon, came about.

Where remote causes end and near causes begin can be a matter of perspective, resolved in part by the purpose and scope of your causal argument. If you are focusing on an event at the end of a week, what happens one day before can be proximate and six days before remote. But in the case of the outcome of an election, for example, what happened a week before or even in the interval since the last election can be seen as proximate compared to a more remote long-term trend developing over many years. Causes can be made to seem more remote if there are intervening factors or events—in time, in place, in kind—that have operated between them and the effect. It all depends on the time frame you construct and the kind of causal argument you are building.

EXERCISE 7.2

Working either alone or with a group of your classmates, use remote and proximate causes to construct accounts of some effects like the ones in the following list, or others you may think of. You may go on to use one of these accounts in a full causal argument.

1. The move of a sports team from one city to another
2. A college student's change in career plans
3. The fall of a leader in any country
4. An outbreak of hostilities between two countries
5. An election outcome that goes against expectations

Frame 3: Necessary and Sufficient Causes

This framework for a causal story is the most common and the most useful when your purpose is either to repeat or to block an effect, that is, to argue not just for a causal explanation but for a way of intervening in a causal process. Here you really want to know only what is required to bring about or prevent an effect. You do not necessarily want to trace causes any further than is required to give you power over them.

Necessary Causes   As the name tells us, a necessary cause is *required* to bring about an effect. It is permanently and in some cases uniquely associated with its effect. For example, oxygen is a necessary condition for a fire; in fact, because its presence is taken for granted, oxygen is rarely mentioned as a cause in an account of how a particular fire came about. But if someone is considering how to stop a fire, oxygen as a necessary and also preventable cause can be an excellent target, as demonstrated in the use of foams that "smother" a fire, cutting off the oxygen.

Similarly, a virus is the necessary cause of a cold. If you can distinguish your symptoms from hay fever or allergy well enough to know that you have a cold, you can be certain that a virus has invaded your mucous membranes. In the case of many infectious diseases, once we have identified the disease correctly, we know exactly what kind of virus or bacteria caused it, a model for how a necessary cause is uniquely associated with its effect.

Thus, the distinguishing characteristic of a necessary cause is that we can reason back to it with conviction. Given an effect, we can assume that certain necessary causes or conditions had to be present to bring it about. If you know, for example, that someone has a valid diploma from a college in the United States, you can infer with near certainty that the diploma-holder passed a required number of courses.

Even though you can reason back with a high degree of certainty from an effect to a necessary cause, you cannot turn the process around, reasoning from the necessary cause to the occurrence of the effect. The presence or occurrence of a necessary cause is not always enough to predict that an effect actually has occurred or will occur. You do not have a fire just because oxygen is present. And the fulfillment of course requirements does not necessarily mean that a person has a diploma. Why? It is possible the individual with the required courses has been disqualified for some reason, such as unpaid tuition, from receiving a degree. For a completely active causal model, you will need, in addition to necessary causes, *sufficient* causes, discussed in the section below.

But first, here is another interesting feature of necessary causes: A necessary cause can always be invented by merely re-describing the effect. The necessary cause of poverty is not having enough money; the necessary cause of a dent in a fender is a dent-producing force; the necessary cause of a famine is not enough food. But these re-descriptions are rarely helpful in the construction of a causal narrative or model in an argument.

Finally, another kind of cause that is always necessary is the absence of anything to prevent the effect (see below). We know that when anything happens, nothing stopped it from happening. If a house burns down, the fire was not detected in time to be put out. Searching for a cause that would necessarily block an effect is useful when you want to argue for reversing a causal process.

Sufficient Causes   Once again, imagine yourself confronting an effect and trying to reason back to its causes. Let us say that the event is, once again, a forest fire. You can be certain that the necessary causes and conditions were present: combustible materials, oxygen, an igniting agent, and the absence of what would have stopped the fire. But though an igniting agent would have to be present, several possibilities could fill that niche: a carelessly thrown match, a bolt of lightning, an imperfectly extinguished camper's fire, a deliberately set fire to clear brush, or carefully planned arson. Given the presence of the necessary conditions, any one of these igniting agents could have started the fire. It would be sufficient to bring about the result. A sufficient cause is one in whose presence the effect must occur, if the necessary causes are also present.

We can work through another example. Suppose you stumble over a dead body. You know that the necessary causes of death are the cessation of breathing and heartbeat and the absence of anything to keep them going artificially, resulting in brain death. But no coroner's report ever recorded the cause of death as cessation of breathing. That is not a sufficient cause. We want to know what caused the breathing to stop.

The coroner called to the scene will test out a number of explanations. Death has many sufficient causes, causes in whose presence it must occur if nothing intervenes: heart failure, stroke, gun shot, strangulation, hemorrhage, poison. Of course, examination of the body will narrow down the list of sufficient causes; if the body is unmarked, then death by violent external means is ruled out. An autopsy will eventually reveal the sufficient cause. We talk about sufficient cause, then, when an event has many possible causes, any one of which is enough to bring it about.

In human affairs, most sufficient causes are not necessary causes. Instead, a combination of necessary and sufficient causes is needed. Take divorce as an example. It can be brought about by a number of things—desertion, adultery, mental cruelty. The law recognizes any of these as a sufficient cause for granting a divorce. But no one of these is both a necessary and sufficient cause. Any or even all three of these can be present in the lives of a married couple and not lead to divorce. The necessary cause of a divorce is filing for one; that is the event in whose absence a divorce cannot occur. But filing itself will not lead inevitably to a divorce unless one of the recognized sufficient causes is also present. The most complete causal explanation, then, is one that uncovers all the causes which are together necessary and sufficient. When they are all present, the effect will occur.

EXERCISE 7.3

Working either alone or with a group of your classmates, build causal narratives to describe each of the following effects in terms of necessary and sufficient causes. You may go on to use these causal narratives in a full causal argument.

1. Getting an A in a college course
2. A recent plane crash
3. The marriage of a particular couple
4. The popularity of a particular movie or kind of movie
5. The capture of a notorious criminal

Considering Other Causal Models

Common usage has given the word *cause* many other meanings that can become important in causal model building and argument. We can use these concepts when we are building a plausible account of how an event or situation came about.

Model 1: Responsibility

Responsibility as a cause exists only in effects involving people. It is a term that often comes up when we examine events that people have helped bring about, and these events include all of history and the subjects of the social sciences, and most of what gets into the daily newspaper. We often hear arguments that acknowledge many contributing factors behind an occurrence but that go on to insist that, no matter what the outside pressures, an individual was responsible for his or her own actions.

We can assign responsibility because of what someone either has done or has not done. For example, a diplomat who initiates contacts and sets up meetings and cultural exchanges can be the cause of improved relations between two countries. On the other hand, a diplomat who makes no overtures to another country—holds no talks and ignores initiatives from the other side—can by such inaction cause deteriorating relations between two countries.

Right away, we can see that in considering a human being who either acts or does not act, we are also considering the idea of intention. What does a person mean to cause by either acting or not acting—and on the other hand to what extent is a person responsible for what he or she does or does not intend? If someone wills a result and acts on that will, then that person is a cause. If, for instance, you want to be physically fit, and you run, do push-ups, and play tennis, your willpower is then as much the cause of improvement in your body as any exercises you do.

To appreciate the importance of intention, consider the enormous difference it makes in deciding punishment for someone's death whether the death was caused intentionally. In the case of accidentally causing another's death, the charge may be manslaughter and the penalty rather slight; in the case of intentional, or premeditated, murder, the perpetrator may receive the death penalty. Thus, the notion of human intention as a cause is crucial in our legal system.

It is also possible to intend not to act, and deliberately doing nothing can also be a cause. Foreign policy, for example, which we assume is largely a matter of human intention, consists as much of actions deliberately not taken as of actions taken. Decision makers in the State Department often resolve not to interfere, not to send letters of protest, not to invade, and not to respond to provocations, and these intended inactions can have effects just as intended acts do.

We are on sure ground identifying responsibility when the acts whose causes we are investigating fall within someone's *domain of responsibility*. Doctors' domain of responsibility is the health of their patients; teachers', the instruction of their students; parents', the welfare of their children. If a patient dies because a disease was misdiagnosed, we do not ask questions about intentions. The result was clearly in the doctor's domain of responsibility and the doctor may be liable to legal action. Whenever we can place an effect within a person's or an institution's domain of responsibility, it may not matter whether the effect was intended or not. In landmark legal decisions in the 1990s, cigarette makers were held responsible for the health problems of smokers, even though packs of cigarettes had carried labels warning of health dangers for over 30 years.

Questions of responsibility can lead us into deep ethical waters. Sometimes it is difficult to decide whose domain of responsibility an action falls under. Is a psychiatrist responsible if a psychotic patient ceases to take a prescribed medication and commits a crime? Is a gun manufacturer responsible if one of its guns is mishandled by a child, causing a death? Or what about the candidate whose aide accepted illegal campaign contributions, supposedly without the candidate's knowledge? When issues like these come up, causal argument may merge into evaluation argument, involving an ethical judgment as well as an assignment of causal agency on the basis of responsibility.

Working either alone or with a group of your classmates, come up with particular instances of each of the following kinds of effects. Then argue for human responsibility for each instance. You may go on to use these instances in a full causal argument.

1. A crime committed by juveniles
2. The harmful side effects of a medication
3. An individual's addiction to gambling, alcohol, drugs
4. An increase or decline in the number of people attending religious services
5. A decline in attendance at X-rated movies

Model 2: Absence of a Blocking Cause

When is the lack of something a cause? How can we say that something that does not happen causes something that does? Imagine a conventional wedding scene. The clergyman looks around and asks, "Is there any reason why these two should not be joined together?" If no one steps forward and the ceremony is completed, we can say that one cause of the marriage was the absence of interference with the ceremony. Something that did not happen helped to bring about something that did. Thus, the absence of restraints, impediments, blocks, inhibitions, or safeguards can actually help to bring about an effect.

The absence of blocking causes is often cited in analyses of public and political trends and events. The spread of the HIV virus in the 1980s is blamed on the absence of an aggressive public health campaign. An increase in juvenile crime is explained by the absence of fathers in families. In combination with the notion of institutional responsibility, we are quick as a society to see the causal role of a lack of action on the part of responsible government officials and agencies.

We can also claim, as we explained in the section above on necessary causes, that a necessary cause is the absence of anything that would have prevented an effect. Although we seldom bother to reckon up all the missing blocking causes when we are trying to explain why an event came about, we certainly do pay attention to possible blocking causes when we want to prevent an effect. For instance, we might say that the cause of a destructive, spreading forest fire, once it had started, was the absence of a firebreak, a clear-cut region, to stop it. If we want to prevent future forest fires from spreading, we will provide a blocking cause like firebreaks.

Below are types of events and trends that might occur, in part because of the absence of causes that could have prevented them. Working either alone or with a group of your classmates, list two potential blocking causes for each of these events and trends. You may go on to use these blocking causes in a complete causal argument.

1. A long-term ecological trend like increasing deserts in North Africa or decreasing rain forests in Brazil

2. A terrorist incident
3. An increase in illegal border crossings
4. An increase in imports of a product
5. An accident occurring during a recreational activity

Model 3: Reciprocal Causes

Informing all our causal narratives or models so far is an image of causes and effects lined up on a one-way street. We begin with a cause at one end and we move ahead to an effect farther down the road, and that effect can be the cause of something still farther down. But this model of a one-way street, though clear and tidy, can oversimplify reality. Instead, we can have a situation in which cause and effect feed each other. We call this *reciprocal causality*. In other words, traffic on the "causeway" can go in two directions; an effect can turn around and influence the cause that caused it.

Here are some familiar examples of reciprocal causality: Higher prices cause increased wage demands, and increased wages cause higher prices. Guerrilla action by ethnic nationalists causes a crackdown by a government, and the crackdown increases guerrilla resistance. In both of these situations, a one-way model fails to represent the actual two-way traffic pattern. A story of reciprocal causality is often used to explain trends and repeating events.

A repeating sequence of causes and effects invites claims of reciprocal causality. For example, sociologists believe that one of the factors leading to child abuse is whether or not a parent was abused as a child. We can look at a sequence of suffering and perpetuating abuse across the generations as a one-way chain of cause and effect.

Abused child in the first generation   → Child abuser as a parent   → Abused child in the second generation   → Child abuser as a parent   → Abused child in the third generation   → Child abuser as a parent

This linear model may be a good representation of events in time. But when we see the same type of event recurring, we can pull the chain around to make a circle that represents reciprocal causality. We often call such cases of reciprocal causality a "vicious circle."

Child abuse

↓   ↑

Abusive parenting

Even when a repeating series is not obvious, you can still try out a reciprocal causal model and see if there is any evidence to make it stick. You may know, for instance, that sunspots interfere with communication satellites. Is it likely that these satellites have any effect on the sun? Of course not. No two-way causality there. But suppose you are analyzing the factors that have influenced a cultural trend like the size of cars Americans buy. You may begin with a argument is to persuade your audience that they are receiving a complete account, that the causes you name are plausible, and that a different version of the events is not as or more plausible. You want to identify the remote causes and contributing conditions, the near and/or precipitating causes, the influences, the responsible agents, the role of chance, and any plausible blocking causes that could have prevented the effect.

Causal arguments are also constructed to emphasize one cause from among many, to nominate it as the most important, as the necessary and sufficient cause in whose presence the effect had to take place. This singling out of a critical cause is usually done to serve other purposes such as finding a way to bring about an effect or to intervene and block it. If you want to bring about an effect, then you look for sufficient causes or influences or precipitating causes that can be created or initiated or charged up to make something happen. If you want to stop or prevent an effect, then you look for a blocking cause to put in place or a necessary cause to remove.

When we want to construct a convincing causal argument, framing a causal narrative is only part of our task. Though a causal story may be convincing in itself, especially if it is similar to other ones known to an audience, readers sometimes also need to be shown that a particular cause could have been connected to an effect, especially since causal arguments usually work in the realm of probability, not certainty. For example, a story about traumatic life experiences leading to drug abuse may sound convincing, but is there any evidence to suggest that such a causal link occurred? To establish the plausibility of the causal connection we are focusing on, we can turn to certain tactics of causal argument, ways of establishing the relationships among the causes in the model we have constructed.

Establishing Causal Relationships

It can be one thing to identify a possible cause, quite another to convince an audience that it operates. Fortunately, arguers and audiences share a whole storehouse of assumptions about what causes what. You draw on these assumptions in causal argument, just as you appeal to shared definitions in arguments about the nature of things. If, for example, you were to argue that "Michael Jordan is an American hero," you would have to evoke a sharable definition of what it means to be a hero. Similarly, if you were to argue the causal claim that "Michael Jordan's heroic accomplishments have had a positive effect on the youth of America," you would appeal to a sharable assumption, namely, that a sports hero can have an effect on admiring kids.

Understanding Agency: Our Basic Assumption
about What Causes What

What convinces us that one thing causes another? Suppose we see a small child fly forward on a swing, the mother pushing from behind. This scene clearly illustrates cause and effect, for we know that the mother's push causes the child's motion on the swing. When we can see the actual push and the forward motion that follows it, we have the most direct kind of evidence of a causal connection between two actions, in this case the push and the swing.

We are going to use the word *agency* for this most basic connection between cause and effect. In a sense, agency is the smallest unit of cause. The simplest kind of agency is direct physical contact: the mother's hand *touches* the child's back; lightning *strikes* a dry tree to ignite it; a car *smashes* into a store window and shatters it.

We intuitively grasp such physical agencies as force, motion, resistance, and reaction. We share a common-sense understanding of how many things work in the natural world. We know that plants need water and sunlight to grow, although they can get too much of either. We know that we need heat to fry an egg, that if we eat too much we gain weight, that cars need fuel to run.

But what about the agencies that operate in individual lives, in social and historical events? In any society, at any time, there are quite a number of accepted agencies whose operation we believe in as readily as we believe in the operation of physical laws. Philosophers, psychologists, anthropologists, and social scientists debate about what to call these agencies—motives, instincts, or learned patterns of behavior. But we all recognize believable appeals to the way human nature works, in the same way that we recognize how physical nature works. We no more accept happiness as a motive for murder than we would accept the plausibility of flying rocks.

What are some of these accepted agencies of human behavior? We believe that people do things to *imitate* one another, and that they also do things *to distinguish themselves* from one another. We believe that people usually act *to maximize their own good* (as they see the good) *with the least amount of effort*. We also believe that people act *to avoid pain*. Certain basic motives, causes, or agencies of human action are widely acknowledged. And these same agencies that move individuals also move groups, communities, and even nations. They too imitate, rebel, seek their benefit, and minimize pain and expense.

We will understand the concept of agency better if we examine some human cause-and-effect relationships and identify the assumed agency in each. If we say that watching violent movies causes violent behavior in children, the assumed agency is imitation. If we say that living in a tract development caused one homeowner to paint a house pink, the assumed agency is the desire to be different. If we say that the citizens of a community voted to increase taxes because they wanted to build a new school, the assumed agency is the desire to maximize their own good. If a nation builds a system of dams to prevent floods, the assumed agency is the desire to avoid disaster. Of course, less obvious agencies may also be operating; the extent to which we argue about them depends on how important it is to elaborate on the springs of human action.

Often when we connect a cause and an effect in argument, as in the cases above, we do not even need to mention the agency between them, just as we do not always need to spell out the warrants in arguments. We assume it. People in the same culture share more or less the same assumptions about causal agency, about what can plausibly cause what. We need to develop our arguments to the point where we and our readers can share basic assumptions about agency. In effect, we want readers to nod and say, "Yes, I believe that could cause that."

With agency in mind, we can distinguish between causal arguments that assume agency and those that do not, those that get the reader's nod easily and those that do not. Let us look first at a causal argument in which agency is so obvious it can be assumed.

Suppose you want to argue that juvenile binge drinking in a community is partly caused by parents' alcohol abuse. Depending on your audience, you could spend much of your time in this argument presenting evidence of the large number of adolescents who binge drink and of the large number of their parents who drink excessively. You can imagine an argument that spent all its time proving the simultaneous existence of the two events you call the cause and the effect. In this case, you might simply bring the cause and the effect into juxtaposition and stop on the assumption that your audience will have no difficulty assuming the agency—in this case, imitation—between them.

Now let us look at an example where agency cannot be assumed so easily. Two types of arguments fall into this category. First, there are implausible agencies. Any argument that assumes an implausible agency is likely to arouse the resistance and incredulity of its audience. If you were to insist in all seriousness that your presence in the stadium as a fan is the cause of your favorite team losing, you would be assuming an unbelievable agency, a causal connection that we don't have any way of accounting for. Most people do not take jinxes seriously because we cannot connect the physical presence of a fan to what happens on the field. There are many other such agencies currently unacceptable to educated audiences, such as the predictive power of horoscopes. Most educated people would not accept the stars as a causal agent. If you seriously wanted to claim that mysterious forces caused something, you would have to move the argument to a different level by arguing for the agency itself. You would have to explain exactly why being born on a particular date makes certain things happen.

The other kind of argument in which agency cannot simply be assumed involves a distant cause, when the cause and the effect are so far apart that we cannot immediately see the agency between them. If we claim that a volcanic eruption on one continent caused a cold summer on another, we are likely to lose our audience of lay people because agency, the meteorological evidence linking cause and effect, is not assumable or known to them. In such cases, agency can be supplied by establishing a chain of causes to unite events distant in time or place.

You can now see the crucial importance of agency in causal argument. In fact, the main task of causal argument is getting down to an assumable agency that your audience will accept. If you have a believable agency, you can simply line up cause and effect by any of the methods we describe in the following section. If you do not have an assumable agency, you will have to establish it. If you cannot establish it, you have no causal argument.

Working either alone or with a group of your classmates, describe the agencies that would plausibly link the following pairs of causes and their effects. Are any of the linkages implausible because no assumption of agency is imaginable? You may go on to use any plausible agencies that you describe in a full causal argument.

1. Parental strictness causes teenage rebelliousness.
2. California high-school students start getting tattoos; a month later, east-coast high school students get tattoos.
3. A ballplayer changes his socks; his hitting streak ends.
4. The salesperson who is physically out of shape has the lowest commissions in the company.
5. France refuses to boycott the 1980 Olympics; the Russians hold a special summit meeting with the French.

Supporting a Causal Relationship

Mill's Four Methods

The English philosopher John Stuart Mill explained in detail how to carry on a causal investigation. He was concerned with identifying potential causes and making the connection between cause and effect as convincing as possible. In the laboratory, once a potential cause-and-effect relationship is identified, it can usually be tested and established with a high degree of certainty. In most ordinary causal arguments, however, certainty is an unreachable goal: we argue about degrees of probability, and we are satisfied when a sufficient degree of probability is demonstrated.

Nevertheless, in supporting a causal argument, we use versions of Mill's basic tactics in two ways. First, they help us find or single out a dominant cause; they are especially useful when we have a number of possible causes to choose from and need something to convince us that a particular one was working. Second, the same tactic that helps us select a dominant cause can also be used to convince a reader. In other words, if one of Mill's tactics convinces us, it will also convince an audience.

The Common-Factor Method The common-factor method works only when the effect we are interested in explaining occurs more than once. Many people catch the same disease, some restaurant patrons become ill, and a few people have difficulty waking up every Monday morning. Investigators looking for the causes of events like these begin by assuming that cause(s) preceded the effect in time. They look at the circumstances or events that came before the effects to see if they have anything in common. Assuming agency, the simplest causal connection, they reason that a factor that all the cases have in common is likely to be the cause.

Here is a fuller example of how the common-factor method works. A literary historian interested in how some prolific novelists accomplished so much looks for something similar in their very different lives. The historian may find that many of them (Charles Dickens, Anthony Trollope, Edith Wharton) set aside a time in the morning for uninterrupted writing. He can then reasonably infer that this common factor, regular morning work habits, was the cause of their productivity rather than some other possible cause such as intermittent inspiration. When he writes his argument and cites his case studies, he can assume that readers will accept the agency linking regular work habits and great productivity.

A search for the cause of food poisoning is a frequently cited example of the common-factor method. If six people come down with the symptoms of botulism, health officials will obtain a list of what the victims ate in the past 24 hours and check for foods in common. They will eliminate the salad or coffee that all six had because they know that Clostridium botulinum grows only in an anaerobic (airless) environment. But when they find that all six ate the canned beans at the local diner, they can be fairly certain that they have found the cause. Health officials looking for the source of botulism have an easy time because they know exactly what they are looking for; botulism has only one necessary and sufficient cause.

Notice the differences among the cases discussed. The health officials' knowledge of the cause of botulism simplified the investigation and led to a firm conclusion. But in the case of the novelists, the conclusion can be no more than probable. Though we know the necessary cause of botulism, no one has yet identified a necessary and sufficient cause of literary productivity (one in whose presence productivity must follow).

Remember that frequently your purpose in causal argument will be to persuade your audience that a dominant cause indeed produced the effect. If you discovered this cause by the common-factor method, you can simply relate that process. You can write it out in your argument like a detective story. The health officials will explain in the local press how they tracked down botulism to the beans. The literary historian will describe the working habits of each novelist and point out the common pattern and the common result. Since such an argument is not scientific, the literary historian may have to refute or concede other possible causes of prolific writing such as insomnia or a need for money. The need for money could be refuted by pointing out that it was not really a common factor, since at least one of the novelists, Wharton, had plenty of money. Or the historian may concede that all the novelists had insomnia, and that is exactly what made them get up early and write every morning. (All the novelists may have had brown hair too, but it is hard to imagine any agency between hair color and literary productivity.)

PROJECT FOR CLASS DISCUSSION

Identify a group of at least five items or incidents or five people who have some effect or condition in common, such as people who have chosen the same unusual major or the best-selling books or CDs or most popular movies of a single year. Look for a common factor shared by all the members of the group. Rejecting any ideas that seem implausible or insignificant, come up with a dominant cause for the effect or condition you have chosen; then, make an argument explaining how you came up with the dominant cause. Which arguments are convincing, and why?

The Single-Difference Method   The single-difference method works only when there are at least two similar situations, one leading to a particular effect and the other not. One seed grows, another doesn't; one president's term is peaceful, another's is full of conflict. You look for the possible cause that was missing in one case and present in the other—the single difference between them. You assume that if everything else is substantially alike in both cases, the single difference must be the cause of the different result—the sunny spot in the garden that one seed was planted in, the international crisis that faced one president.

Here is how the single-difference method works in an extended example. Two students in a course have a B$^+$ average on the exams, but one gets an A and the other a B as a final grade. Both students attended class regularly, both sat in the second row, both were attentive in class; but the one who got the A participated in class discussion, while the other remained silent. If you know that this participation was the single difference between their performances, you can reasonably conclude that it caused the difference between their grades.

When you argue for a cause discovered by the single-difference method, you must first persuade your audience that the two cases being considered are substantially alike. Convincing an audience of such a resemblance is sometimes difficult, for rarely in human events are two situations exactly alike. You can, however, establish likeness in two ways: List all the important elements the two cases have in common, or show how any differences other than the one you are interested in are insignificant or trivial. For instance, if the student who got the B missed one more class than the one who got the A, you may want to argue that such a difference was insignificant in determining their grades.

If you are arguing a case like the one above, you must be especially careful not to overlook any other possibly significant difference. If someone were to point one out, your argument would be weakened. So you have to anticipate any plausible rival difference and refute it. What if someone pointed out that the student who got the A was a man and the one who got the B a woman (or vice versa)? That might be a significant difference. How would you argue that it wasn't?

PROJECT FOR CLASS DISCUSSION

Find pairs of similar situations, one in which an effect occurs and another in which it doesn't, such as two tests in the same subject, one that you do well on, the other less well, or two similar international crises, one resolved peacefully, the other not. Discuss possibilities for the single difference between the two situations. That single difference may be the cause of the effect occurring in one case and not in the other. Which arguments are most convincing, and why?

The Method of Varying Causes and Effects   This method can be used only when an effect persists and varies. Sunspots come and go, SAT scores rise and fall, the cost of living rises, the stock market lurches. Faced with fluctuations and trends, you examine possible causes to find at least one that persists and varies in a way similar to the one you are trying to explain. In doing so, you assume that the correlation between the cause you are supporting and the effect is evidence of their connection. But since correlation is not the same as cause, you can make this assumption only when agency is plausible.

A potential cause-and-effect pair may increase together, decrease together, or one may increase while the other decreases. They may even jolt up and down in absolute harmony. SAT scores may decline while the number of students enrolled in advanced high-school English and math courses declines; the standard of living may rise when family size decreases. In each of these cases, an assumption about agency is as necessary to your argument as the rising and falling patterns you have discerned. That is, your audience must see a plausible connection between the two.

Let's take a look at a case in which the method of varying causes and effects is the key to causal argument. The local booksellers in Centreville keep track of the number of books sold per year. They notice that over a period of 10 years, the number of books sold decreased by half even though the town population increased by 15 percent. Casting around for an explanation, the booksellers notice in the census data that the number of TV sets in the community increased dramatically during this 10-year span. The booksellers conclude, regretfully, that the more time people spend watching TV, the fewer books they buy. In this case, the relationship between potential cause and effect is inverse: As one went up, the other went down.

But in the next 10-year period, the booksellers are pleased to notice a sudden upsurge in the number of books sold. This time there is no single obvious explanation, so they note a number of trends that might have contributed to the increase: a big rise in community enrollment in night-school courses, an increase in the number of senior citizens living in the town, a marked trend toward building bigger houses, an increase in fast-food restaurants, and increased availability of Internet access. None of these is an obvious cause of increased book sales.

Persuading an audience that the increase in the number of TV sets led to a decrease in the purchase of books might not be too difficult: most people cannot read and watch TV at the same time. But arguing for the causal relationship between book buying and any of the other simultaneous trends might be more difficult. If you suspect that an increase in house size and an increase in book buying are causally related and want to convince yourself and others, you would have to construct a chain of causes to connect them. Your argument might go something like this: An increase in the size of houses means that people have more disposable income. People who have more disposable income often have more interest in cultural pursuits. More interest in cultural pursuits means more interest in reading. More interest in reading results in more book buying. This argument, of course, is no stronger than its weakest link.

Arguing a causal connection on the basis of the method of varying causes and effects can depend on forestalling some obvious objections. First, even though trends vary in the same way, they may be unrelated. For example, an increase in the number of fast-food franchises and an increase in book buying probably have nothing to do with one another. Second, both the supposed cause-and-effect trends may really be the effects of yet another cause. Thus increased book buying and an increased number of senior citizens may both be the result of an overall increase in the population. Third, the trends may be the cause and effect of each other—remember reciprocal causality. A rise in continuing-education enrollment could lead to more book buying, which in turn could lead to more continuing-education enrollment. It takes skillful arguing to place causes in a convincing relationship with each other.

PROJECT FOR CLASS DISCUSSION

Think of some trend in your experience that has been either increasing or decreasing over a period of time, such as enrollments in certain kinds of courses at your school, immigration into your community, a change in the divorce rate, or something else. Using the method of varying causes and effects, discuss plausible causes that have increased or decreased in some related way. Which argument is most convincing, and why?

The Elimination Method   Like Mill's three other methods, the process of elimination is both a way of thinking about causes and a way of presenting an argument about them. As a method of investigation, scientists use elimination in controlled experiments, doctors use it in diagnosis, detectives use it to identify suspects, and common sense makes it available to everyone. Using the elimination method we argue for one dominant cause not by proving it happened, but by proving that the other possibilities did not. If your car stalls in traffic, you systematically eliminate all possible causes, beginning with the most obvious, until you find the culprit—you check to see if you ran out of gas, if the temperature gauge has risen, if something in the electrical system failed, and so on. The elimination method works only when an effect can be produced by several possible sufficient causes. We assume that since only one cause was needed to bring about the effect, only one cause operated and you can identify it.

Convincing an audience by this method depends on how complete the initial set of possible causes is and how validly the other members of the set are eliminated. For example, in the story "The Adventure of the Speckled Band," Sherlock Holmes considered all the possible means of entering and leaving a bedroom in order to kill the occupant. The room was sparsely furnished, so no one could hide in it. The door was locked from the inside, so no one could either enter or, once inside, leave without a sign. The window was shuttered from within and could not be opened from outside. After Holmes eliminated these obvious possibilities, he concluded that the only way of getting into the room was through a very small ventilator above the bed, "so small that a rat could hardly pass through." Thus, by the process of elimination, Holmes concluded that he was not dealing with a human intruder. (If you want to know whodunit, read the story.)

Such thoroughness is possible only when the set of causes is limited, as it is by the physical facts of a room. Still, we often use the elimination method loosely. That is, we argue by eliminating the most obvious possible causes—other than the one we are interested in, of course. It is not always necessary to enumerate a complete set of possible causes. Eliminating the most likely is often good enough.

For example, suppose you want to persuade your audience that a widely publicized athletic career was the cause of one candidate's victory in a Senate race. One tactic you could use to support this case would be to eliminate obvious rival causes, such as the candidate's support for a tax cut, a position that usually attracts votes. If the other candidate supported the same tax cut, you could eliminate this cause of your candidate's victory. You could go on to eliminate other possible causes such as the candidate's attractive family, wealth, and dedicated staff, if you are able to. Or you may decide not to bother mentioning all these possible causes—but only if you think some are insignificant and only if your audience is likely to ignore them too. You risk easy refutation if you leave out causes your audience is likely to consider significant.

PROJECT FOR CLASS DISCUSSION

Spend some time brainstorming at least four possible causes for one of the following effects: the stock market rise of the 1990s, the deterioration of Florida's coral reefs, the breakup of the Soviet Union, the rise in the average age of people when they first marry. Discuss the possible causes in class. Then, using the elimination method, remove any causes that could not have been sufficient to bring about the effect and try to arrive at the cause(s) that would have been sufficient. Can the group agree on a single cause? If so, what makes the cause a plausible choice? If not, what is unconvincing about the argument for the sufficiency of each possible cause?

Mill's Methods and Agency

Following Mill's methods can convince an audience that a cause operated whenever agency can be assumed. But what if agency cannot be assumed? If you have some solid evidence that two things are causally connected, but there is still no obvious agency between the cause you have named and its effect, you may need to do some imaginative model building to close the gap. Two principles govern this model building: (1) You must suggest an agency in line with accepted causal laws; no magic is allowed. (2) You should apply the centuries-old wisdom of Occam's Razor, which advises looking for the simplest agency that explains the effect rather than an elaborate, far-fetched explanation with many interlocking steps.

Other Rhetorically Effective Methods of Arguing Causality

Mill's methods make for effective demonstration, but they are complex. In editorials, magazine articles, speeches, and other kinds of writing, we often use simpler, almost shorthand ways of supporting a causal claim. Instead of telling a long story, we may combine several of the techniques listed below to indicate a likely causal connection. These methods may not be as rigorous as Mill's, but they can be convincing ways to present causes.

Chain of Causes   A chain-of-causes argument is a persuasive way to support an improbable or remote causal link. Such a chain divides the big leap between cause and effect into a series of little steps, making it easier for you and your audience to share assumptions about agency.

Here is an example of a chain-of-causes argument. A recent newspaper article announced that the rising human population in a county has led to a large increase in the bear population. That sounds unlikely; one would think that just the opposite would be the case. But here is the explanation. The increased population in the county led to the construction of new neighborhoods. The construction of new neighborhoods brought about the creation of new parks. The new parks brought people into areas that were formerly wilderness. People using these new facilities began leaving signs of their presence, especially garbage. Bears found the garbage and have been feeding heavily on it. The end result is that the bear population has increased because of the increased human population.

This chain of causes looks persuasive. But, like any chain, it is only as strong as its weakest link. It works by appealing to an audience's assumptions about what are plausible causal links.

Working either alone or with a group of your classmates, try to link these remote causes with their effects by describing some plausible intermediate steps between them. You may go on to use one of these chains of causes in a full causal argument.

- A childhood interest   →   a career choice
- A misunderstanding   →   a broken friendship
- A political crisis   →   a war
- Shutdown of a major industry   →   the decline of a town
- Clear-cutting a forest   →   increase of deer population

EXERCISE 7.9

Time Precedence   We are often warned not to assume that one thing causes another just because it came before the other in time. To do so is to commit what is called the *post hoc* fallacy; see p. 66. For instance, a baseball player wears green socks one day and gets four hits. Out of superstition, he may decide to wear green socks every day. But even though this action (green socks) preceded the good effect (four hits) that one time, it did not cause it. (We'll leave aside the question of whether his misplaced—but nonetheless effective—confidence in the socks helps his hitting streak continue!) Although there are many such examples of time precedence without causal connection, causes *do* precede or accompany their effects in time.

This notion of cause first and then effect is our most basic causal assumption. Lightning strikes the transformer and then the electricity goes out. We assume this order of cause followed by effect without bothering to point it out. But mentioning a time sequence does tend to support a causal relationship between two events when the agency is already plausible.

For example, if a rise in interest rates is announced and two days later the stock market falls, commentators may report on the sequence of the two events, assuming that the first caused the second. If we understand the way certain kinds of financial news affect the stock market, we can reasonably assume a causal connection.

EXERCISE 7.10

Identify the causal relationships, if any, between the sequential events in the following pairs.

- The secretary of the treasury predicts recession.
  The stock market declines.
- The president announces he will seek reelection.
  The stock market declines.
- A student takes a study skills course.
  The student's grades improve.
- A student changes roommates.
  The student's grades improve.
- Speed limits are eliminated.
  Automobile accidents decline.
- Speed limits are eliminated.
  Automobile accidents increase.
- Mortgage rates go up.
  The sale of houses declines.
- Mortgage rates go up.
  Unemployment rates go up.

Examples   As you learned in the chapter on definition arguments, generalizations can be supported by examples. Thus, any causal statement that stands for a number of instances can be supported by describing one or more of those instances, assuming, of course, that the instances cited are representative and typical.

Perhaps a social scientist wants to persuade us of the effectiveness of supervised group living for recent parolees. The argument may be more persuasive if it includes some detailed case histories of parolees who return to society successfully under these conditions. Of course, the case histories, no matter how inspiring, may have little to do with the overall statistics of success versus failure for this arrangement. To use this method legitimately, you must back up the examples with either overall statistics or an assessment of the relationship of the examples to the whole and, of course, appeal to a plausible agency.

EXERCISE 7.11

Look at the following common causal generalizations. Find two or more examples to support each.

- Absence makes the heart grow fonder.
- Lying hurts the liar.

- High expectations create success.
- Friendly parents increase the popularity of their children.
- Many hands make light work.

Analogy   Like the use of examples, analogy is a common technique in supporting a causal argument. You use analogy when you establish one cause-and-effect relationship by comparing it with another that is more familiar and acceptable to your audience. FDA scientists, for example, used mice to test the cancer-causing effects of saccharin. When they found that large doses of saccharin produced cancer in mice, they announced that saccharin is dangerous to humans. The persuasive power of their argument depended on the acceptability of the analogy between human and rodent physiology, diet, and metabolism. Most people find such analogies convincing for some kinds of arguments; many theories about human disease, learning, and behavior are based on animal experiments. An analogy will be less persuasive, however, if you fail to take note of any differences that can affect the outcome of the similar situation.

Analogies are often used in prediction arguments. We predict the outcome of one situation by comparing it with a similar one whose outcome is well known. Thus arguments about potential American involvement in wars often make comparisons with wars in the past, whether the Vietnam War, World War II, or the Gulf War in 1991.

Working either alone or with a group of your classmates, choose one of the following possible causal analogies and outline how you would make an extended argument for it. You may go on to use one of the analogies in a full causal argument.

- Ecologists know that even a small disturbance in a delicately balanced ecosystem can lead to its destruction. Think of a neighborhood as a kind of ecosystem and construct a causal argument based on that analogy.
- Historians have argued that many wars (like World War I and the Vietnam War) have resulted from diplomatic blunders and an overriding will to go to war. Could you argue that similar causes have produced a family crisis?
- The second law of thermodynamics, the law of entropy, states that all systems tend to disorder unless energy is invested to maintain their stability. Use this law analogically to argue for a similar tendency toward entropy that you have observed in your own life.
- A classic law of physics states that for every action there is an equal and opposite reaction. Could this law be used analogically to explain trends or phases in history, contrasting, say, the 1950s and the 1960s, or the 1980s and the 1990s?

EXERCISE 7.12

Other Types of Causal Arguments

Sign Arguments
Sometimes a straightforward claim about the existence of a situation can lead to claims about causality, as we argue backward from an effect to its cause.

Ancient rhetoricians called this kind of reasoning a "sign argument." A sign argument claims that if one thing exists, then whatever it is a sign of also exists. We are probably most familiar with sign arguments in the natural world. The presence of certain antibodies in the blood is a sign that a person has been exposed to a particular infection. A trashed bird feeder is a sign that another animal has been present. Indeed, sign arguments may be so convincing to certain audiences that they are taken as establishing facts rather than probabilities, but succeeding generations may undo the sign arguments that once seemed so strong. We no longer believe, for example, that the size of one's cranium is an invariable sign of the size of the cranium owner's intelligence.

In the social sciences and humanities, sign arguments support probabilities. The prosecution in a murder trial, for example, may characterize the accused as angry at the victim in order to support a claim that the murder was premeditated. The prosecution would then make a sign argument, detailing acts and words of the defendant that the jury would take as signs of anger: The defendant shouted at the victim in public, defaced the victim's car, tore up the victim's picture.

The relation between a sign and what it indicates determines how the claim will be supported. It makes a huge difference whether the sign is merely associated with the claim or whether it is causally related to it. These days we believe less in associated signs and more in connected causes. We understand the migration of birds, though a sign of changing seasons, as a consequence of shorter days and the effects of less light on the behavioral "clocks" of birds. Thus, much modern research has replaced mere associations with thoroughly explicated causal pathways. However, we still make sign arguments in areas where precise causal links cannot be traced. Economists, for instance, may not be certain about the precise causal connections between stock market cycles and political events, but they may consider the cycles as signs of events.

Predictions

We all want to know what will happen tomorrow. Fortunetellers and psychics try to appease our curiosity by sharing their divinations and hunches with us. But rational predictions can be supported only by careful argument. To support a prediction, we can forge a chain reaching from the past to the future, or we can use an analogy, showing how a situation in the past resembles one in the future, or we can identify a causal law that has worked in the past and that we are convinced will hold in the future.

A prediction talks about an event or process that is completely in the future—it will probably rain tomorrow; in the next decade, colleges will change the way they offer courses—or about one that exists now and extends into the future—distance education will become more widespread in the next few years; more jobs will switch to the service sector in the future. The only way to argue for something in the future is with a causal argument. If you predict rain tomorrow, it is because a front is approaching now. If you are convinced that college costs will rise in the next decade, it is because they have been rising steadily for a long time. If you think there will be a federal budget deficit in the future, it is because of causes, even causes of causes, that are operating now.

When you argue for a prediction, you try to convince your reader that all the causes needed to bring about an event are in place or will fall into place. In essence, you build a causal model, showing how different kinds of causes come together. You might bring together necessary and sufficient causes, or show how a remote cause constitutes the first link in an inevitable chain, or show how the conditions are ripe for a precipitating cause that is likely to occur, or show how the removal of a blocking cause will bring about some effect.

To argue for the modest prediction "The Nittany Lions football team might win a national championship this year," you might identify a set of causes sufficient to produce a championship: a strong defense, excellent receivers, accomplished running backs, a solid kicking game, and so on. You then show that the Lions have these attributes; if nothing else intervenes, like injury to the quarterback, you have made a good case for the success of the team.

You can also support predictions by analogy. The predicted event can be compared with a similar completed event in the past. The causes of the completed event, the model, should be familiar and acceptable to your readers. After describing the model, you point out the existence of similar causes in the present situation and claim that these similar causes will lead to similar effects. A historian who predicts that Russia will go to war with China may compare the present relationship between Russia and China with the past situation between Russia and Japan that led to war at the beginning of the twentieth century. For an audience of historians, this will be a familiar example. But as usual, the argument is only as good as the analogy, which sometimes must itself be supported.

Working either alone or with a group of your classmates, choose one of the following items and prepare a convincing prediction. You may go on to use this material in a full causal argument.

1. Identify some new product or technology and convince an audience of nonspecialists that it will have important effects.

2. Write a letter to a parent or adviser predicting what you will be doing five years from now, based on what you are doing now and the causal laws of your own personality.

3. Choose a current domestic problem or foreign affairs issue about which you either are or can become fairly knowledgeable. Predict its outcome in a letter to the editor of a newspaper.

4. Predict the state of your favorite sport in five years. Do you think a new sport will catch on or an old one change significantly? Address your prediction to fellow sports enthusiasts.

5. Decide where you think popular music is headed or what artists or types of music will go out of style or be revived. Imagine your prediction as an article in *Rolling Stone*.

EXERCISE 7.13

Cause and Effect for the Eye

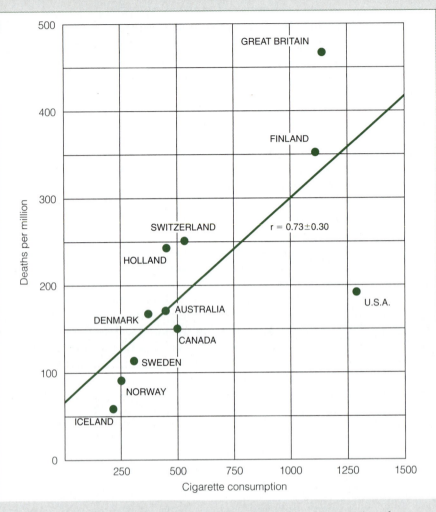

Crude Male Death Rate for Lung Cancer in 1950 and Per Capita Consumption of Cigarettes in 1930 in Various Countries

Writers who are searching or arguing for cause and effect relationships have demonstrated the visual impact of graphs again and again. Graphs can show trends over time in a visual format, or they help determine whether and how two measurable or countable factors are related. When researchers use a graph to test or express a causal relationship, they locate one quantity on the horizontal or "x" axis and the other on the vertical or "y" axis. The researchers then match one with the other: given this value of x, what is the corresponding value of y? Does the value of y increase as the value of x does? Does it decrease? Either of these results could suggest, though by no means prove, that one of these factors is influencing the other. If the y value remains unchanged as x changes, that could suggest the absence of a causal connection.

The two graphs shown here demonstrate the dramatic causal connection between smoking and lung cancer in two ways. The first graph was published in 1964 as part of the

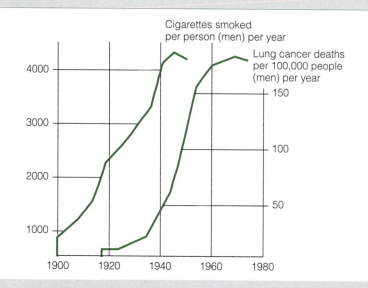

Lag Time Chemicals and radiation that are capable of triggering the development of cancer are called "carcinogens." Carcinogens act through a multistep process that initiates a series of genetic alterations ("mutations") and stimulates cells to proliferate. A prolonged period of time is usually required for these multiple steps. There can be a delay of several decades between exposure to a carcinogen and the onset of cancer. For example, a group of young people exposed to carcinogens from smoking cigarettes generally do not develop cancer for 20 to 30 years. This period between exposure and onset of disease is the lag time.

landmark study from the Surgeon General's Office that first made Americans aware of the link between smoking and cancer. The graph was compiled from statistics published in the 1950s. Two kinds of data are involved. The horizontal axis measures the "per capita consumption of cigarettes in 1930." In other words, the scale along the bottom measures how many cigarettes were smoked in a year "per capita," that is per person in a country. Since there are 365 days in a year, a number like 250 suggests an average of less than one cigarette per day per person; a figure like 1250 indicates roughly three cigarettes per day per person (averaging non-smokers, heavy smokers, etc.). There is certainly no way that anyone could actually measure how many cigarettes all the citizens in a country smoked in a given year. So where do these figures come from? They represent averages that are compiled from cigarette sales and population statistics, and they have to be interpreted accordingly. They do not show that all Swedes smoked less than one cigarette per day in 1930 while all Finns smoked almost three. But they do show that there was generally less cigarette consumption in Sweden than in Finland in 1930, and, we would assume, in the years before and after.

On the vertical axis, the graph records the number of deaths of men from lung cancer per million men in 1950. Iceland has the lowest death rate and Great Britain the highest. At the same time, Iceland had the lowest cigarette consumption per capita in 1930, and Great Britain almost the highest. The results from different countries are plotted with asterisks, and the black line rising from left to right across the graph represents the ideal relationship of the two variables. It is linear. As the x value steadily increases, so does the y value; the more smoking, the more deaths from cancer. The fact that only one of the dots is directly on this line can be explained by the many differences that affect the actual figures. The

–Continued

United States seems to be an interesting exception. It had the highest cigarette consumption in 1930 but not the highest death rate by 1950, perhaps because of better health care. Eventually the death rate caught up.

The second visual, published by the National Cancer Institute, shows two graphs in one. The horizontal axis records the passage of time from 1900 to 1980 in 20-year intervals. The left-hand vertical axis measures the increase in "cigarettes smoked per person per year" and the right-hand vertical axis counts the number of lung cancer deaths per 100,000 people. (A critical piece of information missing from the graph is whether it applies only to the United States or to other countries as well. Since the source is the National Cancer Institutes, we can assume this is U.S. data.) Both graphs together show similar steep increases from 1900 to about 1950 in cigarette consumption and from 1920 to about 1970 in the number of deaths from lung cancer per 100,000 people. (Deaths from mouth, pharyngeal, and esophageal cancer and from emphysema—also caused by smoking—are not included.) The point of combining these graphs, as the legend explains, is to show the 20-year time lag between the cause and its devastating effects. Lung damage from smoking, and the consequent dangers of lung disease, depend on the amount and the length of time that a person smokes. These graphs give the "big picture," the overall public health problem created by a social habit. Data on women are missing from these graphs; women did not smoke in large numbers until after World War II, but recent statistics also show a dramatic increase in lung cancer deaths among women as the 20-year time lag has caught up with them.

The tactic of causal argument used in these graphs is the method of cause and effect varying together or concomitant variation (see pp. 201–203). As one trend changes, so does the other, and a graph is an excellent visual means of summarizing trends and finding patterns in large sets of data. A single graph can suggest a causal relationship when a quantity representing the potential cause (the independent variable) is placed on one axis and another representing the potential effect (the dependent variable) is placed on the other and the result is a clear pattern of increase or decrease. Multiple graphs can suggest a causal relationship if they show similar patterns of fluctuation against the same value on the x axis, usually time. If, for example, the pattern of fluctuations in the U.S. stock market over a year exactly mirrors the pattern in the world stock market index over the same year (as it usually does), that can suggest that the U.S. market drives the international market, or that the international market drives U.S. commodities trading, or that both are responding in the exactly the same way to some other cause.

Critics of this type of causal reasoning, and of visuals like these, have often pointed out that such graphs may show similarities in patterns, or correlations, but they do not necessarily show causal dependence. Other social trends, like the number of telephones in households for example, might show a similar pattern of increase from 1900 to 1950 but not be causally related to lung cancer. This useful caution suggests, once again, the importance of agency in causal reasoning. There is no point in plotting data on a graph unless the investigator is working with plausible connections to begin with.

Writing Your Own Causal Argument

ANSWERING THE QUESTION → "How Did It Get That Way?"

Causal arguments can be part of more complex arguments that evaluate or propose action, or they can be arguments that exist on their own. You may have developed ideas for a causal argument from one of the exercises in this chapter, or you may decide to develop a topic suggested by one of the writing ideas on p. 216. Whether your causal argument will stand alone or be incorporated into another argument, the following steps will help you construct a convincing causal case, shaped for your audience and purpose.

1. Define the Subject Whose Causes You Are Investigating

Are you investigating the causes of a one-time occurrence? A pattern of events? A trend? Is your subject one in which human action is involved?

2. Describe the Purpose of Your Causal Argument

Are you trying to give a full explanation of all the various conditions and factors, actions, and intentions that brought something about? Are you making a prediction? If so, you will want to create as complete a picture as possible of the interaction among many kinds of causes. Your goal may or may not include nominating a single important cause.

Are you investigating causes because you want to make something happen or stop it from happening? If so, you will want to direct your readers' attention to the cause or causes that can be acted on, not causes that are beyond anyone's control.

3. Try Out the Frames for Causal Analysis

After thinking through, and writing down, your answers to items 1 and 2, see if one of the common causal narratives described on pages 184–95 fits the details. Here is a checklist that repeats the possibilities in the form of questions. Try out each of these, and write down your conclusions when you have found a possibility that fits.

- Does it make sense to talk about background conditions and a precipitating cause?
- Can you establish linked events, some remote and some near the effect?
- Can you talk about a complex of necessary causes and a sufficient cause without which the event would not occur?
- Is human responsibility significantly involved, both for acts committed and omitted, whether intentionally or not?
- Is the absence of something the reason for an effect?
- Could you have a case of reciprocal causality?
- Will chance or accident be an important part of your account?

—Continued

The possibility of using these causal narratives may also direct your search for new information that could fill in missing details and complete a satisfying causal account.

4. Consider whether the Causes You Want to Argue For Fit Your Audience's Beliefs about Agency

Is your causal story going to work with or against your audience's beliefs about what can cause what? If you cannot rely on a plausible, established agency, you will have to use other tactics to convince your readers that the causes you are nominating really could bring about the effect you are claiming.

5. Try Out Tactics on Pages 199–209 That Might Help You Link a Cause and Effect

Sometimes cause and effect links can be suggested or established by the evidence, even when no one understands how the link would work. Using the material you have written to answer previous questions, look over this checklist of your options for presenting evidence in a way that suggests a link. These methods can also help establish agency if it is missing or strengthen it even when an agency can be assumed. Write down your observations as you go through the checklist.

Mill's Methods:

- *Common factor:* Are there individual cases that have something in common?
- *Single difference:* Do you have at least two cases, one where the effect occurs and one where it doesn't? What is not the same in the two cases?
- *Varying together:* Are the two things that might be linked as cause and effect varying or changing together? That is, as one increases or decreases does the other increase or decrease in a similar way?
- *Eliminating possibilities:* Can you name all the possible causes that could be reasonably considered and then rule out all, most, or some, leaving a more plausible case for those left?

Other Ways to Support a Causal Argument:

- *Chain of causes:* Are the cause and effect remote from each other? Would it make sense to come up with incremental steps to connect the cause and effect?
- *Time precedence:* Is agency already plausible? Would pointing out that your cause preceded the effect help to support your argument?
- *Examples:* Is your cause-and-effect argument general? Would specific, typical examples add support?
- *Analogy:* Is the cause-and-effect relationship you want to support similar to another case?

6. Choose from the Ideas You Generated under Items 3 and 5 to Construct the Most Plausible Account of Causes Possible

In many cases you will be able to combine techniques from these two lists. For example, eliminating possible causes requires starting with as complete a list of necessary and sufficient causes as possible; finding a single difference goes well with looking at background conditions and the presence or absence of a precipitating cause.

7. Write the Claim That Best Represents Your Causal Account and That Also Fits Your Purpose

Your claim should mention the cause or causes you are nominating and/or suggest the significance of the cause. A complete causal explanation will name several causes; each can then be taken up in turn in separate sections of your paper. Your claim could also specify the most important cause. You can use the claim that you write as a tentative thesis for your paper. If you like, you may sketch out an informal outline of your paper before beginning to draft.

DRAFTING YOUR CAUSAL ARGUMENT

As you write up your causal argument, pay special attention to the claim and the argument that supports it. Be careful not to allow your claim to overstate the case that you actually make. If you are calling for change, make sure that the argument involves a cause that can actually be changed. Consider which parts of your claim can plausibly be assumed and which will need support. Remember, as always, to keep your audience and purpose in mind as you shape your argument.

REVIEWING AND REVISING YOUR CAUSAL ARGUMENT

Once you have completed a draft of your causal argument, put it aside for a while. Then read through it carefully, looking for weaknesses in your argument. The following section will help you analyze your causal argument and solicit helpful comments from your classmates.

Questions to Ask about a Causal Argument

Whether you are reviewing your own causal argument or one written by a classmate, ask yourself the following questions and write down the answers. Make your answers as detailed as possible, pointing out specific places in the draft that are problematic. (Skip any questions that do not apply to the causal argument you are evaluating.) When you have done your own analysis and gone over any comments from your classmates, use these comments and suggestions to revise and refine your causal argument and make it stronger.

1. *Has the causal argument maintained a clear, consistent audience and purpose?* Who is the audience, and what is the purpose of the argument? Does the argument do anything that might confuse or alienate this audience, such as assuming familiarity with a subject that its audience is not acquainted with or spending too much time explaining a common occurrence? Does the purpose seem to vary through the course of the argument? If so, how should the purpose be made more consistent?

2. *Will the audience agree that the effect exists?* If an event, a condition, or a trend is the subject of the investigation, will the audience agree that such an effect is real?

3. *Does the arguer provide an appropriate narrative framework or causal model?* Which framework or model is the arguer using? Does it work with the subject and purpose of the investigation? Why or why not? If not, what other choice might be better?

—Continued

4. *Will the audience agree that agency is believable—that there is a connection between the cause and the effect?* Does the arguer assume agency? If so, is that assumption appropriate—does the assumption of agency agree with natural or physical laws or with a typical view of human nature? If not, is the claim for agency plausibly supported? If not, how could it be?

5. *Is there enough support to convince the audience that a particular cause operated as claimed?* How is the argument supported? Do you see any areas where the support is weak? How might it be strengthened? Does any piece of supporting evidence fail to convince you? What can be done to make it more convincing? Are any pieces of evidence missing?

6. *Are there any obvious problems with the argument that would make it easy to refute?* Does the arguer ignore something obvious? Is there a problem in the argument's logic? If so, what can be done to solve the problem?

7. *Is the argument clear and effectively organized?* Does the argument move in a logical manner from beginning to end? What might be done differently to make the causal argument more effective?

WRITING SUGGESTIONS

A claim about how something happened can be made in any context. Below are some broad suggestions of areas where you can determine an effect and draw conclusions about causes.

1. Environmental/health sciences: Choose an environmental or a health issue or trend and explore its cause(s). (Examples: "Why is the Amazon rain forest disappearing?" "What steps led to the eradication of smallpox?")

2. Social sciences: Explore the cause(s) of a behavior or a social or cultural trend. (Examples: "How can the number of mistaken eyewitness identifications be reduced?" "Why do two-year-olds love Elmo?")

3. Business: Examine the reasons behind the success or failure of a specific business or a type of business or a trend in marketing. (Examples: "Why did dot-com companies first reap huge profits in the 1990s and then go out of business?" "What factors persuade the recipient of a telemarketing call to spend money on the caller's products or services?")

4. History/Political science: Explore the cause(s) of a historical or political event or trend. (Examples: "What are the roots of radical Islamic terrorism?" "What influences contributed to the growth of the movement opposing U.S. involvement in Vietnam?")

5. Arts: Examine a film, theater, or literary character's motivation for action or inaction; a reason for an artistic trend; or the cause(s) of the popularity of an artist, artwork, or art form (whether in film, theater, literature, or music). (Examples: "Why does Othello believe Iago?" "What factors contributed to the popularity of [name a recent box office success of your own choosing]?")

Spandex Nation

HINDA GONCHOR

Hinda Gonchor is a freelance writer. This article was first published in the *New York Times* in June 1999.

Despite knowing about the dangers of obesity and the introduction of a new diet drug every few months, the average American is still overweight. Why are we so fat when we know we should lose weight?

The answer is simple: stretch clothing. With the addition of Lycra or Spandex to fabrics—3 percent, 10 percent, 44 percent, 100 percent—everything always fits. Anyone who so desires—or sees no other way out of a widening problem—need never again button a button, buckle a belt or zip up a zipper.

I haven't worn a garment in 10 years that I couldn't pull up, over or around me without any hardware whatsoever. May I brag? I have put on 10 pounds in the last 10 months and can still get into all of my clothing. No back-of-the-closet wardrobes for me. No Levi's given away to leaner sisters. All of my clothing stretches to accommodate my body of the day.

And I'm not someone who ignores fashion. On casual days, I wear black leggings with a pullover top. For more formal occasions, I throw on a nicer pair of leggings with a little lace at the ankle and a pullover top, maybe with sequins or rhinestones. As for office attire, let me just thank Don Johnson for introducing the T-shirt worn under a suit. That's much more comfortable than a button-bursting blouse.

Yes, of course stretch clothing bulges where there is fat. Sometimes it bulges in 5 front or back or all over the place. But who cares? It still fits.

So listen up, Centers for Disease Control and Prevention, American Heart Association and any other organization that is working to get us fit and trim. Americans are getting fatter because we are missing the telltale signs: the popped button at the board meeting, the snagged zipper in the ladies' room, the burst seam in the seat of the pants. If doctors want us to get thin, they'll have to prescribe a wardrobe that doesn't stretch.

FOR YOU TO ANALYZE

1. Gonchor makes a claim about the reason the average American is overweight. What kind of narrative framework or causal model does she use for her argument? How does she support her claim?

2. Gonchor argues that stretch fabric is responsible for a trend. Do you find her argument persuasive? Why or why not? What tactics could be used to refute Gonchor's claim?

3. The last sentence of Gonchor's argument reads, "If doctors want us to get thin, they'll have to prescribe a wardrobe that doesn't stretch." How seriously do you think Gonchor intends readers to take this conclusion? How does it fit with the tone of her argument? What reasons do you think she might have for adopting this tone?

FOR YOU TO WRITE

1. Gonchor's argument purports to explain the reason that Americans are getting fatter in spite of their knowledge that weight gain is unhealthy. Write a causal argument explaining the reason(s) for people's inability or unwillingness to take action to prevent another avoidable health problem.

2. As an example of the trend toward stretch clothing, Gonchor cites a fairly recent fashion development—"the T-shirt worn under a suit"—and credits the actor Don Johnson with popularizing this look. Choose another past or present fashion trend popularized by a well-known person or group of people and construct a causal argument explaining the causes of the trend's success.

3. Gonchor links a type of clothing and a type of behavior. Write an argument making a plausible causal link between another type of clothing and a pattern of behavior.

FOR YOU TO DISCOVER ONLINE

Search the Internet for information about the sales of clothing made from stretch fabrics (you might begin with a keyword search in Google or another search engine for "textiles" and "sales figures," or you might start at a web site such as www.lycra.com). Then look for information on the web about rates of obesity in the United States (you can start with the National Center for Health Statistics site, www.cdc.gov/nchs). Do you find a correlation between obesity rates and sales of stretch clothing? If so, do you think that this correlation supports Gonchor's argument? Why or why not?

Study: Beer Taxes Reduce STD Rates

DAVID PITT

David Pitt writes for the Associated Press. This article first appeared in the *Washington Post* in April 2000.

Cheap beer is a leading contributor to the spread of sexually transmitted diseases, according to a government report that says raising the tax on a six-pack by 20 cents could reduce gonorrhea by up to 9 percent.

The Centers for Disease Control and Prevention study, released Thursday, compared changes in gonorrhea rates to changes in alcohol policy in all states from 1981 to 1995. In years following beer tax increases, gonorrhea rates usually dropped among young people. The same happened when the drinking age went up—as it did in many states during the 1980s.

"Alcohol has been linked to risky sexual behavior among youth. It influences a person's judgment and they are more likely to have sex without a condom, with multiple partners or with high-risk partners," said Harrell Chesson, a health economist with the CDC.

Beer industry lobbyists, however, said recent statistics show young people are already drinking more responsibly, thanks in part to efforts by brewers.

"Excise taxes have little or nothing to do with alcohol abuse in society," said Lori   5
Levy of The Beer Institute in Washington. "I think that our members understand the

importance of educating young people about how to make responsible choices once they're old enough and they put a lot of money and effort into those programs."

Gonorrhea, one of the most common venereal diseases, was examined in the CDC study because long-term statistics are available and the disease is more evenly spread among states.

The CDC analyzed the drops in gonorrhea rates following different tax increases and came up with the estimate that a 20-cent increase per six-pack would lead to a 9 percent drop in gonorrhea rates.

Chesson cited the example of a 16-cent per gallon—about 9 cents per six-pack – tax increase in California in 1991. Gonorrhea rates in the 15 to 19 age group dropped about 30 percent the following year. Drops in other states were not as dramatic.

During the study, various states raised beer taxes 36 times. Gonorrhea rates among the 15 to 19 age group dropped in 24 of those instances, and rates among those 20 to 24 dropped 26 times.

In both age groups, men seem to be more affected than women by higher beer 10 prices.

Most minimum legal drinking age increases were also followed by a decrease in the gonorrhea rate, especially in the 15 to 19 age group.

"This study suggests these strategies could have a significant impact in reducing sexually transmitted diseases among young people," said Dr. Kathleen Irwin, chief of health services research and evaluation for the CDC's division of sexually transmitted diseases.

About 3 million teen-agers are infected with sexually transmitted diseases each year, Chesson said. Gonorrhea usually can be treated with antibiotics, although some drug-resistant strains have developed.

FOR YOU TO ANALYZE

1. According to Pitt's article, a study by the Centers for Disease Control and Prevention argues that two trends—the price of beer and the rate of sexually transmitted diseases—are causally connected. What chain of causes does the article cite as evidence? How does this lead to a prediction of future events?

2. Do you find the evidence presented in the CDC study convincing? If so, why? If not, could you argue that the supposed cause-and-effect trends are unrelated or that they are both the effects of a different cause?

3. In his fourth and fifth paragraphs, Pitt includes rebuttal information from beer industry lobbyists. Why do you think this information is included? How does it affect your perception of the CDC study's conclusions?

4. An article written for the Associated Press might be expected to reach a general audience. Which specific audiences might be most likely to find the CDC's cause-and-effect claims persuasive? Which audiences would you expect to be unpersuaded by the study? Why?

FOR YOU TO WRITE

1. In Pitt's article, Harrell Chesson of the CDC says, "Alcohol has been linked to risky sexual behavior among youth." Think of another factor that can cause either a portion of the population or a specific person to take unnecessary risks, and then write an argument proposing a way to block that influence.

2. The government study cited in Pitt's article recommends raising taxes on beer. Examine the effects of another legislative change, such as lowering or raising speed limits, lowering the voting age, or increasing penalties for drunk driving, on the problem it was intended to solve.

3. The CDC study proposes a chain-of-causes argument leading from inexpensive beer to increased rates of gonorrhea. Choose a recent societal trend—in entertainment, politics, or any other area that interests you—and argue for a chain linking it to an unexpected or remote cause or effect.

FOR YOU TO DISCOVER ONLINE

Visit the web pages of the Beer Institute (www.beerinstitute.org) and examine their policy briefs for government officials. Then go to the site for the Centers for Disease Control and Prevention (www.cdc.gov) and look at the material on alcohol abuse and sexually transmitted diseases there. Which site do you think contains more convincing material? What makes it convincing?

Expert Report Disputes U.S. on Trade Center Collapse

JAMES GLANZ AND ERIC LIPTON

James Glanz received his Ph.D. in astrophysical sciences from Princeton University. He joined the *New York Times* in 1999 as a science reporter. Eric Lipton is a Pulitzer Prize–winning reporter who covered City Hall for the *New York Times* until September 11, 2001, when he was assigned to cover the attacks and their aftermath full-time. Articles that Glanz and Lipton wrote on the World Trade Center collapse and cleanup were chosen as finalists for the Pulitzer Prize in explanatory journalism in 2002. This article appeared in the *Times* on October 22, 2002.

Experts commissioned in a $4 billion insurance case involving the World Trade Center have come to conclusions that fundamentally contradict a federal investigation into what caused the twin towers to collapse. The new analysis, according to several experts who have examined the confidential findings, holds that the unusual engineering design of the towers did not contribute to the collapses, and that the damage caused by the planes and the resulting fires made the failures of the buildings inevitable.

The analysis, paid for by Larry A. Silverstein, who held the lease on the trade center, finds that there was no structural flaw or weak link that could have led to the collapse. The earlier inquiry concluded that unconventional lightweight floor supports in the twin towers probably softened and then failed, leading to a progressive collapse of the entire buildings. In light of that initial government assessment, some engineers suggested that other buildings might have stood longer or not fallen at all after a similar attack.

Produced by some of the most prominent engineering firms in the country, the analysis is the first to suggest a detailed, step-by-step, alternative explanation for the destruction of the towers. It concludes that the damage to the exterior and interior support columns caused by the hijacked planes, and the devastating fires that erupted inside, rendered vertical steel support columns unable to hold up the weight of the buildings above the floors of impact.

If this view prevails, it could affect judgments in the lawsuits that have been filed against Mr. Silverstein and his landlord, the Port Authority of New York and New Jersey, which built the towers three decades ago. It could also reshape history's reading of whether the construction of the skyscrapers themselves, regarded as revolutionary at the time, should share the blame for the extent of the casualties on Sept. 11.

The new work has impressed some engineers who have learned of it, and elicited 5 skepticism from others, who question how impartial an analysis financed by Mr. Silverstein could be. Some of those skeptical engineers suggest the work amounted to little more than a highly sophisticated exercise in producing just the kind of testimony Mr. Silverstein desired.

A lawyer for Mr. Silverstein, Marc Wolinsky, declined to release any of the documents pending a decision by the judge in the insurance case on whether they should remain confidential. "We will have no comment until the court indicates its preference," Mr. Wolinsky said.

The analysis of the collapse is part of thousands of pages of documentation and expert analysis on the trade center attacks that have been produced for the insurance suit. It was undertaken for Mr. Silverstein by Weidlinger Associates, a Manhattan engineering firm that used tools like a computer program called Flex that it developed with the Pentagon to study the blast effects of bombs.

With Flex, engineers recreated the horrific events of Sept. 11, 2001, on a computer, ramming virtual planes into virtual towers. The Flex program let engineers calculate the number of columns instantly severed deep in the interior of each tower.

From then on, the engineers used much more approximate information, largely from photographs and videos, about the spread of fire throughout the towers. As the fires spread, the interior temperatures rose. The hotter the steel-columns, the softer and less able to support the weight of the towers they became, the Weidlinger report says.

A structure at the top of each tower called a hat truss formed a sturdy connection 10 between the core and the exterior columns. At first, the analysis says, the truss let damaged columns transfer loads to undamaged ones, and the towers stood even though seriously damaged.

But as the heat increased, the columns weakened and became less able to hold up the top of the towers, even with all floors intact. The core of the north tower, hit dead center by the first plane, held out the longest, because the undamaged columns on its outer edges acted like the four legs of a table. But the south tower, struck more asymmetrically, tilted and fell first, like a table with two weakened legs on one side.

There was no need to invoke a failure of the floors to produce a collapse, the study performed for Mr. Silverstein says. The conclusion, this work suggests, is that a collapse was unavoidable, no matter how well constructed the floors were. To support that argument, the study asserts that an analysis of videos of Sept. 11 shows patterns of smoke emerging from trade center windows that are consistent with intact floors rather than fallen ones.

Some engineers who have read the analysis are questioning those conclusions. John Osteraas, director of civil engineering practice at Exponent Failure Analysis in Menlo Park, Calif., and a consultant for the insurance companies, said the computer analysis assumed that the floors stayed intact until the collapse.

Many engineers have pointed out that the floors not only held up acres of office space, but also gave crucial lateral support for the columns—a sideways brace, almost like a flying buttress on a Gothic cathedral—that prevented them from buckling. The federal study concludes that the performance of the floor trusses during the fire was "likely critical to the building collapse," but it conceded that the finding was preliminary.

ADDING IT UP

Contradictory Theories On Towers' Collapse

Some of the most prominent engineering firms in the country provided an analysis of the twin towers' collapse for an insurance case. They came to a conclusion that contradicts a federal report.

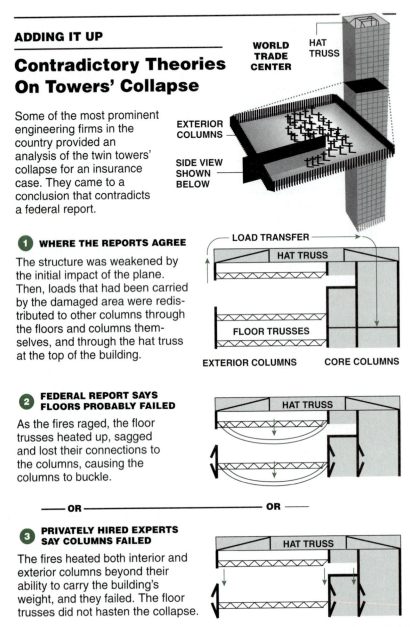

WORLD TRADE CENTER

HAT TRUSS

EXTERIOR COLUMNS

SIDE VIEW SHOWN BELOW

1 WHERE THE REPORTS AGREE

The structure was weakened by the initial impact of the plane. Then, loads that had been carried by the damaged area were redistributed to other columns through the floors and columns themselves, and through the hat truss at the top of the building.

LOAD TRANSFER

HAT TRUSS

FLOOR TRUSSES

EXTERIOR COLUMNS   CORE COLUMNS

2 FEDERAL REPORT SAYS FLOORS PROBABLY FAILED

As the fires raged, the floor trusses heated up, sagged and lost their connections to the columns, causing the columns to buckle.

HAT TRUSS

——— OR ——————————————— OR ———

3 PRIVATELY HIRED EXPERTS SAY COLUMNS FAILED

The fires heated both interior and exterior columns beyond their ability to carry the building's weight, and they failed. The floor trusses did not hasten the collapse.

HAT TRUSS

The New York Times

Because the Silverstein analysis did not allow for the possibility that the floors could 15 give way, the assertion that the floor design played no role was in some ways foreordained, Dr. Osteraas said.

"The mechanism they predict is really the only one they can predict, given the model they use," said Dr. Osteraas, who has seen the study in an exchange of documents between the two sides. "You can't legitimately claim to have looked at all possible collapse scenarios without considering the floors."

If Mr. Silverstein can successfully argue that each tower fell as a result of a chain of events initiated by the impact of a plane, he may have a better chance at sustaining an argument he is waging in Federal District Court in Manhattan: that he is entitled to compensation for two attacks, not just one. If it was one, the maximum coverage for the loss is $3.5 billion; if it is two, that doubles.

Lawyers representing the insurance companies have argued that the insurance coverage question will most likely be decided on the basis of a narrow legal matter related to just what kind of insurance form was used when Mr. Silverstein applied for his coverage. But if Mr. Silverstein prevails in the initial rounds of the case, the testimony by his experts on what caused the collapse could become crucial in determining how much money he will have to rebuild the trade center complex.

Perhaps even more important, the Port Authority has been sued by about 950 families whose loved ones died or were severely injured in the attack. The suits cite safety failures and inadequate evacuation procedures. These liability suits, assuming they go to trial, will almost certainly bring an examination of the design of the towers and a need to decide whether the structural composition of the floors explains why and how the towers fell.

One person who has read the report prepared for Mr. Silverstein made it clear how   20
Mr. Silverstein intends to use the findings.

"The terrorists were the murderers here, not the buildings," the person said.

But two lawyers representing the families said it was too early to reach such a conclusion.

"There isn't any question that the triggering event was the action of the terrorists," said Marc S. Moller, a lawyer. But he added, "Could some of the lives lost have been saved had the design of the building been different?"

FOR YOU TO ANALYZE

1. Although both the federal government and Larry Silverstein, the owner of the World Trade Center, agree that the precipitating event that led to the collapse of the buildings was the impact of two hijacked airplanes, both sides differ radically on the chain of events that began with those impacts and concluded with the collapses. In your own words, reproduce the causal chain of events for both arguments.

2. What are the motives, or exigencies, for Mr. Silverstein's causal argument?

3. What part of Mr. Silverstein's argument has been called into question, and on what basis?

4. Both arguments about the cause of the World Trade Center collapse touch on responsibility—not the obvious assignment of blame to the terrorists, but the responsibility of those who designed and built the Twin Towers. To what, or whom, does each argument assign causal agency? What are the implications of that assignment?

5. Study the accompanying graphic, "Adding it Up." How well does the graphic summarize the two arguments? Is this graphic summary structured differently than the main article?

FOR YOU TO WRITE

1. Describe an immediate effect that the terrorist attacks of September 11, 2001, had on your own life. Your narrative should establish a clear causal relationship using the guidelines in this chapter.

2. Although we live in volatile and unpredictable times, we can use causal analysis to arrive at rational predictions for specific futures (our own, or that of our families and communities). Using analogy, build a causal model that demonstrates the way you or someone you know faced specific local disaster (manmade or natural—the loss of a job, a flood or fire, a devastating illness) that will allow you or that person to overcome future difficulties.

3. One motive for causal analysis is to solve a problem—to establish what went wrong in a specific scenario and determine ways to prevent a repeat of that problem in the future. The information from both arguments in Glanz and Lipton's article will be used to build stronger, safer skyscrapers. Identify a problem on your own campus or in your community. Describe the problem and with the purpose of proposing a solution identify the causes for it that can be acted upon by your readers.

TAKING IT ONLINE

The rebuilding of lower Manhattan most immediately involves the concerns of local residents, businesses, and the families of victims. The Port Authority of New York and New Jersey (which owns the building site) has solicited input on how best to rebuild and renew from many different groups, as well as from politicians, architects, artists, and others. For many perspectives on the site's future, visit the following web sites:

- www.renewnyc.com/plan/concepts.htm (This is the site of the Lower Manhattan Development Corporation, which primarily represents local businesses and economic concerns.)

- www.imaginenewyork.org (This site, organized by the Municipal Art Society, has collected and organized individual comments, proposals, and visions for rebuilding.)

- www.nytimes.com/packages/html/magazine/20020908_911_PLAN/ index.html (This multimedia site features proposals from world-renowned architects for rebuilding lower Manhattan while memorializing the tragedy as well as the winning plan.)

Successful Inner-City Schools Share Common Traits

SAMUEL CASEY CARTER

Samuel Casey Carter works for the Heritage Foundation in Washington, D.C. This article first appeared in the *Chicago Tribune* in June 1999.

Too many educators would have us believe poor children can't learn. Or can't learn well. Or can't learn except at great price. But across the nation dozens of principals of low-income schools are proving that poverty is no excuse for failure.

Take P.S. 161 in Brooklyn. Nearly 100 percent of the children come from low-income families, yet this year's 6th-grade class had the second-highest reading scores in all of New York state. "It's a lot of garbage that poor kids can't succeed," says Principal Irwin Kurz, who came to the school 13 years ago when students were testing in the bottom 25 percent among schools in Brooklyn's District 17. Today they score in the 71st percentile in reading and the 78th percentile in math. Equally dramatic success stories can be found in Chicago, Houston, Detroit and other cities.

I recently interviewed more than 100 principals of high-performing, high-poverty schools like P.S. 161, looking to identify those practices that make a school a center of academic excellence. I wanted to find schools where at least 75 percent of the students come from low-income families but score in the top third on national exams. Typically, schools with this many low-income students score in the bottom third.

The children in the high-achieving schools I found come from typical inner-city neighborhoods. They are predominantly African-American or Hispanic. Many of them even live near failing public schools that draw from the same local population. So what explains their success?

My visits to these schools uncovered seven common traits: 5

- Principals must be free. Effective principals decide how to spend their money, whom to hire and what to teach. They are either given their freedom or take it for themselves. Principals whose schools develop a reputation for academic achievement are usually left alone. But to get there, great principals are often mavericks who buck the system or low-fliers who get the job done quietly.

- Principals use measurable goals to foster achievement. High expectations are one thing—a relentless pursuit of excellence is another. High-performing schools focus on tangible goals. Whether it's calculus by 12th grade, a fluently bilingual school, literacy at the earliest age, or all students working above grade level, great schools set specific benchmarks the whole school must reach.

- Master teachers bring out the best in a faculty. Improving the quality of instruction is the only way to improve overall student achievement, and teacher quality—not seniority—is the key. Effective principals scour the country for the best teachers and design their curriculum around the unique strengths and expertise of their staff. Good principals turn their schools into schools for teachers.

- Rigorous and regular testing improves student performance. Testing is the diagnostic tool that best enforces a school's goals. Regular tests at all levels and in all areas ensure that the prescribed curriculum is being communicated in every classroom. Mock tests are usually administered three or four times a year to prepare for national exams.

- Achievement is the key to discipline. A "command-and-control" approach to discipline is limited to the number of security guards you can hire. When self-discipline and order come from within, every person is part of the solution. Schools must teach by example that self-control, self-reliance and self-esteem—all anchored in achievement—are the means to success. Success, in turn, inspires confidence, order and discipline in students.

- Principals work with parents to make the home a center of learning. A lack of parental involvement is often the first excuse for poor performance. Effective principals overcome this by extending the mission of the school into the home. They establish contracts with parents to support their child's efforts to learn. These principals harness a parent's support and motivation by teaching parents to read to their children and check homework.
- Effort creates ability. Good principals demand that their students work hard. Long days, extended years, after-school programs, weekend programs and summer school are all features of outstanding schools. Effective principals eliminate social promotion. Students must fulfill specific course requirements to advance. No student is promoted without a clear demonstration of mastery.

Outstanding principals know that all children can excel academically regardless of race, income level or family background. Studying their success should be the highest priority of educators in a country where more than half of all low-income 4th-graders cannot even read. Nothing I've described is beyond the reach of any school in America. But if we are to see more such schools, we need to stop making excuses for failure.

FOR YOU TO ANALYZE

1. Carter seeks "to identify those practices that make a school a center of academic excellence." Which of Mill's methods does he apply? What are the results of his application of Mill's method? Do you find these results persuasive? Why or why not?

2. What reasons does Carter provide to explain why successful schools' practices are not more widespread? Why do you think he includes this information? Is the inclusion of this material effective? Why or why not?

3. Carter lists seven traits of schools that he believes lead to good student performance, no matter what the students' backgrounds. Consider each of these traits. Which convince you most? Which convince you least? Why?

4. Carter says that "[D]ozens of principals of low-income schools are proving that poverty is no excuse for failure." Do you agree with Carter's assessment of the effect of principals on a school? Why or why not?

FOR YOU TO WRITE

1. Carter seeks out schools that are exceptions to what he sees as a popular belief that "poor children can't learn." Think of a generalization that you believe to be false about a group—a gender, a racial or ethnic group, a class, a religious community, an age group, or a more specific subset of any of these—and come up with examples that are exceptions to the generalization. What do the examples have in common? Can you argue that your specific examples are proof that the generalization is wrong?

2. When Carter argues, "Improving the quality of instruction is the only way to improve overall student achievement," he hints at widespread dissatisfaction with teachers. Is there a profession—policing, politics, sales, teaching, etc.— that you think is hampered by a high percentage of members who do their jobs

poorly? What causes the problems that you see, and how might these problems be prevented?

3. Carter went to "high-performing, high-poverty schools" to find out what made these institutions successful in spite of apparent obstacles. Look at an institution that is familiar to you—a school, a business, a hospital, a government institution, etc.—that performs better or worse than you would expect it to. Explain the apparent obstacles facing this institution or its apparent advantages, and use one of Mill's methods to discover the causes of its unexpected performance.

FOR YOU TO DISCOVER ONLINE

Carter claims, "Testing is the diagnostic tool that best enforces a school's goals." Try putting keywords such as "school" and "testing" or "standards" into a search engine such as Google (www.google.com). Look at the most promising results of your search. Then search using the keywords "school," "testing," and "backlash" to focus on arguments against school testing. After looking at the best results of that search, do you agree with Carter's statement above? Why or why not? Do you think his article should have made a stronger argument to support this claim? Why or why not?

Evaluation: Is It Good or Bad?

Chapter 8

Why Generation X Is Embracing Morality

Stacey Felzenberg

"For better or worse, marriage hits a low," read a recent headline in *The Washington Post.*

"Americans are less likely to marry than ever before," according to the National Marriage Project at Rutgers University.

I understand the reluctance. Something I read in my freshman year of college convinced me I was not cut out for marriage. "Should I get married?" asked the Beat-era poet Gregory Corso in "Marriage." I answered "No" after reading his description of an unattractive wife "screeching over potatoes" and "five nose-running brats in love with Batman."

With marriage out of the way, I became convinced my future success lay in establishing a career on Capitol Hill and putting a substantial sum in the bank. Sure, having a family some day would be nice, but certainly not necessary. I figured I would be just as well off—perhaps better off—without a husband and children.

Now, as an upperclassman, I'm having second thoughts.

"Married couples have substantial benefits over the unmarried in terms of labor force productivity, physical and mental health, general happiness and longevity," according to the Rutgers study. In other words, married people are generally wealthier, healthier and happier than single people.

Research by Patrick Fagan, a former family counselor, backs this up. Mr. Fagan, a senior fellow in family and cultural issues at the Heritage Foundation, examined the relationship between

marital status and income and found that married couples with children make nearly twice as much as their cohabiting counterparts.

So much for using the thought of a healthy bank account as an argument against marriage. But I'll still have my health if I don't get married, right?

Maybe not. Several studies have shown married people live healthier lives than their unmarried or divorced counterparts.

The most surprising statistic I found came from a University of Minnesota study by William J. Doherty. His research shows the "mortality rates of individuals with poor social relationships are higher than those who smoke cigarettes for many years."

At first I thought, "Hey, if I get married, I don't have to quit smoking." But then I thought about what this finding really means—that poor social relationships, including the failure to marry, could literally kill me faster than smoking.

There goes another argument in favor of remaining a bachelorette. But what about happiness? Surely a woman can live with a man and lead a life just as fulfilling as if she had tied the knot.

Nope—strike three. Once again the National Marriage Project says I'm wrong: "Annual rates of depression among cohabiting couples are more than three times what they are among married couples."

I'm seeing marriage in a different light now. Many of my peers are changing their attitudes on traditional morality. While my generation may

228

not yet be marrying in greater numbers, we are embracing many of the moral values our parents rejected.

Less than 40 percent of college freshmen agreed that "if two people really like each other, it's all right for them to have sex even if they've known each other for a very short time," according to a survey last year by researchers at the University of California at Los Angeles. Quite a leap from the "free love" days of the first Woodstock music festival.

One young person giving voice to this cultural shift is Wendy Shalit. In her book *A Return to Modesty,* Shalit surveys the wreckage of modern feminism. "To the extent that premarital sex is practiced and encouraged," Shalit writes, "to that extent will women who want to wait until marriage find it harder to meet men who will marry them without 'trying them out' first, to have patience with someone with 'hang-ups'—which is to say, hopes." No wonder feminists consider Shalit a traitor to her sex.

It's clear to me now that marriage is not just another lifestyle option—it's the glue binding the moral fabric of American society. Thirty years of soaring divorce rates and cohabiting adults threatened to unravel the nation's moral fabric. But thanks to millions of young people who have examined liberal mores and found them lacking, society may now be on the mend.

ANALYZING "Why Generation X Is Embracing Morality"

The editorial that opens this chapter was written by a college sophomore. It appeared in the *Washington Times* on September 12, 1999, but the relevance of its topic is not limited to the audience of *Times* readers living in the Washington D.C. area. It is of wide general interest because it deals with a newly recognized trend, as its opening sentences explain: the decline in rates of marriage in the United States. This change in a fundamental social pattern has come about quickly, within the last few decades. It is of most interest to the members of Generation X, loosely defined as people in their twenties and thirties in the 90s and 00s, since people in this age group are the ones whose lifestyles have produced the trend.

The author chooses not to ask one obvious question: why has this trend come about? Instead she poses a different question. What can be said for marriage since so many members of her generation are taking a pass? Is it good or bad? How should it be evaluated? Furthermore, the author, Stacey Felzenberg, casts this judgment about the value of marriage as a personal matter. What should *she* think about marriage? Of course posing the question as a personal one does not limit the applicability of the answering argument since most people living in the United States today also face this question (though perhaps members of subcultures in the United States or people in cultures elsewhere do not face it). But as contemporary and immediately relevant as this question on the value of marriage seems, this issue itself is one of the oldest in the Western rhetorical tradition. Indeed, writing about the pros and cons—that is, about the value—of marriage has been a standard essay topic for over two thousand years.

Whenever something is going to be evaluated—that is, judged as a good or bad idea, lifestyle, action, commodity, event, or choice—the evaluator has to have in mind certain **criteria** or **standards** by which to make the judgment. The presence of criteria for evaluation is most obvious when a consumer item is being evaluated. Someone shopping for a toaster has as a basic criterion that the toaster will be able to toast. What are the basic criteria that marriage has to meet? Before we can answer that question, we have to ask ourselves how we would categorize marriage. Of all the possible ways to categorize it (as an evolutionary social adaptation, as a sacramental rite, as a legal state), Felzenberg seems to opt for something like "lifestyle option." Criteria have to be **appropriate** to the category that is being evaluated. If we are evaluating lifestyles, what criteria can we use?

Felzenberg is very explicit about the criteria she uses in the first part of her evaluation. Taking her cue from the Rutgers National Marriage project, she sets her standards for evaluating a lifestyle as wealth, health, and happiness.

These standards—wealth, health, and happiness—are potential **consequences.** We routinely judge actions, events, and choices by their outcomes, by whether or not they have led to good consequences and helped us avoid harmful ones. Our basic argument could be diagrammed as follows:

Reason: Marriage produces good consequences → *Claim:* Marriage is a good lifestyle
↑
Warrant: A lifestyle that produces good consequences is a good lifestyle.

Whenever consequences are part of an argument we are dealing with causes, so, not surprisingly, Felzenberg uses the tactics of causal argument. The single difference method (see Chapter 7) predominates. Felzenberg compares married couples to single people and cohabiting couples (living together but not married). Using ways of measuring that she does not report in her brief argument, Felzenberg presents results suggesting that married people have more income, healthier lives (fewer serious diseases?), and less depression (evidently her working definition of being "happier" is being less depressed). The evidence for these single difference claims is supported in this newspaper piece by references to authoritative sources like a study published by Rutgers University. If Felzenberg had been writing on the same topic for a sociology class, she would have had to handle her evidence much more rigorously and cite her sources precisely. But her method of referring to studies from presumably authoritative sources is fairly routine for an editorial. She assumes her audience will recognize and respect these authorities.

Notably missing from this argument is any **defense of the criteria** themselves. Evidently Felzenberg did not think it was necessary to argue for health, wealth, and happiness as criteria by which to judge a lifestyle. Was that a correct assumption on her part? Would anyone seriously argue against any of these standards? And what about the order she presents them in? Wealth first, and then health, and finally happiness. Does this order accurately reflect the importance of these standards? Although the problem does not come up in this brief argument, sometimes the criteria by which we judge something conflict. We cannot fulfill all of them, so we have to weight the criteria, deciding which is the most important. If wealth is more important than health, for example, then we would have to sacrifice health for wealth if both could not be attained. Weighting the criteria can require another evaluation argument.

So far this evaluation of marriage has been based on consequences, on the good effects that marriage can have when compared with alternative choices. But consequences are not the only bases of evaluation. We also make judgments based on moral standards, that is, on codes of conduct, commandments and laws, cultural norms, and religious principles that tell us what is right or wrong. We absorb these from the culture, and even those who consider themselves outside the established morality of one group will be within the established morality of another.

Judgments based on moral standards can sometimes conflict with judgments based on consequences. Many actions may have neutral or even harmful consequences, but we still choose them because we judge them to be the right thing to do. When we are faced with a novel action or event to evaluate, putting it in a category that is already governed by a moral standard is one way to make a decision about it.

Marriage, however, does not have to be finessed into a moral category. It is already defined by cultural, legal, and religious codes in every society. Felzenberg refers to a pro-marriage judgment as "traditional morality," and notably she does not choose any direct defense of marriage on that basis, nor does she defend the moral standard itself. Defending marriage as a moral standard would require an appeal to a more basic moral standard, or to further consequences. Instead, she chooses what could be called an indirect tactic. She cites evidence that members of her generation are changing their attitudes toward casual sex (presumably as opposed to sex within the commitment of marriage), and she cites one controversial book that discusses pressures on young women in particular. These could be explosive arguments if they were pursued.

Ms. Felzenberg uses her own ethos, her own changing state of opinion, as an appeal in this piece. She begins by characterizing herself as against marriage, influenced by the writings of a Beat poet she was perhaps assigned to read in a class. But she has been having "second thoughts" based on the evidence compiled by the Rutgers National Marriage Project and others. If she can change her mind, or at least rethink her former position, then so might other Gen Xers who now find themselves with similar opinions.

But the closing arguments stray far from matters of one person's decision. Marriage is specifically taken out of the category of "lifestyle option," a choice that faces individuals. It is now seen as the "glue binding American society," as a social institution that society requires. This characterization invokes a serious consequence argument indeed, and Felzenberg is obviously using it here to defend "traditional morality." Just as criteria based on consequences can be defended by appeals to moral standards, so moral standards can be defended by appeals to consequences. Without marriage, Felzenberg warns, the fabric of American society will unravel.

Missing from Felzenberg's positive evaluation of marriage is any refutation of opposing assessments of the evidence or challenges to the criteria. For example, Felzenberg cites the statistic that married couples with children "make nearly twice as much as their cohabiting counterparts." But such couples may need that much income to afford their children. In terms of personal consumption, of buying power dedicated to individual enjoyment, singles, cohabiting or otherwise, may have more purchasing power. Which definition of wealth, then, should be personally desired or socially preferred: total income or income available for personal gratification? The decline in marriage rates may indicate the evaluation made by many young people.

EVALUATION: DETERMINING THE VALUE OF SOMETHING

Once you understand arguments about the nature of things and arguments about causes, you have grasped the basic methods of argument: tying evidence to definitions and linking two occurrences by agency. As you have seen, each of these methods of argument is associated with its own kind of claim. There are two other kinds of claims that also structure arguments—the evaluation and the proposal. Fortunately, these require no new techniques, only a judicious combination of the types of argument already familiar to you.

In this chapter we take up **evaluations,** arguments in support of value judgments. Whenever we label something "good," "right," "beautiful," "bad," "wrong," or "ugly," we are evaluating, and we often need to defend our evaluations for others. To do so, we can use two possible tactics of support. First, we often measure the subject of our evaluation against an ideal definition of what it ought to be, a standard of perfection. This tactic brings us back to the first type of argument. If you say, for example, "I have a wonderful Toyota," that claim looks very much like a simple definition argument, "My Toyota is good." Everything you know about arguing for this kind of claim still works, even though you have characterized the object with a value-judgment term. You may still need to describe the subject for your audience, and your supporting evidence must be fairly representative. And if you cannot count on your audience's immediate understanding of what a "good Toyota" is, you will need to define your standard of "goodness" in a car so that your audience will accept it and your car will fit it.

This definition of "what it means to be good" is called the **criterion** or **standard of judgment,** and there may be several criteria behind any evaluation. The criteria are just as important as the definition in a "what is it?" argument. If the criteria are not acceptable to your audience, you may have to stop and argue for them just as you would have to defend a definition of an important term.

The second tactic for supporting an evaluation is causal argument. Although evaluations look like definitions—characterizations of people, events, things, and policies—they often require causal arguments for support, for the standard we measure our subject against often includes good or bad **consequences.** If one were to argue, for instance, that "properly conducted drill is a good teaching method," the definition of "good teaching method" must include "has good consequences." How else can a teaching method be called good unless students can be shown to learn from it? To show that drill satisfies this criterion of a good teaching method, we would have to first say what we mean by drill so our audience will know what we are talking about, and then we would have to link drill *causally* with certain results. A study could use the single-difference method, showing that students who were drilled in math 15 minutes a day retained more information longer than a similar group of students taught the same material in a less formalized manner. Our criteria for a good teaching method might also include the absence of certain bad consequences like "poor understanding of concepts" as well as positive characterizations like "thoroughly tested," "innovative," or "approved by prominent educators."

CONSTRUCTING A SOUND EVALUATION

Some people think that anyone who makes value judgments in claims like "Mary Cassatt was a wonderful painter" or "Government funding of science is bad policy" expresses a purely personal opinion, a matter of taste that can only be articulated, not argued about. However, when sharable criteria or standards can be identified, evaluative statements can develop into legitimate arguments. Of course, we often express value judgments casually without defending them, venting our pleasure, approval, irritation, or anger and assuming that other like-minded people will agree. But whenever we want to move an audience to judge as we do and to justify our evaluations, we support them with arguments designed to convince others. We do this by appealing to standards we believe our audience shares with us or by working to establish such standards.

Supporting Criteria with a Specific Audience in Mind

You will not need to defend any criteria the members of your audience are likely to share; at most you may remind them of your shared assumptions. If, for example, you want to convince your parents that you are a really good student, you would ordinarily not have to explain to them what a good student is. Just show them the As. But what would you do if they did not automatically accept your criteria? If you wanted to argue that you are indeed a good student even though your grades are not flawless, you might try convincing them that a good student is one who takes a challenging program and does as well as possible, not necessarily one who gets straight As. A number of tactics are available for supporting criteria.

The first tactic for supporting criteria is an appeal to your audience's values. If you can show that your standard of evaluation falls under one of your audience's basic assumptions about what has value, then you have supported your criteria, at least for that audience. In our example above, if you wanted to challenge the common-sense notion that a good student is simply one who gets good grades, you might appeal to your parents' often expressed admiration for those who accept difficult challenges and do their best to meet them. In effect, you would be appealing to what you think are their most dearly held values and trying to get them to place your performance as a student in that category. After all, you may have taken advanced level courses and a heavy load of credits while holding down a demanding job. If they value ambition and perseverance, they may be willing to agree that those qualities characterize a good student, despite some imperfection in the grades.

Second, you can appeal to authority. What if your audience does not automatically acknowledge the higher value you have appealed to, a value you think self-evident? You can remind them that a successful person, a respected leader, a great philosopher, the law, or the Constitution has supported your view. The graduation speaker who offers her experience in the business world as a model for success, despite a rocky and slow start, can serve as a model for those who want to argue that career tracks are not always evident at the beginning of one's college years.

Third, you can make an appeal to consequences, an appeal to the possible good and bad effects of following your standards. Someone might counter your appeal to the authority of the slow-starting career model by citing people who were unable to pursue the careers they wanted because they lacked the necessary training. But you might answer by arguing that the graduation speaker succeeded precisely because she had taken the time to mature and learn about the world through a variety of experiences.

Fourth, sometimes you can create a comparison to support a criterion. You might defend your standard of success as a student by comparing it with a standard of success in character development. You might support this criterion by pointing out that just as one judges character by the internal strength of commitment that a person develops by confronting hardship, not just worldly success, so also should one judge a student's achievement by the determination with which difficulties have been faced and surmounted. Of course, the success of your argument will depend on the degree to which your audience shares the values you have articulated, but if you have accurately assessed and appealed to their most deeply held values, you have a chance of persuading them.

If you think about all these methods of supporting the criteria that support the evaluation, you can imagine going back and back, supporting one appeal with another and that appeal with another, and so on into infinity. If you make an appeal to good consequences, someone might ask how any consequence can be described as "good" except by some prior evaluation that has already labeled it. But you do not always have to go all the way back. At some point—and that point will depend on your audience—you simply call a halt. If you have touched common ground with your readers' values, you should be all right. The skill lies in knowing when you have.

Possible Subjects for Evaluation

Instead of talking abstractly about evaluation, at this point we would like to look at the kinds of things we evaluate and the kinds of arguments we develop to do so. The following sections will help you think about possible subjects for evaluation and will suggest how to go about evaluating using ideal definitions and causal arguments. The subjects of evaluation are divided into four categories: objects, people, actions, and finally abstractions, a special category that in some ways combines the other three.

Evaluating Objects

Objects have material existence, and anything you can trip over you can certainly evaluate. Objects range in size from diamond chips to towering skyscrapers, in duration from the most fleeting to the most lasting. For convenience here we divide them into the natural and the constructed.

Natural Objects   It may seem futile and arrogant to evaluate the givens of the world around us, but we do evaluate natural objects both for their consequences and their beauty. Our notion of the consequences of natural things depends upon our point of view. A child's book says, "Ladybugs are good insects." They are often called the gardener's best friends because they eat the plant-destroying aphids. Actually, ladybugs simply behave like ladybugs, but what they do happens to have good consequences for people. If aphids could write argument textbooks, ladybugs would be really bad insects. Similarly, almost no one has a good word to say in defense of termites, which have very bad consequences for wooden houses, although in a forest they may contribute significantly to the ecological balance. We value all kinds of plant and animal life according to how they affect us for good or for ill, at the same time that concern for the environment has taught us to consider broader kinds of consequence arguments. Spotted owls and frogs may produce no immediate consequence for us and yet may be a vital link in a chain of consequences for other living creatures. A noxious weed in the garden may need to be pulled, but in a meadow it might be called a charming wildflower. The more we know about the natural world, the more complex our evaluations become.

We also evaluate natural objects on aesthetic grounds, labeling them beautiful and ugly from a human point of view. Most people find centipedes and roaches ugly, especially close up, and swans and flamingoes beautiful, especially from a distance. Do we also attach the labels *beautiful* or *ugly* on the basis of consequence? That is, do we call species that are good or at least neutral for our welfare beautiful and whatever harms us ugly? To some extent, yes, although consequences do not completely control aesthetic judgments. The shiver of repulsion we feel at the sight of a poisonous snake like the coral snake can coexist with admiration of its beauty. If something that has hideous consequences can still be beautiful, then the two appeals, the aesthetic and the practical, must be separable. (For a discussion of aesthetic evaluations, see p. 236.)

Constructed Objects   We spend a great deal of time evaluating constructed objects, perhaps because we feel we have some control over them. We choose among them, improve them, reject them. Some of these evaluations are practical, others are aesthetic, and a few are both.

Practical Evaluations   We make practical evaluations of constructed things according to how well they fulfill their functions. We have, as it were, ideal definitions in mind of what good objects of their kinds should do or be, and we measure individual objects against these ideals. For instance, the good refrigerator basically keeps fresh food cold and frozen food frozen with no effort on the part of the owner. We might even add the criteria of silence, energy efficiency, and reliability. Of course, manufacturers and advertisers add other attributes to the ideal definition of the refrigerator—unlimited supply of ice cubes, cold drinks through the door, special storage compartments, and restaurant-style specifications. We always have to decide which criteria we judge most important and which trivial in relation to price and the desire for status. Consumer magazines offer us models for the practical evaluation of everything from pasta sauce to outboard motors.

Practical evaluations offer little challenge to an arguer when the criteria are easy to delineate and win audience agreement for. The problem arises when technical advances suggest new criteria. We can all agree that a television set should offer a sharp picture in natural color, have excellent sound reproduction, require little maintenance, and offer good value for price. But when digital technology and expanding Internet options become available, the standards for evaluation can also shift. Then the question becomes not only "How well does this television set do what television sets usually do?" but also "Does it do these new things well, do I need them, and can I afford them?"

EXERCISE 8.1

Working either alone or with a group of your classmates, establish at least three criteria for evaluating any of the following. You may go on to use these criteria in a full evaluation argument.

1. Microwave oven
2. Sleeping bag
3. MP3 player
4. Personal computer
5. Airport or train station
6. Public washroom
7. Baseball stadium
8. Digital camera
9. Cell phone

Aesthetic Evaluations   Some things we evaluate not for their usefulness but for their beauty and therefore the pleasure they give to the perceiver. We evaluate all kinds of artistic products designed to entertain us, such as movies, concerts, poems, plays, television sitcoms, and the works of artists from Aristophanes to Andy Warhol. Everything we call Art with a capital A is the province of aesthetic evaluation, as well as many other things that contain some element of aesthetic appeal.

You may think that preferring the Beatles to Beethoven or Keats to Stephen King is simply a matter of personal taste, age, or social class and that arguing the superiority of one artist or work over another is futile. It is true that many people refuse to argue any aesthetic issue, choosing to halt with "I know what I like when I see it" or "That's trash to me." It is always possible to cut off discussion by retreating to purely personal grounds of preference.

Nevertheless, vigorous arguments about aesthetic matters persist, as does the attempt to ground aesthetic evaluations in standards other than personal preference. These arguments work just like any other evaluation argument: the object at hand is measured against defined or assumed criteria. But aesthetic criteria may not be as obvious as those used for evaluating useful objects. In fact, the aesthetic evaluations that you are likely to read—reviews of books, movies, music, and art—seldom state their criteria directly. It is simply assumed that people who attend certain kinds of artistic events agree on what makes a good one. Still we can identify and define some common elements in aesthetic criteria. These may be tricky to apply, and some may be incompatible, but knowing what they are can aid your invention as you make your own aesthetic evaluations.

Formal Aesthetic Criteria

- **Proportion:** We often admire an object for the fitness of its parts and how they combine to form a whole. A Greek temple, for example, has columns of fixed proportions, tapered finely to produce an illusion of straightness; the relationship of the size of columns to the size of the whole temple is fixed. In any art, to fulfill an expectation of appropriate proportion or form is to satisfy an aesthetic criterion, while to violate such an expectation can be troubling, whether the violation is intentional or accidental. A popular song without a bridge may be considered imperfect or a picture with everything crowded to one side out of balance. Such works may be considered lacking in proportion, the perfect relation of parts to whole. When we find a work of art satisfying in its proportion, we often praise its unity. To say that a work of art has unity is to say that its parts fit together so well that it becomes one thing.

- **Slight Distortion:** Proportion is easy to understand, but what can it mean to call something appealing because its proportions are slightly exaggerated or distorted? To begin with, when distortion is extreme or constant, we perceive it as ugliness, and most people do not find such complete distortion attractive. In a movie we are surprised and delighted by the occasional odd camera angle, the face reflected in calm water which is then stirred up. But a whole movie with the camera first at knee level, then on a helicopter, then looking in a mirror or through a keyhole, would distort perception beyond the tolerance of most viewers. Extreme distortion can interfere with appreciation—though, of course, audiences differ in their tolerance for it.

  Perfect proportion and slight distortion are rival criteria based on different assumptions about what is preferable. They have never been reconciled, probably never will be, and need not be. The first is often called "classical" and the second "gothic" or "romantic." Both are used as standards of evaluation. The complementary criteria of proportion and distortion can be used in evaluating any art form. For instance, some moviegoers consider Julia Roberts a great beauty, while others think her features exaggerated. Just as proportion pleases by fulfilling the expectation of regularity, so also does slight exaggeration or compression give us the thrill of a ripple in the form.

- **Contrast:** When we appeal to contrast as an aesthetic criterion, we are admiring a juxtaposition, a placing next to each other, of two differing elements of form, color, or content. Some people admire the contrast between the craggy vertical mountains and placid horizontal lake in a landscape painting. Others praise the comic and tragic plots that twine in a Shakespeare play, the sweet and the sour that unite in Chinese cooking. We find it pleasing when vivid differences are brought together, perhaps because each element is intensified by juxtaposition with its opposite. Too much contrast, however, can become an aesthetic defect when it jars instead of pleasing. Again, different individuals and different cultures will have different tolerances for contrast.

- **Harmony:** Just as proportion and slight exaggeration are always in conflict with each other, so too are harmony and contrast in never-ending tension. The appeal to harmony as an aesthetic criterion claims that pleasure can be derived from gentle or subtle rather than extreme variations. When we are not distracted by dramatic contrast, we can admire fine gradations and small details. In the absence of mountain and lake, we can appreciate the subtle undulation of prairie wheat in the wind. The painting we know as *Whistler's Mother* was called by the artist *Arrangement in Grey and Black* to call attention to its delicate harmonies of dark shades, its lack of contrasting bright color.

  There is, of course, such a thing as too much harmony, just as there can be too much contrast. We call the excessive repetition of the same form monotony, a lack of sufficient variety to keep the observer's attention. A film that repeats the same action over and over again (like pornography or cartoons), a housing development that repeats the same model over and over again—all these can be called monotonous.

All of the aesthetic criteria discussed so far are formal; that is, they deal with the disposition of the basic elements of art like shape, color, and sound, rather than content. Now let us mention some criteria that depend on the human maker and perceiver of a work of art.

Aesthetic Criteria Based on Content

- **Craft:** We can also base an argument that something has aesthetic value on the perceivable skill, ingenuity, inventiveness, or persistence of its maker. All these are elements of craft, a criterion of value that can be applied to any made object. How can we judge the skill of the maker? Sometimes a trained eye can infer it from the object itself. If we examine the dense pile and complex design of a handmade rug, we realize how many knots per square inch it contains and therefore how much time and effort it took its weaver.

  How well we infer the skill of the maker from examination of the object often depends on how much we understand of the craft to begin with. Anyone who has ever tried to construct the simplest rhyme will have a much better appreciation of the skill of a rapper who can tell an elaborate story with both rhythmic and verbal precision. When we construct aesthetic evaluations, however, we usually do not judge objects solely on the basis of craft. Any creation may have been difficult to produce, but at some point we ask the question "Was it worth the effort?" Someone may take 20 years to build a miniature castle out of toothpicks, but we may end up marveling more at the artist's patience than the result. On the other hand, we often place great emphasis on the craft of otherwise useful objects, ranging from fancy cars to designer-made clothing.

- **Association:** Like craft, association is another nonformal criterion by which we evaluate art. We often turn to human perceivers and ask what "meaning" a work of art has for them. What ideas does it suggest, what emotions does it arouse, what does it tell them about life? Although some critical approaches discount meaning as a standard of evaluation, most people prefer art whose content has some kind of relevance for them. They want to take something away, in the form of a message, from a work of art. Of course, some works yield a meaning more readily than others, and some messages are more complex than others. It is easier to get the point of Norman Rockwell's depiction of a Thanksgiving feast than to figure out a Picasso painting. And for some people the quality or complexity of the message is related to the ease or difficulty with which it can be extracted.

  What kinds of association do we value in works of art? How can we argue for our evaluation by referring to content? We cannot explore these questions here in the detail they deserve, but we can suggest two basic categories of association:

1. *An appeal to human emotions:* Many people value art most that has strong emotional appeal. The love between mother and child in a Raphael Madonna, the fear evoked in a Stephen King novel, the tenderness between Romeo and Juliet, the hatefulness of the villains in an action movie, the intensity conveyed by heavy metal music, the laughter inspired by Jim Carrey's contortions—such art stirs our feelings.

2. *An appeal to intellectual interest:* Associations can be historical, social, psychological, political, religious—in short, have intellectual rather than (or in addition to) emotional content. We can admire the Chicago skyline not only for its formal characteristics and for the architectural achievement of the buildings, but also for the speculation and associations that skyline evokes as we reflect upon the manifestation of a powerful, technologically adept civilization. Such admiration may have an emotional component, since rational and emotional arguments are not wholly separable, but it is intellectual as well.

   Some people see works of art mainly as vehicles for communicating ideas. People who have strong commitments—political, religious, social—often evaluate works of art according to the extent to which they represent those ideas. Social realists want to read accurate depictions of the lives of the poor or the powerful. Those whose interest is in subjective or "inner" reality value the psychological dimensions of art. Some readers of fiction value works that extend their knowledge and appreciation of ways of life unfamiliar to them, while others seek accurate representations of their immediate and local concerns. If you are evaluating or reviewing a novel, you may find that an appeal to a limited audience will not go over well unless your audience shares your assumptions. A recent novel about quilting, for instance, proved quite popular in rural Pennsylvania but was not of great interest in urban areas. An evaluator who brings a strong ideological commitment may have to back up and argue for the ideology itself, which is no easy matter and may take you far from your original purpose.

Any work of art will spin a web of associations in your mind. A note of caution: some associations will be too personal to use as criteria for aesthetic evaluation. To be useful evaluative criteria, the associations raised by a work of art must be sharable rather than private. Only then can you hope to arouse the same admiration in others.

- **Moral Consequences of Art:** One common form of art criticism bypasses formal criteria entirely, completely assumes the associations that the work arouses, and then goes ahead to evaluate the work on the basis of its possible or actual consequences. This kind of evaluation asks, "What moral effects will this work of art have on the beholder? Will reading this book, seeing this movie, looking at this painting, or watching this television show tend to produce good or bad actions?" According to such a criterion of evaluation, whatever produces good effects is good and whatever produces or has the potential for producing bad effects is bad. That sounds simple, but complicated questions of censorship then arise. How does one decide whether the work of art produces or has the potential to produce bad consequences, and who decides what to do about it? For instance, in the wake of the high school shootings at Littleton, Colorado, a network postponed a television show that depicted the murderous revenge of high school students against their more popular peers for fear of the impact of its depiction of violence on teenagers. While incidents like these give rise to much ongoing debate about policy, we want to stress that any connection between judging a work of art in terms of its moral effects and censorship is not inevitable. Rating systems, for example, label and warn, but do not proscribe. One might conclude that a work of art is immoral and still not censor it; we may still argue about where we think responsibility for action lies.

Using More than One Standard of Evaluation for the Same Constructed Object

A chopping block made of carefully matched end-grain pieces of hardwood, a van with Day-Glo flames consuming its sides and red velour upholstery, a computer screensaver depicting birds in the canopy of a rainforest, a Paul Revere silver teapot—here are objects we can evaluate both practically for their usefulness and aesthetically for their beauty. Beauty and function can be connected in two ways: Sometimes embellishment is obviously added to the functional object, like the decorated side panels of a van. Or sometimes the beauty is in the perfection of the functional design. Think of the sleek and menacing aerodynamic design of a fighter jet.

The following is a list of constructed objects that can be evaluated aesthetically or practically or both ways. Working either alone or with a group of your classmates, decide what criteria of evaluation you would use for each. Then choose one object and write down a list of at least three criteria. You may go on to use these criteria in a full evaluation argument.

1. The photography in a fashion magazine
2. The cover and design of this book
3. The last movie you saw
4. A down-lined coat
5. A salad
6. A supermarket interior
7. A Beatles song
8. A sport utility vehicle
9. Your classroom building
10. A music video
11. An Apache helicopter
12. The lyrics of a popular song

Evaluating People

Though wisdom warns us to "judge not," we constantly evaluate people either in the roles they perform or in their personal lives. In classical rhetoric, such arguments offering praise or blame were called *epideictic*, and in ancient times they were exemplified by funeral orations or speeches praising or blaming public figures. These types of arguments often conveyed and reinforced the most important values held by a culture and still do. We of course make epideictic arguments today, both formally (in eulogies and obituaries) and informally (in intimate conversations, on TV, in books and magazines). Consider the following:

1. My neighbor is a wonderful father.
2. Dr. Bright is a fine scientist.
3. Patton was a great general.
4. My grandmother is a beautiful person.

Evaluations like these use the predictable tactics of definition and causal argument. Once again, if you want to establish that your neighbor is a wonderful father, you have to define what wonderfulness in a father consists of and give evidence from your neighbor's life to show that he fits the definition. Thus, part of your evidence will include certain qualities he possesses, such as warmth and concern for his children. Another part might concern the impact he has had on his family's well-being through his actions and involvement.

Actually, what you are doing is holding an individual up to an ideal definition of a role, and the most contested part of your evaluation might be that ideal definition. What, in our culture, is a good father? That may be a sensitive issue; some fathers are more involved in their children's upbringing than others. You cannot rely on any miscellaneous audience sharing assumptions about fatherhood, as they might have 50 years ago. Defining a "good electrician" would be much easier. And what about the definition of "a good teacher"? One who lectures brilliantly or one who sets students loose on difficult projects? What about a "good doctor"? Or a "good president"? These easily become contentious.

What happens when we turn from the roles and occupations people fulfill and try to evaluate a whole person, praising a life or presenting it in a way that suggests general approval? When you are arguing in the context of a general readership, a vague "good" used to evaluate a person desperately needs definition, like any abstraction. You might appeal to the tenets of one of the major religions to suggest criteria for judging the "good" person: Christianity, Judaism, Buddhism, Islam. Depending on your audience and your topic, even smaller "isms" like socialism, deism, or vegetarianism could offer criteria for evaluating goodness according to their standards. Or, consulting your own moral sense of things, you might set up your own standards. Once again, depending on your audience's assumptions, you may need to argue more for the definition and the standards than for the person you are praising.

EXERCISE 8.3

Working either alone or with a group of your classmates, construct and defend ideal definitions of the following for an audience that you specify. You may go on to compare a particular individual against one of these definitions in a full evaluation argument.

1. A well-behaved child
2. A good sister or brother
3. An excellent musician
4. A competent car mechanic
5. An excellent academic advisor
6. An adequate dentist
7. An outstanding senator
8. A wise counselor
9. An inspiring teacher
10. A first-rate chef

Evaluating Events and Actions

Natural Acts and Events At the mercy of wind, fire, and water, we can do little but hurl our evaluations back into the face of nature. But just as we judge natural objects from our own perspective, so also do we judge natural events and actions by their consequences. We even have the arrogance to evaluate the weather. In one university town, for example, the local weather service grades the weather every day from A to F: "Today will earn only a C in the morning, but will improve to B in the afternoon when the cloud cover breaks." Any evaluation of a natural event will depend entirely on consequence and point of view. The rain that ruins the picnic delights the farmer. From a distant historical perspective, the flooding that deposited rich, alluvial soil in the Nile valley was good, but to the people of Pennsylvania the Great Johnstown Flood that washed away lives and property was a disaster.

Human Acts and Events   The arena of human actions offers enormous scope for evaluation, taking in everything from cheating on an exam to invading Iraq. As in the case of natural events, here also, our heaviest reliance will be on consequence arguments. In effect, when we judge an action we are making two evaluations, one of the situation that precedes it and one of the situation that follows it. A good action improves a situation; a bad one makes it worse. Hiring a new assistant is a good action if messy files get organized and lost letters found. The intervention of the United Nations is good if it stops a war or brings about a cease-fire. But the world is a complicated place, and most actions can have both good and bad consequences: a tax cut can be good if it encourages investment and bad if it feeds inflation. When an action has a mixed effect, an overall positive evaluation will depend on minimizing bad effects and maximizing good ones.

In addition to considering the consequences of action, we also bring in ideal definitions to judge actions or events. We often call an action "wrong" because it violates some ethic, some code or standard of right action, regardless of whether the act has good or bad consequences. Thus cheating on an exam is a form of dishonesty, by definition a wrong action, even though it can temporarily produce good results for a student of hardened conscience.

The Variety of Ethical Appeals   It may be a good idea to pause here and consider how many kinds of ethical appeals there actually are. The word *ethics* may make you think of religion or philosophy, the Ten Commandments, the golden rule—or the kind of moralistic preaching about good behavior that comes down from authorities and seems to have little relation to day-to-day activities. According to one school of thought, we are born with ethics; but it is more generally believed that we are taught them. In any case, we all have a sense of what actions are right or wrong. Ethics affect not only our personal lives, but also our actions as members of groups, professions, and even nations. We all like to see the right thing done, whether that right thing is as personal as visiting a sick friend in the hospital or as national as feeding hungry refugees.

There are many possible ethical warrants, acceptable reasons for evaluating actions and events. Like the paired criteria for evaluating art objects, these ethical warrants that we can invoke for particular audiences and evaluations may sometimes be contradictory. *Self-actualization*, for instance, is usually considered a good thing. It means becoming whatever we can become, even if we must put our own interests ahead of the demands of others. Self-actualization can be used as ethical justification for just about anything from running marathons to studying Greek to taking up a new career. On the other hand, the opposite value of *altruism*, placing the welfare of others above one's own, is held by many as a higher ethical standard.

Family loyalty is another ethical motive for action. You would not sell your relative a lemon of a used car. Even the law respects the loyalty between spouses and does not ask them to testify against each other. And we all belong to larger "families" with their own standards of right and wrong. *Being a stool pigeon* is as ethically wrong to a member of a street gang as *failure to help a partner* is to the police officer. Both groups place a high priority on peer loyalty.

Professions are groups with their own codes of behavior. These codes may be as formalized as *union bylaws* or the *Hippocratic oath;* a teamster considers crossing a picket line unthinkable, and a doctor is supposed to treat anyone in need. The ethical codes of some professions are less formalized, but still powerful. Scholars, for example, swear to nothing and sign nothing, but they share a strict understanding that plagiarizing (using someone else's ideas or work without acknowledgment) or intruding on someone else's declared areas of study is unethical.

Institutions such as hospitals, universities, and corporations also have ethical responsibilities, more or less codified. A hospital should treat the indigent; a corporation has duties to the public that buys its product as well as to its stockholders. Any institution, from country club to nursing home, tries to conform to an ideal definition of its function. Institutions that do so are widely admired, while those that do not run the risk of public disapproval or rejection.

Religions and nations are even larger groups that declare standards of right and wrong behavior, usually in writing. The volumes containing the law of the land fill many shelves, and all religions have their texts and commentaries on morality. Since their standards are written in such detail, we often think of law and religion first when we think of morality or ethical correctness. *Criminal* and *civil law* define what is allowed in human interactions, but we also carry in our minds a sense of what is right for us to do as citizens. People from all nations respect appeals to *patriotism*, or love of country (short of the jingoism that equates love of country with the approval of every national action). As United States citizens, we often find an *appeal to the Constitution* a strong ethical argument, though we may disagree about what actions are or are not consistent with the constitutional precepts.

A few general ethical principles cut across national and religious boundaries. One of the strongest is an appeal to *fairness* or *justice* itself. A desire to be fair is the ethical standard behind many an evaluation, from a good way to share Halloween candy to the proper way of taxing large corporations. Most people also respond to the rightness of *preserving tradition.* We can lament the wholesale leveling of city neighborhoods because the past is being destroyed, or praise the planting of vegetable gardens because they preserve folk culture and our sense of the land.

In contrast, an appeal to *progress*, the opposite of tradition, can also evoke a positive response. Someone might defend the leveling of a neighborhood because the new buildings represent progress for the city. Others defend the importance of circumnavigating the globe in a balloon, climbing previously unscaled mountains, or exploring Antarctica. It may be difficult for us to explain why such acts are "right," but we have a sense that it is fitting for us to extend the capabilities of our species, both because of the potential good consequences and because of the inspiring personal achievement. Here a vague claim of general "rightness" brings us full circle to that most personal of ethical motives, self-actualization. One who takes a giant step for mankind may also be motivated by the desire to take a small step for one's self. All of these ethical standards can be appealed to in argument; which ones work will depend on the values shared by one's audience and how well what is being evaluated fits the particular standard.

Working either alone or with a group of your classmates, consider how you would evaluate the following actions or events. Would you evaluate them by their consequences, by measuring them against an ideal definition, or both? Choose one action or event and write a paragraph about its consequences or sketch out a brief ideal definition. You may go on to use this action or event as the subject of a full evaluation argument.

1. Your performance on your most recent job
2. A rock concert
3. A football game
4. A political campaign
5. A thunderstorm
6. A treaty of some kind (a peace treaty, an environmental treaty, a trade agreement)
7. Buying prewritten term papers
8. Binge drinking
9. Your social life
10. A forest fire

EXERCISE 8.4

Evaluating Abstractions

Abstract terms like "marriage," "management," "professional athletics," and "the government" are really made up of things, people, and actions. Your lifestyle, for example, is certainly characterized by things—cars, sports equipment, an apartment, CDs; people—health-conscious, self-aware, up-to-date friends or colleagues; and actions—taking vacations in a national park, skiing, jogging, dedicated shopping. All of these elements make up a lifestyle and thus will furnish the examples for the evaluation of it. Thus if you want to argue for the value of a certain lifestyle, you will have to assess the merits and consequences of such specific elements.

Once again, you will use ideal definitions and consequences to support the evaluation of any abstraction. Most likely, ideal definition will dominate and will itself often become the focus of the argument. Every society engages in an ongoing debate over the ideal definitions of its most important institutions. What is the ideal Supreme Court—strict constructionist or activist or something else? What is the best kind of municipal government—strong mayor, city council, or regional consolidation? What kind of educational system best serves the needs of students—comprehensive public schools, charter schools, private schools? As these examples suggest, enormous controversies can erupt over ideal definitions of the institutions that affect our lives.

The second concern in evaluating an abstraction is likely to be consequence, the impact it has on people. If, for example, you argue that "The high value we place on constructing new interstate highways is misplaced because it brings development to rural areas," you are appealing to a consequence. But that consequence is negative only because you and your audience have in mind an ideal definition of rural areas as untouched by all that development brings with it.

Clearly consequence arguments predominate when we debate the impact of actions, policies, and useful objects, while ideal definition comes into play more in aesthetic and moral evaluations of things or people. Whatever kind of argument you make, you can strengthen your evaluations by calling on other standbys of support.

First, authority. Why should your audience accept your notion of a good object, person, or institution rather than someone else's? One way of heading off objections is to bolster your definition with appropriate authority. For example, bring in the Constitution to support your definition of the Supreme Court, a reference to Benjamin Franklin to illustrate your notion of a good library, or a quote from a Nobel Prize winner to bolster a concept of good science.

Second, comparison. If you can count on your audience's predictable evaluation of anything as good or bad, you can compare whatever is under scrutiny to whatever is more widely admired or condemned. For example, we have all heard what a magnificent city Paris is. Perhaps Washington, D.C., falls short of that ideal in some respects but approaches it in others. Thus, an evaluation of Washington may be developed by comparing it to Paris.

EXERCISE 8.5

Working either alone or with a group of classmates, evaluate the following list of abstractions. First you will need to define the abstractions as some combination of objects, people, and actions. In your evaluation, appeal to both ideal definitions and consequences and bring in other relevant lines of support. Choose one abstraction and write a brief report of your evaluation to share with the class. You may go on to use this abstraction as the subject of a full evaluation argument.

1. Your institution's student government for an audience of fellow students
2. Your local public library for people who don't use it
3. Adolescence for parents
4. The high school you attended for fellow college students
5. Standard of living to a recent immigrant
6. College life to someone about to enter college
7. Affirmative action to a member of a minority
8. Political advertising to an audience of TV viewers
9. Network television programming to a steady viewer
10. The police (campus, town, state) to the group served

Weighting Criteria

Suppose you are planning to buy a personal computer. If you know something about computers, you will have little difficulty identifying some standards that a good PC must meet.

- Speed
- Expandability
- Memory
- User friendliness
- Internet accessibility
- Software availability
- Price
- Dependability
- Capacity for voice recognition

Two people might nod yes to all these standards, and yet when faced with a real choice among computers, might choose different ones. Why? Because even though they agreed to the same standards, they *weighted* them differently. By "weighting" we mean nothing more complicated than ranking standards in order of importance. One person may put speed at the top of the list; another, user friendliness. Since any real object is unlikely to have all the ideal attributes in the same degree or combination, we have to make a best choice among what is available, and that is why weighting can lead to different choices. If price is important, and the one personal computer that does and has everything you want costs more than you can pay, out it goes.

   In evaluating a consumer product, weighting may be an individual matter. Whenever we are going to spend our own money, an evaluation will take into account our resources and our personal preferences. In buying a computer a technically adept person might put speed and power at the top of the list and not worry about the price, while someone with less money who needs only word processing and Internet access might put price at the top and make do with less speed.

Most of the time when people disagree about an evaluation, then, it is not so much the criteria that they differ about, but the comparative weight they give to them. The weighting of criteria for things and actions other than consumer goods often needs to be defended on more impersonal grounds. Whenever you make an evaluation argument, you not only can but must weight your criteria, and you may even have to defend your weighting. What, for example, is the most important quality of a good administrator—flexibility, sensitivity to employees, an eye on the balance sheet, or the ability to manage detail? If you were the chief executive officer in a company evaluating the managers under you, you would have to decide which quality is most important and defend that emphasis when deciding whom to hire. You might concede the importance of the other standards but emphasize one by claiming that without it the other standards will not work. Such an argument might resemble the following:

> The ability to handle detail is the most important quality of a good manager. A manager can be imaginative in dreaming up new programs, sensitive to handling personnel problems, and know enough accounting to balance the budget, but if this person doesn't answer the mail, return phone calls, and get memos out on time, business will slip into chaos and all the creativity, sensitivity, and bookkeeping skill will go for nothing.

You can also bring in other techniques to support your weighting of criteria, like appeals to authority, comparisons, or examples.

PROJECT FOR CLASS DISCUSSION

Think of a list of standards that a consumer product must meet. It should be a product that every member of the class has purchased at one time or another, perhaps an everyday item such as toothpaste or soap, or a product related to your schoolwork such as a software program or a textbook such as this one. Take a few minutes to think carefully about your list of standards—there may be more of them than you realize at first. Now consider how you would weight your criteria. Don't be surprised if class members disagree on which criteria are most important. Which criteria do most class members rate as most and least important?

Weighting Values: Ethical Argument

Suppose you were a judge faced with the following question requiring your legal evaluation: Is it right for the Amish to refuse state-mandated secondary education on the grounds that any education beyond eighth grade conflicts with the practice of their religion? Here is a case not of clear right versus clear wrong, but of two values in conflict—education and religious freedom. How would you decide which is more important? The United States Supreme Court decided that although a state has the right to insist on compulsory education to the age of sixteen, that right or value was not as significant in this case as freedom of religious practice. So long as the Amish could demonstrate that secondary education disrupted their religious practice (and the Amish of Wisconsin did), the Court's decision was in their favor.

What the Supreme Court did was weight one value over another. Ethical and legal argument often involves making such fine discriminations, ranking values in a hierarchy in order to pass judgment. In many ethical arguments, you and your audience might agree on certain values, but not necessarily rank them in the same way. Your job then is to weight one value, the one that will become the critical criterion of judgment, above others. Evaluating values in this way involves appealing to higher values or to consequences. You might argue, for instance, that faced with a choice, being well educated is better than being wealthy. Though both are good, the first has primacy because education cannot be taken away, has great benefits for the mind and enriches all experience so that life is fuller.

No matter what you are evaluating, from an object to a value itself, most of the time weighting will be the crucial issue for your audience. People are quite likely to agree about the relevance of a set of criteria, but they often disagree about which particular ones are most important in a given situation.

PROJECT FOR CLASS DISCUSSION

Consider an issue involving two conflicting values that is currently in the news, such as the right to publish material on the Internet versus the need to protect children from dangerous messages, or the desirability of increasing the number of jobs available in developing countries versus the concern that such jobs do not pay a decent wage or that they take away jobs from the United States. Discuss which of the two conflicting values is more important than the other one, and why.

Here are five lists of standards for the evaluation of (1) a thing, (2) a person, (3) an action, (4) an abstraction, and (5) an ethical problem. Rank the criteria in each list in two different ways, for two different audiences, and defend each version. You need not work with all the criteria given.

EXERCISE 8.6

1. Thing: an apartment (one-room studio)
   a. amount of rent
   b. security
   c. quiet surroundings
   d. size
   e. convenience of trash disposal
   f. closeness to public transportation
   g. parking facilities
   h. cleanliness/general condition
   i. light and view
   j. maintenance

2. Person: a lecturer
   a. clear speaking voice
   b. sense of humor
   c. command of material
   d. enthusiasm for subject
   e. good organization
   f. writes clearly on board
   g. uses PowerPoint effectively
   h. well-dressed

3. Action: a basketball game
   a. home team wins
   b. close score
   c. full arena
   d. lots of cheering
   e. good pregame party
   f. quality of half-time show
   g. quality of cheerleading
   h. number of fouls
   i. ranking of opponent

4. Institution: a university or college
   a. variety of curricula offered
   b. tuition
   c. number of nationally famous scholars on faculty
   d. adequacy of dorm space
   e. adequacy of parking space
   f. male/female ratio
   g. reputation of sports teams
   h. closeness to an urban center
   i. beauty of campus
   j. closeness to home

5. Ethical or legal problem: gun control
   a. fairness to hunters
   b. effect on manufacturers
   c. fairness to well-qualified potential owners
   d. effect on accident rates
   e. consistency with Bill of Rights
   f. effect on crime rates
   g. impact on those who already own guns

EXERCISE 8.7

Using a list of criteria that you developed for an earlier exercise, rank the criteria in the list for a specific audience, and defend your ranking. You need not work with all the criteria you developed.

All our evaluations so far have taken the simple form of an argument that X is good, bad, or mediocre, and so on. But evaluations can take two other forms, which we will deal with briefly—"better than" or "worse than" arguments; and "best" or "worst" arguments.

Comparative Evaluation

Consider such comparative statements as these:

1. Reba McIntyre is better than Shania Twain.
2. Swimming is better than running.
3. Los Angeles is better than New York.
4. Solitary confinement is worse than physical abuse.

The support for such statements cannot begin until you come up with one or more classes or categories to which the objects of comparison can belong. For example, if you want to argue that Reba McIntyre is better than Shania Twain, no doubt you mean that Reba McIntyre is a better singer or songwriter or concert performer or something else than Shania Twain. Similarly, if you want to make the case for Los Angeles over New York, you might argue that Los Angeles has a better climate, livelier entertainment scene, or greater business opportunities than New York—that is, you choose an area or category in which to compare them. Only if you can come up with one or more categories in which one thing can be better than the other, can you make and organize an evaluation-with-degree argument. Each of the categories of comparison can then be taken care of in its own mini-argument. Some of these might emphasize ideal definitions, while others appeal to consequences. Of course, you might need to weight the elements of your comparison so that ones you think are most important get the most emphasis: "Yes, New York has better business opportunities in some areas, but how could anyone live in such a miserable climate?"

Here are some comparative evaluations. Working either alone or with a group of classmates, generate at least three categories, or areas in which to make an evaluation, that both things can belong to.

1. Jazz is superior to rock.
2. Baseball is better than football.
3. Science fiction is superior to detective stories.
4. E-mail is superior to snail-mail.
5. It is better to have loved and lost than never to have loved at all.

EXERCISE 8.8

Superlative Evaluation

When you argue that something is the best or worst, you will always identify at least one category to which your subject belongs:

1. The Library of Congress is the best library in the United States.
2. The Rolls-Royce is the best car made.
3. Warren G. Harding was the worst president the United States ever had.
4. Traffic in Rome is the worst in Europe.
5. Charity is the greatest virtue of them all.
6. Pride is the worst sin.

The Library of Congress is a library, the Rolls-Royce is a car. Once you have a category, you can construct criteria of evaluation.

For superlative evaluations you have two special tactics of support at your disposal; you can use either one or both. In the first method, you come up with an ideal definition of best library, best car, worst European traffic, greatest virtue, and so on. In effect you create a class that can have only one member, and you go on to show how your subject fits into that exclusive group. If you want to argue that "Pride is the worst sin" you will have to begin by defining worst sin. You might argue that it is the vice that corrupts a person most completely. Of course, you can also appeal to consequence in the same way, arguing that it produces the greatest negative effects, that it is the one sin from which all others flow.

In the second method of superlative evaluation, you define a somewhat larger class, the class of near peers. In other words, you would define not "best library" but "good library." A class like "good libraries" has several members competing for the title "best," so you can now proceed by refutation, showing that the other contenders do not fulfill the criteria as well as yours. To do this you can make a series of "better than" or "worse than" arguments, each of which names a different attribute or a different peer that might be a rival to your claim. Thus you could come up with a series of comparative evaluations that claim the superiority of the Library of Congress over the other good libraries:

1. The Library of Congress is a better manuscript repository than the New York Public Library.
2. The Library of Congress subscribes to more newspapers than the Widener Library at Harvard.
3. The Library of Congress is easier for scholars to use than any other library.

If you have a reasonable, easily acceptable set of near peers, you can bypass discussion of explicit criteria of evaluation and get right into comparison.

Here are some topics inviting superlative evaluations. Defend them by setting up an ideal definition of "best" or "worst" or else a set of near peers for an audience that is likely to name different candidates for praise.

1. What is the best movie you ever saw?
2. Who is the best Republican or Democratic presidential candidate?
3. What is the best way to celebrate a birthday?
4. What is the worst date you ever had?
5. What is the worst insult one could throw at someone?
6. What is the best way to promote equal access to opportunity?

that do not apply to the evaluation you are analyzing.) When you have done your own analysis and gone over any comments from your classmates, use these comments and suggestions to revise and refine your evaluation and make it stronger.

1. *Has the evaluation maintained a clear, consistent audience and purpose?* Does it start out as a simple value judgment and end up arguing for a particular course of action? Is it an abstract or ideal evaluation that does not match its audience's circumstances? If it is evaluating a course of action, for example, it should examine only realistic alternatives, not every possible alternative.

2. *Will the audience agree with the criteria?* List the criteria, whether stated or implied, and consider each one in turn. Do you agree with each criterion? Will the audience agree with it? Are there other criteria that should be included?

3. *Is the subject compared to an ideal definition of its type?* If so, will the audience agree with that definition? If not, how would they change the definition? What definition would they offer in its place?

4. *Has the evaluator weighted the criteria appropriately?* Which criterion does the evaluator consider most important? Do you agree with this ranking? What criterion would you rank higher, and would most audience members agree with your ranking?

5. *Has the evaluator demonstrated that the subject really possesses the qualities of the criteria or of the ideal definition?* Examine the evidence that is provided. Is it appropriate? Can you think of evidence that indicates the subject does not possess this quality? If a causal argument is used, is it appropriate, and are the consequences clearly the result of the cause?

6. *If the evaluation is a comparison, has the evaluator clearly demonstrated that the subject is better than the alternative?* Does the evaluation establish at least one category in which one thing can be better than the other? Is there a strong mini-argument for each category? If it is a superlative evaluation, has the evaluation clearly established an ideal category and then demonstrated that the subject belongs to it, or presented a group of plausible candidates and then demonstrated that the subject is clearly better than they are?

7. *Is the evaluator's judgment of the subject clear?* Is the judgment clearly stated? Or is it ambiguous?

8. *Is the organization effective?* Is the judgment stated right away, or does the argument lead to the judgment, which is given at the end? Do you agree with the order the criteria are given in (if the criteria are explicitly stated rather than implied)? How would you reorganize the evaluation to make it more effective?

WRITING SUGGESTIONS

An evaluation can be written in many different contexts. Below are some broad suggestions of areas in which you can evaluate a subject and form a judgment.

1. Literature or Film: Choose a literary work, an author, a particular film, or a prominent director. (Examples: "Evaluate Arthur Miller's *Death of a Salesman* as a modern tragedy," "Consider the work of Spike Lee and his influence on films made in the last ten years.")

2. The Natural or Social Sciences: Evaluate two competing theories to explain a given phenomenon. (Example: "Which childhood influence—parents or peers—has a stronger effect on a teenager's behavior?")

3. Theater or Music Appreciation: Evaluate a performance, either live or prerecorded. (Examples: "Evaluate Keanu Reeve's performance in *The Matrix Reloaded,*" "Write an evaluation of the recent campus production of Shakespeare's *Twelfth Night,*" "Consider Kiri Te Kanawa's recording of arias by Verdi and Puccini.")

4. Business: For a job you have held or currently hold, evaluate a fellow worker, procedure, policy, existing product, or idea for a new product or service. (Examples: "Is our method of assigning projects working well?" "Is this new brand of snack food better than the competition?")

5. Politics: Evaluate the candidates for a public office at the local, state, or national level and decide which one will pursue the policies you agree with and come closest to your ideal version of a public servant. As an alternative, you might decide whether or not to support a proposition that has been placed on the ballot by an interest group in your area or your state. (Examples: "Will Candidate X make a better governor than Candidate Y?" "Is a cap on school taxes in the best interests of our community?")

Harvest the Whales, with letters to the editor in response

NICHOLAS D. KRISTOF

Nicholas D. Kristof is the associate managing editor of the *New York Times*. With his wife, *Times* reporter Sheryl WuDunn, he won the Pulitzer Prize in 1990 for reporting on the Tiananmen Square uprising in China. Kristof has been at the *Times* since 1984. This editorial appeared in the *Times* on August 20, 2002.

Whale-watching trips off Massachusetts are said to have begun only in 1975, with a pod of elementary school kids taking a boat from Provincetown, but now whale-watching is a $100 million industry in New England. And it's easy to see why: 35-foot humpbacks roll and splash so playfully around the boats that you just want to reach out and hug one.

Whales are so beloved that the authorities spent four months and $250,000 unsuccessfully trying to free a right whale dubbed Churchill from fishing ropes last year, and the stranding of 55 pilot whales near here a few weeks ago prompted a lump in the national throat. The "Save the Whales" ethos is almost unquestioned, and Norwegians and Japanese risk becoming pariahs by continuing to salivate when they see a nice juicy whale.

But it's time to put sentiment aside. The "save the whales" campaign against all commercial whaling was necessary a few decades ago, after whaling had devastated all large species. Even today, there are fewer than 10,000 blue whales worldwide, compared with 200,000 before they were hunted, and right whales may become extinct.

But it is equally true that restrictions on whaling, including a moratorium on all commercial whaling since 1986, have led to a sharp rebound in some whale stocks. The U.S. National Marine Fisheries Service estimated in 2000 that there are more than two million sperm whales worldwide. The International Whaling Commission calculated years ago that there were more than 900,000 minke whales and 780,000 pilot whales worldwide, and the numbers are higher now. Milton Freeman, a whaling expert at the University of Alberta, estimates that the number of minke whales has trebled over 30 years and that humpbacks are exploding at a rate of 12 to 17 percent annually.

Indeed, the number of gray whales (which came off the endangered species list in 5 1994) surged so much in the late 1990's that hundreds of dead ones began washing up on West Coast beaches, so emaciated that their ribs showed. The best guess is that the numbers of grays grew, the food supply shrank and Malthus had his way.

The bottom line is that while most large whales remain at risk, for some species we can no longer argue that we need to "save the whales." They've been saved.

At a time when there's talk about overfishing, it's also worth pointing out that whales now eat at least 300 million tons of marine life, three times as much as humans. There is speculation that rising numbers of minke whales may be holding down the population of blue whales that compete for similar food.

Bruce Mate is a whale specialist at Oregon State University whom I met 23 years ago on a beach where 41 sperm whales had stranded—a devastating scene as the whales thrashed on the sand and watched through sad eyes while a crowd of humans gathered to discuss what to do with them. Dr. Mate, who may know more about the blue whale than any non-cetacean, urges bold new initiatives to protect blues and other whales that are threatened.

But he also says that most biologists would not worry about commercial whaling of minkes and perhaps other populous species so long as quotas were set at a level that would sustain populations.

"Stocks that are in good health condition could have a sustainable commercial take," 10 Dr. Mate said. "Whether you want to do it is a personal moral or ethical matter."

That is the nub of it. There is no longer a "save the whales" imperative for a moratorium on commercial whaling of all species. The only remaining argument to oppose commercial hunting of common species like the minke and perhaps the sperm and gray is to say that whales are such magnificent creatures that no one should be allowed to kill them.

But that is dangerous ground. It is culinary imperialism for us to tell Norwegians and Japanese that because we like whales, they must not eat them. We can disapprove, just as we wince as Koreans or Chinese eat dogs, but what right do we have to forbid them from eating an animal that is not endangered but simply lovable? So are lambs and deer.

So, yes, it makes sense to save the whales that are endangered. Indeed, we should do more to help blue whales, like launching an international initiative to identify and protect their breeding grounds. But it's also time to allow some species to be harvested again.

To the Editor:

Nicholas D. Kristof (column, Aug. 20) is right that many stocks of whales are abundant and could be harvested sustainably. The International Whaling Commission's Scientific Committee has developed a risk-averse method for calculating catch quota for abundant stocks that would ensure long-term sustainability.

While "there is no longer a 'save the whales' imperative for a moratorium on commercial whaling of all species," moving to acceptance of regulated sustainable commercial whaling for food is difficult because politicians have found that an anti-whaling position helps them garner votes from those concerned about our environment without having to address more serious environmental issues.

This situation is perpetuated by political lobbying and intentionally misleading public campaigns by non-governmental organizations that raise millions of dollars a year with their anti-whaling rhetoric.

DAN GOODMAN
Tokyo, Aug. 20, 2002
The writer is a councilor at the Institute of Cetacean Research.

To the Editor:

Re "Harvest the Whales," by Nicholas D. Kristof (column, Aug. 20):

Whaling is now recognized by most of the civilized world as an archaic, barbaric practice, and a call for its return on a wider scale simply boggles the mind.

LEONID KRUGLYAK
Seattle, Aug. 20, 2002

To the Editor:

Re "Harvest the Whales," by Nicholas D. Kristof (column, Aug. 20):

More than 21,000 whales have been killed by Japan and Norway since a moratorium on commercial whaling was established by the International Whaling Commission in 1986. Last year, Japan and Norway killed more than 1,000 whales, and Japan has moved to add endangered sei whales to the Bryde's, sperm and minke whales killed in its annual hunt. DNA analysis of market samples from Japan has found other protected species of whale for sale.

Mr. Kristof says it is "culinary imperialism" to oppose the killing of whales. But whales are highly migratory creatures with special status under international law, and the high seas are not the province of any one country. By what right does Japan continue to kill protected whales in internationally recognized whale sanctuaries?

Commercial whaling is an inherently cruel practice that represents a significant threat to the conservation status of whales, both rare and abundant.

FRED O'REGAN
President, International Fund for Animal Welfare
Yarmouthport, Mass., Aug. 20, 2002

To the Editor:

Re "Harvest the Whales," by Nicholas D. Kristof (column, Aug. 20):

The human race has evolved beyond the point where we need to kill other sentient beings to survive. At least in the so-called developed world, we no longer need to behave like jungle animals or Neanderthal men, deciding which creatures we should or should not kill. It is demeaning to human dignity to debate whether to kill or not kill this or that animal.

CARLTON PARROTT
Newnan, Ga., Aug. 21, 2002

FOR YOU TO ANALYZE

1. How does the author appeal to his audience's shared values in paragraph 7? Are you then surprised by the stance taken in paragraph 9 by whale specialist Bruce Mate? Why?

2. The author makes both an appeal to consequences and an appeal to moral standards in his argument. Are both kinds of appeal effectively supported? Why, or why not?

3. In paragraph 5, the author alludes to the political economist Malthus. The Malthusian doctrine holds that disease, starvation, and war are natural and necessary checks on populations—however cruel the consequences. What kind of appeal does Kristof make by linking Malthusian thought with the plight of starving whales? Is it an effective strategy?

4. What kind of appeal do letter writers Leonid Kruglyak and Carlton Parrott make in response to Kristof's argument? Are the criteria on which they base their appeals adequately supported?

5. How do letter writers Dan Goodman and Fred O'Regan establish their ethos and authority? What kind of appeal do these two writers make in their arguments?

FOR YOU TO WRITE

1. Kristof's point in paragraph 11 is based on the idea of "cultural relativism"— that is, different cultures have different values and moral systems, and it is both hypocritical and biased to judge another culture based on your own belief system. Most Americans, for example, find the idea of eating dogs appalling— but other cultures think it's disgusting to let animals, like dogs, share our kitchens and sofas and beds. But "cultural relativism" becomes a far more serious and complex matter when considering practices like female genital mutilation in sub-Saharan Africa, the abandonment of female babies in China, or the easy availability of firearms in America under the Second Amendment. Think of another controversial American cultural practice or tradition. What makes this practice or tradition uniquely American? Who defends this practice or tradition, and who is challenging it? Whose side are you on, and why?

2. Have you ever taken a specific action based on your concerns about the environment? (For example: you try to shop for organic foods; you bicycle or take public transportation; you volunteer at a community garden.) What were the factors you considered when you decided to take that action? Did you give more weight to the practical consequences of your action, or to considerations of morals and values?

3. Read Carlton Parrott's letter. In your own words, write what you think is Parrott's ideal definition of "human dignity." Do you share his view? What is *your* ideal definition of "human dignity"?

TAKING IT ONLINE

Environmentalists, scientists, and industrialists have disagreed about the definition as well as the implications of "global warming." Visit the following web sites for different perspectives on the phenomenon:

- Yosemite.epa.gov/oar/globalwarming.nsf (site of the National Science Foundation and the Environmental Protection Agency's global warming information).

- www.globalwarming.org (site of the "Cooler Heads Coalition," which is concerned with the economic impact of global-warming treaties and policies).

- www.sierraclub.org/globalwarming (international environmental conservation organization).

Which organizations use their web sites to appeal to consequences? Which organizations appeal to moral standards, or make emotional appeals? Do these organizations use their web sites to educate, to advocate, or both?

Editorial: Leave the Flicks Alone

DES MOINES REGISTER EDITORIAL BOARD

The *Register* is the largest daily newspaper in Des Moines, a city of about 200,000 people that is the capital of Iowa. This editorial appeared on September 28, 2002.

Imagine strolling through the video store and you happen across a movie that looks interesting. There are two versions, though: the original, and a version scrubbed clean of any violence, nudity and foul language.

This is now possible at some video outlets, which prompts cheers from Americans weary of the gratuitous sex and violence in movies. Filmmakers aren't cheering, however. They filed a lawsuit asserting the companies that market videos edited without their permission violate copyright law. All of which raises interesting questions about intellectual property rights in the digital world.

In the old days, the people who made books, music, movies and other media maintained control of content because only a few big companies could afford to mass-produce their work. With off-the-shelf computer software today, however, an ordinary computer user is a few clicks away from a sanitized version of most any recent movie.

This has resulted in a cottage industry that is cleaning up Hollywood's fare and marketing it through commercial video-rental stores, including one in Ames, and through software that allows individuals to "edit" a sanitized version of a movie at home.

The first approach is an obvious violation of movie producers' intellectual property 5 rights. It's one thing to sit at home and delete scenes from a movie for personal use; it's another matter to sell that version on the open market. Steven Spielberg put several minutes of brutal war footage at the beginning of "Saving Private Ryan" for a reason, and for someone to rent or sell a version without those scenes substantially changes his work. That is trespassing on the director's intellectual property.

This is what the law of copyright is intended to prevent. Without it, anyone could change a book, a movie or a song to their liking and sell it as the original creator's work. That may not bother fans of G-rated movies, but how would they feel about someone inserting triple-X-rated scenes into a Disney movie?

Selling computer software that digitally sanitizes movies is a closer question, but it still doesn't pass the copyright test: These computer programs allow consumers to sanitize movies using software pre-programmed to delete select scenes or words from select movies. While this sounds like home editing, it's not: It still is mass-marketing the machinery to alter the creator's work without authorization.

The courts will eventually have to sort out what's permissible and what is not. Meanwhile, the popularity of sanitized movies suggests a compromise: Why doesn't Hollywood put out its own versions of movies (as it does for TV broadcast) without the sex and violence?

FOR YOU TO ANALYZE

1. This editorial makes an aesthetic evaluation not of a specific work of art, but of the nature of creativity. To do so, the authors consider content and craft, but they also link the moral consequences of digitally "sanitized" films to a larger appeal to shared values. What are those shared values to which the writers appeal?

2. In paragraph 6, the authors make an appeal to consequences with a hypothetical scenario. How effective is this appeal to negative consequences? What does this hypothetical scenario suggest about the values of the audience for this editorial?

3. Part of this editorial includes a practical evaluation of software that allows individuals to "edit" DVDs to suit their own tastes. On what criteria is this evaluation based? Do the authors adequately consider other points of view (concerned parents, the software designers themselves, and so on)? Why, or why not?

4. The authors conclude with a rhetorical question. Does this question follow logically from their argument? How does (or doesn't) it build on the appeals and support of the editorial?

FOR YOU TO WRITE

1. Many hip-hop and rap artists are criticized for lurid or violent lyrics. Cable music channels as well as radio stations routinely play "sanitized" versions of these artists' works, and sanitized versions of their CDs are routinely produced and marketed alongside the uncensored versions. Compare a sanitized and an uncensored version of the same recording. Do you agree with the Register Editorial Board that the sanitized version is an "obvious violation" of the artist's "intellectual property rights"? Is the issue the same for movies as it is for music?

2. Is there anything on network (not cable) television now that genuinely shocks you or that you feel would simply not have been broadcast as recently as 10 years ago? Describe a program that you find offensive on moral or aesthetic grounds, being sure to define and clarify those moral or aesthetic criteria precisely.

3. If you had a personal software program that would screen out or eliminate three annoying or offensive things in any media you encounter—any paper you read, web site you visit, television show you watch—what three things would you use it on? Describe what it is about each of the three things that offends you, and evaluate how your daily media experiences would be improved by their elimination.

TAKING IT ONLINE

Visit the Movie Review Query engine at www.mrqe.com and look up a recent popular film that you enjoyed. Compare the criteria used by two or three reviewers to your own reasons for enjoying the film. Are all of you using the same criteria? If so, do you weight your criteria differently than the professional reviewers? If not, do you agree or disagree with the criteria used by the professional reviewers?

The Best

JONATHAN V. LAST

Jonathan V. Last is a reporter and the online editor for *The Weekly Standard,* where this article first appeared in January 1999.

Bobby Knight, who is infallible, says that Michael Jordan is the "best player who's played anything." If there were any argument with the Indiana coach's dictum, consider Jordan's three most impressive statistics: He led the National Basketball Association in scoring 10 times, more than any other player; he won championships in his last six full seasons; in the 1,109 professional games in which he played over the course of 13 seasons with the Chicago Bulls, he was held below 10 points only once (on March 22, 1986, as he was recuperating from a broken foot).

But of course there is no argument. When Jordan retired last week, his dominance, his ability to elevate those around him, and his unearthly consistency were universally acknowledged. For once, the conventional wisdom is right: Jordan was, in fact, the best. But why? Here is where the story gets interesting. The near-beatification of Michael Jordan is a tribute to America's enduring love affair with Success. Yes, we love a winner. What we can't stand these days, though, is the peculiar discipline that produces epic achievement. A fierce desire to win is part of it, but more crucial is the ruthless determination to vanquish your foes. The secret of Michael Jordan's greatness—of all competitive greatness—is not merely, as we now instruct our children, to *do your best*. It is to make *your best* superior to everyone else's. You must cultivate your own talent, yes; but you must also search out and exploit the weaknesses of your opponent. Somebody must lose so you can win.

Needless to say, this stern message has not been featured prominently in the tributes to Jordan. A culture that simultaneously rewards success and averts its eyes from the traits that produce champions must nourish deep illusions. With Jordan, the first of these illusions is embodied in the public persona he has meticulously cultivated for himself—the smiling, lovable super-athlete from television commercials. This is the image *USA Today* must have had in mind when it applauded Jordan's "pride, patience, loyalty, dedication, competitiveness, accountability, and humility." (Humility!) Or the *Philadelphia Inquirer*, when it said that "He smiled and the world was a smaller place." The second illusion is that Jordan merely applied an exceptional set of physical gifts: The "soaring leaps, darting fakes, flawless ball handling" that the *New York Times* hailed as "poetic" were just the product of a body that, as President Clinton put it last week, "would do things no one else's would do."

This is an appealing idea for people who want only to bask in the famous Michael Jordan smile. But it's nonsense. The truth is that dozens of players in recent years were as naturally talented as Jordan—Shaquille O'Neal, Julius Erving, teammate Scottie Pippen, just to name a few. Yet it was Jordan who became the best pro basketball player right out of the University of North Carolina in 1984. And it was Jordan who, in the decade and a half that followed, widened the gulf between himself and everyone else. Jordan defied the immutable law of sports—that time is an athlete's worst enemy. Age felled every other great athlete the world has ever seen. Ali and Mays, Babe Ruth and Mickey Mantle, all of the other greats wilted as their feet became too slow, and their bodies betrayed their minds. Jordan is a better player today, a month from his 36th birthday, than he was ten years ago. The trick is that Michael Jordan was a basketball player the way William Tecumsch Sherman was a soldier and Bill Gates is a businessman.

To be the best means conceiving of one's life as a quest for domination. Jordan has al- 5 ways felt the need not only to win, but to destroy his opponents. And to do this, he has always been on the prowl for sources of motivation. This was easier at first. Jordan was a coltish kid on a University of North Carolina team chock full of future NBA stars, and so he set about trying to earn the respect of his teammates and win something meaningful. It took him six months. As a freshman, Jordan hit the game-winning shot to beat Georgetown for the NCAA title and became a college superstar.

After his junior year, Jordan was drafted by the Chicago Bulls, then one of the worst teams in the league. Rod Thorn, the team's general manager at the time, said, "Jordan isn't going to turn this franchise around. I wouldn't ask him to. He's a very good offensive player, but not an overpowering offensive player." Talk about motivation. Jordan took those comments to heart, and in his ninth game as a professional, scored 45 points against San Antonio. *Washington Post* sportswriter Tony Kornheiser once observed that Jordan "remembers every insult, every innuendo." Thus, in January 1996, a Philadelphia sportswriter said that the 76ers' ballyhooed rookie Jerry Stackhouse might be the second coming of Jordan. Motivation squared. Not long afterwards, an incensed Jordan rang up 48 points playing against Stackhouse and hinted after the game that there was no other Michael Jordan.

During the 1997 season, Jeff Van Gundy, head coach of the New York Knicks, had the sand to say that Jordan was a "con man" who befriended players from other teams off the court so that he could exploit them during games. By all accounts, Van Gundy was right. So at their next meeting, Jordan scored 51 points and leveled his menacing gaze at the Knicks' coach after every single basket.

Jordan's revenge scenarios could be fantasies; that didn't make them any less effective. In May 1993, the Bulls met the Atlanta Hawks in the first round of the playoffs. Jordan's performance was magnificent. At one point, he blocked Hawks star Dominique Wilkins's shot and then hit a jump shot from half-court at the buzzer. After the game, Jordan would write that he had to play harder for that game because Wilkins was "trying to show me up in front of my family." It goes without saying that there's no way Wilkins would have known the whereabouts of Jordan's family, or would have cared had he known. But Jordan needed a reason to throw himself into battle.

Practices, too, were an arena for conquest. At a camp for the 1992 U.S. Olympic team, Grant Hill, a soft-spoken young college player from Duke University, was doing his best to guard Jordan. Jordan was scoring at will, but he still couldn't resist angrily telling his teammate, "Look, man, this ain't Duke. I can get the ball whenever I want, and I can do whatever I want with it."

For all of Jordan's individual brilliance, there's no getting around the fact that bas- 10 ketball is a team sport. His solution? Motivate his teammates, by whatever means necessary. During Jordan's early years with the Bulls, many of his teammates disliked his version of bonding. So he prodded. He once nonchalantly referred to them as his "supporting cast," a bunch of players who weren't "good for much of anything." After workouts, Jordan would challenge people to shooting contests, for money. And despite being the highest paid player on the team, he always collected.

Not surprisingly, Jordan's competitive spirit animates his life off the basketball court, as well. During his college days he was notorious for upending the Monopoly board when defeat was imminent. David Halberstam tells in *Vanity Fair* how Jordan once lost three consecutive games of pool to assistant Tar Heel coach Roy Williams. He wouldn't speak to Williams the next day.

His business dealings, too, have proven to be just another arena in which to compete. *Fortune* recently published a whimsical econometric analysis, estimating that

Jordan is personally responsible for the creation of roughly $10 billion of wealth. This money comes from his salary, ticket sales, television revenues, licensing fees, movies, and product endorsements, of which he is the undisputed king. Dollars, after all, are another convenient way of keeping score. Making more for endorsing Nike shoes than Allen Iverson does for endorsing Reebok; having *Space Jam* (the movie he starred in) gross more than Shaquille O'Neal's movie *Steel*—these are victories to be cherished every bit as much as beating the Knicks.

And Jordan, when he lets down his guard, can be surprisingly clear-eyed about his own single-mindedness. For many pro athletes, the game is a means to an end. Wilt Chamberlain, the dominant player of his era, estimated his sexual conquests in the tens of thousands, and NBA groupies are still legion. For Jordan, on the other hand, the game is the end. He strikes the note of a realist in his glossy autobiography *For the Love of the Game:* "There was a reason for me getting married. That experience of being a husband and a father provided a balance and a focus away from basketball. . . . If I had been single, playing basketball, and making a lot of money, I could have made some wrong decisions." Marriage: another means to becoming the best.

Those who know Jordan are familiar with his ruthlessness and his relentlessness. Doug Collins, his one-time Bulls coach, once observed: "He wants to cut your heart out and then show it to you." Luc Longley, the Bulls' starting center for the last three years and a Jordan booster, was asked to give a one-word definition of his teammate. "Predator," he said.

In a feat almost as remarkable as his athletic exploits, Jordan has managed to sustain a   15
public image as benign and cuddly as the cartoon characters he pals around with on television ads. He prudently allied himself with softdrinks that encouraged us "to be like Mike." He stars in underwear commercials frolicking with his wife and children, and in movies with Bugs Bunny and other animated rascals. He never appears in public wearing anything less formal than a suit. He even went to great pains during games to affect an easygoing jokey manner when the cameras were on him. Off-camera he would grab jerseys, throw elbows, and talk trash with the best. And occasionally, the cameras would capture the warrior, as when, during the 1996 NBA Finals, Seattle's point guard Gary Payton tried to argue a call with the referee. Jordan shouldered his way between the two men and began shouting at Payton, over and over again, "This is the Finals! What's wrong with you?"

The two sides of his game showed his deep understanding of what it takes to become a revered champion. It's not enough to be merely very, very good. To be embraced as heroic, you can't be Dan Marino with record upon record but no Super Bowl, Roger Clemens with no-hitters but no World Series ring, or Greg Norman, the all-time leading money man in golf with only two wins in the major tournaments. You have to win everything, and win it often—but then you have to hide the fierceness. The victorious hero-athlete, 1990s-style, needs to be huggable and lovable, like Mark McGwire, the home-run king with a tear in his eye and an embrace for the children of the man he eclipsed.

But in the end, if you really want to "be like Mike," look at the game tapes and not the commercials. Know that before the games Michael Jordan practiced harder than anyone. And know that after the games, while most of his opponents and teammates kicked back and relaxed, Jordan lifted weights. Look beyond the wagging tongue and the ready smile, and what you see is a man who was never soft, who divided his opponents into potential threats and prey. He was willing to forgo mercy. He never had a second thought about hurting, humiliating, or defeating anyone. It never occurred to him that the 40th or 50th or 63rd point might be overkill, that he didn't need to win this game of pool, that you don't have to humiliate rookies. Embed a deep fear in your opponent, and the next time you meet, you can exploit that fear. The thing that makes a man the best, finally, is his determination to do what other men won't.

On June 14, 1998, in the chaotic twilight of the last game of the championship series, Michael Jordan put the kind of move on Utah's Bryon Russell that destroys a man's career. With 6.6 seconds left and the Jazz clinging desperately to a one-point lead, Jordan faked to his right so hard that Russell actually fell down. With biblical certainty, Jordan took the last shot of his career, and the Bulls won their sixth championship. While people streamed onto the court celebrating and hugging, Jordan ran around the floor, his muscular arms raised, and his hands holding up six fingers. On the tape you can see him yelling the word "six" over and over, a look of vindication and furious anger on his face, and in those delirious moments of what, for him, was jubilation, it became obvious that Michael Jordan had no want or need for love and adoration. What he wanted was to leave his opponents stooped and bowed and to receive the acclaim that is owed the victor.

To afford Michael Jordan the respect he deserves means to acknowledge him as what he is, not what we would like him to be. He is the greatest athlete, the most ruthless competitor—the best—the world has ever known.

FOR YOU TO ANALYZE

1. What does Last mean when he calls Jordan "the best"? How does Last define the ideal? Do you agree with his ideal definition? Why or why not?

2. Last compares two different images of Michael Jordan in this argument. What are the images he chooses? Why do you think he makes this comparison? Does the comparison work effectively in his argument? Why or why not?

3. What kinds of support does Last use for his evaluation argument? What supporting evidence do you find most and least convincing? Why?

4. How do you think Last expects his audience to respond to this argument? What in his argument gives you this impression? Do you think he has anticipated opposition effectively? Why or why not?

FOR YOU TO WRITE

1. Last argues that Jordan is, in fact, "the best," but not for the reasons most people would expect. Choose a public figure who is widely admired and write a brief argument explaining either why the person should not be considered a hero at all or why the person is a hero, but not for the reasons most people believe.

2. Many young Americans respect famous athletes more than any other adults. What do the athletes do to earn their fans' respect? Is an admiring view of athletes in general, or of a particular athlete, good or bad for young fans and for society as a whole? Write a brief evaluation of this trend as either helpful or unhelpful to young people or to society in general. You may want to create a definition of *role model* or look at possible consequences of admiration for sports figures.

3. Have you ever felt that others either admired or disliked you based on an unrealistic perception of who you are? What criteria do others use in judging you? Are these criteria appropriate? Evaluate the inaccurate view that you think others hold of you and argue that it is either better or worse than the "real you."

FOR YOU TO DISCOVER ONLINE

Using your favorite search engine, look for information about a hero of yours. Does the person have a personal web page? If so, what does it contain? Do other fans of this hero have pages devoted to him/her? Can you find chat rooms and other ways to get involved in online discussions about this person? Do you find any dissenting viewpoints about your hero? If so, do they make you reconsider your opinion of him or her? Why or why not?

Yes, Gambling Is Productive and Rational

DAVID RAMSAY STEELE

David Ramsay Steele is an economist and author who writes frequently for *Liberty* magazine, where this article first appeared in September 1997.

"You do not play then at whist, sir! Alas, what a sad old age you are preparing for yourself!"

—Talleyrand

The War on Gambling is about to take its place alongside the War on Drugs as a crusade for decency which no ambitious politician may question. The present movement to legalize gambling, which got under way in the 1960s, is still making some gains, but has become increasingly unpopular. The momentum of legalization has been slowed, and will soon be reversed. Although some gambling is now legal in all but two states (Hawaii and Utah), gambling prohibitionists are confidently predicting absolute nationwide prohibition by early next century, and it's by no means self-evident that they are wrong.

Government policy on gambling has gone through successive cycles of liberalization, backlash, and renewed prohibition. In the U.S., we are currently experiencing the third nationwide backlash—the first was in the middle of the nineteenth century, the second during the 1940s.

The ease with which public opinion can be mobilized against gambling reflects a deep-rooted suspicion. Most people enjoy gambling in moderation, and will gamble occasionally if they can. Yet these same people often oppose further liberalization of the gambling laws. Gambling is one of those things which are obviously harmless when you or I do them, but fraught with menace if millions of other people can do them too.

Why is gambling, enjoyed by the vast majority of people, denounced day in and day out, with hardly any voices to be heard in its defense? The reigning ideology tells us all that gambling is evil, for several reasons. Gambling is selfish; it is addictive; it provides "false hope"; it is a dangerous competitor to some forms of religion because it too offers the prospect of a greatly improved future life at rather long odds.

Yet possibly the single most influential reason for holding gambling to be evil is the belief that it is unproductive and therefore wasteful. Today's hostility to gambling has much in common with the old opposition to "usury" (charging interest on loans) and the current fear of "de-industrialization" (replacement of manufacturing by service jobs).   5

Money-lending, hamburger-flipping, and playing the lottery have all been maligned as essentially sterile pursuits whose expansion bodes ill for the health of the nation.

Simply Sterile Transfers?

Is gambling unproductive? We need to distinguish between the more or less remote *effects* of gambling and its *intrinsic nature*. It is sometimes claimed that gambling encourages people to dream impossible dreams about the future instead of working hard, or that gambling encourages crime at the expense of honest industry. Aside from these alleged effects of gambling, however, it is commonly believed that gambling is intrinsically unproductive—that in gambling, unlike farming or auto manufacture, nothing is produced.

Claims about the injurious *effects* of gambling don't seem to be factually correct. Freedom to gamble encourages hard work on the part of gamblers, especially those with low incomes, just as, broadly speaking, any enhanced opportunity to spend one's earnings as one pleases increases the incentive effect of a given wage. And gambling by itself does not attract crime: it is the illegality of some or all gambling which forces gambling to become a criminal activity.[1]

Is gambling, then, *intrinsically* unproductive? One very popular view was promulgated by Paul Samuelson in his once-canonical textbook: gambling "involves *simply sterile transfers of money or goods* between individuals, creating no new money or goods."[2] A footnote informs the reader that "in all professional gambling arrangements, the participants lose out on balance. The leakage comes from the fact that the odds are always rigged in favor of the 'house,' so that even an 'honest' house will win in the long run." Notice the nasty quotes around "honest," and the use of the word "rigged" to represent the fact that these sneaky casino operators do not provide their services as a charity, but require to be recompensed for their efforts, just like college professors or writers of textbooks.

The Cannibals Are Coming

Before we look at the claim that gambling involves nothing but sterile transfers of money or goods, let's first consider a related charge levelled by anti-gambling propagandists. One of their leaders, Robert Goodman, contends that gambling, when it is permitted after a period of prohibition, displaces or, as he picturesquely terms it, "cannibalizes" other activities.[3]

Goodman continually reiterates this charge, and doesn't seem to notice that it applies equally to any activity which consumes scarce resources—any activity whatsoever. If pizza restaurants were first prohibited and then legalized, the newly legal restaurants would attract some dollars away from other businesses. Buildings, kitchen equipment, tables, delivery vehicles, and employees would be bid away from other kinds of restaurants, and perhaps some resources would be bid away from non-restaurant activities, to cater to the consumers' newly-liberated demand for pizzas. One might then observe that pizza provision grows only by hurting other occupations—that pizzerias "cannibalize" other trades.

If, after being prohibited, a casino is permitted to open, this may well cause people to spend in the casino some money they would formerly have spent in a restaurant. Perhaps that restaurant has to close because of reduced business. Precisely the same would apply in reverse: if casinos were legal, but restaurants prohibited, and then restaurants were legalized, the newly legal restaurants would attract consumers' dollars away from casinos, and some casinos might have to close. Anti-restaurant fanatics could then proclaim that restaurateurs were nothing more than dastardly cannibals, gobbling up legitimate businesses such as casinos.

When a heretofore prohibited but widely desired activity is legalized, the expansion of this activity will necessarily curtail other activities, unless total output increases. This does not mean that the change is unimportant. The fact that people pursue the newly legal activity demonstrates that there is an unsatisfied appetite for that activity. The people who desire to take part in the prohibited activity, and are now free to do so, experience an improvement in their situation, in their own judgment. Their real incomes automatically rise, even though this increase is not captured in national income statistics.

There are two important qualifications to what I have just stated. First, the legalization of a formerly prohibited industry reduces the demand for other industries below what it would otherwise have been, not necessarily below what it has actually been. If total output rises—if there is economic growth—casinos may attract business from restaurants, and yet restaurants may keep the same business as before, or even expand. Second, prohibition of gambling does not succeed in stopping gambling. While prohibition reduces the total amount of gambling, some gambling goes on illicitly. A major part of the expansion of legal gambling following legalization takes away business from formerly illegal gambling rather than from non-gambling activities.

The assertion that gambling subtracts consumer dollars from other industries is precisely as true of gambling as of manufacturing refrigerators, providing health care, or running a church. Why then do anti-gambling zealots make such a fuss about cannibalization? There are two reasons.

First, in recent years politicians who favor legalization of gambling have scored 15 points by appealing to local advantage. They have claimed that the local economy (city, county, state, or Indian reservation) would get a shot in the arm from an increased inflow of visitors. In this case, the money spent on local gambling is not withdrawn from some other local industry; it is withdrawn from industries outside the locality. There is a net gain to business in the locality, at the expense of reduced business elsewhere.

But this only works if gambling continues to be considerably more restricted outside the locality than it is within it. Las Vegas is now established as an exciting vacation center which would easily survive the complete legalization of all gambling in the U.S., but in its formative years Las Vegas would never have taken off if gambling had not been virtually illegal across nearly all of the country. The more gambling is legalized generally, the less any locality can attract visitors by legalization.

There has recently been so much legalization in various parts of the U.S. that any locality which newly legalizes gambling cannot thereby attract many visitors.[4] The bulk of the new gambling business unleashed by a local legalization now comes from people who live nearby.[5] This has led to disappointment at the results of recent legalizations, disappointment which rabid anti-gambling demagogues like Goodman can cynically exploit.

The fundamental argument for legalizing gambling is not that it will bring in business from elsewhere, but rather that people are entitled to do whatever they please with their own lives as long as they don't invade other people's rights. More generally, it is good for people to be free to do what they want to do, so long as this does not impose on anyone else.

The other reason why the "cannibalization" argument is so often made is that many people start with the prejudice that gambling is a waste. If gambling is unproductive, and if the growth of gambling subtracts from some productive activity, then this must, it seems, be bad. But if it is bad for gambling to cannibalize restaurants, yet okay for bookstores to cannibalize drycleaners or for churches to cannibalize bowling alleys, then cannibalization is not what is really being objected to. We come back to the inherent legitimacy of gambling, and the dominant view of that is mightily influenced by the popular theory that gambling is necessarily unproductive.

Production Means Satisfaction of Wants

What does it mean to say that some activity is unproductive? This question was picked   20 over quite thoroughly by economists in the eighteenth and nineteenth centuries. One early view was that only agriculture was productive. Manufacturing (then a small part of total employment) was looked upon as unproductive, since it was obviously supported by agriculture—the manufacturers had to eat. Another idea was that only products which could be turned into gold and silver were truly productive. Later these two theories lost any serious following,[6] but two others remained popular for a while: that anything which did not result in a new physical object was unproductive, and that what we would now call "service" jobs were unproductive. (These two views are not the same, and do not necessarily mesh together well, for a provider of services, such as an architect, may assist in the creation of a new physical object, such as a house.)

Adam Smith contended in 1776 that the labor of domestic servants, government officials, the military, "churchmen, lawyers, physicians, men of letters of all kinds; players, buffoons, musicians, opera-singers, opera-dancers, &c." were unproductive.[7] This contention, and the sloppy argument of which it forms a part, provoked much debate over the next century.

The attempt, by Smith and others, to designate some occupations as unproductive did not lead to convincing conclusions. Those who based productiveness on the making of a physical object were compelled to conclude, for instance, that the performance at a musical concert would be unproductive, whereas printing the tickets and programs for that same concert would be productive.

After the end of the nineteenth century, leading economists no longer paid much attention to the classification of activities as productive or unproductive. The new theory of value based on marginal utility shone a flood of light on the question, and clearly exposed many of the old arguments as fallacious.

The conclusion of the new approach was that "production" means satisfaction of wants. It is productive to make a physical object only insofar as that object enables someone to satisfy a desire. In satisfying desires, the physical object (such as a shirt) yields services. All production is ultimately production of *services* desired by consumers. The musician giving a live performance is being directly productive in the only way in which it is intelligible to be productive: he is satisfying the wants of consumers, in this case of listeners. The producer of a shirt is being productive more indirectly, by making an object which will yield a stream of future want-satisfactions to its wearer. If for some reason the shirt cannot yield these want-satisfactions, whether because everyone undergoes a conversion to an anti-shirt religion or because the shirt falls apart before it can be worn, then the labor of producing it has turned out to be unproductive, despite the fact that a physical object was made.

One way of describing want-satisfaction is to talk about "utility." An activity is   25 productive if it yields utility. According to the modern view, which is no longer controversial among economic theorists, domestic servants, entertainers, priests, and physicians are indeed productive, because they produce services their customers want; they enable those customers to get additional utility.

The same applies to activities in which people may engage either individually or collaboratively. It is productive for a musician to give a recital, assuming that the audience likes it, but it is also productive for a group of friends to get together and perform music for their own enjoyment, or for an individual to perform alone for his own satisfaction.

"Productive" is not a value judgment. If gambling turned out to be productive, that would not show that we would have to approve of it, but it would show that if we disapproved of it, we would have to do so on grounds other than its unproductiveness.

Does gambling satisfy the wants of its participants? Do gamblers enjoy gambling? If they do, then gambling is productive, in much the same way that sports, religious services, or psychotherapy are productive.

Gambling as Recreation

The outstanding theorist of gambling, Reuven Brenner, points out that it comes in two types.[8] There is gambling—call it "recreational"—which takes up a lot of the gambler's time, and gambling which does not. Many people derive considerable enjoyment from recreational gambling. Recreational gamblers do not gamble primarily to gain financially, but to enjoy themselves by playing a game. The possibility of monetary gain or loss adds spice to the game.

Many forms of recreational gambling involve some skill, and these games are therefore not sharply different from games like golf or chess, where there is *some* luck and people pay to play competitively, the winners receiving substantial prizes. In poker, the amount of luck per hand may be high, but this evens out with many hands, so that the element of skill will tend to predominate in the course of a few hours' play.[9] A serious chess game may easily take five or six hours; it is doubtful whether the outcome of five hours' poker is any less governed by skill. Recreational gambling is no less productive than tenpin bowling, ballroom dancing, or barbershop singing—all group pastimes which people pursue because they enjoy them. Samuelson's mistake—a surprising blunder coming from an economist—lies in counting only the monetary transactions. Of course gambling does not create new physical goods; it directly yields utility to the players.

Are Lotteries Productive?

Many people will readily agree that if a concert, a baseball match, or an evening's conversation are considered productive, a poker game might also be judged productive.[10] But there is another kind of gambling: playing the lottery. Surely this can't be primarily an enjoyable way to pass the time. It seems to be done in hope of financial gain, but what if that hope is a product of delusion?

An activity may be anticipated to be productive, but found not to be productive after the fact. Drilling for oil may be unproductive if no oil is found. Technical terms sometimes used for such a distinction are *ex ante* (looking forward before the outcome) and *ex post* (looking backward after the outcome). The anti-gambling ideologue may say: Granted that gambling is productive *ex ante*, it is most often unproductive *ex post*.

Normally we would expect a person to learn from his mistakes, to give up futile endeavors and turn his attention to more successful avenues. Therefore, the mere fact that someone persists with some activity strongly suggests that this activity is productive for that person. It is claimed, however, that the gambler is unable to learn from experience. He is like a driller for oil who keeps coming up dry, but repeatedly pours money into an endless series of unsuccessful drills. Because of a flaw in his thinking, he is unable to learn from experience, despite the fact that he doesn't get what he pays for. Is playing the lottery inescapably irrational? If it is, then lottery playing may perhaps be considered unproductive *ex post*.[11]

Anti-gambling dogmatists usually hold a distinctive interpretation of the motivation for gambling. They maintain that gambling occurs because individuals seek monetary gain, that this desire for monetary gain must be disappointed in most cases, and that therefore the persistence of gambling is irrational—either stupid or involuntary. It is often contended (or just assumed) that a rational person would never gamble. Gambling, on this interpretation, occurs only because gamblers fail to understand elementary probability theory, or, understanding it, cannot bring themselves to act upon it. The cliché that lotteries are "a voluntary tax on the stupid" echoes Sir William Petty (1623–1687), who argued for state management of lotteries on the grounds that the state already had the care of lunatics and idiots.

Gambling prohibitionists are always falling over themselves to "explain" (in the Lardnerian sense) that "gamblers must lose in the long run," that "the odds are stacked against the gambler," that "gamblers as a whole can only lose," and so forth. They pronounce these marvelous insights as though they were gems of wisdom which gamblers must have overlooked. And perhaps a tiny minority of gamblers have indeed missed these earth-shaking commonplaces—after all, people have been known to make silly mistakes in all departments of life, from music to marriage, so there's no reason why gambling should be immune. But I can't see any evidence that the general run of gamblers behave irrationally, or that they would stop gambling if they took a course in probability theory.[12]

Is Gambling Unproductive *Ex Post?*
On the most straightforward level the lottery player gets precisely what he pays for: an equal chance with other players of netting a very large sum of money, of becoming rich. The anti-gambling ideologue, however, will press the point: objectively, the lottery player gets exactly what he pays for, but he is unable to evaluate it correctly, so he never gets what he believes he pays for. He does not appreciate how slim are his chances of becoming rich. His intuitive notion of his chance of winning is unrealistically high because of a peculiar mental defect.[13]

How does the anti-gambling preacher know that the lottery player overrates his chances? Why don't we suppose that, on average, the player rates his chances exactly correctly?[14] Anti-gambling zealots reply that he then would never play the lottery! This argument is fatally circular and therefore worthless. Although anti-gambling zealots often insinuate that rational people would not gamble, there exists no serious argument for any such assumption.

The claim that the gambler overestimates his chances is usually asserted as a blind dogma, with no evidence offered. However, some anti-gambling propagandists mention, as though it were significant, the fact that the whole class of lottery players must lose on balance. In technical terms, playing the lottery is not a "fair" bet; the "expected value" of a lottery ticket is below the price of the ticket.[15]

The expenses of organizing a lottery have to be covered out of sales of tickets. Therefore, the amount returned in prizes is lower than the amount paid for tickets.[16] A technically "fair" lottery would be one in which the total prize money were equal to the total money paid for tickets. In such a lottery, what is called the "expected value" of a ticket would be the same as the ticket price. It is an error to suppose that this offers a criterion of rationality: that it must be irrational to play the lottery when the expected value is below the ticket price. That any such supposition is faulty can be seen upon a moment's reflection.[17]

The proportion of total ticket revenues returned in prizes from lotteries is commonly around 60 percent, though it is sometimes more than 70 percent, and with some of the new state lotteries is little more than 50 percent.[18] If lotteries were purely private and open to competition, this figure would immediately rise to well over 90 percent[19] (except where particular lotteries were openly allied with charitable donation), but it could never reach 100 percent without the lottery's making a loss. Just suppose, however, that a lottery were subsidized, so that 105 percent of the prize money were returned in prizes. Would it then become rational always to buy lottery tickets, and irrational to fail to do so? If so, how many tickets? How much of one's income would it be obligatory, if one were rational, to allocate to lottery tickets? Suppose now that the lottery were hugely subsidized, so that, say, five times the ticket revenues were returned in prizes (but most entrants would still win nothing), what then? At what point, as we increased the subsidy to the lottery, would it become incumbent upon any rational person to buy a ticket?

There is no such point—though there would empirically be a point where the majority of people, or the majority of people with math degrees, would judge that one would have to be a lunatic not to buy at least one ticket. This kind of thing is a matter of personal preference, a matter of one's personality and worldview. It is "subjective" in the sense that there is no single demonstrably correct answer for any rational agent. Such judgments can be influenced by miscalculations or other mistakes, but if all mistakes were eliminated, there would remain a diversity of preferences. Given these preferences, one's behavior is also affected by objective circumstances like one's income.

A lottery player will usually prefer a lottery which returns 90 percent of the ticket revenues to one which returns only 80 percent. Therefore, some will be induced to play at 90 percent who would not play at 80 percent. But someone who plays the lottery buys a chance of being in for a big win, and there is no justification for the assumption that the individual's valuation of this chance, the amount of utility he derives from being aware of it, has to coincide with the "expected value" of a lottery ticket (the prize money multiplied by the chance of winning). There are many cases where it clearly ought not to do so (for example, if the price of a ticket is one's entire income for the next few weeks, so that one will die of starvation unless one wins the prize, it would not be sensible to enter with a one-in-a million chance of winning, even if the prize were so heavily subsidized that the expected value of a ticket were a thousand times the ticket price).

A rational person doesn't have to value a one-in-a-million chance of getting a million dollars at precisely one dollar. You may value such a chance at one cent or at five dollars—either way (though this may tell us something about your personality) there's nothing wrong with you.[20] However, assume for a moment that the "expected value" theory of rational gambling were correct. Suppose that you paid a dollar for a ticket giving you one chance in a million of winning $700,000, with $300,000 of ticket sales going to run the lottery and pay off the state. The expected value of your one-dollar ticket would be 70 cents. Only 30 cents would have to be explained by non-pecuniary elements (a sense of participation, giving something to a good cause, and so forth, or, if we want to indulge in flights of fancy, by "irrational compulsion" or "enhanced daydreaming"). It would follow that at least 70 cents out of each and every dollar spent on lottery tickets would indisputably be rationally allocated. Is this better or worse than the dollars spent on furniture or books? Casual discussion of the rationality of buying a ticket often tacitly assumes that "expected value" is the rule, but then proceeds as though the entire sum spent on tickets would be shown to be irrationally spent, when in fact (on the erroneous assumption that expected value should fix the buyer's valuation of a ticket) only something less than half of the ticket price would then, arguably, be spent irrationally.

The fact that a lottery is not technically "fair" follows automatically from the fact that the costs of running the lottery have to be covered out of ticket sales, and is otherwise a complete red herring from which no conclusions about the rationality of the players may legitimately be drawn. It's a feature of any system for re-allocating existing endowments, such as a subscription to the March of Dimes: organizing a subscription costs something, so the total paid to beneficiaries must be less than the total contributed. This is ineluctable, and in no way sinister.[21] A lottery is simply a way in which a lot of people each put in a small sum, and then a few of those people picked at random get large sums. Nothing in the world could possibly be more harmless or more innocent than this.

Is Insurance Irrational?

Insurance is a negative lottery. In buying insurance, we pay a small sum now to guard against the low probability of losing a large sum in the future, just as, with a lottery, we pay a small sum now to engineer a low probability of winning a large sum in the future. Insurance is always an unfair bet—much less fair than a competitively run lottery, because the costs of running an insurance company greatly exceed the costs of administering a lottery.

Do the ideologues who berate gamblers for their irrational short-sightedness also berate those who, for example, insure the contents of their houses against fire? Quite the contrary! This willingness to pay for insurance more (sometimes vastly more) than its "expected value" is lauded to the skies as the epitome of responsible behavior. *Failure* to take *this* unfair bet is commonly considered thoroughly foolish and even irrational. In the debate over Hillary Clinton's health care plan, it was generally considered a self-evident scandal that an appreciable number of young, fit, comparatively high-income people chose not to buy health insurance, such a scandal that it warranted their being *compelled* to buy it—forced to make this extremely "unfair" bet.[22]

What goes for insurance goes also for precautionary outlays of a non-pecuniary kind, like wearing a car seat belt or getting a polio shot. In a typical recent diatribe against gambling, totally bereft of any serious thought and seething with the malignant compulsion to control other people's lives, one Robyn Gearey blasts the New York state lottery because, *inter alia*, the odds of winning a big prize are less than the odds of being struck by lightning.[23] Aside from the question of whether this is factually correct,[24] Gearey evidently believes that being struck by lightning is a negligibly unlikely event which shouldn't influence a rational person's plans, yet my guess is that Gearey does not inveigh with comparable enthusiasm against the installation of lightning rods.[25]

Lottery Players Are Rational

Some months ago, a thousand-pound man was in the news. He had lain on his bed for years; his main physical exercise was calling the local deli to send round a few dozen sandwiches at a time. The medics had to knock down a wall to get him out of his house and carry him to the hospital.

It would not be sensible, in a discussion of whether to let individuals decide for themselves what to eat, to keep bringing up the case of this thousand-pound monster. Similarly, it would not be appropriate, in a discussion of whether to permit people to attend a church of their own choosing, to endlessly pontificate about the Heaven's Gate suicides.

Yet just such irrelevance is the normal practice with anti-gambling bigots, who compulsively prattle on and on about problem gamblers, people who gamble away their life savings and desert their families for the gaming tables. Such cases are a tiny proportion of gamblers, and most of the people who behave like this would behave just as badly if gambling did not exist. Typically, and overwhelmingly, gamblers practice strict self-discipline and moderation.[26] If they are on low incomes and play the lottery regularly, they often spend less than the price of a six-pack per week. Any freedom of any sort affords the opportunity for foolish behavior by a foolish minority, and that exceptional behavior can never justify clamping iron shackles on the overwhelming majority of people who are sensible and self-disciplined.

The allegation that gamblers are irrational can be tested.[27] We can look at their behavior for signs of irrationality. In all respects which I have seen reported, the vast majority of lottery players behave as if they were rational. They prefer games where the odds are better. (Everyone understands that, to maintain a viable state lottery, private lotteries have to be outlawed.) They bet only a small amount per week. When they win a big prize and become rich, they husband their winnings prudently.[28]

People play the lottery more if they have few other options with lottery-like qualities: the stock market, venture capitalism, an exciting career, a song-writing avocation.[29] Young, talented people with few commitments have many such options, and will respond rationally by playing the lottery rarely. A 55-year-old janitor with ten kids and no equity has hardly any options, and will respond rationally by playing the lottery more frequently. This is just what we observe; it fully corroborates the rationality of playing the lottery. Lottery tickets are the janitor's cattle futures. To blame him for playing the lottery is like reproaching him for not having the good taste to drive a Ferrari.

Lottery players seem to understand the odds quite well (unlike the anti-gambling lobbyists, who demonstrate their innumeracy every time they open their mouths); the players certainly do understand with perfect clarity that it is far more likely than not that if they play every week of their lives they will never win a big prize. They still think it is worth playing, and it is just ignorance to imagine that this judgment of theirs must rest upon a miscalculation.

Lottery players hold that it is better to have played and lost than never to have played at all. Who is to say that they are wrong?

NOTES

1. For some of the evidence for these statements, see the summary in Reuven Brenner, with Gabrielle A. Brenner, *Gambling and Speculation: A Theory, A History, and a Future of Some Human Decisions* (Cambridge: Cambridge University Press, 1990), pp. 37–42. The current anti-gambling campaign has begotten a spate of bogus scholarly "studies" purporting to show that gambling has deleterious consequences for the culture and economy. This literature consists largely of the same writers quoting each other's guesses about the evil effects of gambling, and passing these off as data. When one tracks down the ultimate sources in these works, one finds that they are often anecdotal impressions, for example: the opinions of people like Gamblers Anonymous activists. The methodology of this literature precludes the turning up of any findings other than those assumed at the outset. No studies with any semblance of rigor have yet confirmed the horrific fantasies of the anti-gambling ideologues.

2. Paul A. Samuelson, *Economics: An Introductory Analysis.* Seventh edition (New York: McGraw-Hill, 1967), p. 409. Samuelson's italics.

3. *The Luck Business: The Devastating Consequences and Broken Promises of America's Gambling Explosion* (New York: The Free Press, 1995), passim. The term "cannibalization" seems to have arisen in business corporations, to denote new products which might take business away from a company's existing lines. Its application to gambling is unhappy; the word seems to have been picked up as a vacuous but ominous-sounding instrument of abuse.

4. Gambling is still severely regulated everywhere, so a state or city which simultaneously repealed all restrictions on private gambling would at

once become a shining beacon of affluence. But the restrictive climate of opinion makes such a bold move politically unfeasible.

5. As the anti-gambling enthusiasts succeed in repealing local legalizations, the process will go into reverse. Those localities which are slow to re-impose prohibition will begin to see big gains from visitors. The anti-gambling crusaders are keenly aware of this, hence their strategy of going for a "national gambling policy," in which the federal government takes over the states' and cities' traditional role of regulating gambling.

6. The first is now almost precisely reversed in the minds of many followers of Ross Perot and Patrick Buchanan: only the building of gadgets, preferably of metal, is considered truly productive. "Hamburger flipping"—providing meals for people—has become the very paradigm of unproductiveness.

7. *An Inquiry into the Nature and Causes of the Wealth of Nations*, ed. Edwin Cannan (Chicago: University of Chicago Press, 1976), p. 352.

8. Brenner, pp. 20–21. Brenner's is the best book ever written on gambling. Although I agree with nearly all of Brenner's criticisms of orthodox opinion on gambling, I reject the lynchpin of his own theory: that non-recreational gambling occurs only because people crave an increase specifically in their *relative* income, independent of their desire for an absolute increase in income.

9. Where there is recreational gambling with some skill involved, a resourceful player may win in the long run. There is no reason why the "house" or the "bookie" would necessarily object to some players making consistent gains. The majority of recreational gamblers, whose interest in winning is less predominant, or whose skill is unremarkable, ultimately pay for the winnings of the prize-winners and the gains of the "house." This majority may still be "ahead" in non-pecuniary terms, in the enjoyment they derive from playing. In utility terms, which is all that matters, everybody may be a net winner. An interesting case is that of blackjack, where there is a sure-fire method of winning consistently. Although the existence of this method is very widely known, most blackjack players don't bother to learn it (which takes a few weeks of intensive study), so casinos go on offering a game which they are bound to lose in the long run to any customers who apply the method. See the discussion of this in Willem Albert Wagenaar, *Paradoxes of Gambling Behavior* (Hove, England: Erlbaum, 1988), an interesting book which, however, like so many, never for a moment questions the reigning dogma that gamblers' motivations must involve irrationality.

10. Some writers castigate gambling because there is no "value added." This displays a misunderstanding. Gambling itself occupies the final stage of production: it's a consumer activity, like watching TV or jogging. Manufacturing TV sets, jogging shoes, casinos, lottery tickets, or roulette wheels "adds value." Incidentally, gamblers watch less TV than non-gamblers, though they read more, go to the opera and museums more often, and are more sociable (Brenner, p. 38).

11. Alternatively, the proponent of the irrationality of the lottery might agree that playing is productive both *ex ante* and *ex post*, but insist that the *ex post* judgment is necessarily based on error. The refutation of this position is along similar lines.

12. "Rationality" is a term with a range of senses. I do not use the term here in a sense so weak that any deliberate action, however foolish, would count as rational, nor in a sense so strong that any intellectual mistake would suffice for irrationality. My use of the term here covers any demonstrable mistake which, once understood, would necessarily cause the individual to stop gambling. Gambling is like piloting airplanes: the individuals involved may not always compute everything to perfection, but the very pursuit of the activity in question is not, I am claiming, typically dependent on error.

13. The case of a lottery is unusual, because we cannot simply ask the individual what he thinks of the outcome after it has appeared. The fact that the player has not won does not prove that he was wrong to play (any more than the fact that a person wins proves that he was right to play): the player knew all along, of course, that he very probably would not win.

14. In view of recent evidence that smokers generally *over*estimate the health risks of smoking, we may suspect that lottery players underestimate their chances of winning. The smug, mindless propaganda of anti-smoking bigotry and anti-gambling bigotry, spraying over us day after day from all the major media, with no thought of "equal time" for dissidents, may well be reducing aggregate social utility by causing some people at the margins to misguidedly give up smoking or gambling. The clout of the tobacco industry or the gambling industry, which these bigots routinely revile, is as gossamer compared with the clout of the belligerent prohibitionist lobby.

15. "Fair bet" and "expected value" are technical terms. They have nothing to do with the vernàcular sense of these words. An "unfair" bet may be entirely fair, or vice versa, while an "expected value" is not what anybody expects.

16. Under free competition, the return to investors in all industries, including gambling, will be roughly the same, on average, as the rate of interest.

17. Consider whether you would rather have a dollar or a one-in-50,000 chance of $50,000. The one thing you will not say is that you can see no

difference between these options, that you are indifferent between them. But once a difference in the valuation of these two outcomes is acknowledged, it automatically follows that it may be rational to give up one in exchange for the other.

18. Anti-gambling preachers frequently include in the "costs" of gambling all of the money spent by gamblers, without subtracting the distributed winnings, which at a stroke multiplies the supposed costs several-fold. This is not willful deceit, just the normal intellectual laziness of these anti-gambling rub-thumpers.

19. About 95 percent of the money wagered in Las Vegas casinos is returned as winnings. An appreciable chunk of the remaining five percent goes in taxes.

20. If someone you loved desperately could be saved from a painful and potentially fatal disease only by getting a million dollars, and the only possible way to get a million dollars were to play the lottery, wouldn't you play? Of course you would: it would be contemptible not to do so. The principle is not altered if the person you love so much is yourself, and the disease is not being rich.

21. A lottery is very much like a charitable subscription, and may partake of some of its motivation. Begin with the benevolent idea that you would like someone on a low income to become rich, add the random selection of that person, and you have a lottery which might take place even under pure altruism. (The player would have to make himself eligible for a prize in order not to deny the other participants their share of altruistic utility; restricting the prizes to those who have entered would be justified by the consideration that some minimal level of goodwill, some spark of human decency, would be necessary to qualify. The fact that winners stop playing would be explained by the fact that they can now afford superior ways of being helpful to others.) The altruistic theory of the lottery would explain why players who never win rarely show any resentment against winners, but rather evince sympathetic delight.

22. Some theorists have considered it puzzling that many people both insure themselves against risks and play the lottery. Various solutions have been offered to this supposed paradox. But there is no paradox. It is consistent for a person to pay a small amount to greatly reduce the already small likelihood of a big drop in income and simultaneously to pay a small amount to greatly increase the very small likelihood of a big rise in income. (It is sometimes claimed that the position I take here implies that the rich would not "gamble," and that it is therefore refuted by the fact that the rich do "gamble." But the rich do not play the lottery, a fact of which socialist opponents of the lottery as a devilish capitalist exploitation device remind us *ad nauseam*. The rich gamble recreationally; that's a different matter.)

23. "The Numbers Game," *The New Republic*, May 19th, 1997.

24. The only way to defend this claim would be to suppose that Gearey was comparing, say, one's chance of being struck by lightning in a whole year with one's chances of making a big win by the purchase of one ticket. This would be deceptive in light of Gearey's evident reliance on the stereotype of someone who plays the lottery habitually and heavily. A quick exercise with a pocket calculator will give us some rough idea of the comparison. One estimate of a U.S. resident's chance of being struck by lightning in one year is 606,944 to 1 against (Heron House, *The Odds on Virtually Everything* [New York: Putnam's 1980], p. 181). This means a probability of 1 in 606,945, or .000001648. Suppose a lottery in which a ticket costs $1, each ticket is entered for 1 draw, exactly half the ticket money is distributed in prizes, and each prize is $250,000. The probability of one ticket's winning is then 1 in 500,000, decidedly better than being struck by lightning. Suppose instead that every prize is $500,000; it follows that the chance of winning must be 1 in a million. Now you have to buy two tickets to make the probability of your winning a prize better than the probability of being struck by lightning. If every prize is $5 million, you need to buy 17 tickets, and if every prize is $10 million, you need to buy 33 tickets to improve upon your chance of being struck by lightning. Of course, the picture is complicated by a range of different prizes, and by other factors, but it's clear that anyone who buys several tickets a month for a year has much better prospects than someone who hopes to collect the insurance on being struck by lightning.

25. The main thrust of Gearey's piece is that the New York State Lottery is described misleadingly by its promoters, which is doubtless true—it is, after all, an arm of the government. Yet her very article is filled with misrepresentations, beginning with the line at the top of the first page: "The Lottery: Ticket to Poverty." One only has to substitute some other item of working-class expenditure ("Video Rentals: Ticket to Poverty") to see the utter mendacity of this phrase. Gearey says people play because they believe the state's lies that playing the lottery might really lift them from poverty or drudgery (p. 19). It's a fact well known to Gearey that the lottery not only *might* really lift players from poverty or drudgery but regularly does so. Gearey is so emotionally disturbed by her irrational hatred of ordinary people spending their money as they choose to spend it that she does not balk even at the most ridiculous falsehoods.

26. Brenner, pp. 37–42
27. Abt and her colleagues summarize the research findings as follows:
    "Observations in a wide variety of times and places have shown that gamblers are realistically aware of their chances of winning and conduct their wagering with deliberation and disciplined concentration" (Vicki Abt, et al., *The Business of Risk: Commercial Gambling in Mainstream Amer-* *ica* [Lawrence: University of Kansas Press, 1985], p. 11).
28. Brenner, pp. 42–44
29. The government has effectively eliminated high-risk, high-return opportunities for low-income people, such as the old "bucket shops," which enabled people to speculate on price fluctuations with only a few dollars' outlay.

FOR YOU TO ANALYZE

1. How does Steele categorize gambling? Why do you think he chooses the category he does? How might others categorize gambling?

2. How does Steele define *productive* and *rational?* Are these definitions what you expect? Why or why not? Do you find them reasonable? Why or why not?

3. What kinds of consequences does Steele discuss? Does he address types of consequences that might not support his evaluation of gambling? Do you find his discussion of consequences convincing? Why or why not?

4. Does Steele convince you that his evaluation of gambling is correct? Why or why not? Can you think of opposing (or supporting) arguments that he has neglected? How would you construct an argument that evaluated gambling negatively?

FOR YOU TO WRITE

1. Steele evaluates gambling positively, while many people characterize gambling as a waste of money or even as an addiction. Choose a habit or pastime commonly seen as bad for an individual or for society (such as the consumption of fast food or pornography) and write a brief evaluation of a positive side of it, or choose a habit or pastime commonly seen as good (such as church attendance or exercise) and write a brief argument evaluating it negatively. Why do so many people view this habit or pastime as bad (or good)? How might you weight the ethical considerations differently?

2. Steele criticizes Robert Goodman, whom he identifies as a leader of "anti-gambling propagandists." Choose a person who is or has been identified with a cause, whether on the local, state, national, or international level, and write a brief evaluation of that person's contribution to the cause. Has the person advanced or hurt the cause? Is the cause a worthy one, in your opinion? Do you support or oppose this person's continued involvement in the cause?

3. Steele's perhaps controversial position is that "people are entitled to do whatever they please with their own lives as long as they don't invade other people's rights." What controversial opinion do you support? Can you construct a brief argument that would convince others to evaluate that position positively?

FOR YOU TO DISCOVER ONLINE

The Internet offers sites devoted to gambling, information about attempts to prohibit gambling, organizations to help compulsive gamblers, and nearly every gambling-related subject in between. If you type the keywords "Internet gambling" into your favorite search engine, you are likely to find sites inviting you to make wagers as well as sites explaining problems with gambling or urging prohibition. With Steele's article in mind, look for information about attempts to prohibit gambling altogether: how convincing do you find the arguments available online? Are they more or less convincing than Steele's evaluation? You might also look at a site such as www .gamblersanonymous.org, the home page of the major organization devoted to helping problem gamblers (the people of whom Steele says, "most of the people who behave like this would behave just as badly if gambling did not exist"). Does this or any other organized anti-gambling site offer information that refutes Steele's evaluation in your opinion? Why or why not?

Proposal: What Should We Do about It?

Chapter 9

Hollywood Simply Can No Longer Abdicate Its Responsibility to Kids

An Appeal

Violence: The entertainment industry must curb what's available via TV, movies, music, videos and the Web.

The signatories are announcing this appeal at a press conference today in Washington, D.C.:

American parents today are deeply worried about their children's exposure to an increasingly toxic popular culture. The events in Littleton, Colo., are only the most recent reminder that something is deeply amiss in our media age. Violence and explicit sexual content in television, films, music and video games have escalated sharply in recent years. Children of all ages now are being exposed to a barrage of images and words that threaten not only to rob them of normal childhood innocence but also to distort their view of reality and even undermine their character growth.

These concerns know no political or partisan boundaries. According to a recent CNN-USA Today-Gallup poll, 76% of adults agree that TV, movies and popular music are negative influences on children, and 75% report that they make efforts to protect children from such harmful influences. Nearly the same number say shielding children from the negative influences of today's media culture is "nearly impossible."

Moreover, there is a growing public appreciation of the link between our excessively violent and degrading entertainment culture and the horrifying new crimes we see emerging among our young: schoolchildren gunning down teachers and fellow students en masse, killing sprees inspired by violent films, teenagers murdering their babies only to return to dance at the prom.

Clearly, many factors are contributing to the crisis—negligent parenting, ineffective schools, family disintegration and the ready availability of firearms. But, among researchers, the proposition that entertainment violence adversely influences attitudes and behavior is no longer controversial; there is overwhelming evidence of its harmful effects. Numerous studies show that degrading images of violence and sex have a desensitizing effect. Nowhere is the threat greater than to our at-risk youth—youngsters whose disadvantaged environments make them susceptible to acting upon impulses shaped by violent and dehumanizing media imagery.

In the past, the entertainment industry was more conscious of its unique responsibility for the health of our culture. For 30 years, television lived by the National Assn. of Broadcasters television code, which detailed responsibilities to the community, children and society and prescribed specific programming standards. For many years, this voluntary code set boundaries that enabled television to thrive as a creative medium without causing undue damage to the bedrock values of our society.

283

In recent years, several top entertainment executives have spoken out on the need for minimum standards and, more recently, on the desirability of more family-friendly programming. But to effect real change, these individual expressions must transform into a new, collective affirmation of social responsibility on the part of the media industry as a whole.

We, the undersigned, call on executives of the media industry—as well as CEOs of companies that advertise in the electronic media—to join with us and with America's parents in a new social compact aimed at renewing our culture and making our media environment more healthy for our society and safer for our children. We call on industry leaders in all media—television, film, music, video and electronic games—to band together to develop a new voluntary code of conduct, broadly modeled on the NAB code.

The code we envision would affirm in clear terms the industry's vital responsibilities for the health of our culture; establish certain minimum standards for violent, sexual and degrading material for each medium, below which producers can be expected not to go; commit the industry to an overall reduction in the level of entertainment violence; ban the practice of targeting of adult-oriented entertainment to youth markets; provide for more accurate information to parents on media content; commit to the creation of "windows" or "safe havens" for family programming, including a revival of TV's "family hour" and finally, pledge significantly greater creative efforts to develop family-oriented entertainment.

We strongly urge parents to express their support for this voluntary code of conduct directly to media executives and advertisers with telephone calls, letters, faxes or e-mails and to join us in becoming signers of this appeal via the Internet at www.media-appeal.org. And we call on all parents to fulfill their part of the compact by responsibly supervising their children's media exposure.

We are not advocating censorship or wholesale strictures on artistic creativity. We are not demanding that all entertainment be geared to young children. Finally, we are not asking government to police the media.

Rather, we are urging the entertainment industry to assume a decent minimum of responsibility for its own actions and take modest steps of self-restraint. And we are asking parents to help in this task by taking responsibility for shielding their own children and also by making their concerns known to media executives and advertisers.

Hollywood has an enormous influence on America, particularly the young. By making a concerted effort to turn its energies to promoting decent, shared values and strengthening American families, the entertainment industry has it within its power to help make an America worthy of the third millennium. We, as leaders from government, the religious community, the nonprofit world and the private sector, along with members of the entertainment community, challenge the entertainment industry to this great task. We appeal to those who are reaping great profits to give something back. We believe that by choosing to do good, the entertainment industry can also make good, and both the industry and our society will be richer and better as a result.

STEVE ALLEN

WILLIAM J. BENNETT, co-director, Empower America

DAVID BLANKENHORN, president, Institute for American Values

FREDERICK BORSCH, bishop, Episcopal Diocese of Los Angeles

BILL BRIGHT, founder and president, Campus Crusade for Christ

SISSELA BOK, distinguished fellow, Harvard Center for Population Studies

L. BRENT BOZELL III, chairman, Parents Television Council

SEN. SAM BROWNBACK (R-Kan.)

JIMMY CARTER

LYNNE V. CHENEY, senior fellow, American Enterprise Institute

STEPHEN R. COVEY, co-founder and vice chairman, Franklin Covey Co.

MARIO CUOMO, former governor of New York

JOHN J. DiIULIO, JR., professor of politics, University of Pennsylvania

DON EBERLY, director, the Civil Society Project

AMITAI ETZIONI, professor, George Washington University

VIC FARACI, senior vice president, Warner Brothers Records

GERALD R. FORD

WILLIAM GALSTON, professor and director, Institute for Philosophy and Public Policy, School of Public Affairs, University of Maryland

ELIZABETH FOX-GENOVESE, professor of humanities, Emory University

MANDELL GANCHROW, president, Union of Orthodox Jewish Congregations

NORTON GARFINKLE, chairman, Oxford Management Corp.

ROBERT GEORGE, professor of jurisprudence, Princeton University

GEORGE GERBNER, telecommunications professor, Temple University; dean emeritus, Annenberg School for Communications, University of Pennsylvania

PATRICK GLYNN, director, Media Social Responsibility Project, Institute for Communitarian Policy Studies, George Washington University

OS GUINNESS, senior fellow, the Trinity Forum

ROBERT HANLEY, actor, writer, director, founder and president, Entertainment Fellowship

STEPHEN A. HAYNER, president, Inter-Varsity Christian Fellowship

GERTRUDE HIMMELFARB, professor emeritus of history, City University of New York graduate school

MARK HONIG, executive director, Parents Television Council

JAMES DAVISON HUNTER, professor of sociology and religious studies, University of Virginia

KATHLEEN HALL JAMIESON, dean and communications professor, Annenberg School for Communications, University of Pennsylvania

NAOMI JUDD

JACK KEMP, co-director, Empower America

CAROL LAWRENCE

SEN. JOSEPH I. LIEBERMAN (D-Conn.)

SEN. JOHN McCAIN (R-Ariz.)

E. MICHAEL McCANN, district attorney, Milwaukee County, Wis.

THOMAS MONAGHAN, president, Ave Maria Foundation

RICHARD JOHN NEUHAUS, president, Institute on Religion and Public Life

ARMAND M. NICHOLI, JR., associate clinical professor of psychiatry, Harvard Medical School

SAM NUNN, former U.S. senator from Georgia

NEIL POSTMAN, professor, New York University

ALVIN POUSSAINT, director, Judge Baker Children's Center, Boston

GEN. COLIN POWELL (ret.)

EUGENE RIVERS, co-chair, National Ten Point Leadership Foundation

GEN. NORMAN SCHWARZKOPF (ret.)

GLENN TINDER, professor of political science emeritus, University of Massachusetts

C. DELORES TUCKER, chair and convening founder, the National Political Congress of Black Women

JOAN VAN ARK, actress, producer, director

JIM WALLIS, editor, Sojourners magazine; leader, Call to Renewal program

DAVID WALSH, president, National Institute on Media and the Family

JERRY M. WIENER, emeritus professor psychiatry and pediatrics, George Washington University

ELIE WIESEL, professor in the humanities, Boston University

JAMES Q. WILSON, professor emeritus, UCLA

ALAN WOLFE, professor, Boston University

DANIEL YANKELOVICH, president, the Public Agenda

ANALYZING "Hollywood Simply Can No Longer Abdicate Its Responsibility to Kids"

Proposal arguments call for action. They represent the highest-stakes appeal that an arguer can make since they call upon audience members to give something—time, money, energy—to achieve a goal. Clearly, an audience must be convinced that they will gain some benefit in exchange for what they are asked to give up.

Proposal arguments tend to follow a predictable pattern: they first convince an audience that a problem exists, and then they propose a solution. To achieve their goal, they build on all the previous types we have examined. In the following analysis of a sample proposal argument, we will stress the combination of smaller arguments that together make up the full proposal. Our sample here has the arrangement strategy that, as this chapter will explain, is typical of proposal arguments.

Our proposal comes from the *Los Angeles Times,* where it was published on July 21, 1999, and it offers some special features. To begin with, it has multiple "authors," whose names are attached, including two former presidents (Carter and Ford), two famous generals (Colin Powell, later Secretary of State, and Norman Schwarzkopf), prominent entertainers (Steve Allen and Naomi Judd), figures from both the right and the left of the political spectrum (William Bennett and Mario Cuomo), and a distinguished collection of elected officials, public sector and business leaders, and academics. Everyone whose name might not have wide public recognition has his or her credentials included ("Glenn Tinder, professor of political science emeritus, University of Massachusetts"). Given the galaxy of distinguished voices endorsing this argument, the appeal from ethos is strong and explicit (see Chapter 3).

Also, unlike other Op-Ed pieces, this argument was released nationwide to coincide with a press conference held in Washington, D.C., by representatives of the endorsers. Thus, this argument was intended to have a broad national audience; papers across the country received press releases about the news conference and copies of this argument. The *Los Angeles Times* chose to print the released text in their opinion pages, no doubt because the argument concerns the local southern California entertainment industry, known popularly as "Hollywood." Hence the **audience** for this piece is also a multiple one. The argument is aimed at entertainment executives; the most important action recommended is one that only they can take. But this appeal to the entertainment industry is made *in the presence of* a wider publication.

The **exigence** for this piece is clearly the public shock and the debate about causes and remedies that surfaced after what the text refers to as "events in Littleton Colo.," the school shooting in 1999 in which 12 students and one teacher were killed by two fellow students who then took their own lives. Some of the "signers" of this argument had been outspoken critics of the media long before Littleton. But that horrific incident created a sense of cultural crisis and demands for some kind of curative response, such as the one offered in this proposal.

The **constraints** on this argument include, first of all, length. This proposal argument has a great deal to accomplish, so the support must be condensed and the appeals to widely held beliefs must be strong and sure. Second, as an argument presented in a public newspaper, this proposal cannot go into technical details about how its recommendations could be implemented. Only the broadest supporting appeals can be offered in the most inclusive and inspiring language.

Unlike some of our other sample arguments, this one does not clearly state its overall claim in the title. The heading, "Hollywood Simply Can No Longer Abdicate Its Responsibility to Kids," certainly suggests that Hollywood should do something, and the subheading comes closer ("curb what's available"), but exactly what action should be taken remains unclear until about the middle of the argument (paragraph 7). Some preparatory arguments obviously have to be made before the article comes to the point.

What are these preparatory arguments? Paragraphs 1 and 2 work to **establish a problem.** The first sentence claims that American parents are currently worrying about "an increasingly toxic popular culture," and the third that "Violence and explicit sexual content in television, films, music and video games have escalated sharply in recent years." Both of these statements characterize the current situation (public opinion, media content), and both could be supported with evidence. However, the authors do not back up the claim about increasing media violence. Though researchers have counted the occurrence of "violent" and "sexually explicit" acts from year to year in various media, no reference to such scholarly studies is offered. The authors present the claim about deteriorating content as a widely accepted fact.

The authors do use paragraph 2 to provide evidence supporting their other claim that American parents are concerned about the media. They offer the results of a recent CNN-*USA Today*-Gallup poll showing that a substantial majority of respondents believe the media have negative effects on their children. Most parents polled said that they try to protect their children from media influence, but that they believe doing so is "nearly impossible." The size of the response (running at 75 percent agreement to offered statements) suggests that these results represent American parents across "political and partisan boundaries"; these statistics thus help establish that "[All or most] American parents today are deeply worried about their children's exposure to an increasingly toxic popular culture." To accept the support offered for this claim, readers must of course assume that a poll conducted by the Gallup organization and sponsored by news outlets produces credible results.

To summarize so far, the authors assume their readers will agree that violence and sex have increased in the movies, on TV, and so on, but they do support their claim that American parents are very worried about this state of affairs. The evidence offered in paragraph 2 gives great "presence" to this argument. After all, the public's perception of a media problem is a serious problem for media executives.

Paragraphs 3 and 4 turn to causal argument claiming a link (or at least public perception of a link) between "our excessively violent and degrading entertainment culture and the horrifying new crimes we see emerging among our young." Paragraph 4 acknowledges a complicated causal picture with many factors leading to crimes like Littleton, but it then singles out entertainment violence which "overwhelming evidence" and "numerous studies" link to harmful and desensitizing effects. (In the context of a public argument in a newspaper, the authors can get away with an unspecified reference to the evidence and studies that back up their claim to a causal connection; in an academic argument, such vagueness is unacceptable. The sources would have to be detailed and assessed.)

Where are the authors going in paragraphs 3 and 4? In order for an audience to be moved to action, they have to be convinced that a situation is a problem. Situations are problems when an audience believes they violate an **ethical norm** and/or lead to **bad consequences.** The very terms in which the situation is presented in paragraph 1 suggest a negative evaluation. "Violence" is a negative word, and the loaded phrase "increasingly toxic popular culture" introduces a powerful negative metaphor of a culture that poisons its consumers. The causal argument in paragraphs 3 and 4, sketchy as it is, furthers this negative evaluation by arguing that a very bad consequence, violent crime by the young, is a direct result of violence and sex in the media. Paragraphs 1 through 4 then are, together, a necessary opening subunit. Arguers and audience have a big problem.

Once the problem has been established, however, the arguers do not immediately offer a solution. Instead, they turn in paragraph 5 to history and sketch what was done "in the past" by the television industry, through the National Association of Broadcasters' [NAB] television code, to spell out the industry's social responsibilities and programming standards. Though the authors never say so explicitly, readers infer that this code is no longer in force. If it were, presumably the increase in violence and sexual content would not have occurred. The arguers here have shifted to a **causal analysis** of the situation.

After establishing that a problem exists, they ask, "How did it come about?" Their answer identifies a responsible agent (the entertainment industry itself) and provides a causal story (in this case the absence of an industry code as a blocking cause).

Paragraph 6 opens in contrast to paragraph 5 ("In the past" vs. "In recent years"), and we learn about recent appeals from entertainment executives for a return to such minimum standards and about the need for a "new, collective affirmation of social responsibility on the part of the media industry as a whole." The arguers then present their **specific proposal** addressed to different audiences. Paragraph 7 calls first for a general cultural renewal and next specifies the action proposed: "We call on industry leaders in all media—television, film, music, video and electronic games—to band together to develop a new voluntary code of conduct broadly modeled on the NAB code." Paragraph 8 is even more detailed, expanding the proposal into parts that include not only "minimum standards for violent, sexual and degrading material for each medium, below which producers can be expected not to go" but also the reestablishment of a family hour and family-oriented entertainment. Paragraph 9 is addressed to parents, urging them to contact media executives to express support for the proposal or to sign the appeal on the Internet. It also calls on parents to supervise their children's media exposure.

The main argument provided to convince media executives that the recommended action is feasible could be diagrammed as follows:

Reason: A voluntary code of programming standards was followed for 30 years by the National Association of Broadcasters.   →   **Claim:** The entertainment industry should adopt a voluntary code of conduct prescribing programming standards.

↑

Warrant: A code of conduct in place in the past could be put in place again.

The warrant here is a version of the widely held belief that what was done in the past can be done again. The argument expanded here is just one of many that could be diagrammed to show the interplay of the many claims, reasons, and enabling warrants that make up this argument.

Even if this proposal is feasible, why should it be acted on? Media executives would have to devote considerable resources in time and money to gather together and hammer out a new voluntary code. Parents must phone, write or, at a minimum, access an Internet site; even such minimal action requires energy and commitment. The final three paragraphs, 10–12, offer incentives to action. Paragraph 10 begins with a list of requests that are not being made—for censorship, government control, and media aimed only at children. These are the undesirable alternatives that could be forced on the companies that make up the entertainment industry if they do not police themselves. Thus, paragraph 10 reminds readers in the industry of some of the bad consequences they want to avoid while it stresses the reasonableness of the proposal suggested. Stronger appeals, however, are made on the basis of **ethical rightness** and on the basis of the potential **good consequences.** Paragraph 11 reminds each audience segment of its "responsibility," the duty that comes from its role. Paragraph 12 suggests the good consequences that could follow if the entertainment industry lived up to its ethical responsibilities. The industry is encouraged to believe in its own agency: it "has it within its power to help make America worthy of the third millennium" (a rather vague but high-sounding result); and "by choosing to do good, the entertainment industry can also make good [earn profits?], and both the industry and our society will be richer and better as a result." These are indeed good consequences; both money *and* moral improvement will follow if the arguers' proposal is adopted. In a newspaper editorial, the authors cannot go into the finer points of feasibility (such as how these voluntary associations would police their members into conformity). Instead, they offer overall the satisfying pattern of the proposal—establishing the problem, suggesting a solution, and offering an image of the improvement that will follow.

PROPOSALS: ARGUING FOR ACTION

The desire to make our lives and the world better is a powerful motive for action. We all have schemes for reforming our bodies, our work habits, our neighborhoods, our nation. So strong is our assumption that existing conditions can be made better that we have built regular changes of leadership into many of our institutions, assuming that a new person will mean a new start and a chance for new ideas and policies.

This drive for improvement is even stronger when we sense that something is wrong. We do not endure abuses, either personal or institutional, with patience. Perhaps the Declaration of Independence set the tone for us: after the Continental Congress catalogued the abuses of King George III, they proposed a new nation.

But convincing anyone to take action—whether ourselves or a few colleagues or the public in general—often requires argument. Such an argument "proposes" or urges some action; it says that something should or must be done. We make proposals in every relationship and area of life. Proposal arguments can range from "I should upgrade my modem" or "Our community should build a new indoor swimming pool" to "The United Nations should intervene in any country experiencing a genocidal civil war" or "Humans must preserve the environment for future generations."

Convincing an Audience

If we want to convince an audience to do something, they have to agree with us about two things: that there is a problem that needs to be fixed, and that what we are proposing is a practical solution to the problem. Obviously, an audience must be convinced that a problem exists before they can work up the energy, commitment and resources to do something about it. It takes strong motivation to overcome the stubborn inertia of human nature. But how much an arguer has to do within the argument itself to arouse this perception of a problem and desire for action depends entirely on the situation of the audience. If an arguer addresses an audience immersed in a problem, perhaps even defined by their awareness of that problem, then very little need be done to arouse awareness; the arguer may intensify the audience's beliefs about the problem and then proceed to the proposal. A speaker at the gates of a factory addressing a crowd of employees who have just had their wages cut will not have to do much to remind the audience of the problem; the problem is what brought them together. Such situations are more common in spoken than in written argument. Physical audiences always assemble for a reason, while writers have to construct their potential readers.

On the other hand, an audience can be totally ignorant of the existence of a problem and therefore far from feeling any desire for change. Here the arguer faces a tougher job. First, the arguer has to make the audience aware of the situation that calls for action. This requirement calls for the kind of argument described in Chapter 6, a case for the existence of a situation: the number of right whales has decreased in the last 10 years; the township has just permitted a developer to build 500 new homes in a community.

But convincing the audience that a situation is a problem that needs a solution is a further step. With some audiences, a simple demonstration that a certain situation exists will be enough to move them toward action; with others, more may be necessary. The environmental activists in the Greenpeace movement, for example, will be galvanized into action by statistics on the decline in whale populations; a group of local citizens hearing that 500 new homes are planned in their community may not be convinced they have a problem that needs a solution. The arguer must evaluate the situation negatively before proposing an action.

The preceding chapter described how evaluation arguments are put together. A writer shows the ethical wrongness or the bad consequences of the situation to be corrected. This forceful negative evaluation of an action, event, or policy brings the audience to the brink of wanting to take some action, even when the writer does not suggest exactly what action to take.

Once the audience sees the problem, the proposal arguer can urge a course of action. But here, too, arguments can vary greatly in the kind of action proposed: from an argument that lets the context suggest a patently obvious remedy to one that goes into painstaking detail on the nature and feasibility of specific actions.

After a course of action has been proposed, the proposal itself can receive support from a kind of inverse of the arguments that aroused the audience's desire for some remedy in the first place. If a situation is ethically wrong, for example, then the proposal and its outcome will be ethically right. Or if the problem led to bad consequences, then the proposed action will produce good ones. In other words, the outcome of the proposal receives a positive evaluation; otherwise, why recommend it?

Even if a proposal offers the impetus of ethical results or good consequences, the argument may still have to do more to move an audience to action. After all, most people resist calls upon their time, energy, and money, the very things that proposal makers are usually after. In order to overcome human inertia, the proposal maker often tries to convince readers that the recommended action will be easy to accomplish. But people also tend to suspect that proposals sounding too good to be true are impractical, especially if they are aimed at long-standing problems, familiar evils that people have learned to live with. Given these predictable reasons for skepticism, proposal arguments often launch into elaborate demonstrations of feasibility, showing how action can be realistically taken. Arguing for feasibility involves convincing an audience that the money, time, or cooperative people are available or attainable. Proposal arguments often end with a very precise sequence of steps, starting with an easy first step, that can be followed to achieve a goal.

Sometimes, of course, an arguer cannot reassure an audience that a solution will be easy to accomplish, cost little, take next to no time, and be extremely popular with everyone affected. When these realities intervene, the proposal arguer can engage in trade-offs, showing the audience that although they must make a sacrifice, they will be more than compensated by the resulting benefits or by the extremely worthwhile nature of the proposal's outcome.

KINDS OF PROPOSALS

Before we talk about the contents of the full proposal, we should look at one important way to distinguish one kind of proposal from another. To put it simply, some proposals are more specific than others. We can have vague proposals that do no more than urge some kind of action: "We should do something about this problem," "This situation needs to be improved," "We must not tolerate this state of affairs any longer!" We can also have proposals that are very specific about the course of action recommended: "I should get up at 6:30 tomorrow morning and run three miles around the golf course before breakfast," "We need to install the new OCR software on our office server," "The Secretary of State should meet informally with the Cultural Affairs Minister of Bulgaria in the lobby before the opera."

Actually, we can think of proposals as on a continuum from the vague to the specific: "We need to keep guns out of the hands of children and adolescents in this country" can lead to "Legislation should be passed to make it more difficult to buy guns" and then to "Anyone buying a gun at a gun show should be required to have a background check like that required of purchasers in retail outlets."

Your rhetorical situation (audience, exigence, and constraints) will help you determine how specific your proposal can be. If you are just sitting around complaining about recent events with friends, you probably will get no further than the first proposal above. If someone asks you how that vague goal could be brought about, you might think of the usual solution of "passing a law." But if you are writing to your representative in Congress to urge action, you could be as specific as the third example above, matching your proposal to that of others you may have heard.

How specific the proposal claim is determines the content of the argument supporting it. A more specific claim requires a fuller argument, though not necessarily a longer one. It may not be difficult to convince people that some change is necessary, but if you actually want a practice instituted or a law passed, you need to do some detailed arguing.

CONSTRUCTING A FULL PROPOSAL

The advice in the following sections will help you construct an argument for a specific proposal because that kind requires the fullest treatment. You can adapt this detailed description of a full proposal to meet your needs, choosing the parts you require for audiences and situations where a full proposal is unnecessary or inappropriate.

In its fullest form, the proposal argument breaks into the two parts mentioned above; arguing that there is a problem, and arguing that this proposal offers a practical solution. These two parts flank the proposal claim itself. You can visualize the shape of the full proposal argument as an hourglass, with the recommended action at the neck. Below is a schematic illustrating this idealized arrangement.

Preliminary arguments—convince an audience that a problem exists

**Proposal Claim
(a general or specific
response to the problem)**

**Supporting arguments—convince an audience that a specific action
can and should be taken**

Preliminary Arguments

The Demonstration: "We Really Have a Problem"

What is the aim of a proposal argument? It asks for action from its audience: to change the way something is being done now, to initiate something new, or even to stop something. In most cases, the arguer will begin by pointing out that things are not the way they should be. Therefore, a proposal argument often opens with a demonstration that the present state of affairs is in need of improvement. In effect, the arguer points a finger and says, "Look at that mess!"

Just how much of a demonstration section your proposal needs depends on the obviousness of the problem and the awareness of the audience. If you are standing in a devastated town square the day after a flood and proposing a rebuilding project to the former residents, you will not need much of a demonstration section. But if you are writing to the appropriate agencies in Washington to get funding for this same rebuilding program, you will have to demonstrate just how bad things are in your flood-ravaged town.

If an audience is not at all aware of a problem that needs to be solved, a demonstration section will be a necessary and important part of your argument, maybe even the bulk of it. Imagine, for example, that you want to propose to an audience of typical supermarket shoppers that factory farming should be replaced by more humane methods of raising animals for food and that they should not buy meat from animals raised on factory farms. Since most people are probably not aware of the techniques used in factory farming, any proposal to enlarge cages or to provide straw, light, and fresh air for chickens or a better diet for calves would first have to depict for an uninformed general audience the conditions endured by these animals on factory farms.

An audience can be anywhere between completely ignorant and fully aware of a problem. Sometimes the demonstration section may simply have to provide them with the details of a problem they are already more or less familiar with. For example, the residents of a particular community may have heard about the problems facing senior citizens who live alone, but they may have vague notions rather than specific information. They may not be aware that in their town over 3,000 men and women live alone in substandard housing, that 20 percent of them suffer from malnutrition, and that last winter three old people froze to death in their unheated apartments. You must provide this kind of specific information to make the unaware aware.

As the above example shows, the demonstration section can give an overall picture of a situation, provide trenchant statistics, and bring generalizations alive with specific examples. At the same time that the demonstration section establishes the reality of a situation, it can also appeal to the convictions and emotions that will bring your audience to support your proposal.

You can think about the demonstration section of your proposal as an argument supporting a claim about a state of affairs ("Many old people in our town live in poor conditions"). Remember the steps for supporting such a claim. Do you need to define any terms? How representative is your data? How much evidence might your audience need? These matters are covered in Chapter 6.

Undesirable Consequences of the Situation

The sample situations discussed above involving the mistreatment of animals and the suffering of the elderly would strike most people as problems. However, your demonstration section may convince your audience that a situation does indeed exist but not necessarily that the situation is a problem. To make your audience believe that a situation is a problem, you need to evaluate that situation negatively. As you know from the preceding chapter on evaluation arguments, you can do so by showing that the situation has undesirable consequences or is ethically wrong or both. Let's consider the first method, showing how the situation leads to undesirable consequences. These consequences can be established by causal argument.

Consequences, like situations, may or may not be relatively easy to establish. If they are not obvious, you should certainly trace them for your audience, and if you can bring the bad effects home to your audience and show them how they are affected personally, you will arouse a stronger desire for change.

Why an Audience May Be Unaware of Consequences   First, people may simply be ignorant that any effects exist at all. The public did not know, for instance, that some insecticides irreversibly build up in the fatty tissues of animals in a food chain until Rachel Carson pointed that out in 1962 in *Silent Spring*. The controversial claim that using aerosol sprays depleted the ozone layer was another surprising revelation of a harmful environmental consequence from a seemingly innocuous practice.

Second, consequences may appear bad only from a certain point of view. Machine-dialed commercial phone calls, for example, may be of some benefit to the stores, banks, and credit-card companies that make them, but they can be an intrusive nuisance from the consumer's point of view. Often an arguer needs to show that a group the audience identifies with or has sympathy for is harmed by a situation.

Third, an audience may be aware that consequences exist but not realize their extent. We all know that arson destroys lives and property, but we may be surprised to learn how many lives and how much property. The very extent of a problem can produce its own consequences: The prevalence of arson leads to increased insurance rates and the increased cost of fire protection for everyone.

Evaluating the Consequences

There is one crucial thing to remember about consequence arguments used in proposals. Behind every demonstration of bad consequences stands an evaluation, a judgment that these consequences are indeed bad. Persuading an audience that a situation has consequences can be one thing; showing them that these consequences are bad or undesirable can be another. We may, for instance, agree that the consequence of putting a bounty on wolf pelts is the extinction of the species. But some people may not think that the extinction of wolves is such a bad idea. To substantiate the badness of a consequence that is not self-evidently undesirable to a particular audience may require another consequence argument or an ethical appeal. We may, for example, have to argue further that the extinction of wolves would be bad because their prey, such as deer, would then face overpopulation and starvation. (If your audience needs further convincing, you could explain how this situation affects people—starving deer are vulnerable to diseases that can spread to other animals.)

Informing the Aware

Even when the consequences of a situation are well known to an audience, and they also acknowledge that those consequences are bad, pointing them out may still be worthwhile. Everyone is surely well aware of the potentially harmful effects of cigarette smoking by now, but if you were trying to persuade your father to stop smoking, you would bring them up again. Establishing the harmful consequences of a situation or action when the audience is unaware of them is vital in a proposal argument. Reminding an audience of those consequences even when they are already presumably known can also be convincing. Remember, though, that what everybody knows, nobody cares about, so the art of the arguer is to turn dull acknowledgment into vivid awareness. Any push to action, such as the emotional appeal of reminding the audience about bad consequences, can be useful.

An Ethical Assessment of the Situation

Here is another way to convince your audience that a situation is a problem. You can say that a situation should be remedied not only because of its undesirable consequences, but also because it is simply wrong, no matter what the consequences. Any appeal to an audience's sense of what is right or wrong is an ethical appeal. (See the sections on the variety of ethical appeals and weighting values in Chapter 8.) If you can assume that your audience will immediately agree with your ethical appeal, all you have to do is claim that the situation you want to change is morally wrong.

The Assumable Response   For example, everyone will agree that child abuse is a moral horror. Of course its physical and psychological consequences are damaging too, but even if it had no long-lasting consequences, it would still be wrong in itself. We all agree that slavery is an absolute wrong, even if it had some good consequences for the slave owners. Some audiences will automatically perceive abortion, divorce, the death penalty, gun control, or even their local police department as absolutely wrong in any and all circumstances. You should know when you can expect such a strong response to an ethical appeal from a particular audience. When you can, you do not need to argue ethics; you simply appeal to your audience's preexisting ethical values.

What to Do When an Ethical Response Is Not Assumable   On the other hand, many situations do not call forth an immediate ethical response, and many audiences will not easily see the ethical dimensions of an issue. Whether it is the audience or the issue that will not come around easily, in such cases you have to work for an ethical appeal. The best strategies in this situation are definition and comparison. You can place the situation in an ethical category your audience will react to, or you can compare it to another situation whose ethical dimensions they will recognize.

Suppose that, in an argument addressed to voters, you are proposing to replace our system of graduated income taxes with a flat tax, the same percentage paid by all workers, no matter what they earn. You have to convince your audience that the present situation, increasing the percentage owed with the amount earned, is wrong and should be removed. You can point out the bad consequences of this system (the proliferation of loopholes and deductions), but you may also want to argue that a graduated income tax is simply wrong in itself. Because your audience will probably not assume that tax brackets are ethically wrong, you can try to place this practice into a category that will bring about an immediate ethical response. You might try to define tax brackets as a form of punishment for success. Most people would consider punishing people for doing well to be ethically wrong. You might also try to compare a graduated income tax to another activity that your audience would judge negatively, such as requiring taller people to get on their knees next to shorter people.

Using an ethical category or comparison can be a powerful way to convince an audience that a situation needs to be corrected. Some of these arguments are simpler than others to find, and you should deliberately try to think of appeals in this category: factory farming is a form of cruelty to animals, collecting unemployment compensation is like freeloading, turning off a presidential address on television is unpatriotic. In each of these examples, you are trying to place your subject in a category or make a comparison to which your audience will have an appropriate ethical response.

EXERCISE 9.1

Working either alone or with a group of your classmates, come up with a short argument (one or two paragraphs) convincing an unaware audience that a situation exists and is a problem. Use one of the following choices to help you think of a problem situation, if you like. You may go on to use your paragraphs as part of a full proposal.

1. On your campus:
   a. a safety problem
   b. a housing problem
   c. a problem relating to student recreation facilities
   d. an administrative problem
   e. a course-availability problem
2. In your town or city:
   a. a parking problem
   b. a zoning problem
   c. a transportation problem
   d. an education problem
   e. a crime problem
3. In a course you are taking:
   a. a problem with a text
   b. a problem with the instructor
   c. a problem with the organization of the material
   d. a problem with the amount of work in a course
   e. a problem with the grading

Causal Analysis of the Situation to Be Corrected

Once we have convinced our audience that an undesirable situation exists, they might naturally ask, "How did it get that way?" To answer that question is to find causes, and often to find causes is to find a clue to a solution. It makes sense that one way to correct a situation is to attack the causes that have produced it. A proposal may be designed to alter or eliminate the causes and therefore to alter or eliminate the effect. If we are convinced that violence on TV causes violence in children, we can work to reduce violence on TV; if we know that mosquitoes carry malaria, then we can work to control mosquito populations; if we have evidence that a poor translation caused diplomatic friction, we can make sure that we have a competent translator working for us.

We may, therefore, have to convince our audience that we have identified plausible causes of a problem to make them accept a solution that has been designed to change those causes. The proposal argument will have to incorporate causal argument here, using any of the techniques described in Chapter 7. The causal argument will identify necessary and sufficient causes without which the effect cannot occur, or blocking causes, the kind that will stop the effect. The following example will help you see the place of causal analysis in a proposal argument.

Suppose the river that runs through your town is polluted. As a concerned citizen, you can propose two types of solution. First, you can apply remedies to the effect itself, the pollution, by proposing that a filtration plant be built to purify the water. But notice that remedies that attack only the effect often require continuous application. The filtration plant can never shut down.

Second, you may take a trip upstream and see the enormous industrial complex dumping waste into the river. You may decide to attack this cause of pollution instead of or as well as the pollution itself. You may propose that each factory be required to install its own filtration system or that all the factories dispose of their wastes in another way.

As you can see, in some situations a proposal that attacks the causes of a problem is more convincing than one that attacks effects alone. Attacking causes, when you can get at them, can produce a permanent solution. However, causes are sometimes unreachable. An audience in the United States cannot change the entire political structure of North Africa to prevent the famines caused by civil wars, and no audience on earth can stop storms on the sun to improve radio transmission.

EXERCISE 9.2

Working either alone or with a group of your classmates, work on a causal analysis of the problem whose existence you demonstrated in the first exercise or, if you prefer, a different problem. You should, if possible, identify a dominant cause or one that can be changed. Look in particular for responsible agents or the absence of blocking causes. A factor contributing to the problem may even be the failure of other proposals to solve it. You may go on to use your causal analysis in a full proposal.

Proposal Statement

General Proposals

After you have aroused your audience to awareness of a situation, its bad consequences or ethical wrongness, and its causes, the next step is to suggest what should be done about it. In some cases, you may not know exactly what should be done, or you may think you are not in a position to propose a solution. So you may end after your preliminary argument, which is actually a negative evaluation, with a vague proposal such as "Let's form a committee to study this problem and come up with a solution," or "The people responsible must correct this situation."

Some of these vague suggestions might be called passing the buck, although it is only fair to say that such unspecific proposals have many legitimate uses. A general call for action is one way for an individual with no power to arouse

adopt your proposal. Remember, however, that we are describing an ideal proposal argument. In a real situation, you will pursue only some possibilities and make many alterations in the final arrangement.

The Good Consequences That Will Flow from the Proposal

No one argues for a proposal that would bring about bad consequences. Every proposal, even one to do nothing or to undo something, promises good things to come. Such promises must be substantiated with causal arguments that predict how the course of action you are recommending will bring about good things.

To make these predictions of good things to come from your proposal seem inevitable, two techniques are particularly helpful. These are the *chain of causes* and *analogy*. Let's demonstrate the first of these supporting techniques in the following example. Suppose you make a do-nothing proposal: "Alaskan wilderness areas should not be carved up into any more National Parks." In the "good consequences" section, you will come up with a mini-argument for the following prediction: "If the government refrains from creating parks, the Alaskan wilderness will be preserved." This prediction of what you hope will strike your audience as a good consequence can be supported with a chain of causes.

No parks → No roads → No vehicles → No people → No disturbance →
Wilderness preserved

This argument presents an extended chain, but it is also helpful if you can zero in on agency itself, forging, as it were, a chain with one link in it. You are already familiar with this technique in proposal arguments because you hear it all the time in commercials: Toothpaste X has a whitening agent that causes brighter teeth; bathroom cleaner Y has scrubbing bubbles to make your sink sparkle; shampoo Z has protein to make your hair thicker. Advertisers often claim that agents are present, producing wonderful consequences and hence supporting the unstated proposal that "You should buy this product!"

A prediction of good consequences can also be supported by an analogy if you can find another case where a policy like the one you are proposing has led to the effect you are predicting. You argue that if a similar proposal led to a desirable result there and then, your proposal will lead to a similar result here and now. Suppose, for example, you are proposing a job training program for welfare recipients in your area, and you want to support the prediction that "Job training for welfare recipients will cost taxpayers less in the long run than supporting them at home." You could cite the result of job-training programs versus welfare without training in comparable cities. To support your prediction, you will present evidence that X city, with a training program, spent less per welfare recipient over a certain period of time than Y city, which simply paid welfare recipients who stayed at home. When you can find such a strongly parallel case, it is as though an experiment with your proposal had been performed in another laboratory; you simply predict the same results from similar action.

The Bad Consequences Avoided

Remember that a proposal is usually designed to correct a situation that has led to undesirable consequences. You probably demonstrated the existence of this bad situation and traced its bad consequences earlier in your argument, before you made your full proposal. The desire to eliminate a situation and its harmful effects provided a strong motive to begin with, when your purpose was simply to make your audience receptive to change. Now, after you have revealed your specific proposal, you may want to remind your audience of all the evils that will be avoided if your solution is adopted. For example, when an automobile manufacturer recalls a defective model, the probability of accidents caused by the defect will decrease. When processed meats are eliminated from the diet, harmful nitrate levels in the blood will go down.

If you have not already traced bad consequences in your preliminary arguments, you might want to do so now. If you have already done this, you may simply mention again briefly what your proposal will eliminate. In some circumstances, a fuller discussion of the problem to be ended, even if it is repetitive, emphasizes this crucial appeal. But if you have already traced the bad consequences thoroughly and do not think that repeating them will lend any persuasive force to your argument, this whole section need not exist.

What kind of claim do you have to support here? Again, a causal one. If you argue that certain bad consequences will be avoided, you are, in effect, claiming that your specific proposal will break a chain of causes or remove or block a sufficient cause. You will argue that once a critical cause is removed or blocked, bad consequences will disappear and good ones will take their place.

Suppose you are proposing extended hours at your campus library on the weekends. In your preliminary arguments, you traced the bad consequences when students have no place to study on Friday and Saturday evenings when the library is closed. After disclosing your plan for extended hours, you could remind officials of the rate of students leaving the school because of poor academic performance and argue that extended library hours will help reduce this bad consequence.

The Ethical Appeal for the Proposal

In the first half of your full proposal argument, when all the attention was focused on a problem, you may have appealed to your audience's sense of what was wrong. Now you may want to appeal to their sense of what is right. If slavery is wrong, then freedom is right. If child abuse is wrong, then nurturing care for children is right. Again, if you think you can count on your audience's immediate response to an ethical appeal, you simply make that appeal. But if you cannot count on it, you must place your subject in a category or construct an analogy to which your audience will respond.

A new line of argument is also possible in specific proposals that urge action from an institution or official with responsibility for the issue you are addressing. You may point out that in adopting your proposal, the person or institution responsible will fulfill an ethical obligation. Because institutions and people have responsibilities, showing how action on your proposal fulfills such a responsibility can be a strong ethical appeal. The zoning board, the school principal, the mayor, and the religious leaders who act within their spheres often do so from a moral sense of fulfilling their responsibilities.

EXERCISE 9.4

Working either alone or with a group of your classmates, try your hand at inventing supporting arguments for the proposals below. Do not overdo it; you will almost certainly not need all three types of supporting arguments just outlined. Decide what kind of audience you want to persuade and choose the one or two arguments that would be appropriate for that audience.

1. This county should offer incentives to small farmers to ensure that some land here will continue to be used for agriculture.
2. The county should encourage real-estate development of unprofitable farmland.
3. The city should build a commuter rail system to the suburbs and penalize those who continue to commute by car.
4. The city should build more highways to connect the city center with outlying suburban areas.
5. The college should eliminate its foreign language requirement.
6. The college should require every graduate to complete two years of foreign language study.
7. The federal government should legalize marijuana.
8. The federal government should offer stiffer penalties, including jail time, for marijuana use.

Feasibility: "It Can Be Done"

If you are recommending a specific course of action and want people to get out of their chairs and shake off their apathy, then you must convince them that your proposal is feasible, that it can be done. Feasibility means workability. It is one thing to dream up pie-in-the-sky proposals and quite another to argue that they are actually doable. Arguing feasibility is often a matter of anticipating the questions a skeptical reader is likely to ask about the details. The following sections show how to answer the kinds of questions audiences usually have about feasibility.

Can We Afford It?

Action costs money. So it is not surprising that for most people feasibility comes down to economics. How fully you answer this most predictable of all questions—"How much?"—depends on your proposal and audience. If you are applying to the government for a research grant, you must submit an itemized budget. If you propose that the School Board open the high school in the evening for adult education, you should show that tuition will offset the increased operating costs. Even when you cannot predict costs down to the last penny, you should still show readers that you have considered money by giving a generally correct assurance that your proposal is affordable.

And, of course, if you are actually proposing something that will save more than it costs, make a big point of that good consequence. If your proposal to recycle glass, wood chips, used motor oil, cocoa bean hulls, or autumn leaves will create income where there was once only waste, that is a benefit too great to be overlooked.

Will It Take Too Long?

People tend to be as thrifty of their time as of their money. They will resist a proposal that takes too much of either. The exercise routine of a ballet dancer may keep the body in perfect physical shape, but if it takes eight hours a day and the "body" works in an office all week, it is hardly feasible.

Sometimes the goal of a proposal can also seem to take too long to come to fruition. As a society, for example, we are eager to open professions and influential positions to under-represented groups because doing so is ethically right. But we have been impatient with solutions that wait years for changes in education and hiring to make a measurable difference.

You can try to answer the time question the same way you answered the money question, with detailed schedules or with arguments that amount to general assurances: "It won't take too much time" or "It cannot be done any faster." And, of course, if your proposal can actually save time, you have a strong feasibility argument. Microwave ovens cook a potato more quickly than conventional ovens, and computerized turnstiles process subway passengers more quickly than human ticket collectors. This kind of time-saving has a strong appeal for most audiences.

Can We Get People to Do This?

"It's a fine idea," your reader says, "but how are you going to get people to go along with you?" Human nature resists change. If your proposal involves getting people to move, to act, to invest energy, you may have to convince your audience that you can get people moving. Let's imagine that you are proposing to managers of your company that office personnel be trained to use new software. You point out to them all the time that will be saved once the switchover is accomplished. Nevertheless, they want to know how you get personnel to commit themselves to the arduous training required. You note that employees are usually eager to upgrade their skills, you suggest a modest wage increase as an incentive, and you advise that anyone who refuses to go along be left to do basic data entry. Your audience of managers is convinced when they see how you will convince others.

Suppose your proposal involves moving the general public or a large, varied group of people to action. Such general appeals are common: A governor asks citizens to conserve water; the Surgeon General campaigns against smoking. Common sense tells us that no one will ever convince everyone to stop smoking or wasting water. When defending a proposal addressed to the general public, you have to concede that the entire populace will not go along with it. But a significant number may respond when good and bad consequences and ethical rightness and wrongness are pointed out to them. We can imagine the Governor of California defending a conservation appeal to advisors by arguing that though some people will be too selfish to cut back on water consumption, most Californians will respond to an appeal to the public good if they can see that it is also in their self-interest.

The question "Can we get people to do it?" can have another meaning in a feasibility argument. In the examples above, it means "Can we motivate them?" It can also mean "Do we have the personnel? Can we find them? Can we hire them?" You may feel like the playwright who has a great role for an elderly woman who can tap-dance and sing opera, but can the part be filled? When money is not an object, personnel may be easier to find or train, but in more ordinary situations, the question becomes "Can we find the people we need at our price?"

What Trade-Offs Are Needed?

In any proposal, a separate, satisfactory answer to each of the above questions may be possible. But what if your answer to one or more of the questions will dismay your audience: Your proposal will be expensive, take time, and meet with great resistance. How do you get around such stumbling blocks? Imagine how a successful salesperson would get someone to buy a car that leaks oil. The salesperson admits the car does leak a little oil, but then points out its rust-free body, its custom upholstery, and its low mileage. In the same way, an arguer whose proposal has problems engages in trade-offs. You persuade your audience to accept the defect in your proposal because of its greater overall benefits. Yes, frozen spinach soufflé is expensive, but convenience foods save time in the kitchen. Yes, your plan to convert the old train station into a recreation center will take hours of volunteer work, but once they see the benefits, enough people will turn out to help.

How Can We Do It?

Even if you have the time, money, and people, your audience may still withhold assent until you show them exactly how your proposal will be accomplished. The end looks great, but far off. "What steps, what parts, what processes must we go through to get there?" You can anticipate such predictable questions by going into the details of your proposal in an orderly, sequential fashion. Just showing your audience that you have thought your proposal through, that you have a fully worked-out plan in mind, is in itself persuasive.

Suppose you send a letter to the parents of nursery-school children in your area, proposing piano, violin, and cello lessons for three- and four-year-olds. Time, money, teachers, and equipment are all available. But you have to persuade the parents that teaching such tiny children to play an instrument is possible. The only way to do so is to explain the process, the sequential teaching method you will use. First, the children learn basic rhythms, which they then combine into longer patterns. Next, they are introduced to the instrument, and finally they put all their skills together into a simple song like "Twinkle, Twinkle, Little Star." Once they've mastered one song, they learn another that recombines the same elements and introduces some new ones. In this way, the children build up a repertoire of songs. When parents can see the steps for bringing a three-year-old from clapping to mastering a song, they are more likely to be convinced to the point of enrolling their children. (We have just described the famous Suzuki method of music instruction.)

What's the First Step?

Your audience can acknowledge your proposal's merit, agree that it is feasible, and understand the process required to bring it about, but still be unmoved to action because they do not clearly see the first step to take. You cannot overcome human inertia, even when your audience is favorably disposed, without very precise instructions for an initial action. Without specific guidance into that first step, the audience's commitment will fade away. You may have filled your nursery-school parents' heads with visions of little Jessica as the next Yo Yo Ma, but unless you specify the first organizational meeting for next Thursday night at 8:00 at the school, the visions will evaporate.

Not only should the first move be clear, it should also be easy. Wise advertisers simplify the first move when they include a postage-paid addressed card with their ad or mailing or a simple step-by-step procedure online. All you have to do is drop the card in the mail or respond to the prompts on the screen, and in three weeks a large and expensive package arrives. That first step was so simple!

Has It Been Done Before?

One of the most convincing ways to show that something can be done is to show that it already has been done. If your proposal has been tried elsewhere and worked successfully, you have a case history of its feasibility to bring in as support, as an analogy to predict its workability. Your main challenge will be to show that "elsewhere" is similar to "here" in all essential ways. If another community the same size mounted a successful anti-vandalism campaign, if another supermarket installed computerized deli ordering, then why not your community or your supermarket? This appeal is even stronger when you have more time, more money, or better facilities than your model.

PROJECT FOR CLASS DISCUSSION

Select an editorial from a local newspaper that proposes a solution to a problem. Discuss the ways the writer demonstrates the feasibility of the proposal. Does the class agree that the proposal seems feasible, or not? If so, why? If not, why not? What would make the proposal seem more feasible? What would be a good way to refute the writer's demonstration of feasibility?

Anticipating Difficult Questions

Anyone who makes plans for other people—and that is exactly what you do when you make a proposal for anyone other than yourself—should anticipate some hostile questions: "Who asked you?" "What business is it of yours?"

"Who are you working for?" But if you know what to expect from your audience, you can prevent such questions from forming in their minds. Some of the techniques used to forestall such questions are the accommodation tactics that work with all arguments. But here we will look at a few objections that proposal makers are particularly vulnerable to.

If Your Idea Is So Good, Why Hasn't Anyone Done It Before?

This question has two roots. First, it can come from a suspicion that you have overlooked some fatal flaw that has kept others from proposing your solution. If your proposal has truly never been tried or even suggested before, the best defense against the suspicion that it is too good to be true is a very thorough feasibility section, showing that you have not overlooked anything vital.

Second, this question may reflect honest puzzlement as to why such a good solution never occurred to anyone else working on the problem. You may want to answer, "Because no one else was smart enough to think of it before." But that statement is too boastful and blunt. A better defense here could take one of the following forms.

New Circumstances   You may argue that the situation has changed so that now a solution like yours is possible. For example, your cure for inflation may work only when inflation goes over 10 percent; when the problem is that serious, public motivation will work for you.

A Blocking Cause Removed   One special new circumstance is the disappearance of something that had previously prevented a solution to a problem. The old boss has retired, so now you can finally propose revamping the outdated procedures of the complaint department. Or now that the old bridge has become unstable, you can think of building a new and larger one.

New Knowledge   It may be possible for you to forestall a lethal question by attacking it head on. You may argue that your proposal is not really a new, harebrained idea at all. It's an old idea applied in a new way, or one that was proposed before but never given a fair hearing. Anything that gives your proposal a history can give it authority. For example, your proposal to use soybean derivatives as a protein source to improve school lunches may not be as far-fetched as it sounds. The supermarkets already sell ground meat enriched with soy protein, and Japanese and Chinese cuisines feature soy protein.

What's in It for You?

Even people who don't ask this very impolite question out loud may be thinking it. The motives of do-gooders are always suspect. If no one has authorized you to come up with a proposal, if the problem is not in your domain of responsibility, if you apparently have nothing to gain, then people will wonder why you went to all the trouble. They will suspect that you are going to profit in some hidden way.

How do you forestall this suspicion? First, if you are going to benefit, you should admit it, as long as what benefits you helps others as well. Benjamin

Franklin's many proposals for Philadelphia provide us with models of what has been called "enlightened self-interest" in action. The free public library he proposed certainly was in Franklin's interest. He was an avid reader and it was difficult to obtain books in colonial America. But the public library benefited everyone else in his circle as well. So did his fire company, his inventions, like bifocals and the lightning rod, and the University of Pennsylvania, which he founded.

What if there really is nothing in it for you? Say you are a graduating senior proposing an improvement in a high school you will never attend again, or a math student who got an A in calculus suggesting that the course's multiple-choice tests be replaced by "show-all-work" exams. In situations like these, the benefits of your proposal are for others, not for you. Should you point out what a good person you are? You may be wonderful, but no one wants to hear about it; it is best not to include a passage in praise of your own unselfishness.

Yet some justification is necessary when you have been neither authorized to make a proposal nor led to it naturally by self-interest. Most audiences will accept proposal making from certain ethical motives. The graduating senior could bring up school loyalty; most people are attached to the schools they attended and want to see them prosper. The math student could identify with other students. And both the graduating senior and the math student could boost their credibility by identifying their unique positions as "one who has been through it." It is as though they looked around and said, "No one else is in a better position to make this proposal than I am, so I'll do it."

What's Wrong with the Other Proposal?

Unless you are the only one making a proposal, you are in competition with others, and in a competition it is unwise to ignore the existence of your opponents. Better to acknowledge them and take them on, to show you are aware of the other proposals and refute them where logically possible.

You will probably have to defend your proposal against others that are not very different from your own and that may seem, on the surface, just as plausible as yours. Here is where your knowledge of the parts of the full proposal will be useful. By comparing your proposal to others part by part, you can uncover your competitors' deficiencies.

PROJECT FOR CLASS DISCUSSION

As a class, come up with a local or national problem to which several people or groups have proposed solutions. Working individually or in small groups, locate different proposals that provide solutions to this problem. Compare the proposals in class, working through each one part by part. Can you reach a consensus about which proposal is most effective? What makes it better than the other proposals? If the class disagrees on the best proposal, what reasons do you have for disagreeing? How would you convince a classmate who prefers a different proposal?

Before and After: The Visual Proposal

What is the most powerful incentive for taking action? Undoubtedly, we are more willing to respond to a proposal when we are convinced that we will be better off for doing so (or, in some cases, worse off for not doing so). To provide this incentive, proposal arguments are usually structured as follows: before doing x, the situation is bad; after doing x, the situation is better.

Advertisers have always taken advantage of this very simple before-and-after structure by delivering the argument for a product in terms of a stark visual contrast. For example, to advertise a certain brand of face cream, an ad offers in a "before" picture a frowning person with a dull and blemished complexion; the "after" picture shows a smiling model with smooth, radiant skin. Before trying a miracle diet, the person in the picture is overweight; after, the person is slim. Before working out at the gym, love handles; after, six-pack abs. Before and after contrasts offer a strong reason for change. And the magic "agent," the force that brings about change, is taking the recommended action, or, in the case of advertising, buying the product.

Thus the advertisement for Allegra-D, an allergy drug, shown here can be seen as a proposal. The pictures make a "before and after" argument. On the left, the woman in the

Side effects with Allegra-D were similar to Allegra alone and may include headache, insomnia, and nausea. Due to the decongestant (pseudoephedrine) component in Allegra-D, this product must not be used if you: are taking an MAO inhibitor (a medication for depression) or have stopped taking an MAO inhibitor within 14 days; retain urine; have narrow-angle glaucoma; have severe high blood pressure or severe heart disease. You should also tell your doctor if you have high blood pressure, diabetes, heart disease, glaucoma, thyroid disease, impaired kidney function, or symptoms of an enlarged prostate such as difficulty urinating. Allegra-D is for people twelve and older.

Multi-Symptom Relief:

The stuffy nose and sneezing from seasonal allergies can make any drive hard to take. Only Allegra-D has fexofenadine plus pseudoephedrine. So it provides real relief from allergies and congestion, without the drowsiness that can be caused by many other antihistamines.

Talk to your doctor about Allegra-D, and get on the road to relief today.

For more information, visit allegra.com or call 1-800-allegra.

Real relief. For real living.

car is driving with her left hand while wiping her eye with her finger. Her forehead is furrowed, her eyebrows drawn upward and together, her mouth open (as if to breathe more easily) and its corners turned down. She has a problem, and the text offers two possible interpretations for her obvious discomfort: "Unbearable Commute? or Unbearable Congestion?" These two alternatives conceal a double meaning. Is her "congestion" physical or internal, the congestion of an allergy or a cold, or the "congestion" of traffic? The picture offers no evidence to answer that question. All we know is that the woman looks miserable, whether she has brought her congestion with her or experienced it on the road. Her state is one that most people can identify with. Who, after all, would want to put up with itchy watery eyes and nasal congestion anywhere, let alone while driving?

The ad offers a solution to this problem, however, and the picture on the right shows what happens when the problem is solved. Here the woman is happy. Her head is thrown back, her right hand is on the wheel, and her left arm rests casually on the window frame. Her brow is smooth, her smile broad, and, most important, she is now looking directly out of the picture, making eye contact with the viewer. As viewers, we are brought into a more personal, engaged relationship with her. Whatever congestion (of any kind) she had been experiencing has disappeared, and she is clearly enjoying her car trip. Even her hair looks bouncy rather than bedraggled. The writing on the picture removes both possible causes of the congestion. The answer to "unbearable commute or unbearable congestion" is "neither." We don't have to choose between possible explanations. Whatever is causing the congestion is removed, and a picture of well-being replaces the picture of misery.

The placement of these two pictures is critical. We are conditioned to read the picture of happiness as replacing or coming after the picture of misery because our usual "reading frame" for text is from left to right. Our eyes take in the pictures in that order, just as they would scan text. If we came from a culture where people read from right to left, we would interpret this visual quite differently: we would see a picture of happiness succeeded by a picture of discomfort.

Whenever we see such a graphic before and after, depicting a situation that is unacceptable and then one that is desirable, we naturally assume that something must have happened to cause the change. The text on the right side of the page tells us what solved the problem and thus supplies the missing link in this visual argument. In this case it is the drug Allegra-D. Notice how the presentation of the text corresponds with the representation of the pictures; the right side of the page is the "happy side." Under the positive picture we are told that Allegra-D offers "multi-symptom relief" from "seasonal allergies" that "can make any drive hard to take." No one is claiming that Allegra-D will clear up the environmental causes of congestion or make a daily commute bearable, but we are told that it will provide relief "from allergies and congestion, without the drowsiness that can be caused by many other antihistamines." On the left or "unhappy side" of the ad, we see the familiar list of potential side effects or bad consequences that the medication might cause. This entire paragraph presents the conditions under which the proposal should be set aside. In an ad for something like socks, we would never see a list of warnings and qualifications, but the sale of socks is not federally regulated in the way the sale of prescription drugs is. Advertisers for prescription drugs are required by law to acknowledge the situations in which their product should not be used or be used only with caution.

The contrasted pictures convey the misery of the "before" and the pleasure of the "after," and the prominent text tells us what we need to do to achieve the good consequences. But an advertisement for a prescription drug also has to address the issue of feasibility. The required first step, highlighted visually in bold text, is to "Talk to your doctor." The prominent letters reinforce the picture: like the woman in the car, you will be "on the road to relief." The text returns the reader to what remains most memorable on this page, the argument conveyed by the before and after pictures.

Writing Your Own Proposal

> ## "What Should We Do About It?"

You may have developed ideas for a proposal argument for one of the exercises in this chapter, or you may decide to develop a topic suggested by one of the writing ideas on p. 313. Whatever topic you choose, the following steps will help you construct a successful proposal.

1. Define the Problem, the Audience, and Your Proposed Solution

Writing a successful proposal argument requires answers to three critical and connected questions:

- What exactly is the problem or challenge you want to address?
- Who is your audience?
- What exactly do you want them to do?

These questions depend on each other. Write down your possible topic(s). For each problem or challenge, consider what solution you would propose. Then consider the different audiences you could possibly address to bring your plan about. While some appeals would be the same for all audiences, others would be different, tailored to the precise group and what you want from them. If you have several possible topics at this point, use your analysis of solutions and audiences to focus on the topic that you could argue most persuasively.

2. Plan the Parts of Your Argument

Once you have identified your problem and a precise audience and decided what you want from them, you can begin to plan the parts of your argument. A full proposal includes preliminary arguments that convince an audience that the problem exists, a proposal statement responding to the problem, and supporting arguments explaining that a specific action can and should be taken. Not every argument requires all three parts, so jot down some notes as you consider your plan. The following questions will help you think in more detail about each of the sections of your proposal.

3. Think of Ways to Convince Your Audience That They Face a Problem or a Challenge

What is the situation that needs to be changed or addressed? This is an essential step. Unless your audience is convinced there is a problem or challenge, they will have no motivation for the effort that any proposal requires. Will your audience know that the situation exists? Even if you think your audience is aware of the pressing problem you want to address, your argument will still have to remind them. Can you assume that your audience will agree that the situation is a problem? If not, how can you convince them that the situation is bad?

Since your audience's motivation depends on their ___
is, an effective proposal argument dramatizes the nega___
quences and moral wrongness. Can you use a striking ___
imaginary story of what could happen unless someth___
part of your argument. Testimony from victims or ___

4. Consider the Causes of This Problem Si___

Once you have established that a situation is a problem, your ne___
caused it. Proposals that can address the causes of a situation and ___
more persuasive because they seem permanent and final. (For detailed he___
causes, look at Chapter 7.) But some causes cannot be touched, and some challeng___
as raising money for a charity, do not need causal analysis. So this section of a full propos___
is not always needed.

5. Make Sure That the Action You Recommend Is One That Your Audience Can Accomplish

Some proposals are vague because they are addressed to audiences that cannot take direct action. If you plan to argue for a general audience, you may simply want them to put pressure on those who can actually take action; much arguing in the mass media works this way. More often, however, you will actually want your audience to do what you recommend. In that case, you can tailor your recommendation to what your audience can accomplish, though you will probably also have to convince them that they can accomplish it.

6. Plan Convincing Supporting Arguments

What good consequences and moral improvement will follow from your proposal? Since the source of a proposal is a problem, its result will be a solution. You can fill out your proposal argument by linking your recommendations to these good results. It's even better if you can argue that your proposal will have additional good consequences, beyond fixing the problem or meeting the unmet challenge.

Proposal arguments ask their audiences to sacrifice time, money, or energy. You must, therefore, work hard in proposal arguments to motivate or even inspire your audience. Can you think of ways to create a positive emotional appeal for the solution? Can you emphasize this appeal with vivid writing, narrative, or illustrations?

7. Think of Ways to Assure Your Audience That the Proposal Is Feasible

A successful proposal argument convinces its audience that the change it wants to bring about is desirable and doable. Convincing people they can do something can involve the following details. See if any apply to your topic.

- Is your recommendation practical in terms of the time it will take, the money it will cost, and the people who have to cooperate?

- Can you present your audience with examples of persons or places that have already put your proposal into action? This last tactic is the most convincing if the circumstances in your example are not too different from your own and your audience's.

8. Try to Defend Your Proposal from Competitors and Objections

If you are addressing a crisis or a long-standing problem, there will probably be other proposals out there. What other solutions have been recommended? Why is your proposal better?

—Continued

uld also note possible answers to the following common objections.

 idea is so good, why hasn't anyone done it before?

 at's in it for you?

Write a Brief Statement of the Solution You Are Proposing

After you have decided on a topic, your audience, and your proposed solution and planned the parts of the argument that your proposal should include, write a statement outlining your proposal. You can use this statement as a tentative thesis for your paper. If you like, you may sketch out an informal outline of your paper before beginning to draft.

DRAFTING YOUR PROPOSAL

As you write up your proposal, pay special attention to shaping your argument in the most convincing way. As you consider preliminary arguments, plan ways to demonstrate the problem effectively; make sure that your proposal statement asks for something that the audience can deliver and when you write supporting arguments, think of the best possible ways to support your points vividly and to fend off opposition. Remember, as always, to keep your audience and purpose in mind as you shape your argument.

REVIEWING AND REVISING YOUR PROPOSAL

Once you have completed a draft of your proposal, put it aside for a while, Then read through it carefully, looking for weaknesses in your argument. The following section will help you analyze your proposal and solicit helpful comments from your classmates.

Questions to Ask about a Proposal

Whether you are reviewing your own proposal or one written by a classmate, ask yourself the following questions and write down the answers. Make your answers as detailed as possible, pointing out specific places in the draft that are problematic. (Skip any questions that do not apply to the proposal you are evaluating.) When you have done your own analysis and gone over any comments from your classmates, use these comments and suggestions to revise and refine your proposal and make it stronger.

1. *Has the proposal maintained a clear, consistent audience and purpose?* Is the proposal aimed at a general or specific audience? Is this the best possible audience for the proposal? If not, what audience would be a better choice? Is more than one type of audience addressed? If so, is the action each is expected to take clear to you? Could the audience for this proposal realistically take the action proposed? If not, what changes would you suggest?

2. *Will the audience agree that the problem exists?* Is the audience likely to be aware of the problem already? Why or why not? If the audience is not aware of the problem, does the proposal effectively prove the existence of the situation? Will the audience agree that the situation is a problem? Why or why not?

3. *Does the writer appeal to the audience effectively?* Does the writer offer an overall picture, provide statistics, or describe specific examples of the problem that make it vivid for the audience? Is there a demonstration that the problem creates bad consequences or unethical results? If so, what are they? Is there an appeal to the audience's emotions or convictions? How could this appeal be made more effective? What parts of the appeal are most and least convincing to you?

FOR YOU TO DISCOVER ONLINE

Novak's proposal looks at the historical background of the school prayer issue, discussing the views of "Founding Fathers" John Adams and Thomas Jefferson. Research Adams's and Jefferson's views online and see for yourself what these men thought and wrote about the role of religion in the public life of the United States. You might begin by entering terms such as "role of religion" and "John Adams" and "Thomas Jefferson" into your favorite search engine. Pay attention to the views espoused by the sponsors of the pages you look at; notice how the excerpts from Adams's and Jefferson's writings differ according to the views of those sponsors. After you have done some research on other sites, look at the web site of Novak's organization, the American Enterprise Institute (www.aei.org). How would you characterize the organization with which he is affiliated? Do you think that Novak represented Adams's and Jefferson's views fairly? Why or why not?

My 60-Second Protest from the Hallway

EMILY LESK

Emily Lesk graduated from Thomas Jefferson High School for Science and Technology in Virginia in 2001. This article first appeared in *Newsweek* in June 2001.

It's 8:32 A.M. School began two minutes ago. My bulging book bag is inside my first-period classroom saving my favorite seat. I am standing in the near-empty hallway, leaning against a locker right outside the classroom. I should be in class, yet my teacher has never objected to my minutelong absence, which has become a daily routine. I trace around the edges of the floor tiles with the toe of my running shoe, pausing several times to glance up at the second hand of the standard-issue clock mounted across the hall.

Although I have casually checked this clock countless times during my high-school career, this year looking at it has made me think about how significant 60 seconds can be. Last spring, the Commonwealth of Virginia passed a law that requires every public school in the state to set aside one minute at the beginning of each day during which students must remain seated while they "meditate, pray, or engage in any other silent activity." Every morning, at around 8:31, a resonant voice echoes over the school intercom, "Please rise for the Pledge of Allegiance." I stand up straight and salute the flag. After the pledge the voice commands me to "pause for a minute of silence." I push my chair under my desk and stride out of the classroom.

My objection to Virginia's Minute of Silence law is very simple. I see the policy as an attempt to bring organized prayer into the public schools, thus violating the United States Constitution. Last June at a statewide student-government convention, I spoke with state lawmakers, who confirmed my suspicion that the minute of silence is religiously motivated. One delegate proudly told me that she supported the law because reciting the Lord's Prayer had been a part of her own public-school education.

I agree with the law's strongest critics, who argue that it promotes religious discrimination because many faiths do not pray in the seated position mandated by the legislation. How would a Muslim third grader react to those students (and maybe a teacher) who might fold their hands and bow their heads to pray? Would she feel pressured to join in just to avoid criticism?

My opposition to this law is ironic because I consider myself religious and patriotic. 5
I recite the Pledge of Allegiance daily (including the "one nation under God" part,
which to me has historical, not religious, implications). As a Reform Jew, I get peace
and self-assurance from religious worship and meditation, both at my synagogue and
in my home. But my religious education also taught me the importance of standing up
against discrimination and persecution.

In a school of 1,600 students, fewer than two dozen have joined me in protest. I usually walk out of class with one or two kids, sometimes none. Most days, when I glance
back into the classroom, I see several students praying, heads bowed or eyes closed,
while others do homework or daydream. Although I have not encountered any outright opposition, I often overhear classmates making sarcastic comments or dismissing
the protest as futile. When I see that so many of my peers and teachers find no reason
to question something I feel so strongly about, I wonder if my objection is justified.
What do my 30 extra daily paces accomplish?

In contemplating that question, I've come to realize that taking a stand is about
knowing why I believe what I do and refusing to give in despite the lack of support. My
decision to protest was largely personal. Though I stayed in class the first morning the
law was implemented—because I was caught off guard and because I was curious to see
how others would respond—sitting there felt like a betrayal of my values. I also felt an
obligation to act on behalf of the students all over Virginia who found their own beliefs violated but don't attend schools that allow them to express their opinions.

Deep down, I know this issue will be decided in a courtroom, not in my corridor.
On May 8, the Fourth U.S. Circuit Court of Appeals heard oral arguments from
ACLU lawyers representing seven families who are challenging the law, and will probably reach a decision over the summer. But for now I'll walk out of class each day to
show my school community that an easy alternative to complacency does exist. This
year I will have spent approximately three hours standing in the hallway in protest,
watching the second hand make its 360-degree journey. As a senior about to graduate,
I've thought a lot about the impact I've had on my school. I hope that my protest inspired other kids to use the time to think, not about a beckoning test, but about their
views—even if those views differ from my own.

FOR YOU TO ANALYZE

1. What audience(s) is Lesk writing for, and what action does she want them to take? How effectively does she appeal to her chosen audience(s)?

2. Lesk says, "I consider myself religious and patriotic." How does this statement affect your view of her argument? Why?

3. After reading both Novak's proposal (the previous reading, "With Liberty and Prayer for All") and Lesk's, compare the problems they see and the ways they try to convince their audiences that the problem exists. Which one is more likely to convince you that there is a problem? Why?

4. Lesk says that her objections to the Minute of Silence law are based on the potential for the majority to pressure members of the minority. How does her view of the problem compare with Leon Botstein's discussion of the problems in American high schools in "Let Teen-Agers Try Adulthood" (see below)?

FOR YOU TO WRITE

FOR YOU TO WRITE

1. Lesk mentions that "fewer than two dozen" of her 1,600 classmates have pro-tested the minute of silence in the classroom. Choose an issue on which your views are in the minority, and write a proposal trying to convince the majority that your views are best.

2. Lesk protests a law that she believes is unconstitutional. How would you pro-test a law or rule that you oppose? Propose a way to convince others to object to this rule or law.

3. Lesk discusses the Minute of Silence law with a legislator who said that she supported the law "because reciting the Lord's Prayer had been a part of her own public-school education." Think of a tradition that persists (in your com-munity, your family, your job, or elsewhere) largely because people with power over the situation have "always done it this way." Write a brief proposal argu-ing for abolishing or changing the tradition.

FOR YOU TO DISCOVER ONLINE

Look more deeply into the controversy over school prayer in the United States. You might start with the web site of the American Civil Liberties Union (www.aclu.org), which is seeking to change the Virginia law Lesk discusses in her article. To find out specific information on the Virginia case, you can search their site (try typing in "Minute of Silence" or "Virginia"). How would you characterize the views of the ACLU? To find information from sources on the other side of this issue, put the phrase "school prayer" into a search engine and look at a selection of likely sites. How do the two sides present their arguments? Which side makes the more persuasive case, in your view? Why? If you like, take part in an online discussion of this topic, and try to convince others of your views.

Vote, or Else

JOHN SOLOMON

John Solomon is a freelance journalist. This article was first published in the *New York Times* in October 1998.

The returns are in, and they're pathetic. Of the 36 states that held statewide primaries for both parties this year, 16 set new lows for how many citizens showed up to vote, according to the Committee for the Study of the American Electorate. Overall, only 17 percent of the voting age population cast ballots in this year's primary elections.

It's easy to find excuses for this disturbing trend—the winners in some races were forgone conclusions and there was no presidential contest to draw people to the polls. But the fact remains that voter turnout is continuing to plummet, as it has for several decades. Many experts are predicting that the upcoming general election will see a record-low turnout for mid-term balloting.

Is the anemic participation primarily the result of apathy? Contentment? Cyni-cism? The candidate choices? None of those, if you believe the results of one new survey. "Too busy" was the top reason given by non-voters in a recent U.S. Census Bureau report. But I think the answer is much simpler. A majority of Americans do not vote because they are legally allowed not to do so. While citizens face punishment for failing to pay income taxes, register for the draft or, in many states, to serve jury duty, there is no penalty for neglecting to vote. There should be.

Two years ago, I served jury duty for the first time, though I had been eligible for more than a decade. Like many fellow New Yorkers, I had always found ways to postpone service. But New York City's jury selection system has been streamlined, reducing exemptions and virtually eliminating excuses. The law allows for no-shows to be fined or forced to perform community service.

Not surprisingly, jury attendance is up. If a bit of coercion works at the courthouse, 5 why not use the same idea to improve turnout for another important civic duty? Instituting some kind of sanction—even a small fine—would not only guarantee a higher percentage but also would make the point that voting should be viewed as a responsibility of citizenship rather than an option. Mandatory voting has been adopted by a number of other democracies, including Australia, Italy and Brazil.

No citizen should be forced to cast a vote. There must be an opportunity to abstain or choose a "none of the above" lever. But most no-shows don't have a moral objection to the act of voting. Like many called for jury duty, they just find it a bother.

My jury pool was filled with people who had never served before—either those in previously exempt groups (practically one out of every two seemed to be a lawyer) or others like myself who had continually postponed service. As the Census Bureau study shows, non-voters often cite inconvenience as their reason for not going to the polls. But is being too busy a reasonable excuse for not voting? How could a majority of Americans have had something so pressing to do on Election Day that they couldn't spare half an hour to vote? Even more remarkable is that so many of us countenance that kind of priority setting by our fellow citizens.

While working for a cable television network in 1992, I helped produce a series of "get out and vote" public service announcements. They were among the multitude of PSAs that advocacy groups, companies and the media create around election time. Yet no matter how clever the images, how popular the celebrity spokespeople or how targeted the messages, at best only half of all Americans would ultimately heed our advice.

I looked enviously at the PSAs being produced simultaneously for the U.S. Selective Service, which were "encouraging" those turning 18 to register for the draft. The ads weren't perhaps as creative as ours, but they had quite a compelling tag line: "Register, it's the law." Not surprisingly, 99 percent of eligible men complied by filling out a registration form at the post office. If voting is viewed as an obligation of citizenship, then why not use the straightforward ("Vote, it's the law") approach?

Some argue that we should not be alarmed about the low participation numbers, that if citizens decide they do not want to vote—whatever the reason—it should not be the concern of others. I disagree. Society has decided that the justice system cannot perform effectively unless the bulk of its adult population is available to serve on juries. Similarly, our political process needs to have its voting-age citizens take an active part—even if that activity is just a matter of throwing a lever.

Surprisingly, amid all the doom-and-gloom talk about voter turnout, the idea of 10 compulsory voting does not receive much attention. I think that's largely because it is not viewed as a politically acceptable solution. Republicans have not been eager to pursue "no-shows," who tend to hail from traditionally Democratic groups. In 1992, then-President George Bush had similar concerns when he vetoed the so-called "Motor Voter" legislation. Yet when it comes to electoral policy, sometimes the free market can surprise. The law, approved in 1993 by President Clinton, has not caused the rolls to bulge with new Democratic registrants. And in Washington state, an innovative vote-by-mail process has unexpectedly ended up helping Republican candidates in the last two elections.

Election officials should continue to look at new ways to make participation easier such as expanding voting hours and/or days as well as considering postal and electronic mail balloting. But experience tells us that these measures won't make a significant enough difference. Americans should be brought to the ballot box the same way that I was brought to the jury box—by law.

FOR YOU TO ANALYZE

1. What parts of a full proposal argument does Solomon use, and what parts does he eliminate? Why do you think he chose to structure his proposal in this way? Do you agree with his choices? Why or why not?

2. What audience(s) do you think Solomon is targeting with this article? How does he appeal to his audience(s)? How effective do you find this appeal?

3. What analogy does Solomon choose to support his proposed solution? Do you think this analogy is effective? Why or why not?

4. Does Solomon's proposal anticipate objections and answer questions about feasibility? How would you refute his argument? How would you strengthen it?

FOR YOU TO WRITE

1. Solomon's article responds to what he sees as a failure of citizens to do their civic duty. Write a short proposal suggesting a solution for another problem that occurs when people avoid their responsibilities.

2. Solomon assumes that his audience will agree that low voter turnout is a "disturbing trend." Write a demonstration section for his proposal explaining why this is a problem. Try to convince an audience made up of the people Solomon describes in paragraph 10, who "argue that we should not be alarmed about the low participation numbers, that if citizens decide they do not want to vote—whatever the reason—it should not be the concern of others."

3. Choose a segment of the American voting-age population as your audience and write a proposal for a public-service announcement aimed at convincing this specific group to vote.

FOR YOU TO DISCOVER ONLINE

Spend some time online searching for possible causes of declining voter turnout in U.S. elections. You might begin by searching for the phrase "voter turnout" and seeing what kinds of sites turn up, or you can start with web sites and links from such organizations as the Center for Voting and Democracy (www.fairvote.org), MTV's Rock the Vote (www.rockthevote.org), or the Alliance for Better Campaigns (www.bettercampaigns.org) to learn about some problems that discourage would-be voters. What information do you find, and do you think it explains anything about low voter turnout? Why or why not? Should Solomon have discussed possible causes in more depth? Why or why not?

Let Teen-Agers Try Adulthood

LEON BOTSTEIN

Leon Botstein is the president of Bard College in Annandale-on-Hudson, New York. This article first appeared in the *New York Times* in May 1999.

The national outpouring after the Littleton shootings has forced us to confront something we have suspected for a long time: the American high school is obsolete and should be abolished. In the last month, high school students present and past have come forward with stories about cliques and the artificial intensity of a world defined by insiders and outsiders, in which the insiders hold sway because of superficial definitions of good looks and attractiveness, popularity and sports prowess.

The team sports of high school dominate more than student culture. A community's loyalty to the high school system is often based on the extent to which varsity teams succeed. High school administrators and faculty members are often former coaches, and the coaches themselves are placed in a separate, untouchable category. The result is that the culture of the inside elite is not contested by the adults in the school. Individuality and dissent are discouraged.

But the rules of high school turn out not to be the rules of life. Often the high school outsider becomes the more successful and admired adult. The definitions of masculinity and femininity go through sufficient transformation to make the game of popularity in high school an embarrassment. No other group of adults young or old is confined to an age-segregated environment, much like a gang in which individuals of the same age group define each other's world. In no workplace, not even in colleges or universities, is there such a narrow segmentation by chronology.

Given the poor quality of recruitment and training for high school teachers, it is no wonder that the curriculum and the enterprise of learning hold so little sway over young people. When puberty meets education and learning in modern America, the victory of puberty masquerading as popular culture and the tyranny of peer groups based on ludicrous values meet little resistance.

By the time those who graduate from high school go on to college and realize what 5 really is at stake in becoming an adult, too many opportunities have been lost and too much time has been wasted. Most thoughtful young people suffer the high school environment in silence and in their junior and senior years mark time waiting for college to begin. The Littleton killers, above and beyond the psychological demons that drove them to violence, felt trapped in the artificiality of the high school world and believed it to be real. They engineered their moment of undivided attention and importance in the absence of any confidence that life after high school could have a different meaning.

Adults should face the fact that they don't like adolescents and that they have used high school to isolate the pubescent and hormonally active adolescent away from both the picture-book idealized innocence of childhood and the more accountable world of adulthood. But the primary reason high school doesn't work anymore, if it ever did, is that young people mature substantially earlier in the late 20th century than they did when the high school was invented. For example, the age of first menstruation has dropped at least two years since the beginning of this century, and not surprisingly, the onset of sexual activity has dropped in proportion. An institution intended for children in transition now holds young adults back well beyond the developmental point for which high school was originally designed.

Furthermore, whatever constraints to the presumption of adulthood among young people may have existed decades ago have now fallen away. Information and images, as well as the real and virtual freedom of movement we associate with adulthood, are now accessible to every 15- and 16-year-old.

Secondary education must be rethought.

Elementary school should begin at age 4 or 5 and end with the sixth grade. We should entirely abandon the concept of the middle school and junior high school. Beginning with the seventh grade, there should be four years of secondary education that we may call high school. Young people should graduate at 16 rather than 18.

They could then enter the real world, the world of work or national service, in 10 which they would take a place of responsibility alongside older adults in mixed company. They could stay at home and attend junior college, or they could go away to college. For all the faults of college, at least the adults who dominate the world of colleges, the faculty, were selected precisely because they were exceptional and different, not because they were popular. Despite the often cavalier attitude toward teaching in college, at least physicists know their physics, mathematicians know and love their mathematics, and music is taught by musicians, not by graduates of education schools, where the disciplines are subordinated to the study of classroom management.

For those 16-year-olds who do not want to do any of the above, we might construct new kinds of institutions, each dedicated to one activity, from science to dance, to which adolescents could devote their energies while working together with professionals in those fields.

At 16, young Americans are prepared to be taken seriously and to develop the motivations and interests that will serve them well in adult life. They need to enter a world where they are not in a lunchroom with only their peers, estranged from other age groups and cut off from the game of life as it is really played. There is nothing utopian about this idea; it is immensely practical and efficient, and its implementation is long overdue. We need to face biological and cultural facts and not prolong the life of a flawed institution that is out of date.

FOR YOU TO ANALYZE

1. What audience is Botstein writing for? How does he structure his appeal for this audience? Is the appeal effective? Why or why not?

2. What problems with U.S. high schools does Botstein assume the audience will understand and agree with? Do you think he is right in his assumptions? If so, why? If not, how would you change his proposal argument?

3. Analyze Botstein's proposal for restructuring American high schools. Has he anticipated all of the objections you can think of? If not, what has he missed? How feasible does his solution seem to you?

4. Botstein's article is entitled "Let Teen-Agers Try Adulthood." What assumptions does he make about the idea of adulthood? Do you agree with them? Why or why not? Does his proposal really offer teens a way to "try adulthood"?

FOR YOU TO WRITE

1. Botstein talks about the dominance of team sports in the high school environment and identifies a chain of causes growing out of that phenomenon. Identify a chain of causes that leads to or grows out of a problem in your school or community, and briefly propose a solution.

2. Botstein argues that high schools have outlived their usefulness because teen-agers reach physical maturity earlier than they did a century ago and because they have ready access to information once available only to adults. Write a proposal for changing (or resisting change in) an institution that was designed in a different era.

3. Botstein mentions "the tyranny of peer groups masquerading as popular culture." Write about an aspect of popular culture that you believe tyrannizes a segment of the population and propose a solution to the problem.

FOR YOU TO DISCOVER ONLINE

Botstein's article, like the article at the beginning of this chapter, refers to the school shootings in Littleton, Colorado. Since that event, many people have made suggestions about how to re-form high schools. Look for more information online about post-Littleton education reform (you might try entering keywords such as "Littleton" and "education reform" into your favorite search engine and see what articles come up). What kinds of suggestions do you find? What suggestions are similar to Botstein's, and which ones differ dramatically? After researching the issue, do you find yourself more or less in agreement with Botstein's proposal? Why?

Researching Arguments

Part Three

10. Finding Sources to Support Your
    Claim 327

11. Using Sources to Support Your
    Claim 372

Finding Sources to Support Your Claim

Chapter 10

When we make or defend claims casually in everyday conversation, we often rely on widely held beliefs or on information that we have heard or read about "somewhere." But when an issue arouses our interest and we decide to investigate it thoroughly in order to write or speak about it with authority, then we need a different approach. It is not enough to repeat facts that may or may not be verified or to ignore relevant information and expert assessments. In the same way, when we offer arguments in more formal situations—in a professional setting or in a paper written for a college course—the stakes are high and our credibility is on the line. Our arguments have to represent our best efforts and be put together from the best available resources.

AN OVERVIEW OF SOURCES

Whether you are researching an issue with no idea what your final position will be or are beginning with a potential claim and looking for support or refutation, you must investigate your subject as thoroughly as possible. What sources of information and interpretation are available? Where and how can you begin to look? How reliable are the sources you find, especially online sources? The following discussion will give you an overview of the three types of sources that you may need to call upon as you explore an issue, decide on your claim, and gather support and counterarguments:

1. Primary sources that serve as basic evidence in different fields
2. Secondary sources that offer analysis, interpretation, evaluation, and commentary
3. Sources that help you answer questions of fact: general reference materials

---

Chapters 10 and 11 were written by Sonya Brown and Elizabeth Colson.

Primary Sources That Serve as Direct Evidence in Different Fields

Most fields of inquiry distinguish between two broad categories of sources, called primary and secondary sources. **Primary sources** include information that you experience firsthand; documents or works that you locate in archives, museums, or other collections; or data that you actively gather or construct using interviews, surveys, experiments, or other means of direct observation. **Secondary sources,** discussed on pages 333–34, are derived from the experiences or primary research of others. The following is a list of common primary sources.

A GENERAL LIST OF PRIMARY SOURCES

- Original works of art and literature
- Videotapes, audiotapes, or transcripts of television and radio programs and films
- Diaries and letters
- Interviews (conducted by phone, letter, or e-mail, or given as court testimony)
- Results of surveys and polls
- Original documents (such as birth and death certificates, and trial transcripts)
- Patents
- Proceedings from meetings, conferences, and symposia
- Legal proceedings
- Original web pages
- Museum collections of artifacts
- Business records and documents

Doing research with primary sources often requires your active efforts. Arguments that use primary sources as evidence can be very persuasive because firsthand information is frequently considered more reliable than information that is relayed through secondhand sources. Which would you be inclined to judge a better argument about the causes of a crime: one supported by interviews with witnesses and an examination of the crime scene itself, or one supported by interviews with people who had heard witnesses talking about the crime and an examination of photographs of the crime scene? Similarly, if you support an argument with evidence derived from your own interaction with the people, places, and items that are directly involved with the issue, your argument is likely to be highly persuasive. While secondary sources will often be important to your research as well, and in some situations may be the only evidence that is available to you, doing research with primary sources means you are building your own argument on direct experience rather than relying solely on the arguments and experiences of others.

As a college student, you will most likely use the following types of primary sources in constructing arguments for your courses:

- Materials from museums, archives, and special collections
- Interviews
- Surveys and Polls

Museums, Archives, and Special Collections

Museums and archives store a wide variety of materials of interest to researchers, from important documents to works of art to collections of fossils to everyday objects from the past. While most people think of libraries as places that let patrons use or borrow print materials, like museums they can also harbor relics and objects related to the theme of a "special collection." Such special collections are often of regional and historical interest: The Minneapolis Public Library, for example, has a collection of approximately 10,000 photographs of the city, its landmarks, and citizens, spanning from the 1850s to the 1960s. The Julia Davis Branch of the St. Louis public library, which contains a collection of books on African-American Literature and Culture, is another example of a special collection arranged by theme, as is Duke University's collection of advertisements for health and hygiene products, "Medicine and Madison Avenue." These special collections are usually housed within the library but may not be available during all of the regular library hours. More and more libraries are "digitizing" some of their materials, however: the Minneapolis photography exhibit and the Duke advertisement collection described above are also available online. Some archives are government-related; government archives include the presidential libraries and the National Archives, located in Beltsville, Maryland.

If you plan to do research in a museum, an archive, or a library, you will usually need to contact the institution in advance for permission and to learn its rules. As you plan your research project, keep in mind that retrieving items from storage at museums, archives, and special collections in libraries may take some time. Do not expect to look at too many items in one visit. You should know in advance, by searching print or online catalogs, whether the items you wish to see are available, and you should contact the museum, archive, or library well ahead of time by mail, by phone, or by e-mail to find out what the hours and restrictions are. Depending on the archive, some materials may not be available to the general public. Photographs, video and audio tapes, and other recording devices may also be similarly restricted. Note taking pictures or photocopying may be permitted only under special circumstances.

Interviews

Interviews with authorities on your issue or with people who have relevant experience can often provide you with crucial support for your claim. In order to get the most out of an interview, there are several important steps to take before, during, and after your meeting with your subject.

- **Set up the appointment.** When you call or write to ask for an interview, explain who you are, the topic you are researching, and your purpose in conducting the interview. Also tell your subject approximately how long your interview will last, propose some possible times for your meeting, and invite the interviewee to set a convenient time.
- **Develop a list of questions and decide how you will record the answers.** For a successful interview, it is essential that you know enough about the topic in advance to ask stimulating questions and carry on a conversation. Think of questions that are likely to generate answers more complex than merely "yes" or "no." If you would like to record the session with a tape recorder or video camera, you should obtain the interviewee's permission in advance. Keep in mind that such devices may inhibit your subject. Alternatively, you could take notes during the interview or listen carefully and make notes immediately afterwards. Although note taking may slow down your interview, careful, accurate notes will allow you to be more certain that you are recording information accurately. If you are taking notes during the interview, you might wish to check the accuracy of any direct quotations you plan to use, with permission, by reading them back to the interviewee.
- **Immediately after the interview, check your notes.** You may want to flesh out your notes as necessary with additional information you remember from your conversation.
- **Write a brief, timely thank-you note.** Be sure to thank the person again for sharing his or her time and knowledge with you. Also share with the interviewee the final product of your research.

If it is impossible to conduct an interview in person, you can send a list of questions through the mail or by e-mail, or ask for a phone interview. These options require the same etiquette as in-person interviews.

TIPS ON CONDUCTING INTERVIEWS

- *Act professionally.*   Arrive on time for the interview and dress neatly and appropriately. Greet your respondent by saying "Hello, I'm____. Thank you for taking the time to meet with me today." And make sure that you emphasize the purpose of the interview before you begin to ask questions.

- *Listen carefully.*   Allow the respondent to speak freely, and ask follow-up questions such as

    What more can you say about _____?

    How do you think that happened?

    Could you define _____?

    Could you clarify what you meant by _____?

- *Take summary notes.* Do not try to write down every word your respondent says; otherwise, you may miss some important points to follow up on. Instead, try to write down key words or phrases that you can then expand on later.
- *Keep the interview on track.* Prepare a list of questions or topics to cover—an "interview plan"—ahead of time, and redirect the discussion if necessary.
- *Conclude well.* Ask respondents if they would like to add any information. Ask for a follow-up interview if you feel that one may be necessary. Tell respondents that you will e-mail your notes if they would like to review what they have said, and thank them for their time. Write a complete version of the interview for your notes immediately after you leave.

Surveys and Polls

Surveys and polls are designed to get information from people whose opinions are relevant or who have day-to-day experience, rather than expertise, with an issue. Essentially, researchers formulate a question or set of questions on a given topic or issue and ask people to answer, often by choosing from among predetermined answers. You may find the results of preexisting surveys and polls on the issue you are investigating, especially if the issue is of national or regional importance. If you are using an already published survey, be sure that you have examined how the research was conducted: What percentage of the relevant population was measured, and did the population sample reflect the characteristics of the larger population whose views the researchers claim to present? What questions were the respondents asked? Were the questions worded in a way that might lead to a particular answer? If the same question or questions were worded differently, would the respondents have answered differently? If the sample seems inadequate or the questions unclear or misleading, you should discount the results.

If you are collecting information on a local population—say, the students on your campus—and need to design your own survey, you will want your sample to represent a range of individuals and to reflect, as closely as possible, the characteristics of the larger population you are interested in learning about. One common way to obtain a representative group of respondents is to use a **random sample,** in which the respondents are chosen arbitrarily—for example, by picking every tenth name on a list. Keep in mind, though, that getting a truly random sample can be difficult, and the size of the larger population and the information you are seeking are important considerations. A survey of 20 people, randomly selected, who live on 113th Street in Largo, Florida, might fairly represent the views of people living in that neighborhood on such topics as their satisfaction with their particular suburban housing development or nearby park. Those same 20 people, however, would not adequately represent "Floridians," or "Americans," or "suburbanites." You should describe your survey methods in your final paper to help your audience judge the reliability of your survey.

Depending on the type of information you are seeking, you will also want to choose the appropriate type of question. Your questionnaire can contain open-ended questions, multiple-choice questions, two-way questions that might be answered with "true or false," or "yes or no," questions requiring a specific, "correct" answer. Often, questionnaires will include more than one type of question.

Examples of open-ended questions include "What do you think of the airport security bill currently being debated in the House of Representatives?" or "What is your opinion of mandatory school uniforms in public schools?" Open-ended questions may generate some interesting answers you were not expecting, but keep in mind that you are also likely to get vague answers or answers that are difficult for you to interpret or tally.

If you use multiple-choice questions, you can avoid vague, difficult-to-interpret answers, but for the most accurate results the answer choices need to be easy for respondents to understand and must not overlap. For a survey on student employment, for example, you might use the following question:

If you have a job, how many hours do you work each week?
a. Less than 10 hours
b. 11–20 hours
c. 21–35 hours
d. More than 35 hours

Of the four possible answers, each respondent could choose only one.

Multiple-choice questionnaires can also enable you to gauge respondents' attitudes by presenting them with a range of responses, from "disagree strongly" to "agree strongly," from "poor" to "excellent," and so on. This type of question is known as a **Likert scale.** A range of five responses is most popular, followed by three; you can, however, provide as wide or as limited a range as you choose, as long as you offer an odd number of possible responses.

You can also design multiple-choice questions that deal with specific behaviors:

How often do you shop on the Internet?
a. Every day
b. Four to six times a week
c. Two to three times a week
d. Once a week
e. Once every few weeks
f. Never

Be wary of asking questions that respondents may be embarrassed to answer, such as, "How often do you do illegal drugs?" Such emotionally laden questions, often called *loaded questions,* may predispose your audience to exaggerate or limit their answers to what they think is acceptable.

Like multiple-choice questions, two-way questions are focused and easy to tabulate:

Do you approve of the President's tax bill? Yes ☐ No ☐

Two-way questions do not allow respondents to express ambivalence, however, so responses to them can be misleading.

Finally, if you wish to discover how much people of different ages know or remember about a subject, you might design a series of questions asking about it and provide multiple-choice answers, only one of which is correct. For example, a series of questions such as this one would help you learn how much your respondents know or remember about the administration of President Jimmy Carter:

What year was President Carter elected?
a. 1972
b. 1976
c. 1980
d. 1984

Questionnaires can be distributed or conducted in person, or you can conduct them by phone or distribute them by mail or e-mail. If you use mail, you will need to provide a stamped, self-addressed envelope to encourage responses.

TIPS ON CONDUCTING SURVEYS

- *Determine what kind of data you are searching for.* This information will help you decide how to administer and collect the data. It will also help you decide on the types of questions to use.

- *Consider what kind of questions you will ask.* You can ask open-ended questions:

    How would you change this assignment?

  Or you can ask close-ended questions:

    Did you enjoy coming to this class? ___Yes ___No

- *If you are trying to learn respondents' attitudes or opinions, consider using Likert scales in your questions.*

    Did you find the textbook effective?

    1—not at all effective   2—somewhat effective   3—very effective

  This kind of scalable survey is easy for respondents to read, and it will generate hard data for you to analyze. For best results, design the survey so that you always provide an odd number of possible responses on the scale.

- *Let your respondents know the purpose of the survey.* Make sure that the respondents feel that their answers are important.

- *Avoid asking embarrassing or loaded questions.*

Secondary Sources That Offer Analysis, Interpretation, Evaluation, and Commentary

Secondary sources are the kinds of sources that often bring issues to our attention in the first place. They include newspaper and magazine articles, TV programs, websites, and most published books, including the many histories, biographies, and commentaries produced by scholars and journalists. These sources provide summaries, analyses, interpretations, commentary, and sometimes evaluations or judgments of primary sources. A newspaper article, for example, is often based on the testimony collected or interviews conducted by journalists. A history or biography is based in part on the primary sources—documents, records, and artifacts—examined by the author. A sociologist's study of a trend can be based on survey or census data. A scientist's research report is usually based on experimental results compiled in a laboratory or on careful observations in the field. A study of an artist by an art critic is based on the critic's firsthand inspection of the artist's work in museums and private collections. Many sites on the World Wide Web are interpretive summaries of material on a topic with links to other sites where researchers can retrieve documents or additional secondary sources. (For more on web sources, see pages 349–71.)

Secondary sources are indispensable. You must use them to give yourself an overview of a subject or an issue and to sample informed opinion, and they often contain the facts and quotations that are the building blocks of all arguments. And their interpretations and assessments need not be discounted. After all, the judgment of a journalist, historian, scientist, or critic who has spent a lifetime studying a subject is a valuable resource. But because all secondary sources inevitably represent one author or institution or time period or perspective, you should always be careful to consult multiple secondary sources. Secondary sources also differ considerably in their reliability; some are based on a much more thorough assessment of primary materials than others.

The sources listed on page 338 that help you find sources will lead you to secondary sources. The sections on pages 349–71 will help you conduct online searches and guide you in evaluating the sources you find on the Internet.

A GENERAL LIST OF SECONDARY SOURCES

- Newspaper and magazine articles
- Biographies
- Histories and commentaries
- Books, book chapters, and journal articles written to analyze or condense a primary source
- Theses and dissertations

Sources That Help Answer Specific Questions

Another type of source includes such publications as encyclopedias, dictionaries, thesauruses, almanacs, fact books, directories, maps, and atlases. You turn to such **general reference** sources to decide questions of fact or to find a quick overview of a topic. In many libraries these sources are found in the general reference section, and they are usually noncirculating.

Encyclopedias and **dictionaries** may be either general or field-specific. General encyclopedias and dictionaries contain entries on a variety of subjects, while specialized encyclopedias and dictionaries, such as the *A.D.A.M. Health Illustrated Encyclopedia*, the *Stanford Encyclopedia of Philosophy*, *Merriam Webster's Medical Dictionary*, and the *Grove Dictionary of Music*, contain more detailed entries on terms within a specific field and eliminate the meanings of the term that fall outside the field's usage. Specialized reference materials that introduce the key figures, terms, and concepts exist for every discipline. Whether you use general or field-specific dictionaries, they can help you discover not only word meanings, but also word origins, historical examples of usage, and changes in meaning over time. Those available on CD-ROM will also pronounce words for you. General and specialized encyclopedias are often the best sources for the kind of information that is not open for debate: When was the Hoover Dam built? Who invented the electron-scanning microscope? They can also give you a quick, reliable overview of a topic, and bibliographies at the ends of entries can lead you to additional resources.

When you are searching for quantitative information or the kind of data compiled from year to year, consult specialized **almanacs, yearbooks,** and **atlases.** Both almanacs and yearbooks are compendiums of facts, statistics, or other data for a specific year. You may have had your photograph taken for your high school yearbook, which included a collection of photographs for each class as well as photos of various school activities for the year and lists of participants, sports team records, and so on. Somewhat similarly, *Congressional Quarterly* publishes the *Supreme Court Yearbook* for those interested in the activities of the court each year. *Almanacs* are often arranged in the form of charts and tables that make it easy to compare data. *The World Almanac and Book of Facts,* compiled since 1868, is an excellent source for comparative data on the exports, educational systems, and governments of different countries. Again, you will find these specialized compilations for almost any area of interest. Finally, *atlases* are more than just collections of maps featuring unchanging terrain; they also provide information on shifting political boundaries, population, annual rainfall, mineral resources, average temperatures, and so on, and can be quite useful to researchers of many topics.

To discover facts about a famous person, or even a not-so-famous person, you can consult one of the many **biographical dictionaries** that collect brief biographies about people according to their nationality (for example, *Dictionary of American Biography*), profession (*Contemporary Authors*), gender (*International Women in Science*) or ethnicity (*Biographical Dictionary of American Indian History to 1900*). The research collections of most libraries also maintain useful **directories** that provide names and profiles of institutions, associations, corporations and so on, along with addresses and sometimes phone numbers. Many of these sources are also available online.

WIDELY USED REFERENCE MATERIALS

Encyclopedias

- The *Encyclopedia Britannica,* and its searchable partner, *Britannica Online,* is one of the most respected general encyclopedias.
- The *Columbia Encyclopedia* offers over 80,000 cross-referenced entries and 40,000 bibliographic citations.

—Continued

- *Encarta* is a well-known CD-ROM and online encyclopedia with 40,000 plus articles and 12,000 plus illustrations.

Dictionaries

- The *Oxford English Dictionary*, with its 22 print volumes, available in their entirety in its online version, is an authoritative guide to the English language and its evolution over the last thousand years. It provides examples of usage from a variety of historical documents as well as word roots and pronunciation guides.
- The *American Heritage Dictionary* has entries for over 90,000 words. Notes for many of the entries explain the development of American English in various regions and among various ethnic and cultural groups. It can tell you who first used the word *bandwagon* and what foreign language the term *gung ho* is derived from.
- *Merriam Webster's Collegiate Dictionary*, related to *Encyclopedia Britannica* and *Britannica Online*, provides guides to pronunciation, etymologies, examples of historical usage, synonyms and antonyms, and hundreds of images to aid your imagination.

Almanacs and Yearbooks

- *World Almanac and Book of Facts* is the standard print almanac, providing geographical, cultural, political, and historical information on regions of the world.
- *World Almanac Online* incorporates information from the *World Almanac and Book of Facts*, *World Almanac of the United States of America*, *World Almanac of United States Politics*, and *World Almanac Knowledge Source*.
- *World Fact Book*, under the aegis of the Central Intelligence Agency (CIA), provides basic information on all of the world's countries.

Biographical Dictionaries

- *American National Biography* covers Americans and non-Americans who died before 1996 and who had a significant impact on American culture or history.
- *Biographical and Genealogical Master Index* is an online index to current and retrospective biographical dictionaries.
- The *World Biographical Index* contains over 2 million brief entries, as well as citations to reference works on each biographical subject.

Atlases

- The *National Atlas of the U.S.A.* has been a standard resource. Its new online version allows you to choose a spot on a map and overlay information on that town or territory on such diverse topics as population, water resources, and history.
- The *Global Gazzetteer* offers geographical and meteorological information on more than 3 million non-U.S. cities and towns.

EXERCISE 10.1

What kinds of primary, secondary, and general reference sources might you use to research the following:

1. How woodlands in your region have been affected by climate trends over the last 50 years.
2. The life of Elvis Presley.

3. The potential benefits of mandatory school uniforms in public schools.
4. The history behind the foundation of East Timor.
5. The rise of grunge rock in the early 1990s.

LOCATING SOURCES

Indexes, catalogs, abstracts, and bibliographies are the most helpful tools you can use to locate primary and secondary resources.

- **Indexes** are published listings of published material; familiar examples that are available in print include *Books in Print* and the *Reader's Guide to Periodical Literature.* There are also a host of specialized indexes that pertain to particular fields, and some contain brief descriptions of the content of each entry they list.
- **Catalogs** are comprehensive lists of specific collections, for example, of a particular library or museum or archive.
- **Abstracts** are lists of sources that include a brief summary of each book, article, or other resource listed, such as *Physics Abstracts* or *Dissertation Abstracts.* Many indexes and catalogs have versions available in print, on CD-ROM, and online, but many are only available online.
- **Bibliographies** are lists of works published on a given topic. Sometimes bibliographies also provide summaries of books and articles, commentary on their potential usefulness from experts in the field, and information on how to find the rare materials listed. There are also bibliographies of bibliographies for nearly every subject of interest.

As you begin your research, you should seek out indexes and databases that may help you find sources of information and opinion on your topic. **Databases** are regularly updated files of digitized information, made searchable using database management systems software. Usually a database reflects print information: the database producer *(The Modern Language Association)* organizes the content into a format *(The MLA Bibliography),* then allows a vendor *(EBSCOhost,* for example) to provide a computer-readable version on CD-ROM and/or online. Different vendors allow different search criteria or categories, so your library may subscribe to two or more versions of the same online database, which allows you to select the format you feel most comfortable with. For example, both *OCLC First Search* and EBSCOhost provide access to *ERIC,* a periodicals index in education.

You can, therefore, access many indexes and other search tools online as well as in print. Check the list of databases to which your library subscribes, and think about which general and field-specific databases may contain information on your topic. General indexes and databases usually cover both general news magazines and also some field-specific magazines and journals. Field-specific indexes and databases limit the periodicals they cover to magazines, journals, newsletters and trade publications within one field of study. For example, WilsonSelect offers full texts of multidisciplinary and general journals, whereas

PAIS International covers only international journals on public policy and social issues from 1972 to the present. General indexes cover a wider variety of publications and issues, but perhaps with less depth, so searching both general and specialized indexes is often a good strategy. Education issues, for example, are likely to be discussed in national and local newspapers as well as in journals written by and for scholars in that field, and the different types of sources can provide you with multiple points of view on the issue you are researching.

As you scan indexes, catalogs, abstracts, and bibliographies for relevant sources on your topic, you may need to consider when potential sources were published or posted: for some issues, you will need the most up-to-date information in order to construct an effective argument; for others, you may need current information bolstered by substantial research into the history of the issue.

GETTING STARTED: SOME HELPFUL TOOLS FOR GENERAL RESEARCH

Your library probably subscribes to one or more of the following databases.

Lexis-Nexis Academic

This database provides full text for national and international newspapers. *Lexis-Nexis* also has databases that cover U.S. history, the U.S. Congress, statistics, business, and U.S. case law.

Academic Search Elite

Provided by the vendor *EBSCOhost,* this database provides abstracts for over 3,000 general, social science, science and humanities journals, and covers approximately one-third of these in full text.

WilsonSelect Full Text

This database indexes 800 social science, science, humanities, and business journals, from 1994 to the present.

Alternative Press Index

This database covers 380 "alternative," left, radical publications, many of which are not covered by other databases, from 1991 to the present.

Reader's Guide and Reader's Guide Abstracts

The original print source and its online counterpart cover popular magazines.

Congressional Quarterly and CQ Researcher Database

Another pair of resources that are available in print and online, these cover current events in some depth, providing history, background, bibliographies, pro/con articles, and more on controversial public issues from 1992 to the present.

WorldCat

This mammoth database, provided by OCLC First Search, is the largest source of bibliographic information in the world, with over 48 million records. Most citations include a physical description of the object and its contents, and all indicate which member libraries own the item, making this a helpful resource for obtaining hard-to-find items through interlibrary loan (see page 346).

ArticleFirst

Another OCLC First Search offering, ArticleFirst provides information about articles on a wide variety of subjects from nearly 12,500 journals.

Dissertation Abstracts Index (DAI)

Provides information about master's theses and doctoral dissertations from 1861 to the present in every field from approximately 1,000 graduate schools and universities. With full text for nearly 100,000 dissertations, this is a rich resource for otherwise unpublished documents. Fees may apply for some services.

Searching for Sources by Keyword

All types of sources—primary, secondary and general reference—may be available in print, on CD-Rom, on the Internet, or in some combination of these media. While it is certainly possible to support an argument solely with primary sources, and to locate them without even touching a computer, savvy researchers have the ability to search for all of these materials using computer databases, including online library, museum, and archive catalogs, periodical indexes, and the World Wide Web. Variations in the way computer databases are searched exist, and this section will discuss some of those variations, but most of the technology used to make databases searchable works in much the same way, whether you are searching the CD-ROM version of an encyclopedia, a computerized library catalog, or the Internet.

Developing Keywords

Whenever you are searching an online database, you will need one or more **keywords**—important words, phrases, or names that relate to your topic or issue—that you can enter into the database's search engine. The same keyword search skills will help you explore most of the online information resources that are available to researchers.

Any database search works by scanning for the word or words you enter within the title, abstract, subject descriptors, and perhaps even the full text of the material itself. For example, if you are searching a library's catalog for books and other materials on *gambling*, you may find *Without Reservation: How a Controversial Indian Tribe Rose to Power and Built the World's Largest Casino*. Even though the word *gambling* doesn't appear in the title, the word *gambling* appears in a description of the book's contents, or as a *subject heading*. On page 340, for example, is a sample catalog entry for the book above, showing author, title, and subject headings, which here reflect those assigned by the Library of Congress.

Author	Jeff Benedict
Title	Without Reservation: How a Controversial Indian Tribe Rose to Power and Built the World's Largest Casino
Subject(s)	Pequot Indians Gambling
	Gambling on Indian Reservations Connecticut
	Casinos Connecticut
	Pequot Indians Government Relations
	Pequot Indians Economic Relations

As you can see, the first and second subject headings include the keyword *gambling*, and the database has therefore retrieved this record. For more information on searching by subject, see page 341.

If you are familiar with your topic, you may already know the important terms that can serve as keywords. To get the best results, however, you should think of keyword searching as an activity that you refine as your research progresses. To start, think of your topic as a phrase or sentence. For example, you might say "I want to find information about the legalization of gambling in the United States." If you simply enter the word *gambling* in the periodical database Lexis-Nexis, you will receive a message telling you that "your search has been interrupted" because too many records matched your query. Similarly, if you enter *gambling* as a search query in the Internet search engine Alta Vista, you will have over 3 million hits (for more on search engines, see page 354). This huge quantity of information is neither useful nor efficient; also, most of the items retrieved would be of little or no use to you because although they contain the word *gambling*, they may have nothing to do with legalized gambling in the United States.

At this point, you should go back to your statement of your topic, think about what you are trying to find out, and decide which words in the sentence are of key importance. Because you are interested in learning about legal gambling in a particular country—the United States—it appears that *legalization* and *United States* will be key terms, in addition to *gambling*. To develop your list of keywords further, you should think of synonyms for the key terms. General reference materials such as encyclopedias can assist you, and you can also consult the *Library of Congress Subject Headings (LCSH)*. The Library of Congress assigns each published item a description, or set of descriptions, pertaining to its subject. The "big red books," as librarians call them, list items published under each of the subject headings recognized by the Library of Congress. Print versions of these are available in most libraries' reference sections. The catalog entry above, for example, shows five Library of Congress Subject Headings for the book *Without Reservation*. The library's online catalog may also allow you to search by subject using the LCSH system or another one; most databases also allow some form of *searching by subject*. When you are conducting an online search using keywords, you can incorporate words from subject descriptions when you find them useful, or you can often choose to search a subject heading by clicking on it.

After adding keywords from Library of Congress Subject Headings and reference works, then, our keyword list is expanded:

Legalization	**Gambling**	**United States**
policies	gaming	America
	casinos	specific state?
		specific city or cities?

EXERCISE 10.2

Develop a list of keywords for three of the following topics.

1. Affirmative action policies in college admissions
2. The relationship between learning to play an instrument and intellectual development in children
3. The benefits of organic gardening
4. Reintroduction of predators into national parks
5. Day care for children of working parents

Using Boolean Operators

Your next step in refining your search will be to combine your search terms using Boolean operators. **Boolean operators** include both words (*and, or, not*) and symbols (*, ?, !). Most databases use some combination of Boolean operators to facilitate searching. Some of these operators limit your search by decreasing the amount of information the database will retrieve for you. If you connect two or more terms with *and* (or sometimes + or &), the search will turn up only material that contains all of the words connected by *and*. For instance, if you enter

legalization **and** gambling

you will retrieve a list of all the materials in the database that have those two words present in their full text, in their title, or in the description of the item. Entering

legalization **and** gambling **and** United States

will eliminate all materials from the previous search that do not also refer to the United States.

United States is a two-word term, of course. Many databases will search for words that are not joined by a Boolean connector as a phrase: that is, the database searches for items that have the words *United* and *States* side by side in that specific order, rather than for the two individual words in any order. If you enter

the legalization of gambling

only items that contain those exact words in that order will be retrieved. In the first example, the limitation works to your advantage because you are looking for information on legalized gambling in the United States. In the second example, though, you may find this limitation too restrictive.

In the same way, if you are searching for sources on substance abuse, using the keyword search

substance **and** abuse

will retrieve items that contain both words in any order; most people refer to substance abuse using that specific phrase, however, so it would be a more useful limitation to look for the specific phrase. To do this, you would enter

substance abuse

Some databases, however, automatically supply the Boolean connector *and* between words entered in the keyword search box. If you are searching for a phrase, these databases require you to enclose the phrase in quotation marks, as seen here.

"substance abuse"

Other Boolean connectors also help you to expand your search. *Or* allows you to search for alternative words or synonyms. If you are trying to find general information on gambling, for instance, you might search for

gambling **or** gaming **or** casinos

It is usually more efficient, however, to combine *and* and *or* phrases:

legalization **and** (gambling **or** gaming **or** casinos) **and** (United States **or** America **or** New Jersey)

This search asks the database to retrieve materials containing the word *legalization* and any of the three terms within the first set of parentheses and any of the three terms within the second set of parentheses. Using parentheses to organize search terms in this way is called *nesting*. Many databases provide advanced search options that make the parentheses unnecessary. It is a good idea to switch from the basic search page to the advanced search page of any database in order to conduct an efficient search on a complex issue (for more on basic and advanced searches, see page 343).

Another Boolean connector used to limit searches is *not* (sometimes −). *Not* eliminates materials that contain the word that follows it. For example, if in your research about legalized gambling in the United States you were not interested in Las Vegas, you might try the following search query:

legalization **and** gambling **and** United States **not** Las Vegas

Be wary of using *not* too liberally, however, as the search will eliminate all potential sources that contain the words *Las Vegas*, even if the source refers to Las Vegas seldom or only peripherally.

Wildcard symbols allow you to search for multiple spellings of a word. Wildcard symbols vary from database to database; check the search help or tips screens for information about which symbols function as wildcards in the database you are using. Often, the asterisk (*), question mark (?), or exclamation point (!) will function as the wildcard symbol. Let's say you are searching for works by and about the Russian author Fyodor Dostoyevsky and you discover that his last name is sometimes spelled Dostoievsky in English. You could run a search using *or:*

Dostoyevsky **or** Dostoievsky

If you are using a database that uses the asterisk as a wildcard symbol, however, you might run a search on

Dosto*evsky

Finally, **truncation symbols** are wildcard symbols that end the search term, making it possible to search for multiple variations on a word. In our search above, for example, we looked for materials related to the legalization of gambling, but words that are related to *legalization*—such as *legal, legalization, legalized, legality* and so on—might be used in relevant articles. To find articles that use these variations, determine the root word or figure out which letters are present at the beginning of all the words. Then type only that root followed by a truncation symbol. Consider whether each word in your search has variations that might occur in potential sources on your topic. Note that some databases allow you to search for multiple forms of all the words in your search by clicking a button.

A final form of the keyword search for our researcher might look like this:

legal* and (gambling **or** gaming **or** casino*) **and** (United States **or** America **or** New Jersey)

where the asterisk functions as a truncation symbol.

Use Boolean operators to prepare a keyword search for one of the topics for which you developed a list of keywords in Exercise 10.2 on page 341.

EXERCISE 10.3

Simple and Advanced Searches

Before you run any online search in any database, whether you are searching a library catalog at a small town library or searching the Web using a giant search engine, you should spend a few minutes familiarizing yourself with exactly which Boolean operators and special functions the database allows. Each database should have a link (a word underlined or highlighted) that takes you to a help page explaining the search functions available for that database. This link may be the word *help*, or *tips*, or something similar.

Most databases provide two methods for searching: a simple search and an advanced search. Understanding the differences between these two options can mean the difference between a frustrating and a fruitful search, so it is useful to explore both options in any database you consult. A simple search screen is your best choice when you are using a small number or keywords and Boolean operators, or you are proficient in using the Boolean operators discussed in the previous section, including the parentheses. Most simple search screens include one box for data entry and a "search" button below or beside this box.

Here, for example, the simple search screen allows you to fill in keywords, after which you click on the Go! or Search button to retrieve matching items. Advanced search screens, however, usually include three or more boxes for entering data, and you can select the Boolean operators you would like to use before you search.

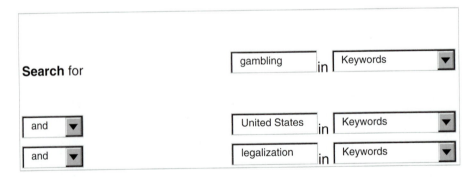

In this case, you could put one keyword in each empty box:

You could also adjust the search by changing the Boolean operator: click on the downward-pointing arrow beside "and" in either box and you will see the range of other Boolean operators provided by the database (usually *or* and *not*):

Search for | gambling | in | Keywords ▼ |

| or ▼ | | gaming | in | Keywords ▼ |
| and ▼ | | legalization | in | Keywords ▼ |

Advanced search screens such as this one also allow you to change from keyword searching to searching by subject, title, or date. To find out what the database allows you to alter, you can click the downward-pointing arrow beside "Keywords." Another alternative is to enter several keywords, which are themselves connected with Boolean connectors:

Search for | gambling or gam | in | Keywords ▼ |

| and ▼ | | United States or | in | Keywords ▼ |
| and ▼ | | legalization | in | Keywords ▼ |

A number of other possible search strategies using Boolean operators are available. Before you use any database, consult the help screens, or the list of Frequently Asked Questions (FAQs), to find out if it provides one or more of the following options that may help you limit your search.

Sorting results by relevance.   A database that sorts by relevance will rank the possible sources it turns up by the number of times the keyword occurs in each one.

Sorting by date.   A database that sorts by date organizes the list of possible sources to show you the most recent material on your topic first.

Limiting date.   This option allows you to enter the dates between which you want the material you find to have been published. For example, suppose you are looking for

—*Continued*

material published on the prevention of terrorism in the United States after September 11, 2001. You would set the date restriction for September 11, 2001, to the present date.

Searching by publication source. Many periodical indexes and databases can search for articles in only one source, or in a limited number of their indexed sources. If you want to limit your search to articles from *The New York Times,* for example, you can type this title into the "publication source" section, providing the database covers this newspaper.

Limit to specific languages. Most databases cover material written in English and a variety of other languages. If the database allows, you can refine your search to find only articles in languages you are able to read.

Finally, especially if you are researching a historical topic, you may want to make sure your database covers the time period you need. Few online databases cover materials published before 1980, though some are expanding their information backward in time as well as forward.

Searching for Library Sources

To find books, journal and newspaper articles, news wires and transcripts, and government documents on your topic, you can use a variety of different search tools that are available in your college library, including library catalogs and periodical indexes and databases. Most libraries have converted their card catalogs into online catalogs. Although your library may still retain its old card catalog, it probably no longer adds new entries to it. For most searches, then, you will need to use your library's online catalog. While most people think primarily of books when they think of the library, the online catalog will tell you not only what books, journals, and reference materials the library contains, but also what audio and video tapes, CDs, DVDs, government documents, photographs, works of art, and other materials are in the library's collections. It will tell you where items are located, and often whether or not the item is already checked out or not. Online library catalogs will almost always offer you the opportunity to search by keyword as well as by using other search methods, including searching by title, by author, by subject, and by call number. You should select the option that will help you retrieve the material you need most efficiently. For example, if you already know the title of a book you wish to use in your research, it is most efficient to search by title.

Many libraries are linked with other libraries in a network, which means that from a terminal in one library you can search through the catalogs of several other libraries, often simultaneously. The advantages of this type of system are clear, and sometimes libraries linked in this way will also offer **interlibrary loan,** which allows you to request that books and other materials be sent to your home library from another, for you to check out. Sometimes libraries will send photocopies of articles to your home library; you may be required to pay a small photocopy and shipping fee for this service. Some libraries post articles that have been requested on a web page, which is accessible to the requester for a limited number of uses. In some cases, a request for an interlibrary loan may take a week or more, so budget your research time wisely.

FIND THE RIGHT EDITION

While obtaining a book or article on your topic might seem relatively straightforward, there are still some factors to consider when you are looking for the appropriate text to use. Remember that books, like all texts, are subject to revision. Revisions may occur because the original edition had errors, or because the author has revised his or her position, or because new information has become available, or for a number of other possible reasons. Charles Dickens rewrote the conclusion to *Great Expectations* because his audience of Victorian readers complained about the first ending, but many contemporary readers feel that his original ending was the "true" one. As a result, many contemporary editions print the original ending first, then supply the second version as an appendix. No matter what kind of text you are considering as a source, be aware of the variations and revised editions that may be in existence, and the potential merits of each, before you begin formulating an argument based on them.

The following guidelines will help you determine which edition of a book you should use:

1. Check for an author's, translator's, or editor's preface, foreword, or afterword, which may provide information about the differences between the original and revised texts.

2. For historical editions especially, you should also look for a "Textual Note," or "A Note on the Text," which usually contains information about what edition the current editor worked from, as well as what additional editorial changes were made.

3. When you are using the library catalog to find books, examine all of the bibliographic information that is available about it. The catalog will tell you what year the book was published and what edition it is.

4. Check the copyright page at the front of the book (usually the page immediately following the title page) to see the edition number and the year published.

5. Use a scholarly bibliography, if possible, to see which edition researchers rely on most heavily.

In addition to the online catalog, most libraries subscribe to one or more of the hundreds of *periodical indexes* currently available, and these indexes may be consulted in print, on CD-ROM, and/or online. The print versions of these indexes provide lists of citations of articles by topic, along with enough bibliographic information for you to find the articles you want from the list. The *Reader's Guide to Periodical Literature* is a standard print index for general research subjects. Online periodicals indexes, or *periodicals databases*, also make it possible for you to search for articles from a wide variety of periodical publications, such as newspapers, magazines, and scholarly journals. These databases provide essentially the same service as print indexes, but many of them also offer researchers important advantages over print versions. Unlike print indexes, which are usually available in monthly or yearly volumes, making it necessary to search several volumes separately, online databases search through whatever dates you select from their records, all at once. Online databases are also more flexible. You can tailor the types of information you find to your individual search needs by altering search criteria, such as keywords and date limitations (see above).

Because you can usually gain access to the library's catalog and to the databases the library subscribes to from the same computer terminals, you will often find yourself using the same computer to look for articles in databases and for books and other library resources in the library's catalog, a situation that can lead to some confusion. It is therefore important to remember that, while a library's online and card catalogs include the items the library owns, periodical indexes and databases canvas materials that are not identical to the holdings of the libraries that subscribe to them. As a result, when you search a periodicals index or database, you may find abstracts or citations of articles in journals that your library does not subscribe to. You may need to use interlibrary loan, discussed on page 346, to get such articles.

A number of online databases, however, offer some or all of the articles they index in their entirety, in what is called *full text*. For example, your library may subscribe to and receive print copies of the *New York Times* and the *Chicago Sun-Times* but may not have print copies of the *Denver Post* or the *Financial Times*, a London-based paper. The periodicals index Lexis-Nexis will provide articles from these newspapers and many more that your library may not subscribe to. You can then print out articles in the library or send text to your personal e-mail account. For the most part, you need not be concerned that the version of an article that is available from a periodicals database is different from the original, print version. Keep in mind, though, that the print version may include charts, graphs, photographs and other visuals that the periodicals index does not reproduce.

While several large periodicals databases, such as Lexis-Nexis and Wilson Select, offer full text services, most do not. Some provide full-text articles from only some of the periodicals they cover. Most of the databases designed for special fields also do not cover their full range of periodicals in full text. But these databases are still enormously useful, and you can usually find the article with little difficulty once you have the citation and a bit of know-how.

When you use a periodicals database that does not offer full texts of the articles it indexes, and you find citations and abstracts for articles that look useful, you will need to find the articles in their entirety. To find out whether your library has the issue of the periodical you need, search the library catalog for the title of the magazine, newspaper, or journal in which the article appears. To do this, follow these steps:

1. Note the title of the journal or newspaper (sometimes labeled "source") that published the article you want to find.
2. Note the date, volume, and issue number for the article.
3. Using your library's catalog, do a title search, not a keyword search, for the complete title of the journal or newspaper.
4. When you find the catalog entry for your source, check to see if the date, volume and issue number are within the library's holdings. Your

library may store older issues in bound volumes, or on microfilm or microfiche.

5. Note the complete call number, which will help you locate the journal.

Some vendors (OCLS First Search, for example) make finding articles in your library easier by formatting their material so that you can check to see which member libraries own the source publication for the article citations you retrieve.

As an alternative, you might search a full-text database to see if it covers the periodical:

1. Set the search criteria for title search rather than a keyword search.
2. Use the title of the article as a query.
3. Set the date limitations for the exact date of publication.

You might also see if the source publication has a website with a searchable archive of past articles. The *Washington Post*, for example, has a searchable archive on its website, www.washingtonpost.com. Many newspapers and other periodicals will charge a small fee for downloading an article from their websites.

Choose one of the topics from Exercise 10.2 and do the following:

1. Find two books on the topic in your library's catalog.
2. Find two citations for articles on the topic using a periodicals index or database.
3. If the full text of one or both of the articles you found in 2 is not available from the database, use the library catalog to find out if the library owns the periodicals you would need to read the articles.

EXERCISE 10.4

Searching for Electronic Sources

The world-wide computer network known as the **Internet** offers a broad spectrum of primary and secondary sources—from the lyrics to the 1960s *Spiderman* theme song to the British Library's manuscript version of the ancient epic *Beowulf*, from the U.S. National Library of Medicine's (NML) home page to the constitution for the National Organization for the Reform of Marijuana Laws (NRML). But searching for electronic resources is not as simple as it seems. Although information on a topic may be just a click away, it may not be accurate or credible. In other words, just because electronic information is free and available without even visiting a library, that does not mean it's a good bargain. So while the Internet can be a promising research tool, you should plan your search carefully and use the information that you obtain judiciously.

Of the different ways to access information on the Internet, the **World Wide Web** is the most recent and the fastest growing. Many people incorrectly think that the Internet and the World Wide Web, or "Web," are the same thing. In fact, the World Wide Web is only one part of the Internet. The Web is an application that runs on top of the Internet; more specifically, it is an application containing hypertext (http) or linked formats that allow you to move from one location to another by clicking on a link. The Internet also offers access to **newsgroups,** which can enable you to read the opinions of—and communicate with—other people in a particular field or with a specific interest.

Even if you have used the Internet before to do research, you still may not know the difference between a search engine and a site directory, or you may not know how to access a newsgroup. The sections that follow will provide you with a better understanding of how to search the World Wide Web and of how to decide which web sources to use. Following this chapter is a helpful list of subject-specific directories and websites of research interest.

Searching the World Wide Web

To search the Web successfully, you will need to call on your critical thinking skills. According to *Super Searchers Do Business*, a research manual for information specialists, "people who like to solve puzzles make good online searchers—anything that involves a stepwise process toward an end that isn't just jumping from here to there." In fact, most research librarians agree that searching for information on the World Wide Web is one of the most difficult research tasks, partly because of the nature of the Web itself: information is added to and deleted from the Web every day. Often a researcher will discover that what he or she found on one day cannot be found the next.

The Internet began during the 1960s in the Department of Defense as a computer network that allowed researchers to communicate with each other using a common computer language. Now anyone with a computer (or even a television) and Internet access can be linked to this network. However, as the Internet evolved from a closed communication system to a global and somewhat democratic information network, the hardware and communications technology that operate this network have had trouble keeping pace with its tremendous growth. That is why it often takes so long for you to download a web page and why it is sometimes difficult even to connect to a page.

You may be tempted to think of the Web as an information warehouse, but that metaphor does not really fit because there is no one central storage unit for every bit of digital information. In fact, it is better to think of it as an enormous "net," as its name suggests, with no beginning or end. It is a loose network of millions of computers, and these individual computers are what hold the bits of digital information.

If you have already used the Web, then you know that it contains information that is linked, known as **hypertext,** allowing you to move from one page to another. To access a website, you might click on a link—a word, phrase, or picture—in another website, or you might type a Uniform Resource Locator (URL) into your web browser (a software program such as Netscape or Microsoft Explorer that allows you to view web pages). Each website has a distinct URL, an address that directs you to a particular website or home page.

For example, the URL for the National Criminal Justice Reference Service home page is http://www.ncjrs.org (shown below).

PARTS OF A WEB ADDRESS		
Type of Access	**Name of Site**	**Domain**
http	www.ncjrs	.org

At the end of this URL, the three letters that make up the domain name, ".org," indicate the type of organization that is hosting this web page. You should always note the domain names of the sites that you turn up on your searches because they are clues to a site's reliability. For example, the domain name ~/al indicates that the site is a personal web page. The information posted on such a site may not be as trustworthy as that found on a government or educational site. The most commonly used domain names are listed below, with examples of each type of organization.

URL	**Designation**	**Example Site**
.com	Commercial or company site	Facts on File http://www.facts.com
.edu	Educational	University of Maryland http://www.inform.umd.edu
.gov	Government or government agency	National Institutes of Health http://www.nih.gov
.mil	Military	Department of Defense http://www.defenselink.mil
.net	Network of computers	A Shopping Network www.shoppingring.net
.org	Not-for-profit organization	The National Criminal Justice Reference Service http://www.ncjrs.org
.uk	Country-sponsored site	The British Library http://www.bl.uk

In addition to knowing the type of organization that publishes the site, you should also determine the general character and purpose of each site you visit. The following types of sites can be useful in different ways.

- Subject-specific sites focus on a particular subject or theme and contain links to similar sites. Envirolink (www.envirolink.org) is one example of a subject-specific site. It offers information or links to information on topics of interest to the environmental community, and it is maintained by a nonprofit organization. Envirolink contains articles on subjects ranging from endangered species to global warming, and it can direct you to other environmental sites.

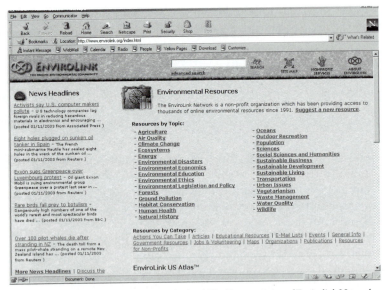

Source: Envirolink Network. www.envirolink.org/index.html. Used by permission of Envirolink Network; Netscape browser window © 2002 Netscape Communications Corporation. Used with permission. Netscape Communications has not authorized, sponsored, endorsed, or approved this publication and is not responsible for its content.

Many of these sites are searchable; they have a search program that allows you to search the site in much the same way you would use a search engine. The National Criminal Justice Reference Service website, for example, is another site with a search feature.

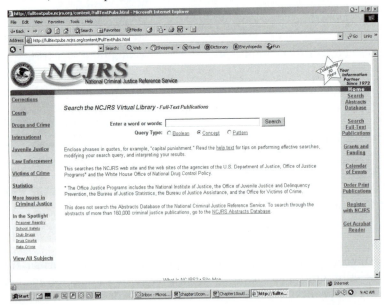

Source: National Criminal Justice Reference Service. www.ncjrs.org. Used by permission of NCJRS. Netscape browser window © 2002 Netscape Communications Corporation. Used with permission. Netscape Communications has not authorized, sponsored, endorsed, or approved this publication and is not responsible for its content.

- FAQ or "frequently asked questions" sites give answers to popular questions asked about a particular topic. You could, for example, go to the Ask-An-Earth-Scientist website (**www.soest.hawaii.edu/GG/ASK/askanerd.html**) and find the answers to questions on such topics as volcanoes, earthquakes, or sedimentary rock. This site actually links you to experts from the University of Hawaii's Geology and Geophysics Lab.

Source: University of Hawaii, School of Ocean & Earth Science & Technology. www.soest.hawaii.edu/GG/ASK/askanerd.html. Used by permission. Netscape browser window © 2002 Netscape Communications Corporation. Used with permission. Netscape Communications has not authorized, sponsored, endorsed, or approved this publication and is not responsible for its content.

- Electronic journals/newspapers give you access to articles in online journals and to articles from print sources. The *New England Journal of Medicine*, for example, can be found in an online version as well as a print version.

In fact, websites such as the NCJRS site or the one maintained by the *New England Journal of Medicine* contain some of the most up-to-date and authoritative information you can find on a subject. The NCJRS site, for example, is maintained by the U.S. Department of Justice and by the Office of National Drug Control Policy and gives researchers access to hundreds of well-researched, well-documented texts. To find a subject-specific site, a FAQ site, or an electronic journal in your field of interest, consult the list of "Web Pages of Interest" on pages 360–71.

To search the World Wide Web effectively, you will need to think about the kinds of information you are looking for and how you plan to use that information. You will also need to formulate search terms—also known as keywords—that are related to your topic. (See pages 339–46 for advice on formulating keywords and using Boolean operators.) Finally, you will need to decide which search engine or site directory will be the most useful for your search.

Search engines (indexes) compile their listings using programs called "spiders" or "crawlers" that search the Web and record the text and topics of pages. A search engine will index millions of pages in this way. By entering keywords into the search site's user interface, you can retrieve lists of Web pages that contain your term. Most well-known search engines such as Alta Vista, Google, Lycos, and MSN Search claim to have a large web database and to be able to help you find exactly what you need. While the first claim may be accurate, the second claim is less so. In fact, no one search engine is going to be able to find everything that you need. Most research librarians know that they can conduct the same search on two different days or on two different search engines and gather two different sets of information.

When you use a search engine, you should ask the following basic questions about the site and how it works:

- When was the last time this search engine searched the net for new sites?
- How does the search engine rank the sites it retrieves?
- Why is the first site listed first? Is it because it is the most relevant to your topic or because its web designer has tricked the search engine into ranking it first?
- Was the search done using exactly the words you typed, or did the search engine expand the search to related concepts as well?
- Does the search engine have the ability to cluster searches so that only one page per site can be listed in your top results?

You can find the answers to most of these questions simply by reading the information that the search engine site provides its users on how to conduct a simple or advanced search. If you are looking for more detailed information about a particular search engine, you might want to consult *PC Magazine* online to find out about the most recent changes to the major search engines.

Listed below are the major search engines you can use. Keep in mind that all search engines update their features regularly, and information about them dates quickly. To find out about the latest innovations in search engine technology or the most up-to-date strategies to use, consult Danny Sullivan's *Search Engine Watch* (http://searchenginewatch.com).

- *Alta Vista* (http://www.altavista.com) Alta Vista indexes the full texts of more than 90 percent of all websites, according to their own information, as well as a million newsgroup messages. It allows users to search by keyword and also by category, and it allows users to screen out personal web pages and limit searches by dates. Because its reach is so vast, for best results you will need to limit your keywords using

Boolean operators to avoid being inundated with thousands of hits. Moreover, Alta Vista does not allow online searchers the ability to cluster their searches.

- *Google* (http://www.google.com)   One of the most popular search engines today, Google began as a student project at Stanford University. Google's crawler allows you to search by keyword or phrase—and it also allows you to find exact matches to text passages. For example, if you are searching for a quote by Martin Luther King, you can type in what you can remember of the quote (e.g., ". . . one day this nation will rise up . . ."), and Google can quickly find the entire "I Have a Dream" speech. Google is the search engine of choice, even among research librarians, primarily because it is comprehensive and because it allows you to search for images, newsgroups, and old versions of web pages easily.

- *HotBot* (http://www.hotbot.com)   HotBot has been a favorite tool of online researchers because it offers users the ability to cluster search results and it has "stemming capability," which allows it to search for variations on a word. For example, if you enter the word *prevent*, the search engine might also search for pages that contain the term *prevention* or *preventing*.

- *Lycos* (www.lycos.com/network)   Lycos offers users the ability to do clustering, stemming, and related searches. It sometimes reads more into users' queries than necessary though, returning sites that feature none of the original search terms.

- *MSN Search* (www.search.msn.com)   MSN Search is a site worth considering because it offers users both edited search results and crawler-based results. According to Search Engine Watch, MSN uses editors to "monitor the most popular searches being performed and then hand picks sites that are believed to be the most relevant." MSN also uses the LookSmart directory and Inktomi's search engine to provide users with a thorough searching tool.

- *Ask Jeeves* (www.ask.com)   This site uses "natural language processing," which allows users to type a question and click on "ask." The site offers answers and search suggestions in response. For example, if you type in "Who was the fifth president of the United States," the site responds with links to information about James Monroe, as well as links to other presidents and a list of related searches.

Site directories are lists of websites devoted to various topics. Unlike other search tools, they are edited and maintained by people. Compared to search engines, site directories seem to access a relatively small number of web pages. But because these directories are created by individuals rather than computers, they often contain recommendations or reviews of sites. Moreover, you will be less likely to find as many web pages that lack credibility using a directory than you will when you use one of the search engines listed above. *Yahoo!*

(www.yahoo.com), probably the most widely known directory, began as an on-line bibliography developed by two students and has now expanded into a directory with hundreds of thousands of pages in its databases. Because it has an online editorial board that reviews the sites listed, the quality of the information that you receive from a Yahoo! search is high. It is also a good idea to use a directory such as Yahoo! when you are looking for information about a broad category to start your research; for example, you might start with a Yahoo! search if you are looking for information about Maine.

EXERCISE 10.5

Using a search engine and a directory, locate five websites on one of the topics from Exercise 10.2 on page 341.

Advantages and Disadvantages of Using Web Sources

As with any type of source, web sources offer researchers advantages and disadvantages, and you need to be aware of both.

Advantages of Using Web Sources   The web is one of the best means of accessing raw data such as census reports issued by the government, stock reports for a corporation, or new statistics on breast cancer rates. It is also helpful when you are searching for an obscure or unusual document or piece of information such as the manuscript version of the *Magna Carta*. The web is also a ready source of recent news, press releases, biographical information, and company facts. And you can tap into anecdotal information by connecting with people in chat rooms who may be willing to share their experiences with you. But the main advantage of information that you obtain from the Web is that it is often the most up-to-date information you can find.

Disadvantages of Using Web Sources   One of the main advantages of using sources from the web—their timeliness—can also be a disadvantage. Websites may become quickly outdated if they are not maintained, and sites often disappear overnight. Moreover, it can take you a great deal of time to find the right keywords to use in search engines, to search links in websites for further information, and to wait for pages to download.

The most serious disadvantage for student researchers, however, is the lack of quality control on the web. Traditional media outlets such as scholarly journals and newspapers have peer reviewers and editors who watch for inaccurate data, unreliable sources, and other content problems. Editors also correct problems with grammar, punctuation, and spelling. While the content on some websites is also subject to these controls, the content on others is published without any kind of editorial input. As Lida Larsen, the coordinator for online information resources at the University of Maryland at College Park, reminds students, "The Web is not an encyclopedia. Encyclopedias have subject experts writing refereed articles that pass through editors before publication. The Web has these same experts, and many non-experts, creating non-refereed Web pages on a vast array of topics at a vast range of quality and depth." The guidelines on pages 358–60 will help you to evaluate the information you locate on the Web.

As a researcher, you also need to bear in mind that while every year more Americans gain access to computers and to the Internet, that access still seems to be limited. In a report published in 1999, the National Telecommunications and Information Industry Administration (NTIA) found that high-income white and Asian/Pacific Islander households were most likely to have Internet access. The NTIA has in fact found what it calls a "digital divide"—a divide between classes and sometimes races in Internet access. This divide is significant for researchers who use the Web. Because the main audience for the Web is not diverse, many web pages, and commercial sites in particular, are often tailored to one audience and biased toward that audience's interests.

Finally, the international telecommunications infrastructure is not always as well developed as the infrastructure in the United States. Some international sources may not be accessible to you simply because their pages cannot be downloaded or because your search engine fails to recognize them. If you are working on a topic that is international in scope, you will probably need to use traditional search tools and sources such as library catalogs and databases and communications with experts in addition to web-based materials.

Usenet/Newsgroups

Usenet is a unique conference system that hosts thousands of online newsgroup discussions. Next to e-mail and the Web, Usenet, according to Internet researchers, is the third most popular way for users to interact on the Internet. **Newsgroups** allow subscribers to "meet" electronically and discuss a wide range of issues with a group of people who share a particular interest. Newsgroups, however, are not **chat rooms**—forums in which participants discuss a topic in real time. A newsgroup discussion may go on for several days or even years. A newsgroup participant posts a question or a document to the group, which is then posted to different news servers. The question or document remains in this archive of posts, and people can then read it and respond to it if they wish.

Some long-running newsgroups have hundreds of participants or posters, and many of them have thousands of regular readers. Many newsgroups are also moderated. In a moderated newsgroup, a reviewer reads and evaluates all contributions before posting the material on the Web. Therefore, moderated groups are more reliable sources of information than unmoderated newsgroups, although postings to unmoderated groups may contain some interesting anecdotal evidence.

One of the easiest ways to find a newsgroup on a particular topic is to search a newsgroup directory on the Web. For example, Foorum.com (**www.foorum .com**) offers users access to thousands of newsgroups. It allows you to search the newsgroup directory using a keyword search or to browse through the newsgroup files, ranging from French language newsgroups to newsgroups devoted to science issues.

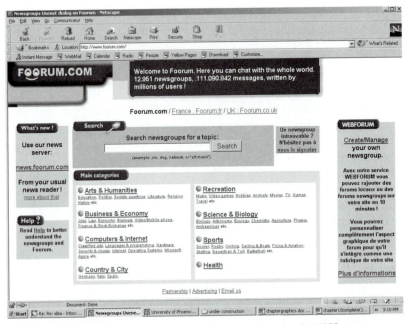

Source: Foorum.com. Screen shot of www.foorum.com; Netscape browser window © 2002 Netscape Communications Corporation. Used with permission. Netscape Communications has not authorized, sponsored, endorsed, or approved this publication and is not responsible for its content.

Newsgroups can be valuable research tools because they can give you access to experts on particular topics and they allow you to survey people with similar interests. You can also post questions about your research methods. For example, you could post the following query to a newsgroup on computer security: "What sort of firewalls are the most vulnerable to hackers?" In response, you might receive direct answers as well as references to articles on the subject. Newsgroups, in fact, often function as online annotated bibliographies.

If you use information from a newsgroup posting, however, you should be careful to (1) investigate the author's sources and academic background and (2) cite any material that you use in your paper just as you would cite information that you obtained from an interview or through personal communication. (For more information on citing these kinds of sources, see Chapter 11.)

Evaluating Internet Sources

You need to evaluate the credibility of any source you plan to use, of course, but evaluating and establishing the credibility of sources on the Web can pose a significant problem because virtually anyone can post material to the Web and make it look authoritative. How can you tell if an Internet source is credible? One quick way to evaluate a source is to ask some of the basic questions you would ask about any source:

- Who is the author?
- What is the author's background or credentials?

- What organization is the author associated with?
- What are the author's goals?

In addition, for any website you should also ask these two questions:

- Who sponsors this website or owns the server (host computer) that stores the site?
- When was the information last updated?

Check the Site's Author

Establishing the qualifications of the author(s) or custodian(s) of a web page is not always easy. Authors of Internet documents do not always make their names visible. If the name of the person or organization responsible for the source is not stated clearly at the beginning or end of the document, try the following approaches before labeling the source "anonymous."

- Look for the source's e-mail address. If the address is not clearly visible, use your browser's Find or Search function to locate the @ symbol (which appears in every Internet e-mail address).
- Consult your browser's Document Information window for the author or source's name or e-mail address.

If you cannot identify the author—be it a person or an organization—you should not rely on that source for expert testimony in your paper. If you are able to identify the author, and he or she is not familiar to you, check for biographical information on the site itself, or do a search using the author's name as a keyword.

Determine Who Published the Web Page

You would certainly not consider information from the *Weekly World News* next to your supermarket's checkout counter as reliable as information from the *Washington Post*. The same reliability issues extend to websites. As noted earlier, the domain name in a site's URL gives you an important clue about the type of organization that publishes the site (see page 351). You should always check the links that brought you to a web page as well as the publishing body—the server on which the file is stored—for a web document. The server, however, cannot guarantee the reliability of the information it stores.

More important than the server's name are any names or logos appearing within the document that represent the organization that may stand behind the site. Always view such names or logos with skepticism. Just because an author includes NIH (the acronym for the National Institutes of Health) in a document, that does not necessarily mean that the NIH stands behind that particular work. Finally, if you have been linked to a web page from another page, go to the site's home page to find information on the organization that publishes it. Most legitimate organizations will provide a link on their site's home page to information about themselves and their goals.

Check the Publication Date

It is often difficult to determine when a website was first posted or most recently updated. A website that does not provide this information is significantly less reliable than one that lists its posting date or the dates of revisions.

Check the Site's Use of Other Sources

Just as you would do with a printed source, make sure the author of a web page uses, quotes, cites, and represents other sources accurately. If you have any doubts, seek out the sources the author cites to see if he or she has represented them accurately and has considered enough alternative views. For example, one group of female students who were researching anorexia found two seemingly authoritative websites containing fact sheets about bulimia. However, not only did they find that a university health center's site had a different definition of the term than that provided by a national women's center, but they also discovered that the university definition did not accurately cite the definition that they had reprinted from the *Diagnostic and Statistical Manual of Mental Disorders*.

Check for Bias

Any site will represent a source's point of view or bias, and finding out what people from different perspectives are thinking about an issue can be a very valuable addition to your research. But the Internet is also filled with personal rants and outrageous charges. If a site contains obviously inflammatory language or outrageous accusations, that is a clear sign that the source is not credible. For any site that you are evaluating, ask yourself the following questions:

- Does the author have anything to gain from the position argued?
- What organized financial, political, or other interests are backing the site, and who stands to profit financially or otherwise from it?

EXERCISE 10.6

Use the guidelines above to evaluate two of the websites you found for Exercise 10.5. Write a paragraph or two about each website in which you give your evaluation and explain the reasoning behind it.

WEB PAGES OF INTEREST TO RESEARCHERS

Arts and Humanities

Site/URL	Contents
Academic Info's Humanities Directory. http://www.academicinfo.net/subhum.html	A site that is searchable by keyword or by subject index
Art History Resources on the Net http://witcombe.sbc.edu/ARTHLinks.html	A comprehensive guide to art and culture resources on the

*Web addresses (URLs) are subject to change. If the site is no longer available at the address given here, try searching for it using a search engine such as Google.

Site/URL	Contents
	Web. Covers any art-history era or subject, and has links to recent research and articles on topics ranging from prehistoric to modern.
Artforum http://www.artforum.com	A monthly art journal covering modern and contemporary art.
Art Institute of Chicago http://www.artic.edu	A subject specific website that indexes the works at the museum.
Humbul Humanities Hub http://www.humbul.ac.uk	Offers a searchable catalogue of evaluated online resources in humanities research, on subjects ranging from archeology to classics to Russian and Slavonic studies.
The Labyrinth: Medieval Studies Web http://www.georgetown.edu/labyrinth	Provides comprehensive access to electronic resources in medieval studies, including art, history, literature, and philosophy.
Metropolitan Museum, New York http://metmuseum.org	A subject-specific site that indexes works at the museum.
National Gallery, Washington, DC http://www.nga.gov	A subject-specific site that indexes works at the museum.
Open Directory's Arts Directory http://dmoz.org/Arts	Offers a large subject index with links to categories such as dance, animation, body art, and literature.
Voice of the Shuttle http://www.vos.ucsb.edu	One of the most comprehensive searchable web directories.
WWW Virtual Library Humanities http://www.hum.gu.se/w3vl/w3vl.html	Includes links to archaeology, history, philosophy, religion, languages and literature resources.
World Wide Art Resources http://wwar.com	Provides links to artist portfolios and arts resources and services.

Biology, Medicine and Health Sciences

Biosciences Index http://mcb.harvard.edu/BioLinks.html	A comprehensive site covering such subjects as biochemistry, molecular biology, biochemical databases, evolution, and

Site/URL	Contents
	immunology. Also contains links to online biological journals.
Journal of the American Medical Association http://jama.ama-assn.org	Contains articles, editorials, and reviews on medical and public health issues.
Journal of Cell Biology http://www.jcb.org	A refereed research journal with links to other related sites.
Links to the Genetic World http://www.ornl.gov/TechResources/ Human_Genome/links.html	A comprehensive site searchable by subject, including such topics as the Human Genome Project, cloning, genetic testing, protein research, bioinformatics, computational biology and many others.
National Institutes of Health http://www.nih.gov	Contains links to and information on NIH research projects.
National Library of Medicine http://www.nlm.nih.gov	Offers information on research programs such as AIDS/HIV, on current research news, and on links to MEDLINE—the search engine for the library.
National Science Foundation: Biology http://www.nsf.gov/home/bio/start.htm	A searchable site containing information about research programs and funding in the biological sciences.
The New England Journal of Medicine http://content.nejm.org	A refereed medical journal with links to articles and other sites related to medical research.
@Nursing http://www.atnursing.com	A keyword searchable site indexing resources for medical professionals and for patients.
WWW Virtual Library of Medicine http://www.ohsu.edu/cliniweb/wwwvl/	Provides links to online medical journals, government research, and academic research resources.

Business and Finance

The BizTech Network http://www.brint.com	A directory for information on business and technology issues. Provides free newsletter service. Also contains *A Business Researcher's Interests* (http://www.brint.com/interest.html)

Site/URL	Contents
BusinessWeb http://www.businesswebsource.com	Contains links organized by industry.
Business Week Online http://www.businessweek.com	An online edited business journal.
Dow Jones Industrial Average http://averages.dowjones.com	Includes 30 selected industrial firms.
Economist http://www.economist.com	A weekly periodical covering international business and finance news.
Emerald Press (formerly MCB University Press) http://www.mcb.co.uk	Offers current management news and information.
Federal Reserve Board http://www.federalreserve.gov	Provides access to information and publications.
Harvard Business Review http://www.hbsp.harvard.edu/hbr	A bimonthly journal featuring articles in business and economics.
International Business Resources on the WWW http://ciber.bus.msu.edu/busres.htm	An index of international business resources on the Web. Includes resources on countries, governments, statistics, and news.
Rutgers Accounting Web http://accounting.rutgers.edu	A comprehensive directory searchable by keyword containing links to accounting resources on the Web and all major accounting organizations.
The Virtual Library: Business and Economics http://vlib.org/BusinessEconomics.html	A directory that links to university-maintained resources in such areas as arbitration, electronic commerce, finance, labor and business history, marketing, economics, and transportation.
The World Bank http://www.worldbank.org	Contains links to the bank's policies, initiatives, current research, data and statistics, and upcoming events.
The World Trade Organization http://www.wto.org	Offers links to WTO publications, resources, and news.

Communication

American Communication Association http://www.americancomm.org/	Provides information about the ACA, a collection of materials on communication law and First Amendment issues, and resources

Site/URL	Contents
	for teaching and research in communication studies.
Columbia Journalism Review http://www.cjr.org	A journal published by Columbia University's Graduate School of Journalism. Also offers a resource guide.
Communication Monographs http://natcom.org/Publications/ JOURNALS/CM/cm.htm	A quarterly journal featuring articles and research reports on communication issues.
Communication Studies Resources http://www.uiowa.edu/%7Ecommstud/ resources/index.html	Provides links to resources on such topics as advertising, cultural studies, digital media, film studies, rhetorical studies, and visual rhetorics.
Film and History http://www.h-net.msu.edu/~filmhis	A scholarly journal devoted to film studies.
The First Amendment Handbook http://www.rcfp.org/1stamend	A site maintained by the Reporters for Freedom of the Press.
International Communication Organization http://www.icahdq.org	Offers information to scholars interested in the study, teaching, and application of all aspects of human-mediated communication.
Journalism Resources http://bailiwick.lib.uiowa.edu/journalism/	Offers links to resources on such topics as cyberjournalism, gender and race in mass communication, and media law.
WWW Virtual Library: Broadcasters http://archive.museophile.sbu.ac.uk/ broadcast/	Contains a list of national and international TV and radio broadcasters, together with other relevant links.
WWW Virtual Library: Journalism http://209.8.151.142/vlj.html	Provides links to web pages devoted to journalism issues. Contains a subject-specific index that ranges from broadcasting to Internet communication.

Computer Sciences and Engineering

Academic Info's Mechanical Engineering Directory http://www.academicinfo.net/ engringme.html	Offers a reference guide and information on engineering standards.

Site/URL	Contents
American Society for Civil Engineering http://www.asce.org	Features information on the professional society, research projects, and civil engineering news.
Argonne National Laboratory Mathematics and Computer Science Division http://www-unix.mcs.anl.gov/LANS/computational-science.html	Includes links to research projects at the laboratory.
Association for Computing Machinery http://www.acm.org	Offers a digital library of ACM publications. Provides links to special computing interest groups and to *Communications of the ACM—* a periodical covering news and research.
The Computing Research Repository http://xxx.lanl.gov/archive/cs/intro.html	Offers a database that is searchable by a combination of author, title, keyword, journal, subject class, and report number; or it may be perused by subject class. Sponsored through a partnership of the ACM, the Los Alamos e-Print archive, and Networked Computer Science Technical Reference Library (NCSTRL).
Carnegie Mellon University School of Computer Sciences Research Projects Page http://www.cs.cmu.edu/research/projects/	Provides information about and links to the school's research projects—ranging from algorithims to robotics to language acquisition.
IEEE Computer Society http://www.computer.org/	Contains a range of information about conferences, standards, publications, activities, education certification, and employment. The subscription-based Digital Library includes full text of articles from its transactions and magazines, and papers from selected proceedings.

Site/URL	Contents
The Internet for Civil Engineers: iCivilEngineer http://www.icivilengineer.com/	A web directory that exclusively indexes and catalogs web sites of civil engineering knowledge and technology. Covers all disciplines of civil engineering.
MIT Laboratory for Computer Science http://lcs/mit.edu	A hub for research projects at MIT; also provides links to other computer research projects of interest.
Open Directory's Electrical Engineering Directory http://dmoz.org/Science/Technology/ Electrical_Engineering	Offers links to electrical engineering sites. Provides subject headings for searching.
Wired Magazine http://www.wired.com	A journal covering the most recent computing news.
The WWW Virtual Library: Computing http://src.doc.ic.ac.uk/	Provides links to pages devoted to computer science research, news, and projects.

Criminology and Law

CataLaw http://catalaw.com/	Offers a listing of all catalogs of law and government.
Columbia Law Review http://columbiareview.org/	A journal published by the Columbia School of Law.
Find Law http://findlaw.com	Provides a comprehensive search tool for legal research.
Internet Legal Resource Guide http://www.ilrg.com	Indexes legal resources on a wide range of topics.
The Justice Information Center http://www.ncjrs.org	A service of the National Criminal Justice Reference Service (NCJRS). Contains links to information on juvenile justice, law enforcement, crime prevention, courts, corrections, and criminal justice statistics.
The Legal Information Institute http:www.law.cornell.edu/topics	A directory maintained by Cornell University Law School containing an encyclopedic reference tool with links to other law-related sites.
The National Law Journal http://ljextra.com/nlj	Provides weekly updates for the legal profession.

Site/URL	Contents
The Supreme Court Decisions http://www.cornell.edu/supct/	Contains a searchable index of Supreme Court Decisions.

Education

AskERIC http://www.askeric.org/Eric/	Offers more than 1 million abstracts of documents and journal articles on education research and practice.
Education Index http://www.educationindex.com/	An annotated guide to education-related sites on the Web. Allows you to search for educational information and links in over 50 categories.
The ERIC Clearinghouse on Disabilities and Gifted Education (ERIC EC) http://ericec.org/	Contains professional literature, information, and resources on the education and development of individuals of all ages who have disabilities and/or who are gifted. Provides access to the ERIC database of educational materials, which has more than 1,000,000 citations.
Harvard Educational Review http://gse.harvard.edu/~hepg/her.html	A journal devoted to education research.
The National Library of Education http://www.ed.gov/NLE/	Acts as the federal government's main resource center for education information.
U.S. Department of Education http://www.ed.gov	Offers access to the National Library for Education and links to department research and reports.

English Language and Literature

Academy of American Poets http://www.poets.org/	Contains links to specific poets, text databases, journals, poetry resources, conferences, arts advocacy, and literary organizations online. Also offers the Online Poetry Classroom and the Poetry Audio Archive.

Site/URL	Contents
The Brown University Women Writers Project http://www.wwp.brown.edu/texts/ wwoentry.html	Provides links to texts written by women prior to 1830. It is a long-term research project devoted to early modern women's writing and electronic text encoding. All texts can be browsed and searched using tools that provide access to the full SGML encoding.
EServer http://www.eserver.org	A searchable web directory with links to resources in cultural theory, early modern culture, drama, film studies, gender studies, rhetoric, and other categories.
The Institute for Advanced Technology in the Humanities http://jefferson.village.virginia.edu/	A research unit of the University of Virginia, IATH's goal is to explore and expand the potential of information technology as a tool for humanities research. Projects include the Melville Electronic Library, The Rossetti Archive, The World of Dante, and the Walt Whitman Hypertext Archive.
Literary Resources on the Net http://andromeda.rutgers.edu/~jlynch/Lit/	A searchable site organized by category. Covers such areas as classical and biblical, medieval, renaissance, romantic, twentieth-century British & Irish, American, theatre and drama, and theory.
National Council for Teachers of English http://www.ncte.org	Features information on the professional society. Contains links to the organization's journals, standards, teaching ideas, research foundations, and conferences.
Postcolonial and Postimperial Literature http://www.postcolonialweb.org/	Offers links to topics in postcolonial theory and is organized by countries.
The Rhetoric Society of America http://rhetoricsociety.org/	Features information on the professional society. Provides links to rhetoric research resources.

Site/URL	Contents
The Victorian Web http://www.victorianweb.org/	A searchable index of Victorian authors, topics, and links to other sites covering the Victorian period.
Voice of the Shuttle http://vos.ucsb.edu	One of the most comprehensive searchable web directories. Offers literature links organized by genre, nation, and period.
The William Blake Archive http://www.blakearchive.org/	An international public resource that provides access to major works of visual and literary art. Archive contains fully searchable and scalable electronic images.

Government

Centers for Disease Control and Prevention http://www.cdc.gov	Provides updates on public health issues. Offers facts sheets on disease prevention and health information on topics such as anthrax, cancer, drownings, and so on. Contains CDC health data standards, scientific data, surveillance, health statistics reports, and laboratory information.
The Department of Agriculture http://www.usda.gov	Contains updates on agricultural news, a search feature, an e-mail directory, and links to agencies such as food safety and regulatory programs.
The Department of Defense http://www.defenselink.mil	Provides a directory of defense sites as well as links to sites such as the U.S. Air Force Radio online.
The Department of Justice http://www.usdoj.gov	Provides access to department press releases, speeches, and other publications.
The Environmental Protection Agency http://www.epa.gov/	Offers links to environmental laws and regulations, educational resources and information resources. Covers such topics as pesticides, pollutants, ecosystems, international

Site/URL	**Contents**
	cooperation, and environmental management.
The Food and Drug Administration http://www.fda.gov	Offers a Google-driven search engine. Contains links to product regulations, information for consumers, product approvals, safety reports, fact sheets, and the latest FDA news.
The House of Representatives http://www.house.gov	Provides a search index as well as information on bills, roll call votes, and the congressional schedule. Also links to the *Congressional Record*.
National Technical Information Service http://www.ntis.gov	Contains technical and research reports from the NTIS.
The Senate http://www.senate.gov	Offers a bill search feature as well as information on the hearing schedule, committees, legislative activities, and senators.

History

American Historical Association http://www.theaha.org/	Features information on the professional association. Contains links to the organization's journals, grants, teaching ideas, research, and conferences.
The History Guide http://www.HistoryGuide.de/index.html	An Internet-based subject gateway to information relevant to scholars in history with a focus on Anglo-American history and the history of Central and Western Europe.
History On-line http://www.ihrinfo.ac.uk/search/welcome.html	Provides information resources for the teaching and learning of history. Contains over 40,000 records providing details of books and articles, UK university lecturers, UK current and past research, and evaluated links to websites and online resources.
National Archives Records and Administration http://www.archives.gov/	Offers researchers the opportunity to search selected archival databases directly through the Internet. Provides access to

Site/URL	Contents
	personal papers of U.S. Representatives and U.S. Senators that are archived at institutions around the nation.
WWWVL The World Wide Virtual Library: History http://www.ku.edu/history/VL/	Contains the History Catalogue maintained by the University of Kansas. Provides hundreds of links to network sites on historical periods for many different countries.

Philosophy

American Association of Philosophy Teachers http://aapt-online.dhs.org/	Features information on the professional association. Contains links to the organization's journals, grants, teaching ideas, research, and conferences.
The American Philosophical Association http://www.apa.udel.edu/apa/index.html	A professional organization for philosophers in the United States. Offers a comprehensive list of web resources online.
The Internet Encyclopedia of Philosophy http://www.utm.edu/research/iep/	An edited virtual encyclopedia.
The WWW Virtual Library: Philosophy http://www.bris.ac.uk/Depts/ Philosophy/VL/	Offers access to thousands of philosophy resources, each selected and described by academic librarians and subject specialists. These pages serve as a philosophy-specific view into the larger *Social Science Information Gateway* catalogue.

Using Sources to Support Your Claim

Chapter 11

Chapter 10 covered ways of finding sources of evidence to use in your arguments. This chapter will cover strategies for effective note taking and for integrating your notes into your own prose gracefully and without inadvertently plagiarizing your sources. Finally, it will present two professional systems of documentation, the MLA style, developed by the Modern Language Association, and the APA style, developed by the American Psychological Association, with sample research papers in each style.

TAKING EFFECTIVE NOTES

The computer has made note taking easier than it used to be. Where once researchers had to write out individual note cards for each quotation, paraphrase, or summary, now they can download the texts of entire articles, cutting and pasting paragraphs into their own documents without having to copy anything by hand. But while using the computer and the Internet can save time, it can also lead to sloppy note taking or worse—plagiarism (the presentation of other people's work as your own). As you begin to read through your sources, then, it is important to develop and follow a standard procedure for note taking that will help streamline your writing process, make checking your references easier, and help you avoid inadvertent plagiarism.

You may already have developed a way of taking notes that involves highlighting or underlining significant passages within a text and incorporating those highlighted sections into your paper. But this method can lead to a paper that is little more than a string of quotations, often inadequately documented, and at worst a plagiarized text. To enhance your credibility, you need a way of recording exactly where a point that is not common knowledge comes from or precisely where you found each quote that you use. If you use the old-fashioned method of writing out individual note cards, as shown in the sample note card below, you have a foolproof—though cumbersome—way of recording and acknowledging each quote, paraphrase (an idea given entirely in your own words and sentence structure), or summary (a condensed version of the main points in a paragraph or article, given in your own words).

SAMPLE BIBLIOGRAPHY NOTE CARD WITH QUOTATION

Larson   264

"Galveston counted its dead. The city conducted a census and in October reported a tally of 3,406 confirmed deaths."

Larson, Erik. Issac's Storm. New York: Vintage Books, 1999.

These days, however, most students find it easiest to type their notes into a computer file. You can organize your notes by source or by topic.

- To organize by source, simply summarize, paraphrase, or quote from a document as you read it. Type the material into a numbered list, indicating the order in which the information appears in the original document.

- To organize by topic, you first need to identify the topics that will be important to your argument and create a file for each one. As you take notes from your sources, categorize them by topic, writing them into the appropriate files. You will also need to prepare a separate list with complete bibliographic information for all of your sources. While categorizing your notes by topic takes more time initially, it makes writing your draft easier because the ideas and information you need will already be grouped under headings. The sample notes that follow illustrate both methods of note taking.

TIPS ON TAKING NOTES

- *Begin the research process early*—if you wait to begin your research, you may end up rushing note taking, taking notes on sources that you may not use or producing notes that are of little use.

- *Take notes only after you have evaluated your source's credibility*—for more on evaluating a source's credibility, see pages 37 and 41 in Chapter 2 and page 358–60 in Chapter 10.

- *Make note taking a part of your invention process*—summarize and paraphrase material as you read (see p. 377–81 for guidelines for paraphrasing or summarizing). If you are working with printouts, write marginal notes as you read through your sources—these can then be typed or copied into a computer file.

- *Make copies of original articles* (either in electronic or hard copy form) for later reference checks.

—Continued

- *Note all the bibliographic information* for a source (including author, title, date, editor, publisher, page number, and complete URL, if necessary) either on your note cards or in your computer files.
- *Record all page references* and add links to any URLs if you are using a computer to take notes.
- *Consider using a personal bibliographic software package.* This kind of software allows you to record bibliographic information into a database and may even format the material for you (check with your school reference librarian to see if such software (like Pro-Cite) is available on campus).
- *Recheck your references* after you've written your draft.

SAMPLE NOTE FILE GROUPED BY SOURCE

Lion and Rappeport. "They Do What They See." *Washington Post,* 9/12/99, p. B01

1. Intense media coverage of the Columbine school massacre may provoke similar attacks.
2. Following Columbine, several juvenile patients were admitted to Sheppard Pratt Hospital (a psychiatric facility) because they made up similar "hit lists."

SAMPLE NOTE GROUPED BY TOPIC

Media's Influence on Juveniles

Sheppard Pratt patients "seemed not only susceptible to media stories, but enchanted by them . . ." (WP 9/12, p. 3)

Gallup poll indicates that "76% of adults agree that TV, movies, and popular music are negative influences on children." (*LA Times,* 7/21, p. 1)

INTEGRATING SOURCES

As writers and as researchers, we have an obligation to our sources, to our readers, and to ourselves to represent fully, accurately, and fairly information that we have borrowed. Readers should be able to find our sources for themselves, if they choose, to verify their accuracy and to collect more information. When you use other writers' work, whether you are presenting their ideas in your own words or theirs, you must make it clear to your audience that you are doing so. As we have mentioned, the three methods of incorporating the work of others into your text are *quoting, paraphrasing,* and *summarizing.* Writers use each of these methods for different reasons, and they require different integration techniques.

Quoting

When you **quote,** you use another person's exact words and phrases. An occasional quotation can be effective, but beware of the temptation to quote more often than is necessary or desirable. Your writing should be controlled by you and dominated by your voice. It should not be a hodgepodge of quotations linked by a few sentences that you have written. Consider this passage:

> A lot of people deeply enjoy rock music. However, "There are lots of people who don't feel this way about rock-and-roll. Some of them don't understand it," according to Anna Quindlen. These include "the Senate wives who said that records should have rating stickers on them so that you would know whether the lyrics were dirty." In response to such criticisms, Tipper Gore wrote, "I can't even count the times in the last three years, since I began to express my concern about violence and sexuality in rock music, that I have been called a prude, a censor, a music hater, even a book burner. So let me be perfectly clear: I detest censorship." Gore advocates "a candid and vigorous debate about the dangers posed for our children by what [she] call[s] the 'exploitation industry.'"

While the quoted passages above may be interesting and may even make sense, the voice of the writer is overwhelmed by the noise from the sources.

There are, however, some important strategic reasons to use an occasional quotation. In argument, quotes are often used to show that the views or research of others support the author's claims. Choosing appropriate sources is thus one way to build your ethos, and making the appropriateness of your choices evident to your readers by quoting your sources effectively is another way. To quote your sources effectively, you need to tell your audience why you believe the source has credibility on the issue at hand by providing supplementary information about the source's experiences or credentials, as in the examples that follow.

> According to psychiatrist Ernest Montgomery, "Children of alcoholics are much more likely to be alcoholics themselves later in life than those whose parents drink only moderately or not at all" (153).

> Bill Howard, manager of the McDonald's on Main Street, says that "sales have been increasing lately due to increased customer flow resulting from the widening and repaving of the street. It's been a great thing for restaurants in the area."

You should also make sure that every quote in your argument is serving your purpose and strengthening your case. The box that follows provides some good reasons to use quotes.

GOOD REASONS TO QUOTE

- *The language of the original is striking.* If you cannot think of a better, or perhaps a worse, way of wording an idea, and you therefore want to call attention not just to the content of the original but also its style, then quoting is a good choice.

- *You will be analyzing the exact phrasing of the original.* To do a critique of your source, you will need to quote the relevant passage so that your audience can see, as much as possible, the precise wording of the passage you are examining.

- *The original was written or spoken by someone likely to be significant to your audience.* The source you are using may seem credible, or not at all credible, to your audience. In either case, it may be worth your while to quote from that source. In an argument on human rights, readers may be inspired by a quote from Martin Luther King, Jr., or Mahatma Gandhi. On the other hand, they may also react strongly, but in the opposite way, to a quote from Adolf Hitler or Osama bin Laden.

Punctuating Quotations

- *Include all of the quoted material within quotation marks.* In English, we signal that we are quoting by surrounding the words, phrases, or sentences taken from our sources with quotation marks. All of the quoted material—and only what is quoted—should be within the quotation marks. In the examples that were given above, everything written or spoken by Ernest Montgomery and Bill Howard falls within the quotation marks.

- *Indent longer quotations an additional 10 spaces.* If you are using MLA style, you should indent quotations that take up more than five lines of text 10 spaces from the left margin. This type of quote is called a *block quotation* and does *not* need to be enclosed in quotation marks, as shown in the following example:

  Poet Mary Oliver explains how breathing is analogous to poetic meter in this way:

  > A cardinal attribute of breath (or breathing) is, of course, its repetition. The galloping footbeats of the heart, that spell fear. Or the slow and relaxed stretch of breath of the sleeping child. In either case, by their repetition, they make a pattern. Truly this pattern is as good as a language. It reveals a great deal: the depth of sleep, the stress or ease of the breather. If the pattern changes, we know it reflects something important—mood has plunged, or health has been touched by crisis, or the inner life, without being seen externally, has pressed upon the heart, has tightened or loosened the lungs. *It is as good as a language.* We sigh. We pant. We reveal ourselves. (3–4)

- All of the material included in the indented block quotation above was written by Mary Oliver, and the quotation preserves her parenthetical remarks and her use of italics. Notice that a colon is used to introduce the block quotation, and a page reference follows it. (If you are following APA style, you should use block form for quotations over 40 words long, and you should indent them 5 spaces.)

- *Use a comma or a colon to introduce a quotation that includes material that can stand alone as a grammatical unit.*
  Lily Tomlin spoke truly when she said, "If you win the rat race, you're still a rat."
  or
  Remember the words of Lily Tomlin: "If you win the rat race, you're still a rat."

- *When you integrate the quotation into the phrasing of your own sentence, do not add extra punctuation.*
  David Messaris argues that visual literacy is important because it "might make a viewer more resistant to the manipulations attempted by TV commercials, magazine advertising, political campaigns, and so on" (3).

- *If you integrate the quotation into your sentence by supplying or altering words, you must put the additions and alterations in brackets.*

  According to Ellen Ullman, "Physicists and mathematicians created the [computer] industry just after World War II and became the first programmers."

- Note that the original passage did not contain the word "computer." So that the passage will make sense to other readers, the writer has inserted the word "computer" and surrounded it by brackets (not parentheses); the brackets tell readers that the word has been inserted by the person using the quotation. Similarly, if you need to change the form of a word to make it fit your sentence grammatically, surround your change with brackets.

  ORIGINAL:

  "I recall the day when I turned eighteen very well, as Hurricane Elena passed through my hometown and ripped the roof off of our family home."

  QUOTED:

  Raphael Velasquez remembers that on his eighteenth birthday "Hurricane Elena passed through [his] hometown and ripped the roof off of" his family's house.

- Here, the brackets indicate that "his" is not included in the original quote but is an alteration of the original passage. Note that the bracketed term does not supplement but replaces the language of the original.

- *Use ellipses (three spaced periods) to indicate that material has been excluded from a quotation.*

  M. F. K. Fisher writes about the importance of our feelings and prejudices concerning word use:

  > I know a man who finally divorced his wife because, even by indirection, he could not cure her of "calling up." She called up people, and to her it meant that she used the telephone—that is, she was not calling across a garden or over a fence, but was calling up when she could not see her friends. . . . Her phrase continued to set his inner teeth, the ones rooted directly in his spiritual law, on such an edge that he finally fled. She called up to tell me.

- The ellipses here are included in addition to the period that ends Fisher's sentence after the word "friends"; they indicate that a portion of Fisher's writing has been excised.

- Remember that when you quote you must pay conscientious attention to what your source actually said or wrote, and *you must not exclude important information* that will affect how your audience perceives the source's meaning. In short, *never alter a passage without indicating that you have done so.*

Paraphrasing

When you **paraphrase,** you take someone else's ideas and put them in your own language. When done correctly, paraphrasing preserves the meaning of the original; when done well, paraphrasing allows you to express a source's ideas in your own style and in a way that fits in with the rest of your paper. You should paraphrase when a significant portion of the source material is useful but the style is not striking and there is no reason to quote at length.

Because you are using another person's ideas, you must still document the source of the ideas even though you are expressing them in your own language. You should indicate to your audience what content is derived from a source either by acknowledging the source within your prose or by a parenthetical citation at the conclusion of your paraphrase. (For more on in-text citations, see pages 385–86 and 400.)

Quite unlike quoting, when paraphrasing, you change the words and the sentence structure of the original as *much* as possible, making the style your own. If you reproduce exactly any phrases from the source, you are actually quoting (and then you'd need quotation marks), not paraphrasing. Of course, you can safely use any standard words or common phrases that would inevitably be used in the debate, or words for which there are no suitable synonyms.

For an example, first read the following paragraph, which is an excerpt from a section entitled "Stuff That Moves" from *Nightwatch: A Practical Guide to Viewing the Universe,* by Terence Dickinson.

> The prime time to look for satellites is during the first hour of darkness on spring and summer evenings. Try a reclining lawn chair, and watch the overhead region. Within a few minutes, you should see several starlike dots march through the constellations. One might be the space shuttle, another a secret military satellite, a third simply a spent rocket still in orbit. A satellite easily visible to the unaided eye is typically the size of a delivery van, travels at 28,000 kilometers per hour and crosses the sky in two to three minutes at an altitude of 300 to 500 kilometers (Dickinson 35).

Now have a look at a poor paraphrase of this paragraph, which follows.

FAULTY PARAPHRASE:

First dark is the best time to search for earth-orbiting satellites. Sitting back and watching the sky, you will probably be able to see pinpoints of star-like light moving overhead within minutes. A satellite glimpsed by the naked eye is likely to be about the size of a delivery van, to move at a rate of approximately 28,000 kilometers every hour, and to range from 300 kilometers to 500 kilometers from the earth (Dickinson 35).

This paraphrase has a few problems. First and most seriously, it reproduces exactly the image and phrase "the size of a delivery van." No doubt it is a useful image, but to reproduce it exactly as it appears in the original is to borrow not merely Dickinson's idea but his exact words and phrasing. *Failure to put that phrase in quotation marks constitutes plagiarism,* however accidental. To correct this problem, the writer could either omit the comparison altogether or find another that accurately gauges the size of such satellites. Since it is such a striking image, however, if the paraphraser decides that the comparison is needed

Integrating Sources **379**

weight cl
peers (L[
Solovay]
1995 stu[
as less de
obese re[
adequate
suffer dis
Mayer 1[

The overa
"Aversion
thirty-five
tion date f
in phrases
ence will a
were publi
friends an[
rate summ

The passag
sides from t[

Residen[
accomm
spring a
go cano[
ing in N
Many, a[
on the s
flies tor[
weight,

With a gr[
difficult, an
phrase? W
Now tr[
pesticides,
of pestici[
group. Wh
to most of
pesticides-
If you r[
the passag
mologists]
trol black [
favor of its
source in f

and that no comparison works as well as the one given by Terence Dickinson, then the phrase must be enclosed in quotation marks.

A second problem is that the paraphrase excludes the information about which seasons of the year (spring, summer) are most appropriate for this type of skywatching and what types of satellites are on display: The space shuttle? A "secret military satellite"? A "spent rocket"? As these omissions suggest, it can be hard to decide what constitutes crucial information. Consider the paraphrase again. How important do you feel these omissions are?

Finally, the paraphrase does not call attention to the source of the information. Although it is not an error to cite Dickinson in parentheses following the paraphrase as is done, indicating the source within the sentence itself is better and can help to demonstrate the credibility of the information.

A revised paraphrase, with all three problems addressed, appears below.

ACCEPTABLE PARAPHRASE:

According to Terence Dickinson, author of *Nightwatch: A Practical Guide to Viewing the Universe*, the first dark of spring or summer is the best time to search for earth-orbiting satellites. Sitting back and watching the sky, you will probably soon be able to see pinpoints of star-like light moving overhead. A satellite glimpsed by the naked eye is likely to be about the size of a UPS truck, to move at a rate of approximately 28,000 kilometers per hour, and to range from 300 kilometers to 500 kilometers from the earth. What is it? It may be the space shuttle, a cast-off rocket, or a mysterious military satellite (35).

Note that this paragraph, though it reorders the potential satellite types in the last sentence, still reproduces the terms "space shuttle" and "military satellite." It also includes the measurements that are given in the original. Because the terms have no close synonyms, and the measurements are simple facts, these phrases are necessary and their use here does not constitute plagiarism, although you could carefully convert the measurements to miles instead of kilometers, a change that might be beneficial for an audience of Americans who are not scientists. Also notice that the writer has substituted the word "mysterious" for "secret" before the term "military satellite," thus changing the connotations of the phrase. What would be the effect if, instead of "mysterious," the writer of the paraphrase had substituted "covert"?

Summarizing

When you **summarize,** you extract the major ideas in another writer's work and put them into your own terms. Summaries are broader in scope than paraphrases. While a paraphrase translates one person's words and sentence structure into another's, a summary condenses material to its essential points. You can summarize a paragraph, a whole page, a whole chapter, or even a whole book in a few sentences or even one sentence.

The amount of detail you include in your summary will depend on the needs of your audience. For example, suppose you and a friend are in a bookstore, and he picks up Charlotte Brontë's novel *Jane Eyre* and asks if you have read it, and what it is about. You might answer, "It's about the struggles of its title character, an orphan and governess in nineteenth-century England." Your summary condenses hundreds of pages into a few words, leaving out what

other readers m
not to tell your
because doing s
book with some
your summary i
Such a short
few elements o
Suppose your f
"This novel is (
erness in a spoc
crazy first wife
friend's summa
respond, "Not
Victorian wom
century, includ
of plot where :
Charlotte Bro
school—which
As this imag
biases of their :
first summary
ments of the p
ments of the te
to your audien
Thus a summa
when you sum
that you are d
text citations, :

1. After readin
   supporting p
2. Put the mair
   just as in pa
3. If you are su
   original in y
4. Incorporate
   summary m
5. Finally, cite
   an introduc

You may even
your own poi

Aversion to
thirty-five y

school students. Which of the following statements do you think you will need to document?

1. Anorexia nervosa, an eating disorder, is usually found in adolescent females.
2. More than 80 percent of the cases of anorexia involve adolescent girls aged 13 to 18 years old.
3. Most teen girls diet to conform to strong social pressures that declare thin as ideal and necessary for popularity.
4. The number of anorexia cases has risen in the past 20 years.
5. Anorexia nervosa usually starts with normal dieting to lose weight, but the girl then eats less and less every day.
6. Of those teenagers who develop the disease, up to 15 percent die.
7. Girls with anorexia nervosa tend to come from families that frequently think and talk about the "right" amounts or kinds of things to eat.

Why did you choose the statements that you did? Did you consider the audience's knowledge to be the determining factor? Or did you consider how new or specific the information seemed? In general, information that is available from a number of different popular or scholarly sources, such as the fact that anorexia usually affects adolescent girls (statement 1) or the way anorexia nervosa starts and its usual course (statement 5), can be considered common knowledge. Information that was gathered by a particular researcher, such as statistical information about trends (statements 2 and 4), should be documented.

Documenting sources does not suggest dependence on others or diminish your own contribution and credibility—on the contrary. As you decide which sources to document in your paper, keep in mind that acknowledging well-respected sources strengthens your argument. It shows you are wise enough to find good support. By offering supporting information from reliable sources, you are demonstrating that you have "done your homework" and that you understand the issue. On the other hand, if you fail to cite any sources, you will diminish your credibility because it will appear that you are not familiar with the literature on your topic. No reader wants to waste time reading an argument written by an uninformed writer.

Documenting Ideas

As noted earlier, the sources of the ideas, hypotheses, and theories that underlie your arguments must be acknowledged just as you acknowledge the specific quotations you use. Many students worry that if they cite the sources of their ideas, their work may not seem "original." To this fear most teachers would reply, "On the contrary, acknowledging the sources for your ideas only serves to strengthen your ethos." In fact, most articles that appear in scholarly journals begin with a review of the literature that serves as a background for the researcher's work.

Let's say you are writing a paper on preventing juvenile violence in the Washington, D.C., area, and you identify one of the major causes of juvenile violence as the lack of adequate mental health care for at-risk youths. You are proposing that the city institute in-school mental health programs as early as kindergarten. If you present this idea as wholly new, your readers may be less likely to accept it. But suppose you can show that this idea is not new by providing specific information about another school district that either inspired or supports your proposal. Such evidence, which you document so that readers can verify it if they wish, will give you strong support for your proposal.

Documenting Online and Copyrighted Material

The ease of researching, and of copying and pasting, on the World Wide Web can be deceptive. Keep in mind that much of the material that appears on the Web is copyrighted, just as most print materials are. According to the Legal Information Institute, the Copyright Act has been expanded to include "architectural design, software, the graphic arts, motion pictures, and sound recordings" (1999). You can borrow brief quotations and ideas from Internet sources so long as you treat them like print sources by mentioning them in your paper, or in a parenthetical reference, and documenting them adequately.

When you are composing a Web page, the same rules apply. In addition, if you incorporate copyrighted material (whether a graphic or an HTML source code) from another site on your own site, you must obtain the author's permission and give him or her credit.

CITING SOURCES IN YOUR PAPER

All researchers need to follow standard formats for documenting their sources so that their peers and readers can easily find the information cited in their work. When you write for college, you will probably use either the style recommended by the Modern Language Association (MLA) or the style recommended by the American Psychological Association (APA). The MLA sets the standard for publishing in the humanities. The APA sets the standard for publishing in many of the social sciences. Both styles use in-text parenthetical citations and a works-cited list at the end of a paper.

Using MLA Style

The MLA guidelines for documenting all types of sources are explained in detail in the *MLA Handbook for Writers of Research Papers* (6th edition, 2003) and in the *MLA Style Manual and Guide to Scholarly Publishing* (2nd edition, 1998). You can also find information about MLA format at **www.mla.org/main_stl.htm**.

In-Text References

Parenthetical references should appear in the text after each use of a source. Include the author's name and the page number from which your information comes, as shown below.

Lavender, roses, and olive and lemon trees are typical plants found in Provencal gardens (Hanley 37).

If you include the author's name in the sentence that introduces the paraphrase, summary, or quote, you need only put the page number in parentheses.

According to Laura Hanley, an American landscape architect who has studied French gardens, typical plants in a Provencal garden include lavender, roses and olive and lemon trees (37).

If the name of the author is not known, put an abbreviated form of the title and the page number in parentheses.

Racially-motivated attacks occurred on campus three times in one week last February ("Rage" B4).

Works-Cited List

At the end of your paper, you must include a works-cited list that shows the full sources you have cited in the course of your argument. The following examples provide you with some guidelines for citing sources both within your paper and in your list of works cited. For each type of source, the first entry shows how the source should appear in your list of works cited, and the second one shows how it should be cited within your text as a parenthetical reference. However, these examples may not cover every type of source you may use. For the most complete information, refer to the MLA books and website mentioned on page 385.

Books

BASIC FORMAT FOR CITING BOOKS USING MLA STYLE

1. Author's name (last name first)
2. Title
3. Place of publication (list the first city if several are listed)
4. Name of the publisher, shortened
5. Date of publication (located in the copyright notice)

Book by One Author

Pinker, Steven. The Language Instinct: How the Mind Creates Language. New York:

Morrow, 1994.

(Pinker 63)

Two or More Books by the Same Author

Pinker, Steven. The Language Instinct: How the Mind Creates Language. New York:

Morrow, 1994.

---. Language Learnability and Language Development. Cambridge: MIT P, 1984.

(Pinker, Instinct 124)

(Pinker, Learnability 256)

Book by Two Authors

Kostelnick, Charles, and David D. Roberts. Designing Visual Language: Strategies for
Professional Communicators. Boston: Allyn, 1998.

(Kostelnick and Roberts 55)

Edited Book

Smith, Marc A., and Peter Kollock, eds. Communities in Cyberspace. New York:
Routledge, 1999.

(Smith and Kollock 1)

Selection in an Anthology or Chapter in an Edited Collection

Gurak, Laura. "The Promise and the Peril of Social Action in Cyberspace."
Communities in Cyberspace. Eds. Marc A. Smith and Peter Kollock. New York:
Routledge, 1999. 243–63.

(Gurak 245)

Book Published in a Reprinted Edition

Brontë, Anne. The Tenant of Wildfell Hall. 1848. New York: Penguin Books, 1985.

(Brontë 45)

Book Published in Several Volumes

Kazhdan, A. P., et al., eds. Oxford Dictionary of Byzantium. 3 vols. Oxford: Oxford UP,
1991.

(Oxford 67)

One Volume in a Set

Kors, Alan Charles. Atheism in France, 1650–1729. Vol. 1. Princeton: Princeton UP,
1990.

(Kors 100)

Government Publication

United States. Cong. House. Committee on the Judiciary. Transcripts of Eight Recorded
Presidential Conversations. 93rd Cong., Serial No. 34. Washington: GPO, 1974.

(United States XX)

Translation

Erasmus, Desiderius. The Praise of Folly. Trans. Clarence H. Miller. New Haven:

Yale UP, 1979.

(Erasmus 67)

Corporate Author

Families USA. Healthcare in the United States. Washington: Families USA, 2000.

(Families USA 45)

Introduction, Preface, Foreword, or Afterword

Miller, Clarence H. Introduction. The Praise of Folly. By Desiderius Erasmus. Trans.

Clarence H. Miller. New Haven: Yale UP, 1979. ix–xxxi.

(Miller xxi)

The Bible

According to the MLA, you do not need a bibliographic listing when you use the King James version, and your parenthetical in-text citation should read as follows: book of the Bible (abbreviated) chapter. verse(s). However, if you are quoting notes from the King James version, or if you are using another version, then you must give a full citation.

New International Version of The Holy Bible. Grand Rapids: Zondervan, 1986.

(New International Version, Matt. 1.2–4)

Encyclopedias and Dictionaries

"Cheetahs." Encyclopedia Britannica: Micropaedia. 1990 ed.

("Cheetahs")

Periodicals

BASIC FORMAT FOR CITING PERIODICAL ARTICLES USING MLA STYLE

1. Author's name (last name first)
2. Title of article, in quotation marks
3. Title of periodical, underlined
4. Volume number, issue number (if applicable), date
5. Page number(s)

Article in a Scholarly Journal—Continuous Pagination

> Lighthall, Frederick. "Launching the Space Shuttle Challenger: Disciplinary Deficiencies in the Analysis of Engineering Data." IEEE Transactions on Engineering Management 38 (Feb. 1991): 63–74.
>
> (Lighthall 66)

Article in a Scholarly Journal—Pagination by Issue

> Grice, Roger A. "Focus on Usability: Shazam!" Technical Communication 42.1 (1995): 131–33.
>
> (Grice 132)

Article in a Monthly Magazine

> Alva, Walter, and Christopher B. Doonan. "Tales from a Peruvian Crypt." Natural History May 1994: 26–36.
>
> (Alva and Doonan 27)

Article in a Weekly Magazine

> Hafner, Kate. "Have Your Agent Call My Agent." Newsweek 27 Feb. 1995: 76–77.
>
> (Hafner 76)

Newspaper Article

> Fahri, Paul. "Nasdaq 'Casino' Had Few Safeguards." The Washington Post 11 Nov. 2002, home ed.: A1.
>
> (Fahri A1)

Letter to the Editor

> Glandorf, Joe. Letter. Washington Post 11 Nov. 2002, home ed.: A24.
>
> (Glandorf A24)

Editorial

> "How to Fix Wall Street." Editorial. Washington Post 11 Nov. 2002, home ed.: A24.
>
> ("How to Fix Wall Street")

Online Sources

BASIC FORMAT FOR CITING ONLINE SOURCES

1. Author's name (last name first)
2. Title of the work, web page, or posting to a discussion list
3. Publication information for any print version of the source

—Continued

4. Title of the scholarly project, database, periodical, or professional or personal site (underlined); for a professional or personal site with no title, description such as "Home page"

5. Name of the editor of the scholarly project or database

6. Version number of the source (if not a part of the title) or, for a journal, the volume number, issue number, or other identifying number

7. Date of electronic publication, of the latest update, or of posting

8. For a posting to a discussion list or forum, the name of the list or forum

9. Number or range of pages/paragraphs

10. Name of any sponsoring institution or organization

11. Date when researcher accessed the source

12. Electronic address or URL of the source in angle brackets

Article in a Scholarly Journal on the Web

Eisenberger, Claus. "Diagnosis of Renal Cancer by Molecular Analysis." Journal of the National Cancer Institute 91 (1999): 2028–2032. 10 Nov. 1999 <http://jnci .oupjournals.org/current.shtm#ARTICLE>.

(Eisenberger)

Document from a Government or an Organization Site

National Telecommunications and Information Administration (NTIA). "Falling Through the Net: Defining the Digital Divide." Americans in the Information Age: Falling Through the Net. 8 July 1999. 18 Aug. 1999 <http://www.ntia.doc.gov/ntiahome/ digitaldivide/>.

(NTIA)

Scholarly Web Site

The William Blake Archive. Eds Morris Eaves, Robert Essick, and Joseph Viscomi. 15 Sep. 1998. Library of Congress. 24 Sep. 1998 <http://jefferson.village.edu/ blake/main.html>.

(William Blake Archive)

Professional or Commercial Web Site

"What's New at Alta Vista?" 20 Oct. 1999. Alta Vista. 25 Oct. 1999 <http:// www.altavista.com/av3/promo/ads_newav.html>.

("What's New at Alta Vista?")

E-Mail

McDermott, Rebecca. "Re: Healthcare Credits." E-mail to the author. 10 May 2001.

(McDermott)

Online Posting

Mopsick, Don. "Favorite Jazz Quotes." Online posting. 17 Mar. 2000. Big Band-Music
Fans. 17 June 2000 <http://www.remarq.com/list/4755?nav+FIRST&rf+1&si+
grou>.

(Mopsick)

Other Sources
Personal or Telephone Interview

McAdams, Katherine. Personal interview. 8 March 2001.

(McAdams)

Fenyvesi, Lizou. Telephone interview. 7 Nov. 2001.

(Fenyvesi)

Unpublished Dissertation

Jasiniski, James. "Rhetorical Practice and Its Visions of the Public in the Ratification
Debate of 1781–1788." Diss. Northwestern U, 1986.

(Jasiniski 12)

Work of Art

Carpeaux, Jean-Baptiste. Girl with Shell. National Gallery of Art, Washington.

(Carpeaux)

Film

List the film first if that is your subject.

Sahara. Dir. Zoltan Korda. Perf. Humphrey Bogart, Lloyd Bridges, and Dan Duryea.
Columbia Pictures, 1943.

(Sahara)

List the director first if that is your subject.

Korda, Zoltan, dir. Sahara. Perf. Humphrey Bogart, Lloyd Bridges, and Dan Duryea.
Columbia Pictures, 1943.

(Korda)

Audio Recording

Talking Heads. Talking Heads: Fear of Music. Audiocassette. Sire Records, 1979.

(Talking Heads)

Lecture

Hess, Charlotte. "Untangling the Web: The Internet as a Commons, 1996." Reinventing
the Commons Workshop. Transnational Institute. Bonn, Germany. 4 Nov. 1995.

(Hess)

A Student Paper in MLA Style

O'Keefe 1

Meaghan O'Keefe

Instructor Rosalia Saklas

English 391

10 December 2001

Add a New Clause to the American Society for Interior Designers'
Code of Ethics

*Writer establishes
the exigence for
her argument.*

    As part of their profession, interior designers keep abreast of
trends in culture and style. They are certainly aware that American
interest in art from the developing world has grown tremendously in
the last thirty years. In the past two decades, the Metropolitan
Museum of Art in New York and the Smithsonian Institution in
Washington, D.C., have both opened major galleries dedicated to

*In-text citation
of author and page
number, appearing
in parentheses at
the end of the sen-
tence. Subsequent
citation of source
requires only page
number.*

African art (Labi and Robinson 50). Even smaller, less well-known
museums are "echoing this trend" (50). The Neuberger Museum in
Purchase, New York, has recently created a major traveling exhibi-
tion of African art.

    Interest in ethnographic art has moved into the private sector
as well. David Brook notes that the homes of the new elite contain
a "mélange of artifacts . . . Amazonian figures, Native American
totems, Egyptian deities, animistic shells, or Shinto statuettes. . . .
An African mask will sit next to an Incan Statue" (95, 96). However
the growing market in ethnographic art presents not just design
challenges but also serious ethical ones. An increasing number of
artifacts sold on the art market are either looted or forged.

*Writer states
the scope of the
problem and
supports claim
with expert
testimony.*

    Gloria Goodale of the Christian Science Monitor estimates that
nearly 80 percent of the artifacts on the international antiquities market are "plundered, illegally exported, or fake," a jump from 60 percent in the late seventies (Elia 247). Thomas Hoving, former director

*Writer introduces
quote with expert's
credentials.*

of the Metropolitan Museum of Art in New York, goes further, stating, "Almost every antiquity that has arrived in America in the past
ten to twenty years has broken the laws of the country from which it

O'Keefe 2

came" (Elia 247). Official sources concur with this assessment. According to the International Council of Museums, there has been "a dramatic increase in the illicit traffic and looting of cultural heritage" over the last twenty years. Interpol states that it is difficult to obtain exact statistics on the number of works looted each year because many developing countries do not provide much information, nor do they track statistics on these crimes (Interpol). However, Interpol estimates, "The illicit trade in cultural property [looted artifacts] is worth $4.5 billion, up from $1billion a decade ago" (Labi and Robinson 51), putting it just behind drug smuggling and arms dealing.

The number of forgeries on the market is also rising. Michel Brent of <u>Archaeology Magazine</u> estimates that "Since the 1980's, nearly 80 percent of the allegedly antique terra cottas that have left Mali have been counterfeit" (2). In his book, <u>The Lie Became Great</u>, art scholar Oscar White Muscarella estimates that 25,000 forgeries enter the art market each year (iv). Anecdotal evidence from a U.S. Customs Service special agent at the new Cyber-Smuggling Center also reflects this disturbing trend. The agent stated in a telephone interview that artifacts purchased recently by the Customs Service for investigative purposes are "mostly turning out to be fake."

There are a number of reasons for the increase in looted and forged artifacts on the art market today. Wars in developing countries have weakened their governments' ability to protect the countries' cultural heritage. In addition, trading in looted artifacts and manufacturing forgeries provide much-needed sources of income for the poverty-stricken communities of the developing world. Finally, in the countries that import artifacts, not only has interdiction been a low priority, detection is difficult.

When war breaks out, civil chaos ensues and protection of cultural heritage becomes a low priority. As George Abungu, chairman of the International Standing Committee on the Traffic of Illicit Antiquities, remarks, "Lack of order is the perfect breeding ground for people who collect art. For starving, unpaid soldiers anything is good for sale" (Labi and Robinson 52). The Associazione Internazionale di Archeologia Classica echoes this statement: "Dislocations

---

Annotations (right margin):

The source of the quotation from the International Council of Museums is their website named in the sentence.

Website citation contains only the author's identity—in this case a government agency.

Writer puts her addition to quoted material in brackets.

Writer demonstrates growing trend using expert testimony and statistics.

Writer summarizes the causes of the problem.

Writer establishes background conditions (war and poverty) as causes of the problem.

of war . . . have led to dramatic increases in theft and illegal exports"
(Harvey 19). This source is also reflected in the fact that most of the
items on the International Council of Museums' "Red List" (a list of
artifacts most likely to have been looted) are from war-torn nations.
Niger, for instance, has experienced a five-year rebellion, an over-
throw of the elected government, and a military coup all in the last
ten years (McGeveran 827). Chad was embroiled in a fourteen-year
border war with Libya and is now in the midst of a civil war (774).
There are ongoing clashes between the government forces and civilians in the northern states of Nigeria, which in 1999 elected its first
civilian government in fifteen years (828).

    The story in Central Asia is much the same. Robin Thorne, of
the J. Paul Getty Trust, asserts, "The National Museum in Kabul lost
90 percent of its collection during the civil war in that country" (2).
To paraphrase John Malcolm Russell, even Iraq, which has devoted
considerable resources to prevent art theft, has been unable to
protect its cultural heritage in the aftermath of the Gulf War (44).

    Thirty years of war and civil strife have nearly destroyed the
temples at Angkor Wat in northern Cambodia. According to
Douglass Preston of National Geographic, the site was host to a
number of sieges and firefights, which caused immense damage,
but looting soldiers did even more damage (85). He states, "At
Angkor Wat scarcely a freestanding statue retains its head, while
many statues have disappeared entirely" (86).

    In Peru the activities of terrorist groups, such as the Shining
Path, have made it difficult to protect more remote archeological
sites. In 1987 looters broke into a previously undiscovered Moche
tomb in a remote community on Peru's coastal plane. Although the
looters were quickly arrested when one of them turned the others in,
archaeologists were forced to wait for months for an armed military
escort to accompany them to the site. According to archaeologist
Walter Alva, by the time they arrived, "little was left except a boot
shaped hole" (26). In an article for Natural History, Alva described
the site as the, "richest grave offerings ever to be excavated . . . in
the Western Hemisphere" (28).

O'Keefe 4

Another factor in the trade of illicit cultural objects is the poverty that afflicts the developing world. Patrick O'Keefe, in his report for the United Nations Education, Science and Culture Organization (UNESCO), explains, "For many people with little resources, the taking of antiquities from sites and monuments for sale may be a way out of an economic stranglehold for them and their children" (6). It is not just the money, but the kind of money these sales provide, that makes looting and forging an attractive prospect. According to Interpol, most dealers in illicit antiquities pay in dollars. Given the inflation prevalent in most developing nations, the infusion of hard currency from art dealers provides stability in an uncertain economy.

It is important to compare the economic realities of the developing world with the profits of trading in illicit and forged cultural property. In Mali, where the ancient Jenne terra-cotta figures originate, the average per capita income is $790 (McGeveran 820). The starting price of an undocumented Jenne statue is $550 (820). A Peruvian Madonna figure recently seized by the U.S. Customs Service (Press release # 01-015) was offered for sale on E-bay starting at $15,000, more than triple the average Peruvian income of $4,300 (832). According to Labi and Robinson, a Nok figure from Nigeria, where the average annual income is $960 (McGeveran 828), can "command tens of thousands of dollars" (52).

Although the International Council of Museums contends that most of this profit ends up in the hands of middlemen (3), a farmer in Nigeria can double his monthly income by selling just one statue (Labi and Robinson 50). In northern Cambodia a farmer can feed his family for several years on the profits from selling one Angkor Wat sculpture (Preston 85). Statistics on forgeries are difficult to obtain; however, Brent describes a booming industry in Mali, with potters turning out hundreds of copies annually of "ancient" terra-cotta pieces (2).

The countries that import other nations' cultural patrimony have not been terribly successful in combating the trade in looted and forged artifacts. Although UNESCO banned the international trade in items of cultural heritage in 1970, interdiction by customs agents in

Writer documents the absence of blocking causes.

the industrial world is difficult. One reason is that, although it is commendable to interdict illicit art shipments, countries give a higher priority to stopping drug traffic or weapons smuggling by international terrorists. This concern is reflected in the monies allocated to investigate art smuggling. The U.S. Customs Service opened its Cyber Smuggling Center in September of 2000. Designed to counter Internet trading of illicit materials, the Center has an operating budget of $2.4 million, a small fraction of the Customs Service overall budget of $1.7 billion (Shear).

In addition to inadequate funding and low prioritization, there is another problem facing customs agents: It is extremely difficult to distinguish modern copies from actual antiquities. It is perfectly legal to import contemporary art rendered in an ancient style. The problem arises when a dealer imports what he or she claims are modern pieces but that are actually ancient artwork. Although there are no statistics available on the prevalence of this practice, it is clear that copies often fool even experts. In 1991, Sotheby's New York branch auctioned a Khun Ram for $275,000. Brent reports that although thermoluminescence tests indicated that the figure was over 500 years old, subsequent investigation revealed it as a forgery (1). The Smithsonian's African Art Curator, Bryna Freyer, admits, "I can't always spot a phony" (Labi and Robinson 52).

Writer begins an evaluation argument by making an appeal to consequences.

The trade in illicit cultural property has serious and irreparable consequences. Artifacts are damaged and even destroyed by looting and forging. The historical context of the objects is lost forever. Professional reputations and personal lives can be ruined when people, even unwittingly, deal in forged and looted artifacts.

Ancient artifacts are often damaged during the looting process. Michel Bessieres of the UNESCO Courier reports, "The tombaroli of southern Italy are ransacking archaeological sites with earth moving equipment. In Central America, they have electric generators and circular saws to steal Mayan stele. In China, underwater sites off the Xisha islands are attacked with dynamite" (17). Though such destructive excavation takes a toll on delicate artifacts, there are other factors that contribute to degradation. Looters are either unaware of

O'Keefe 6

or simply are not concerned about the need to provide a suitable environment for the artifact, or they lack the resources to do so. To paraphrase Steven Weintraub of Art Preservation Services, an environment with a relative humidity of over 60 percent can destroy terra cotta. Sixteenth-century Japanese lacquer boxes can crack if kept in a relative humidity of less than 50 percent. As Gary Thomson points out in his book The Museum Environment, high relative humidity also "suit[s] the growth of mold and fungi" which causes immense damage to plant and animal materials (66). Heat and light can also do an enormous amount of damage in a relatively short time. According to Lizou Fenyvesi, a textile conservator specializing in Pre-Columbian objects, just a few days of exposure to sunlight will irreparably fade fragile vegetable dyes.

Forgers often dismember artifacts in order to incorporate an authentic piece in an area most likely to be tested. In the case of the Kuhn Ram, the core samples that were tested indicated that the figure was over 500 years old (Brent 3). The samples were taken from an area behind the front legs, where a hole is less visible. Unfortunately, the forgers had placed authentic shards in the area tested (6). The original sculpture these shards came from can never be reassembled and that piece of the world's heritage is lost forever.

The destruction of the historical context that accompanies forging and looting is appalling. Forgers muddy the historical record by creating a false picture of the past. When scholars cannot distinguish between fakes and artifacts, they may draw flawed conclusions about their historical context. Even true antiquities ripped from their original site can often tell us precious little about the cultures they came from. On the "Red List" web site the International Council of Museums explains:

> Whole sections of our history have been wiped out and
> can never be reconstituted. These objects cannot be
> understood once they have been removed from their
> archaeological context and divorced from the whole to
> which they belong. Only professional archaeological

Writer introduces a long quote with a colon and indents the quoted material ten spaces.

O'Keefe 7

excavations can help recover their identity, their date
and their location.

Often, looters take only the artifacts that are valuable or easily
transported. Fenyvesi says that when Inca tombs are raided the looters will often "just throw away the textiles." According to Fenyvesi
these textiles are "the alternative literacy of the Inca culture," and
their system of knots and symbols has yet to be deciphered. Karen
Tubb, an archaeological conservator, describes the wreckage left by
looters in the following passage:

> Those of you who have never seen a site destroyed
> by plunderers have no idea the amount that gets de-
> stroyed. I would say roughly that what comes out of a
> commercial dig is between five and ten percent of
> what was to be found, without even considering the
> destruction of documentation, which is, of course, a
> catastrophe. (256)

If looting continues, we may lose our only chance at understanding ancient cultures. The Rosetta stone of the Inca may have
already wound up in a garbage heap in Lima.

On a professional and personal basis, trading in undocumented
artifacts can have disastrous consequences. If a designer acquires
an artifact for a client that later turns out to be a forgery, he or she
may be sued for fraud. Further, if an artifact without provenance
turns out to be illicit cultural property, the legal penalties are considerable. Carol Carnett of the Legal Aid Bureau of Maryland notes
that under the Archaeological Resources Protection Act, penalties
for trafficking in illicit cultural property "include up to $250,000 in
fines and up to five years imprisonment" (1). According to the United
States Department of State, individuals in possession of illicit cultural property may also be prosecuted under the National Stolen
Property Act (Public Law 97-446, see appendix 4).

Recent actions testify to the fact that these laws are being enforced. U.S. Customs Today reports that Frank Stegmeier, who has
been arrested for importing illicit cultural property, has had his house
and possessions seized and is awaiting further criminal charges

O'Keefe 8

(Miles). In a related story, the New York Times reports that Marc S. Garrison of Salt Lake City has lost his Russian art collection to the United States Customs Service by order of forfeit (Bohlen).

New agreements with foreign governments provide additional impetus for aggressive enforcement. Guy Gugliotta of the Washington Post reports, "The United States and Italy signed a far-reaching agreement [recently] prohibiting unlicensed imports of Italian antiquities." The United States has signed similar agreements with nine other nations, including Peru, Bolivia, and Mali. The United States Department of State notes that the provisions of these agreements allow the Customs Service to investigate any artifact without provenance; in other words, it is up to the owner to prove that it has been legally acquired.

By a purely ethical standard, trading in illicit cultural property is wrong. We would not insist that a starving man sign away his inheritance for a loaf of bread. In the same way, taking advantage of wars that leave people dead, maimed, and homeless in order to secure valuable artifacts at a low price is morally reprehensible.

Writer argues for ethical criteria.

Today in Peru 100,000 tombs, or half the known sites, have been looted (Brodie and Watson 3). In Belize 73 percent of the sites have been looted (3). It is imperative that we preserve the past for future generations. If this pillage continues we will destroy our chances to understand not just our own heritage, but also the world's.

Solving the problem of world poverty and ending war are clearly beyond the scope of interior designers. However, designers can contribute to the efforts to preserve the world's cultural heritage. I propose that the American Society of Interior Designers add a new clause to their code of ethics. The wording may be adapted from other professional codes of ethics, but it would cover three main points.

Writer limits the argument's scope and then states her proposal.

1) Interior designers will not help obtain, nor purchase, any artifact that they have reasonable cause to believe has been stolen, looted, or forged.

2) Interior designers will provide appropriate documentation (provenance) for any artifact acquired for a client.

O'Keefe 9

3) Any violations of this code will be rigorously investigated and reported to appropriate authorities.

Writer uses an analogy to support her proposal.

Similar clauses have been added to the codes of ethics for
many institutional and professional organizations. In 1986 the
International Council of Museums, made up of over 750 museums
in more than 140 countries, added a section prohibiting the acquisi-
tion of illicit cultural objects. Christie's, Sotheby's, the Society of
Fine Art-Auctioneers, the Antiquarian Booksellers' Association, and
the International Association of Dealers in Ancient Art, to name just
a few, have all adopted codes of ethics to help prevent trade in
looted artifacts. As the oldest and largest organization of design professionals, the American Association of Interior Designers (ASID)
can lead the way in expanding the scope of preventive efforts.

UNESCO advocates the adoption of relevant codes of ethics
as a means of reducing the destruction and theft of cultural patrimony (O'Keefe 44). As Patrick Boylan points out, "the removal of a
significant part of a potential market, whether financial, legal or ethical, can drastically affect the market" (99). As an example he cites
the collapse of trade in looted Chinese art when major investors
pulled out of the market. The large client base of ASID members
constitutes a significant part of the trade in decorative antiquities,
and refusing to buy artifacts of questionable origin will have an
impact on this trade.

Writer points out good consequences.

Adding the proposed items to the Code of Ethics would
publicize the problem and educate the public in a number of ways.
The ASID web site displays its code of ethics prominently. The
thousands of hits it receives from members of the public will provide
much needed exposure. The literature produced by the ASID
includes copies of the code, which will draw even more attention to
the problem. On a more personal level, designers will be able to educate their clients about the dangers of the illegal trade in cultural
property. Awareness of the danger facing our cultural heritage is imperative if the trade in looted or forged artifacts is to be stopped.

The proposed changes to the code will give designers the authority to take a moral stance. If a client insists on acquiring artwork

that appears on the ICOM "Red List" (a list of artifacts most likely to be looted), a designer can point to the Code of Ethics and assert his or her authority to refuse. The public image of designers will only be enhanced as a result of this ethical stand.

On a more pragmatic level, designers will be able to avoid the legal consequences of trading in forged or illicit cultural goods. Demanding clear and unambiguous proof that the seller has legal title to the artifact being sold is good practice. After all, as Mark Rose points out, "you wouldn't buy your car from a stranger standing on a street corner—even if [he or she wears] a suit and stand[s] on a swank street corner—who doesn't have title to it" (3).

A long-term benefit for clients is that artifacts with legitimate provenance are rising in value. Souren Melikan describes this phenomenon in a recent article in the International Herald Tribune. Melikan points out that "buying antiquities that *might* be suspected of having been illicitly dug up recently will henceforth be seen as a huge commercial risk" (1). In recent auctions, artifacts with provenance are fetching higher than expected prices. At Christie's a small (about 9 inches tall), heavily damaged Egyptian Stele went for twice the top estimate, selling for £97,250 (approximately $150,400) (3). It had an unquestionable provenance, having been in Europe since the early 1800s. The British Museum recently paid a "phenomenal" 1.6 million dollars for an early Celtic piece with a good provenance (2).

It is important to note that even while these sales were going through, many lots with questionable provenance did not even make minimum bid. Other sources, including UNESCO, expect this phenomenon to continue as restrictions get tighter. Buying artifacts with impeccable provenance will provide clients with good investments in the long term. In addition, clients will not be saddled with worthless forgeries. As we have seen with the Khun Ram forgery, scientists can be fooled by clever forgers, but to create a credible provenance is beyond the scope of most forgers.

We in the United States can no longer see the destruction of the world's heritage as a victimless crime. We all suffer when our

O'Keefe 11

past is destroyed. It is morally untenable to purchase or trade in looted goods. In addition, it is impractical, as well as unfair, to expect impoverished villagers to take a moral stand at the expense of their families. We in the industrial world must take an ethical stand. Including the proposed additions in the American Society of Interior Designers Code of Ethics will be an important step in rendering the purchasing of looted art socially and morally unacceptable.

O'Keefe 12

Works Cited

Alva, Walter, and Christopher B. Doonan. "Tales from a Peruvian
 Crypt." Natural History May 1994: 26–36.

Elia, Ricardo. "Conservators and Unprovenanced Artifacts:
 Preserving Cultural Heritage or Servicing the Antiquities Trade."
 Antiquities Trade or Betrayed: Legal and Conservation
 Issues. Ed. Kathryn Tubb. London: Archetype Publications,
 1995.

Bessieres, Michel. "Indiana Jones Has No Future." UNESCO
 Courier Apr. 2000: 16–21.

Bohlen, Celestine. "34 Smuggled Icons Are Returned to the Russian
 Church." New York Times 18 May 2001: B3.

Brent, Michel. "Faking African Art." Abstract. Archaeology Magazine
 54 (Jan./Feb. 2001). 13 Oct. 2001 <http://www.archaeology.org/
 cgi-bin/site.pl?page=index/index>.

Brodie, Neil, and Peter Watson. "Illicit Antiquities: the Destruction of
 the World's Archeological Heritage." The Newsletter for Illicit
 Antiquities Research Centre Autumn 1999.

Brooks, David. Bobos in Paradise: The New Upper Class and How
 They Got There. New York: Simon, 2000.

Carnett, Carol. "Legal Background for Archeological Resources Protection." Technical Brief. Archeology and Ethnology Sep. 1991:
 section 1.

Fenyvesi, Lizou. Telephone Interview. 7 Nov. 2001.

Goodale, Gloria. "Central American Sleuths Target a Hot Black Market." Christian Science Monitor 23 Oct. 1996: 1, 3c.

Gugliotta, Guy. "U.S., Italy Act to Halt Pillage of Antiquities." Washington Post 20 Jan. 2001: A22.

Harvey, Archer St. Claire. "Art, Antiquity and the Law." AIAC News
 Dec./Mar. 1998–1999: 19–20.

International Council of Musuems. "The Illicit Traffic of Cultural
 Property Around the World." ICOM home page. 2001. 11 Nov.
 2001 <http://www.icom.org/traffic.html>.

Works-cited list arranged alphabetically begins at the top of a new page.

Second line of citation is indented five spaces.

O'Keefe 13

---ICOM RED LIST. 2001. 11 Nov. 2001 <http://www.icom.
 org/redlist/indexRedList.html>.

Interpol. Interpol home page. Dec. 2001. 5 Dec. 2001
 <http://www.interpol.int/>.

Labi, Aisha, and Simon Robinson. "Looting Africa." Time 30 June
 2001: 50–52.

McGeveran, William A. Jr., ed. The World Almanac and Book of
 Facts, 2001. Mahwah, New Jersey: World Almanac Books, 2001.

Melikan, Souren. Untitled. International Herald Tribune. 5 May
 2001: 9d.

Miles, Cherise. "Seattle Case Gives Treasures Back to Mexico."
 US Customs Today Online Sept. 2000. 31 Oct. 2001.
 <http://www.customs.ustreas.gov/hot-new/pressrel/ 2000/
 0922-00.htm>.

Muscarella, Oscar White. The Lie Became Great. New York: Styx,
 2000.

O'Keefe, Patrick. Trade in Antiquities: Reducing Destruction and
 Theft. Paris: UNESCO Pub. London: Archetype, 1997.

Preston, Douglass. "The Temples of Angkor." National Geographic
 Aug. 2000: 82–104.

Rose, Mark. "Stealing History." Archeology Online News, 21 June
 2000. 31 Oct. 2001. <http://www.archaeology.org/online/
 news/stealhist.html>.

Russell, John Malcolm. "Stolen Stones: The Modern Sack of Nin-
 eveh." Online Feature: Archeological Institute of America.
 30 Dec. 1996. 13 Oct. 2001. <http://www.archaeology.org/
 online/ features/nineveh/index.html>.

---. "Robbing the Archaeological Cradle". Natural History Feb. 2001:
 44–56.

Shear, Michael D. "Cyber-Crime Center Opens; Computer Investigation Offices in Fairfax Have Global Impact." The Washington
 Post 5 Oct. 2000: V1.

Thomson, Garry. The Museum Environment. Cornwall, Eng.: Hart-
 nolls, 1986.

O'Keefe 14

Thorne, Robin. "The Making of an Object ID." Protecting Cultural
    Objects In The Global Information Society. London: Getty Trust,
    1999.

Tubb, Kathryn. "The Antiquities Trade: An Archeological Conserva-
    tor's Perspective." Antiquities Trade or Betrayed: Legal and
    Conservation Issues. Ed. Kathryn Tubb. London: Archetype,
    1995.

United States. U.S. Customs Service. "Customs Returns Artifact to
    Peru." Press Release # 01-015: 20 Nov. 2000.

---. ---. Special Agent ---. Telephone interview. 9 Nov. 2001.

---. Department of State: Bureau of Educational and Cultural Affairs.
    "U.S. Federal Cultural Property Legislation." Department of
    State Online, Nov. 2001. 11 Nov. 2001 <http://exchanges.
    state.gov/education/culprop/uslaws.html>.

---. ---. "International Cultural Property Protection: Implementation."
    Department of State Online, Nov. 2001. 11 Nov. 2001
    <http://exchanges.state.gov/education/culprop/>.

Weintraub, Steven. Telephone interview. 7 Nov. 2001.

Using APA Style

The APA guidelines for documenting all types of sources are explained in detail in the *Publication Manual of the American Psychological Association* (5th edition, 2001).

In-Text References

Parenthetical references should appear in the text after each use of a source. Include the author's last name and the date of the source.

> When bipolar patients are misdiagnosed as having major depressive disorder and treated with antidepressants, the drugs often have a negative effect (Bowden, 2001).

If you are quoting from the source, you should also include a page number, preceded by a comma, using the abbreviation *p.* for *page:* (Bowden, 2001, p. 52). If the source has two or more authors, put an ampersand (&) before the final author's name: (Pope & Hudson, 1984).

If you include the author's name in the sentence that introduces the paraphrase, summary, or quote, you should put the date in parentheses following the author's name. For a quote, you should include both the date and the page number.

> Bowden (2001) notes that when bipolar patients are misdiagnosed as having major depressive disorder and treated with antidepressants, the drugs often have a negative effect.

If the name of the author is not known, put the first few words of the title in parentheses:

> ("Difficulties in diagnosis," 2000).

References List

At the end of your paper, provide a full list of sources for your parenthetical references throughout your paper. In the following example the first entry shows the style for your references list and the second the style for in-text references. For further questions refer to the APA Manual mentioned above.

Books

BASIC FORMAT FOR CITING BOOKS USING APA STYLE

1. Author's name(s) (last name first followed by the author's initials)
2. Date of publication in parentheses
3. Title in italics—only the first word, the first word in the subtitle, and proper names are capitalized
4. City of publication, followed by a colon
5. Name of publisher

Book by One Author

Hirschfield, L. A. (1996). *Race in the making: Cognition, culture, and the child's construction of human kinds.* Cambridge, MA: MIT Press.

(Hirschfield, 1996)

Two or More Books by the Same Author

Torrey, E. F. (1988). *Nowhere to go: The tragic odyssey of the homeless mentally ill.* New York: Harper.

Torrey, E. F. (1997). *Out of the shadows: Confronting America's mental illness crisis.* New York: Wiley.

If you are citing both works: (Torrey, 1988; 1997)

Book with Two to Six Authors

Pope, H. G., & Hudson, J. I. (1984). *New hope for binge eaters: Advances in the understanding and treatment of bulimia.* New York: Harper.

(Pope & Hudson, 1984)

If the book has seven or more authors, use *et al.* after the sixth author's name.

Edited Book

Shafii, M., & Shafii, S. L. (Eds.). (1998). *Melatonin and psychiatric and neoplastic disorders.* Washington, D.C.: American Psychiatric Press.

(Shafii & Shafii, 1998)

Selection in an Anthology or Chapter in an Edited Collection

Reiter, R. S. (1998). The structure and evolutionary development of the pineal gland. In M. Shafii & S. L. Shafii (Eds.), *Melatonin and psychiatric and neoplastic disorders* (pp. 38–56). Washington, D.C.: American Psychiatric Press.

(Reiter, 1998)

Revised Edition

McIlwain, J. (1972). *Biochemistry and the central nervous system.* (Rev. ed.). New York: Churchill.

(McIlwain, 1972)

Government Publication

Social Security Administration. (2000). *Social security: Working while disabled: A guide to plans for achieving self-support.* Baltimore, MD: Author.

(Social Security Administration [SSA], 2000)

Translation

Shayegan, Daryush. (1992). *Cultural schizophrenia: Islamic societies confronting the west.* (J. Howe, Trans.). London: Saqi.

(Shayegan, 1992)

Corporate Author

Human Settlements Programme, International Institute for Environmental Development. (1999, April). *Environment and urbanization.* London: Author.

(Human Settlements, 1999)

Encyclopedias and Dictionaries

"Dyslexia." (1999). *American Heritage Dictionary* (4th ed.). New York: Houghton Mifflin.

("Dyslexia," 1999)

Periodicals

BASIC FORMAT FOR CITING PERIODICAL ARTICLES IN APA STYLE

1. Author's name(s) (last name first with first initials only)
2. Date, in parentheses
3. Title (capitalize the first word of the title, the first word of the subtitle, and proper names only)
4. Title of periodical, in italics
5. Volume number (in italics), issue number in parentheses (if applicable), and page number(s)

Article in a Scholarly Journal—Continuous Pagination

Hatton, D. C. (2001). Homeless women's access to health services: A study of social networks and managed care in the U.S. *Women and Health, 33,* 149–79.

(Hatton, 2001)

Article in a Scholarly Journal—Pagination by Issue

Blum, S. F. (2002). Not in my world: Media representations and sympathy for the homeless. *Journal of Social Work, 29*(4), 131–74.

(Blum, 2002)

Article with More than Six Authors

Boada, R., Willcutt, E. G., Tunick, R., Chabildas, A., Olson, R., DeFries, J. et al. (2002, December). A twin study of the etiology of high reading ability. *Reading and Writing 15*(7–8), 683–707.

(Boada et al., 2002)

Article in a Monthly Magazine

Shell, E. R. (2001, June). New world syndrome. *Atlantic Monthly 287*(6), p. 50.

(Shell, 2001)

Article in a Weekly Magazine

Quindlen, A. (2002, November 14). Young in a year of fear. *Newsweek 140*(19), p. 68.

(Quindlen, 2002)

Newspaper Article

Wells, R. M. (2002, August 5). Welfare reform. *Seattle Times,* p. B1.

(Wells, 2002)

Editorial or Letter to the Editor

Indicate the document type in brackets after the title.

Califano, Joe. (2002, September 23). Get real about welfare [Editorial]. *Capital Times,*
    p. B8.

(Califano, 2002)

Online Sources

BASIC FORMAT FOR CITING ONLINE SOURCES IN APA STYLE

1. Author, if known. If not known, put title in author position
2. Date (use the date posted or date of last revision)
3. Title
4. Retrieval date
5. URL, or database used to retrieve information. Do not end web addresses with a period

Article in a Scholarly Journal on the Web

Weir, J. P., Mahoney, K. P., Haan, K. G., Davis, A. (1999, July 3). Influence of electrode
    orientation on electromyographic fatigue indices of the vastus lateralis. *Journal of
    Exercise PhysiologyOnline, 2*(3) Retrieved February 11, 2002, from www.css.edu/
    users/tboone2/asep/WEIR6-99.PDF

(Weir et al., 1999)

Document from a Government or an Organization Site

Department of Health and Human Services. (1999, August). *Health care for the
    homeless (HCH).* Retrieved December 6, 2001 from http://aspc.hhs.gov/progsys/

homeless/Programs.htm#HCH

(Department of Health and Human Services, 1999)

Scholarly Web Site

Autism Research Program. (2002, November 10). Retrieved December 28, 2002 from

http://www.pitt.edu/~nminshew

(Autism Research Program, 2002)

Professional or Commercial Web Site

National Law Center on Homelessness and Poverty. (2002). Retrieved January 15,

2003 from http://www.nlchp.org/

(National Law Center, 2002)

E-mail

Include an in-text reference for e-mail messages and other personal correspondence, but do not include an entry in the list of references.

According to G. Fuller (personal communication, July 26, 2002) . . .

or

(G. Fuller, personal communication, July 26, 2002)

Online Posting

Bennett, C. (2001, February 20). Dependence on online-friendship: the future?

Message posted to http://behavior.net/cgi-bin/nph-display.cgi?MessageID=

61&Top=9&Config=job&uid+nC1M8.user&new=0&adm+0

(Bennett, 2001)

Other Sources

Personal or Telephone Interview

Include an in-text reference for conversations that you conducted in person or by telephone, but do not include an entry in the list of references.

As P. Quiksetta explained (personal communication, March 4, 2000) . . .

or

(Quiksetta, personal communication, March 4, 2000)

Unpublished Dissertation

Treat an unpublished dissertation as you would a published book.

Alden, A. F. (2002). *A critical analysis of the concept of resilience: Inquiry into the lives

of female adolescents.* Unpublished doctoral dissertation, State University of New

York, Binghamton.

(Alden, 2002)

Video Recording

Wohl, I. (Producer/Director). (1996). *Diagnosis according to the DSM-IV* [Video recording]. Princeton, NJ: Brooks/Cole.

Audio Recording

Gross, M. L. (March 28, 1978). *The failure of the psychological revolution* [Sound recording]. New York: Encyclopedia Americana/CBS News.

A Student Paper in APA Style

Daniel M. Pulver

English 391

Professor Brown

University of Maryland, College Park

October 23, 2002

Include title, name, affiliation, and any other information specified by the instructor.

Manic Depression: A Diagnostic Challenge

Summer, a twenty-three-year-old saleswoman with a thin build, has bipolar, or manic-depressive, disorder. During her manic phases, she is the life of the party, staying out all night at dance clubs and bars. She has a penchant for cocaine, ecstasy, and other amphetamines; entertains her friends with her grandiose plans and stories; and sleeps for a maximum of four hours a night yet feels endlessly energetic. Sometimes Summer hears voices and talks to people who exist only in her imagination. During her depressive phases, however, Summer is a loner, rarely leaving her apartment. She is sometimes too low-spirited even to eat, and she can barely summon the energy to visit the doctor for her depression.

The author uses an example to introduce the disorder to his audience and create exigence with pathos.

Summer's account demonstrates the diagnostic difficulties of bipolar or manic-depressive disorder. Bipolar disorders are characterized by the patient's dramatic and sometimes frequent ups and downs, otherwise known as mania and depression. The symptoms of these vary widely. Most psychological disorders are diagnosed on the basis of what clinicians observe when patients come into the office, but some bipolar patients may be so clouded by their current emotions that they are unable to recall a time, however recent, when they felt anything other than their present state. As a result, patients with bipolar disorder are being misdiagnosed with other disorders that have properties similar to one phase or the other, and they are, therefore, often given inadequate treatment.

The author shows why the disorder described in the introduction is hard to diagnose, setting up the problem.

Manic 2

This widespread misdiagnosis is a serious problem for the psychiatric community. It is estimated that as many as 15–20% of untreated manic-depressive patients eventually commit suicide (Ghaemi, Sachs, Chiou, Pandurangi, & Goodwin, 1999), making proper diagnosis and treatment for Summer, and others like her, an urgent problem.

The recent discovery of the frequent misdiagnosis of bipolar disorder may help to explain why many patients currently being treated either for major depressive disorder or for schizophrenia are not responding well to their treatment. Patients with bipolar disorder respond best to a treatment consisting of therapy and mood stabilizing drugs. When bipolar patients are misdiagnosed as having major depressive disorder and treated with antidepressants, the drugs often have a negative effect (Bowden, 2001). Dr. Charles L. Bowden, professor and chairman of the Department of Psychiatry at the University of Texas, believes that treatment of bipolar disorder with antidepressants alone is counterproductive, often causing a more profound level of mania and speeding up the cycle of the disease (2001).

A recent study on the over-prescription of antidepressant medication showed that 43% of patients with bipolar disorder were not diagnosed with the disease until 7.5–9.8 years after their first visit to a psychiatric facility. Up to that point, the majority of those patients had been diagnosed with unipolar major depressive disorder and treated accordingly. After being treated with antidepressants, those patients reported a much higher and more frequent level of mania (Ghaemi et al., 1999). Another study, conducted by Dr. Dwight L. Evans, found similar problems; this study, which aimed to find better diagnostic tactics and treatment options for patients with bipolar disorder, found a common trend of early onset and late treatment for bipolar disorder. Of the 500 patients involved in the study, the peak age of onset was between 15–19 years of age; however, most of the participants reported that their disease went untreated for an average of 5 years after onset. Of those who were not immediately diagnosed, over one-third were diagnosed as having either major

The names of the five listed authors and the date of publication for the source of this statistic are cited in parentheses.

The author explains the results of misdiagnoses.

Continues to explain effects of misdiagnosis with specific study.

Two sources are cited to support the argument that bipolar patients are misdiagnosed consistently.

Manic 3

depressive disorder, schizophrenia, attention deficit/hyperactivity disorder, or a substance abuse problem (Evans, 2000). The discrepancies in diagnosis were due to the state of the patient at the time of the initial interview. It is more common for adolescents with bipolar disorder to be diagnosed with attention deficit disorder (E. Weller, R. Weller, & Fristad, 1995), and more common for the elderly to be diagnosed with secondary mania disorder, because these diseases are more prevalent in their respective age brackets (Evans, 2000).

Though many patients with bipolar disorder respond positively to treatment for schizophrenia, as the drugs are chemically similar, these fail to cover the totality of bipolar symptoms, and so can only be temporarily effective. One specific case of this problem was detailed by Dr. Kathleen T. Brady (2000). Mr. C., an African-American construction worker, was diagnosed with schizophrenia and drug abuse when first interviewed at age 21. He was treated with haloperidol and benzodiazephines, and released from the hospital when his symptoms resolved. Mr. C. remained stable for three years before his next episode and was readmitted with symptoms similar to his first visit. This pattern of re-emergent symptoms continued for 10 years; each time he was treated for schizophrenia with minimal benefit. It was not until his mid-thirties and after an attempted suicide that doctors explored the possibility of bipolar disorder (Brady, 2000).

The low diagnosis rate for bipolar disorder may also have to do with the diagnostic criteria in the *DSM-IV,* perhaps indicating that this standard diagnostic guide needs further modification. A recent study aimed to test the reliability of *DSM* criteria for diagnosing bipolar disorder found troubling results: a survey was conducted to assess the *DSM-IV* by evaluating patients with known bipolar disorder strictly according its criteria. The results showed that 33% of the sample with bipolar disorder would have been diagnosed with major depressive disorder if the diagnosis were based solely on the *DSM-IV* (Bowden, 2001). While Dr. Bowden, who oversaw the survey, stresses the importance of a meticulous sensitive assessment on

The argument moves to examining the effects of treating bipolar disorder with medications for schizophrenia.

Here the author shows a step that might be taken to help reduce misdiagnosis.

Manic 4

the part of the diagnostician, he believes that there should be improvements in the *DSM-IV* criteria.

Considering the difficulties in diagnosing bipolar disorder, it is no wonder that many patients diagnosed as depressed or schizophrenic are showing negative, if any, response to their medications. Patients with bipolar disorder usually respond best to treatment with mood stabilizers, which are widely available for clinical use. The breakthroughs in medication of the last decade do no good without proper prescription. The psychiatric community must take a step back and work on its diagnostic techniques by revising the *DSM-IV* and working to ensure that those responsible for diagnosing patients are more aware of the difficulties of accurately assessing bipolar disorder.

The argument concludes by showing what the author thinks should be done and who should do it (a general proposal).

Manic 5

References

Bowden, C. L. (2001, January). Strategies to reduce misdiagnosis of bipolar depression. *Psychiatric Services, 52* (1), 51–55.

Brady, K. T. (2000). Difficulties in diagnosis and management of bipolar disorder: Three case presentations. *Journal of Clinical Psychiatry, 61* (Suppl 13), 32–37.

Evans, D. L. (2000). Bipolar disorder: Diagnostic challenges and treatment considerations. *Journal of Clinical Psychiatry, 61* (Suppl 13), 26–31.

Ghaemi, S. N., Sachs, G. S., Chiou, A. M., Pandurangi, A. K., Goodwin, F. K. (1999, March). Is bipolar disorder still under-diagnosed? Are antidepressants overutilized? *Journal of Affective Disorders, 52* (1–3), 135–144.

Weller, E. B., Weller, R. A., Fristad, M. A. (1995, June). Bipolar disorder in children: Misdiagnosis, underdiagnosis, and future directions. *Journal of the American Academy of Child & Adolescent Psychiatry, 34* (6), 709–14.

An Anthology of Arguments

Part Four

12. The Promise and Perils of Globalization 419

13. The Revolution in Biotechnology 435

14. The Challenge of Dealing with Juvenile Crime 465

15. The Meaning of Sports in Our Society 493

16. Public Taste 508

17. The Debate on the Meaning of the First Amendment 528

The Promise and Perils of Globalization

Chapter 12

I Love Global Capitalism—and I'm under 30

AARON LUKAS

An analyst for the Cato Institute, Aaron Lukas has written articles for the *Wall Street Journal*, the *Washington Times, USA Today,* and the *New York Times*. He has also been an elections supervisor in Bosnia-Herzegovina. The following article was first published in April 2001 on the Cato Institute's home page.

"Fight corporate power and greed!"

Thus runs the refrain of the perpetual-protest set. From Seattle to Washington, D.C., from Prague to Davos, and soon in Quebec, street-bound "carnivals against capitalism" have become a political lollapalooza that no deeply caring, shallow-thinking young person can afford to miss. If you aren't protesting, you aren't cool.

Well, for you politicians and journalists out there, I have an announcement: I'm in my '20s and I like global capitalism. And here's some more news: Most people my age agree with me.

Yet you won't hear much about my views at this weekend's Summit of the Americas in Quebec. Instead, you'll see members of my generation trumpeting their passionate concern for the environment, the world's poor, Mumia Abu-Jamal, organic farming and a laundry list of other causes.

Honestly, I'm not sure what planet these kids are living on. They look at the world and see only exploitation and repression, as if such evils were the bane of multinational corporations and not the norm throughout history.

In contrast, I see a flowing of human liberty and material prosperity. I see the move toward economic freedom that has swept through the Communist and developing worlds over the past decades for what it is: a recognition on the part of national leaders that their state-dominated systems have failed—failed in absolute terms as billions of people remained mired in grinding poverty, and failed in relative terms by comparison with the prosperous West and the relatively open and thriving Pacific Rim. Free trade has not been imposed from the top down; it has emerged from the bottom up.

Trade is also a matter of freedom here at home; the freedom to spend your own money on whatever you wish, regardless of the skin color or language of the person you decide to buy from; the freedom to invest your savings where you choose, even if that choice is on the other side of the planet. We have no more right to tell our fellow citizens what brand of clothing or car they must buy than we have the right to tell them what they can say or think.

Free trade has been good for both workers and the environment. By promoting economic growth, it enables less-developed countries to afford higher environmental standards and helps create an educated middle class to support them. A similar story exists with wages and labor conditions, which are improving in those places where globalization has taken hold.

The institutions that govern trade, like the Free Trade Area of the Americas to be discussed in Quebec, are no threat to sovereignty or democracy. Such agreements are nothing but contractual arrangements between sovereign nations to mediate trade disputes according to rules agreed upon by consensus. And despite the talk of "secret" negotiations, the Summit of the Americas is more democratic than the people it drives to apoplexy. After all, the negotiators at Quebec represent elected governments from throughout the hemisphere. Who elected the purple-haired sign-waver on the street in the black mask? The disruption and damage left in the wake of these protests are more akin to mob rule than democracy.

Puppet-bearing students in Quebec will speak of a "global corporate coup d'etat." 10 But let me let you in on a little secret: Most young people don't hate corporations. In fact, many of us either work in one, know someone who does, or even own stock in one. Corporations are nothing more than voluntary associations of people who are trying to achieve some common business goal. So the "evil, sinister, greedy corporation" mantra doesn't jibe with our life experiences. It's propaganda, and we know it.

Hurtling oneself against a police barricade in protest of free trade may be fun. But it's hardly a brave act for spoiled children of affluence—though ask any protester and you'll inevitably hear a tale of "hardship" (I had to work and go to school!)—to rail against the instruments of their own prosperity. Doubtless many of the Quebec marchers will be concerned for the world's poor. Yet through their opposition to open markets they make themselves the enemies of the poor.

Hey kids, want to help make the world a better place? Then grow up: Start a business or get a job. Want to help the poor? Hire them. "Corporate greed" has helped far more people than big puppets ever will.

French Food vs. Fast Food

MICHELLE MARTIN

A resident of Albuquerque, New Mexico, Michelle Martin writes on environmental issues. The following article was published in 1999 on the web site *Environmental News Network.*

Making headlines around the world, French sheep farmer Jose Bové, 46, led some of 1 his Farmers' Confederation followers in an August 12 attack on a McDonald's under construction in the southern French town of Millau. In what Bové calls "a festival atmosphere" that included children and singing, they ransacked the unfinished restaurant and used tractors to tear down the roof.

When the wiry farmer with the fu man chu mustache found himself arrested for his actions, M. Bové quickly became France's newest national hero.

Bové chose to remain behind bars for 20 days, thus enhancing his image as a "martyr" to the country's growing revolt against industrialized food production. He was finally released on the $17,000 bail his supporters and Roquefort cheese producers had raised on his behalf. Bové remains "under examination," a step short of being charged with a crime.

In an attempt to defuse the situation, Denis Hennequin, the President of McDonald's France, has said the company won't press charges against Bové and the others for the $113,000 in damages done to the Millau franchise.

It may not be enough. Bové's imprisonment has made him and the 500-member   5 Farmers' Confederation—which he founded in 1987—famous and increasingly powerful as sympathizers around the country send the Confederation their financial support.

It Started with Beef
Standing at the heart of Jose Bové's actions and his national and even international popularity are American cows.

Earlier this year, the European Union banned imports of U.S. hormone-treated beef, claiming it causes cancer. The World Trade Organization declared that the ban had no medical basis and was therefore illegal. The European Union refused to budge from its position.

President Clinton's administration responded by placing punitive U.S. sanctions on 100 French food products, including Roquefort cheese, foie gras, and other traditional foods dear to French hearts. Towns like Millau, in southern France, and the gastronomic Larzac region where Bové lives and raises his sheep for milk and meat, have been particularly hard hit by duties on products like ewe's cheese.

Bigger than Beef
But Jose Bové and the Farmers' Confederation are protesting much more than the U.S. sanctions. They are fighting what Bové calls "a global problem," which is why he is considered a hero and why his and the Confederation's actions have won the support of the Community Party, the Green Party, French labor unions, ecologists, and much of the French public.

That "global problem" includes industrialized food production, which is crowding   10 out France's small farmers and their distinctive products, and the growing domination of big retail distributors, like the recent merger of France's Carrefour and Promodes retail chains, which created the world's second largest retailer.

Finally, there is the pressure of economic globalization, which is perceived as an American threat to French livelihoods and to traditional ways of life. "There is a certain allergy in Europe to the extent of American power accumulated since the cold war's end," says French political analyst Allain Duhamel.

Citing the "invasion of France by American food," and the tyranny of "American imperialism," Bové and the Farmers' Confederation have struck a chord with French citizens by claiming they fight "to defend the right of people to feed themselves with their own food in their own way and against the determination of the United States to impose their way of eating on the whole planet."

Targeting the Golden Arches
The "global problem" sparked waves of protests throughout France in the summer and fall. McDonald's, more often than not, has been the national scapegoat.

Protestors around France have dumped home-grown fruits and vegetables on the counters of some of the nation's 750 McDonald's restaurants. On October 16, Jose Bové led 150 Farmers' Confederation members in a sit-in at the same McDonald's restaurant he had vandalized in August. The protestors picnicked on traditional French cuisine.

McDonald's has done nothing overt to warrant these protests and attacks. As 15 McDonald's spokeswoman Alessandra di Montezemolo has said, "We are attacked because we are a Number One global American brand." McDonald's has 24,500 restaurants in 116 countries.

In September, McDonald's responded to protests and attacks with a "Born in USA, Made in France" public relations campaign proclaiming that the French franchises are owned by the French, that they employ French workers, and that 80 percent of the products sold in its French restaurants are French-produced, thus supporting thousands of French farmers and local economies.

But this is a nation of gourmets and McDonald's is considered a guilty pleasure at best. Few will admit to actually eating at McDo ("Mac-doh"), as the French call it. Graffiti like "End McDomination" covers many buildings in Millau, the town Jose Bové made famous. But since the Millau McDonald's finally opened, it has enjoyed strong business.

Tampering with Mother Nature

Adding fuel to the fire Jose Bové ignited is the growing European reaction against genetically engineered or modified foods. Compounding European concerns are the several food scares it has weathered recently, including the 1996 outbreak of "mad cow" disease in Great Britain, supposedly contaminated bottles of Coca-Cola in France and Belgium, and the discovery this year of dioxin-laced animal feed that created dioxin-polluted chicken in Belgium, provoking what the *New York Times* calls a "widespread fear of any 'tampering' with nature." U.S. hormone-enhanced beef falls under that purview.

The European Union insists that, under WTO rules, it isn't bound by majority scientific opinion in its assessment of potential health risks, and that it will probably regard with equal concern imported genetically modified foods. Nevertheless, it has offered a compromise. It will pay the U.S. the $117 million in damages levied by the WTO. The U.S. wants the money to go to beef producers affected by the European ban.

Meanwhile, Jose Bové plans to attend the World Trade Organization conference 20 in Seattle, Wash., next week, which will address many issues dear to his heart. "My struggle remains the same," Bové has said. "The battle against globalization and for the right of peoples to feed themselves as they choose."

▌ *A World Not Neatly Divided*

AMARTYA SEN

A master of Trinity College at Cambridge University in England, economist Amartya Sen was born in India. He has taught at Harvard, Oxford, and the London School of Economics. In 1998 he was awarded the Nobel Prize for economics for his work on social welfare and the causes of famines. The following article was first published in the *New York Times* op-ed page in November 2001.

When people talk about clashing civilizations, as so many politicians and academics do 1 now, they can sometimes miss the central issue. The inadequacy of this thesis begins well before we get to the question of whether civilizations must clash. The basic weakness of the theory lies in its program of categorizing people of the world according to a unique, allegedly commanding system of classification. This is problematic because civilizational categories are crude and inconsistent and also because there are other ways of seeing people (linked to politics, language, literature, class, occupation or other affiliations).

The befuddling influence of a singular classification also traps those who dispute the thesis of a clash: To talk about "the Islamic world" or "the Western world" is already to adopt an impoverished vision of humanity as unalterably divided. In fact, civilizations are hard to partition in this way, given the diversities within each society as well as the linkages among different countries and cultures. For example, describing India as a "Hindu civilization" misses the fact that India has more Muslims than any other country except Indonesia and possibly Pakistan. It is futile to try to understand Indian art, literature, music, food or politics without seeing the extensive interactions across barriers of religious communities. These include Hindus and Muslims, Buddhists, Jains, Sikhs, Parsees, Christians (who have been in India since at least the fourth century, well before England's conversion to Christianity), Jews (present since the fall of Jerusalem), and even atheists and agnostics. Sanskrit has a larger atheistic literature than exists in any other classical language. Speaking of India as a Hindu civilization may be comforting to the Hindu fundamentalist, but it is an odd reading of India.

A similar coarseness can be seen in the other categories invoked, like "the Islamic world." Consider Akbar and Aurangzeb, two Muslim emperors of the Mogul dynasty in India. Aurangzeb tried hard to convert Hindus into Muslims and instituted various policies in that direction, of which taxing the non-Muslims was only one example. In contrast, Akbar reveled in his multiethnic court and pluralist laws, and issued official proclamations insisting that no one "should be interfered with on account of religion" and that "anyone is to be allowed to go over to a religion that pleases him."

If a homogeneous view of Islam were to be taken, then only one of these emperors could count as a true Muslim. The Islamic fundamentalist would have no time for Akbar; Prime Minister Tony Blair, given his insistence that tolerance is a defining characteristic of Islam, would have to consider excommunicating Aurangzeb. I expect both Akbar and Aurangzeb would protest, and so would I. A similar crudity is present in the characterization of what is called "Western civilization." Tolerance and individual freedom have certainly been present in European history. But there is no dearth of diversity here, either. When Akbar was making his pronouncements on religious tolerance in Agra, in the 1590's, the Inquisitions were still going on; in 1600, Giordano Bruno was burned at the stake, for heresy, in Campo dei Fiori in Rome.

Dividing the world into discrete civilizations is not just crude. It propels us into the absurd belief that this partitioning is natural and necessary and must overwhelm all other ways of identifying people. That imperious view goes not only against the sentiment that "we human beings are all much the same," but also against the more plausible understanding that we are diversely different. For example, Bangladesh's split from Pakistan was not connected with religion, but with language and politics.

Each of us has many features in our self-conception. Our religion, important as it may be, cannot be an all-engulfing identity. Even a shared poverty can be a source of solidarity across the borders. The kind of division highlighted by, say, the so-called "antiglobalization" protesters—whose movement is, incidentally, one of the most globalized in the world—tries to unite the underdogs of the world economy and goes firmly against religious, national or "civilizational" lines of division.

The main hope of harmony lies not in any imagined uniformity, but in the plurality of our identities, which cut across each other and work against sharp divisions into impenetrable civilizational camps. Political leaders who think and act in terms of sectioning off humanity into various "worlds" stand to make the world more flammable—even when their intentions are very different. They also end up, in the case of civilizations defined by religion, lending authority to religious leaders seen as spokesmen for their "worlds." In the process, other voices are muffled and other concerns silenced. The robbing of our plural identities not only reduces us; it impoverishes the world.

A New Ethics for a New World

PAUL R. EHRLICH

Paul R. Ehrlich is the Bing Professor of Population Studies at Stanford University. He has written extensively on the dangers of overpopulation; his books include The Population Bomb **(1968),** The Population Explosion **(1990),** The Stork and the Plow **(1995), and** Human Natures: Genes, Cultures, and the Human Prospect **(2000). He is the cofounder of the field of coevolution and an expert on butterfly populations. The following article appeared in 2002 in** Newsday, **a newspaper for Long Island, New York.**

In the wake of the horrors of Sept. 11, it is well to remind ourselves that people   1
evolved, culturally and genetically, as small-group animals. For millions of years human groups consisted of a few dozen individuals, mostly close relatives with the same skin color and other obvious physical characteristics. Each adult individual possessed essentially the entire culture of the group—its store of non-genetic information housed in the brains and simple artifacts of the group's members. And that group had a uniform set of ethics: rules for governing the conduct of members and making moral judgments of right and wrong.

In 10,000 years, an evolutionary eye-blink, humanity has been transformed from an extremely clever great ape living in groups of six to 600 individuals, to the very same ape dominating Earth, living in a global group of 6 billion. And those billions are tied together by instant electronic communication and high-speed transport systems. That transformation was an example of extraordinarily rapid cultural evolution (changes in humanity's store of non-genetic information) in the area of technology. But, sadly, cultural evolution in the area of ethics didn't keep pace.

Consider a few of the ethical issues raised for Americans by the terrorist atrocities (I'll mostly skip the profound ethical questions that the people involved in, or sympathetic to, those horrific acts should be addressing). Some of us have long been concerned with the basic causes of terrorism. Anne Ehrlich and I wrote 15 years ago: "Its roots in poverty, despair, greed, racism, religious prejudice and unfulfilled economic and political ambitions are hardly novel. . . . Population growth, differential population growth and dashed expectations are . . . watering the roots of terrorism as they have never been watered before."

Were we right? Has the large size of the U.S. population and its profligate consumption played some role in creating the conditions that led to Sept. 11? Has it been ethical for a giant nation to consume a vastly disproportionate share of Earth's resources? Were Americans in the past century obliged to consider how designing their nation and lives around automobiles would affect people in the Middle East? Do they have an obligation now? What about the massive destruction of tropical forests and indigenous societies caused by America's related thirst for rubber, or for that matter, its high consumption of beef, coffee or sugar?

Becoming a large-group animal has raised new kinds of ethical questions. Ethics in   5
our ancestral small groups dealt almost exclusively with in-group members; out-group

individuals were seldom considered worthy of ethical treatment (just 150 years ago many Europeans still considered Africans subhuman). Today people have ethical concerns about the direct treatment of people in other groups, as evidenced by attempts to avoid "collateral damage" in the bombing campaigns in Afghanistan.

But a more vexing question is, what should be our ethical position today about indirect impacts—such as those generated through purchasing hamburgers or an espresso—on poor people in other nations? How much might our devotion to gas-guzzling SUVs have contributed to the deaths of innocent fellow citizens slaughtered in New York and Washington by aligning us with repressive regimes sitting on vast oil reserves? Indeed, how do the ethics of individual citizens relate to the actions of their own nation's government? Are individuals who are unaware of subtle ethical issues (or out-voted in democracies or intimidated in dictatorships) devoid of responsibility for actions taken in their names? When ethical views differ among citizens or groups, how are people to decide who is right?

The few young Saudis who killed thousands of Americans doubtless thought they were acting ethically because they believed policies and actions of the U.S. government had caused the deaths and misery of many innocents. And retrospection suggests that even decisions of democratic governments, such as terror bombings aimed at German and Japanese civilians in World War II, were hardly ethical.

These questions may seem hypothetical now, but consider some current ethical dilemmas. Should Americans change their views on the death penalty so Spain will extradite its terrorist prisoners? Was the treatment of women by the Taliban one legitimate reason to intervene militarily in Afghanistan? To what degree are short-term American policies in the past and today threatening the quality of life, or even the very lives, of our grandchildren? Is it our duty to bequeath our descendents functioning societies and sound life-support systems? Or can we simply assume that technological progress will solve future problems regardless of today's behavior? Can an ethical American couple have more than two children, when their additional consumption may well help reduce the options of their grandchildren or great-grandchildren? Can we make truly ethical decisions if we are ill-informed or required to make judgments under conditions of great uncertainty?

The questions are myriad; the answers barely explored in public. The lack of leadership from Washington on such ethical issues is disturbing, especially following the recent heart-breaking events. Blind patriotism is not a substitute for careful consideration of our actions. If the people killed, injured or psychologically damaged by the terrorist attack are not to have suffered in vain, we need to do much more than hunt down some of the individuals responsible. Americans need to think hard about the ethical issues brought to the fore by Sept. 11.

The world is increasingly divided between a very rich globalizing minority and a diverse majority that ranges from the reasonably well-off to the desperately poor, the latter often in nations riven by ethnic, religious or economic strife. In such a world, what are the "right" things for a lone superpower to do? We all need to consider how to reinvent ourselves as a large-group animal, with ethics that will enable human beings to cooperate in solving the horrendous environmental and social problems confronting our species. As individuals and nations, we will not always behave ethically, but it's important to try to reach some agreement on what such behavior should be. Some level of ethical consensus was obviously an important part of the "glue" that kept our small groups functional. Now we need to work toward some form of global ethical superglue.

We have the tools to communicate with each other about moral decisions, modern analogues of the campfire consultations that established norms when a few dozen people constituted a society. And we have forums that can serve as partial models. In the Intergovernmental Panel on Climate Change, for example, the world's governments, climate scientists, corporations and non-governmental organizations concerned with global warming debate the issues of costs and remedies in open meetings, and provide society with the results of their deliberations. If the media covered the deliberations more closely, the panel might be a model mechanism for helping to democratically guide the cultural evolution of one area of ethics.

Based on the best possible scientific scenarios, the Panel on Climate Change has generated an ethical debate over allocating the responsibility for avoiding climatic disaster, forming a basis for the also open negotiations over the Kyoto Protocol. If the World Trade Organization deliberations had followed this model of openness and participation, its troubled progress, not to mention the outcomes, might have been very different.

In a panglossian dream, one could imagine many such forums that, unlike today's more limited ones, would garner substantial media attention. Panels could be constituted on valuing human and biological diversity, on when a human individual deserving of rights comes into existence, on the circumstances in which state violence might be justified, on our reproductive and consumption behavior and its consequences for people today and for future generations, and so on. Such panels could catalyze widespread debate and better solutions to global problems, as the Panel on Climate Change has done.

We are not going to create a utopia. But we could do a much better job of consciously, democratically, and with mutual respect, guiding the cultural evolution of ethics. It will take more than smart bombs and special forces to secure our future, it will take smart charismatic leaders with special concern for the evolving moral values of society. If we are successful, our descendents will bless us for it.

Veil of Fears

STANLEY KURTZ

Stanley Kurtz has a doctorate in social anthropology and has been a Dewey Prize Lecturer in the social sciences at the University of Chicago. He is currently a research fellow at the Hoover Institution. He is also an editor at *National Review Online* and has written articles for the *Wall Street Journal*, the *Weekly Standard*, *Policy Review*, *Commentary*, and the *Chronicle of Higher Education*. The following article was published in the *National Review* in January 2002.

Last month's dramatic pictures of Afghan women shyly peeking out from beneath freshly lifted veils set off a torrent of commentary on the meaning and aims of the war. Although Afghanistan's new rulers quickly abolished the Taliban's draconian codes of womanly conduct, some Americans called for a government-imposed program of feminist reform. Feminists, like *Vagina Monologues* author Eve Ensler, even tried to spin the war as a crusade against a global "patriarchy."

Meanwhile, the mainstream press was busy detailing the horrors of the Taliban's treatment of women, focusing on the veil. "It was like being in jail," said one Afghan woman of her years under the veil. But now, proclaimed the *New York Times*, "the prisoners have been set free." In a cover story on Muslim women, *Time* magazine dubbed the Afghan burka "a body bag for the living."

But the "veil as body bag" notion is both mistaken and dangerous. There is no surer way to drive the Islamic world into the arms of the fundamentalists than to force Western feminism on a newly conquered Muslim country. It is no coincidence that the two Muslim fundamentalist regimes of our day—Iran and Afghanistan—arose in nations that had systematically attempted to root out traditional Islamic practices regarding women. (Those efforts were sponsored by the shah in Iran and the Soviets in Afghanistan.) Instead of being damned as a senseless outrage, veiling deserves a qualified defense. The practice has undoubtedly slowed the Muslim world's path to modernity, and that is a serious problem. But that difficulty would never have arisen in the first place if veiling hadn't accomplished something important. Veiling is embraced by millions of Muslim men and women as one of the keys to their way of life. They are not mistaken.

The conflict between modernity and the traditional Muslim view of women is one of the most important causes of this war. The tiresome claim of the leftist academy that poverty causes terrorism misses the point. So far from being poor, Muslim fundamentalists tend to come from a relatively wealthy modernizing class. The terrorists and their supporters are generally newly urbanized, college-educated professionals from intact families with rural backgrounds. They are a rising but frustrated cohort, shut out of power by a more entrenched and Westernized elite. True, the new fundamentalists often find themselves stymied by the weak economies of Muslim countries, but as a class they are relatively well off. Like many revolutions, the Muslim fundamentalist movement has been spurred by increased income, education, and expectations. But it is the clash between traditional Middle Eastern family life and modernity that has decisively pushed so many toward fundamentalism. And women are at the center of the problem.

Although the puzzle of "modernity and the Muslim woman" is one of several keys 5 to this war, the feminist sensibility of the American press has rendered the connection between terrorism and the Islamic sexual system all but invisible. The press has been obsessed with the relatively small number of modernized women in Afghan cities who were indeed viciously oppressed by the Taliban's infamous policies. Women who had once been accustomed to Western skirts were not only forced to cover themselves entirely and forbidden to leave home without a male relative, they were banned even from making noises with their shoes as they walked through the streets of the city.

The world has justly condemned these policies, but this picture of government-imposed veiling does not accurately describe the situation of most Afghan women under the Taliban, much less the lives of the many educated women throughout the Middle East who have enlisted in the Muslim fundamentalist movement through their decision to don the veil.

Town and Country
The Taliban's code of womanly behavior was intentionally directed toward the cities. The aim was to "purify" those areas of Afghanistan that had been "corrupted" by modernization. But the Taliban never bothered to enforce its rules in traditional areas. Actually, in most Afghan villages, women rarely wear the burka. That's because villages in Afghanistan are organized into kin-oriented areas, and the veil needs wearing only when a woman is among men from outside of her kin group. A rural woman puts on a burka for travel, especially to cities. Yet just by exiting her home, a woman in a modern city inevitably mixes with men who are not her kin. That's why the Taliban prohibited the modernized women of Kabul from so much as stepping onto the street without a male relative. So the real problem with the veil in Afghanistan was the Taliban's attempt to impose the traditional system of veiling on a modernizing city.

Yet, remarkable as it may seem, many modernizing urban women throughout the Middle East have freely accepted at least a portion of the Taliban's reasoning. These educated women have actually taken up the veil—and along with it, Muslim fundamentalism. To see why, it is necessary to understand what makes traditional Muslim women veil in the first place.

Life in the Muslim Middle East has long revolved around family and tribe. In fact, that's what a tribe is—your family in its most extended form. For much of Middle Eastern history, tribal networks of kin functioned as governments in miniature. In the absence of state power, it was the kin group that protected an individual from attack, secured his wealth, and performed a thousand other functions. No one could flourish whose kin group was not strong, respected, and unified.

In the modern Middle East, networks of kin are still the foundation of wealth, security, and personal happiness. That, in a sense, is the problem. As we've seen in Afghanistan, loyalty to kin and tribe cuts against the authority of the state. And the corrupt dictatorships that rule much of the Muslim Middle East often function themselves more like self-interested kin groups than as rulers who take the interests of the nation as a whole as their own. That, in turn, gives the populace little reason to turn from the proven support of kin and tribe, and trust instead in the state.

So from earliest youth, a Middle Eastern Muslim learns that his welfare and happiness are bound up in the strength and reputation of his family. If, for example, a child shows a special aptitude in school, his siblings might willingly sacrifice their personal chances for advancement simply to support his education. Yet once that child becomes a professional, his income will help to support his siblings, while his prestige will enhance their marriage prospects.

The "family" to which a Muslim Middle Easterner is loyal, however, is not like our family. It is a "patrilineage"—a group of brothers and other male relatives, descended from a line of men that can ultimately be traced back to the founder of a particular tribe. Traditionally, lineage brothers will live near one another and will share the family's property. This willingness of a "band of brothers" to pool their labor and wealth is the key to the strength of the lineage.

But the centrality of men to the Muslim kinship system sets up a problem. The women who marry into a lineage pose a serious threat to the unity of the band of brothers. If a husband's tie to his wife should become more important than his solidarity with his brothers, the couple might take their share of the property and leave the larger group, thus weakening the strength of the lineage.

There is a solution to this problem, however—a solution that marks out the kinship system of the Muslim Middle East as unique in the world. In the Middle East, the preferred form of marriage is between a man and his cousin (his father's brother's daughter). Cousin marriage solves the problem of lineage solidarity. If, instead of marrying a woman from a strange lineage, a man marries his cousin, then his wife will not be an alien, but a trusted member of his own kin group. Not only will this reduce a man's likelihood of being pulled away from his brothers by his wife, a woman of the lineage is less likely to be divorced by her husband, and more likely to be protected by her own extended kin in case of a rupture in the marriage. Somewhere around a third of all marriages in the Muslim Middle East are between members of the same lineage, and in some places the figure can reach as high as 80 percent. It is this system of "patrilateral parallel cousin marriage" that explains the persistence of veiling, even in the face of modernity.

By veiling, women are shielded from the possibility of a dishonoring premarital affair. But above all, when Muslim women veil, they are saving themselves for marriage

10

to the men of their own kin group. In an important sense, this need to protect family honor and preserve oneself for an advantageous marriage to a man of the lineage is a key to the rise of Islamic revivalism.

Covering Up

Most people think of the Iranian revolution of the late 1970s as the beginning of the contemporary Muslim fundamentalist movement, but it was in Egypt in the mid 1970s that modern Islamic fundamentalism really took off. The movement was started by students—men and women—at Egyptian universities who spontaneously adopted a code of Islamic decorum in mixed company. In keeping with that code, and despite government attempts to forbid it, Egyptian college women began to don the veil. The practice soon spread (and along with it, the ideology of Islamic fundamentalism) to legions of educated working women in Egypt's cities. 15

Oddly, these willing wearers of the veil were precisely the sort of educated career women on whom the Taliban would ruthlessly force the burka. The difference was that these women, unlike those who later fell victim to the Taliban, had free access to education and modern careers. They put on the veil precisely as a way of enjoying these modern innovations—without also endangering their marriage prospects, or their family's honor, in the new, mixed-sex environment.

The last three decades have seen a tremendous increase in the number of Egyptians receiving an education. Many of these young people are fresh from villages, where the traditional marriage system is still strong. These are the grown children whose parents, uncles, brothers, and sisters sacrificed to make them into professionals. By veiling, they are fulfilling their end of the bargain; they are promising not to destroy—by a shameful affair, or by marriage to a stranger—the honor or prosperity of their families. Of course, not all Muslim women are young or waiting to marry relatives, but the preferred marriage pattern shapes a wider ethos. Some modernized office workers decide to veil only after they marry, to reduce jealousy, and protect the honor of their husbands and families.

The veil was never the nightmare American feminists make it out to be. In a world where satisfaction in life is predicated on the honor, strength, and unity of the kin group, the veil makes sense. Although the oppressive impositions of the Taliban have rightly been abolished, the United States ought not to be in the business of browbeating Muslim women out of their veils, much less reforming the Middle Eastern kinship system. Instead, we need to encourage the separation of traditional Muslim family practices from the political ideology of Islamic fundamentalism. By far the best way to do this is to roundly defeat the fundamentalists on the battlefield.

Once military and political failure has broken fundamentalism's appeal as an ideology, traditional family practices will be free to gradually adapt to modernity. Modernizing Egyptian women may still veil, but if they drop the theocratic fundamentalist baggage, that will be enough. Can we really get modernizing Muslim women who veil to drop their support for fundamentalist theocrats? It won't be easy, but nothing is more likely to produce a disastrous backlash against the United States than the conviction that an American victory will lead to a feminist-directed assault against veiling and the family. And many Muslim women in rural areas veil without being followers of the fundamentalist theocrats.

When the United States governed Japan after World War II, we forcibly reconstructed the country as a democracy, without being so foolish as to seriously challenge its traditional family or sexual system. That system has remained far more "traditional" than our own, yet today Japanese family and sex roles (for better, and for worse) are 20 slowly changing and adapting to modernity. With luck, the pattern will someday repeat itself in the Middle East.

Muslim fundamentalists have turned on America as a convenient scapegoat for the agonies and contradictions of modernization in their own society. Yet distorted and unjust though it is, their logic contains a kernel of truth. The Western movies, television shows, and other media that now reach the Middle East tell of a world in which premarital sex and love-marriages are the norm—a world in which the extended family counts for little, and the lineage for nothing. This is what most alarms Muslim traditionalists. Western family norms may someday gain a foothold in the Middle East, but historically, family change lags behind and adapts to changes in political and economic life. So it is to the economic and political spheres that we ought to apply our pressure.

The veiling question cuts across conventional political lines. The Left, of course, is split between feminists and multiculturalists: The former camp says, "Such practices as veiling are impermissible, for anyone"; the latter camp says, "Well, this is what *they* do, and who are we to object?" But conservatives are divided as well. Conservatives are eager to spread Western values across the globe, and when it comes to democracy and the free market, they have a point. But the conservative "realist" tradition in foreign policy warns against endangering ourselves through attempts to remake the world in our image.

Burke's conservatism is the model here. Burke was a critic of the excesses of British rule in India, and he also favored American independence when few of his fellows did. Burke was never the diehard opponent of reform he's often made out to be, but he did respect the wisdom embodied in custom. Burke believed that gradual change—from within the framework of custom—was the best policy, not only for England, but also for the nations England ruled. When it comes to veiling, Burke's policy should be our policy.

Beauty and the Beast of Intolerance

WOLE SOYINKA

Born in Nigeria, Wole Soyinka has written plays, poetry, and novels, including political satire. He was jailed by the Nigerian government from 1967 to 1969 and subsequently left his native country for over five years in the 1970s. In 1986, he became the first African writer to be awarded the Nobel Prize for literature.

The article that follows was first published in November 2002 in the *Houston Chronicle*. It was written after deadly riots took place in Kaduna, a city in northern Nigeria, following journalist Isioma Daniel's commentary on the 2002 Miss World contest, which was to be held in Nigeria. Daniel, who suggested that the prophet Mohammed would probably have approved of the contest, was subsequently sentenced to death by the state of Zamfara and fled the country. In response to the riots, in which over 200 people lost their lives, the Miss World contest was moved to London.

In order to stop the Miss World pageant from taking place on Nigerian soil, the fundamentalist agenda mounted a rampage of frustration. It was not sufficient that the organizers agreed to shift the date for the finale out of respect for the season of Ramadan, the Muslim season of fasting and purification and—lest it be forgotten—peace. It was not sufficient that, as yet another concession, the absurd decision was taken that the competitors would not appear in swimsuits in the finale. Additionally, the head of state, President Olusegun Obasanjo, had earlier agreed to receive the contestants in a courtesy call; he withdrew in deference to Muslim sensibilities. All these merely whetted the appetite of the beast of intolerance, to whom a superficial loss of face can only be assuaged by a loss of lives.

The newspaper that allegedly committed the offense, *ThisDay*, published fulsome apologies and retraction of the publication that gave offense. This apology was sententiously accepted by Muslim leaders and the Supreme Islamic Council, laying emphasis that the newspaper in question showed contrition and remorse.

Nothing in the statement of the Muslim leaders, however, considered an expression of remorse necessary for the loss of innocent lives nor administered a stern rebuke to the fanatic hordes that swept through the streets of Kaduna, burning and butchering.

The pattern has become wearisomely familiar—an imagined slight or disrespect, even governmental failure to promptly acquiesce in unreasonable demands that infringe on the civic rights of others, and the response is violence unleashed on an unsuspecting populace!

I shall withhold comment for now on the appropriateness of the apology of *This- 5 Day*, the indicted newspaper, since my intention is not to fan awake the embers of mayhem whose flare-up now appears to have been temporarily doused. Sooner or later, the issue of the freedom of expression must be addressed within societies such as mine, and the nature of due response that is permissible when such freedoms are held to have wounded the sensibilities of others. A society that tolerates the murder of innocents, or incitement to murder, as the interpretation of due and legitimate response is a society that is breaking apart beyond all remedy.

For now, let this be clearly understood: The alleged offense by the newspaper— which merely reported the comment made by a citizen—was only an excuse. Anything at all, anything or nothing, would have served as the trigger of a predictable rioting. If an "offending statement" had not conveniently appeared, the rioters would have invented one or rioted without one. The minds that we are dealing with feel obliged to prove, time and time again, that they would go to any lengths to impose their concept of appropriate human conduct on their immediate society and even on the world.

The parameters of "offense" are now totally without definition and have turned infinitely expansible. While they deny others the right of freedom of expression, they exercise theirs in the form of bloodletting. The streets of the ancient city of Kaduna are awash with blood because of a group of bigoted murderers who will not accept that it is the right of others to express themselves in the glorification of the human body.

Perhaps at this point it is necessary for me to repeat my views on beauty pageants in general. I have always considered them a frivolity that does nothing to enhance the condition of womanhood. However, this 2002 edition, its originally scheduled location in a nation whose mostly peaceful secular coexistence has been brutally shattered, not once but repeatedly in recent times, has been a critical event. Nigeria, in case anyone has forgotten, is that nation of more than 30 states where a calculating political animal suddenly unsheathed the sword of religious fundamentalism for purely political gains, setting a dangerous example that has been followed by eight other states.

The governor of that state, Zamfara, declared his intention to rule the state on strictly *Sharia* principles. This, as I stated repeatedly, was an act of secession, and the various violent manifestations that we have witnessed since then, stemming from that declaration, mostly engineered, have been a pursuit of a secessionist political agenda that attempts to disguise itself in religious robes. The amputation of the hands of thieves followed shortly, in defiance of the provisions of the nation's criminal code which—let this be emphasized—does grant *Sharia* laws their legitimacy, but sets unambiguous limits on their application in the administration of justice.

The most notorious punitive measure of the *Sharia* states, however, has been the   10
sentencing of two women to death for alleged adultery. The first was acquitted on appeal, on a technicality, while the latter, Safiyat, remains under that threat of judicial
murder of the utmost sadism—to be buried up to her neck and stoned to death. This
will not happen, however.

No, the sentence will not be carried out. The Nigerian government has assured the
world that it will not, and the *Sharia* states understand this. To kill Safiyat is to step beyond the line of no return and, for a number of reasons, none of the seceding states is
prepared to go that far. So what we are witnessing are simply sanguinary incursions
into the cohesion of the Nigerian nation, acts of defiance intended to warn the government that the rebellious states are determined to assert a degree of autonomy that
is not enjoyed by the rest of the member states and need not be compatible with the
provisions of the constitution that define the state known as Nigeria. When a state acts
outside a constitution, it has effectively seceded from the entity that is governed by
that constitution.

Yes, a beauty pageant is a trivial indulgence, and some may argue that it even di-
minishes the status of womanhood. However, given a choice between the bearded
wannabe Taliban face of any protagonist governor of *Sharia*, uttering his imprecations
against the beauty contest on television, and the sight of sylphid aspirations of femininity on parade, I have no hesitation in opting for the latter. Unfortunately, our world
is infested by minds to whom lissome limbs only evoke dreams of amputation. A lovely
face makes them fantasize, even salivate on the messy pulp that will be left at the end
of some Stone Age stoning ritual.

In any case, Mr. Universe contests are equally ludicrous exercises in exhibitionism,
and I have yet to hear of any riots taking place on account of the exposure of those
grotesque abdominal muscles and the flexing of improbable biceps. Mr. Universe competitors wear skimpy pants with recognizable bulges, only slightly less assertive and
literal than the tightly packaged crotches of the male ballet dancer.

From the moment that I learned of sectarian opposition to the female Universe
version being held in Nigeria, it became something other than a beauty contest and
assumed serious sociopolitical dimensions. Whenever my travels took me to any
place where a boycott was threatened—such as South Africa, Italy and the United
States—I deliberately took time off to argue against the boycott. Never has a frivolity
acquired such profundity in the pluralist character that is the very essence of the
Nigerian nation.

Destruction of property and human massacres are always traumatic events in a   15
community, saddening and enraging, but the organizers of the beauty contest, as well
as the participants, must understand that they are totally free of guilt. The guilty are
the storm troopers of intolerance, the manipulators of feeble-minded but murderous
hordes of fanaticism.

The nation will mourn the dead and render aid to the maimed and bereaved, but
that same nation must understand that it will itself join the graveyard of nations if it
fails to uphold the principles of plurality, choice and tolerance. The phenomenon of
intolerance is eating up a world that can only survive on peaceful coexistence. The accommodating are in retreat on so many fronts, little understanding that every abandoned space of coexistence is immediately occupied by the aggressive agenda of fanatics. They advance again and again to demand and seize more concessions, more
demands on the way of life of others. The mind of the zealot is an insatiable dark hole,
engorging all that makes life light and bearable.

QUESTIONS FOR DISCUSSION

1. **Making Connections:** In the wake of 9/11 and the War against Terror, there has been talk of a "clash of civilizations" between the Muslim and Western worlds. Considering the issues discussed in the Kurtz and Soyinka readings, how is the status of women at the heart of this debate?

2. **Analyzing Strategy:** How does Amartya Sen try to undo the various group and cultural identities that drive dissension around the world? What is his main argumentative tactic?

3. **Analyzing Strategy:** Soyinka, Lukas, and Ehrlich all refer to themselves in the first person ("I") at different points in their arguments. Identify the different uses of these self references. (See Chapter 5 for an overview of the different uses of "I".)

4. **Making Connections:** Aaron Lukas and Paul R. Ehrlich have opposing positions on the role of capitalism and consumption on the global distribution of wealth. Which author supports his position more effectively? Which position do you agree with?

5. **Analyzing Strategy:** Issues of definition are central to many of the arguments in this set of readings, such as "free trade" or "corporations" in the Lukas piece or "patrilineage" in the Kurtz piece or "global ethical superglue" in the Ehrlich piece. How are these key terms, and others like these, defined in these pieces? Or do the authors assume that their readers will understand these terms without further definition?

6. **Making Connections:** McDonald's has been a target of violence not only in France but also in Indonesia and India in 2002. What does the fast food chain symbolize to those attacking it? Have Americans reacted in reciprocal ways to any foreign imports? Why are cultural practices involving food and dress so often the flash points of cultural disagreement? What areas of global exchange are seldom targeted?

7. **Analyzing Strategy:** Look at the series of rhetorical questions that Paul Ehrlich uses in his fourth, sixth, and eighth paragraphs. Try rephrasing these questions as claims. When these questions take the form of claims, are they more or less likely to be accepted by an audience of U.S. readers?

8. **Making Connections:** What is the "cultural evolution of ethics" that Ehrlich calls for? Would it apply to the practices of controlling women described by Kurtz? To what extent is economic prosperity connected to the ethical treatment of women and children?

WRITING SUGGESTIONS

1. Find an issue of *Time* or *Newsweek* magazine published in the 1950s. Compare its advertisements with those in a current issue. Does this comparison provide evidence of increasing globalization?

2. Multiculturalism is sometimes defined as an acceptance and tolerance of the beliefs and practices of all groups, and it is often seen as a necessary consequence

of globalization. Select a practice regarding child-raising, marriage, and family that you do not think should be tolerated in the name of multiculturalism. (This practice can even be one that is accepted in the United States.) Write a negative evaluation of this practice, based on consequences and moral principles, for an audience that does not engage in this practice. Or try to address your negative evaluation to an audience that does engage in the practice.

3. Can any of the trends toward globalization be reversed? Select one aspect of globalization such as ease of communication or increasing world trade or cultural exchange and construct an argument identifying the causes that could reverse these trends.

4. Write a personal essay in which you examine your own material surroundings, your own patterns of personal consumption, your own leisure activities, and your own work or school environment and assess how many items or elements have their origins in other countries and cultures.

5. Find examples of a foreign language newspaper. If you can read the language, fine. If you can't, find a person who can and who will go through the newspaper with you. How many articles and advertisements refer to events or products from the United States?

The Revolution in Biotechnology

Chapter 13

Closing In on Cloning

WESLEY J. SMITH

Wesley J. Smith has been a lawyer, writer, and public advocate. He collaborated with Ralph Nader on four books, including *Collision Course: The Truth about Airline Safety* (1993) and *No Contest: Corporate Lawyers and the Perversion of Justice in America* (1996). His most recent book is *Culture of Death: The Assault on Medical Ethics in America* (2001). The following article was first published in the *Weekly Standard* in January 2002.

The brave new world order is hurtling toward us at Mach speed. With the announce- 1 ment by Advanced Cell Technology that it has created the first human clones and developed them into six-cell embryos, the country finds itself at an ethical point of no return. Either Congress will ban human cloning, or human cloning will soon be a fait accompli.

With cloning—and its first cousin, embryonic stem cell research—biotech companies are embarked upon a radical enterprise. They intend to make vast fortunes by patenting and marketing products derived from the destruction of human life. If they succeed, certain categories of humanity will be reduced to a commodity with no greater moral standing than penicillin mold. For those who doubt the objectifying intent of this research, note the language of an October 1, 2001, press release by the Geron Corp., crowing that one of its recent research breakthroughs "greatly facilitates the development of scalable manufacturing processes to enable commercialization of hES (human embryonic stem) cell-based products."

How did we get this far down the slippery slope this fast? After all, it has been only a few months since President Bush supposedly settled the stem cell debate by permitting limited federal funding of research using existing stem cell lines derived from human embryos. But as the Spanish Civil War was really just the opening engagement of World War II, the controversy over embryonic stem cell research can now be seen as merely a precursor to the greater clash over cloning about to unfold.

The struggle over embryonic stem cell research began less than two years ago when biotech companies and their allies within the bioethics movement convinced President Clinton to open the spigot of federal funding. Clinton was willing, but he had a significant legal problem to overcome. Extracting stem cells kills embryos and federal law (the Dickey Amendment) explicitly prohibits federal funding for destructive embryonic research.

What to do? Clinton's bioethics commission recommended a Clintonian approach: Simply use private money to pay for destruction of the embryos and the extraction of their stem cells. After that, the federal government could pick up the tab. Clinton signed the order shortly before leaving office, and in doing so plopped George W. Bush right onto the hot griddle of an unwanted moral controversy.

Fulfilling his campaign promise to oppose embryonic stem cell research, President Bush promptly suspended Clinton's executive order, sparking a furious, three-pronged political counterattack. First, making a strong appeal to the pragmatism that is central to the American character, promoters of embryonic stem cell research promised that only unwanted embryos left over from in vitro fertilization procedures and due to be destroyed would be used in the research. Since these embryos were doomed in any event, the argument went, we might as well get some use out of them.

The second prong consisted of junk science. Proponents of embryonic stem cell research, such as Senator Orrin Hatch, argued that the embryos in question weren't really the early stages of human life because they would never be implanted. "Life begins in a womb, not in a Petri dish," Hatch said. Others assured squeamish Americans that these frozen humans "no larger than the period at the end of this sentence," as the pro-stem cell research propaganda had it, were actually "pre-embryos," cells of no significant moral concern.

The third prong was an intensely emotional appeal—typically featuring testimony from celebrity disease or injury victims such as Christopher Reeve, Mary Tyler Moore, and Michael J. Fox—promoting embryonic stem cell research as a veritable cornucopia of miraculous medical cures. We were told that if the government would only fund such research, quadriplegics might walk, Parkinson's patients would regain control over their bodily movements, and diabetics would be liberated from insulin.

This well-coordinated campaign was successful. Polls soon showed growing support for federal funding—so long as only doomed, leftover in vitro embryos were used. By last summer, the pressure to fully fund embryonic stem cell research had grown white hot, with more than 60 senators and 260 congressmen—including some of the president's closest political allies—publicly vowing to overturn a decision by President Bush to prohibit federal funding. Pushed into this very tight political corner, the administration let it be known that President Bush had entered a season of deep moral contemplation.

In early August, in his first televised policy speech to the nation, Bush announced his decision. Informing the nation of the importance of the moral issues involved in the debate, Bush announced that he would permit limited federal funding of research involving stem cell lines extracted from embryos—but only from cell lines already in existence. In other words, no federal money would fund research on stem cell lines taken from embryos that were not already dead.

Proponents of embryonic stem cell research howled at having their agenda substantially thwarted. Americans were warned, hyperbolically, that a new "dark age" in scientific research was descending. Some scientists spoke of pulling up stakes and moving overseas. At least one prominent researcher did just that.

Opponents, on the other hand, were divided. Some, including this writer, applauded the decision, believing that President Bush's "compromise" had the virtue of being politically defensible and was thus the best decision possible under difficult circumstances. Others denounced the decision on principle, worrying that by permitting federal funding of research on cell lines that had been derived from the taking of embryonic human life, the imprimatur of the United States would be placed on the entire enterprise, making it almost impossible to prevent further encroachments by the Brave New World Order. That judgment will be tested in the attempt to outlaw human cloning.

It may well be more difficult to outlaw human cloning than it was to restrict federal funding of embryonic stem cell research. The earlier debate was essentially a struggle to win over the heart and mind of one man: President George W. Bush. But the president cannot settle the cloning dispute with the stroke of a pen on the signature line of an executive order. It will require legislation that the Republican House and the Democratic Senate can agree upon. That will be no easy task, considering the awesome lobbying and public relations power of the biotech industry, which is now fully engaged and determined to keep human cloning legal.

Still, opponents of human cloning would appear to have a strong hand. The American people are very squeamish about cloning. President Bush supports a ban, and he is a far more popular leader today than when he announced his stem cell decision. Moreover, the House of Representatives already passed a strong ban last year in a lopsided bipartisan vote.

But a formidable hurdle remains: the United States Senate. Majority Leader Tom 15 Daschle has prevented S 790, legislation virtually identical to that which passed the House, from coming to the floor of the Senate before this spring. But all signs are that the Human Cloning Prohibition Act of 2001 is in for a very bumpy ride. One indicator: The Senate recently refused to enact a six-month legal moratorium in the wake of ACT's cloning announcement.

And so the fight is on. If a ban on human cloning is to pass in the Senate, its supporters will have to surmount the following series of tactics by cloning enthusiasts.

- **The false distinction between "reproductive cloning" and "therapeutic cloning."** To keep human cloning legal, cloning advocates seek to distinguish between "reproductive cloning," which they are willing to prohibit, and so-called "therapeutic cloning," which they urge remain legal. According to this argument, reproductive cloning consists of implanting a cloned embryo into a willing woman's womb for the purposes of gestation and birth. Outlaw this activity to your heart's content, cloning proponents argue, because bringing a cloned embryo to term can't yet be safely accomplished. But don't prohibit the creation of human embryonic clones destined to be experimented upon, because to do so would unduly interfere with medical research.

  But the distinction is false. The act of cloning does not take place when a baby clone is born. It takes place when an egg, which has had its nucleus removed and replaced with genetic material of the individual to be cloned, is stimulated to begin embryonic growth. Once that process begins, a human clone exists.

  At this point, a clone that will be used in research is no different in kind or nature from one destined for implantation in a uterus. To put it another way, a clone is a clone is a clone. The only question remaining is the fate of the new cloned human life. Merely banning clones for use in reproduction would free biotech companies to make all of the human clones they desire, without limit—so long as they destroy them rather than bring them to birth.

- **The threat that medical breakthroughs will not happen without cloning.** 20 Only six months ago the country was most earnestly assured by supporters of embryonic stem cell research that all we need to achieve our miraculous medical future are the stem cells of doomed in vitro embryos. Now, some of these same advocates argue—and just as earnestly—that all we need to achieve our miraculous medical future are the stem cells taken from human clones.

What happened to limiting research to IVF embryos? It turns out there may be a hitch that could prevent stem cells harvested from normal human embryos from being used in future medical therapies: A patient's immune system could reject tissues grown from embryonic stem cells that are injected into the body in the same way the body strives to reject transplanted organs. But, the theory goes, if the stem cells were extracted from a clone of the patient, the body would not reject the treatment because the tissues would be virtually identical to the patient's.

Of course promoters of federal funding of embryonic stem cell research knew this during the earlier debate. They just didn't talk about it, realizing that if the American people suspected embryonic stem cell research would lead directly to human cloning, their cause might be lost. Now, with the stem cell debate behind them, it is as if the earlier assurances about limiting embryonic research never happened. This raises an important question: Why should Americans believe the new assurances that human clones will not be used for reproductive purposes, when the former promises about embryonic stem cell research were disingenuous?

It's also the case that the "promise" of research cloning is wildly speculative. Researchers don't even yet know whether they can maintain a human clone long enough to extract stem cells. (Cloning experiments on primates seem to indicate that maintaining a human clone may be exceedingly difficult.)

Nor do they know whether embryonic stem cell therapy itself will be able to cure diseases and overcome disabilities. In this regard, it is worth noting that the same level of enthusiasm existed about using tissues from aborted or miscarried fetuses a few years ago. Yet, that research has been generally disappointing and, in one experiment, devastating to the human subjects suffering from Parkinson's disease who were injected with such tissues.

- **Junk science, squared.** Pretending that in vitro embryos weren't really human life during the stem cell debate pales in comparison with the junk science being shoveled in the cloning debate. One argument is that clones aren't distinct human organisms but mere cells, akin to those that fall off your body when you scratch your nose. "To commit ourselves morally to protecting every living cell in the body would be insane," Ronald Green, the Dartmouth bioethicist and long-time promoter of destructive embryonic research, told *U.S. News and World Report*. (It wasn't by chance that ACT selected Green to be on its corporate ethics committee.) In the same article, Robert Lanza, ACT's medical director, made the equally ludicrous mirror-image argument that "all cells are embryonic" because now DNA can be extracted from any cell in the body for use in the construction of a clone. Pro-cloning propaganda thus asserts both that individual somatic cells are akin to embryos and that embryonic clones are nothing but mere (somatic) cells.

Each of these assertions is wrong. Somatic cells, such as those your toothbrush destroys during your morning brushing, are minute parts of the greater organized whole that is a human being. On the other hand, clones in the early stage of development are no different in kind or nature from normal embryos at the same stage of growth. Each is an individual, self-contained form of human life, with a specific genetic makeup and gender.

Nor are individual body cells any more "embryonic" than are ovum or sperm that have not joined in fertilization. Just because a cell has the potential to contribute to the creation of a new human life, that does not ipso facto transform the cell into the realization of the potential before it actually happens. Until that time, it is merely a cell, no more and no less.

Here is the biologically accurate truth about what would happen if I submitted to embryonic stem cell therapy derived through cloning:

- My DNA would be extracted from one of my somatic cells.

- The nucleus of an egg that had been purchased from an anonymous young woman by the biotech company holding the patent to my treatment modality would be removed.

- My DNA, consisting of 46 chromosomes, would be inserted into the area of the egg that formerly contained the nucleus.

- The genetically modified egg would then be stimulated to begin embryonic development.

- The resulting embryo would essentially be my identical twin brother. His biological parents would be my parents.

- When my twin brother reached about 14 days of embryonic development, he would be destroyed for his stem cells.

- These stem cells would then be coaxed into differentiating into the type of tissue I needed for my medical treatment.

- A line of these now differentiated cells would be maintained and nurtured until enough tissue existed to be injected into my body.

- My dead twin brother's tissues would then be injected into me, to treat my illness.

These are the facts that should be the subject of the cloning debate, not junk science and euphemistic pro-cloning propaganda that blurs vital distinctions and deconstructs precise scientific definitions.

- **The claim that viable alternatives do not exist.** Promoters of cloning/embryonic stem cell research either pooh-pooh the potential of an alternative source of stem cells or damn it with faint praise. But scientists who have been researching the medical uses of adult and alternative sources of stem cells have already made tremendous strides toward the development of effective stem cell therapies for a wide variety of illnesses and disabilities—without having to resort to embryonic sources. For example, Canadian researchers have discovered that stem cells in the bone marrow of adults can apparently repair organs without being rejected by the patient's immune system. These cells even appear to be safely transplantable between species. If this breakthrough pans out, the alleged need for cloning could utterly disappear.

  Meanwhile, the *Journal of the American Heart Association* recently published a study involving stem cells found in human umbilical cord blood. When the umbilical cord blood was injected into the tails of rats, within hours the cells migrated into the animals' brains and began repairing stroke damage. Even rats treated one week after a stroke demonstrated some improvement, according to the report. These are the scientific breakthroughs that promoters of cloning/embryonic stem cell research can only hope will begin to be achieved years from now.

30

The stakes could not be higher in the struggle to ban cloning. But proponents of a ban will not succeed without confronting the false distinctions, bad science, and misleading propaganda of cloning enthusiasts. When the Senate takes up the cloning debate later this year, we will confront the most fundamental of issues: Does individual human life have inherent value simply because it is human? If the answer is yes, then we will ban human cloning as an immoral objectification and unethical commodification of human life.

Fatalist Attraction

VIRGINIA I. POSTREL

An editor and columnist, Virginia Postrel has written extensively on technology issues for the *New York Times*, the *Washington Post*, *Wired*, *Forbes*, and the *Wall Street Journal*. She was the editor of *Reason* magazine from 1989 to 2000 and is currently editor-at-large for that publication. Her book *The Future and Its Enemies: The Growing Conflict over Creativity, Enterprise, and Progress* was published in 1998. The following article was published in *Reason* in July 1997.

Twenty years ago, the bookstore in which I was working closed for a few hours while   1
we all went to the funeral of one of our colleagues. Herbie was a delightful guy, well liked by everyone. He died in his 20s—a ripe old age back then for someone with cystic fibrosis. In keeping with the family's wishes, we all contributed money in his memory to support research on the disease. In those days, the best hope was that scientists would develop a prenatal test that would identify fetuses likely to have C.F., allowing them to be aborted. The thought made us uncomfortable. "Would you really want Herbie never to be?" said my boss.

But science has a way of surprising us. Two decades later, abortion is no longer the answer proposed for cystic fibrosis. Gene therapy—the kind of audacious high-tech tool that generates countless references to *Brave New World* and *Frankenstein*—promises not to stamp out future Herbies but to cure them.

This spring I thought of Herbie for the first time in years. It was amid the brouhaha over cloning, as bioethicists galore were popping up on TV to demand that scientists justify their unnatural activities and Pat Buchanan was declaring that "mankind's got to control science, not the other way around."

It wasn't the technophobic fulminations of the anti-cloning pundits that brought back Herbie's memory, however. It was a letter from my husband's college roommate and his wife. Their 16-month-old son had been diagnosed with cystic fibrosis. He was doing fine now, they wrote, and they were optimistic about the progress of research on the disease.

There are no Herbies on *Cross-fire*, and no babies with deadly diseases. There are   5
only nature and technology, science and society, "ethics" and ambition. Our public debate about biotechnology is loud and impassioned but, most of all, abstract. Cowed by an intellectual culture that treats progress as a myth, widespread choice as an indulgence, and science as the source of atom bombs, even biotech's defenders rarely state their case in stark, personal terms. Its opponents, meanwhile, act as though medical advances are an evil, thrust upon us by scheming scientists. Hence Buchanan talks of "science" as distinct from "mankind" and ubiquitous Boston University bioethicist George Annas declares, "I want to put the burden of proof on scientists to show us why society needs this before society permits them to go ahead and [do] it."

That isn't, however, how medical science works. True, there are research biologists studying life for its own sake. But the advances that get bioethicists exercised spring not from pure science but from consumer demand: "Society" may not ask for them, but individual people do.

Living in a center of medical research, I am always struck by the people who appear on the local news, having just undergone this or that unprecedented medical procedure. They are all so ordinary, so down-to-earth. They are almost always middle-class, traditional families, people with big medical problems that require unusual solutions. They are not the Faustian, hedonistic yuppies you'd imagine from the way the pundits talk.

And it is the ambitions of such ordinary people, with yearnings as old as humanity—for children, for health, for a long and healthy life for their loved ones—of which the experts so profoundly disapprove. As we race toward what Greg Benford aptly calls "the biological century," we will hear plenty of warnings that we should not play God or fool Mother Nature. We will hear the natural equated with the good, and fatalism lauded as maturity. That is a sentiment about which both green romantics and pious conservatives agree. And it deserves far more scrutiny than it usually gets.

"Nobody wants to stand around and point a finger at this woman [who had a baby at 63] and say, 'You're immoral.' But generalize the practice and ask yourself, What does it really mean that we won't accept the life cycle or life course?" Leon Kass, the neocons' favorite bioethicist, told *The New York Times*. "That's one of the big problems of the contemporary scene. You've got all kinds of people who make a living and support themselves but who psychologically are not grown up. We have a culture of functional immaturity."

It sounds so profound, so wise, to denounce "functional immaturity" and set one- 10
self up as a grown-up in a society of brats. But what exactly does it mean in this context? Kass can't possibly think that 63-year-olds will start flocking to fertility clinics—that was the quirky action of one determined woman. He is worried about something far more fundamental: our unwillingness to put up with whatever nature hands out, to accept our fates, to act our ages. "The good news," says Annas of human cloning, "is I think *finally we have a technology that we can all agree shouldn't be used.*" (Emphasis added.) Lots of biotech is bad, he implies, but it's so damned hard to get people to admit it.

When confronted with such sentiments, we should remember just what Mother Nature looks like unmodified. Few biotechnophobes are as honest as British philosopher John Gray, who in a 1993 appeal for greens and conservatives to unite, wrote of "macabre high-tech medicine involving organ transplantation" and urged that we treat death as "a friend to be welcomed." Suffering is the human condition, he suggested: We should just lie back and accept it. "For millennia," he said, "people have been born, have suffered pain and illness, and have died, without those occurrences being understood as treatable diseases."

Gray's historical perspective is quite correct. In the good old days, rich men did not need divorce to dump their first wives for trophies. Childbirth and disease did the trick. In traditional societies, divorce, abandonment, annulment, concubinage, and polygamy—not high-tech medicine—were the cures for infertility. Until the 20th century, C.F. didn't need a separate diagnosis, since it was just one cause of infant mortality among many. Insulin treatment for diabetes (highly unnatural) didn't exist until the 1920s. My own grandmother saw her father, brother, and youngest sister die before she was in middle age. In 1964 a rubella epidemic left a cohort of American newborns deaf.

These days, we in rich countries have the wonderful luxury of rejecting even relatively minor ailments, from menstrual cramps to migraines, as unnecessary and treatable. "People had always suffered from allergies. . . . But compared to the other health problems people faced before the middle of the twentieth century, the sneezing, itching, and skin eruptions had for the most part been looked at as a nuisance," writes biologist Edward Golub. "In the modern world, however, they became serious impediments to living a full life, and the discovery that a whole class of compounds called antihistamines could control the symptoms of allergy meant that allergic individuals could lead close to normal lives. The same story can be told for high blood pressure, depression, and a large number of chronic conditions."

Treating chronic conditions is, if anything, more nature-defiant than attacking infectious diseases. A woman doesn't have to have a baby when she's 63 to refuse to "accept the life cycle or life course." She can just take estrogen. And, sure enough, there is a steady drumbeat of criticism against such unnatural measures, as there is against such psychologically active drugs as Prozac. We should, say the critics, just take what nature gives us.

In large part, this attitude stems from a naive notion of health as the natural state of the body. In fact, disease and death are natural; the cures are artificial. And as we rocket toward the biological century, we will increasingly realize that a bodily state may not be a "disease," but just something we wish to change. Arceli Keh was not sick because her ovaries no longer generated eggs; she was simply past menopause. To say she should be able to defy her natural clock (while admitting that mid-60s parenthood may not be the world's greatest idea) doesn't mean declaring menopause a disease. Nor does taking estrogen, any more than taking birth control pills means fertility is a sickness.

"The cloned human would be an attack on the dignity and integrity of every single person on this earth," says German Research Minister Juergen Ruettgers, demanding a worldwide ban, lest such sub-humans pollute the planet. (The Germans want to outlaw even the cloning of human cells for medical research.) Human cloning is an issue, but it is not *the* issue in these debates. They are really about whether centralized powers will wrest hold of scientists' freedom of inquiry and patients' freedom to choose—whether one set of experts will decide what is natural and proper for all of us—and whether, in fact, nature should be our standard of value.

Ruettgers is wildly overreacting and, in the process, attacking the humanity of people yet unborn. As Ron Bailey has noted in these pages, human cloning is not that scary, unless you're afraid of identical twins, nor does it pose unprecedented ethical problems. No one has come up with a terribly plausible scenario of when human cloning might occur. Yet judging from the history of other medical technologies, the chances are good that if such a clone were created, the parents involved would be ordinary human beings with reasons both quite rare and extremely sympathetic. We should not let the arrogant likes of Ruettgers block their future hopes.

Growing More Food

COUNCIL FOR BIOTECHNOLOGY INFORMATION

The Council for Biotechnology Information was founded in 2000 by biotechnology companies and trade associations such as Dow AgroSciences, DuPont Biotechnology, and Monsanto in order to provide information about biotechnology and promote its acceptance. The following article was published on its web site in 2002.

The world's population more than doubled in the last half century and topped 6 billion in 1999.[1] Each year, it is adding about 73 million people—a population nearly the size of Vietnam's. By 2030, it is projected to reach around 8 billion, and nearly all of that increase is expected to occur in developing countries,[2] which are also expected to see higher incomes and rapid urbanization.

At the same time, the world's hungry and chronically malnourished remain at about 840 million people, despite global pledges and national efforts to improve food security.

These trends mean the world will have to double its food production and also improve food distribution over the next quarter century.[3] These pose staggering challenges for the world's farmers: Much of the world's land suitable for farming is already cultivated and natural resources are under pressure. Soil degradation is widespread, agriculture has already razed 20 to 30 percent of the world's forest areas[4] and water tables in many areas are falling. Agriculture consumes about 70 percent of the fresh water people use every year and, at the current consumption rate, two out of three people will live in water-stressed conditions by 2025.[5]

By 2050, some 4.2 billion people may not have their daily basic needs met.[6]

These projections and complex challenges facing the world's future food supply are 5 prompting international food and agricultural experts and policymakers—including the U.N. Food and Agriculture Organization and the World Health Organization— to call plant biotechnology a critical tool to help feed a growing population in the 21st century.

Governments need to develop policies to ensure greater investment in research and regulatory oversight that's needed to manage the health, environmental and socioeconomic issues associated with biotechnology, according to the Human Development Report 2001, an annual report commissioned by the U.N. Development Programme.[7]

Biotechnology: An Eco-Efficient Option

World crop productivity could increase by as much as 25 percent[8] through the use of biotechnology to grow plants that resist pests and diseases, tolerate harsh growing conditions and delay ripening to reduce spoilage, according to the Consultative Group on International Agricultural Research (CGIAR). All this could be achieved on existing farmland and customized to meet local needs.

Biotechnology also offers the possibility for scientists to design "farming systems that are responsive to local needs and reflect sustainability requirements," said Calestous Juma, director of the Science, Technology and Innovation Program at the Center for International Development and senior research associate at the Belfer Center for Science and International Affairs, both at Harvard University.[9]

Scientists are developing crops that resist diseases, pests, viruses, bacteria and fungi, all of which reduce global production by more than 35 percent at a cost estimated at more than $200 billion a year.[10] For instance, test fields in Kenya are growing sweet potato varieties that are resistant to a complex set of viruses that can wipe out three-fourths of Kenyan farmers' harvest.

In the United States, crops with built-in insect protection and that tolerate a 10 specific herbicide have helped farmers improve yields and reduce costs. In 2000, direct benefit to growers of insect resistant corn, cotton and potatoes exceeded $300 million, according to the Environmental Protection Agency.[11]

In a study to be released in 2002, the National Center for Food and Agricultural Policy quantified biotechnology's benefits for U.S. farmers through 44 case studies that covered 30 different crops, including papaya, citrus, soybeans and tomatoes. For instance, it found that herbicide tolerant soybeans helped farmers reduce their annual production costs by $15 an acre, which totals $735 million across 49 million acres. Virus-resistant papaya is credited with saving Hawaii's papaya industry, which produces 53 million pounds of the fruit valued at $17 million a year.[12]

Biotechnology: Getting the Most from Poor Growing Conditions

Scientists are developing crops that can tolerate extreme conditions, such as drought, flood and harsh soil. For instance, researchers are working on a rice that can survive long periods under water [13] as well as rice and corn that can tolerate aluminum in soil. [14]

A tomato plant has been developed to grow in salty water that is 50 times higher in salt content than conventional plants can tolerate and nearly half as salty as seawater. [15] About a third of the world's irrigated land has become useless to farmers because of high levels of accumulated salt.

Biotech crops "could significantly reduce malnutrition, which still affects more than 800 million people worldwide, and would be especially valuable for poor farmers working marginal lands in sub-Saharan Africa," the Human Development Report stated.

Technology in a Seed

While the Green Revolution kept mass starvation at bay and saw global cereal production double as a result of improved crop varieties, fertilizers, pesticides and irrigation, its benefits bypassed such regions as sub-Saharan Africa. The new hybrids needed irrigation and chemical inputs that farmers there couldn't afford.

In contrast, the benefits of biotechnology are passed on through a seed or plant cutting, so that farmers anywhere around the world can easily adopt the technology. That's why biotechnology is particularly attractive to scientists and rural development experts in poor countries where most of the people farm for a living.

Biotech crops are "tailor-made for Africa's farmers, because the new technology is packaged in the seed, which all farmers know how to handle," said Florence Wambugu, a Kenyan plant scientist who helped develop a virus-resistant sweet potato. [16]

Agreeing with Wambugu, the International Society of African Scientists issued a statement in October 2001 calling plant biotechnology a "major opportunity to enhance the production of food crops." [17]

NOTES

1. United Nations Population Fund (UNFPA), "Population Numbers and Trends," <www.unfpa.org/modules/briefkit/05.htm>.

2. International Food Policy Research Institute, "World Food Prospects: Critical Issues for the Early Twenty-First Century," October 1999, p. 9.

3. United Nations Population Fund (UNFPA), "State of World Population 2001 Report," November 7, 2001, <www.unfpa.org/swp/swpmain.htm>.

4. "New Study Reveals That Environmental Damage Threatens Future World Food Production," World Resources Institute, February 14, 2001, <www.wri.org/press/page_agroecosystems.html>.

5. Global Environment Outlook, 2000—UN Environment Programme, <www.unep.org/geo2000/>.

6. "State of World Population 2001 Report," United Nations Population Fund (UNFPA), November 7, 2001, <www.unfpa.org/swp/swpmain.htm>.

7. "The Human Development Report 2001," United Nations Development Programme, July 2001, <www.undp.org/>.

8. Prakash, C.S., (October 4, 2001). In a media presentation sponsored by the American Medical Association (AMA), cited Consultative Group on International Agricultural Research (CGIAR) as source. See <www.ama-assn.org> media briefings.

9. Calestous, Juma, director of the Science, Technology and Innovation Program at the Center for International Development and senior research associate at the Belfer Center for Science and International Affairs, "Appropriate Technology for Sustainable Food Security—Modern Biotechnology," both at Harvard University, *2020 Focus* 7, International Food Policy Research Institute (IFPRI). August 2001.

10. Krattiger, Anatole, "Food Biotechnology: Promising Havoc or Hope for the Poor?" Proteus, 2000.

11. "Bt Plant-Pesticides Biopesticides Registration Action Document—Executive Summary,"

United States Environmental Protection Agency, <www.epa.gov/pesticides/biopesticides/other docs/bt_brad2/1 overview.pdf>.

12. Gianessi, Leonard, (October 4, 2001). "The Potential for Biotechnology to Improve Crop Pest Management in the United States," In a media presentation sponsored by the American Medical Association (AMA). See <www.ncfap.org> and <www.ama-assn.org> media briefings.

13. "Food in the 21st Century: From Science to Sustainable Agriculture," CGIAR, p. 36, <www .worldbank.org/html/cgiar/publications/shah book/shahbook.pdf>.

14. Ibid.

15. Owens, Susan, "Genetic engineering may help to reclaim agricultural land lost due to salina-

tion," European Molecular Biology Organization (EMBO) Reports 2001, Vol. 2/No. 10, p. 877–879, <www.emboreports.oupjournals .org/cgi/content/full/2/10/877>.

16. "Biotech 'Tailor-Made' for Africa, Researcher Tells Tufts Conference" Council for Biotechnology Information, Washington, D.C., November 19, 2001 <index.asp?id=1156&redirect= con 1309mid17%2Ehtml>.

17. "Position Statement on Agricultural Biotechnology Applications in Africa and the Caribbean," International Society of African Scientists, <www.monsantoafrica.com/reports/ISAS/ ISAS.html>.

A Personal Note

JEREMY RIFKIN

The president of the Foundation on Economic Trends, Jeremy Rifkin has a degree in economics from the Wharton School of Finance and Commerce of the University of Pennsylvania and a degree in international affairs from the Fletcher School of Law and Diplomacy at Tufts University. He has written over fourteen books on science and technology and their impact on society, including *The Biotech Century: Harnessing the Gene and Remaking the World* (1998), and has appeared on a number of news programs, including *Nightline*, the *Today Show*, the *News Hour with Jim Lehrer*, and *Good Morning America*. He has also testified before Congress and been involved in litigation against the government. The following selection is the final chapter of *The Biotech Century*.

Over the past twenty years I've expressed growing concern about many aspects of the emerging biotech revolution, leading many in the scientific community, and in the general public, to ask if, in fact, I'm simply opposed to science and the introduction of new technologies. The question is not whether one is in favor or opposed to science and technology writ large, but rather, what kind of science and technology does one favor. I am reminded of the denunciation of critics by the Vatican at the dawn of the modern era. Any views that appeared to challenge the official Church orthodoxy were branded as ungodly and blasphemous, the clear message being there is only one way to believe in God.

The fact is, just as there are many ways to celebrate God, so too are there many ways to celebrate science. We have become so accustomed to thinking of science in strictly Baconian terms that we have lost sight of other approaches to harnessing the secrets of nature. . . . Bacon viewed nature as a "common harlot" and urged future generations to "tame," "squeeze," "mould," and "shape" her so that "man" could become her master and the undisputed sovereign of the physical world. Many of today's best-known molecular biologists are heirs to the Baconian tradition. They see the world in reductionist terms, and view their task as grand engineers, continually editing, recombining, and reprogramming the genetic components of life, to create more compliant, efficient, and useful organisms that can be put to the service of humankind. In their research, they often favor isolation over integration, detachment over engagement, and the exercise of applied force or penetration over stewardship and nurturance.

Others in the field of biology, although equally rigorous, exercise a more integrative, systemic approach to nature. The ecological sciences, which are gaining in stature and importance, view nature as a seamless web made of myriad symbiotic relationships and mutual dependencies, all embedded in larger biotic communities that together make up a single living organism—the biosphere. Ecologists favor more subtle forms of manipulation designed to enhance rather than overpower and sever existing relationships, always with an eye toward preserving ecological diversity and maintaining community bonds.

Each of these approaches to the biological sciences leads to very different kinds of practices. For example, in agriculture . . . molecular biologists are experimenting with new ways to insert genes into the biological code of food crops to make them more nutritious and more resistant to herbicides, pests, bacteria, and fungi. Their goal is to create a self-contained, safe haven, fortressed away from the large biotic community. Many ecological scientists, on the other hand, are using the new flow of genomic data to better understand the relationship between environmental influences and genetic mutations to advance the science of ecologically based agriculture. Their goal is to combine the wealth of new genetic information being collected with the knowledge being gained on how ecosystems function to establish a more integrative approach to agriculture—one that relies on integrated pest management, crop rotation, organic fertilization, and other sustainable methods designed to make agricultural production compatible with the ecosystem dynamics of the regions where the crops are being grown.

Similarly, in medicine . . . molecular biologists are fixing their attention on somatic 5 gene surgery, pumping altered genes into the patient to "correct" disorders and arrest the progress of disease. Their efforts are designed to cure people who have become ill. Other researchers, however, including a small but growing number of molecular biologists, are exploring the relationship between genetic mutations and environmental triggers with the hope of fashioning a more sophisticated, scientifically based understanding and approach to preventive health. More than 70 percent of all deaths in the United States and other industrialized countries are attributable to what physicians refer to as "diseases of affluence." Heart attacks, strokes, breast, colon and prostate cancer, and diabetes are among the most common diseases of affluence. While each individual has varying genetic susceptibilities to these diseases, environmental factors, including diet and lifestyle, are major contributing elements that can trigger genetic mutations. Heavy cigarette smoking, high levels of alcohol consumption, diets rich in animal fats, the use of pesticides and other poisonous chemicals, contaminated water and food, polluted air, and sedentary living habits have been shown, in study after study, to cause genetic mutations and lead to the onset of many of these high-profile diseases.

The Human Genome Project is providing researchers with vital new information on recessive gene traits and genetic predispositions for a range of illnesses. Still, little research has been done, to date, on how genetic predispositions interact with toxic materials in the environment, the metabolizing of different foods, and lifestyle to effect genetic mutations and phenotypical expression. The new holistic approach to human medicine views the individual genome as part of an embedded organismic structure, continually interacting with and being affected by the environment in which it unfolds. The effort is geared toward using increasingly sophisticated genetic and environmental information to prevent genetic mutations from occurring. (It needs to be noted, however, that a number of genetic diseases appear to be unpreventable and immune to environmental mediation.)

It might be asked, in the case of agriculture and medicine and any number of other fields, why both approaches to applied science can't live side by side, each complementing and augmenting the other. In reality, the commercial market favors the more reductionist approach for the obvious reason that for now, at least, that's where the money is to be made. While there is certainly a growing market for organic produce and preventive health practices, programs, and products, far more money is invested in biotech agriculture and "illness"-based medicine. That could change, but it would require a paradigm shift in the way we think about science and its applications, with awareness of and support for a science founded in systems thinking and sensitive to the twin notions of diversity and interdependence.

Each of the visions of science I've outlined are based on different sets of values, although I suspect that most molecular biologists continue to entertain the notion that their approach is unbiased, objective, value-free, and the only true science. Their remonstrances notwithstanding, what you see ultimately depends on what you're looking for. The search is always preconditioned by the biases of the researchers.

Of course, science goes hand in hand with technology. Here again, it is amazing how unexamined has been our approach to the new gene-spliced biotechnologies. The fatalistic attitude that if it can be done, it will be done, speaks volumes to our current understanding of and relationship to technology. We've come to view technological "advances" much the way we view the evolution of nature, as if each is fated and irrepressible, the implicit message being that to oppose their introduction is as ill-advised and futile as opposing nature's own steady advance. I know molecular biologists who sincerely believe that their ability to make changes in the genetic code of living things represents the inevitable next step in the evolutionary process and is as unstoppable as natural selection itself. For more than a century we have also labored under the preposterous but nonetheless deeply held belief that technologies are neutral and value-free. The very notion that technological innovations might be socially constructed projections of a particular world view, nurtured by market forces and made current by the prevailing social milieu, would be unthinkable to most scientists.

By vesting every new technology with neutrality and inevitability, the many special interests who have so much to gain from the speedy introduction and acceptance of their "inventions" free themselves of any responsibility for having to ponder the merit, wisdom, or appropriateness of their "contributions." Technologies, however, are not value-free, nor are they inevitable. The fact is, technologies are amplifications and extensions of our biological bodies, appendages we create out of the stuff of the Earth to help inflate ourselves so that we might more easily overcome spatial limitations, minimize temporal constraints, and better expropriate and consume the world around us. A bow and arrow is an extension of our throwing arm. Automobiles extend our legs and feet. Computers amplify our memory. Every tool we've ever created represents increments of power, a way to exercise an advantage over the forces of nature and each other. The exercise of that power is never neutral, for in the act of utilizing the power inherent in each new tool we fashion, someone or something in the environment is compromised, diminished, or exploited to enhance or secure our own well-being. The point is, power is never neutral. There are always winners and losers whenever power is applied.

The question, then, that should be asked of any new technology being readied for society is whether the power being exercised is appropriate or inordinate in scale or scope. Are there technologies whose inherent power is so immense and overshadowing that the unleashing of that power will result in greater diminution than enhancement and more harm than good? Does the technology ultimately drain rather than sustain the labyrinth of relationships that sustain our lives? Nuclear power is a good example of a technology whose inherent power is so utterly overwhelming and beyond

appropriate scale that it inflicts more harm than good. The ever-present danger of nuclear meltdowns and the long-term threat of accumulating radioactive wastes makes
any short-term market benefits pale in comparison. Nuclear power drains rather than
sustains the environment and, therefore, ought not be used as an energy source.

The splitting of the atom and the unraveling of the DNA double helix represent the
two premier scientific accomplishments of the twentieth century, the first a tour de
force of physics, the second of biology. Both, when applied in the form of new technologies, represent unparalleled potential power to alter both the physical and natural
worlds. In the case of nuclear technology, in the form of the bomb and nuclear energy,
some nations belatedly chose to reduce and even discontinue their production and use,
concluding that the risk in deployment, both to the environment and current and future generations, exceeded any potential benefits. Only two atomic bombs have been
dropped on human populations in more than a half century. Nuclear energy, once considered the greatest source of power ever developed, has been partly or largely abandoned in many countries for financial and environmental reasons. In both cases, it was
the public that forced the change in policy. Most of the physicists involved in the research as well as the industries that financed and profited from the development and
introduction of these two powerful nuclear technologies continue to champion their
development to this very day.

If the century just passing was the age of physics and nuclear technology its crown
jewel, then the century just coming into view will belong to biology and its premier
technology will be genetic engineering. It seems altogether reasonable then, on the
cusp of this new century, to ask the critical threshold question that ought to be asked
of any new technology revolution. Is the power inherent to the new genetic technologies an appropriate exercise of power? Does it preserve and enhance rather than desta-
bilize and deplete the biological diversity of the planet? Is it easily manageable or ultimately uncontrollable? Does it protect the options or narrow the opportunities for
future generations and the other creatures who travel with us? Does it promote respect
for life or diminish it? On balance, does it do more good than harm?

While it might seem highly improbable, even inconceivable, to most of the principal players in this new technology revolution that genetic engineering, with all of its
potential promise, might ultimately be partially rejected, we need remind ourselves
that just a generation ago, it would have been just as inconceivable to imagine the partial abandonment of nuclear energy which had for years been so enthusiastically embraced as the ultimate salvation for a society whose appetite for energy appeared nearly
insatiable. It is possible that society will accept some and reject other uses of genetic
engineering in the coming Biotech Century. For example, one could make a solid case
for genetic screening—with the appropriate safeguards in place—to better predict the
onslaught of disabling diseases, especially those that can be prevented with early treatment. The new gene-splicing technologies also open the door to a new generation of
life-saving pharmaceutical products. On the other hand, the use of gene therapy to
make corrective changes in the human germ line, affecting the options of future generations, is far more problematic, as is the effort to release large numbers of transgenic
organisms into the Earth's biosphere. Society may well say yes to some of the genetic
engineering options and no to others. After all, nuclear technology has been harnessed
effectively for uses other than creating energy and making bombs.

Even a rejection of some genetic engineering technologies does not mean that the   15
wealth of genomic and environmental information being collected couldn't be used in
other ways. While the twenty-first century will be the Age of Biology, the technological application of the knowledge we gain can take a variety of forms. To believe that

genetic engineering is the only way to apply our newfound knowledge of biology and the life sciences is limiting and keeps us from entertaining other options which might prove even more effective in addressing the needs and fulfilling the dreams of current and future generations.

It needs to be stressed that it's not a matter of saying yes or no to the use of technology itself and never has been—although many in the scientific establishment like to frame the issue this way, leaving the impression that if one is opposed to their particular technological vision, one is anti-technology. In this sense their position on technology mirrors their position on science, in both cases taking a fundamentalist view that there is only one "true path" to the future.

Rather, the question is what kind of biotechnologies will we choose in the coming Biotech Century? Will we use our new insights into the workings of plant and animal genomes to create genetically engineered "super crops" and transgenic animals, or new techniques for advancing ecological agriculture and more humane animal husbandry practices? Will we use the information we're collecting on the human genome to alter our genetic makeup or to pursue new sophisticated health prevention practices?

Human beings are tool makers by nature. We are continually rearranging and altering our environment to secure our well-being and enhance our prospects for a better way of life. We are also risk takers. How then, do we know which tools to use and what risks to take? Since it is impossible to be clairvoyant and know all of the potential ramifications and consequences that might accompany the many new technologies we might want to introduce, we should attempt to minimize regrets and keep open as many options as possible for those who come after us—including our fellow creatures. This means that when choosing among alternative technological applications, we are best served by taking the less radical, more conservative approach—the one least likely to create disruptions and externalities. "First, do no harm" is a well-established and long revered principle in medicine. The fact is, the more powerful a technology is at altering and transforming the natural world—that is, marshaling the environment for immediate, efficient, and short-term ends—the more likely it is to disrupt and undermine long-standing networks of relationships and create disequilibrium somewhere else in the surrounding milieu. Which of the two competing visions of biotechnology—genetic engineering or ecological practices and preventive health—is more radical and adventurous and most likely to cause disequilibrium and which is the more conservative approach and least likely to cause unanticipated harm down the line? The answer, I believe, is obvious.

We may decide, in the final analysis, to shift technological priorities altogether. Now, the genetic engineering technologies are the dominant mode of application of the new biological sciences. The more integrative and embedded technological applications, the ones more sensitive to ecosystem dynamics and interrelationships, remain marginal to the unfolding of the Biotech Century. However, it is not difficult to imagine a turnaround of sorts, in the years ahead, with the more ecological and sustainable biotechnologies taking precedence, and with some genetic engineering technologies being abandoned and others used in a limited fashion and only as options of last resort. For example, in those cases where prevention and holistic health practices are insufficient to ward off seriously debilitating or deadly genetic diseases, somatic gene surgery may be an appropriate remedy.

We should also consider the very real possibility that the new genetic engineering 20 technologies may not, in the final analysis, deliver on many of their promises. The reason I say this is because most molecular biologists, while they use the language of the new cosmological narrative, are still wed to the older, industrial frame of mind.

They continue to try to force living processes into linear contexts, believing it possible to manipulate development, gene by gene, as if an organism were merely an assemblage of the individual genes that make it up. This old-fashioned reductionist approach to biotechnology, with its emphasis on sequentiality and strict causality, is likely to meet with only limited success. The Biotech Century will ultimately belong to the systems thinkers, those who see biology more as "process" than "construction" and who view the gene, the organism, the ecosystem, and the biosphere as an integrated "super organism," with the health of each part dependent on the health and well-being of the whole system. That is why the genetic engineers might eventually lose their dominant position to the ecologists whose thinking is more in tune with a biosphere consciousness. If that were to happen, alternative biotechnologies might yet triumph over gene-splicing techniques in the Biotech Century.

Unfortunately, most of the discussion of the biotech revolution, thus far, has centered less on the weighty issues at hand, and more on the "claims" of the scientists conducting the research and the "motivations" of the critics challenging their work. The stereotyping on both sides of the debate has done little to advance the larger questions that need to be asked as we journey into the Biotech Century. My own sense is that most of the molecular biologists engaged in gene research are motivated as much by their desire to make a meaningful contribution to science and enhance the human condition as they are by dreams of financial rewards. Similarly, while most of the companies pursuing this new economic frontier are driven by the prospect of reaping commercial gain, I have talked to enough business leaders in the biotech industry to know that they too believe that their efforts will improve the lot of life for millions of people and make the world a better and more secure place for future generations.

The fact is, many of the new products and processes of the fledgling biotech revolution are of potential benefit. If they weren't, they wouldn't find a commercial market. Companies aren't in business to make products and provide services people don't want. And that's exactly the point. The issue is not simply the motivation of the scientists or the companies financing the research, but, rather, the motivation of the rest of us whose expectations, desires, attitudes, and biases set the cultural parameters for the kind of future we chart as a civilization.

Some will argue that it's not as simple as saying we get the future we want and expect. After all, most people have little control over the kind of research being pursued and even less ability to influence decisions made in corporate boardrooms over which kinds of products and services should be produced and marketed. Nor do most people have any effective way of countering or turning away from the barrage of mass media and advertising that are such pervasive forces in shaping societal values. All of this is true. Still, consumers create markets as much as markets create consumers. Despite the overwhelming pressure of these institutional forces, in the final analysis, I believe that each of us is responsible, in some way, for determining the collective future we share together as a species. To think otherwise would be to suggest that most of us are little more than passive observers of our own destinies, our fate always in someone else's hands. In some ways, it's easier to think that way, since it absolves each of us from having to take responsibility for the world we inherit, experience, and pass on.

The biotechnology revolution will affect each of us more directly, forcefully, and intimately than any other technology revolution in history. For that reason alone every human being has a direct and immediate stake in the direction biotechnology will take in the coming century. Until now, the debate over biotechnology has engaged a narrow group of molecular biologists, industry executives, government policy makers, and critics. With the new technologies flooding into the marketplace and into our lives, the moment has arrived for a much broader debate over the benefits and risks of the new science, one that extends beyond professional authorities and "experts" on both sides of the issue and includes the whole of society. The discussion will need to be as deep as it is broad. The biotech revolution raises fundamental questions about the nature of science, the kinds of new technologies we introduce into the marketplace, and the role of commerce in the intimate affairs of biology. . . .

Skeptics will say it's naive to believe that most people either care about or desire to 25 participate in "abstract" issues far removed from their day-to-day lives. Yet, the questions surrounding the new technologies are neither abstract nor remote. Quite the contrary, they are the most intimate and pressing ever to face humanity and are of concern to every human being living on Earth. This point came home to me recently on a visit to a medium-size city, Ribeirão Prêto, deep in the interior of Brazil. My hosts, none of whom were involved in the biotech revolution, told me that the news of the birth of Dolly, the cloned sheep, had come as a shock and became a topic of intense discussion and debate among local farmers and townspeople. Friends and neighbors wondered out loud in beer halls, at social gatherings, and around kitchen tables about the implications of this startling new development and sought to understand its potential benefits and risks and how it might affect both their lives and their children.

The biotech revolution will affect every aspect of our lives. The way we eat; the way we date and marry; the way we have our babies; the way our children are raised and educated; the way we work; the way we engage in politics; the way we express our faith; the way we perceive the world around us and our place in it—all of our individual and shared realities will be deeply touched by the new technologies of the Biotech Century. Surely, these very personal technologies deserve to be widely discussed and debated by the public at large before they become a part of our daily lives.

The biotech revolution will force each of us to put a mirror to our most deeply held values, making us ponder the ultimate question of the purpose and meaning of existence. This may turn out to be its most important contribution. The rest is up to us.

Remarks by the President on Stem Cell Research

GEORGE W. BUSH

George W. Bush is the forty-third president of the United States. He delivered the following address on television to a national audience in August 2001.

Good evening. I appreciate you giving me a few minutes of your time tonight so I can 1 discuss with you a complex and difficult issue, an issue that is one of the most profound of our time.

The issue of research involving stem cells derived from human embryos is increasingly the subject of a national debate and dinner table discussions. The issue is confronted every day in laboratories as scientists ponder the ethical ramifications of their work. It is agonized over by parents and many couples as they try to have children, or to save children already born.

The issue is debated within the church, with people of different faiths, even many of the same faith coming to different conclusions. Many people are finding that the more they know about stem cell research, the less certain they are about the right ethical and moral conclusions.

My administration must decide whether to allow federal funds, your tax dollars, to be used for scientific research on stem cells derived from human embryos. A large number of these embryos already exist. They are the product of a process called in vitro fertilization, which helps so many couples conceive children. When doctors match sperm and egg to create life outside the womb, they usually produce more embryos than are planted in the mother. Once a couple successfully has children, or if they are unsuccessful, the additional embryos remain frozen in laboratories.

Some will not survive during long storage; others are destroyed. A number have 5 been donated to science and used to create privately funded stem cell lines. And a few have been implanted in an adoptive mother and born, and are today healthy children.

Based on preliminary work that has been privately funded, scientists believe further research using stem cells offers great promise that could help improve the lives of those who suffer from many terrible diseases—from juvenile diabetes to Alzheimer's, from Parkinson's to spinal cord injuries. And while scientists admit they are not yet certain, they believe stem cells derived from embryos have unique potential.

You should also know that stem cells can be derived from sources other than embryos—from adult cells, from umbilical cords that are discarded after babies are born, from human placenta. And many scientists feel research on these types of stem cells is also promising. Many patients suffering from a range of diseases are already being helped with treatments developed from adult stem cells.

However, most scientists, at least today, believe that research on embryonic stem cells offers the most promise because these cells have the potential to develop in all of the tissues in the body.

Scientists further believe that rapid progress in this research will come only with federal funds. Federal dollars help attract the best and brightest scientists. They ensure new discoveries are widely shared at the largest number of research facilities and that the research is directed toward the greatest public good.

The United States has a long and proud record of leading the world toward ad- 10 vances in science and medicine that improve human life. And the United States has a long and proud record of upholding the highest standards of ethics as we expand the limits of science and knowledge. Research on embryonic stem cells raises profound ethical questions, because extracting the stem cell destroys the embryo, and thus destroys its potential for life. Like a snowflake, each of these embryos is unique, with the unique genetic potential of an individual human being.

As I thought through this issue, I kept returning to two fundamental questions: First, are these frozen embryos human life, and therefore, something precious to be protected? And second, if they're going to be destroyed anyway, shouldn't they be used for a greater good, for research that has the potential to save and improve other lives?

I've asked those questions and others of scientists, scholars, bioethicists, religious leaders, doctors, researchers, members of Congress, my Cabinet, and my friends. I have read heartfelt letters from many Americans. I have given this issue a great deal of thought, prayer and considerable reflection. And I have found widespread disagreement.

On the first issue, are these embryos human life—well, one researcher told me he believes this five-day-old cluster of cells is not an embryo, not yet an individual, but a pre-embryo. He argued that it has the potential for life, but it is not a life because it cannot develop on its own.

An ethicist dismissed that as a callous attempt at rationalization. Make no mistake, he told me, that cluster of cells is the same way you and I, and all the rest of us, started our lives. One goes with a heavy heart if we use these, he said, because we are dealing with the seeds of the next generation.

And to the other crucial question, if these are going to be destroyed anyway, why 15
not use them for good purpose—I also found different answers. Many argue these embryos are byproducts of a process that helps create life, and we should allow couples to donate them to science so they can be used for good purpose instead of wasting their potential. Others will argue there's no such thing as excess life, and the fact that a living being is going to die does not justify experimenting on it or exploiting it as a natural resource.

At its core, this issue forces us to confront fundamental questions about the beginnings of life and the ends of science. It lies at a difficult moral intersection, juxtaposing the need to protect life in all its phases with the prospect of saving and improving life in all its stages.

As the discoveries of modern science create tremendous hope, they also lay vast ethical mine fields. As the genius of science extends the horizons of what we can do, we increasingly confront complex questions about what we should do. We have arrived at that brave new world that seemed so distant in 1932, when Aldous Huxley wrote about human beings created in test tubes in what he called a "hatchery."

In recent weeks, we learned that scientists have created human embryos in test tubes solely to experiment on them. This is deeply troubling, and a warning sign that should prompt all of us to think through these issues very carefully.

Embryonic stem cell research is at the leading edge of a series of moral hazards. The initial stem cell researcher was at first reluctant to begin his research, fearing it might be used for human cloning. Scientists have already cloned a sheep. Researchers are telling us the next step could be to clone human beings to create individual designer stem cells, essentially to grow another you, to be available in case you need another heart or lung or liver.

I strongly oppose human cloning, as do most Americans. We recoil at the idea of 20
growing human beings for spare body parts, or creating life for our convenience. And while we must devote enormous energy to conquering disease, it is equally important that we pay attention to the moral concerns raised by the new frontier of human embryo stem cell research. Even the most noble ends do not justify any means.

My position on these issues is shaped by deeply held beliefs. I'm a strong supporter of science and technology, and believe they have the potential for incredible good—to improve lives, to save life, to conquer disease. Research offers hope that millions of our loved ones may be cured of a disease and rid of their suffering. I have friends whose children suffer from juvenile diabetes. Nancy Reagan has written me about President Reagan's struggle with Alzheimer's. My own family has confronted the tragedy of childhood leukemia. And, like all Americans, I have great hope for cures.

I also believe human life is a sacred gift from our Creator. I worry about a culture that devalues life, and believe as your President I have an important obligation to foster and encourage respect for life in America and throughout the world. And while we're all hopeful about the potential of this research, no one can be certain that the science will live up to the hope it has generated.

Eight years ago, scientists believed fetal tissue research offered great hope for cures and treatments—yet, the progress to date has not lived up to its initial expectations. Embryonic stem cell research offers both great promise and great peril. So I have decided we must proceed with great care.

As a result of private research, more than 60 genetically diverse stem cell lines already exist. They were created from embryos that have already been destroyed, and they have the ability to regenerate themselves indefinitely, creating ongoing opportunities for research. I have concluded that we should allow federal funds to be used for research on these existing stem cell lines, where the life and death decision has already been made.

Leading scientists tell me research on these 60 lines has great promise that could 25 lead to breakthrough therapies and cures. This allows us to explore the promise and potential of stem cell research without crossing a fundamental moral line, by providing taxpayer funding that would sanction or encourage further destruction of human embryos that have at least the potential for life.

I also believe that great scientific progress can be made through aggressive federal funding of research on umbilical cord placenta, adult and animal stem cells which do not involve the same moral dilemma. This year, your government will spend $250 million on this important research.

I will also name a President's council to monitor stem cell research, to recommend appropriate guidelines and regulations, and to consider all of the medical and ethical ramifications of biomedical innovation. This council will consist of leading scientists, doctors, ethicists, lawyers, theologians and others, and will be chaired by Dr. Leon Kass, a leading biomedical ethicist from the University of Chicago.

This council will keep us apprised of new developments and give our nation a forum to continue to discuss and evaluate these important issues. As we go forward, I hope we will always be guided by both intellect and heart, by both our capabilities and our conscience.

I have made this decision with great care, and I pray it is the right one.

Thank you for listening. Good night, and God bless America.   30

The Political Control of Biotechnology

FRANCIS FUKUYAMA

A member of the President's Council on Bioethics, Francis Fukuyama is dean of the faculty and the Bernard L. Schwartz Professor of International Political Economy at Johns Hopkins University. His bestselling book *The End of History and the Last Man* (1992) garnered a great deal of attention and won the *Los Angeles Times's* Book Critics Award in the category of current interest books. The following is a chapter from his book *Our Posthuman Future: Consequences of the Biotechnology Revolution*, which was published in 2002.

Some new technologies are frightening from the start and create an instant consensus 1 on the need to establish political controls over their development and use. When the first atomic bomb was detonated at Alamogordo, New Mexico, in the summer of 1945, not one of the witnesses to the event failed to understand that a terrible new potential for destruction had been created. Nuclear weapons were thus from the start ringed with political controls: individuals could not freely develop nuclear technology on their own or traffic in the parts necessary to create atomic bombs, and, in time, nations that became signatories to the 1968 nonproliferation treaty agreed to control international trade in nuclear technology.

Other new technologies appear to be much more benign, and consequently subject to little or no regulation. Personal computers and the Internet are examples: these new forms of information technology (IT) promised to create wealth, spread access to information and therefore power around more democratically, and foster community among their users. People had to look hard for downsides to the Information Revolution; what they have found to date are issues like the so-called digital divide (that is, inequality of access to IT) and threats to privacy, neither of which qualify as earth-shaking matters of justice or morality. Despite occasional efforts on the part of the world's more statist societies to try to control the use of IT, it has blossomed in recent years with minimal regulatory oversight on either a national or international level.

Biotechnology falls somewhere between these extremes. Transgenic crops and human genetic engineering make people far more uneasy than do personal computers and the Internet. But biotechnology also promises important benefits for human health and well-being. When presented with an advance like the ability to cure a child of cystic fibrosis or diabetes, people find it difficult to articulate reasons why their unease with the technology should stand in the way of progress. It is easiest to object to a new biotechnology if its development leads to a botched clinical trial or to a deadly allergic reaction to a genetically modified food. But the real threat of biotechnology is far more subtle, and therefore harder to weigh in any utilitarian calculus.

In the face of the challenge from a technology like this, where good and bad are intimately connected, it seems to me that there can be only one possible response: countries must regulate the development and use of technology politically, setting up institutions that will discriminate between those technological advances that promote human flourishing, and those that pose a threat to human dignity and well-being. These regulatory institutions must first be empowered to enforce these discriminations on a national level, and must ultimately extend their reach internationally.

The state of the debate on biotechnology is today polarized between two camps. 5 The first is libertarian, and argues that society should not and cannot put constraints on the development of new technology. This camp includes researchers and scientists who want to push back the frontiers of science, the biotech industry that stands to profit from unfettered technological advance, and, particularly in the United States and Britain, a large group that is ideologically committed to some combination of free markets, deregulation, and minimal government interference in technology.

The other camp is a heterogeneous group with moral concerns about biotechnology, consisting of those who have religious convictions, environmentalists with a belief in the sanctity of nature, opponents of new technology, and people on the Left who are worried about the possible return of eugenics. This group, which ranges from activists like Jeremy Rifkin to the Catholic Church, has proposed banning a wide array of new technologies, from in vitro fertilization and stem cell research to transgenic crops and human cloning.

The debate on biotechnology has to move beyond this polarization. Both approaches—a totally laissez-faire attitude toward biotech development, and the attempt to ban wide swaths of future technology—are misguided and unrealistic. Certain technologies, such as human cloning, deserve to be banned outright, for reasons both intrinsic and tactical. But for most other forms of biotechnology that we see emerging, a more nuanced regulatory approach will be needed. While everyone has been busy staking out ethical positions pro and con various technologies, almost no one has been looking concretely at what kinds of institutions would be needed to allow societies to control the pace and scope of technology development.

It has been a long time since anyone has proposed that what the world needs is more regulation. Regulation—and particularly international regulation—is not something that anyone should call for lightly. Before the Reagan-Thatcher revolutions of the 1980s, many sectors of the economies of North America, Europe, and Japan were vastly over-regulated, and many continue to be so today. Regulation brings with it many inefficiencies and even pathologies that are well understood. Research has shown, for example, how government regulators develop a self-interest in promoting their own power and position, even as they make claims to speak in the public interest.[1] Poorly thought out regulation can drive up the costs of doing business enormously, stifle innovation, and lead to the misallocation of resources as businesses seek to avoid burdensome rules. A great deal of innovative work has been done in the past generation on alternatives to formal state regulation—for example, the self-regulation of businesses, and more flexible models for rule generation and enforcement.

The inefficiency of any scheme of regulation is a fact of life. We can try to minimize it by designing institutions that seek to streamline the regulatory process and make it more responsive to changes in technology and social needs, but in the end there are certain types of social problems that can only be addressed through formal government control. Schemes for self-regulation tend to work best in situations in which an industry doesn't produce a lot of social costs (negative externalities, in economists' terminology), in which the issues tend to be technical and apolitical, and in which industry itself has strong incentives to police itself. This is true in international standards setting, coordination of airline traffic routes and payments, product testing, and bank settlements and was at one time true for food safety and medical experimentation.

But it is not true of present-day biotechnology, or of the kinds of biomedical technologies that are likely to appear in the future. While the community of research scientists has in the past done an admirable job in policing itself in such areas as human experimentation and the safety of recombinant DNA technology, there are now too many commercial interests chasing too much money for self-regulation to continue to work well into the future. Most biotechnology companies will simply not have the incentives to observe many of the fine ethical distinctions that need to be made, which means that governments necessarily have to step in to draw up and enforce rules for them.

Many people today believe that biotechnology should not and cannot, as a practical matter, be controlled. Both of these conclusions are wrong, as we will see.

Who Gets to Decide?

Who gets to decide whether we will control a new biotechnology, and with what authority?

During the debate in the U.S. Congress on bills to ban human cloning in 2001, Congressman Ted Strickland of Ohio insisted that we be guided strictly by the best available science, and that "We should not allow theology, philosophy, or politics to interfere with the decision we make on this issue."

There are many who would agree with this statement. Opinion polls in most countries show the public holding scientists in much higher regard than politicians, not to mention theologians or philosophers. Legislators, as we well know, like to posture, exaggerate, argue by anecdote, pound the table, and pander. They often speak and act out of ignorance and are at times heavily influenced by lobbyists and entrenched interests. Why should they, rather than the disinterested community of researchers, have final say on highly complex and technical issues like biotechnology? Efforts by politicians to limit what scientists do in their own domain evoke memories of the medieval Catholic Church branding Galileo a heretic for saying the earth revolves around the sun. Since the time of Francis Bacon, the pursuit of scientific research has been seen to carry its own legitimacy as an activity that automatically serves the broader interests of mankind.

This view is, unfortunately, not correct.

Science by itself cannot establish the ends to which it is put. Science can discover vaccines and cures for diseases, but it can also create infectious agents; it can uncover the physics of semiconductors but also the physics of the hydrogen bomb. Science qua science is indifferent to whether data are gathered under rules that scrupulously protect the interests of human research subjects. Data, after all, are data, and better data can often be obtained . . . by bending the rules or ignoring them altogether. A number of the Nazi doctors who injected concentration camp victims with infectious agents or tortured prisoners by freezing or burning them to death were in fact legitimate scientists who gathered real data that could potentially be put to good use.

It is only "theology, philosophy, or politics" that can establish the ends of science and the technology that science produces, and pronounce on whether those ends are good or bad. Scientists may help establish moral rules concerning their own conduct, but they do so not as scientists but as scientifically informed members of a broader political community. There are very many brilliant, dedicated, energetic, ethical, and thoughtful people within the community of research scientists and doctors working in the field of biomedicine. But their interests do not necessarily correspond to the public interest. Scientists are strongly driven by ambition, and often have pecuniary interests in a particular technology or medicine as well. Hence the question of what we do with biotechnology is a political issue that cannot be decided technocratically.

The answer to the question of who gets to decide on the legitimate and illegitimate uses of science is actually pretty simple, and has been established by several centuries of political theory and practice: it is the democratically constituted political community, acting chiefly through their elected representatives, that is sovereign in these matters and has the authority to control the pace and scope of technological development. While there are all sorts of problems with democratic institutions today, from special-interest lobbying to populist posturing, there is also no obviously better alternative set of institutions that can capture the will of the people in a fair and legitimate way. We can surely hope that politicians make decisions that are informed by a sophisticated understanding of science. History is full of cases where laws were made based on bad science, such as the eugenics legislation passed in the United States and Europe in the early twentieth century. But in the end, science itself is just a tool for achieving human ends; what the political community decides are appropriate ends are not ultimately scientific questions.

When we turn to the question of establishing a regulatory regime for human biotechnology, we face a rather different problem. The issue is not whether it should be scientists or politicians who make choices regarding scientific research, but whether what is best in terms of reproductive decisions should be decided by individual parents or the government. James Watson has argued that it should be individual mothers and not a group of male regulators:

> My principle here is pretty simple: just have most of the decisions made by
> women as opposed to men. They're the ones who bear children, and men, as
> you know, often sneak away from children that aren't healthy. We're going to
> have to feel more responsible for the next generation. I think women should be
> allowed to make the decisions, and as far as I'm concerned, keep these male
> doctor committees out of action.[2]

Counterposing the judgment of male bureaucrats against the concerns of loving mothers is a clever rhetorical strategy, but it is beside the point. Male judges, officers, and social workers (as well as a lot of female ones) already interfere in the lives of women all the time, telling them they can't neglect or abuse their children, that they have to send them to school rather than making them go out to earn money for the family, or that they can't give them drugs or arm them with weapons. The fact that most women will use their authority responsibly doesn't eliminate the need for rules, particularly when technology makes possible all sorts of highly unnatural reproductive possibilities (like cloning) whose ultimate consequences for children may not be healthy.

. . . [T]he automatic community of interest that is assumed to exist between parent 20 and child under natural forms of reproduction may not exist under the new ones. Some have argued that we can presume the consent of a yet-to-be-born child to be free of birth defects or of mental retardation. But can we presume the consent of a child to be a clone, or to be born the biological offspring of two women, or to be born with a non-human gene? Cloning in particular raises the prospect that the reproductive decision will suit the interests and convenience of the parent rather than those of the child, and in this case, the state has an obligation to intervene to protect the child.[3]

Can Technology Be Controlled?

Even if we decide that technology should legitimately be controlled, we face the problem of whether it can be. Indeed, one of the greatest obstacles to thinking about a regulatory scheme for human biotechnology is the widespread belief that technological advance cannot be regulated, and that all such efforts are self-defeating and doomed to failure.[4] This is asserted gleefully by enthusiasts of particular technologies and by those who hope to profit from them, and pessimistically by those who would like to slow down the spread of potentially harmful technologies. In the latter camp, particularly, there is a kind of defeatism as to the ability of politics to shape the future.

This belief has become particularly strong in recent years because of the advent of globalization and our recent experience with information technology. No sovereign nation-state, it is said, can regulate or ban any technological innovation, because the research and development will simply move to another jurisdiction. American efforts to control data encryption, for example, or French efforts to enforce a French-language policy on French Web sites, have simply hobbled technological development in these countries, as developers moved their operations to more favorable regulatory climates. The only way to control the spread of technology is to have international agreements on technology-restricting rules, which are extraordinarily difficult to negotiate and even harder to enforce. In the absence of such international agreements, any nation that chooses to regulate itself will simply give other nations a leg up.

This kind of pessimism about the inevitability of technological advance is wrong, and it could become a self-fulfilling prophecy if believed by too many people. For it is simply not the case that the speed and scope of technological development cannot be controlled. There are many dangerous or ethically controversial technologies that have been subject to effective political control, including nuclear weapons and nuclear power, ballistic missiles, biological and chemical warfare agents, replacement human body parts, neuropharmacological drugs, and the like, which cannot be freely developed or traded internationally. The international community has regulated human experimentation effectively for many years. More recently, the proliferation of genetically modified organisms (GMOs) in the food chain has been stopped dead in its tracks in Europe, with American farmers walking away from transgenic crops that they had only recently embraced. One can argue about the rightness of this decision on scientific grounds, but it proves that the march of biotechnology is not an unstoppable juggernaut.

Indeed, the common assumption that it is impossible to control pornography or political discussion on the Internet is wrong. It is not possible for a government to shut down every objectionable Web site around the world, but it is possible to raise the costs of accessing them for ordinary people who live in their jurisdictions.

The Chinese authorities, for instance, have used their political power effectively to force Internet companies like Yahoo! and MSN to restrict publication of unsympathetic stories on their Chinese-language Web sites by simply threatening to revoke their right to operate in China.

Skeptics will argue that none of these efforts to control technology has been suc- 25 cessful in the end. Despite the huge diplomatic effort that the West, and especially the United States, has put into non-proliferation, for example, India and Pakistan became the sixth and seventh powers to test nuclear devices openly in the 1990s. While nuclear power for energy generation was slowed down after Three Mile Island and Chernobyl, it is now back on the table because of rising fossil fuel costs and concerns over global warming. Ballistic missile proliferation and the development of weapons of mass destruction continue in places like Iraq and North Korea, while there is a large underground market in drugs, spare body parts, plutonium, and virtually any other illicit commodity one cares to name.

All of this is true enough: no regulatory regime is ever fully leak-proof, and if one selects a sufficiently long time frame, most technologies end up being developed eventually. But this misses the point of social regulation: no law is ever fully enforced. Every country makes murder a crime and attaches severe penalties to homicide, and yet murders nonetheless occur. The fact that they do has never been a reason for giving up on the law or on attempts to enforce it.

In the case of nuclear weapons, vigorous nonproliferation efforts on the part of the international community were in fact very successful in slowing down their spread and keeping them out of the hands of countries that might at different points in their histories have been tempted to use them. At the dawn of the nuclear era, in the late 1940s, experts routinely predicted that dozens of countries would possess nuclear weapons in a few years.[5] That only a handful have developed them, and that none of these weapons had been detonated in conflict by the end of the twentieth century, was a remarkable achievement. There are any number of countries that could have developed nuclear weapons but refrained from doing so. Brazil and Argentina, for example, harbored nuclear ambitions when they were both military dictatorships. The nonproliferation regime in which they were enmeshed, however, forced them to keep these programs secret and slowed their development; when both returned to democracy in the 1980s, the programs were shut down.[6]

Nuclear weapons are easier to control than biotechnology for two reasons. First, nuclear weapons development is very expensive and requires large, visible institutions, making their private development very unlikely. Second, the technology is so obviously dangerous that there was a rapid worldwide consensus on the need to control it. Biotechnology, by contrast, can be carried out in smaller, less lavishly funded labs, and there is no similar consensus on its downside risks.

On the other hand, biotechnology does not pose high enforcement hurdles the way nuclear weapons do. A single bomb in the hands of a terrorist group or rogue state like Iraq will pose significant dangers to the world's security. By contrast, an Iraq that can clone Saddam Hussein does not pose much of a threat, unappetizing as that prospect may be. The purpose of a law banning human cloning in the United States would not be undermined if some other countries in the world permitted it, or if Americans could travel abroad to have themselves cloned in such jurisdictions.

The argument that regulation cannot work in a globalized world unless it is inter- 30 national in scope is true enough, but to use this fact to build a case against national-level regulation is to put the cart before the horse. Regulation seldom starts at an international level: nation-states have to develop rules for their own societies before they can even begin to think about creating an international regulatory system.* This is particularly true in the case of a politically, economically, and culturally dominant country like the United States: other countries around the world will pay a great deal of attention to what the United States does in its domestic law. If an international consensus on the regulation of certain biotechnologies is ever to take shape, it is very difficult to see it coming about in the absence of American action at a national level.

In pointing to other cases where technology has been regulated with some success, I do not mean to underestimate the difficulty of creating a similar system for human biotechnology. The international biotech industry is highly competitive, and companies are constantly searching for the most favorable regulatory climate in which to do their work. Because Germany, with its traumatic history of eugenics, has been more restrictive of genetic research than many developed countries, most German pharmaceutical and biotech companies have moved their labs to Britain, the United States, and other less restrictive countries. In 2000, Britain legalized therapeutic or research cloning and will become a haven for this type of research should the United States join Germany, France, and a number of other countries that do not permit it. Singapore, Israel, and other countries have indicated an interest in pursuing research in stem cells and other niches if the United States continues to restrict its own efforts out of ethical concerns.

The realities of international competition do not mean, however, that the United States or any other country has to fatalistically jump into a technological arms race. We do not know at this point whether an international consensus on the banning or strict regulation of certain technologies, such as cloning and germ-line modification, will emerge, but there is absolutely no reason to rule out the possibility at this early stage in the game.

Take the issue of reproductive cloning—that is, the cloning of a human child. As of this writing (November 2001), twenty-four countries had banned reproductive cloning, including Germany, France, India, Japan, Argentina, Brazil, South Africa, and the United Kingdom. In 1998 the Council of Europe approved an Additional Protocol to its Convention on Human Rights and Dignity with Regard to Biomedicine, banning human reproductive cloning; the document was approved by twenty-four of the council's forty-three member states. The U.S. Congress was just one of a number of other legislatures deliberating on similar measures. The French and German governments have proposed that the United Nations enact a global reproductive cloning ban. Given that Dolly the sheep had been created only four years earlier, it is not surprising that it has taken time for politicians and the law to catch up with technology. But at the moment it appears that much of the world is heading toward a consensus on the illegitimacy of human reproductive cloning. It may be that in a few years, if some crackpot cult like the Raelians wants to clone a child, they will have to travel to North Korea or Iraq to do so.

What are the prospects for the emergence of an international consensus on biotech regulation? It is hard to say at this early point, but it is possible to make some observations about culture and politics with regard to this issue.

There is a continuum of views in the world today concerning the ethicality of certain types of biotechnology and particularly genetic manipulation. At the most

---

*There are some exceptions to this general rule, such as the case of new or transitional democracies that appeal to international rules on human rights to promote the observance of these rules in their own societies. This analogy is not appropriate in the case of rules for biotechnology, however. International conventions on human rights were established at the instigation of countries that observed these rights and had them codified in their legal systems already.

restrictive end of this continuum are Germany and other countries in continental Europe that, for historical reasons already mentioned, have been very reluctant to move too far down this road. Continental Europe has also been home to the world's strongest environmental movements, which as a whole have been quite hostile to biotechnology in its various forms.

At the other end of the spectrum are a number of countries in Asia, which for historical and cultural reasons have not been nearly as concerned with the ethical dimension of biotechnology. Much of Asia, for example, lacks religion per se as it is understood in the West—that is, as a system of revealed belief that originates from a transcendental deity. The dominant ethical system in China, Confucianism, lacks any concept of God; folk religions like Taoism and Shinto are animistic and invest both animals and inanimate objects with spiritual qualities; and Buddhism conflates human and natural creation into a single seamless cosmos. Asian traditions such as Buddhism, Taoism, and Shinto tend not to make as sharp an ethical distinction between mankind and the rest of natural creation as does Christianity. That these traditions perceive a continuity between human and nonhuman nature has allowed them to be, as Frans de Waal points out, more sympathetic to nonhuman animals.[7] But it also implies a somewhat lower degree of regard for the sanctity of human life. Consequently, practices such as abortion and infanticide (particularly female infanticide) have been widespread in many parts of Asia. The Chinese government has permitted practices abhorrent in the West, such as the harvesting of organs from executed prisoners, and passed a eugenics law as recently as 1995.

Between continental Europe and Asia on the continuum lie the English-speaking countries, Latin America, and other parts of the world. America and Britain never developed the phobia for genetic research that Germany and France did, and are by virtue of their liberal traditions more skeptical of state regulation. The United States in particular has always been addicted to technological innovation and, for a host of institutional and cultural reasons, is very good at producing it. The American fondness for technology has been strongly reinforced by the information technology revolution of the last two decades, which has convinced many Americans that technology inevitably promises to be individually liberating and personally enriching. Balanced against this is the strength of conservative religious groups in the United States—Protestant, Catholic, and, increasingly, Muslim—that have up to now acted as brakes on uncontrolled technological advance.

Britain has always been closer to America, with its liberal traditions, than to Germany, but it has paradoxically been home to one of the strongest environmental protest movements opposed to GMOs and agricultural biotechnology. There are probably no deep cultural reasons for this; British skepticism about GMOs is more likely traced to the massive regulatory failure represented by mad cow disease, a failure that has left Britain with the largest population of victims to date of the human form of bovine spongiform encephalopathy (BSE), Creutzfeldt-Jacob disease. BSE has nothing to do with biotechnology, of course, but it did reasonably raise doubts in people's minds about the credibility of governments that pronounce on the safety of food products. A generation ago, Americans were much more concerned with threats to the environment and eager to regulate them, based on their recent experiences with Love Canal and other environmental disasters.

If there is any region of the world that is likely to opt out of an emerging consensus on the regulation of biotechnology, it is Asia. A number of Asian countries either are not democracies or lack strong domestic constituencies opposed to certain types of biotechnology on moral grounds. Asian countries like Singapore and South Korea have the research infrastructure to compete in biomedicine, and strong economic incentives to gain market share in biotechnology at the expense of Europe and North America. In the future, biotechnology may become an important fracture line in world politics.

An international consensus on the control of new biomedical technologies will not simply spring into being without a great deal of work on the part of the international community and the leading countries within it. There is no magic bullet for creating such a consensus. It will require the traditional tools of diplomacy: rhetoric, persuasion, negotiation, economic and political leverage. But in this respect the problem is not different from the creation of any other international regime, whether in air traffic, telecommunications, nuclear or ballistic missile proliferation, and the like.

The international governance of human biotechnology does not inevitably mean the creation of a new international organization, expanding the United Nations, or setting up an unaccountable bureaucracy. At the simplest level it can come about through the effort of nation-states to harmonize their regulatory policies. For members of the European Union (EU), this harmonization will presumably already have occurred at a European level.

Take, for example, the international regime governing pharmaceuticals. Every industrialized country has a science-based regulatory agency comparable to the American Food and Drug Administration to oversee the safety and effectiveness of drugs. In Britain it is the Medicines Control Agency, in Japan the Pharmaceutical Affairs Council, in Germany the Bundesinstitut für Arzneimittel und Medizinprodukte, and in France the Agence Française du Médicament. The European Community has sought to harmonize the drug-approval process of its member states since 1965 to avoid the duplication and waste involved in filing multiple applications in different national jurisdictions. This led to the establishment in London in 1995 of the European Medicines Evaluation Agency, which was supposed to provide one-stop drug approval shopping at a European level.[8] At the same time, the European Commission convened a multilateral meeting to broaden harmonization beyond Europe (called the International Conference on Harmonization). Although some Americans have criticized this as an effort by Eurocrats to extend their reach to the United States, it remains a voluntary regime that has received strong support from the pharmaceutical industry because it could lead to substantial increases in efficiency.[9]

NOTES

1. The self-interestedness of public officials is the starting premise of the Public Choice school. See James M. Buchanan and Gordon Tullock, *The Calculus of Consent: Logical Foundations of Constitutional Democracy* (Ann Arbor, Mich.: University of Michigan Press, 1962); and Jack High and Clayton A. Coppin, *The Politics of Purity: Harvey Washington Wiley and the Origins of Federal Food Policy* (Ann Arbor, Mich.: University of Michigan Press, 1999).

2. Quoted in Gregory Stock and John Campbell, eds., *Engineering the Human Germline: An Exploration of the Science and Ethics of Altering the Genes We Pass to Our Children* (New York: Oxford University Press, 2000), p. 78.

3. For a general theory of where the state can legitimately intervene in family matters, see Gary S.

Becker, "The Family and the State," *Journal of Law and Economics* 31 (1988): 1–18. Becker argues that the state needs to intervene only in cases where the interests of children are not adequately represented, which would seem to be the case with cloning.

4. I myself have been guilty of this kind of thinking. See Francis Fukuyama, Caroline Wagner, et al., *Information and Biological Revolutions: Global Governance Challenges—A Summary of a Study Group* (Santa Monica, Calif.: Rand MR-1139-DARPA, 1999).

5. See, for example, P. M. S. Blackett, *Fear, War, and the Bomb* (New York: McGraw-Hill, 1948).

6. Etel Solingen, "The Political Economy of Nuclear Restraint," *International Security* 19 (1994): 126–169.

7. Frans de Waal, *The Ape and the Sushi Master* (New York: Basic Books, 2001), p. 116.

8. Drugs can also be approved at the nation-state level, and across jurisdictions, under a mutual-recognition procedure.

9. Bryan L. Walser, "Shared Technical Decision-making and the Disaggregation of Sovereignty," *Tulane Law Review* 72 (1998): 1597–1697.

QUESTIONS FOR DISCUSSION

1. **Making Connections:** Both Rifkin and Fukuyama question the ability of scientists to regulate or make decisions about the direction of cloning research. What is the basis of their doubt? Do you agree? How does this particular issue raise the general question of the right of experts versus the public to make decisions on issues involving technology?

2. **Analyzing Strategy:** Definitions are critical in these arguments addressed to different audiences on different aspects of biotechnology. How consistent are the definitions of the following key terms in the different readings: *clone; human clone; embryonic stem cell; recombinant DNA.* Do you see a difference in how these terms and other synonyms are used depending on the position of the writer?

3. **Making Connections:** Why do spokespersons from different sides of the political spectrum (Rifkin the liberal and Smith the conservative) agree in their skepticism about biotechnology in general and human cloning in particular?

4. **Making Connections:** How would you assess (or measure) the state of public knowledge on biotechnology as it is applied to agriculture or to medicine or to other areas? You might do an informal survey of your friends, asking them if they can define some of the key terms or issues. How could the public become better informed? What sources should nonexpert readers trust on these issues?

5. **Analyzing Strategy:** Which authors use appeals to pathos, particularly to their audience's fears, hopes, prejudices, or other emotionally charged beliefs? Do any of these appeals seem inappropriate given the issue and audience?

6. **Analyzing Strategy:** Select one of the readings and discuss the underlying warrants it appeals to on issues like progress, government responsibility, religious beliefs, individual rights.

7. **Analyzing Strategy:** Why does the phrase "brave new world" appear in several of these readings? Where does this phrase come from? What are the possible persuasive effects of using it?

8. **Making Connections:** Why is the issue of human cloning treated differently from the application of biotechnology in other areas?

9. **Analyzing Strategy:** Why do opponents of human cloning use the term "eugenics" and recall this movement from the early twentieth century?

10. **Analyzing Strategy:** Characterize President Bush's position on stem cell research, as laid out in his speech in August 2001. What is the predominant line of argument in this speech?

11. **Analyzing Strategy:** The reading supporting the application of biotechnology comes from the "Council for Biotechnology Information," a group supported by the biotech industry. Rikfin, an outspoken critic of biotechnology,

is supported by his own think tank with the generic title, "The Foundation on Economic Trends." How should readers consider these sources? Is an argument "invalidated" because the source is not neutral?

WRITING SUGGESTIONS

1. Write an argument based on ethical principles alone for or against the application of biotechnology in a specific area such as (a) genetically modified crops, (b) pollution abatement, (c) a genetic disease such as cystic fibrosis, or (d) human reproduction.

2. Write an argument for your own reasoned position on the involvement of religious principles in the debate on issues of scientific research.

3. Identify one of the readings in this section, or another on this issue that you have found, whose position you agree with for the most part. Despite this agreement, criticize any weaknesses you find in the way the argument is made, and suggest better arguments.

4. If you find that your position on the application of biotechnology to agriculture or medicine or reproduction has changed in the course of your reading, write a personal account of the process by which your position changed and the reasons for the change. What was the appeal that affected you the most?

The Challenge of Dealing with Juvenile Crime

Chapter 14

The Killer Narcissists

BARBARA LERNER

A writer and a psychologist, Barbara Lerner lives in Chicago. She has published articles in the *National Review,* including the following essay, which appeared in May 1999.

The questions won't go away. The recent shooting spree—the eighth in two years— 1
forces us to face them again. Why all these wanton killings by schoolboys, this senseless spiral of schoolhouse slaughter? Who are these kids? Why are they doing it? What
can we do? In the '90s, most parents look to psychology for answers, but psychology
doesn't have one set—it has two: pre-'60s answers and post-'60s answers. And they
conflict.

Every sensate American knows the post-'60s answers. You hear them from all the
talking heads. Not just establishment experts, but mainstream teachers, preachers,
politicians, and journalists. All subscribe to the conventional wisdom of the '90s: Kids
who kill are in great distress, they've been neglected, rejected, and abused, their self-
esteem is low, they are crying out for help. They need more love and understanding,
more communication and parental attention, more early intervention, professional
counseling, and anger-management training. And the reason we have more of these
kids today is that we have more absent parents, more media violence, more guns.

Will the Colorado killers fit this profile? Were they the abused offspring of harsh,
uncaring parents and a cold, indifferent community, desperately unhappy beings with
nowhere to turn for help? It doesn't look like it. Eric Harris and Dylan Klebold both
came from intact middle-class families variously described by neighbors as "solid,"
"sensitive," and "utterly normal," and both had already been through the therapeutic
mill. Each boy had gotten individual counseling; each got anger-management training
as well. Both finished their therapy in February, two months before the crime, and
both got glowing reports from their counselors.

Maybe, when all the facts are known, Harris and Klebold will turn out to be a lot
more like Kip Kinkel, the 15-year-old Oregon shooter who vanished from the news as
soon as his life story began to emerge because it didn't fit the profile at all. Kinkel was
a problem for the conventional wisdom because he had it all, everything '90s experts

recommend. His parents were popular teachers, one of them was always there for him when he came home from school, and both did their best to make him happy, spending time with him, taking him on family vacations, helping him get whatever he wanted, even when the things he wanted unnerved them. They made few demands, rejected firm discipline as too harsh, and sought professional help, early and often. They were in counseling, along with Kip, when, in May 1998, he shot them both dead, killed two of his many school friends, and wounded 22 others.

Looking at cases like this, psychologists in the 1950s and earlier had a set of answers   5 you don't hear much anymore. Here's an updated sample: We have more wanton schoolboy killers today because we have more narcissists, and the step from being a narcissist to being a wanton killer is a short one, especially in adolescence. A narcissist is a person who never progressed beyond the self-love of infancy, one who learned superficial social skills—narcissists are often charming—but never learned to love another and, through love, to view others as separate persons with an equal value. To the narcissist, other people have no intrinsic worth; their value is purely instrumental. They are useful when they satisfy his desires and enhance his self-esteem, disposable as bottle caps when they don't.

Only the narcissist matters, and because his sense of self-importance is so grossly inflated, his feelings are easily hurt. When they do get hurt—when others thwart him or fail to give him the excessive, unearned respect he demands—he reacts with rage and seeks revenge, the more dramatic the better. Take guns away from kids like these, and many won't settle for knives and baseball bats: They'll turn to deadlier weapons—to explosives, as that overgrown schoolboy, Ted Kaczynski did, or to environmental poisons, as the young subway saboteurs of Japan did. Kip was on his way— police found five bombs at his house. And the Colorado killers upped the ante: They made more than 30 bombs and used shrapnel as well as bullets to blow away their victims.

Will more counseling and anger-management classes help? At best, they are palliatives, in cases like these. They can put a patch over the hole at the core of these kids, the moral void, but they cannot fill the hole. No brand of psychology can, and earlier brands—Freud's especially—had the humility to recognize that. He saw the hole for what it is, a moral hole that only moral training can fill. Not just calm, rational, smiley-face, didactic lessons, but the kind of intense, gut-level experiences children have when their parents draw a sharp moral line and demonstrate a willingness to go all out to defend it.

Through experiences like these, normal children learn that the parental love they could take for granted as infants and toddlers can no longer be taken for granted. That love is no longer unconditional; it can be withdrawn. And to avoid that frightening outcome, the child learns to see his parents as more than human piñatas, full of goodies he has only to bang away at to get. He learns to see them as moral beings with standards and values that are more important than his own immature wishes, and he begins to internalize those standards and values, making them his own, and developing a conscience.

Many '90s experts don't understand this process. They focus only on self-esteem, not on esteem for others, and they obsess about the methods parents use to teach their kids, ignoring the content, the moral lessons they are trying to teach, insisting that any physical punishment, however infrequently and judiciously applied, is child abuse. These experts have no real solutions to offer, when the problem is overindulgence rather than abuse, as it now so often is. They are part of the problem. And the sooner we recognize that, the better.

Violence by Young People: Why the Deadly Nexus?

ALFRED BLUMSTEIN

Alfred Blumstein is the director of the National Consortium on Violence Research as well as the J. Erik Jonsson University Professor of Urban Systems and Operations Research at Carnegie Mellon University and the former dean of the H. John Heinz III School of Public Policy and Management there. The following article first appeared in the August 1995 issue of the *National Institute of Justice Journal*.

Despite evidence that aggregate rates of crime have been leveling off or even declining in the past two decades,[1] there continues to be widespread concern about the issue on the part of policymakers and the public. Indeed, among all issues, crime may be the one perceived by Americans as most pressing.[2] When aggregate crime data are broken down by certain demographic and other variables, however, the otherwise flat trend shows major distinctions, indicating that the concern is understandable. Although gender and race account for much of the differences in crime rates, age is the variable whose effect has been changing significantly in recent years. And while many of the national trends have remained strikingly flat, there has been some dramatic change in violent crime committed by young people.

The Rise in Juvenile Crime

Data gathered from a variety of sources indicate that after a period of relative stability in the rates of juvenile crime, there was a major turning point in about 1985. Then, within the next seven years, the rate of homicides committed by young people, the number of homicides they committed with guns, and the arrest rate of nonwhite juveniles for drug offenses all doubled. The sudden upward surge in all three of these indicators, beginning with the increased drug trafficking of the mid-1980's, is the topic of this article.

Particularly relevant to future crime, and to consideration of prevention and intervention strategies, is the size of the current teenage population. The age cohort responsible for much of the recent youth violence is the smallest it has been in recent years. By contrast, the cohort of children ages 5 to 15, who will be moving into the crime-prone ages in the near future, is larger. This suggests that if current age-specific rates do not decline, planning needs to begin now to address the increase in crime likely to occur as this group grows older.

The Age Factor

That young people commit crime at a high rate is no revelation. Age is so fundamental to crime rates that its relationship to offending is usually designated as the "age-crime curve." This curve, which for individuals typically peaks in the late teen years, highlights the tendency for crime to be committed during an offender's younger years and to decline as age advances.

For example, figures on rates of robbery and burglary, broken down by age, indicate that for both these crimes, the peak age of offending has been about 17, after which there is a rapid decline as the offender gets older. For burglary, the rate falls to half the peak by age 21, whereas the falloff for robbery is somewhat slower, reaching half the peak rate by age 25. The age-specific patterns are about the same for the most recent year data are available (1992) as they were in 1985.

Young people and murder. The age-specific patterns for murder present quite a different pattern; the trends for this crime have changed appreciably in the past

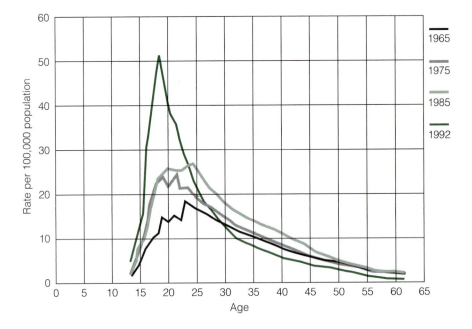

FIGURE 1   Age-Specific Murder Rate: 1965–1992. (Source: *Age-Specific Arrest Rates and Race-Specific Arrest Rates for Selected Offenses, 1965–1992,* Uniform Crime Reporting Program, Federal Bureau of Investigation, Washington, D.C.: December 1993.)

decade. First, the peak is much flatter. For a fairly long period—1965 to 1985—the age at which the murder rate was highest remained fairly stable, with a flat peak covering ages 18 to 24. In other words, during this 20-year period, people in this age group were the most likely to commit murder, and it was in the age group of the mid-30's that the rate dropped to half the peak. Then, in 1985, an abrupt change began to take place, with the murder rate moving to a sharp peak at age 18 instead of the more traditional flat peak covering the entire 18-to-24 age group. (See figure 1.)

The change over time in the age-specific murder rate is striking, especially for the peak ages 18 to 24. (See figure 2.) Following an initial increase from 1965 to 1970, the rate remained stable (and about the same for all ages in this group) for about 15 years—from 1970 through 1985. Among people at the older end of this age spectrum—the 24-year-olds—there has been no strong trend since 1970. But beginning shortly around 1985, murder by people under 24 increased, with the rate of increase inversely related to age. For people age 18, the increase was dramatic—it more than doubled.

For people at all ages under age 18, the increase was equally dramatic—it too more than doubled. For 16-year-olds, for example, whose murder rate before 1985 was consistently about half that of the 18-to-24 peak rate, the increase between 1985 and 1992 was 138 percent. By contrast, for ages older than 24, there has been no growth, and even a decline for ages 30 and above.

"Excess" murders committed by young people. The increase in murder by very young people after 1985 has not at all been matched by increases among the older groups (ages 24 and over). Among them murder rates have even declined. Thus, much

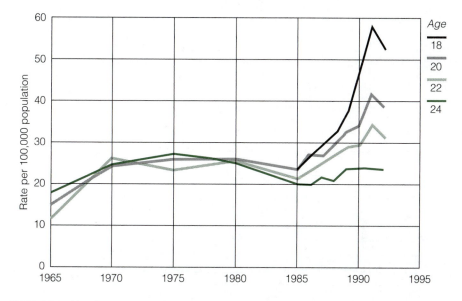

FIGURE 2   Trends in Age-Specific Murder Rate: Trends for Individual Peak Ages. (Source: *Age-Specific Arrest Rates and Race-Specific Arrest Rates for Selected Offenses, 1965–1992.* Uniform Crime Reporting Program, Federal Bureau of Investigation, Washington, D.C.: December 1993.)

of the general increase in the aggregate homicide rate (accounting for all ages) in the late 1980's is attributable to the spurt in the murder rate by young people that began in 1985.

One can calculate the "excess" murders attributable to the rise in murder by young people over and above the average rate that prevailed for each of the young ages in the period 1970–85. In other words, this figure represents the number of murders that would not have been committed had the youth murder rate remained at its earlier, flat average. For the eight ages, 15 through 22, in the 7 years of 1986 through 1992, the number of "excess" murders is estimated to be 18,600. The number is a significant component of the overall number for that period; it accounts for 12.1 percent of the annual average of about 22,000 murders in those years.

Race

There are important race differences in involvement in murder, both in the rate itself and the change since 1985. Among African-American males ages 14 to 17, murder rates have been about four to five times higher than among white males of the same age group, although for both groups the rates had remained fairly stable from the mid-1970's until the mid-1980's. (See figure 3.) Then, beginning about 1985, the rates rose for both groups, though the growth rate was much faster among blacks. For white males in this age group, their annual rate for murder was 8.1 per 100,000 in the period 1976 to 1987, after which it almost doubled in the next four years (from 7.6 in 1987 to 13.6 in 1991). In those four years, the arrest rate for murder by black males in this age group rose even faster, more than doubling (from 50.4 to 111.8 per 100,000).

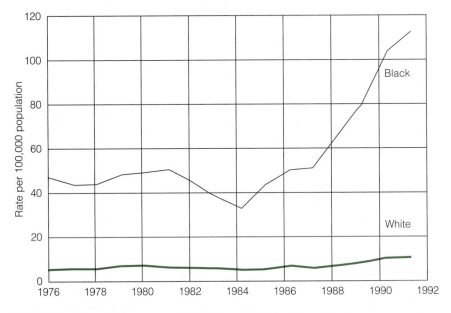

FIGURE 3 Homicide Arrest Rate of 14–17-Year-Old Males. (Source: The data were generated by Glenn Pierce and James Fox from the FBI's Supplementary Homicide Reports, which are based on reports of individual homicides submitted by the nation's police departments.)

Factors Generating Fear

Strangers. Persistent fear of crime is not caused by reviewing the aggregate rate of homicide and noting the absence of a trend. Rather, distinctive incidents or changing patterns of crime stimulate the anxiety levels. In particular, because young people are generally perceived to be more reckless than their elders, the growth in youth homicide conveys a sense that their killing is random. This is confirmed by the greater extent to which homicide by the young is committed against strangers. When victims seem to be selected at random, vulnerability is heightened: anyone can be a target. For example, the FBI's Supplementary Homicide Report for 1991 noted that 28 percent of the homicides committed by people under 25 were against strangers, whereas only 18 percent of those committed by offenders age 25 and above were against strangers.

Guns. Also intensifying the fear of crime is the increasing involvement of guns in homicides committed by young people. This factor generates fear because of the recognition that young people are less likely to exercise the restraint necessary to handle dangerous weapons, particularly rapid-fire assault weapons. Data on the use of weapons in homicide reflect the same patterns described above: after a period of stability came an abrupt increase in the mid-1980's. Thus, from 1976 to 1985, a very steady average (59 percent) of homicides committed by juveniles involved a gun. Beginning in 1985, there was steady growth in the use of guns by juveniles in committing murder, leading to a doubling in the number of juvenile murders committed with guns, with no shift in the number of non-gun homicides. (See figure 4.)

Juvenile Violence and the Drug-Crime Connection

The public also has a vague sense of a link between the growth in juvenile violence and drugs. In part, this derives from recognition that, especially in the past decade, a major factor affecting many aspects of criminal behavior has been the illicit drug industry and

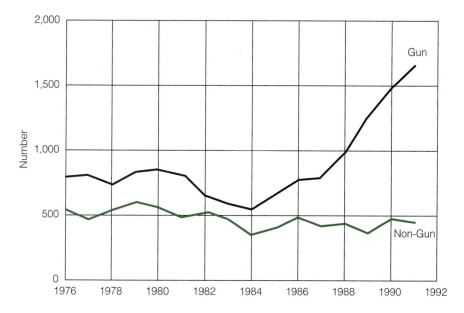

FIGURE 4 Number of Gun and Non-Gun Homicides: Juvenile Offenders. (ages 10–17) (Source: The data were generated by Glenn Pierce and James Fox from the FBI's Supplementary Homicide Reports, which are based on reports of individual homicides submitted by the nation's police departments.)

its consequences. Beyond the offenses of drug sale or drug possession, the drug-crime link has been described as taking several forms:

- Pharmacologically/psychologically driven crime, induced by the properties of the drug. (The most widely recognized connection is between alcohol and the violence it induces.)
- Economic/compulsive crimes, committed by drug users to support their habit.
- Systemic crime, which includes the crimes committed as part of the regular means of doing business in the illicit drug industry. (An example is the violence used to resolve disputes between competing traffickers.)[3]

There is a fourth, still broader connection of drugs to crime: the community dis- 15 organization effect of the illicit drug industry and its operations in the larger community. This effect includes the manner by which the norms and behaviors of the industry, which can become a significant activity in some communities, influence the behavior of people who themselves have no direct connection to drug trafficking. The effect could, for example, include the influence on others of the widespread possession of guns by drug sellers. When guns are so prevalent, people in the community might arm themselves, perhaps for self-defense, perhaps to settle disputes that have nothing to do with drugs, or perhaps just to gain respect. In other words, once guns are used within the illicit drug market, they become more prevalent in the larger community, and used for purposes unrelated to buying and selling drugs. Hence, they add to community disorganization well beyond what happens as a direct result of the drug industry.

Juveniles and illicit drug marketing. Drug arrest rates, especially for nonwhites, began to move upward in the early 1980's, and then accelerated appreciably after 1985

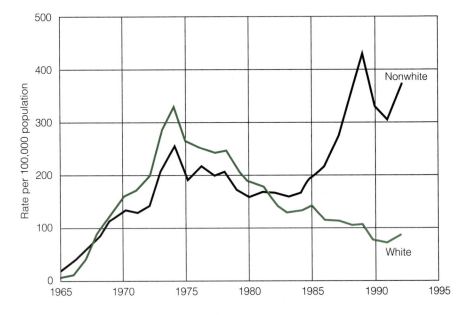

FIGURE 5   Drug Arrest Rate—Juveniles. (Source: *Age-Specific Arrest Rates and Race-Specific Arrest Rates for Selected Offenses, 1965–1992*, Uniform Crime Reporting Program, Federal Bureau of Investigation, Washington, D.C.: December 1993.)

as the distribution of crack cocaine became widespread, particularly in inner-city areas. Among nonwhite juveniles, drug arrest rates were lower than those of whites in the 1970's, and were also fairly constant, until they began a very rapid acceleration until about 1985, doubling by 1989. This pattern contrasted with that of the 1960's and 1970's, when the rate at which young whites were arrested for drug-related offenses followed the pattern of whites, but stayed somewhat low. The arrest rate of whites then peaked in 1974 and then began a steady decline. (See figure 5.)

The acceleration in drug arrests of young nonwhites (primarily blacks) reflected a major recruitment of sellers to market crack, which required many more street transactions. The racial differences in arrest rates indicate the extent to which drug enforcement has focused on blacks more than on whites. The black-white difference is magnified also because black drug sellers tend much more often to operate in the street, where they are vulnerable to arrest, whereas white sellers are much more likely to operate indoors. The amenability of inner-city nonwhite juveniles to recruitment into the illicit drug industry was undoubtedly enhanced by their pessimism—or perhaps even hopelessness—as they weighed the diminishing opportunities available to them in the legitimate economy.

A Proposed Hypothesis

This striking array of changes in juvenile crime since 1985—a doubling of the homicide rate, a doubling of the number of homicides committed with guns, and a doubling of the arrest rate of nonwhites for drug offenses, all after a period of relative stability in these rates—cries out for an explanation that will link them all together. The explanation that seems most reasonable can be traced to the rapid growth of the crack markets in the mid-1980's. To service that growth, juveniles were recruited, they were armed with the guns that are standard tools of the drug trade, and these guns then were diffused into the larger community of juveniles.

Recruitment. The process starts with the illicit drug industry, which recruits juveniles partly because they work more cheaply than adults, partly because the sanctions they face are less severe than those imposed by the adult criminal justice system, and partly because they tend to be daring and willing to take risks that more mature adults would eschew. The plight of many urban black juveniles, many of whom see no other comparably satisfactory route to economic sustenance, makes them particularly vulnerable to the lure of the profits of the drug industry. The growth in the drug arrest rate of nonwhite juveniles is evidence of this recruitment.

Guns as a means of self-protection. These juvenile recruits, like all participants 20 in the illicit drug industry, are very likely to carry guns for self-protection, largely because in that industry guns are a major instrument for dispute resolution as well as self-defense. People involved in the drug industry are likely to be carrying a considerable amount of valuable product—money or drugs—and are not likely to be able to call on the police if they are robbed.

The diffusion of guns. Since a considerable number of juveniles can be involved in the drug industry in communities where the drug market is active, and since juveniles are tightly "networked," at school or on the street, other juveniles are also likely to arm themselves. Again, the reason is a mixture of self-protection and status-seeking. Thus begins an escalation: as more guns appear in the community, the incentive for any single individual to arm himself increases, and so a local "arms race" develops.

The violent outcome. The recklessness and bravado that often characterize teenage behavior, combined with their lack of skill in settling disputes other than through physical force, transform what once would have been fist fights with outcomes no more serious than a bloody nose into shootings with much more lethal consequences because guns are present. This sequence can be exacerbated by the socialization problems associated with extreme poverty, the high proportion of single-parent households, educational failures, and the pervasive sense of hopelessness about one's economic situation.

It does appear, however, that by the time these young people move beyond their early twenties, they develop a measure of prudence. It may be that the diffusion process is far slower because adults are less tightly networked and less prone to emulate each other's behavior. Even within the drug industry, they appear to act more cautiously when they are armed, and to otherwise display greater restraint. However, there is some concern that the restraint that normally comes with age may not materialize in this particular age group. It is possible that a cohort effect may be occurring, with the possibility that the 18-year-olds currently responsible for the higher homicide rates may continue their recklessness as they get older. This possibility needs to be monitored and explored.

Evidence of the diffusion. The possibility that guns are diffused from drug markets to the larger community through juvenile recruits is further confirmed by the pattern of white and nonwhite arrests for murder. Since 1980, the murder arrest rates for adults, both white and nonwhite, have followed the same downward trend, and have shown no growth since 1985. (See figure 6.) By contrast, among juveniles the murder arrest rates for whites and nonwhites have grown markedly between 1985 and 1992. The increase among nonwhite juveniles was 123 percent (from 7.1 to 15.8 per 100,000). Among white juveniles the murder arrest rate also increased markedly, although by a lesser amount—80 percent (from 1.5 to 2.7 per 100,000). (See figure 7.)

What is notable in these figures is that the murder rate rose among white as well as 25 nonwhite juveniles since 1985, at a time when the drug arrest rate for nonwhites alone

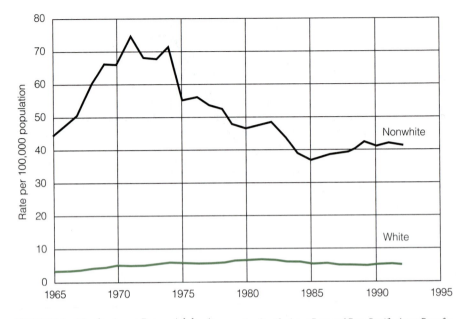

FIGURE 6   Murder Arrest Rate—Adults. (Source: *Age-Specific Arrest Rates and Race-Specific Arrest Rates for Selected Offenses, 1965–1992*, Uniform Crime Reporting Program, Federal Bureau of Investigation, Washington, D.C.: December 1993.)

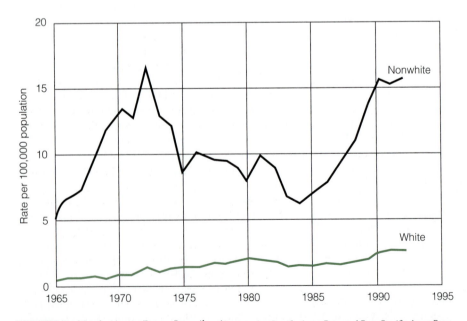

FIGURE 7   Murder Arrest Rate—Juveniles. (Source: *Age-Specific Arrest Rates and Race-Specific Arrest Rates for Selected Offenses, 1965–1992*, Uniform Crime Reporting Program, Federal Bureau of Investigation, Washington, D.C.: December 1993.)

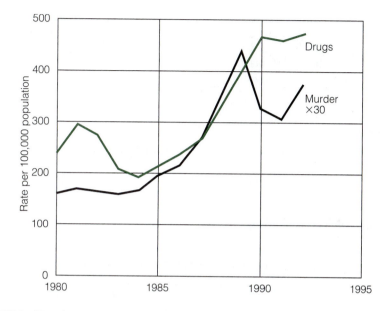

FIGURE 8　Nonwhite Juvenile Murder/Drug Arrest Rates. (Source: *Age-Specific Arrest Rates and Race-Specific Arrest Rates for Selected Offenses, 1965–1992,* Uniform Crime Reporting Program, Federal Bureau of Investigation, Washington, D.C.: December 1993.)

began to climb. Thus, the apparent absence of significant involvement of white juveniles in the drug markets during this time (figure 5) has not insulated them from the growth of their involvement in homicide, possibly through the suggested process of the diffusion of guns from drug sellers into the larger community.

When the arrest trends of young nonwhites for homicide and drug offenses are compared (figure 8), it is evident that both rates climbed together from 1985 through 1989, suggesting the relationship between the two. The drug arrest rate declined somewhat after 1989. There was a flattening out, but no corresponding decline in the murder arrest rate. In other words, the continued high rate of murder arrests seems to demonstrate that once guns are diffused into the community, they are much more difficult to purge.

Reversing the Trends

If the explanation outlined above is at all valid, it implies the need for solutions, some immediate and others longer range. One immediate approach would involve aggressive steps to confiscate guns from juveniles carrying them on the street. Laws permitting confiscation of guns from juveniles are almost universal, but they require more active and skillful enforcement. The need is particularly urgent in communities where homicide rates have risen dramatically, probably co-incident with the appearance of drug markets. James Q. Wilson has made some concrete proposals for pursuing such efforts, including better devices for detecting guns from a distance.[4]

Also, in contrast to the intense pursuit of drug markets by law enforcement over the past 15 years, very little attention has been paid to the illegal gun markets through which guns are distributed to juveniles. This issue clearly needs much greater attention. More complex in its implications for policy are the links among the magnitude of the criminal drug market, the use of guns in drug markets, and the juvenile homicide rate—the subject of this discussion. The presence of guns in drug markets results from the fact that these markets are criminalized. This does not, of course, warrant an immediate call for legalization of drugs. Any policy in the broad spectrum between full prohibition and full legalization involves carefully weighing the costs of criminalization (of which homicide is but one) against the probable consequences of greater use of dangerous drugs. The complexity of this issue prohibits its discussion here. However, if the diffusion hypothesis is correct, the impact on juvenile homicide represents one component of the cost of the current policy.

To the extent that efforts to diminish the size of the illegal drug market could be pursued (through greater investment in treatment, more effective prevention, or other health care initiatives responsive to addicts' needs), then although illegal markets would continue, the demand for drugs and the volume of drugs sold in the markets would diminish. A cost-benefit comparison of current policies and possible alternatives is needed but has yet to be made. Perhaps concern about the recent rise in the juvenile homicide rate might lend urgency to the issue.[5]

NOTES

1. *Criminal Victimization in the United States: 1973–92 Trends—A National Crime Victimization Survey Report*, Washington, D.C.: U.S. Department of Justice, Bureau of Justice Statistics, July 1994:1. In the period 1973–92, the highest rate of violent victimization was 35.3 per 1,000 persons, reported in 1981. That number fell until 1986, then started to climb, reaching 32.1 in 1992 (pp. 1, 9). National Crime Victim Survey data do reveal a 5.6 percent increase between 1992 and 1993 in victimization for violent crime, principally because of a rise in attempted (as opposed to completed) assaults. "Crime Rate Essentially Unchanged Last Year," press release, U.S. Department of Justice, Bureau of Justice Statistics, October 30, 1994. Homicide rates show a flat trend similar to that for violent victimization (homicide figures are not included in the victimization survey). The homicide rate per 100,000 people was 9.5 in 1993, but the historical high occurred in 1980, when the rate was 10.2. *Crime in the United States, 1993: Uniform Crime Reports*, Washington, D.C.: U.S. Department of Justice, Federal Bureau of Investigation, December 4, 1994: 13, 283.

2. A New York Times/CBS nationwide poll reported early in 1994 indicated crime or violence as the leading issue (cited by 19 percent of respondents), followed by health care—the subject of considerable public discussion at the time—with 15 percent. See Richard L. Berke, "Crime Joins Economic Issues as Leading Worry, Poll Says," *New York Times*, January 23, 1994.

3. This taxonomy of the drug-crime connection was developed by Paul Goldstein in "The Drug/Violence Nexus: A Tripartite Conceptual Framework," *Journal of Drug Issues* 15 (1985):493–506.

4. James Q. Wilson, "Just Take the Guns Away," *New York Times*, March 20, 1994. NIJ is now sponsoring research to aid in detecting concealed weapons. See page 35 of this Journal.

5. In my presidential address to the American Society of Criminology in November 1992, I suggested proposing establishment of a Presidential Commission to examine the costs and benefits of our current zero-tolerance policy and to contrast that with various possible alternatives. Such an assessment would require major research support from the National Academy of Sciences. (See Alfred Blumstein, "Making Rationality Relevant," *Criminology* 30: 1–16.)

They Do What They See

JOHN R. LION AND JONAS R. RAPPEPORT

John R. Lion is on the faculty of the University of Maryland School of Medicine in Baltimore, where he is a clinical professor of psychiatry. Jonas R. Rappeport is a retired psychiatrist and is a former chief medical officer for the Circuit Court of Baltimore. The following article appeared in the *Washington Post* in September 1999.

Protecting schools from violence is more than a matter of installing metal detectors and hiring additional security guards. School authorities, law enforcement agencies and journalists covering the issue need to grapple with another question, too: Might not the immense publicity given to troubled youths who kill or wound classmates—and perpetrators of other kinds of mass violence—actually spawn further attacks?

We think the answer is clearly yes. After two disturbed teenagers killed 12 other students, a teacher and themselves in Littleton, Colo., in April, young people across the country who showed signs of potential copycat behavior were brought to hospitals for psychiatric evaluation. Approximately a dozen such youngsters, all but one of them boys and ranging from elementary school age to the late teens, were admitted during the ensuing months to Sheppard Pratt Hospital in Baltimore, where one of us consults. These were children and adolescents who had come to the attention of authorities when they made public threats to bomb a school or talked openly about killing acquaintances who had wronged them. Several had constructed "hit lists." In most cases, they were first reported to the police, then taken to a local emergency room and brought from there, either by police or their parents, to Sheppard Pratt.

Within certain of these patients, the boundary between good and bad was thin, but even more gauze-like was the separation between hurting and playing, between toy pistols and real guns, between cartoon annihilations and real explosions. We speculate that there exists a population of fantasy dwellers who contemplate revenge for past wrongs. Some are children, but many are children in full-grown bodies, and age would appear to make a difference only insofar as the procurement of artillery is concerned.

Further, the more they are exposed to images of wounding and killing, the more legitimacy their violent broodings are given. For those struggling with urges to harm or kill, saturation coverage of violent events—especially on television—becomes a disinhibitor, like alcohol.

We are not talking about robberies or drug trafficking or family violence; ordinarily, people who become involved in these crimes are not affected by the media. The group we describe—and these can be adults prone to erupt in the workplace, as well as kids nursing fantasies of violent attacks in a school—are isolated beings who are already immersed in media images and infected by their immediacy and glamour. These folks can interpret those images as a personal signal to act on their impulses in any setting.

The contagiousness of violence and threats of violence are well known in other settings. When we interviewed police and fire officials concerning the handling of bomb threats, for example, we found that they already knew that certain behaviors follow the rules of infection. If firefighters follow their standard practice of emptying out a school, there will typically be further bomb threats made by those who seek the thrill of forcing an evacuation. In cases where there is no evacuation, because authorities have enough evidence to be satisfied that there is no bomb, there are likely to be fewer copycat threats. Similarly, Federal Aviation Administration officials told us that airlines deal with bomb threats very quietly, on the theory that giving publicity to one threat will bring on more. The Secret Service never reveals threats against public officials for much the same reason.

We learned back in the '60s that riots feed heavily off media attention, and most responsible journalists in that era eventually developed less inflammatory ways of reporting riot stories. In the '80s, when hostage situations were frequently encountered in domestic quarrels or failed robberies, hostage takers were often given the microphones they demanded until negotiators realized that this encouraged more hostage taking, not less.

It is not an exact parallel, but history does offer an example of how a change in news coverage successfully combated a different group of copycat predators.

In the mid-1980s, we were retained by the Grocery Manufacturers of America to study the phenomenon of individuals who engaged in product tampering. Beginning with the poisoning deaths of seven people in the Chicago area when someone laced Tylenol pills with cyanide in 1982—a crime that has never been solved—product tampering became first a sensational news story and then a national problem as a wave of actual or threatened poisonings hit other over-the-counter medications and foodstuffs.

Tamper-proof packaging was not yet in general use, and when callers used food or drug manufacturers' toll-free phone lines claiming to have poisoned a product, or saying that they had found glass shards, metal splinters or some other dangerous material in food or medicine, the manufacturer usually had no choice but to remove the product from certain stores, unless the call could be traced and proven to be a prank. Even a bogus tampering claim could be financially disastrous. 10

It did not take long for all involved to realize that tamperings and threats came in waves, and appeared to be driven by coverage in the news media. Intense media attention gave a great sense of power to the person who had tampered with a product or phoned in a threat and could then turn on the television and see pictures of store shelves being emptied.

As the dynamic became more evident and a consensus grew that restraint was needed, local media generally cooperated. National media responded more slowly but eventually came around. Some journalists publicly bristled at the notion of censorship while privately acknowledging the reasonableness of restraint.

Slowly, tampering stories drifted to inside pages and the epidemic ended, only to reappear a few years later in England. In 1990, a spate of tainting threats occurred in London. The British tabloids leapt on the story. Tampering episodes made bold front-page headlines: "POISON CHOCS ALERT," or (referring to a popular snack food) "GLASS IN QUAVERS."

The British Food and Drink Federation implored tabloid editors to play down the story. At one meeting we attended, a major European meat producer was on the verge of tears as he begged for less sensational coverage of alleged tampering with chicken, which threatened to wipe out his company. The tabloids resisted, raising the traditional arguments about the public's right to know, but in the end, as U.S. media had done, they toned down their coverage and the crisis subsided.

One of the recurring requests put to us was to pin down a profile of the tamperer or those making false threats. Who were these people? Where did they hide? Were tamperers simply extortionists seeking money from large companies? Was this a quest for a bizarre fame? What kind of discontents drove a person to derive gratification from placing metal filings inside a package of crackers? 15

There were few answers; indeed, few threateners were caught, let alone psychiatrically examined. Nearly a decade later, similar questions could be asked about youngsters who might be harboring fantasies of killing teachers or bombing classrooms.

The young people who came in for evaluation at Sheppard Pratt after the Littleton bloodbath provided some clues. While diagnoses varied, the patients as a group were angry, helpless and socially immature. Assessing which of them might be truly dangerous was difficult because the nurturing milieu of the hospital typically softened their resentments, but some remained overtly full of rage and were hence seen as greater risks. Others came from (and would return to) chaotic households where domestic violence or emotional trauma could easily cause a child to fall back into anger and violent fantasies. Evaluating these youngsters always left a lingering doubt about what they might have done if a school principal had not seen a hit list, or if a parent had not happened to overhear a homicidal threat.

Most of the threats made by these patients seemed quite obviously to have been unleashed by the publicity surrounding Littleton and the school shootings that preceded it. Some youths seemed not only susceptible to media stories but enchanted by them; a crime that might make a healthy person wince they embraced as empowering.

The potential for media-inspired contagion of school violence is significant enough that editors and news directors need to reconsider how the subject should be covered, and how they can adequately inform their audience about one tragedy without provoking another one somewhere else.

Stories about bomb threats belong on the inside pages of newspapers, if they are 20 published at all. Ideally, bomb scares in a school, particularly repeated threats, should be kept out of the media entirely—not to keep the news from parents, who should be informed by other means, but to deny the perpetrator the thrill of seeing his exploit capture a headline or broadcast time. Those who commit sensational acts of violence should be profiled on inside pages, not given inverted glory by being trumpeted in headlines. If possible, some coverage should show individuals in jail after being convicted of similar crimes.

The breathless sound bites and highly dramatized visual teasers that local television stations use to promote their broadcasts should be eliminated in favor of calm, factual reporting. Particularly pernicious is the tendency of broadcasters to keep replaying tapes of previous acts of violence, thus conveying to the potential copycat a sense of the destructive power and attention he might command.

Visual imagery is, we think, particularly captivating for immature persons. Interviews with experts and commentators and other ancillary reporting should be done without incessantly replaying video scenes of the carnage. Generally speaking, the less graphic the television exposure of the results of violence, the better. The public can be adequately informed without so many shots of bloodstains, casualties on stretchers being rushed from a shooting scene, destroyed furniture or buildings, or other images that only serve to heighten drama rather than provide information.

We recognize that when children are wounded or killed in a school, or when lives are lost in any other violent outbreak, it's more newsworthy than, say, a telephone threat claiming to have tampered with some brand of headache pills. School shootings will be covered, and should be. But in view of the media's clear capacity to spread the contagion of violence, is it so unreasonable to ask for some restraint, some willingness to forgo maximum dramatic effect in reporting the event? This is not incompatible with either the freedoms or the responsibilities of journalists covering these tragic stories.

The start of another school year brought with it another set of images to think about: scenes of children filing past security guards or through metal detectors, or SWAT teams and emergency rescue squads rushing onto campuses in simulated shooting crises, rehearsing for the real outbreaks that, the scene suggests, probably lie ahead. Doesn't this all convey a terribly wrong message of violent expectations?

Some sense of responsibility must eclipse the armed-camp vision that is thrust be- 25 fore us. Weapons screening may become an American way of life, but equipping schools as if in preparation for war—and advertising that war—will only bring out the disturbed souls who are lurking in the shadows nearby.

Preventing School Violence: No Easy Answers

LYNNE LAMBERG

A medical journalist and the author of six books, Lynne Lamberg is a frequent contributor to the *Journal of the American Medical Association*, where the following article first appeared in August 1998.

Psychiatrists and other mental health professionals know how to identify and treat young people at risk for violent behavior, and they have a good handle on primary prevention of violence, too, presentations at the annual meeting of the American Psychiatric Association (APA) in Toronto, Ontario, in June and interviews afterward suggest. Implementing this knowledge is the tough part: that takes money, a network of support services, and physicians and others committed to voluntary service in their communities.

Last year, the National Institutes of Health budgeted only $10 million for research in childhood violence, said Harold Eist, MD, a psychiatrist practicing in Washington, D.C. and immediate past president of the APA. "This is a minuscule amount of money for this issue," Eist said in an interview. "It's as if Congress doesn't want to admit the seriousness of the problem."

"Violence is the leading public health problem in America," Eist asserted, "and we're doing virtually nothing about it."

Whence the Escalation?

The bruises, black eyes, and bloody noses of playground clashes a generation or so ago now prompt nostalgia. In the 1997–1998 school year, children as young as 11 years old have gunned down classmates and teachers in mass shootings at schools in Pearl, Mississippi, West Paducah, Kentucky, Jonesboro, Arkansas, Edinburgh, Pennsylvania, and Springfield, Oregon (*JAMA.* 1998;279:1853), leaving 13 dead and 45 wounded,

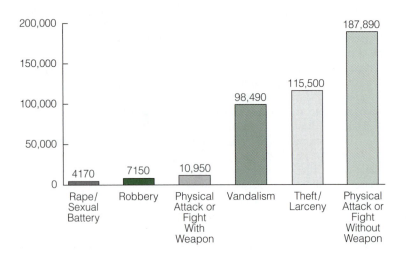

The *Principal/School Disciplinarian Survey on School Violence*, conducted by the U.S. Department of Education, National Center for Education Statistics, Fast Response Survey System, documented the number of violent crimes occurring in public schools in the United States in the 1996–1997 school year. (Credit: Courtesy of Joan Kinlan, MD.)

according to Ronald Stephens, EdD, executive director of the National School Safety Center, a nonprofit organization based in Westlake Village, California.

Such youngsters undeniably represent the far end of the violence spectrum, said 5 Richard Harding, MD, APA vice president and clinical professor of pediatrics and psychiatry at the University of South Carolina School of Medicine, Columbia. In hindsight, signs of their disturbance may have been apparent, he said, but it takes a system sensitized to such signals to pick them up and to respond appropriately.

"Other children often distance themselves from peers who are irritable, angry, and talk of 'blasting someone away' or other scary or extreme acts. Most children don't want to think about the things these children are thinking about," Harding said. "Yet they rarely report the danger to adults," he noted. "There's peer pressure not to tell."

The troubled youngster becomes increasingly isolated, Harding said, leaving him—the typical offender is male—with no counterbalance for his violent thoughts. He wants to make people pay attention to him. If he has seen enough examples of violence and bizarre behavior on television and in movies, video games, and comic books, Harding said, similar feats may seem a good way to impress others. Being kicked out of class may trigger an impulsive act of aggression.

"This is why locking up guns saves lives," Harding said. "If a person doesn't have ready access to a gun, the passage of time may permit him to reorganize and calm down."

"The recent school shootings are headline-grabbing events because of their rarity," Joan Kinlan, MD, a child and adolescent psychiatrist practicing in Washington, D.C., said at an APA workshop on school violence. But the possibility of such violence in schools, she said, is appallingly common. In a national survey of nearly 22,000 students in public and private schools, nearly 13% of schoolchildren reported knowing another student who brought a gun to school in the 1995–1996 academic year (*Students' Reports*

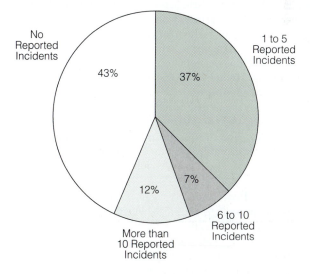

The same U.S. Department of Education survey cited [above] showed the percentage of public schools reporting various crimes in the 1996–1997 school year. The number of reported incidents of crime at a school is based on the total number of the following crimes for which the school reported that the police were contacted: murder, rape or other sexual battery, suicide, physical attack or fight with and without a weapon, robbery, theft or larceny, and vandalism. Percentages do not total 100 because of rounding. Credit: Courtesy of Joan Kinlan, MD.

of School Crime. Washington, D.C.: U.S. Dept of Education; 1998, publication NCES 98-241; available at: http://www.nces.ed.gov). The Centers for Disease Control and Prevention found that 7.6% of a representative sample of nearly 11,000 students in grades 9 through 12 reported carrying a gun during the 30 days preceding the survey (Youth Risk Behavior Surveillance—United States, 1995. *MMWR.* 1996:45 (SS-4):1–86).

Some of those who carry guns belong to gangs. Others are those whom teachers 10 would not suspect of violence. They often feel insecure, Kinlan said, and see the world as a dangerous place. They avoid fights. They are the ones who are bullied. "But because the gun is there," she said, "they may use it."

Stephens of the National School Safety Center said that from July 1, 1992, when the organization began keeping records, to July 1, 1998, there have been 226 school-associated violent deaths. Of these, 175 were shootings, 33 were stabbings or slashings, and the remainder were attributed to beatings, hangings, or asphyxiations. In the past school year alone, there were 40 violent deaths in the nation's schools.

The National Center for Education Statistics reported that 10% of U.S. public schools experienced at least one serious violent crime in the 1996–1997 school year. These incidents included murder, rape or other type of sexual battery, suicide, physical attack or fight with a weapon, or robbery. There were nearly 190,000 physical attacks or fights without a weapon, as well as high numbers of thefts or larceny and vandalism (*Violence and Discipline Problems in U.S. Public Schools 1996–97.* Washington, D.C.: U.S. Dept of Education; 1998, publication NCES 98-030; available at: http://www.nces.ed.gov).

These statistics do not include other pervasive and disturbing events that create an atmosphere conducive to violence that occurs in schools on a daily basis, Kinlan said, citing "verbal harassment, graffiti in bathrooms that identifies kids by name, and sexual harassment of both boys and girls, such as butt holding and breast touching." A visitor to almost any public high school who spends just 5 minutes in the hall, she said, will see numerous examples of such violence.

Moreover, incidents of violence in schools probably are underreported, according to Lois Flaherty, MD, clinical associate professor of psychiatry at the University of Pennsylvania School of Medicine, Philadelphia, and chair of the APA workshop on school violence. School administrators want to downplay violence, she said, and may not report such events as assaults on teachers and fights in lunchrooms.

Violence occurs most often in unstructured time, she said, when classes are chang- 15 ing, at lunchtime, recess, and dismissal, for example. Having clear rules for students about what is and is not acceptable behavior and having teachers who are viewed as fair and consistent, Flaherty said, help reduce violence.

Children Need Rules, Protection

Children who have witnessed violence or been victims of violence feel let down by the adult protective system, said Carl Bell, MD, chief executive officer of the Community Mental Health Council and professor of psychiatry and public health at the University of Illinois College of Medicine, both in Chicago. These children often have generalized anxiety and depression, he said at the APA workshop. They are afraid of being victimized again and may carry knives or guns to school for self-protection. "The solution is to reestablish the adult protective shield," he said in an interview. "The school must be clear about security. Children need to feel safe at school."

Some schools have eliminated lockers and even book bags, he said, providing one set of books to be used in class and another to be left at home. Others require that students use see-through book bags. Although some schools have used metal detectors at doors like those in airports, there are easy ways to stymie this system, he said: children may bring tin cans to set off the alarm, especially on test days, causing long delays. Handheld detectors may be more practical, he said, because they can be used for spot checks on, say, every second child or on different days of the week. Some schools employ uniformed security guards. Hallway cameras may serve as a deterrent. Signs can make the rules explicit, Bell said: "No guns; no alcohol; no fighting. Violators will be prosecuted. Do your part to make our school a safe place."

The school principal must make safety a prime mission, he said, by involving students and teachers in a collaborative partnership to work toward their shared goal. In a mission-driven system, he said, students are asked to take personal responsibility for how they resolve conflicts with one another. Students who buy into the mission of keeping their school safe learn that it sometimes is necessary to snitch on someone whose behavior is subverting that goal.

Schools need gun safety drills, Bell said. "Every school has procedures for a fire drill," he noted, "but few have plans for what to do if a student walks into school with a gun." Most, he said, have an "It won't happen here" mentality. Schools, he said, should adopt public address codes for emergencies like those hospitals use: "Mr Strong, report to the auditorium." Teachers should lock doors to their classrooms and stay with students until an all-clear signal sounds, not send students fleeing from the building. This tactic, he said, keeps them from becoming targets.

Students who are caught carrying weapons or are otherwise disruptive, Bell said, 20 need counseling. They may need to go to an alternative school. They should not just be expelled and put on the street. "Behind all anger, usually, is some form of hurt," he said. "A child who tries to commit suicide," he noted, "gets a lot of attention. Disruptive children need intensive services, too. Schools need support from the social service system and the psychiatric system. Violent children may have treatable psychiatric illnesses."

Some Need In-School Help

A contemporary approach to reducing youth violence is to reverse the traditional model of referring troubled youngsters out to treatment and bring both treatment and prevention services into the school. The mental health program affiliated with the University of Maryland School of Medicine, Baltimore, started in 1989 under Flaherty's direction, is an example.

According to its present director, Mark Weist, PhD, a clinical psychologist and associate professor in the Department of Psychiatry, the in-school program sees proportionally more youngsters with internalizing disorders such as depression and posttraumatic stress, while community mental health centers see proportionally more youngsters who had to act out to get treatment and have been diagnosed with disorders involving oppositional defiance, antisocial behavior, and conduct.

In some inner-city communities, the majority of children could benefit from some mental health services, Weist said in an interview. Studies show that fewer than one-third of those who have such needs nationally receive appropriate services (Dryfoos J.G. *Full-Service Schools*. San Francisco, Calif.: Jossey-Bass; 1994; *Adolescent Health*. Washington, D.C.: Office of Technology Assessment; 1991). In-school programs, Weist said, not only minimize the stigma of seeking care, but also avoid financial, transportation, and other barriers, as well as long waiting lists and long intake procedures.

Kindergarten teachers, he said, can identify highly aggressive children, the ones at risk for later dropping out and engaging in violence and criminal behavior.

"But schools often don't know what to do with these youngsters," he noted. Frequently the only way to get mental health services is to refer the child to special education, a cumbersome process that often leads to unwarranted labeling.

About one-third of Baltimore's 183 schools now have expanded mental health services, provided by five separate programs. The one Weist directs serves 19 schools, offering brief focused intervention throughout the school years from providers with whom children feel comfortable. "After I'm finished wearing my clinician hat," said Weist, who spends part of his time working directly with high school students, "I can put on my mentoring hat." Students drop by his office for help with filling out college applications or studying for tests. In this context, he said, he continues to provide therapeutic services.

The program offers all students classroom training in ways to manage anger, develop cognitive skills, improve self-control, and reduce aggressive behaviors. Such programs also give youngsters the opportunity to talk about violence they've experienced. Having a classmate killed, for instance, understandably upsets the others. In this situation, Weist said, the mental health group forms a team, makes an announcement about what happened, asks for a moment of silence, and holds a series of meetings to let students know adults are concerned about them and are there to help them cope.

Without outside concern, Weist said, children may develop a sense that life is cheap, and whole communities may be numbed and feel beaten down by violence. Children who undergo traumatic experiences that are not processed, he noted, are more likely to become violent themselves.

Weist said the mental health program seeks parental consent for most of those who participate because the school wants the parents to become involved. In Maryland, youths over 16 years of age may independently receive mental health services. When substance abuse is involved, services may be provided to youths younger than 16 years without parental consent.

Involve the Parents

Paul Fink, MD, professor of psychiatry at Temple University School of Medicine, Philadelphia, Pennsylvania, speaking at the APA workshop on school violence, described a kind of psychological autopsy he conducts as the voluntary head of the Philadelphia health department's youth homicide committee. Annual reviews of the killings of all persons in the city under the age of 22 years, he said, showed that the earliest marker for killing or being killed was truancy.

This finding, he said, prompted lowering the threshold at which parents are brought into truancy court from 50 days to 25 days and increasing the court's sessions from twice a month to 4 days a week. Some 30,000 of the 215,000 students in the Philadelphia school system are absent on any given day, he said, and often parents are unaware that their children are skipping school. This year the court will handle 10,000 cases of youngsters absent from school 25 days or more, up from 2,000 when the cutoff was 50 days. The court also has been decentralized and moved into the community, holding sessions in schools. This raises the embarrassment for parents on the local level, Fink said, and also brings them into the school.

The committee found that ninth grade is a critical time: the majority of youngsters who murdered or were murdered had truancy problems or dropped out in that academic year. The transition to high school may be more perilous than previously suspected, Fink said, suggesting that a longer and more in-depth orientation period may prove a useful violence prevention strategy.

Is Media Violence to Blame?

The statistics are familiar but still chilling: By 18 years old, the APA reports, the typical American child will have seen 16,000 simulated murders and 200,000 acts of violence while watching 28 hours of television a week. The perpetrators of violence went unsanctioned in 73% of these violent scenes, according to the National Television Violence Study in 1996. The most effective way to quell imitation, the study said, is to show punishment for such acts. Failure to show consequences desensitizes viewers and promotes identification with aggressors. The APA's fact sheet on the psychiatric effects of media violence may be found at the APA web site: http://www.psych.org.

Fink also directs a child-centered community collaboration that aims, he said, "to identify at-risk children before they kill someone or are killed themselves." Once a month, he meets at an inner-city middle school serving grades 5 through 8 with the school principal, nurse, counselors, and other faculty members, along with representatives from the department of human services, local community mental health center, and other service agencies or organizations—about 20 to 25 participants on average. A school counselor presents cases of disturbed or distressed children, including those engaging in violent behavior.

Typically, Fink said, a school system has three ways of dealing with disruptive children: transfer them, suspend them, or expel them. All, he said, "are punitive and useless." But now, he said, everyone works together to try to improve the situation. One child was getting an "A" in math, but flunking all other subjects. The math teacher became his mentor. Other children were facing difficult family situations that home visitors from the mental health center helped resolve. Treatment of a parent with a substance abuse or other problem may be the key to improving a child's behavior.

Fink, a past president of the APA, volunteers his services. The project, he said, takes only a modest amount of his time: 90 minutes for the monthly meeting, travel time, and occasional other visits to the school. He would like to see more physicians assume a similar role. "With 650,000 physicians in this country," he said, "there must be a few others who understand the need to bring more and more people into the room. The community has to acknowledge that schools can't do their job all alone."

Juvenile Offenders: Should They Be Tried in Adult Courts?

MICHAEL P. BROWN

Michael P. Brown is an associate professor of criminal justice and criminology at Ball State University. The following article first appeared in *USA Today Magazine* in January 1998.

Children have been described as our future, our greatest resource, and our hope for a better tomorrow. For many Americans, though, children invoke fear. They represent violence, a segment of society lacking in self-control and devoid of ethics and morals, and the failure of the family to instill traditional values—chief among them being the value of human life and respect for others.

Fear of crime, especially random violence perpetrated by young Americans, is among the nation's greatest concerns. It has served as the motivation for countless numbers of people to change their lifestyles, take self-defense classes, install home security systems, and carry handguns for protection. Moreover, fear of crime has influenced politicians and laypersons to adopt the position that a conservative justice system, which seeks to punish and deter, holds the most promise in curtailing juvenile crime. Waiving juveniles to criminal (i.e., adult) court and imposing criminal penalties, according to the conservative position, are effective ways for society to express outrage for the transgressions of "out-of-control" youth and to placate its desire for retribution. Others, however, contend that treating juveniles as adults is going too far. Although many of these juveniles are incarcerated for their crimes, which the law allows, they often are the easy victims of homosexual rape and other forms of violence at the hands of hardened adult criminals.

The criminal sanctioning of juvenile offenders is not a contemporary phenomenon. Juveniles have been punished as adults for centuries. Prior to the 17th century, for instance, children were seen as being different from adults only in their size. Hence, they were held essentially to the same behavioral standards as adults. Youngsters were perceived of as being miniature adults and, therefore, subject to the same punishments as offenders who were decades their senior. Childhood was considered to end at about age five.

It was not until the 17th century that European church and community leaders successfully advanced the notion that children were weak and innocent and in need of the guidance, protection, and socialization of adults. Consequently, childhood was prolonged, education became a priority, and societal norms emerged specifying age-appropriate behavior. Youngsters no longer were viewed as miniature adults. For the first time in recorded history, they were a separate and distinct group.

By the 18th century, English common law characterized those under the age of seven as being incapable of forming criminal intent. For an act to be considered criminal, there must be actus reus (the criminal act itself), mens rea (the intent to commit the criminal act), and corpus delecti (the interaction between the act and the intent to commit it). Therefore, since youths were considered to be incapable of forming mens rea, they were legally unable to commit a crime or be criminally sanctioned. Between the ages of seven and 14, children were presumed to be without criminal intent unless it could be proven that they knew the difference between right and wrong. At age 14, they legally were considered adults, capable of forming criminal intent and therefore justly sentenced to serve time in jail and prison alongside other adults.

By the early 1800s, there was the belief that juvenile and adult offenders should be incarcerated separately. At that time, special correctional institutions for youthful offenders were established in the U.S. It was not until 1899, though, that the first juvenile court was established. This uniquely American institution was based on the premise that youthful offenders should be treated differently than their adult counterparts. Instead of deciding guilt or innocence, the court would ascertain whether youths were in need of treatment. Under the driving philosophy of the new court, parens patriae, it would serve as the benevolent parent—all-knowing and all-loving, wanting only that which is in the best interest of children. Consequently, instead of harsh, punitive sanctions that sought to deter, the court would seek long-term behavioral change by providing the guidance youths so woefully lacked from their natural parents. Sentences were to be customized to meet the needs of each juvenile so as to optimize the rehabilitative effects of court intervention.

For most juveniles, the parens patriae doctrine still serves as the foundation upon which their sentences are based. Such an orientation is not deemed appropriate, however, for those juveniles waived to criminal court. Provisions that allow juveniles to be waived are, on the one hand, in contrast with the original intent and purpose of the juvenile justice system. On the other, they are consistent with the manner in which youthful offenders were sanctioned in the past.

The present-day controversy surrounding waivers appears to be a consequence of at least two factors converging. First, the definitions of childhood and age-appropriate behavior are in a state of flux. Young people are said to be more predisposed toward violence today than they were in the past. National crime data sources seem to support this notion. Violent juvenile crime has increased by nearly 70% since 1986. Moreover, the violence perpetrated by juveniles is portrayed by the mass media as being more heinous than at any other time in history. People are fearful of falling victim to a generation that seemingly holds beliefs and values that diverge drastically from those of normative society.

Second, the "get tough" approach to dealing with law violators—as seen throughout the criminal justice system—increasingly is being applied to juvenile offenders as well. Although a conservative approach to juvenile crime is not new, it is in sharp contrast to the predominant way in which the juvenile justice system has responded to youthful offenders in the U.S. for nearly 100 years. While it is true that waivers have been in existence for more than 70 years, they are used more today than in the past. This has drawn attention to how society's response to juvenile offenders is changing from primarily being oriented toward rehabilitation to increasingly becoming prone to subjecting juveniles to conservative criminal court practices.

"Legal Adults"

Every state and the District of Columbia have at least one provision (some states have 10 as many as three) to waive certain juveniles to criminal court. Juveniles may become "legal adults" through judicial waiver, prosecutorial discretion, or statutory exclusion. A judicial waiver involves the juvenile court waiving jurisdiction over a case and sending it to criminal court for prosecution. In all but three states, juvenile court judges have been entrusted with the power to waive juveniles to criminal court. Prosecutorial discretion (also known as concurrent jurisdiction) refers to the prosecutor deciding in which court—juvenile or criminal—charges will be filed. Ten states and the District of Columbia give prosecutors this authority. Statutory exclusion involves state legislatures designating certain offenses for which criminal prosecution is required. Thirty-six states and the District of Columbia have enacted legislation that excludes certain offenses from juvenile court jurisdiction.

Age and offense seriousness traditionally have been the criteria by which juveniles are waived to criminal court. Twenty-one states and the District of Columbia have no minimum age requirements for transferring juveniles to criminal court. Among the remaining 29 states, minimum age requirements range from seven to 16. The largest proportion of cases waived to criminal court are serious crimes such as murder; offenses involving serious personal injury (such as aggravated assault); property crimes; public order offenses (such as disorderly conduct, obstruction of justice, and weapons offenses); and drug offenses. Additionally, some minor offenses (such as fish and game violations), which do not fall within the jurisdiction of the juvenile court, are tried in criminal court. Moreover, some states permit juveniles to be waived if their current charge is a felony and there is evidence of prior felony convictions. Furthermore, most states have a provision that allows juveniles to be waived to criminal court if there is reason to believe that offenders are not amenable to treatment.

Using the most recent available data, the Office of Juvenile Justice and Delinquency Prevention (OJJDP) reports that, from 1985 to 1994, the number of delinquency cases waived to criminal court rose from 7,200 to 12,300, a 71% increase. Despite this growth, the percentage of cases waived to criminal court during this 10-year period remained relatively constant, ranging from a low of 1.2% to a high of 1.5% of all formally handled delinquency cases.

Over this span, the types of offenses waived to criminal court have changed considerably. While 54% of the cases waived in 1985 were for property crimes, the percentage dropped to 37% by 1994. Cases involving murder and personal injury rose from 33 to 44%. The percentage of drug offenses more than doubled, from 5 to 11%. Public order offenses remained relatively constant—9 percent in 1985 and 8 percent in 1994.

The percentage of cases involving youthful offenders under the age of 16 increased from 6 to 12%. Males consistently have comprised the majority of cases waived to criminal court—95% in 1985 and 96% in 1994. Of the juveniles waived to criminal court in 1985, 57% were white, 42% black, and 2 percent of other racial and ethnic groups. By 1994, the percentage of white and black juvenile offenders became more similar (49 and 48%, respectively), and youths from other racial and ethnic groups increased to 4 percent. (Figures have been rounded off to nearest full percentage point.)

Waiving juveniles to criminal court often is justified on the grounds that they are 15 deserving of more punitive criminal court sanctions and that the "get tough" approach to fighting crime will serve to deter future criminal conduct. Decades of research have yielded mixed findings regarding whether juveniles are sentenced more harshly by criminal courts and are less likely to recidivate. Most studies indicate that juveniles waived to criminal court do not receive substantially more punitive sanctions. In fact, many studies have reported that juveniles are more likely to receive probation instead of incarceration. Of those incarcerated, most receive terms of confinement comparable to those imposed in juvenile court. Moreover, research has revealed that juveniles waived to criminal court are no less likely to recidivate than those sanctioned in juvenile court.

The methods by which the justice system responds to unlawful conduct are not determined in a vacuum. They are a reflection of societal attitudes. In the past, waiving juveniles to criminal court was considered an option after all other avenues of treatment in the juvenile court had been explored. Today, the situation is drastically different. The conservative environment that currently exists not only makes it more acceptable, it is an expectation that judges and prosecutors will act decisively by waiving certain juveniles to criminal court. Hence, waivers no longer are viewed as a last resort. In fact, the use of waivers has been expanded to include first-time juvenile offenders. The establishment of exclusionary statutes, requiring certain juveniles to be waived automatically, eliminates the possibility of the exercise of discretion by those who know youngsters best—juvenile court judges and prosecutors. It is estimated that exclusionary statutes have resulted in more juveniles waived to criminal court than judicial waivers and prosecutorial discretion combined.

Waiving juveniles to criminal court is not the answer to the crime situation. At best, waivers are a short-term solution to a complex social condition that will not be simplified by transferring juveniles to the jurisdiction of the criminal court. At best, they merely serve to mollify the public's desire for retribution. After all, the majority of those juveniles waived to criminal court will re-enter society stigmatized by their criminal label and, in all likelihood, more dangerous than they were before being sanctioned as adults. This is especially true of youths who have served time in prison alongside adults.

Nevertheless, it is unlikely that waivers will be repealed. Therefore, it is incumbent upon decision-makers to make an informed, socially responsible use of waivers. In so doing, they would be restricted to those who pose the greatest risk to the safety and security of society—violent youth such as murderers, rapists, and robbers who show no apparent promise for reformation.

As for the others, juvenile court intervention holds the most promise for transforming troubled youths into productive, law-abiding adults. The OJJDP, based upon the results of numerous studies, has proposed a multifaceted strategy for dealing with youthful offenders:

Strengthen the family unit. Parents are primarily responsible for instilling in their   20
children socially redeeming morals and values. Parenting classes may be necessary when mothers and/or fathers lack the skills, abilities, and maturity to socialize their offspring properly. When a functional family is nonexistent, a surrogate one should be established to fill that void in a child's upbringing.

Support core social institutions. Capable, productive, and responsible youths are influenced positively by schools, religious institutions, and community-based organizations. Social institutions impart law-abiding beliefs and values and offer youths legitimate opportunities for economic gain.

Promote delinquency prevention. Communities must be proactive by responding to children who are at risk of committing delinquent acts. Although youths have a responsibility to live within the boundaries of the law, social institutions have a similar responsibility to engage youngsters in activities that encourage productive, law-abiding behavior.

Encourage an effective and immediate justice system response to delinquency. When delinquency occurs, the justice system must respond immediately to prevent future such actions and suppress escalation in their seriousness. The justice system should act in concert with conventional social institutions to enlist the influences that the family and religious organizations, for instance, have on the lives of youths.

Identify and control those youths who already are serious offenders. Youths who have not responded to traditional juvenile court intervention efforts or have demonstrated an unwillingness to abide by the rules of nonsecure community-based treatment efforts should be isolated in secure juvenile facilities for the protection of society. Deviating somewhat from the OJJDP's proposal, this intervention effort would be restricted to nonviolent offenders.

The alternative to waiving juveniles to criminal court is a comprehensive commu-   25
nity response to juvenile unlawfulness that views juvenile and criminal justice as components of a larger whole—society. Moreover, it sees crime as a community problem with a community solution, instead of viewing it solely as a justice system problem with a justice system solution.

Many people will resist the notion of instituting alternatives to criminal court waivers. A community response to juvenile crime requires the commitment of the entire society. Therefore, it needs more effort than simply waiving juveniles to criminal court. Nevertheless, it holds the promise of returning children to their natural and rightful position as our future, our greatest resource, and our hope for a better tomorrow.

Injustice and Ice Cream

BOB HERBERT

A columnist for the *New York Times* since 1993, Bob Herbert has been a reporter since he began his career at the *Newark Star-Ledger* in 1970. Before joining the *Times*, he was a reporter and editor at the *New York Daily News* and a correspondent at NBC. He writes frequently about problems with the justice system, especially in its treatment of defendants who are members of minority groups. The following column appeared in the *New York Times* in 1993.

As crimes go, it was not one of the great ones. No gunshots, no victims writhing in ₁
pain, no hysterical witnesses.

Supposedly a box of ice cream bars was taken. But weary investigators, perspiring
in the Southern heat, were uncertain even about that. Some of the evidence melted.
The rest of it, presumably, was eaten.

The only thing noteworthy about the case was the astonishing sentence ultimately
imposed on the alleged perpetrator, a 17-year-old boy.

Three years, said the judge. Three years hard time.

Three hideous years in prison for stealing ice cream. ₅

The lunacy started on a Sunday back in July in Thomaston, a small town in central
Georgia. Seventeen-year-old Dehundra Caldwell, his 15-year-old brother, Marcus,
and a juvenile whose name has not been released were on their way to play basketball
when they stopped by the Upson-Lee Middle School.

Dehundra Caldwell said they went into the school through an open door to use the
bathroom.

An employee discovered Dehundra inside the school and called police. All three
boys were arrested.

The law enforcement authorities in Thomaston are not quick. Some still believe
that Poirot is a billionaire from Texas. But they're pretty tough to fool once they get
their investigatory apparatus rolling.

After careful study, they concluded that the boys had broken into the school. This ₁₀
was serious, they told themselves.

Dehundra was charged with burglary. The two younger boys were charged with
juvenile offenses.

Investigators do not know for sure who took the Snickers ice cream bars, which
were discovered missing from the school cafeteria. But that never mattered much.
What mattered was upholding the law. In Thomaston, there is no such thing as a
minor offense. Once it was discovered that the ice cream was missing, all necessary
forces were mobilized to insure that somebody pay, and pay dearly.

A statement was taken from Dehundra Caldwell, who had never before been in
trouble with the law. He confessed to entering the school. The law enforcement
elders of Thomaston congratulated themselves for bagging a dangerous felon.

Only then was young Caldwell assigned an attorney, a man named Richard Bishoff.
That was not a cause for celebration. It was more like getting a lump of coal in your
Christmas stocking.

Mr. Bishoff, at least in this case, kept his talents carefully hidden. He didn't even ad- ₁₅
vise his client to object to an agreement, explained in advance, under which he would
plead guilty to burglary and be sentenced to three years in prison.

The sentence was handed down by Superior Court Judge Andrew Whalen on
Aug. 23.

No probation. No community service. No first-offender status. Three years hard
time.

Mr. Bishoff, the attorney, was not even in the courtroom with his client when the
sentence was imposed. He said in an interview yesterday that at the time of the
sentencing he was busy with another case.

"I had a trial starting at 1 o'clock," he said. Another lawyer filled in for him at the
sentencing.

I asked Mr. Bishoff if Judge Whalen (who has not been available for comment) was ₂₀
aware that only ice cream had been taken from the school.

Mr. Bishoff replied, "I don't know what the judge did or did not know."

Dehundra Caldwell served 10 days of his three-year sentence. By that time the media and the N.A.A.C.P. were on the case and Thomaston was in danger of becoming a laughing stock.

Even the Chamber of Commerce was concerned.

An arrangement was made for Dehundra to be freed on $15,000 bail and now he's back in school. A hearing will be held on Oct. 15, when Judge Whalen plans to rule on whether his first sentence was unduly harsh.

Of course it was. But there are other questions. Why weren't alternatives to a crim- 25 inal charge explored? And what do we do about the felony conviction that's a permanent part of Dehundra's record?

More importantly, what do we do about a criminal justice system that readily opens up a cell for Dehandra Caldwell while waving goodbye to murderers and rapists because of overcrowding?

And the scariest question of all: How many Dehundra Caldwells are there that we don't know about?

QUESTIONS FOR DISCUSSION

1. **Analyzing Strategy:** Bob Herbert's editorial argues through a single, detailed, example. What can he accomplish with this tactic that the other articles relying on statistics cannot? How does his perspective differ from that in the other readings?

2. **Making Connections:** Consult the National Center for Education Statistics of the U.S. Department of Education or the Uniform Crime Reporting Program of the FBI. Has the trend in juvenile crime from the eighties through the nineties changed recently?

3. **Analyzing Strategy:** The articles by Blumstein and Lamberg are addressed to professional readers in the criminal justice and medical communities. How do their arguing strategies differ from those in the articles by Lerner, Lion and Rappeport (both psychiatrists), and Brown that appeared in general circulation publications?

4. **Analyzing Strategy:** Blumstein's article moves carefully through the issues. Identify the sections of his argument that establish a trend, examine causes, and suggest solutions. Why is an evaluation section not necessary?

5. **Making Connections:** Has school violence, emphasized in the Lerner and Lamberg articles and the Lion and Rappeport piece, had a greater impact on public opinion than the general increase in violent juvenile crime described by Blumstein? If so, why? Are different kinds of juvenile crime being confused by the focus on these sensational cases?

6. **Analyzing Strategy:** Drs. Lion and Rappeport argue strongly for imitation of media images as a cause of violence. How do they establish their casual generalization? Does this generalization offer an explanation for the increase in violent offenses by the young?

7. **Making Connections:** Lerner and Brown differ greatly in their explanations of the causes of violence by youthful offenders. Are their explanations mutually exclusive? How do their different explanations lead to different recommendations?

WRITING SUGGESTIONS

1. Cases of juvenile crime often come to national attention. In 2002, for example, two brothers in Florida, aged eleven and thirteen, were tried as adults for murdering their father. Select a recent or local case, not mentioned in the readings, and argue that the case should/should not be waived to criminal court (see the article by Michael P. Brown) and that the juvenile defendants should or should not be tried as adults.

2. The authors of these articles are convinced that an increase in violent offenses by juvenile offenders is a real trend. They therefore turn to causal explanations for the increase. Compare the causal explanations offered in the readings and establish which you find the most convincing and why. Or offer a causal factor that the authors sampled in this section have not considered.

3. You may have had a personal experience with an outbreak of violent behavior by one or more young people. This episode may or may not have led to serious consequences for the victims or perpetrators. Write a narrative of the event and follow it with an analysis of the causes behind it and possible actions that could have prevented it.

4. Recommendations to decrease violent juvenile crime range from see-through school bags to confiscating guns, eliminating violent video games, altering local news coverage, and changing the way parents teach their children esteem for others. Imagine that you are an advisor to the President of the United States and you have been asked to write a policy speech in which you lay out a series of feasible initiatives for reducing violent crime by juveniles.

The Meaning of Sports in Our Society

Chapter 15

Where Have All the Young Men Gone?

PAUL AUSTER

Paul Auster is a novelist, poet, essayist, and translator. He is the author of *New York Trilogy* (1987), a collection of detective stories, and the novels *Moon Palace* (1989), *Leviathan* (1992), and *Timbuktu* (1999), as well as collections of poems and essays and the screenplay for the film *Smoke* (1995). The following essay was published in 1999 in the *New York Times Magazine*.

This past summer, more than a million people gathered on the Champs-Elysées to cel- 1
ebrate France's victory in the World Cup. By all accounts, it was the largest demonstration of public happiness seen in Paris since the liberation from the Germans in 1944.

One could only gape at the significance of the event. It was just a sports victory, and
by no stretch of the imagination could it be compared to the end of the Nazi occupation. And yet there it was for everyone to see: on the same street in the same city, the
same joy, the same outpouring of national pride that had greeted De Gaulle 54 years
earlier.

What to make of this? When I was asked to write something about the millennium,
the first word that came to me was "Europe." The term itself is a European idea, after
all, and when I cast about in my mind for a dominant image or fact that might sum up
the past 10 centuries of European history, the word that kept coming back to me was
"bloodshed." And by that I mean the metaphysics of violence: war, mass destruction,
the slaughter of the innocent.

This is not to denigrate the glories of European civilization. But in spite of Dante
and Goya, in spite of Chartres and the Declaration of the Rights of Man, scarcely a
month has gone by in the past 1,000 years when one group of Europeans has not been
intent on killing another group of Europeans. Country has fought against country (the
Hundred Years' War), alliances of countries have fought against other alliances of
countries (the Thirty Years' War) and the citizens of a single country have fought
against one another (the French Wars of Religion). When it comes to our own much-
vaunted century of progress and enlightenment, just fill in the appropriate blanks.

Mercifully, there has been peace among the major European powers since the end 5
of World War II. That doesn't mean they like one another and it doesn't mean that

the carnage has stopped everywhere, but for once it seems that the vast majority of Europeans have found a way to hate one another without hacking one another to pieces. This miracle goes by the name of soccer.

Legend or not, the first reference to football playing in this millennium stems from an incident of war. In the year 1000 or thereabouts, the British supposedly celebrated their victory over an invading Danish chieftain by removing his head from his body and using it as a football.

We don't have to believe that story, but we do know that by the 1100's, Shrove Tuesdays were celebrated in England with football matches that pitted entire towns against one another. Five hundred players on a side. A field that could be up to several miles long. And games that lasted all day, with no fixed rules. It came to be known as mob football, and the mayhem that resulted from these semiorganized brawls led to so many injuries that in 1314 Edward II banned the game.

Further bans were issued by Edward III, Richard II and Henry IV. These kings were not just disturbed by the violence of the sport; they worried that too much "meddling in football" had cut into the time previously devoted to archery practice and that therefore the Kingdom would not be militarily prepared in the event of an invasion. But by the late 17th century, archery ceased to be a required skill among soldiers, and football was actively encouraged by Charles II. Standard rules were introduced in 1801, and after 1863, when the rules of present-day soccer were drawn up at Cambridge University, the game spread throughout Europe and the rest of the world. Since then, it has developed into the most widely played and popular sport in history.

Countries now wage their battles on the soccer field with surrogate armies in short pants. It's supposed to be a game, and it's supposed to be fun, but an eerie memory of past antagonisms hovers over each match, and every time a goal is scored, one hears an echo of old victories and old defeats. Holland versus Spain. England versus France. Poland versus Germany. When I watched the World Cup last summer and saw the supporters of the various national teams waving their country's flag and singing patriotic songs, I understood that the Europeans had finally found a substitute for war. Yes, I am aware of the football hooligans, and I know about the riots that occurred in France during the World Cup. But still, we are able to count the casualties on the fingers of our two hands. A generation ago, we counted them in the millions.

Celebration or Exploitation? Women Athletes Pose Question

LINDA ROBERTSON

Linda Robertson writes a column on sports for the *Miami Herald,* which she joined in 1983. She has also covered the Summer and Winter Olympics for the *Herald.* The following column first appeared in January 2000.

Amy Acuff considers herself an athlete, not a sex goddess.

As both Olympic high jumper and fashion model, it might seem she leads a double life: aggressive competitor vs. passive poser.

But the 6-2 Acuff, who was not always comfortable with her self-image, has found a way to reconcile those roles. In fact, she decided to celebrate the beauty of the athletic body by publishing a calendar of female track and field athletes in provocative, semi-nude photographs.

She is one of a growing number of female athletes who are no longer shy about showcasing the muscles they worked hard to build. Call it sweat equity, or part of the evolution of the female form from the pillowy Rubenesque ideal of the 17th century to the full-figured, full-of-fun Marilyn Monroe gals of the mid-20th to the chiseled Venus (as in Williams) look of the 21st.

When Brandi Chastain ripped off her jersey in a spontaneous expression of joy at winning the World Cup, the photo of her ripped torso became emblematic of a larger victory for women—the sports bra over the Wonder bra. Even before the World Cup, Chastain had posed nude for *Gear* magazine, with soccer balls hiding her private parts. 5

Sports fans may not readily acknowledge it, but a great deal of the appeal of physical contests is the inherent sensuality. Powerful NBA players on a fast-break waltz. Butterfly swimmers undulating through the water. Graceful 400-meter hurdlers skimming around the track.

The Greeks were the first to admire the nude as art form. Athletes are our modern-day Davids in uniform.

But for women, the question of how much skin to show and how to show it is always more problematic than it is for men. And more political. In her book *Femininity*, Susan Brownmiller accentuates the intertwining of image and equality by pointing out that during the campaign for women's right to vote in England, a suffrage activist walked into the National Gallery and smashed the glass that protected the Rokeby Venus painting. The painting depicts an (ample) backside view of a reclining woman looking at her naked body in a mirror. Then, in 1968, the Women's Liberation Movement staged a protest at the Miss America contest in Atlantic City.

While women have progressed from corsets and swim bloomers and ankle-length tennis dresses to Lycra athletic apparel, there remains a level of skepticism—or disapproval or fear—about women's display of strength. Recall the uproar over the Gulliver High girls' cross-country team four years ago. The runners were disqualified at the state meet not because they cheated but because their shorts were too short. A couple of chauvinist state athletic officials took it upon themselves to give a running event an X rating.

Acuff and other female athletes in revealing photos realize they are walking a thin line—even though Acuff doesn't think her calendar contains anything racier than the annual *Sports Illustrated* swimsuit issue. What some see as exploitative others see as an expression of power and independence. The courts have faced the same sort of difficulty in defining pornography. 10

But there is a difference between Acuff posing pridefully with an American flag, her breasts covered by body paint of the stars and stripes, and Katarina Witt posing in high heels and sheer nightgown for *Playboy* under the headline "the gold medal skater goes from 5.9 to a perfect 10."

"The women in our calendar come across as strong, not as sex objects," Acuff said. "I've turned down *Playboy* three times. Their photos portray women too submissively."

Demeaning, meek, malleable: Those qualities don't apply to the calendar photo of distance runner Nnenna Lynch, an artsy shot of her wearing angel wings.

"I always thought the main purpose of femininity was to appreciate a woman for all her traits," Acuff said. "Nnenna Lynch is a Rhodes scholar, a world-class athlete and she's gorgeous. I think what women really want is to be accepted for being intelligent, hard-working and nice-looking and not have one be exclusionary of the other."

A calendar of Australian women's soccer team players in full frontal nude poses was much more controversial, as was a layout of a Romanian gymnast in *Playboy*. 15

Basketball player and model Lisa Leslie, who regrets posing semi-nude for a Nike ad campaign, thinks such displays are a step backward.

"I think it's unfortunate women have to go so far to grab the public eye," she said. "It shows that sexism still exists. Women have a tendency to use their bodies to get attention."

Unfortunately with women's sports, there's always a subtext to success, some misgivings about the muscles. Americans still prefer petite gymnasts and figure skaters to big-shouldered swimmers or tall basketball players. They loved seductive Laura Baugh but aren't quite sure what to make of strong Serena Williams. When Martina Navratilova lifted weights she was "manly." When rival Chris Evert followed Navratilova's lead, she was "in terrific shape."

The U.S. women's soccer team would not have been such a sensation had the players not been promoted as the "babes of summer." Fringe fans found it easy to embrace the pony-tailed, attractive, all-American bunch.

"I do not think women are lagging so far behind in popularity that they have to   20 do something for attention," Acuff said. "Women's tennis and soccer are bigger than men's. Eventually, I think in all but football, basketball and baseball, women's sports will surpass men's sports in popularity."

Don't Call Jocks Sports "Heroes"

GEORGE J. BRYJAK

George J. Bryjak is a professor of sociology at the University of San Diego and the co-author of *Sociology: Changing Societies in a Diverse World,* Fourth Edition (2000), along with other textbooks. The following article appeared in *USA Today* in February 2002.

When U.S. snowboarders swept their event in Salt Lake City, many of the media re-   1 sponses were as predictable as ice at a winter Olympics: The three young men were "genuine American heroes" . . . "the most recent U.S. Olympic heroes" . . . "the most unlikeliest of heroes" . . . "treated like national heroes." One writer even gushed: "No, this was not your average day on the slopes, unless your average day ends with an Olympic hero saying, 'I've never tried to pick up a girl using a silver medal.'"

One would think that after Sept. 11 we would finally realize that "athlete" and "hero" don't belong in the same sentence. For all of the passions that surround the games we play and watch, they are just that: games with limited social relevance beyond entertainment.

Designating athletes as heroic because of the strength, speed and physical agility they exhibit as competitors makes about as much sense as confirming that lofty status on racehorses or acrobatic dolphins at Sea World.

Athletic participation at the elite level is an egoistic, self-centered activity, as athletes must continually hone their bodies to play to the limits of their abilities. While athletes are routinely injured, their impairments are suffered in the pursuit of fame, fortune and championships. By contrast, heroism is altruistic behavior performed from a strong sense of love, duty and commitment, and often entails placing oneself in life-threatening situations.

Many Forms of Valor
There are three types or categories of heroism: 5

- Active heroes risk injury or death during the course of their actions: the firefighters who charged up the World Trade Center to render aid while everyone else was trying to escape (some who perished were off-duty at the time); the police officer hoping for a non-lethal resolution who waits that extra second before firing on an armed assailant; Doctors Without Borders physicians who may contract fatal diseases from the very people they are trying to help.

- Accidental heroes rise to the occasion during extraordinary circumstances: the passengers who confronted the terrorists on the flight that crashed in Pennsylvania and prevented another suicide attack.

- Passive heroes are those whose selfless work contributes to the betterment of society: the recent college graduate who turns down a lucrative position and joins the Peace Corps; the single mother who works two jobs, supports three children and still finds time to do charity work.

Athletes should be accorded the respect and admiration they deserve. However, to speak of All-Pro quarterbacks or home-run hitters as heroes trivializes the activity of those truly deserving of the title.

Some athletes appreciate the difference. "We're not heroes," San Francisco Giants shortstop Rich Aurilia said after Sept. 11. "We're playing a game. The real heroes are the people who are out there clearing the rubble and the people who gave their lives to save others."

Heroism off the Field

That said, athletes can become heroes. Jackie Robinson suffered years of blatant dis-   5
crimination that would have caused lesser men to lash out at their tormentors and postpone the racial integration of Major League Baseball. Hall of Fame outfielder Roberto Clemente lost his life in a plane crash bringing food and supplies to earthquake victims in Nicaragua. After serving in World War II, baseball legend Ted Williams returned to active duty in the Korean conflict, where he flew 39 combat missions. The three men are heroic figures because of the courage and exemplary behavior they exhibited as human beings, not as athletes.

In the bygone days of myth and legend, heroes were thought to be favored by the gods, and, in part, descended from them. If so many of today's self-indulgent, egotistical athletes are descendants of supernatural beings, then, as the title of the movie suggests, the gods must be crazy.

What Tiger Does Best Is Golf

JOSEPH H. BROWN

Joseph H. Brown is an editorial writer for the *Tampa Tribune*. The following article appeared in the *Tampa Tribune* in November 2002, during a controversy over whether champion golfer Tiger Woods should take a stand on the exclusion of women from the Augusta National Golf Club, where the prestigious Masters Tournament is held every spring.

Back when "The Cosby Show" was in its heyday, Bill Cosby was asked during an in-   1
terview why he didn't break even more barriers by having a member of his TV family date a white person. Cosby said he wouldn't do it for a lot of reasons, the most prominent being that he was tired of "blacks bearing most of the burden of integration."

To make his point, he suggested that characters played by Mary Tyler Moore and Bob Newhart date outside their race, since they had been on TV longer than he had.

Or that one of the children on the popular show "Family Ties" go out with a black kid. The interviewer seemed shocked by his suggestion, which proved his point.

I thought of that last week when the *New York Times*, in an editorial on the ongoing controversy over the all-male membership of the Augusta National Golf Club, suggested that golfer Tiger Woods skip next year's Masters.

"A tournament without Mr. Woods would send a powerful message that discrimination isn't good for the golfing business," said the *Times*.

But a tournament without Phil Mickelson, David Duval or Davis Love III wouldn't   5 send a message?

Why Only Tiger Woods?
When interviewed last week, Woods stated that he was becoming annoyed by the call for him to skip next year's Masters because of the all-male membership at Augusta National. I don't blame him.

"It's frustrating because I'm the only player they are asking," said Woods. "They're asking me to give up an opportunity no one has ever had—winning the Masters three years in a row."

And he added that no one has boycotted the Masters before. So why must he be the only one with a social conscience? And why doesn't the *Times* follow its own advice and boycott the event?

Indeed, I doubt that anyone asked golf greats Ben Hogan, Arnold Palmer and Jack Nicklaus to boycott the Masters when the club's membership was all white. But that goes back to what Cosby talked about—who should be the initiators in bringing about change?

Let Tiger Be A Golfer—Period
The most revealing thing about this whole episode is the double standard placed on   10 black athletes in the spotlight, like Woods and Michael Jordan. White athletes are never asked to "speak out" on issues or expected to "give back" to their communities, as almost all black athletes are.

(Asians I've talked to say Woods shouldn't be considered black, since his mother is Thai. They're probably right, but that's a subject for another column.)

In 2000, the NAACP asked Woods to boycott a PGA Tour event in South Carolina in support of the group's protest of the Confederate flag. Woods wouldn't go along, saying: "I'm a golfer. That's their deal, not mine."

For his independence, he was viewed as arrogant and uncaring. I viewed him as secure in who he is.

Woods' self-assurance showed at his first appearance at the Masters as an amateur, when Jim Nantz of CBS asked him whether he had a special obligation to be a role model for "minority kids."

"No. I have an obligation to all kids," replied Woods. (Again, how many white ath-   15 letes are asked about their obligations to kids?)

Still, few athletes in history have been more of a force for change than Tiger Woods. Since he came on the scene, the sport has become more popular and inclusive. He's proved that you can be an agent for change without being a social activist or a racial spokesman.

So everybody needs to quit hounding him about this Augusta mess or any other social issues. His only obligation is being the best golfer he can be, and he's fulfilling it just fine.

The Indian Wars

S. L. PRICE

S. L. Price is a writer for *Sports Illustrated*, where the following article appeared in March 2002.

"The campaign against Indian nicknames and mascots presumes that they offend Na- 1
tive Americans—but do they? We took a poll, and you won't believe the results."

Solve this word problem: Billy Mills, the former runner who won the gold medal
in the 10,000 meters at the 1964 Olympics, is on a commercial airliner hurtling somewhere over the U.S. It is August 2001. Because Mills's father and mother were three-
quarters and one-quarter Native American, respectively, he grew up being called *half-
breed* until that was no longer socially acceptable. As sensibilities shifted over the years,
he heard a variety of words and phrases describing his ethnic background, from Indian
to Sioux to Native American to the one with which he is most comfortable, the age-
old name of his tribal nation: Lakota.

Mills is sitting in first class. A flight attendant—the words *steward* and *stewardess* are
frowned upon today—checks on him every so often. The man is African-American, the
preferred designation for his racial background; before that, society called him *black* or
colored or *Negro*. The man is friendly, doing his job. Each time he addresses Mills, he calls
him Chief. Mills doesn't know if the flight attendant realizes that he is Lakota. Maybe
he calls everyone Chief. Maybe he means it as a compliment. Mills motions him over.

"I want to tell you something," Mills says. The man leans in. "I'm Native American, and you calling me Chief, it turns my stomach. It'd be very similar to somebody
calling you Nigger."

The flight attendant looks at Mills. He says, "Calling you Chief doesn't bother 5
me . . . Chief."

Who is right and who is wrong? Whose feelings take precedence? Most important,
who gets to decide what we call one another?

If you've figured out an answer, don't celebrate yet. The above confrontation is only
a warmup for sport's thorniest word problem: the use of Native American names (and
mascots that represent them) by high school, college and professional teams. For more
than 30 years the debate has been raging over whether names such as Redskins, Braves,
Chiefs and Indians honor or defile Native Americans. Whether clownish figures like
the Cleveland Indians' Chief Wahoo have any place in today's racially sensitive climate
and whether the sight of thousands of non–Native Americans doing the tomahawk
chop at Atlanta's Turner Field is mindless fun or mass bigotry. It's an argument that,
because it mixes mere sports with the sensitivities of a people that were nearly exter-
minated, seems both trivial and profound. It's further complicated by the fact that for
three out of four Native Americans, even a nickname such as Redskins, which many
whites consider racist, isn't objectionable.

Indeed, some Native Americans who purportedly object to Indian team nicknames
wear Washington Redskins' paraphernalia with pride. Two such men showed up in late
January at Augustana College in Sioux Falls, South Dakota, for a conference on race
relations. "They were speaking against the Indian nicknames, but they were wearing
Redskins sweatshirts, and one had on a Redskins cap," says Betty Ann Gross, a member of the Sisseton-Wahpeton Sioux tribe. "No one asked them about it. They looked
pretty militant."

Gross's own case illustrates how slippery the issue can be. She grew up on a reservation in South Dakota and went to Sisseton High, a public school on the reservation

whose teams are called the Redman. Gross can't recall a time when people on the reservation weren't arguing about the team name, evenly divided between those who were proud of it and those who were ashamed. Gross recently completed a study that led the South Dakota government to change the names of 38 places and landmarks around the state, yet she has mixed feelings on the sports issue. She wants Indian mascots and the tomahawk chop discarded, but she has no problem with team names like the Fighting Sioux (University of North Dakota) or even the Redskins. "There's a lot of division," Gross says. "We're confused, and if *we're* confused, you guys should be really confused."

Indeed, a recent SI poll suggests that although Native American activists are virtu- 10 ally united in opposition to the use of Indian nicknames and mascots, the Native American population sees the issue far differently. Asked if high school and college teams should stop using Indian nicknames, 81% of Native American respondents said teams should not stop using Indian nicknames, mascots, characters and symbols. Opinion is far more divided on reservations, yet a majority (67%) there said the usage by pro teams should not cease, while 32% said it should.

"I take the middle ground," says Leigh J. Kuwanwisiwma, 51, director of the Hopi Cultural Preservation Office in Kykotsmovi, Arizona, and an avid devotee of the Atlanta Braves. "I don't see anything wrong with Indian nicknames as long as they're not meant to be derogatory. Some tribal schools on Arizona reservations use *Indians* as a nickname themselves. The Phoenix Indian High Schools' newspaper is *The Redskin*. I don't mind the tomahawk chop. It's all in good fun. This *is* sport, after all. In my living room, I'll be watching a Braves game and occasionally do the chop."

Native American activists dismiss such opinion as misguided ("There are happy campers on every plantation," says Suzan Harjo, president of the Morning Start Institute, an Indian-rights organization based in Washington, D.C.). This may be evidence that Native Americans' self-esteem has fallen so low that they don't even know when they're being insulted. American Indians—unlike, say the Irish Catholics who founded Notre Dame and named its teams the Fighting Irish—had no hand in creating most of the teams that use their names; their identities were plucked from them wholesale and used for frivolous purposes, like firing up fans at ball games.

"This is no honor," says Michael Yellow Bird, an associate professor of social work at Arizona State. "We lost our land, we lost our languages, we lost our children. Proportionately speaking indigenous peoples [in the U.S.] are incarcerated more than any other group, we have more racial violence perpetrated upon us, and we are forgotten. If people think this is how to honor us, then colonization has really taken hold."

Regardless, the campaign to erase Indian team names and symbols nationwide has been a success, though Native American activists have made little progress at the highest level of pro sports. Officials of the Atlanta Braves, Chicago Blackhawks, Cleveland Indians and Washington Redskins, for example, say they have no intention of changing their teams' names or mascots. Their single-minded pursuit of the issue has literally changed the face of sports in the U.S. Since 1969, when Oklahoma disavowed its mascot Little Red (a student wearing an Indian war bonnet, buckskin costume and moccasins), more than 600 school teams and minor league professional clubs have dropped nicknames deemed offensive by Native American groups.

What's more, the movement continues. On Jan. 9 the Metropolitan Washington 15 Council of Governments, which represents 17 local governments in D.C., south Maryland and northern Virginia, voted 11-2 to adopt a resolution calling the Redskins name "demeaning and dehumanizing" and asking team owner Dan Snyder to change it by next season. A week earlier former Redskins fullback Dale Atkeson had been told by the California Department of Motor Vehicles to remove his vanity plates reading 1 REDSKIN. The word *Redskin* was banned on plates by the DMB in 1999.

"We consider ourselves racially sensitive," says D.C. council member Carol Schwartz, who introduced the resolution against the Redskins, "yet in this one area we are so hypocritical. Since when is a sports team's name more important than the sensitivities of our fellow human beings? For decades we had the Washington Bullets and [owner] Abe Pollin on his own changed the name [in 1997, because of the high murder rate in D.C.]. Guess what? The world did not stop spinning. Why we would keep this racist term is beyond me."

While those who support names such as Seminoles (Florida State) and Braves can argue that the words celebrate Native American traditions, applying that claim to the Redskins is absurd. Nevertheless, Redskins vice president Karl Swanson says the name "symbolizes courage, dignity and leadership and has always been employed in that manner"—conveniently ignoring the fact that in popular usage dating back four centuries, the word has been a slur based on skin color. Swanson trots out research that traces the term *redskin* to Native Americans' custom of daubing on red paint before battle. Many experts on Native American history point out that the red paint was used not for war but for burial, and that whites that paid and received bounties for dead Indians first used the word redskin. "If you research the origin of *redskin*, no one would want that associated with his team," says pro golfer Notah Begay III, who is half Navajo and half Pueblo. "Trading post owners used to offer rewards for Indians' scalps. Signs would say something like, 'Redskin scalps, worth so much.'"

However, what's most important, Swanson counters, is intent: Because the Redskins and their fans *mean* nothing racist by using the nickname, it isn't racist or offensive. "This has been the name of our organization for 70 years," Swanson says. "We believe it has taken on a meaning independent of the word itself—and it's positive."

Not so, says Harjo: "There's no more derogatory word that's used against us, about us, in the English language. Even if it didn't have such heinous origins, everyone knows that it has never been an honorific. It's a terrible insult."

Harjo is not alone in her thinking. A slew of dictionaries agree that *redskin* is con- 20 temptuous, and so do Native American academics, nearly every Native American organization and three judges on the U.S. Trademark Trial and Appeal Board. In April 1999, responding to a lawsuit brought by Harjo and six other Indian leaders, the board stripped the Washington Redskins of federal protection on their seven trademarks. If the decision stands up under appeal, the team and the NFL could lose an estimated $5 million annually on sales of licensed merchandise.

Even though no team name is under more sustained attack, there's evidence that for the Redskins, a name change would be good for business. In 1996, after much pressure from alumni threatening to withdraw their financial support, Miami (Ohio) University acceded to the Miami tribe's request that it change its team name from Redskins to Redhawks. The following year alumni gave a record $25 million to the school. "Someday it will change," Miami spokesman Richard Little says of the Washington Redskins name. "And you know what? There'll still be a football team there, and there'll still be those ugly fat guys in dresses cheering for it."

Swanson says the vast majority of Redskins fans like the name, and indeed, beyond the protests of politicians, there's no groundswell of outrage against it in D.C. This is a city so racially sensitive that an aide to Mayor Anthony Williams was forced to resign in 1999 for *correctly* using the nonracial term *niggardly*. However, there's nothing hotter than the mass pilgrimage of 80,000 fans to Landover, MD, on Sundays in autumn to sing *Hail to the Redskins* at FedEx Field. Williams mentioned changing the name at a press conference once, but "no one really paid attention," says his aide Tony Bullock. "It's not something that anyone is really talking about." Nevertheless, Bullock says, "the mayor believes it is time to change the name."

That the name is offensive to Native Americans is easy for non-Natives to presume. It resonates when an Olympic hero and former Marine Corps captain such as Mills speaks out against Indian names and mascots at schools around the country. He insists that a team named Redskins in the capital of the nation that committed genocide against Native Americans is the equivalent of a soccer team in Germany being called the Berlin Kikes. Says Mills, "Our truth is, *redskin* is tied to the murder of indigenous people."

Somehow that message is lost on most of Mills's fellow Native Americans. Asked if they were offended by the name Redskins, 75% of Native American respondents in SI's poll said they were not, and even on reservations, where Native American culture and influence are perhaps felt most intensely, 62% said they weren't offended. Overall, 69% of Native American respondents—and 57% of those living on reservations—feel it's O.K. for the Washington Redskins to continue using the name. "I like the name Redskins," says Mark Timentwa, 50, a member of the Colville Confederated Tribes in Washington State who lives on the Tribes' reservation. "A few elders find it offensive, but my mother loves the Redskins."

Only 29% of Native Americans, and 40% living on reservations, thought Snyder 25 should change his team's name. Such indifference implies a near total disconnect between Native American activists and the general Native American population on this issue. "To a lot of the younger folks the name Redskins is tied to the football team, and it doesn't represent anything more than the team," says Roland McCook, a member of the tribal council of the Ute tribe in Fort Duchesne, Utah.

The Utes' experience with the University of Utah might serve as a model for successful resolution of conflicts over Indian nicknames. Four years ago the council met with university officials who made it clear that they would change their team's name, the Running Utes, if the tribe found it objectionable. (The university had retired its cartoonish Indian mascot years before.) The council was perfectly happy to have the Ute name continue to circulate in the nation's sports pages, but council members said they intended to keep a close eye on its use. "We came away with an understanding that as long as the university used the Ute name in a positive manner that preserved the integrity of the Ute tribe, we would allow the use of the name and the Ute logo [two eagle feathers and a drum]," says McCook. Florida State, likewise, uses the name Seminoles for its teams with the express approval of the Seminole nation.

Like the Ute tribe, most Native Americans have no problem with teams using names like Indians and Fighting Illini—or even imposed names like Sioux. "People get upset about the Fighting Sioux, but why?" Gross says. "We're not Sioux people, anyway. The French and the Ojibway tribe gave us that name and they're our hereditary enemies. We're not braves, and we're not really Indians. I know the history. For me those names are not a problem." Many Native Americans are offended, however, by mascots such as Illinois's Chief Illiniwek and others that dress up in feathers and so-called war paint. "Just do away with the imagery—the dancing, the pageantry," says Gross.

Which brings us to the point at which the word problem becomes a number problem. Say you are a team owner. You kiss Chief Wahoo goodbye. Stop the chop. Dump the fake Indian garb, the turkey feathers and the war paint. Get rid of, say, the Redskins name because it's got a sullied history and just sounds wrong. Rename the team the Washington Warriors—without the Indian-head logo—and watch the new team hats and jackets hit the stores. Money is going to pour in, you see, and someone will have to count it.

Polls Apart

ANDREA WOO

SI polled Native Americans and sports fans in general on the use of Indian nicknames, and got some surprising answers.

Although most Native American activists and tribal leaders consider Indian team names and mascots offensive, neither Native Americans in general nor a cross-section of U.S. sports fans agree. That is one of the findings of a poll conducted for SI by the Peter Harris Research Corp. The pollsters interviewed 351 Native Americans (217 living on reservations and 134 living off) and 743 fans. Their responses were weighted according to U.S. census figures for age, race and gender, and for distribution of Native Americans on and off reservations. With a margin of error of ±4%, 83% of the Indians said that professional teams should not stop using Indian nicknames, mascots or symbols, and 79% of the fans agreed with them. Surprisingly, there is a greater divergence of opinion between Native Americans who live on reservations and those who don't. Sixty-seven percent of Indians on reservations do not object to the use of Indian images, against 87% of those off the reservations. When pollsters asked about the Washington Redskins, they found no great resentment toward the name. Instead, they again found agreement between Native Americans and fans (69% of the former and 74% of the latter do not object to the name), and less agreement between Indians on and off reservations (57% and 72%, respectively). Other results appear [in the tables below].

Asked whether the use of Native American team names and mascots contributes to discrimination against Indians, respondents said:

	TOTAL FANS%	TOTAL INDIANS%	INDIANS LIVING ON/ OFF RESERVATIONS	
			ON%	OFF%
Contributes to discrimination	12	23	45	17
Does not contribute	88	75	53	81
Undecided	0	2	2	2

Asked what they thought of the tomahawk chop at Atlanta Braves games, respondents said:

	TOTAL FANS%	TOTAL INDIANS%	INDIANS LIVING ON/ OFF RESERVATIONS	
			ON%	OFF%
Like it	28	28	11	33
Find it objectionable	21	23	39	18
Don't Care	51	48	46	49
Undecided	0	1	4	0

Asked their opinions of team nicknames derived from other ethnic groups—Celtics, Fighting Irish, Ragin' Cajuns, Flying Dutchmen—respondents said:

	TOTAL FANS%	TOTAL INDIANS%	INDIANS LIVING ON/OFF RESERVATIONS	
			ON%	OFF%
Like them	49	25	16	27
Find them objectionable	4	12	14	12
Don't care	47	62	68	60
Undecided	0	1	2	1

SOURCE: Peter Harris Research Group, Inc.

Mascot Supporters Insult Native Peoples

REBECCA L. ADAMSON

Rebecca L. Adamson, a Cherokee, writes a monthly column for *Indian Country Today* and is president of First Nations Development Institute. An activist for over 30 years, she has served on the boards of philanthropic organizations and investment funds and has worked to foster tribal investment and development. The following editorial appeared in *Indian Country Today* in March 2002.

New and more sophisticated ways of insulting Native peoples and depriving them of   1
their voices are on the march, and we must greatly increase our efforts to confront them. Of course, we have seen this sort of backlash before. Remember when fishing and hunting groups first organized against tribes for "perceived special treatment"?

The same is happening with gaming. Efforts continue by states and private interests to undermine this important new tool for Native economic development. The resentment and animosity are building, though often hidden. One open example is the campaign of the Texas Attorney General to deny tribes in that state the right to operate casinos. Shades of Slade Gorton!

In the media, two recent, egregious examples of this recent trend demeaning to Native people surfaced in articles in *Sports Illustrated* and *Crain Business* magazine. The latter highlighted the continued use by the Tootsie Roll Corp. of the Indian wrapper legend and "Chief Shooting Star."

The *Sports Illustrated* issue of March 4 contains a story, "The Indian Wars," that says the general public—mostly sports fans—and large percentages of Natives, both on and off the reservation, see nothing wrong in the use of Native mascots and logos. The piece implies that American Indian leaders and activists are on one side of the issue and Indian peoples are on the other. The interviews chosen, combined with the limited polling data offered, paint a picture of Native confusion in relation to the mascot issue. We have serious doubts about the polling process and numbers. And I agree with Suzan Harjo's comment that there are always "happy campers on every plantation."

Despite the considerable progress in changing the Indian names and logos of high   5
school and lower-level professional teams in the past decade or so, the top-level professional teams still resist. The Washington Redskins is the classic example of a team trying desperately to justify a name, one that no one believes has been anything but

derogatory to Native peoples over the centuries. But, there is lots of money in Washington Redskins merchandise.

As for the Indian wrapper legend and "Chief Shooting Star" of Tootsie Pop fame, an article in *Crain Business* asks what's the big deal about "Chief Shooting Star." To Native peoples, plenty. The legend of how the Tootsie Pop came to be is a parody of Indian storytelling and insulting to all Indian people. The Tootsie Roll folks, of course, see nothing wrong in the story and justify its continued use. It doesn't matter, you see, what Indian peoples think. Again, as in the case of the Washington Redskins and other professional sports teams, money stands in the way of doing what's right.

Unfortunately, Tootsie Roll isn't content with defending its bogus legend and insulting story. A more sophisticated move is afoot. Tootsie Roll has approached the Securities and Exchange Commission trying to get shareholder activism stopped on the grounds it interferes with the management of its business.

This move is very dangerous. It not only attempts to stop the free speech of American Indian peoples, but, if approved by the SEC, it would seriously hamper the growing movement of socially responsible investing. This movement has begun to reap important results for tribes as their voice in how companies treat Indian issues is being heard more and more. This progress is based on what is, apparently, the most important thing to companies—the bottom line. In fact, a number of such companies are beginning to see that treating all peoples with dignity is just good business.

The use of polling and backroom deals at the SEC to stop the movement against the derogatory and demeaning use of Indian names, logos and mascots can only be called what it is—greedy racism. These newer sophisticated ways of demonizing Indian leaders, activists and those who don't approve of the use of Indian mascots are just different ways of keeping our voices silent. For too long, Indian voices have been silent. Because various tribes and socially responsible investors, like the Calvert Social Investment Fund, have been making inroads in favor of taking Indian issues seriously, the status quo must find newer ways to stop us.

This all reminds me of what my respected colleague, Elsie Meeks, has gone through 10 just for standing up for all Native people. Elsie, the first American Indian member of the U.S. Civil Rights Commission, sponsored a resolution that opposed the use of American Indian names and images as sports symbols. The resolution passed on April 13, 2001. Since then, Elsie has received many, many hate letters opposed to her and the resolution she sponsored. When I hear this, I wonder: why are these people so angry? What are they afraid of? Native people having their own voice? Anti-Native racism is still within the psyche of too many Americans, but we can not allow it to silence us.

Now is the time for all Indian leaders and peoples to respond even more forcefully against the greedy racism perpetuated by the use of offensive Indian mascots and logos. To begin with, *Sports Illustrated* and the Tootsie Roll Corp. need to hear what all Indian peoples really think about the demeaning use of our images and symbols. The backlash needs to be met forcefully and quickly. The *Sports Illustrated* poll is wrong. Speak up for yourselves and your children and grandchildren. Now is the time to buttress the progress that has been made on the mascot issue on so many levels. Speak out!

QUESTIONS FOR DISCUSSION

1. **Analyzing Strategy:** Rebecca L. Adamson is writing in *Indian Country Today*, a journal for Native Americans. S. L. Price is writing in *Sports Illustrated*, a mass circulation magazine. How do their arguments reflect the audiences they are addressing?

2. **Analyzing Strategy:** How was the survey cited in the Price article conducted? Why does Adamson find it unacceptable? How does Price state his position? Would his argument be stronger if he identified himself as a Native American?

3. **Making Connections:** Joseph H. Brown, an African-American writer, claims that black athletes are expected to fill exemplary social roles in a way that white athletes are not. Do you agree? If Brown is correct, is this imposed standard justified? (Find the original *New York Times* editorial that Brown was responding to and see how they made the case for Tiger Woods's responsibility to boycott the Masters since the sponsoring golf course, the Augusta National, admits only male members.)

4. **Analyzing Strategy:** Bryjak's argument depends on a definition of "heroism" and a discussion of three types of heroism. Find the overall definition. Is it readily believable? Could a different but still plausible definition of "heroism" be constructed that would include many professional athletes?

5. **Making Connections and Analyzing Strategy:** Auster suggests that soccer (football to the rest of the world) is a replacement for or a form of warfare in Europe. Is this an analogy or something else? Would his case be stronger if he took a global perspective and argued about the place of soccer in non-European countries? Does the United States also use sports competition as a disguised form of warfare? Is there any significance in the fact that, until recently, the most popular sports in the United States, football and baseball, were not played internationally?

6. **Making Connections:** Robertson claims that the appeal of sports is celebration of the body (ambivalent for women), Auster that soccer is sublimated warfare, and Bryjak that athletes fall far short of heroism, and some Native Americans, like Adamson, find the naming of sports teams a matter of deep offense. All of these authors insist on the emblematic or symbolic importance of sports, far beyond its entertainment value. Can you identify other symbolic and cultural values in sports? What meanings are possible when local and children's sports activities are considered?

7. **Analyzing Strategy:** How do Price and Robertson use quotations in their arguments? Which one is more effective in the use of quotations?

8. **Making Connections:** Brown wants to celebrate Tiger Woods purely on the basis of his extraordinary golfing ability. Others would make him a cultural role model and demand representative social responses. What effect does the appearance of some sports figures in advertisements have on their cultural stature?

9. **Making Connections:** Why have Native American terms and names been used for sports teams while those of most other ethnic groups in the United States have not? (Are the "Fighting Irish" of Notre Dame and the "Boston Celtics" in the same category as the "Washington Redskins" or not?)

| WRITING SUGGESTIONS |

1. Critics of sports have cited the enormous salaries paid to sports figures and the many players who have been arrested for serious crimes. Considering these issues, the perspectives on sports offered by the readings, and your personal

experience, does professional sports on the whole have a positive or negative effect on contemporary American culture?

2. George J. Bryjak lists three athletes who did achieve the status of hero: Jackie Robinson, Roberto Clemente, and Ted Williams. Write an evaluation in which you argue for a fourth true sports "hero" who fits Bryjak's requirements.

3. Write a constrasting persuasive account of two sports so that one is understood as a symbolic form of warfare while the other is not.

4. Has the standard for depicting women as athletic versus feminine changed in the United States over the last five or six decades? Select a magazine or newspaper that has been in publication for several decades (like *Sports Illustrated* or *Time*). Collect a representative sample of images of women sports figures and compare them, arguing for your interpretation of whether there has been a change and what kind of change there has been.

Public Taste

Chapter 16

Statement Concerning the Recent Actions of Abercrombie and Fitch

JAMIE CHAN, DARREN JOE, AND JUNG JU

The authors of this statement were students at Princeton University when it was published in 2002.

Racism can be very subtle, often disguised as humor or excused as a facet of pop culture. Last week, Abercrombie and Fitch, a popular clothing label with over 200 stores nationwide, issued a new line of Asian-themed graphic T-shirts that display racially charged slogans such as "Wong Brothers Laundry Service: Two Wongs Can Make it White" alongside stereotypical caricatures of slanted-eyed Asians wearing rice paddy hats. In reaction to protests initiated by Asian American student college groups across the country, Abercrombie recalled the controversial attire and company spokesman Hampton Carney issued a statement expressing regret that the T-shirts may have offended some people.

We responded this week by presenting an information table located at Frist Campus Center with statements denouncing the "ethnic" T-shirts and petitions demanding that Abercrombie take further corrective measures for their insensitive act. Since the company has already issued a recall of the T-shirts, some may find this protest unnecessary. However, we believe that it is imperative to press the issue for the following reasons:

First, Abercrombie has refused to acknowledge the racially offensive nature of the T-shirts. According to company spokesman Hampton Carney, the company thought "everyone would love [the shirts], especially the Asian community . . . they were cheeky, irreverent, funny . . . [and] designed with the sole purpose of adding humor and levity to our fashion line." Nowhere in their formal statement of apology does the company acknowledge or address the racial implications of the T-shirts or the corporate actions that led to their design and approval. Instead, Abercrombie issued a half-hearted apology, defending their position that the shirts were humorous and witty without any mention or explanation of how their stereotypical depictions were harmful and insensitive. Abercrombie has yet to take responsibility for their mistakes by failing to address the racist caricatures and slogans in their shirts.

It is especially necessary for a company like Abercrombie to take corporate responsibility for its actions. The company promotes a certain image and lifestyle directed at its young and easily influenced consumer base, in effect dictating what is "cool" not only in clothing, but also in mindset and attitude. With such a powerful influence on American youth, what message does Abercrombie convey about cultural diversity, minority issues, racism, and stereotypes when it issues racially offensive shirts and then excuses them merely as an attempt at humor? The company fails to realize that by condoning its racially insensitive remarks and caricatures, it prompts its young customers to disregard the stereotypes implicit in the shirts and take them for humor and amusement.

Second, Abercrombie actually benefits from this latest controversy. As in prior notable controversies, such as a sexually provocative advertising campaign and the publishing of alcoholic drink recipes in their quarterly catalogue, the company thrives on sensational publicity. For example, when news that the T-shirts would be pulled from stores reached the general public, a consumer frenzy led to a mad rush to buy the shirts before they were pulled from the shelves. The leftover supply of these shirts is currently selling for $500 apiece on eBay, generating greater hype for the company. Furthermore, the company is receiving praise from the media for its quick response to its consumers as they pulled the shirts. It is a crime that Abercrombie gains greater name-recognition and garners praise for their irresponsible actions.

Lastly, the Princeton community should be educated on why many find the shirts themselves offensive. The caricatures used by Abercrombie are similar to propaganda circulated in the late nineteenth century used to ignite widespread hostility and fear of Chinese immigrant laborers, many of whom owned and worked in laundromats. The depictions helped fuel xenophobia towards Chinese immigrants, contributing to the passage of the 1882 Chinese Exclusion Act, which prohibited the entrance of Chinese laborers into the country for 61 years. The shirts are insensitive to the historical legacy of Asian Americans' experience here in the United States. The stereotypical caricatures—slanted-eyed laundry service and restaurant workers who speak broken English—are historically demeaning depictions of Asian Americans, ones that have been used to emphasize their foreignness and outsider status in American society.

Even if one is not aware of the history behind these depictions, the content of the shirts is still offensive. The statement, "Two Wongs Can Make it White" is a play on the saying "Two wrongs make it right" [sic]. This not only implicitly equates Wong with wrong and White with right, but also suggests the physical inferiority and diminished worth of Asians, as it takes two Asians to equal the value of one White. The emphasis on the mispronunciation and misspelling of words by the Asian characters in the slogan "You love long time" and "1-888-GOO-PEZA" implies that Asian Americans cannot speak English properly.

One shirt even has a line reading, "Buddha Bash—get your Buddha on the floor." Abercrombie must have forgotten that Buddhism is an actual religion practiced by millions worldwide. How disrespectful would a shirt saying, "Christ Bash—get your Christ on the floor," be? When a stereotype is cast over an entire group of people, it not only trivializes their culture and heritage, but also undermines the very identity of the individuals it ridicules. Many Asian Americans, including our own grandparents, relatives, family friends, and even parents work or have worked in laundromats and restaurants and speak broken English. By reducing the existence of real individuals to slant-eyed, subserviently smiling caricatures, Abercrombie trivializes and disrespects the lives and occupations of many Asian Americans—those who have already fought racism and discrimination to establish themselves in America, and those who are still fighting today. Their daily struggle to survive and to find a place in society as Americans is taken a step backward as Abercrombie encourages the acceptance of their mockery. We find this to be degrading, offensive, and not at all "cheeky."

As a result, we would like to issue the following demands to Abercrombie:

1. Permanently remove the entire line of offensive "Asian" T-shirts from all market venues.

2. Issue an official apology from the Abercrombie and Fitch CEO Michael S. Jeffries to be published in the form of a one-page advertisement in all major newspapers and to be posted on the main page of the company web site, the next quarterly catalogue, and in all Abercrombie and Fitch stores.

3. Encourage the return of previously bought "Asian" T-shirts with guaranteed unconditional refund and incentives (i.e. vouchers or discount on future purchases).

4. Donate the already made profits from the T-shirts to national Asian American organizations that encourage understanding of diverse cultures and histories and hire an Asian Pacific–American consultant team to ensure sensitivity to minority issues.

A Small Plea to Delete a Ubiquitous Expletive

ELIZABETH AUSTIN

The winner of an award for magazine journalism from the National Mental Health Association, Elizabeth Austin has published articles in *Self*, *Time*, *Psychology Today*, and *U.S. News and World Report*, where the following article appeared in April 1998.

Oh, f——.

The "F" word, as it's called in more polite circles (including magazines such as this one), is increasingly hard to escape. Those who rarely use it themselves nonetheless hear it frequently—on the street, on the job, at the health club, at the movies—anywhere two or three disgruntled citizens might gather. Most people have uttered the word; everyone can define it. But even those who aren't particularly shocked by it don't want to hear it all the time. The toughest of tough guys cringes inwardly when somebody says it in front of his mother. Becoming a parent induces instant hypersensitivity to the word's ubiquitous presence in movies, on cable TV, in music, and in the loose talk of childless friends.

In its simplest and oldest usage, the "F" word refers to copulation. This usage has a long, frequently jolly, occasionally distinguished history. Shakespeare made glancing puns about it, and Scottish poet Robert Burns included it in his racier verses. More commonly today, though, the "F" word is used to express not desire but derision, not heat but hostility. Even when used as a kind of verbal space holder, a rougher, hipper equivalent of "you know" (as in "I f——ing love that f——ing movie," or in the Army patois that has been common for decades), it carries a rude message. It is both a gauge and an engine of our ever plummeting standards of civility. Yet enough people are fed up with it that it's possible to erase the "F" word from public parlance and civil discourse.

Last word. A couple of generations back, calling for a public elimination of the "F" word would have been preposterous, since the word was never uttered in polite company (loosely defined as anywhere middle-class women were likely to hear it). In the late '60s, however, the loud, open use of the "F" word became a true shibboleth, dividing the student radicals from the Establishment "pigs" they delighted in tweaking. In Jerry Rubin's words, the "F" word was "the last word left in the English language. Amerika cannot destroy it because she dare not use it."

But America took that dare. From the early '70s on, the "F" word started turning up with increasing regularity in movies, literature, and real life, according to Jesse Sheidlower's exhaustive volume, *The F-Word.* Many linguists and social critics celebrated the "F" word's coming out as a healthy abandonment of prudishness; a few still do. But civic virtuecrats today make a stronger case that public use of the word is a prime example of the "broken window" theory of social decay. When we put private frustrations and the right to be foulmouthed ahead of public order and civility, we coarsen society and risk an avalanche of rage and violence. Despite its near universality, the "F" word remains a fighting word. 5

So let's get rid of it. Scholars of social norms say all that's necessary to remove offensive language from public speech is a critical mass of people willing to take up cudgels against it. University of Chicago law Prof. Randal Picker describes such sudden overthrows of social standards as "norms cascades." If society is ripe for change, he contends, a single, powerful catalyst can engineer swift, widespread transformation. Picker cites Jesse Jackson, whose call for a switch from "black" to "African-American" changed the nation's nomenclature almost overnight. A more subtle but equally effective norms cascade was engineered by a handful of feminist writers in the early 1970s. Author-activist Robin Morgan remembers furiously listing words then commonly used to describe women, both in conversation and in print. "Produce and animals is what we were," she recalls. "We were 'chicks' and 'lambs' and 'birds' and 'bitches,' and there was always the infamous 'cherry.'" When Morgan and other feminist leaders publicly insisted on being called women, they started a norms cascade that eventually erased not only chick and bitch but girl and lady as well.

The "F" word seems like a particularly ripe target for a new generation of linguistic activists from both sides of the ideological divide. Erasing the word from civil discourse is one goal that Phyllis Schlafly could share with Andrea Dworkin. Here are a few modest proposals to help make that happen:

Police should start ticketing drivers who use the "F" word (or the correlating hand gesture), thereby boosting civility and calming road rage simultaneously. Although this could raise some First Amendment hackles, keep in mind that "fighting words" are not protected speech. One simple test of the fighting-words concept is whether a fight actually ensues. Slapping a $100 ticket on a driver whose uplifted finger sparked a collision should pass any constitutional test.

The Motion Picture Association of America movie rating system should be overhauled to give an automatic NC-17 rating to any film that uses the "F" word even once. An NC-17 rating all but guarantees diminished viewership. Writers and directors who considered the word necessary to their artistic expression could still get their movies made; they'd just have to make the decision to trade lucrative ticket sales to teenagers for their artistic license.

Authors who salt their books with gratuitous "F" words should get the same critical treatment as those who sprinkle their prose with casual racial epithets. Certainly, there are times when the "F" word expresses precisely what a writer means to convey. But we need literary critics who understand the distinction between necessary frankness and the adolescent desire to shock. 10

Most important, we must delete the "F" word from our own lives. The most lasting shifts in social standards are those that begin at cocktail parties and around water coolers. We can wipe out the "F" word simply by refusing to use it ourselves and quietly but firmly objecting when others use it within earshot. The next time someone uses the "F" word in casual conversation, Judith Martin, better known as Miss Manners, suggests responding: "I'm not used to that sort of language." (If you can't say that line with a straight face, try: "We don't use that word anymore.")

Objecting to the "F" word isn't censorship. You can still use it as a punch line, if you like. You'll just risk the freezing silence and icy glares now reserved for white people who use the "N" word in public. Similarly, you're free to use it among your intimates, as a term of (in Sheidlower's words) "endearment, admiration, [or] derision." The rules of public civility have always included the naked-and-sweaty exemption. How you talk in the locker room or bedroom is up to you.

Ultimately, a social norm is nothing more, and nothing less, than the sum of individual decisions. In reconsidering the "F" word, you may prize your right to say it above your neighbor's right not to hear it. But personally, I'm swearing off.

A Parent's View

JOHN A. YAHNER

John A. Yahner is a freelance writer who lives in Washington, D.C. The following article first appeared on the website of the Recording Industry Association of America (RIAA) in 2002. A note that follows the posting indicates that "this column represents Yahner's own views and was not paid for by the RIAA or any other entity."

That night at the dinner table decades ago, we were especially excited. Only minutes before we had peeled the plastic off the new Woodstock album and placed it on the turntable. We knew we were taking a risk listening to it for the first time with the parents present, but we were teenagers, and in the spirit of the '60s we wanted to open up dinner—or shut it down.

As we settled in to the meal and banter, Country Joe and the Fish started the fight song. The lyrics exploded much too loud and all too clearly, "Give me an F!" After the "U" it didn't take a linguist to figure out what word was forming. It wasn't fun. All the kids bolted for the record player. My older brother got there first, I can still hear the skid marks of the needle viciously ripping across the vinyl. Before the age of hip-hop this was quite an unwelcome sound. It meant skippage, severe, deadly skippage. The album was ruined, dinner too.

The parents had never heard such trash; we were never to buy or listen to it again. They didn't want us to get high or by with a little help from our friends, didn't care if we were talking about our generation, blah blah blah.

I survived the sixties. I am not sure whether I'll survive being a parent. It is without a doubt the toughest job I've ever had—and the best job too. Now, my wife and I must face the music chosen by our three "tween" children. (I can almost feel my parents smiling down from heaven.)

Thirty years after our kitchen Woodstock concert, I went to a record store in Washington, D.C., with my ten-year-old son Kyle. He wanted a CD by some artist named Eminem. I had no idea who he was so I decided to check with the sales people behind the counter, who happened to have a lot of facial body piercing. So much so that it looked like if they drank a glass of water it would spill out onto the floor. I asked about the CD. They looked at me, looked at Kyle and both said, "No way." Then they proceeded to help us.

They explained to both of us what the Parental Advisory label meant. They asked Kyle what kind of music he liked. They showed us other albums that might be acceptable. In short, they couldn't have been more accommodating. But for the threat of puncture, I could have kissed them.

Was all this acceptable to Kyle? Heck no. He wanted Eminem. I took a deep breath. I told him to look around the store at all the CDs, rows and rows of them. Then I explained that he could choose from thousands of CDs, but not the dozen or so that had the parental advisory label. He had to compromise. It took some time, but finally he chose an acceptable CD.

It is every generation's mission to defy, reject, and alienate the previous generation. Parents are the closest targets. Before you leave the nest empty, you scream and slam the door on your way out. So, in a sense I understand the rebellion. The form it takes is often difficult to swallow. I don't mind the clothes so much (I can't believe polyester is back!), I balk at the body piercing, and yes, some of the music is so offensive I can't stand it. Nothing tests my free speech principles more than some of the lyrics I hear. Violent, mysognistic, exploitive junk.

Yet, one person's junk is another person's jewel. So who's to decide what music is acceptable? In our house, with our kids, my wife and I. We are the censors; we set the limits. That's our job. It is not the government's job. We're not ready to sacrifice our first amendment rights to protect our kids from the minuscule amount of offensive music available on the market.

We tell our kids two things. (1) They can have all the freedom that they can handle 10
responsibly. (2) TV, radios, and movies are privileges, not rights, and they can be taken away. We talk about "hate speech" and offensive lyrics and the rights of others. Violate the rules and you lose privileges.

We're bracing for the teen years. We know we can't and won't be with them all the time in the future. We're trying to raise them to be able to make sound judgments on their own.

It's difficult being parents; it must be twice as difficult being a single parent. Parents need all the help they can get. The industry must continue to help with warning labels, the stores must post them prominently and assist ignorant parents with hip kids. But the government has to stay out of the way. Censorship is a job the government is decidedly unsuited for. We learned that in the 1950s.

Nietzsche was wrong about God being dead, but he was right when he wrote, "Without music, life would be a mistake." There's a galaxy of beautiful music kids and parents can choose from and talk about.

In our family, we all agree on the Beatles and Fleetwood Mac. My wife and I still like Hanson even though the kids are on to *NSYNC, and 98 Degrees. After a lifetime of hating country music, my daughters played the Dixie Chicks and I now admit to liking them because I love the song where Earl has to die. (I have to play Earl when they all sing it.) When our kids were taking piano lessons, I played Bud Powell, Keith Jarret, and Mozart's piano concertos for them. They're on to different instruments now, and they're all active in their public school's music program. When they're a little older maybe they'll appreciate Mahler's Fifth Symphony. Whatever we listen to, I don't want the government telling me we can't hear Miles Davis's *Bitch's Brew* because there's a nasty word in the title.

Music Censorship Limits Rights

JENNY LEETE

Jenny Leete was a staff writer for the *Crusader Online,* the online student newspaper for Susquehanna University, where the following article was published in 2001.

It is the responsibility of parents and the government to make sure children at a young   1
age are not purchasing and listening to music with offensive lyrics. I do not believe in censorship of music for the sole reason that we as Americans have rights.

Wal-Mart sells CDs that bleep out profanity and any kind of foul language that society deems derogatory in each and every song. To me, this is ridiculous, stupid and simply unfair to the artist who is attempting to express himself or herself.

I am not saying there are not offensive lyrics out there in the world, because obviously that would be a fallacy. If you do not want to hear certain artists, then you do not have to listen to them. It is your choice.

Now, I understand the concern when it comes to children listening to artists such as Eminem, Rage Against the Machine, Limp Bizkit or Marilyn Manson at a young age. It can definitely affect how a kid grows up, interprets his or her surroundings and acts and reacts to specific situations in life.

Parents are expected to discipline their children and make sure they are not watch-   5
ing MTV and buying CDs that are not appropriate for kids at certain ages.

Now, I know children naturally tend to be rebellious and can always find ways to obtain CDs behind their parents' backs or watch MTV when they are not home.

This is where the government comes into play. Some CDs that have offensive lyrics in their songs also have tags on them that say "explicit lyrics."

As for MTV and VH1, parents need to lay the rules down and not permit their kids to watch these two channels if they find the music played extremely distasteful.

A call to the cable company would shut off undesirable channels. You would still have to pay the same amount of money as if you had all the cable channels. But if it has to be done to prevent your kids from viewing insulting music videos, then it is worth it.

When children become adults, they gain the option of listening to whatever their   10
hearts desire.

Children who are raised properly know better than to apply corrupting lyrics to real life and society. If they choose to listen to offensive music, it is simply for pleasure, and nothing bad comes of it. There is no harm in enjoying one's favorite type or style of music.

It would be unrealistic to assume that all parents are going to take appropriate care of their children and that every worker in a music store is going to comply with the laws and not permit young kids to buy offensive music.

And, even if this ideal situation were somehow possible, there are always going to be kids who can get their hands on stuff they know they are not supposed to have.

But the point is that the two factors I named above would definitely help and make a significant difference in how children grow up in our society, but only if people make a conscientious effort.

Music censorship is absurd. First of all, it goes against our right to speak what we   15
feel and to express ourselves as we please. Music is one of the many aspects in life that help create individuals, and it is unjust to take the right to be different away.

If parents strictly observed their children and carefully paid attention to what their kids were listening to and the government created laws about purchasing music and actually abided by them, music censorship would not be necessary or even discussed as an option to begin with.

The censorship of music is a heinous idea; it is a cop-out and simply ignores the leading reasons children are able to easily acquire debasing music.

If you do not wish to hear certain artists, then simply do not buy their music. And above all, do not complain about kids listening to offensive music when there are ways to prevent that from happening in the first place.

Breaking a Taboo, Editors Turn to Images of Death

FELICITY BARRINGER

A media reporter for the *New York Times,* Felicity Barringer covers the newspaper industry. Before joining the *Times* in 1993, she worked for the *Bergen Record* and the *Washington Post.* The following article was published in the *Times* in October 1998.

One spring afternoon in 1994, a University of Wyoming freshman was shot in the head at point-blank range and left to die. A day or two later, The *Laramie Daily Boomerang* shoved the event in the community's face, printing a front-page photograph of the young man's body as it lay near his dormitory. The figures of police officers partly blocked the view. But only partly.

"Writing a story about somebody being gunned down in the busiest intersection of town in cold blood didn't have the same impact as seeing it," said Robert Wilson, the managing editor, whose daily newspaper has a circulation of about 8,000. "I wanted people to feel that horror. I particularly wanted young people to see that this isn't a movie we're playing here. This is real."

Outrage was what Mr. Wilson wanted. Outrage was what he got—directed not against the killers or the crime, but against the newspaper.

Increasingly, if inconsistently, images of the dead are finding their way into print and onto television. There are corpses without shrouds, without the comfort of a soft focus. There are slack bodies, bloated bodies, frozen, frightened faces that make viewers turn away. "This is not something I wish to see alongside my breakfast," an angry reader wrote to the *New York Times* three weeks ago when the newspaper ran a photograph of a massacre victim in Kosovo, his face contorted.

In fits and starts, the reflexes that made graphic death a rarity in newspapers in the generation after the Vietnam War are being supplanted by a willingness to use such images for their emotional impact.

Taking Sides
An uncomfortable fact for journalists is that their use has an editorial tone at odds with the buttoned-down objectivity of news columns. But images from Rwanda, Kosovo and Algeria have focused popular outrage. The larger the point to be made, the more willing editors have been to use visual horror to make that point.

That does not mean there has never been graphic death in newspapers. In the first decades of the 20th century, pictures of dead mobsters and suicides filled the tabloids. But in the last two decades, along with the rise of graphic violence on television and in the movies, both the grittier tabloids and the more restrained broad-sheets took a different approach. Instead of embracing all disturbing images, editors waited until a particularly visceral image captured a visceral moment.

"Bombing victims in Kosovo look the same as bombing victims 10 years ago in Iran," said Eric Meskauskas, photo editor of the *Daily News.* "You wind up trying to look for something that has something else in it that makes it more powerful."

He added, "Since we've seen almost everything there is to see in this age, what photo editors are trying to do is make you feel something."

Some photographs have "outrage quality," said Michael Smith, a deputy picture 10 editor at the *New York Times.*

"Take the baby in the Oklahoma City bombing," he said, speaking of the photograph by Charles H. Porter IV, an amateur, showing a firefighter cradling the dead body of one-year-old Baylee Almon. "Yeah, people agonized over it because it was a baby. Nobody wants to put a baby in the paper. But it so symbolized the loss of innocence, the fact that we were as vulnerable to terrorism as anyone else."

Editors who chose to run photographs of charred corpses in a Nairobi morgue after this summer's embassy bombing, or the face of an old Albanian man killed in a Kosovo massacre, made the same argument. At a panel discussion at the Newseum in New York recently, Mr. Meskauskas said, "I think you have to use it because it tells you something about terrorism and what the people were feeling like."

The visible dead tend to have two things in common. For one, they have usually died at human hands. With the exception of the youth whose ash-covered body was photographed from the air after the explosion at Mount St. Helen's in 1980, dead victims of natural disasters, as well as victims of airplane crashes, tend not to be shown in the news media. As a senior photo editor described it, without a moral lesson to be drawn, there is no point in showing corpses.

Death Far Away

"When you look at a war," said Vincent J. Alabiso, the executive photo editor of the Associated Press, "one image can somehow define a story and crystallize your feelings some way or another, and can force you to decide on a point of view you might take. That's different from looking at a hurricane picture."

A second factor common to many images of the dead in newspapers is their distance 15 from readers. While no generalization is foolproof, it is safe to say that the farther away the dead person is, physically or psychologically, the more likely that the image will find its way into print. "I don't think people really want to look at highly disturbing photographs, and the closer to home, the more disturbing the images," said Gail Buckland, a photo historian and an associate professor at Cooper Union.

"Dead bodies in Africa are more tolerated," she added.

Others, like Mr. Meskauskas, have a simpler explanation: Crime scenes in the West are tightly controlled. None of the editors interviewed had seen images of the bodies of James Byrd Jr., the black man dragged to death in Jasper, Texas, last summer, or Matthew Shepard, the gay college student tied to a fence, beaten and left to die two weeks ago in Laramie, Wyoming.

No Faces, Please

The rollicking, anything-goes photojournalism of the 1920's and 1930's changed during World War II, according to John G. Morris, a former photographer and picture editor for *Life* magazine, "The rule was: We can show enemy dead but not our own people. Especially faces."

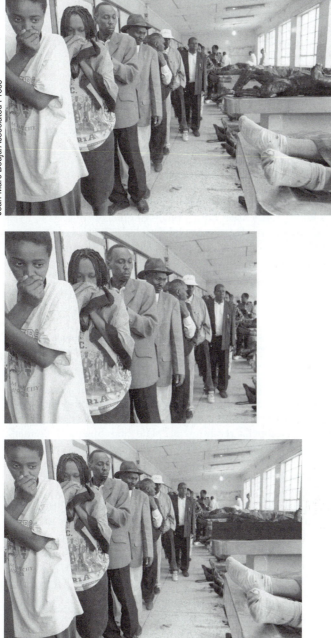

Jean-Marc Bouju/Associated Press

A photograph of the morgue in Nairobi last August after the bombing of the American Embassy there posed questions of ethics and taste for editors. At top, the *Los Angeles Times* ran the full picture, but on page 14. The *New York Times*, center, used part of it on the front page, leaving out the burned bodies. At bottom, the *San Francisco Examiner* blurred the image of a corpse; its editors said later they should not have done so.

"The first big breakthrough occurred in 1943," added Mr. Morris, who was also picture editor at the *New York Times* in the 1960's and 1970's. "*Life* ran a photo from Buna Beach in New Guinea. That picture was held up in censorship in Washington for about eight months before it was released. It showed two or three American bodies face down in the sand."

Censorship was eased during the Vietnam War, but returned during the Persian 20 Gulf war; the *Detroit Free Press*'s photographer, David Turnely, had to argue and cajole the military censors to approve a photograph of a soldier crying next to a body bag.

But censorship had little role to play in 1993 during the ill-fated American military involvement in Somalia. The *Toronto Star*'s image of a dead American serviceman dragged through the street by mobs went around the world. "We ran the poor American soldier who was dragged through the streets in Mogadishu," said Michele Stephenson, the director of photography for *Time* magazine. "We felt we needed to do that to show what was going on there."

Despite his decision to put the corpse of a murdered college student before his readers, Mr. Wilson, of the *Laramie Daily Boomerang*, would not quickly do it again. Even had photos of Mr. Shepard tied to the fence existed, he said, the cruelty of the crime was such that "I don't think I or anyone else could have faced a photograph of it."

The Kitschification of Sept. 11

DANIEL HARRIS

Daniel Harris is the author of *Cute, Quaint, Hungry, and Romantic* (2000), a critique of consumer culture, as well as *The Rise and Fall of Gay Culture* (1997). The following article appeared in the online magazine *Salon* in January 2002.

Within minutes after the collapse of the World Trade Center, inspirational songs, 1 propagandistic images designed to feed the fires of patriotic fury, and poetry commemorating the victims began to proliferate on radio, television and the Internet. The Dixie Chicks performed an a cappella rendition of "The Star Spangled Banner"; car-window decals appeared featuring a lugubrious poodle with a glistening tear as large as a gum drop rolling mournfully down its cheek; refrigerator magnets of Old Glory flooded the market ("buy two and get a third one FREE!"); and the unofficial laureates of the World Wide Web brought the Internet to a crawl by posting thousands of elegies with such lyrics as "May America's flag forever fly unfurled,/May Heaven be our perished souls' 'Windows on the World'!" Gigabytes of odes to the lost firemen and celebrations of American resolve turned the information superhighway into a parking lot:

My Daddy's Flag

Arriving home from work and a trip to the store,
My 5 year old daughter greeted me at the door.
"Hi daddy!" she smiled, "what's in the bag?"
"Well, daddy has brought home the American flag."

With a puzzled look she asked "What does it do?"
I answered, "it's our country's colors, red, white and blue.
This flag on our house will protect you my dear,
It has magical powers to keep away fear."

Does an event as catastrophic as this one require the rhetoric of kitsch to make it less horrendous? Do we need the overkill of ribbons and commemorative quilts, haloed seraphim perched on top of the burning towers and teddy bears in firefighter helmets waving flags, in order to forget the final minutes of bond traders, restaurant workers and secretaries screaming in elevators filling with smoke, standing in the frames of broken windows on the 90th floor waiting for help, and staggering down the stairwells covered in third-degree burns? Perhaps saccharine images of sobbing Statues of Liberty and posters that announce "we will never forget when the Eagle cried" make the incident more palatable, more "aesthetic" in a sense, decorated with the mortician's reassuringly familiar stock in trade. Through kitsch, we avert our eyes from tragedy, transforming the unspeakable ugliness of diseases, accidents and wars into something poetic and noble, into pat stories whose happy endings offer enduring lessons in courage and resilience.

And yet while kitsch may serve to anesthetize us to the macabre spectacle of perfectly manicured severed hands embedded in the mud and charred bodies dropping out of windows, it may conceal another agenda. The strident sentimentality of kitsch makes the unsaid impermissible and silences dissenting opinions, which cannot withstand the emotional vehemence of its rhetoric. It not only beautifies ghoulish images, it whitewashes the political context of the attack which, when portrayed as a pure instance of gratuitous sadism, of inexpiable wickedness, appears to have had no cause, no ultimate goal. Four months into Bush's "crusade," despite clear successes, we remain far from certain about what, in the long run, we hope to achieve.

Ignoring geopolitics, we sealed the incident off in an ideologically sterile vacuum, the perfect incubator for kitsch, which thrives on irrational simplifications of moral complexities. Rather than making sincere efforts to understand the historical origins of the event in a protracted international conflict, we erect a schematic narrative that pitted absolute evil against absolute good, our own unwavering rationality against the delirium of crazed fanatics. On the electronic bulletin boards on the Internet, the terrorists became cartoon villains whose "insane and beastly acts" were both unmotivated and unaccountable, the result of nothing more explicable than "malevolence," of the "dastardly cowardice" of "an inhuman . . . group that has no place in the universe." These "depraved minions of a hate-filled maniac" who subscribed to "the toxic theology [of] suicidal barbarism," "watched from a distance/And laughed in a hauty [sic] tone" at this "ungodly intrusional [sic] violation of human life," this "psychotic" prank ostensibly staged out of sheer spite.

If the perpetrators are monsters, the victims are not just innocent but angelic, 5 diaphanous seraphs with harps who, after being crushed in the collapse, "rose again,/ Through the smoke, and dust and pain./To fly. To play above again/In the blue American sky./The perfect, blue American sky." R&B vocalist Kristy Jackson has hit the charts with a commemorative single entitled "Little Did She Know" about a woman who, on the morning of Sept. 11, sent her fireman husband off to work with a peck on his cheek, heedless of the fact that he would never return:

Little did she know she'd kissed a hero
Though he'd always been one in her eyes
But when faced with certain death
He'd said a prayer and took a breath
And led an army of true angels in the sky

Little did she know she'd kissed a hero
Though he'd always been an angel in her eyes

Putting others first, it's true
That's what heroes always do
Now he doesn't need a pair of wings to fly

The kitsch of extreme innocence also emerges in the selectivity of the roll call of the martyrs. We found the deaths of the emergency personnel far more riveting than the deaths of the office workers, even though the latter outnumbered the former by a ratio of approximately 12 to 1. It is difficult to make a martyr out of someone who is run down in the street by a bus, as the casualties in the two buildings essentially were, dying, not while manning gun turrets or lobbing grenades, but while filing expense reports and faxing spreadsheets. Such an unglamorous, clerical fate is not suited to instant martyrdom and hence our attention shifted away from secretaries and CEOs, who did nothing more intrepid than attempt to save their own lives, and gravitated toward a group that more adequately satisfies our folkloric requirements for heroism. The whole story was reshaped so that the narrative focus fell squarely on those whose bravery in the face of death allowed us to superimpose on the chaos and panic of that incomprehensible hour a reassuring bedtime story of valiant knights charging into the breach, laying down their lives for their countrymen as they fought against "the forces of darkness."

Much as the skies above New York were immediately "sterilized" to prevent further attacks, so debate was sterilized to prevent further discussion of the disaster. Many patriotic stalwarts seemed to believe that dissent amounted to a disavowal of one's American citizenship, a McCarthyite accusation that created an atmosphere of fear and paranoia, a self-consciousness hardly conducive to the effective discussion of an emergency. Moreover, uncritical defenders of our foreign policy made liberal use of such words as "tasteless," "inappropriate" and "untimely" to describe the statements of anyone who questioned the wisdom of carpet-bombing Afghanistan, including the unfortunate host of the television program "Politically Incorrect," who was forced to retract remarks deemed offensive to the Pentagon after his outraged sponsors, Sears and Fed-Ex, summarily yanked their advertisements. Because other more despotic forms of repression have been outlawed in democracies, we now rely heavily on a lawful form of censorship, social pressure, a subtle method of coercion that legislates conformity by stigmatizing marginal opinions as the indiscretions of ill-mannered boobs who, while they may not literally break the law, trample on the more elusive statutes of "decency." It is ironic that, during a time in which we seem so preoccupied with the "tastefulness" of people's remarks, we exhibit an appalling insensitivity to the tastelessness of kitsch, which repeatedly and unapologetically rides roughshod over all aesthetic standards.

Instead of conducting open and uninhibited discussions, we state our opinions through symbols, through saber-rattling images of American eagles sitting on stools sharpening their claws; screen savers of rippling flags captioned "these colors don't run"; computer-manipulated photographs of the tear-streaked face of the Man of Sorrows superimposed on the Statue of Liberty; and votive candles that morph into the burning buildings themselves. It is appropriate that President Bush, a man known for the endlessly inventive infelicities of his speech, should communicate to the American public largely by means of symbols, by displaying the badges of dead policemen and staging photo-ops in which, bull horn in hand, he hugs firemen on piles of rubble and leads squirming first-graders in the Pledge of Allegiance after admiring a bulletin board of their drawings titled "The Day We Were Very Sad."

Symbols are the language spoken by those who are uncomfortable with words. Our leaders use them when they seek to stimulate, not thought, but adrenaline. They are the weapons of emotional obscurantism, paralyzing dialogue before we are plunged into war where doubts and hesitations have potentially disastrous consequences and where our actions must be swift, decisive and unthinking. So much of the "discussion" of the World Trade Center is based on button-pushing, on a barrage of symbols designed to trigger reflexive, Pavlovian reactions, bringing us to our feet against our wills to salute the flag and burst as one into song, our intellectual independence shot down by salvos of patriotic kitsch.

In the course of the imagistic orgies that flared up after Sept. 11, a brand new American symbol was invented: the towers themselves. Poets and commentators anthropomorphized the skyscrapers as, on the one hand, "pillars of strength," which, like Atlas, seemed to support the weight of the entire United States; and, on the other, as wavering ghosts, which, like Hamlet's murdered father, seemed to call out for revenge, especially when they were superimposed on top of sympathy card images of disconsolate angels. The buildings quickly lost their material reality as architecture and became living beings; "two brothers" endowed with the capacity to move, to "reach," "stretch," and "stand tall." We even cast this prime piece of Manhattan real estate as Christ in a resurrection scene: No sooner do the buildings collapse than, like phoenixes, they rise again from their ashes, often in the form of the American eagle, soaring skyward out of the smoking rubble: "As the Eagle lay on the ground, In awe I witnessed a miracle, a rebirth! The eagle rose triumphant."

The transformation of the World Trade Center from a physical location into a turn of phrase, a "vibrant symbol of the bounty and pride of democracy," gave both terrorism and dissent a new dimension, that of heresy, of the desecration of holy idols, of buildings that quickly acquired the mystique of temples and, in many images, of New Age crystals, which, like gigantic prisms, emanated a throbbing aura of iridescent energy. As a result, those who advocated restraint became more than just opposing voices but iconoclasts and flag-burners, blasphemers who inflicted physical harm on objects that our high-flown rhetoric treated as sacred relics. We left the realm of reason, of bricks and mortar, and entered the realm of faith, of sacraments and graven images, of flags that have "magical powers to keep away fear." We scoff at the extremism of terrorists who are willing to die in the name of Allah, but we ignore the religious dimension of our own behavior which we justify not by carefully reasoned defenses but by animistic symbols as hallowed as the Koran or the Kaaba. Both the Islamic fundamentalist and the American patriot may share more than they care to admit.

Economic as well as political factors contributed to the proliferation of kitsch after Sept. 11. Kitsch is frequently associated with fundraising, especially fundraising for diseases that afflict children, whether it be the doe-eyed poster children of the first muscular dystrophy campaign, or Ryan White, the heroic young AIDS victim who, after being railroaded out of his bigoted hometown, was canonized as the patron saint of AIDS charities, largely by means of the attention lavished on him by *People* magazine. And yet, appearances notwithstanding, AIDS affects far fewer children than it does adults. Similarly, on Sept. 11, only three victims were below the age of 13 (all passengers on the hijacked planes). That's a surprising statistic, given the disproportionate number of relief agencies that, after the attacks, were launched specifically to help children, the cash cows of the tragedy's nonprofits, which have primed the pumps of American generosity with ad campaigns featuring images of bereft toddlers superimposed on apocalyptic photographs of the ruins. Even during an event in which children are only indirect casualties, they are the ones brought in to shake the tin cans. They, and not adults, are easiest on the eyes, the most photogenic of panhandlers, issuing importunate entreaties with a mere kiss on the cheek or squeeze of the hand. Children are the unpaid workmen of kitsch, its drudges and slave laborers. Many did, of course, lose a parent, but many parents lost something equally important: their lives. Once again, the primary victims of the tragedy were shuffled off to the sidelines to make room for a cast of more narratively appealing objects of compassion, much as the rescue workers were elevated into the starring roles of this "Towering Inferno," since their deaths were more dramatic than the banal denouements of file clerks collapsing at the water cooler and stockbrokers suffocating in bathroom stalls.

What distinguishes the professional fundraiser from any other sort of commercial advertiser is that he has nothing to sell other than his complimentary toasters and his tote bags, his "Never Forget" T-shirts and his American flag car window clings. Because the altruist receives nothing commensurate with the money he gives, nonprofit organizations must ensure that they provide an adequate emotional boon to their benefactors, an intangible feeling of pride, a "warm glow," the sole "product" that the fundraiser really "sells." Charities must induce the consumer to do something that goes against his capitalistic instincts, to give something for nothing, a dilemma that leads them to employ the full rhetorical arsenal of kitsch, providing a particularly rich and satisfying spiritual reward in the complete absence of a material one. Charities are so kitschy precisely because they are an industry that packages the warm glow, the well-earned satisfaction we experience after limping to the finish line of an the AIDS walkathon sponsored by AmFAR or adopting a wide-eyed Central American waif through the Save-the-Children Fund.

But in the midst of epidemics and natural disasters, many Fortune-500 companies try to pass themselves off as charities, to slip into wallets already lubricated by the grease of legitimate, fundraising kitsch, such as Burger King, which is helping to "rebuild the American way of life" by selling $1 flag decals with their shakes and fries. After Sept. 11, the airwaves were flooded with corporate condolences from firms that should perhaps have donated to the FDNY's Widows and Orphans Fund the millions they squandered on prime-time television spots advertising their good Samaritanship, expressing their "horror," and dispensing their "thoughts and heartfelt prayers." Charity impersonators infiltrated the ranks of the Red Cross and the Twin Towers Fund, camouflaging their commercials as public service announcements, while hordes of unscrupulous entrepreneurs set up shop by promising to donate to the orphans of dead firemen 20 percent, a full one-fifth, of the proceeds they collected from the sale of their WTC coffee mugs and their "United We Stand" posters of the towers wrapped like an enormous Christo work in 110-story flags ("please support our country, every purchase helps. God Bless America"). Even a pornographic Web site that offers paying clients images of big-busted Asian women promised to donate 10 percent of its proceeds to relief agencies.

If there was something duplicitous about Wendy's asserting its intentions of selling   15 hamburgers to make "our beloved nation stronger than ever," Coca-Cola blowing its own horn about the fruit juices it supplied the rescue workers, and Chase Manhattan Bank hanging a four-story American flag on the facade of its Midtown offices, there was something equally duplicitous about the consumers who responded to these blandishments and shopped up a storm under the thin pretense that, given a company's outpouring of concern, they were "giving" rather than "buying," donating their hard-earned dollars to a caring, compassionate organization that offered something a little more enticing than a thank-you note, a toaster, and a tax break. We discovered that we could have our cake and eat it too, enjoy that laptop or that surround-sound stereo system and simultaneously bask in the warm glow. If corporations engaged in charity impersonation, consumers engaged in a similar fraud: benefactor impersonation, with both parties participating in a mutually beneficial game of self-flattery.

The marketing of self-congratulation finds a particularly susceptible consumer niche in a culture permeated with pop psychology, with its ever-more clamorous calls for emotional candor and its dire warnings about the dangers of bottling up potentially explosive feelings of anger, pain and grief. Soon after the attack, Oprah's Oxygen Media posted on its Web site a video of Cheryl Richardson, a self-styled "life coach," who advised viewers to "get your feelings up and out of your body in order to assist in the healing process," as if our emotions were toxic substances or medieval "humours," which exert damaging pressure on our internal organs, poisoning our systems if they are not purged or drawn out by professional blood-letters. Throughout the crisis, the constant refrain of politicians, celebrities, and even housewives was the necessity of beginning the process of "healing," which, in the current context, has nothing to do with recuperation, but precisely the opposite: with wallowing, indulging in the unnecessary prolongation of our misery, in the drama of living in a state of high alert.

What's more, the word "healing" promiscuously extends the status of victim to the general public and hence the privilege of being coddled, consoled and pitied, as if we were all casualties and had all narrowly escaped being crushed in the collapsing towers, rather than merely sat safely in our living rooms glued to our television sets.

The mandate to "allow yourself to cry the wounded animal sounds and write in your grief journal," to quote one of several mourning "rituals" Oprah offered her audience after Sept. 11, shows how the contemporary notion of mental health has weakened the inhibitions that once held our sentimentality in check, our sense of shame about self-disclosure, about losing control in public. We have reached unprecedented levels of mawkishness, levels that exceed even those attained by such lachrymose Victorians as Dickens and his devoted readers who wept copiously over the untimely death of Little Nell, a tragedy that would appear to bear some resemblance to the Sept. 11 attack, which, according to one commentator, was so moving that it "burst the clogged, stereotypical male tear duct wide open."

Our belief in the putative healthiness of creating external embodiments of internal states through "art" and "play" therapies, activities that lead to a proliferation of folk ceremonies and homemade tchotchkes: commemorative quilts, the largest hug ever staged in human history (thousands linked arms in a field after the tragedy), and the work of the so-called "Crayola Coalition," a group of school children nationwide who commit their hopes and fears to paper and send them to the rescue workers (often with the help of McDonald's, which includes original artwork—surely an indication of how highly such drawings are prized—in each bag of Big Macs and French fries it distributes at ground zero).

We are now taught that it is detrimental to our peace of mind, indeed, to our sanity, to experience emotion apart from its communication, its "release," and must therefore never remain alone with our feelings but seek out an audience to receive our discharges, our cathartic unburdenings, the messy, unhygienic ruptures of our blockages. What we are witnessing in the kitschification of the World Trade Center is how the pressure to externalize, to emote, "to get your feelings up and out of your body" results in emotional exhibitionism, emotional pornography, a need to play to the galleries and ham up our shock and horror as histrionic spectacles that we relish in and of themselves. Internal states retain their authenticity only if they retain some of the solitude in which they are originally experienced, only if there is no audience that needs to be entertained by the trembling of our chins, only if our real responses remain inaccessible to others in the privacy of our consciousness.

The Internet bulletin boards provide one of the most unrestrained examples of the emotional exhibitionism that pop psychology sanctions. The anonymity of the Web eliminated any need for a censoring mechanism to contain the exuberance of our grief and the result was a crying contest to see who could utter the loudest lamentations, the most piercing keens:

"I felt . . . disbelief, horror, sadness, and the relentless shedding of tears . . . Would I ever be able to enjoy a sunrise again? . . . Would food ever taste good to me again?"

"I flipped the tv to the news early Tuesday while putting a workout video in the vcr . . . needless to say, i never did work out that day . . . Every time i hear or see the news, i cry . . . the flags flying all over my city make me cry . . . hearing our national anthem through various media makes me cry . . . hearing people going around trying to find their loved ones makes me cry . . . knowing how many lives were directly affected . . . makes me cry . . . i've been crying since Tuesday."

When the crying subsided, bulletin board contributors offered each other a profusion of papal blessings ("may God bless each & every one of you," "may the Lord cause His Countenance to shine upon you") and engaged in one of the most complex and disingenuous acts of mourning seen in the aftermath of the World Trade Center tragedy: They posted condolences to the victims' families, electronic sympathy cards in which they told the orphaned children of firemen that "I just wanted you all to know I cared" and wrote poetry to the bereaved husbands and wives and despairing mothers and fathers:

"We care that you are lonely and blue,
So we are sending this hug especially for you."

One unnerving thing is missing from this soothing murmur of comforting words: 25 the people being comforted. It is doubtful that the survivors of the tragedy spent the hours after Sept. 11 poring over the thousands if not millions of notes that appeared on the Web and one must therefore conclude that we posted them for our own benefit, that we were both the senders and receivers of these love letters, and that we took turns playing for each other an audience of devastated widows and orphans. We were acting as aesthetes of grief, competing to see who could utter the windiest sighs, who could beat their breasts and gnash their teeth most piteously. Kitsch was created as the ante was steadily upped and the emotional pornography of an exhibitionistic culture reached its climax, its money shot. Just as Puritans once vied with each other in demonstrations of their piety, so we competed to prove who could *feel* the most, who could "express" the most intensely, showing off a new type of secular piety as unctuous as the zealotry of 17th century religious purists.

The Internet samizdat offered not only a talent contest for the self-appointed pall-bearers of the tragedy but an art gallery in which grass-roots designers displayed their click-and-drag doodles and daubs. The images in this electronic museum are based on what might be called the aesthetic of jumble, the haphazard look that results when pre-existing images available in such computer programs as Clip Art are carelessly juxtaposed or even rendered transparent and placed on top of each other, forming an arty if often illegible mess. With a click of the mouse, files can be copied and pasted so that the same American eagle can be endlessly recycled and combined in countless permutations with the same angel, the same candle, the same red-white-and-blue ribbon, and the same dove carrying the same olive branch. The deadening unoriginality of Internet kitsch is largely the result of the computer's capacity to clone pictures and photographs, thereby minimizing the user's need to invent his own graphics and reducing his role to that of a collector, the rag picker of the World Wide Web who scavenges through various databases in order to assemble a collage of ready-made imagery.

The aesthetic of jumble and the prefab look that it creates become a metaphor of the intellectual vacuity of the Internet samizdat where opinions are replicated and then pasted in like Clip Art, the same denunciations of the terrorists' "evil" appearing cheek-by-jowl with the same panegyrics of the firemen's selfless heroism, the same expression of American indomitability with the same torrential spate of tears. As an experiment in democracy, the Internet has failed, for while it is true that the voiceless may have found their voices in a forum in which it is always open-mike and people are free to say virtually anything they'd like, in fact they do little more than repeat the clichés of their leaders, mouthing slogans that are the literary equivalent of the graphics created in the wake of the attacks. The photo-ops of President Bush and the inflammatory symbol-mongering that has dominated the discussion of the attack become the editorial Clip Art of the bulletin boards, the source of the generic patriotism and jingoistic hawkishness that the contributors right-click and copy, presenting them to the public as revelations. Much is made of the radical potential of the Web, which has restored to common people the means of being heard above the deafening corporate voices of the media, but when we really listen to these quieter, uncensored voices, what we hear is smiley faces and little red cabooses, Santa Clauses and carved pumpkins. The Internet is the grave of free speech, a monument to our lack of thought and autonomy. Freedom to speak amounts to freedom to repeat, to select a pictograph from an archive of icons, here a whimper of stereotyped anguish, there a defiant cry of militaristic fury.

The same voice echoes from server to shining server. The response to the World Trade Center attack was a celebration of consensus, of the exhilarating unanimity of what one bulletin-board contributor aptly characterized as "Americans banning [sic] together, soaring [sic] flags, showing pride." People from every corner of the globe weighed in with their expression of sorrow and solidarity, from the residents of "the little Inupiaq Eskimo village on the shores of the Bering Sea in Deering, Alaska" to the Australian chapter of the Jackie Chan Fan Club: "on behalf of the members of the Australian Jackie Chan Fan Club, our thoughts, prayers, and hearts are with all of our brothers and sisters in the United States."

Within a matter of days, memories of the tragedy seemed to fade as horror gave way to the unadulterated joy of togetherness, which lent the bulletin boards an air of morbid conviviality, the stately funeral procession quickly lapsing into a riotous Irish wake. "How I wish I could embrace you all!" one contributor bursts forth, while another shouts "we love you all!!!" and still another recommends hugging as a palliative to grief, for "a hug heals more pain than the eye alone can see." One contributor was so overwhelmed by the spirit of good will created by the tragedy that she wrote a poem in which she imagined the victims of the attack "choosing" to die in the World Trade Center well before their birth, volunteering in heaven for a divine mission, that of rallying all nations together in a common cause against evil:

"In the halls of Heaven an offer
was made to thousands
of angels one day:

'You can go to the earth and help unite the world
But you won't be able to stay.'
The angels stepped forward."

Behind the kitsch of our grief is a horrible, seemingly inhuman fact: We are not as 30 dejected as we profess but in fact excited, a repulsive notion that we hide from ourselves, burying our euphoria deeper and deeper in sentimentality, becoming all the more long-faced the more gleeful we are at having come together as one.

Why do we experience pleasure during such crises? Surely not because we are sadists at heart, prurient, unfeeling ghouls who gloat over the sufferings of others. Instead, such an inappropriate reaction is the natural outcome of the fact that we no longer consciously experience on a daily basis a very acute sense of belonging to any community, even though the infrastructure of a highly complex society lies behind our most insignificant actions, from opening a tap and raising the thermostat, to flushing a toilet and flipping on a light. And yet, the communities we live in have become invisible, despite their omnipresence; the thousands who work in our water departments are never seen, we have no contact with those who keep our furnaces running, and the electric company appears only when the meter reader rings our bell. What's more, our government operates so efficiently that it has all but disappeared from our lives, leaving us with an eerie sense of being free agents acting alone in an unpopulated wilderness full of automated amenities. A society that seems to run by itself, that does not require us to perform any civic duties, is plagued by feelings of isolation and is particularly prone to bouts of pathological collectivity in which we hold old-fashioned neighborhood socials around a centerpiece of mangled corpses, a hideous incongruity that we hide behind a tearful mask of kitsch. In an atomized society, any crisis becomes a catalyst for instant togetherness in which the pleasure of companionship far exceeds the depths of sorrow and our fierce tribal instincts reemerge with a vengeance, having been thwarted by the curse of autonomy that afflicts advanced Western cultures.

QUESTIONS FOR DISCUSSION

1. **Making Connections:** Why is the public display of potentially offensive material considered so much worse than the private consumption of it? Should music with offensive lyrics escape censure?

2. **Analyzing Strategy:** John Yahner uses anecdotes to present a reciprocal case: my musical tastes once offended my parents, and my children's musical tastes now offend me. Could he have made the same argument without the personal anecdotes?

3. **Analyzing Strategy:** Are there internal inconsistencies in the arguments of Yahner and Leete about not censoring music but prohibiting access by minors?

4. **Making Connections:** The Princeton students were offended by the images and slogans displayed on clothing. Are there cases of similar images and slogans that have been accepted in public displays without comment? (In what sense is clothing a private expression?)

5. **Making Connections:** Do you agree that it is "every generation's mission to defy, reject, and alienate the previous generation" ("A Parent's View")? Does such generational change happen more often in music than in other forms of artistic expression? Is there a commercial payoff for some in encouraging generational revolutions in taste?

6. **Analyzing Strategy:** How does Harris define *kitsch?* Can you offer an example other than those he offers that would fit his definition? Look closely at the

language Harris uses to depict items memorializing 9/11 that he considers in bad taste. How does he try to construct the reader's agreement with his value judgments?

7. **Making Connections:** The articles by Harris on public responses to 9/11 and by Barringer on newspapers' practices with images of the dead both strongly suggest that there are political motives and consequences to such depictions or the lack of them. What are these consequences? What is the opposite argument about the effect of saturation with painful images?

8. **Making Connections:** Harris is offended by items of popular culture widely endorsed by many people. Is there an element of class bias in his evaluation? How does he rely on his audience having a sense of identity to make his case? Would Harris recommend censoring the presence of items he finds disturbing? What response would be appropriate?

9. **Making Connections:** Which is worse? Verbal offenses like the "F" word or sadistic and misogynistic song lyrics, or visual offenses like the display of mutilated bodies?

WRITING SUGGESTIONS

1. Many recent exhibitions of contemporary art in public museums, and many individual works of art, especially of performance art, have been criticized in the last few years as offensive to public taste and therefore not worthy of public funding, either indirectly through public support of museums or directly through funding from the National Endowment for the Arts. Investigate one of these cases (for example, Robert Mapplethorpe, Andres Serrano, Damien Hirst) and write an argument supporting or denying public funding, direct or indirect, for such artistic expression.

2. Freedom of speech and offensive public display are often at odds. Select any of the cases discussed in the readings, or another case with which you are familiar, and argue either for or against the freedom to be offensive. You may also recommend a compromise, a mixed response.

3. If you have ever had the experience of being offended by someone else's depiction of your religion, ethnicity, or moral standards, describe the experience in such a way that a person who does not share your identity and beliefs will nevertheless understand what it is like to experience such an offense.

4. Elizabeth Austin makes a "few modest proposals" to diminish the public presence of the "F" word. Formulate your own list of "modest proposals" (serious or satiric) to diminish the public practice or display of something you find offensive.

The Debate on the Meaning of the First Amendment

Chapter 17

Bill of Rights

THE FIRST TEN AMENDMENTS TO THE U.S. CONSTITUTION

Amendment I

Congress shall make no law respecting an establishment of religion, or prohibiting the free exercise thereof; or abridging the freedom of speech, or of the press; or the right of the people peaceably to assemble, and to petition the government for a redress of grievances.

Amendment II

A well regulated militia, being necessary to the security of a free state, the right of the people to keep and bear arms, shall not be infringed.

Amendment III

No soldier shall, in time of peace be quartered in any house, without the consent of the owner, nor in time of war, but in a manner to be prescribed by law.

Amendment IV

The right of the people to be secure in their persons, houses, papers, and effects, against unreasonable searches and seizures, shall not be violated, and no warrants shall issue, but upon probable cause, supported by oath or affirmation, and particularly describing the place to be searched, and the persons or things to be seized.

Amendment V

No person shall be held to answer for a capital, or otherwise infamous crime, unless on a presentment or indictment of a grand jury, except in cases arising in the land or naval forces, or in the militia, when in actual service in time of war or public danger; nor shall any person be subject for the same offense to be twice put in jeopardy of life or limb; nor shall be compelled in any criminal case to be a witness against himself, nor be deprived of life, liberty, or property, without due process of law; nor shall private property be taken for public use, without just compensation.

Amendment VI

In all criminal prosecutions, the accused shall enjoy the right to a speedy and public trial, by an impartial jury of the state and district wherein the crime shall have been committed, which district shall have been previously ascertained by law, and to be informed of the nature and cause of the accusation; to be confronted with the witnesses against him; to have compulsory process for obtaining witnesses in his favor, and to have the assistance of counsel for his defense.

Amendment VII

In suits at common law, where the value in controversy shall exceed twenty dollars, the right of trial by jury shall be preserved, and no fact tried by a jury, shall be otherwise reexamined in any court of the United States, than according to the rules of the common law.

Amendment VIII

Excessive bail shall not be required, nor excessive fines imposed, nor cruel and unusual punishments inflicted.

Amendment IX

The enumeration in the Constitution, of certain rights, shall not be construed to deny or disparage others retained by the people.

Amendment X

The powers not delegated to the United States by the Constitution, nor prohibited by it to the states, are reserved to the states respectively, or to the people.

Sometimes Freedom Is a Necessary Nuisance

CLARENCE PAGE

The winner of the 1989 Pulitzer Prize for commentary, Clarence Page is a nationally syndicated columnist and an essayist and a frequent panelist on the Public Broadcasting program *The Newshour with Jim Lehrer.* He is a member of the editorial staff of the *Chicago Tribune,* which he joined in 1984. The following article appeared in his column in September 2002.

Want to have a little fun at a party? Ask people if they can name all five of the freedoms   1
in the 1st Amendment.

If you cannot quite do it, you're not alone.

In the latest of their annual polls on our freedoms to be taken by the First Amendment Center and the American Journalism Review, only 2 percent of Americans could name all five.

What I find more disturbing is that no more than 58 percent could name even one! That was the percentage that named freedom of speech.

After that, the responses dropped way off. Freedom of religion was mentioned by   5
18 percent. Then came freedom of the press (14 percent), right of assembly (10 percent) and the one that almost everyone forgot (including me), the right to petition the government (2 percent).

For a parlor game, such responses are amusing, revealing and sometimes frightening.

For example, the Nashville-based First Amendment Center's most recent poll found that nearly half of Americans think that our constitutional freedoms of speech and press, among others, go too far.

About 49 percent of those surveyed said they think the 1st Amendment gives us too much freedom, up from 39 percent last year and 22 percent in 2000.

More than 40 percent said newspapers should not be allowed to freely criticize the 10 U.S. military's strategy and performance.

About half said the news media have been too aggressive in asking government officials for information about the war on terrorism.

More than 40 percent said they would limit the academic freedom of professors and bar criticism of government military policy.

About half said the government should be able to monitor religious groups in the interest of national security, even if it means infringing upon our religious freedoms.

More than four in 10 said the government should have greater power to monitor the activities of Muslims living in the United States than it does other religious groups.

What this poll tells me is that a lot of Americans are afraid. Very afraid in the 15 aftermath of the Sept. 11 terror attacks.

"Fear can short-circuit freedom," writes Ken Paulson, executive director of the center. "From Abraham Lincoln's suspension of civil liberties during the Civil War to the internment of Japanese-Americans in World War II to the McCarthyism of the 1950s, our nation sometimes has lost sight of its commitment to freedom. Fear does that."

People don't want to be troubled by too many questions when they are scared. I have received quite a few letters and e-mails from readers who quote the old World War II line, "Loose lips sink ships," as if it were gospel to justify self-censorship and the obsessively excessive government secrecy sometimes practiced by the Bush administration.

Sorry, folks, but democracy doesn't work that way.

Benjamin Franklin tried to tell that to the Pennsylvania governor in 1755, when he wrote, "Those who would give up essential liberty to purchase a little temporary safety deserve neither liberty nor safety."

Indeed. We all have a responsibility to keep our leaders accountable because we will 20 all share the blame when our leaders mess up.

Some people apparently do not wish to be troubled by too many facts. They would rather live with the questions. It is no wonder, then, that the news-and-opinion media are so unpopular in polls. It is a big part of our job as news and opinion writers to provoke people, to try to get answers or try to encourage our audiences to think.

After all, what good is the 1st Amendment if we don't use it?

Some people seem troubled to see reporters questioning government officials about sensitive matters.

I have a different feeling. I am reassured by it. To face reporters' questions shows me that our leaders are trying, at least, to look and sound accountable. There are no stupid questions, in my view, only stupid answers.

Nevertheless, I am optimistic that when Americans think these issues through they 25 will come out for more freedoms, not less.

About 40 percent of the 1,000 adults who were surveyed said we have too little access to information about the government's war on terrorism, while only 16 percent believe we have too much.

And when asked how important they thought each right to be, 68 percent gave the right "to be informed by a free press" the top rating of "essential," which is what an even larger 75 percent called the freedom of speech.

That sounds about right. First Amendment freedoms sound like a nuisance some-times but they are a nuisance that we Americans really don't want to do without.

The (No) Free Speech Movement

JULIE BOSMAN

Julie Bosman was a journalism major and the editor in chief of the *Badger Herald*, the student newspaper at the University of Wisconsin–Madison, when the following article was published in the *Wall Street Journal* in March 2001.

One hundred screaming protesters outside the doors of a small newspaper office can   1
be intimidating, especially for the editor who is the main target of their abuse.

The protesters swarmed outside the office of my paper, the *Badger Herald*, at the University of Wisconsin–Madison, after first marching across campus brandishing placards that read "*Badger Herald* Racist." They demonstrated for more than an hour, demanding my resignation as editor, because the *Herald* had run a paid advertisement entitled "Ten Reasons Why Reparations for Slavery Is a Bad Idea—and Racist Too." The ad was written and placed by David Horowitz, a conservative author, and had ap-peared on the last day of Black History Month, a full six days before the demonstra-tion, which took place March 6.

The 10 anti-reparations reasons listed ranged from the commonplace ("There is no single group clearly responsible for the crime of slavery," or "Only a tiny minority of white Americans ever owned slaves") to the very controversial ("What about the debt blacks owe to America?"). But our decision to publish was based on the straight-forward view that our paper believes in free speech.

The Horowitz ad was published elsewhere too, and the hostile response to it was as disturbing as the mobbing of our offices. Angry protesters confronted staffers of the *Daily Californian* at the University of California, Berkeley, after the ad had run. The *Daily Cal*'s editor, Daniel Hernandez, printed a front-page apology for running the ad, calling his paper "an inadvertent vehicle for bigotry" and acknowledging, in a mea culpa wrung from him by the protesters, that the ad had not passed through the proper channels.

We were also under pressure to abase ourselves. But the *Herald* editorial board re-   5
fused to run an apology. Instead, we published an editorial saying that "at the *Badger Herald*, we only regret that the editors of the *Daily Californian* allowed themselves to give in to pressure in the manner that unfortunately violated their professional in-tegrity and journalistic duty to protect speech with which they disagree."

The issues raised here go to the heart of a critical question: Are American univer-sity campuses free and open to a spirit of inquiry, or closed places where activist co-horts can determine what is, or isn't, acceptable? Signs of rot can be detected in the fact that at least 15 college newspapers—including those at Harvard, Columbia, Notre Dame, the University of Washington, Georgia Tech and the University of Virginia—have rejected the Horowitz ad on grounds that it was politically unacceptable.

This is not to say that newspapers must print all advertisements submitted. The *Herald* does not prints ads that are completely false. The ad submitted (and rejected) last weekend by the Multicultural Student Coalition calling the *Herald* a "racist pro-paganda machine" would fall into this category. But the Horowitz ad is well within the bounds of political discourse.

One student (and student-government representative) at the *Badger Herald* rally shouted, "This isn't free speech, it's hate speech." Really? Most people outside of college campuses no doubt would be amazed to find that reparations for slavery has become, for some, a nondebatable subject.

On a traditionally liberal campus like ours, any opinions originating from the right tend to be stomped out with a vengeance. Rather than rebut Mr. Horowitz's arguments, the protesters simply tried to drown out his message with name-calling directed at the *Herald*. It's woefully apparent that the same campuses that once stood for idealistic causes in the '60s and '70s now tolerate only political hyper-correctness and unchallenged "progressive" thought. Though the students who protested at the doors of the *Herald* say they demand "diversity"—UW–Madison's latest buzzword—they appear not to accept that principle when it comes to expression or beliefs.

The most consistent criticism of the *Herald*'s action in printing the Horowitz ad has   10
been our alleged lack of sensitivity to students of color on campus. While I do not deny the passionate reaction by many students to the advertisement, this is one of the painful and inescapable by-products of the free-speech principle by which ethical journalists must abide.

Shamefully for the culprits, the most recent maneuver in the speech wars at UW–Madison is an illegal and cowardly one. Several students have witnessed others throwing away stacks of *Heralds* from their racks in university buildings, while several *Herald* staff members have retrieved heaps of bundled papers from garbage cans in the same buildings. How ironic it is that the diversity of viewpoints the activists are demanding is trashed along with the open forum in which it can be represented.

Once Nailed to the Door, Now Shuffled Out of Sight

HOWARD TROXLER

Howard Troxler's column on Florida politics appears three times a week in the *St. Petersburg Times*. The following column appeared in August 2001.

One of the great protesters of all time was a German guy named Martin Luther. Back   1
in the 1500s, he got fed up with the excesses of the Catholic Church. Luther wrote and circulated a list of 95 points of debate. According to legend, he posted his "Ninety-Five Theses" right smack on the door of the church at Wittenberg University.

A mighty movement arose from Luther's words. The Reformation split the Catholic Church from this new wave of breakaway protesters—called Protestants. If today you are a Baptist or a Methodist or a Presbyterian or an Episcopalian or any number of other forms of Christian, you owe part of your freedom of choice to Martin Luther.

It is a good thing that back in Luther's day they didn't have Designated Protest Areas.

Modern spin doctors would have fenced off Luther out of sight, several blocks away, where he wouldn't bother decent people. There would have been no nailing of anything on the church door, nosiree.

"Hey, look at me!" I can hear poor Luther shouting, his voice echoing across the   5
empty cobblestones. "Look, I have some Theses!" Everybody would figure he was a nut. All the big scribes would be blocks away over at the university. At most, Luther would get a tiny, it-takes-all-kinds photo back on page 7B of the *Wittenberg Daily Bugle* ("Lone Protester Fails To Spoil Leo X's Day").

Location is everything.

So when today's government claims that it has the power to keep dissent at a remote physical distance from the thing being protested—and when the police claim the power to arrest citizens who refuse to obey—it is an anti-American suppression of free speech.

We should support the right of the anti-Castro protesters of the Latin Grammy Awards in Miami not to be banished, out of sight and out of camera range, so they won't upset the pretty little celebrities.

We should support obstreperous grandmothers from Clearwater who demand the right to wave a sign of protest against the president of the United States in a baseball park (a baseball park bought with MY tax dollars for Mr. Steinbrenner!) without getting hauled off by the Tampa police.

We should support protesters against the Democratic and Republican national 10 conventions. We should support protesters at the Salt Lake City Olympics. We should support the so-called anti-globalization protesters who will gather yet again in Washington next month.

We should oppose attempts by the government, by special event organizers and by commercial developers of places such as Centro Ybor to designate public or publicly subsidized areas as "private" property so they can kick out undesirables. We should support the right of citizens to protest abortion clinics peacefully, up until the instant that they interfere with the rights of others.

When it's the feds, everybody throws up their hands and says, "You can't argue with the Secret Service." But each mayor should tell the Secret Service, if you won't let our citizens be citizens, then we won't stage your dog-and-pony show. Go away.

Advocating free protest is not advocating anarchy or crime. The government certainly can enforce neutral rules of the road.

Trespassing on truly private property is still illegal, sure. Arrest the trespassers.

Violence is still illegal. Arrest anybody who breaks the law.   15

Nobody has the right to silence anybody.

But the premise behind out-of-sight "designated protest areas" is that politicians and big shots can use the government to force citizens who disagree to disappear. Does this make it easier for police to enforce "security"? You bet it does. Lucky for us, the primary purpose of the Bill of Rights is not to make life easier for the police.

I like to think that Luther, despite taking 95 theses himself, would have admired our First Amendment's economy: freedom of religion, of speech, of the press, of assembly and the right to petition for redress of grievance, all in one package. The sentiment would not have seemed too out of place, nailed to the door of the Wittenberg Castle Church.

The "Separation of Church and State" Myth

LINDA CHAVEZ

Linda Chavez is the former director of the U.S. Commission on Civil Rights (1983–85) and a columnist for *USA Today*. She has written for a number of publications, including the *Washington Post*, the *Wall Street Journal*, and the *New Republic*. She has also appeared on *The McLaughlin Group* and *The Newshour with Jim Lehrer*. She is the author of the book *Out of the Barrio: Toward a New Politics of Hispanic Assimilation* (1991). The following article was published in the *Jewish World Review* in July 2002, after a federal appeals court in California ruled that the words "under God" in the Pledge of Allegiance violated the First Amendment.

As soon as the Ninth Circuit Court of Appeals handed down its decision on the Pledge   1
of Allegiance last week, the e-mails started pouring into my mailbox. Most railed
against the idea that a couple of judges on "the Left Coast," as one person put it, could
strike down the words "under God," which Congress added to the pledge in 1954. But
a few, mostly from readers of my column, suggested that if I didn't like the decision,
maybe I should try thinking about how I'd feel if Congress had inserted the words
"under no God" instead—a sentiment echoed by the Ninth Circuit. In order to protect religious liberty, they implied, we have to make sure government divorces itself
from any expression of religious belief.

"Why did the Founding Fathers, a group of basically conservative, property-
owning religious men find it necessary at all to put the separation of Church and State
into the Constitution, if not because of the persecution suffered in the lands they left
from those who felt that only they knew the truth?" wrote one of my interlocutors.

Good question, because it exposes one of the most widely held myths in modern
America.

Ask most Americans what the First Amendment says about religion, and you'll get
the standard reply (if you're lucky enough to get any answer at all) that it guarantees
the separation of church and state.

It says no such thing, of course. What it says is careful and precise: "Congress shall   5
make no law respecting an establishment of religion, or prohibiting the free exercise
thereof."

The First Amendment guarantees the freedom of religion, not from religion.

The Founders understood that religious belief was not incidental to the American
experiment in liberty but was the foundation on which it was built. The whole idea that
individuals were entitled to liberty rests on the Judeo-Christian conception of man.
When the colonists rebelled against their king—an action that risked their very
lives—they did so with the belief that they were answering to a higher law than the
king's. They were emboldened by "the laws of nature and nature's God," in Thomas
Jefferson's memorable phrase to declare their independence.

"We hold these truths to be self-evident that all men are created equal and that they
are endowed by their Creator with certain unalienable rights," he wrote.

It is impossible to overstate how important the Judeo-Christian tradition was guiding the Founders' deliberations. Yet, in recent years, we've virtually ignored this aspect
of our history.

As scholar Michael Novak points out in his excellent little book *On Two Wings:*   10
Humble Faith and Common Sense at the American Founding, "Professor Donald Lutz
counted 3,154 citations in the writings of the founders; of these nearly 1,100 references (34 percent) are to the Bible, and about 300 each to Montesquieu and Black-
stone, followed at considerable distance by Locke and Hume and Plutarch."

Perhaps the most eloquent argument on behalf of the role of religion in preserving
our democracy was George Washington's, who cautioned in his Farewell Address on
Sept. 19, 1794, that virtue and morality were necessary to popular government.

"And let us with caution indulge the supposition, that morality can be maintained
without religion" he said. "Whatever may be conceded to the influence of refined education on minds of peculiar structure, reason and experience both forbid us to expect
that national morality can prevail in exclusion of religious principle."

The Constitutional Convention of 1787 opened with a prayer, as does each session
of Congress today. The motto "In God We Trust" is on our currency, and similar
expressions adorn public buildings across the Nation. Even the U.S. Supreme Court,
which has been the locus of so much recent confusion on the First Amendment,

begins its proceedings with the phrase "God save the United States and this honorable court."

Perhaps our plea should be "God save us from the courts."

As Jefferson, perhaps the least devout of our Founders, once said to the Rev. Ethan 15
Allen, as recorded in Allen's diary now in the Library of Congress, and quoted by Michael Novak: "No nation has ever yet existed or been governed without religion. Nor can be."

Let us hope the Supreme Court in reviewing the Ninth Circuit's opinion does not insist on testing whether Jefferson was right.

Going Overboard, with letters to the editor in response

St. LOUIS POST-DISPATCH

The following editorial appeared in the *St. Louis Post-Dispatch* on June 27, 2002, after a federal appeals court in California ruled that the words "under God" in the Pledge of Allegiance violated the First Amendment to the Constitution. The letters that follow the editorial were published in the *Post-Dispatch* on June 28, 2002.

The federal appeals court in San Francisco exhibited an astonishing lack of legal rea- 1
soning, common sense and timing when it ruled Wednesday that Congress violated the First Amendment by inserting "under God" in the Pledge of Allegiance.

The Pledge's reference to God is one of those minimal, ceremonial references to religion clearly permitted by the First Amendment—such as legislative prayers, the motto "In God We Trust" and government recognition of Christmas and Thanksgiving as national holidays. Even the most committed separationists, such as the late Justice William J. Brennan Jr., have said that the Pledge's reference to God is such a part of the nation's fabric that it is clearly constitutional.

That should be the end of it. But the 9th U.S. Circuit Court of Appeals in San Francisco likes to poke its finger in the eye of the more conservative U.S. Supreme Court, which doesn't shrink from poking back. What is extraordinary, and a real testament to life tenure, is that the court issued the decision so close to July 4 during a time of war.

The reaction was swift. U.S. House members recited the Pledge on the steps of the Capitol. Hopefully, the issue won't become a political football like flag-burning.

The Pledge of Allegiance did not contain the words "under God" until 1954 when 5
Congress inserted them to stress the contrast between the United States and "godless communists." The government can't force a school child to recite the Pledge. But an atheist from Sacramento said his daughter was injured by having to listen to her teacher and classmates recite the reference to God.

Veteran U.S. District Judge Alfred T. Goodwin, a Nixon appointee, agreed. He concluded that Congress had inserted the reference for a solely religious purpose and that it amounted to an unconstitutional endorsement of one form of religion—monotheism. Reciting the Pledge, he wrote, is to "swear allegiance to the values for which the flag stands: unity, indivisibility, liberty, justice, and—since 1954—monotheism."

Judge Goodwin's argument is not incoherent. Some Americans might feel more comfortable pledging their allegiance—and the nation might be more indivisible—if the Pledge did not contain the reference to God. Nor should Americans be tempted to think that God is always on our side.

But even cherished legal principles, such as the separation of church and state, can be taken to absurd lengths. To follow the court's reasoning, as a dissenter pointed out, we'd have to change the motto on our currency, stop the singing of "God Bless America" and "America the Beautiful" at public occasions and censor the third stanza of the "Star Spangled Banner" and the fourth stanza of "My Country 'Tis of Thee." Questions might also be raised about the president's standard speech closing, "May God Bless America."

Such absolutism would impoverish our public ceremonies and preclude leaders from calling upon spiritual values to address national challenges.

LETTERS TO THE EDITOR: RELIGIOUS FREEDOM AND THE PLEDGE

At a time when patriotism has reached an all-time high and democracy worldwide is engaged in a struggle against terrorism and aggression, there could be perhaps no more anti-American statement made than that of the 9th U.S. Circuit Court of Appeals' ruling that the phrase "under God" is unconstitutional.

The "Pledge of Allegiance" is as American as the national anthem, the song "America the Beautiful" and even—dare I say—baseball and mom's apple pie.

The concept of separation of church and state has been blown out of proportion and into a monumental waste of the courts' time.

One of this nation's greatest strengths is its diversity. It is known for its tolerance of all peoples, regardless of race or religion. As stated in the Pledge, this land is one that offers "liberty and justice for all."

Unfortunately, the court chose to enforce "justice for all" by attacking a symbolic statement of the liberty they seek to preserve.

Jay Perry, St. Louis

Under the guise of a separation of church and state, our courts have progressively silenced our religious expression. The court ruling that the phrase "under God" in the Pledge of Allegiance is unconstitutional only underscores this point.

The Constitution does not mention the much-touted "separation of church and state." The concept was partly based on the First Amendment in the Bill of Rights, which plainly states that the government is not to restrain or regulate religious expression.

Since this is the case, why have we allowed the courts to rule that prayer in school is unconstitutional, that churches and ministers may not speak too directly about political matters without jeopardizing their tax status, that a judge cannot display the Ten Commandments on his courtroom wall and that cities must remove everything from simple crosses to holiday manger scenes from public property?

A country that was founded by the God-fearing has been robbed at the hands of the godless. This nation exists only because a handful of men turned to God for courage and strength. God help us if we turn away.

Darin Stratton, Joplin

Despite what we may be led to believe by the media, some of us support the federal court decision on the Pledge of Allegiance.

I have no problem understanding that "under God" is a religious term. Setting aside time in our public schools in which children are encouraged to say the Pledge, with the words "under God," constitutes a government endorsement of religion, in violation of the establishment clause of the First Amendment.

There is no reference to God anywhere in the Constitution, despite such references in most, if not all, state constitutions at the time. This was a deliberate decision on the part of our Founding Fathers. They were trying to tell us something.

It seems many of us have not yet gotten the message.

Michael E. Nolan, Brentwood

If we cannot "force" our children to say the word "God" while reciting the Pledge of Allegiance, then American citizens should not be forced to use our currency, considering that each unit includes the words "In God We Trust."

Does this mean the federal government has been trampling our constitutional rights?

Angie Anderson, Lemay

Removal of the words "under God" from the Pledge of Allegiance is clearly an example of the minority ruling over the majority.

Atheism is a religion unto itself as much as Christianity, Judaism, Islam or any other, because it is a belief. Atheists who preach to us about their belief are as offensive to us as we are to them when they try to take away our right of freedom of religion.

This nation was founded under God by our ancestors, and that is reflected in our currency, our oath for taking a public office and our opening prayers in Congress. The majority must rule in this democracy.

Audrey Jagels, St. Louis

Bravo to the 9th U.S. Circuit Court of Appeals for saying what has needed to be said for a long time: The phrase "one nation under God" amounts to a government endorsement of religion in violation of the separation of church and state. Shame on the politicians who lashed out at the decision as ridiculous without reading its full meaning.

When did we become a nation that cared more about its symbols of democracy than the truths those symbols represent? When did the words of a sincere pledge to the ideals of freedom become more important than that most basic of freedoms: the freedom to believe in any god, in many gods or in no god at all?

The god in which I believe is not vain enough to desire the shallow and hollow pledges of second-graders who have learned to recite words without understanding their meaning. He does not need the idle flattery of mandated faith. He hears the words of sincere prayer from those who choose to believe, not those who are compelled by force or subtle intimidation to utter the words.

We must aggressively defend the separation of church and state. If we are truly people who live under god, we do not need to be "one nation under god."

Brian Clay Luedloff, Wentzville

While not surprised, I am shocked and saddened at the actions of the federal appeals court in San Francisco. What nonsense!

The two judges who feel that our Pledge of Allegiance is unconstitutional should pack their bags, buy one way airline tickets to whatever godforsaken country they wish, and get the heck out of the United States. I would be more than happy to escort them to the airport!

Mike Macauley, Ballwin

In accordance with the federal appeals court ruling, I can only conclude that it is also unconstitutional to pay federal income taxes with any currency containing the words: "In God We Trust."

James Jacobi, Chesterfield

If atheists do not believe in the existence of God, what are they afraid of? Let the rest of us proudly pledge our allegiance to our country . . . under God.

Ed Carlson, Salem, Ill.

Free Speech in the Sky

ROBIN CHARLOW

Robin Charlow is an associate professor of law at Hofstra University in Hempstead, New York. The following article appeared in *Newsday,* the newspaper for Long Island, in 2002.

My family's lovely summer day at the beach recently was marred by a strange, disturb- 1 ing event. As my husband and 3-year-old twins looked on, a plane flew by towing a huge banner displaying 10-week-old aborted fetuses. I missed it, but my husband's description—"Disgusting!"—kind of summed it up.

We weren't the only ones offended. The press reported that many irate citizens questioned whether the appalling banner could be outlawed. We live in a pretty un-civil society, I thought, but this just goes too far. Subjecting unsuspecting toddlers to grossly horrific visual images crosses the line.

Well, some kind of line. But, as a constitutional law professor, I had to admit, not the legal line. To paraphrase a Supreme Court justice, one man's vulgarity is another's free speech.

Nevertheless, my initial impulse was to ban the banners. I learned that they were the first ads in a campaign by abortion foes to shock those at various pleasurable ven-ues. The group had a legitimate point to make, whether or not I agreed with it. But the ends didn't justify the means.

The problem is that, under the First Amendment, government cannot outlaw 5 speech based on its disagreeable content. The Federal Aviation Administration moni-tors safe use of the airways and had licensed this plane operator to tow banners. But the FAA does not oversee good taste. Attempts to remove only repulsive pictures of fe-tuses from the skies would surely be unconstitutional. In fact, the message—that abor-tion is ugly—concerns a central political issue, and political speech is at the core of the First Amendment's protection.

I recalled a Supreme Court case allowing the Federal Communications Commis-sion to ban a limited number of "dirty words" on the radio when kids might be listen-ing. How about banning "sickening signs" at the beach? This wouldn't work, I real-ized, partly because the government has special leeway in regulating use of very limited broadcast airwaves, unlike the more unlimited airways.

Nor would it help to argue that the signs were dangerously distracting to pilots and boaters. Another Supreme Court decision rejected a town's attempt to bar nudity in films at drive-ins, dismissing a nearly identical argument about hazards to passing motorists.

Perhaps beachgoers are a "captive audience." The Court once ruled that municipal-ities can censor signs on city buses because riders are stuck there, unable to look away.

But the air is more like the street than the bus. The street is the ultimate public forum, where free speech is at its freest. Just as we are expected to tolerate street demonstrations complete with atrocious posters, we have to avert our eyes and shield our babies from nauseating banners.

Maybe we could ban all overhead signs as visual clutter, regardless of their message. Aesthetically minded towns can prohibit even political campaign posters when barring all signs from public property.

This, too, would probably fail. The federal government exclusively regulates the nation's airspace, so the area is federally preempted and off-limits to local lawmakers. Congress would need to pass a law, signed by President George W. Bush, banning all sky-based expression. Even if we defeated the commercial advertising lobby, I wouldn't bet on that happening.

My search for legal ammunition ended when I came across Justice John Marshall Harlan's words in ruling that a protester could not be punished for wearing "—the Draft" on his jacket in a courthouse. Free speech, said Harlan, means not only that we can make a point, but also that we can make it in the most emotionally effective way.

He was right. Absorbed in my own personal affront, I had lost sight of the fact that speech isn't truly free if people can't shock or offend you.

There's an old adage in constitutional circles that one should fight speech with more speech. I envisioned a war of counter-banners, but of what? Unwanted children dead from drugs or violence? The connection to abortion was too thin. Maybe one of those pre-Roe vs. Wade, bloody, back-alley abortion photos. It didn't take long to realize that filling the skyways with competing horrors was not an acceptable solution.

Yet there is an ironic justice here, I think. Pro-choicers were not the only ones who complained. Repulsing middle America's parents and frightening their kids is not likely to win friends to the anti-abortion cause. So, let the air be free, and let those who would abuse it shoot themselves in the foot.

QUESTIONS FOR DISCUSSION

1. **Analyzing Strategy:** The readings in this chapter all suggest the importance of paying attention to the precise wording of a statement. Reread the First Amendment at the beginning of the chapter. Are there any phrases that surprise you? Are there any phrases that could be interpreted in more than one way? Do the same with the remaining amendments in the Bill of Rights.

2. **Analyzing Strategy:** *The Oxford English Dictionary* is available online through most college libraries. Select several key terms from the First Amendment (for example, *press, establishment, petition, respecting, grievance*) and investigate their meanings in the eighteenth century, the time when the amendment was written. Paraphrase any of the phrases in the amendment informed by the eighteenth-century senses of its key term (e.g., "redress of grievances"). How could an argument based on historical definition be used when arguing for a contemporary application of the First Amendment?

3. **Analyzing Strategy:** Look over the *St. Louis Post Dispatch* editorial and responding letters on the suit against the pledge of allegiance. Make a list of the arguments used. What line of argument is missing from either side?

4. **Analyzing Strategy:** Several of the readings in this chapter (for example, Chavez, Troxler) use arguments from historical practices. How are those arguments relevant to contemporary applications of the First Amendment?

5. **Making Connections:** The freedoms defended in the First Amendment are tied to issues of public taste (see the readings in chapter 16), as the Charlow article points out. No culture is without limitations on public speech, display, assembly, and publication. If you are familiar with the practices in another country, explain the differences in tolerance to other members of your class.

6. **Making Connections:** In what way has Troxler extended the right "peaceably to assemble" and the right to freedom of speech? On what grounds can the right to assemble be controlled?

7. **Making Connections:** Compare the U.N.'s Declaration on Human Rights with the U.S. Bill of Rights.

8. **Making Connections:** Are freedom of speech and freedom of the press synonymous, as the Bosman piece suggests?

9. **Making Connections:** Perform the same test that Clarence Page did. Ask a group of at least 10 people if they can name the five "freedoms" in the first amendment. Why is the right to "petition" relatively unknown? Can you cite a recent instance of its use?

WRITING SUGGESTIONS

1. The First Amendment was written before technologies for disseminating ideas like television or the Internet were ever dreamed of. As a result, there have been many debates over "freedom of speech" in these media. Select one narrow issue (for example, publication of bomb-making instructions; hate speech against a religious or ethnic group) and argue for your reasoned final position (for, against, or nuanced) on control of freedom of expression on that issue in that medium.

2. An amendment to the constitution has been proposed for protecting/instituting the pledge of allegiance with the words "under God." Such an amendment would require ratification by the state legislatures of three-fourths of the states. Write speeches for *and* against such an amendment to be delivered before your state's legislature. Argue both sides with conviction, with appeals to your audience's sense of identity and to their strongly held beliefs.

3. The Bill of Rights is considered fundamental to U.S. government and culture. Other nations do not embrace these freedoms (for example, China rigorously censors the Internet and the press and Saudi Arabia does not allow freedom of religious expression). How tolerant should the United States be toward the "intolerance" of other cultures? Write an argument proposing a code of conduct for Americans with nationals of another country who do not recognize the same freedoms (for example, Saudi Arabia supports the building of mosques in the United States but allows no Christian churches or synagogues to be built in Saudi Arabia; the Cuban government organizes anti-American rallies but does not allow anti-Castro rallies).

4. Begin a movement to petition Congress to redress a grievance. Write the argument that would be circulated along with pages for signatures.

CREDITS

Adamson, Rebecca L. "Mascot Supporters Insult Native Peoples," posted March 24, 2002, on Indiancountry.com (editorial from *Indian Country Today*). Used by permission of the author.

Advisory Committee to the Surgeon General. "Crude Male Death Rate for Lung Cancer in 1950 and per Capita Consumption of Cigarettes in 1930 in Various Countries." Reprinted from Report of the Advisory Committee to the Surgeon General, *Smoking and Health* (Washington, D.C., 1964), p. 176; based on R. Doll, "Etiology of Lung Cancer," *Advances in Cancer Research* 3 (1955), 1–50. Copyright © 1955, with permission from Elsevier.

Anderson, Angie. "Religious Freedom and the Pledge" [Letter to the Editor], *St. Louis Post-Dispatch*, June 28, 2002.

Associated Press News Service. "Scientists Determine Chimpanzees Have 'Culture'" from *Raw News*. Copyright © 1999 Associated Press News Service. Reprinted with permission of The Associated Press.

Auster, Paul. "Where Have All the Young Men Gone," *New York Times Magazine*, April 18, 1999, p. 143. Used by permission.

Austin, Elizabeth. "A Small Plea to Delete a Ubiquitous Expletive," *U.S. News & World Report*, April 1998. Copyright © 1998 U.S. News & World Report, L.P. Reprinted with permission.

Barringer, Felicity. "Breaking a Taboo, Editors Turn to Images of Death," *New York Times*, October 25, 1998. Copyright © 1998 The New York Times Company. Reprinted with permission.

Blumstein, Alfred. "Violence by Young People: Why the Deadly Nexus?" *National Institute of Justice Journal*, August 1995.

Bosman, Julie. "The (No) Free Speech Movement," *The Wall Street Journal*, March 14, 2001. Copyright © 2001 Dow Jones & Company, Inc. All rights reserved. Used by permission of the author.

Botstein, Leon. "Let Teen-Agers Try Adulthood," *New York Times*, May 17, 1999. Copyright

© 1999 The New York Times Company. Reprinted with permission.

Brown, Joseph H. "What Tiger Does Best Is Golf," *Tampa Tribune*, November 24, 2002, editorial. Printed by permission of The Tampa Tribune and Joseph Brown.

Brown, Michael P. "Juvenile Offenders: Should They Be Tried in Adult Courts?" *USA Today Magazine*, January 1, 1998. Copyright © 1998 by the Society for the Advancement of Education Inc. (SAE). Reprinted with permission.

Bryjak, George. "Don't Call Jocks Sports 'Heroes,'" *USA Today*, March 18, 2002, p. A13. Reprinted by permission of the author.

Carlson, Ed. "Religious Freedom and the Pledge" [Letter to the Editor], *St. Louis Post-Dispatch*, June 28, 2002.

Carter, Samuel Casey. "Successful Inner-City Schools Share Common Traits," *Chicago Tribune*, June 17, 1999. Copyright © Knight Ridder/Tribune Media Services. Reprinted with permission.

Centre Daily Times, May 27, 2000; *Centre Daily Times*, Sunday, June 4, 2000. Used by permission of the publisher.

Chan, Jamie, Darren Joe, and Jung Ju. "Statement Concerning the Recent Action of Abercrombie and Fitch" at www.cs.Princeton.edu/~savraj/af/statement.html.

Charlow, Robin. "Free Speech in the Sky," *Newsday*, August 11, 2002. © Robin Charlow 2002. All rights reserved. Reproduced with permission.

Chavez, Linda. "The 'Separation of Church and State' Myth," *Jewish World Review*, July 3, 2002.

Connerly, Ward. "Subsidizing Illegal Residents," retrieved from Townhall.com, March 8, 2002. Copyright © 2002 American Civil Rights Institute. Used by permission of the author.

Council for Biotechnology Information, "Growing More Food," at www.whybiotech.com Copy-

Lerner, Barbara. "The Killer Narcissists," *National Review*, May 17, 1999. © 1999 by National Review, Inc., 215 Lexington Avenue, New York, NY 10016. Reprinted by permission.

Lesk, Emily. "My 60-Second Protest from the Hallway," *Newsweek*, June 11, 2001. Copyright © 2001 Newsweek. All rights reserved. Reprinted by permission.

Lion, John R., and Jonas R. Rappeport. "They Do What They See: That's Why We Should Tone Down Violent Images," *Washington Post*, September 12, 1999, p. B1. Used by permission of the authors.

Los Angeles Times, "Hollywood Simply Can No Longer Abdicate Its Responsibility to Kids," July 21, 1999. Copyright © 1999 Los Angeles Times. Reprinted with permission.

Luedloff, Brian Clay, "Religious Freedom and the Pledge" [Letter to the Editor], *St. Louis Post-Dispatch*, June 28, 2002. Used by permission of the author.

Lukas, Aaron. "I Love Global Capitalism—and I'm Under 30," The Cato Institute 2001. Used with permission.

Macauley, Mike. "Religious Freedom and the Pledge" [Letter to the Editor], *St. Louis Post-Dispatch*, June 28, 2002.

Martin, Michelle. "French Food vs. Fast food," retrieved from www.enn.com/enn-features-archive/1999/11/112299/mcdomination_7192.asp. Copyright © 1999 Michelle Martin 1999. Reprinted with permission.

McCaffrey, Barry R. "Don't Legalize Those Drugs," *Washington Post*, June19, 1999, p. A15. Used by permission of the author.

Newsweek, caption for "1000 Words," August 11, 2002, pp. 20–21. Copyright © 2002 Newsweek, Inc. Reprinted with permission.

Nolan, Michael. "Religious Freedom and the Pledge" [Letter to the Editor], *St. Louis Post-Dispatch*, June 28, 2002. Reprinted by permission of the author.

Novak, Michael. "With Liberty and Prayer for All," *New York Times*, June 18, 1999. Copyright © 1999 Michael Novak. Used by permission.

O'Regan, Fred. "Harvest the Whales" [Letter to the Editor], *New York Times*, August 20, 2002. Used by permission of the author.

Page, Clarence. "Sometimes Freedom Is a Necessary Nuisance," *Chicago Tribune*, September 25, 2002. Copyright © 2002 Tribune Media Services, Inc. All rights reserved. Reprinted with permission.

Parrott, Carlton. "Harvest the Whales" [Letter to the Editor], *New York Times*, August 20, 2002. Used by permission of the author.

Perry, Jay. "Religious Freedom and the Pledge" [Letter to the Editor], *St. Louis Post-Dispatch*, June 28, 2002.

Pitt, David. "Study: Beer Taxes Reduce STD Rates," *Associated Press*, April 27, 2000. Reprinted with permission of The Associated Press.

Pitts, Leonard. "A Letter to the Terrorists," *Miami Herald*, December 9, 2001, p. 2A. Republished with permission of the *Miami Herald*; permission conveyed through Copyright Clearance Center, Inc.

Postrel, Virginia I. "Fatalist Attraction," *Reason*, July 1997. Reprinted, with permission, from the July 1997 issue of *Reason* magazine. Copyright © 2003 by Reason Foundation, 3415 S. Sepulveda Blvd., Suite 400, Los Angeles, CA 90034. www.reason.com.

Price, S.L. "The Indian Wars," *Sports Illustrated*, March 4, 2002. Reprinted courtesy of Sports Illustrated. Copyright © 2002 Time Inc. All rights reserved.

Rifkin, Jeremy. "A Personal Note" from *The Biotech Century* by Jeremy Rifkin. Copyright © 1998 Jeremy Rifkin. Used by permission of Jeremy P. Tarcher, an imprint of Penguin Group (USA) Inc.

Robertson, Linda. "Celebration or Exploitation? Women Athletes Pose Question," *Miami Herald*, January 31, 2000. Republished with permission of the *Miami Herald*; permission conveyed through Copyright Clearance Center, Inc.

Rock-Richardson, Audrey. "Pay Your Own Way! (Then Thank Mom)," *Newsweek*, June 11, 2000. Copyright © 2000 Newsweek. All rights reserved. Reprinted by permission.

Rosenthal, A.M. "While the Children Sleep," *New York Times*, September 22, 1995. Copyright © 1995 by The New York Times Company. Reprinted with permission.

Samuelson, Robert J. "The Spectre of Global Aging," *Washington Post*, February 28, 2001, p. A25. Copyright © 2001 Newsweek. Reprinted with permission.

Santas, Shawntelle. "The Face of Welfare: Not Quite What You Pictured, Am I?" *Woman's Day*, April 1999. Copyright © 1999 Shawntelle Santas. Used by permission.

Sen, Amartya. "A World Not Neatly Divided," *New York Times*, November 23, 2001. Copyright

© 2001 by The New York Times Company. Reprinted with permission.

Shiner, Josette. "Crucifix Can Reflect on Good Moral Character of School," *News Journal*, November 8, 1997. Copyright © Scripps Howard News Service. Reprinted with permission from United Media.

Simon, Richard Keller. "Much Ado About *Friends*: What Pop Culture Offers Literature," *Chronicle of Higher Education*, June 16, 2000. Copyright © 2000 by Richard Keller Simon. Reprinted by permission.

Smith, Wesley J. "Closing in on Cloning," *The Weekly Standard*, January 14, 14, 2002. Used by permission.

Solomon, John. "Vote, or Else," *The Washington Post*, October 11, 1998. Used by permission of the author.

Soyinka, Wole. "Beauty and the Beast of Intolerance in Nigeria," *Houston Chronicle*, November 25, 2002. Copyright © 2002 by Wole Soyinka. Reprinted by permission of Melanie Jackson Agency, L.L.C.

Steele, David Ramsay. "Yes, Gambling Is Productive and Rational," *Liberty Magazine*, vol. 11, no. 1 (September 1997), pp. 27–34. Reprinted from Liberty with permission. Copyright © 1997 Liberty Magazine. All rights reserved.

St. Louis Post-Dispatch, "Going Overboard," June 27, 2002, editorial. Copyright © 2002 St. Louis Post-Dispatch. Reprinted with permission of the St. Louis Post-Dispatch.

Stratton, Darin. "Religious Freedom and the Pledge" [Letter to the Editor], *St. Louis Post-Dispatch*, June 28, 2002.

Tolbert, Kathryn. "Japan's Modern Women Living Single and Loving It," *Washington Post Sunday News Journal*, February 13, 2000. Copyright © 2000 The Washington Post. Reprinted with permission.

Troxler, Howard. "Once Nailed to the Door, Now Shuffled Out of Sight," *St. Petersburg Times*, August 22, 2001. Copyright © 2001 St. Petersburg Times. Reprinted with permission.

Trusty, Lance. "College Students: Test-Taking Advice for the Wise," *The Christian Science Monitor*, October 2, 1978. Used by permission of the author.

Williams, Patricia J. "Better Safe . . . ?: Diary of a Mad Law Professor," *The Nation*, March 11, 2002. Copyright © 2002 The Nation Company, L.P. Reprinted with permission from the March 11, 2002 issue of *The Nation*.

Woo, Andrea. "Polls Apart," *Sports Illustrated*, March 4, 2002. Reprinted courtesy of Sports Illustrated. Copyright © 2002 Time Inc. All rights reserved.

Yahner, John A. "A Parent's View," published on the website for the Recording Industry of America in 2002, at www.riaa.org/Parents-View.cfm. Used by permission of the author.

Photo Credits

Chapter 2—Figure 2.1, ad for Purina Beef Jerky Strips. Courtesy of Purina ONE™ brand pet food, page 16. Figure 2.2, AP photo of people in market. AP/Wide World Photos, page 39. Figure 2.3, ad for Kleenex Cold Care. © KLEENEX COLDCARE Tissues, page 42.

Chapter 5—Figure 5.1, Uncle Sam recruiting poster. © Swim Ink/CORBIS, page 122.

Chapter 6—Figure 6.1, photo of Neil Armstrong stepping onto the moon's surface. AP/Wide World Photos/NASA, page 158.

Chapter 7—Figure 7.1, AP photo of Los Alamos National Lab on fire. © Reuters NewsMedia Inc./CORBIS, page 180.

Chapter 8—Figure 8.1, photo of the eye of a dying whale that appeared in Newsweek (date and page no. to come). © S. Heaslip—Cape Cod Times—Gamma, page 255.

Chapter 9—Figure 9.1, ad for Allegra-D. Advertisement courtesy of Aventis Pharmaceuticals. Photo © Catherine Ledner, page 308.

Chapter 16—Figure 16.1, AP photo of Nairobi morgue (full picture). © AP/Wide World Photos/Jean-Marc Bouju, page 517. Figure 16.2, AP photo of Nairobi morgue (as cropped for the NY Times). © AP/Wide World Photos/Jean-Marc Bouju, page 517. Figure 16.3, AP photo of Nairobi morgue (as blurred for the SF Examiner). © AP/Wide World Photos/Jean-Marc Bouju, page 517.

INDEX

Abstractions:
   in definition arguments, 140
   evaluation of, 245–247
Abstracts (as sources), 337
Academic arguments, definitions in,
     145–146
Action(s):
   evaluation of, 242–245
   incentives for, 308
   questions about, 86, 92 (*See also*
     Proposals)
Ad hominem appeals, 70
Ad populum arguments, 70
Adamson, Rebecca L., 504–505
Aesthetic evaluations, 137, 236–240
Agency:
   in causal arguments, 181, 196–198
   definition of, 183
   and distant cause, 198
   implausible, 198
   models for establishing, 204
All, 141–143
Almanacs, 335, 336
Almost all, 141
Analogies, 207
   false, 67–68
   in predictions, 209, 300
APA style, 406–416
Appeal(s):
   to emotion, 70–71 (*See also* Pathos)
   ethical, 243–245, 295–296,
     301–302
   expressing (*see* Voice)
   to groups, 120–121
   sources of, 19
Archives (as sources), 329

Argument(s):
   basic elements of, 4–7, 19–21
   contexts for, 8–11
   definition of, 8
   expansion of, 22–24, 27–29
   goals of, 7–8
   one-part, 21
   purpose of, xxvi
   rhetorical situation of, 11–15
   schematizing, 20
   skills needed for, xxvi–xxvii
   three-part, 20–23
   two-part, 21–22
Aristotelian logic, 20
Aristotle:
   and basic parts of argument, 22
   on character of arguer, 49
   and intellectual virtues, 56
   and mistakes in reasoning, 65
   and sources of appeal, 19
Art works:
   arguments interpreting, 137
   MLA style for citing, 391
Arts, research Web pages for, 360–361
Association (as aesthetic criterion),
     239–240
Assumptions, implicit, 5
Atlases, 335, 336
Attitudes (of readers), 5–6
Audience:
   attitudes and feelings of, 5–6
   convincing, 289–291
   evaluation criteria specific to,
     233–234
   and goal of argument, 4
   implicit beliefs and assumptions of, 5

Audience (*continued*)
  inducements presented to, 4–5
  and pathos, 19
  as rhetorical element of argument,
    12
  voice for creating, 109–110
Audio recording citations:
  APA style for, 411
  MLA style for, 391
Auster, Paul, 493–494
Austin, Elizabeth, 510–512
Authority(-ies):
  appeals to, 233
  in evaluating abstractions, 246
  facts from, 36–37
  interviews with, 329–331
  and use of *I*, 105

Barringer, Felicity, 515–518
Beauty and the Beast of Intolerance
    (Wole Soyinka), 430–432
Begging the question, 68
Beliefs, implicit, 5
Bibliographies, 337
Bill of Rights, 528–529
Biographical dictionaries, 335
Biology, research Web pages for,
    361–362
Bitzer, Lloyd, 11
Blocking causes, 182, 192, 306
Blumstein, Alfred, 467–476
Book citations:
  APA style for, 406–408
  MLA style for, 386–388
Boolean operators, 341–345
Bosman, Julie, 531–532
Branching support, 22–23
*Breaking a Taboo, Editors Turn to Images
    of Death* (Felicity Barringer),
    515–518
Brown, Joseph H., 497–498
Brown, Michael P., 485–489
Bryjak, George J., 496–497
Building arguments (*see* Logos)
Burke, Kenneth, 55

Bush, George W., 451–454
Business, research Web pages for,
    362–363

Catalogs, 337, 346–347
Categorizing arguments, 137, 146
Causal arguments, 85, 179–227
  agency in, 196–198, 204
  analogy in, 207
  chain of causes in, 205
  establishing relationships in,
    196–199
  fitting narrative to purpose in,
    195–196
  framing narratives for, 184–190
    conditions, influences, and pre-
      cipitating causes, 184–186
    near and remote causes, 186–199
    necessary and sufficient causes,
      188–190
  models for, 190–195
    absence of a blocking cause, 191
    chance, 194–195
    reciprocal causes, 193–194
    responsibility, 190–191
  predictions as, 208–209
  in proposals, 287–288, 296–297
  sign arguments as, 207–208
  supporting relationships in,
    199–207
    common-factor method,
      199–201
    elimination method, 203–204
    Mill's four methods for,
      199–204
    single-difference method, 201
    varying causes and effects
      method, 201–203
  time precedence in, 205–207
  visual support for, 210–212
  writing, 214–217
Causes:
  false, 66–67
  questions about, 85, 91–92 (*See also*
    Causal arguments)

Celebration of Exploitation? Women Athletes Pose Question (Linda Robertson), 494–496
Chain(s):
  of causes, 203–204, 300
  of events, 181, 187
  of support, 23–24
Chan, Jamie, 508–510
Chance, 184, 194–195
Character:
  of arguer (*see* Ethos)
  attacks on, 70
Charlow, Robin, 538–539
Chat rooms, 357
Chavez, Linda, 533–535
Circular arguments, 68
Circumlocution, 62
Citing sources, 385–416
  APA style for, 406–416
  MLA style for, 385–405
Claim-reason pairs, 26–27 (*See also* Enthymemes)
Claim(s), 19–21
  in one-part arguments, 21
  from reasons/warrants, 18
  sources supporting (*see* Sources)
  in two-part arguments, 21–22
  (*See also* Generating arguments)
Closing In on Cloning (Wesley J. Smith), 435–440
Common-factor arguments, 199–201
Communication, research Web pages for, 363–364
Comparative evaluations, 51
Comparison(s):
  and contrasts, 164
  in definition arguments, 134, 153–157, 164
  with degree, 156–157
  in evaluating abstractions, 246
  evaluation as, 251
  with points of similarity/difference, 154–156
  to support criteria of judgment, 234

Competition:
  conceding points to, 57–58
  understanding, 56–57
Complex questions, 69
Computer sciences, research Web pages for, 364–366
Concessions, 57–58
Conclusion, 20 (*See also* Claim(s))
Conditions (in causal arguments), 184–185
Consequences:
  of abstractions, 246
  appeals to, 233–234
  audience's unawareness of, 293–294
  avoidance of bad, 301
  evaluation of, 294–297
  in evaluations, 230, 232
  moral, of art, 240
  predictions of good, 300
  in proposal arguments, 287, 288, 293–297
  questions about, 85, 91–92
  (*See also* Causal arguments)
Constraints:
  in proposals, 286
  as rhetorical element of argument, 14–15
Contrast arguments, 164
Contrast (as aesthetic criterion), 237–238
Contrast definitions, 151
Conviction, 59
Convincing an audience, 289–291
Copyrighted material, documenting, 385
Council for Biotechnology Information, 442–445
Counterarguments, 7, 28–29
Couple, 141
Craft (as aesthetic criterion), 238
Credibility:
  of arguer (*see* Ethos)
  and sources for argument, 6
Criminology, research Web pages for, 366–367

Criteria of judgment, 229, 232
  aesthetic, 237–240
  appropriateness of, 229–230
  defense of, 230
  specific to audience, 233–234
  weighting, 247–248

Databases, 337, 347–349
Definition arguments, 84–85,
    131–178
  about nature of things, 135–137
  for categorizing or labeling, 137
  comparisons in, 153–157, 164
    and contrasts, 164
    with degree, 156–157
    with points of similarity/
      difference, 154–156
  definitions in, 133, 143–153
    accepted definitions, 145
    evidence vs., 144–145
    explicit definitions, 145–147
    placement of, 147–148
    tactics of definition, 148–153
  documentary photography in,
    158–159
  examples in, 133, 138–143
    modifying subject to fit evidence,
      140–143
    specific/iterative examples,
      138–139
  for existence of things, 137
  to identify trends, public taste or
    opinion, 136
  interpreting works of art, 137
  for reality of events, 136–137
  writing, 160–163
Definition(s):
  accepted, 145
  as basic question, 84–85, 91
  in definition arguments, 133,
    143–153
  evidence vs., 144–145
  explicit, 145–147
  placement of, 147–148
  tactics of, 148–153
Degree, comparisons with, 156–157

Demonstration (of problems), 292–293
Descriptive language, 63
Dialogue building, 115–117
Dictionaries, 334–336
Dilemmas, false, 68
Direct address, 102–103, 112–113,
    123
Directions, giving, 110–111
Directories, 335, 355–356
Disclaimers, 59
Dispersed definitions, 147–148
Dissertation citations (unpublished):
    APA style for, 410
    MLA style for, 391
Distortion (as aesthetic criterion), 237
Documentary photography, 158–159
Documenting sources, 383–385
Domain of responsibility, 191
Don't Call Jocks Sports "Heroes"
    (George J. Bryjak), 496–497

Education, research Web pages for,
    367
Effects (*see* Causal arguments)
Ehrlich, Paul R., 424–426
Either/or fallacy, 68
Electronic sources, 349–358
    evaluating, 358–360
    usenet/newsgroups, 357–358
    Web searches, 350–357
    (*See also* Online sources)
Elimination (causal arguments),
    203–204
Emotional appeals, 70–71 (*See also*
    Pathos)
Encyclopedias, 334–336
Engineering, research Web pages for,
    364–366
English language, research Web pages
    for, 367–369
Enthymemes, 22
Epideictic arguments, 241
Equivocation, 69–70
Ethical appeals, 243–245, 295–296,
    301–302
Ethical argument, 248–250

Ethical norms, 287

Ethical rightness, 288

Ethos, 48–53

and claims of authority, 105

and conviction vs. moderation, 59

definition of, 19

and disclaimers, 59

elements of, 49–50

establishing, 46–47

extrinsic, 51

in identification, 55

intrinsic, 51–52

and reasonableness, 56–58

Etymological definitions, 150

Euphemisms, 61–62

Evaluations, 85, 228–282

of abstractions, 245–247

comparative, 251

criterion/standard of judgment for, 232

of events and actions, 242–245

of Internet sources, 358–360

of objects, 234–241

constructed, 235–241

natural, 234–235

of people, 241–242

superlative, 252–253

supporting criteria and audience for, 233–234

visual rhetoric for, 254–255

weighting criteria for, 247–248

weighting values for, 248–250

writing, 256–259

Events:

arguing reality of, 136–137

chain of, 181, 187

evaluation of, 242–245

initiating, 181

precipitating, 181, 185–186

random, 195

Evidence:

definition vs., 144–145

documenting, 383–384

Example(s):

in definition arguments, 133, 138–143

and modification of subject to fit evidence, 140–143

specific/iterative examples, 138–139

definition by, 150

for evoking pathos, 63–64

typicality of, 139

Exigence:

in definition arguments, 135

in proposals, 286

as rhetorical element of argument, 12–13

Expanding arguments:

with branching support, 22–23

with chains of support, 23–24

with Toulmin model, 27–29

Explicit definition, 145–147

Extremism, 56

Extrinsic ethos, 51

Factors (in causal arguments), 182, 184

Facts, 32–37

definition of, 33

documenting, 383–384

questions about, 84–85, 91 (*See also* Definition arguments)

stating, 34

verifying, 34–37

Fallacies, 65–71

False analogy, 67–68

False causes (*post hoc*), 66–67

False dilemma (either/or), 68

Fatalist Attraction (Virginia I. Postrel), 440–442

Faulty emotional appeals, 70–71

Feasibility (of proposals), 302–305

Feelings (of audience), 5–6

Few, 141

Figurative definitions, 151–152

Film, MLA style for citing, 391

Finance, research Web pages for, 362–363

First person, 102, 103 (*See also I; We*)

Free Speech in the Sky (Robin Charlow), 538–539

French Food vs. Fast Food (Michelle Martin), 420–422
Fukuyama, Francis, 454–463
Full text databases, 348

General proposals, 297–298
Generalizations, hasty, 66
Generating arguments, 77–100
    by answering questions with claims, 81–82
    four basic questions for, 83–86
        combining, 88
        finding key questions, 88–90
        reading for, 92–97
        as research strategy, 90–92
        and type of warrants, 86–88
Genetic definitions, 150–151
Genre, 14
Genus/difference definitions, 149–150
Goals of argument, 4, 7–8
God in a Labcoat: Can We Control the Biotech Revolution before It Controls Us? (Jeremy Rifkin), 445–451
Going Overboard (and Letters to the Editor in Response) (St. Louis *Post Dispatch*), 535–538
Good sense, 49
Good will, 49–50, 108–109
Government Web sites, 369–370
Graphs, 210–212
Groups:
    creating/appealing to, 120–121
    emotional appeals to, 53–54
    undefined, 103
    voice for creating, 118–119
Growing More Food (Council for Biotechnology Information), 442–445

Harmony (as aesthetic criterion), 238
Harris, Daniel, 518–526
Hasty generalizations, 66
Health sciences, research Web pages for, 361–362
Herbert, Bob, 489–491

Historical definitions, 150–151
History, research Web pages for, 370–371
Hostile questions, anticipating, 305–307
Humanities, research Web pages for, 360–361
Humans:
    evaluating events/actions related to, 243–245
    evaluation of, 241–242
    responsibility of (as cause), 182, 184, 190–191
Hypertext, 350

I, 102, 104–108
I Love Global Capitalism—and I'm under 30 (Aaron Lukas), 419–420
Ideas, documenting, 384
Identification, 55
Ignorance, appeals to, 70
Images (*see* Visual rhetoric)
Impersonal voice, 121
Implicit beliefs and assumptions, 5
Indexes, 337
    periodical, 347
    search engines as, 354–355
Indian Wars, The (S. L. Price), 499–502
Inducements, 4–5
Influences (in causal arguments), 181, 185
Initiating events, 181
Injustice and Ice Cream (Bob Herbert), 489–491
Intellectual virtues, 56
Intention, 191
Interlibrary loan, 346–347
Internet, 349
    arguments on, xxvii
    evaluating sources on, 358–360
    origin of, 350
    reliability of information from, 37, 41
    World Wide Web vs., 350 (*See also* World Wide Web)

Interpersonal arguments, 9
Interviews:
    APA style for citing, 410
    MLA style for citing, 391
    as sources, 329–331
In-text reference citations:
    APA style for, 406
    MLA style for, 385–386
Intrinsic ethos, 51–52
Invisible universals, 142–143
Isolated definitions, 147
Iterative examples, 138–139

Joe, Darren, 508–510
Jung Ju, 508–510
*Juvenile Offenders: Should They Be Tried
    in Adult Courts?* (Michael P.
    Brown), 485–489

Key questions, 88–90
Keyword searches, 339–346
Killer Narcissists, The (Barbara Lerner),
    465–466
Kitschification of Sept. 11, The (Daniel
    Harris), 518–526
Kurtz, Stanley, 426–430

Labeling, 120, 137, 146
Lamberg, Lynne, 480–485
Law, research Web pages for, 366–367
LCSH (*see* Library of Congress Sub-
    ject Headings)
Lectures, MLA style for citing, 391
Leete, Jenny, 514–515
Lerner, Barbara, 465–466
Less, 156–157
Library of Congress Subject Headings
    (LCSH), 340–341
Library sources, 346–349
Likert scale, 332
Lion, John R., 476–479
Literature, research Web pages for,
    367–369
Loaded questions, 332
Logos, 16–44
    claim in, 19–21

claim-reason pairs in, 26–27
definition of, 19
expanding arguments, 22–24, 27–29
facts in, 32–37
images in argument, 38–40
for one-part arguments, 21
reason in, 19–21
sources for
    reliability of, 37, 41
    verifying facts, 34–37
testing other positions in, 29–31
Toulmin model, 27–29
for two-part arguments, 21–22
values in, 32–33
visual communication of, 39–40
warrant in, 20–21
Lot, 141
Lukas, Aaron, 419–420

Major premise, 20 (*See also* Warrants)
Many, 141–142
Martin, Michelle, 420–422
Mascot Supporters Insult Native Peoples
    (Rebecca L. Adamson),
    504–505
Medicine, research Web pages for,
    361–362
Mill, John Stuart, 199
Minor premise, 20 (*See also* Reason(s))
MLA (*see* Modern Language
    Association)
MLA style, 385–405
Moderation, 59
Modern Language Association (MLA):
    citation style of, 385–405
    database of, 337
Moral character, 50
More, 156–157
Most, 141, 142
Museums (as sources), 329
Music Censorship Limits Rights (Jenny
    Leete), 514–515

Narratives, causal, 195–196
Natural events/actions, evaluating,
    242–243

Natural objects, evaluating, 234–235
Near causes, 186–187
Necessary causes, 188–190
Negative definitions, 151
Nesting, 342
New Ethics for a New World, A (Paul R. Ehrlich), 424–426
New Rhetoric, The (Chaim Perelman and Lucie Olbrechts-Tyteca), 32
Newsgroups, 350, 357–358
(No) Free Speech Movement, The (Julie Bosman), 531–532
Non sequiturs, 68–69
None, 142
Note taking, 372–374

Objects, evaluation of, 234–241
    constructed objects, 235–241
        aesthetic evaluations, 236–240
        more than one standard for, 240–241
        practical evaluations, 235–236
    natural objects, 234–235
Occam's Razor, 204
Olbrechts-Tyteca, Lucie, 7, 32, 33
Once Nailed to the Door, Now Shuffled Out of Sight (Howard Troxler), 532–533
One-part arguments, 21
Online sources:
    APA style for citing, 409–410
    documenting, 385
    MLA style for citing, 389–391
    (*See also* Electronic sources)
Operational definitions, 152–153
Ostensive definitions, 152

Page, Clarence, 529–531
Paraphrasing, 377–379
Parent's View, A (John A. Yahner), 512–513
Pathos, 47–48, 53–55
    choosing examples to evoke, 63–64
    choosing words to evoke, 61–63
    definition of, 19

in identification, 55
in images, 72–73
People (*see* Humans)
Perelman, Chaim, 7, 32, 33
Periodicals:
    APA style for citing, 408–409
    databases of, 347–349
    indexes of, 347
    MLA style for citing, 388–389
Periphrasis, 62–63
Personal arguments, 8–9
Personal experience:
    facts from, 35
    and use of *I,* 104–105
Personification, 122–123
Philosophy, research Web pages for, 371
Photography, documentary, 158–159
Place constraints, 14–15
Plagiarism, 378, 382–385
Plato, 12
Political Control of Biotechnology, The (Francis Fukuyama), 454–463
Polls Apart (Andrea Woo), 503–504
Polls (as source), 331–333
Positions, testing, 29–31
Post hoc fallacies, 66–67, 205
Postrel, Virginia I., 440–442
Practical evaluations, 235–236
Precipitating events, 181, 185–186
Prediction arguments, 207–209
Preliminary arguments (proposals), 292–294
Premises, major vs. minor, 20
Preventing School Violence: No Easy Answers (Lynne Lamberg), 480–485
Price, S. L., 499–502
Primary sources, 328–333
Professional arguments, 9–10, 145–146
Pronouns, 102–103 (*See also specific words*)
Proportion (as aesthetic criterion), 237
Proposal statements, 297–299

Proposals, 86, 283–324
  anticipation of hostile questions in, 305–307
  consequence arguments in, 294–297
  convincing an audience with, 289–291
  feasibility of, 302–305
  kinds of, 291–292
  preliminary arguments in, 292–294
  proposal statement in, 297–299
  supporting arguments in, 299–302
  visual, 308–309
  writing, 310–313
Proximate causes, 186–187
Public arguments, 10–11
Public taste:
  arguments identifying, 136
Publication Manual of the American Psychological Association, 406 (*See also* APA style)

Qualifiers, 27–28
Questions, 81–86
  anticipating hostile, 305–307
  begging the question, 68
  combining, 88
  complex, 69
  dialogue building with, 115–117
  finding key questions, 88–90
  to involve readers, 103
  raised/answered in reading, 92–97
  as research strategy, 90–92
  rhetorical, 103, 115–116
  structuring, 115
  for surveys/polls, 331–333
  warrants and type of, 86–88
Quoting sources, 374–377

Random events, 195
Random samples, 331
Rappeport, Jonas R., 476–479
Readers (*see* Audience)
Reasonableness, 56–58
Reason(s), 19–21
  as claims, 18
  in two-part arguments, 21–22

Rebuttal condition, 28
Reciprocal causality, 182, 193–194
Red herrings, 69
Reference list, APA style for, 406
Reference materials, 335, 336
Relationships:
  causal
    analogy support method for, 207
    chain of causes support method for, 203–204
    common-factor support method for, 199–201
    elimination support method for, 203–204
    establishing, 196-199
    predictions of, 208–209
    sign arguments for, 207–208
    single-difference support method for, 201
    supporting, 199–207
    time precedence support method for, 204–207
    varying causes and effects support method for, 201–203
    you for establishing, 108-109
Reliability (of sources), 37, 41
Remarks by the President on Stem Cell Research (George W. Bush), 451–454
Remote causes, 187–188
Repetitive examples, 138–139
Research:
  basic questions as strategy for, 90–92
  sources for (*see* Sources)
Responsibility (as cause), 182, 184, 190–191
Rhetorical questions, 103, 115–116
Rhetorical situation, 11–15, 135
Rifkin, Jeremy, 445–451
Robertson, Linda, 494–496

St. Louis *Post Dispatch*, 535–538
Search engines, 354–355
Secondary sources, 328, 333–334
Sen, Amartya, 422–424

"Separation of Church and State" Myth, The (Linda Chavez), 533–535

Several, 141

Sign arguments, 207–208

Silent universals, 142–143

Similarity, points of, 154–156

Single-difference arguments, 201

Site directories, 355–356

Slippery slope fallacy, 67

Small Plea to Delete a Ubiquitous Expletive, A (Elizabeth Austin), 510–512

Smith, Wesley J., 435–440

Socrates, 12

Some, 141

Sometimes Freedom Is a Necessary Nuisance (Clarence Page), 529–531

Sources, 327–416
  to answer specific questions, 334–336
  for arts and humanities, 360–361
  for biology, medicine, and health sciences, 361–362
  for business and finance, 362–363
  citing, 385–416
    APA style for, 406–416
    MLA style for, 385–405
  for communication, 363–364
  for computer sciences and engineering, 364–366
  and credibility of argument, 6
  for criminology and law, 366–367
  documenting, 383–385
  for education, 367
  electronic, 349–358
    evaluating, 358–360
    usenet/newsgroups, 357–358
    Web searches, 350–357
  for English language and literature, 367–369
  evaluating, 358–360
  government, 369–370
  for history, 370–371
  integrating, 374–381

  keyword searches of, 339–346
  in libraries, 346–349
  locating, 337–339
  note taking from, 372–374
  paraphrasing, 377–379
  for philosophy, 371
  and plagiarism, 382–385
  primary, 328–333
  quoting, 374–377
  reliability of, 37, 41
  secondary, 333–334
  summarizing, 379–381
  for verifying facts, 34–37

Special collections (as sources), 329

Specific examples, 138–139

Specific proposals, 288, 291–292, 298

Standard of judgment, 232

Standards, evaluation, 229

Statement Concerning the Recent Actions of Abercrombie and Fitch (Jamie Chan, Darren Joe, and Jung Ju), 508–510

Straw man fallacy, 67

Structuring questions, 115

Subjects:
  for arguments (*see* Generating arguments)
  with definite numbers, 140–141
  for evaluations, 234–247
    abstractions, 245–247
    events and actions, 242–245
    objects, 234–241
    people, 241–242
  with indefinite numbers, 141–143
  individual, 140

Sufficient causes, 181, 189–190

Summarizing, 379–381

Superlative evaluations, 252–253

Support:
  branching, 22–23
  chains of, 23–24
  (*See also specific topics*)

Surveys (as source), 331–333

Syllogisms, 20

Synonyms, 148–149

Testimony of others, facts from, 35–36

They, 103

They Do What They See (John R. Lion and Jonas R. Rappeport), 476–479

Things:
arguing existence of, 137
arguments about nature of, 135–137

Third person, 103

Three-part arguments, 20–23

Time constraints, 14

Time precedence arguments, 204–207

Topics for argument (*see* Generating arguments)

Toulin, Stephen, 20

Toulmin model, 27–29

Trends:
in causal arguments, 186
definition arguments identifying, 136

Troxler, Howard, 532–533

Truncation symbols, 343

Two-part arguments, 21–22

Uncertainty, acknowledging, 58

Undefined groups, 103

Uniform Resource Locators (URLs), 350–351

Universal statements, 142–143

Unpublished dissertation citations:
APA style for, 410
MLA style for, 391

URLs (*see* Uniform Resource Locators)

Usenet, 357

Usually, 141

Value(s):
appeals to, 233
questions of, 85–86, 92 (*See also* Evaluations)
as sources of agreement, 32–33
weighting, 248–250

Varying causes and effects arguments, 201–203

Veil of Fears (Stanley Kurtz), 426–430

Verification of facts, 34–37

Video recordings, APA style for citing, 411

Violence by Young People: Why the Deadly Nexus? (Alfred Blumstein), 467–476

Virtues, intellectual, 56

Visual rhetoric:
for cause and effect, 210–212
documentary photography, 158–159
emotion in images, 72–73
for evaluation, 254–255
and personification, 122–123
for proposals, 308–309
supporting logos, 38–40

Voice, 104–114, 117–121
I, 104–108
impersonal, 121
we, 117–120
you, 108–113
(*See also* Pronouns)

Warrants, 20–21
agents as, 181
as claims, 18
ethical, 243–245
in three-part model, 22–24
and type of questions raised, 84–88

We, 103, 117–120

Web (*see* World Wide Web)

Weighting (in evaluation), 247–250

What Tiger Does Best Is Golf (Joseph H. Brown), 497–498

Where Have All the Young Men Gone? (Paul Auster), 493–494

Wildcard symbols, 343

Woo, Andrea, 503–504

Word choice, 61–63 (*See also* Voice)

Works-cited list, MLA style for, 386

World Not Neatly Divided, A (Amartya Sen), 422–424

World Wide Web, 349–357
advantages of using, 356
disadvantages of using, 356–357

World Wide Web (*continued*)
    documenting information from,
        385
    evaluating sources from, 358–360
    newsgroups on, 357–358
    research sites on, 360–371
    searching, 353–356
    types of sites on, 351–353

URLs for, 350–351
Usenet on, 357
Woyinka, Wole, 430–432
Writing, exigence in, 13

Yahner, John A., 512–513
Yearbooks, 335, 336
You, 102–103, 108–113